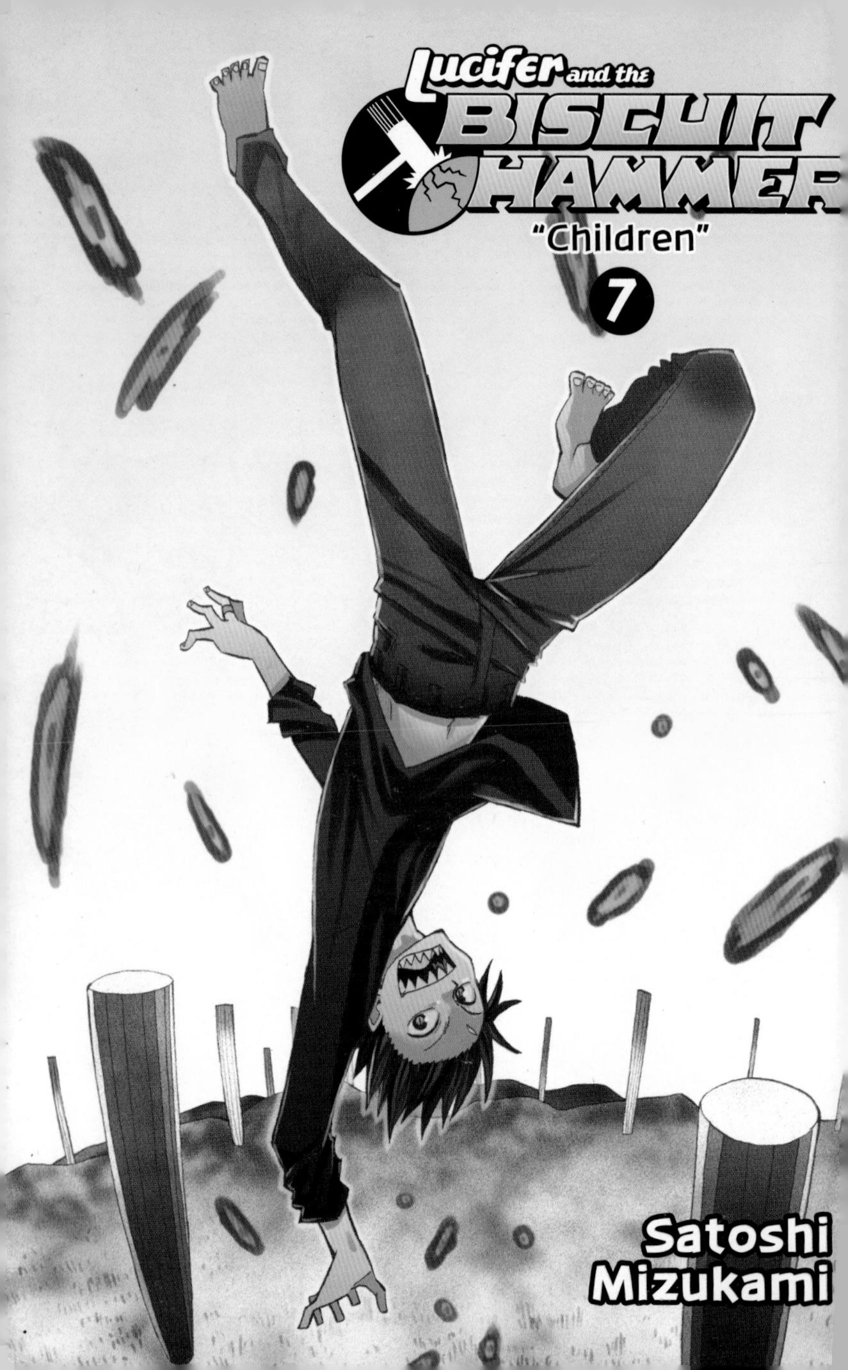
Lucifer and the
BISCUIT HAMMER
"Children"
7
Satoshi
Mizukami

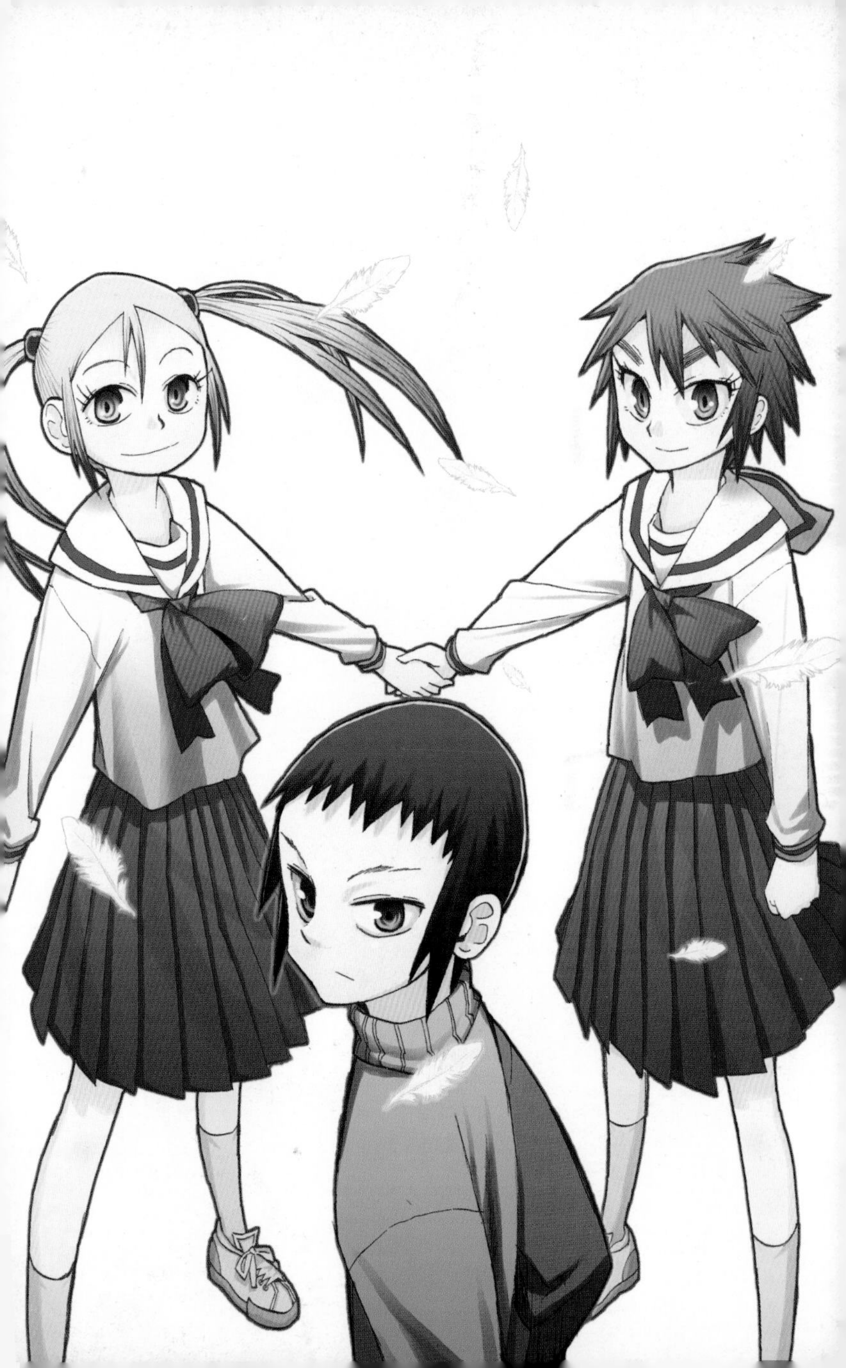

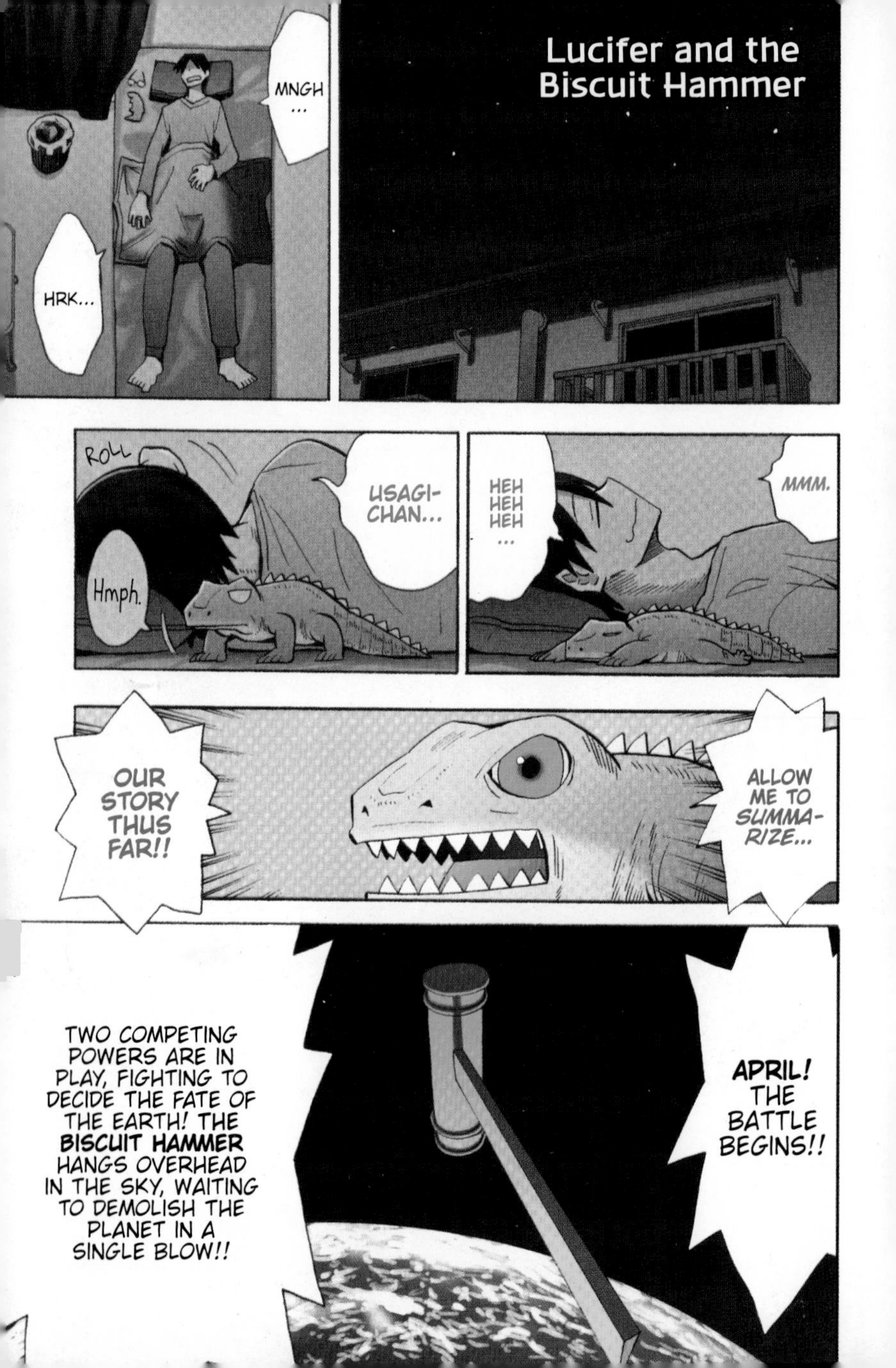
Lucifer and the Biscuit Hammer
MNGH ...
HRK...
MMM.
HEH HEH HEH ...
ROLL
USAGI-CHAN...
Hmph.
ALLOW ME TO SUMMARIZE...
OUR STORY THUS FAR!!
APRIL! THE BATTLE BEGINS!!
TWO COMPETING POWERS ARE IN PLAY, FIGHTING TO DECIDE THE FATE OF THE EARTH! THE BISCUIT HAMMER HANGS OVERHEAD IN THE SKY, WAITING TO DEMOLISH THE PLANET IN A SINGLE BLOW!!

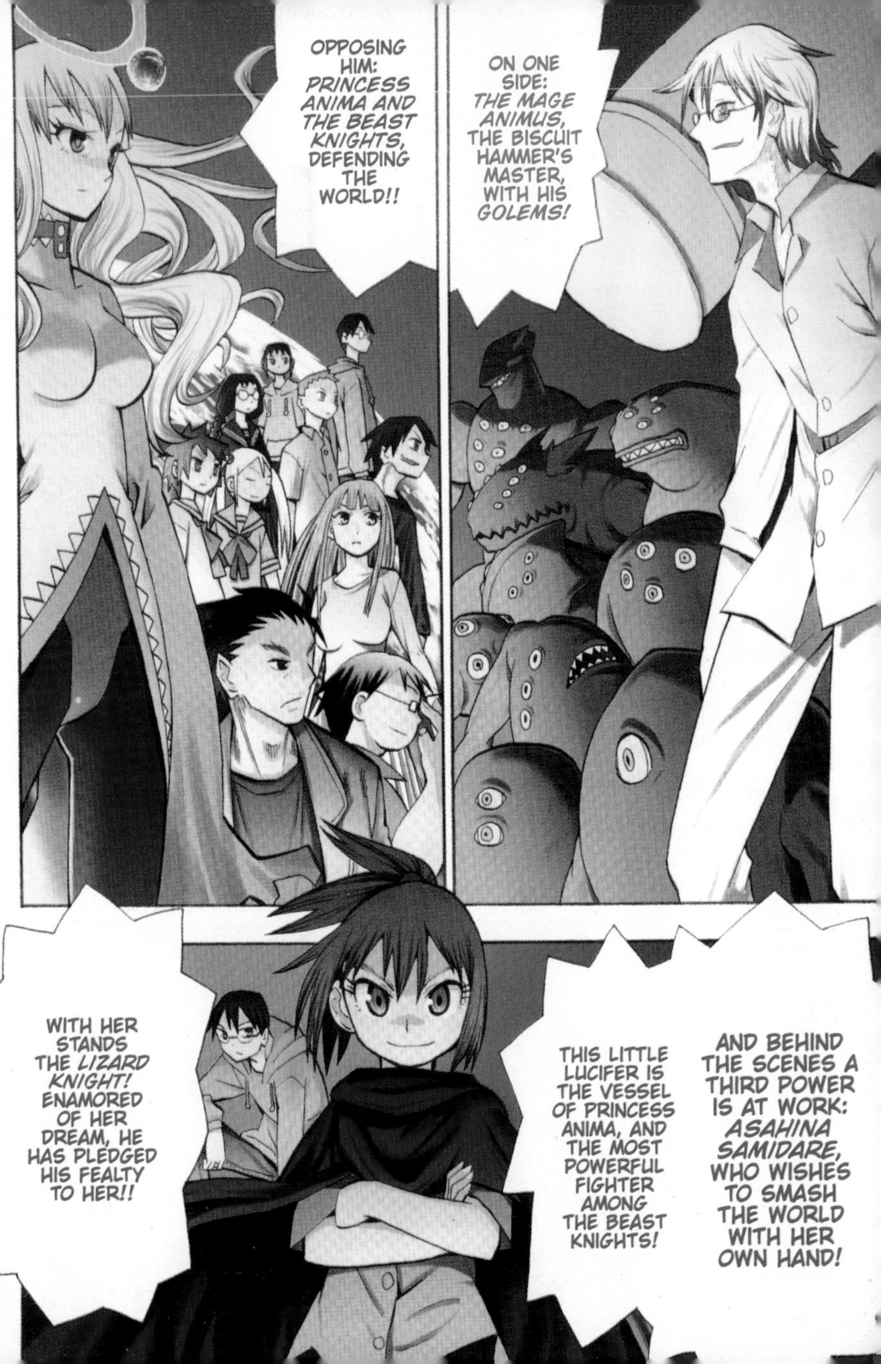
ON ONE SIDE: THE MAGE ANIMUS, THE BISCUIT HAMMER'S MASTER, WITH HIS GOLEMS!
OPPOSING HIM: PRINCESS ANIMA AND THE BEAST KNIGHTS, DEFENDING THE WORLD!!
AND BEHIND THE SCENES A THIRD POWER IS AT WORK: ASAHINA SAMIDARE, WHO WISHES TO SMASH THE WORLD WITH HER OWN HAND!
THIS LITTLE LUCIFER IS THE VESSEL OF PRINCESS ANIMA, AND THE MOST POWERFUL FIGHTER AMONG THE BEAST KNIGHTS!
WITH HER STANDS THE LIZARD KNIGHT! ENAMORED OF HER DREAM, HE HAS PLEDGED HIS FEALTY TO HER!!

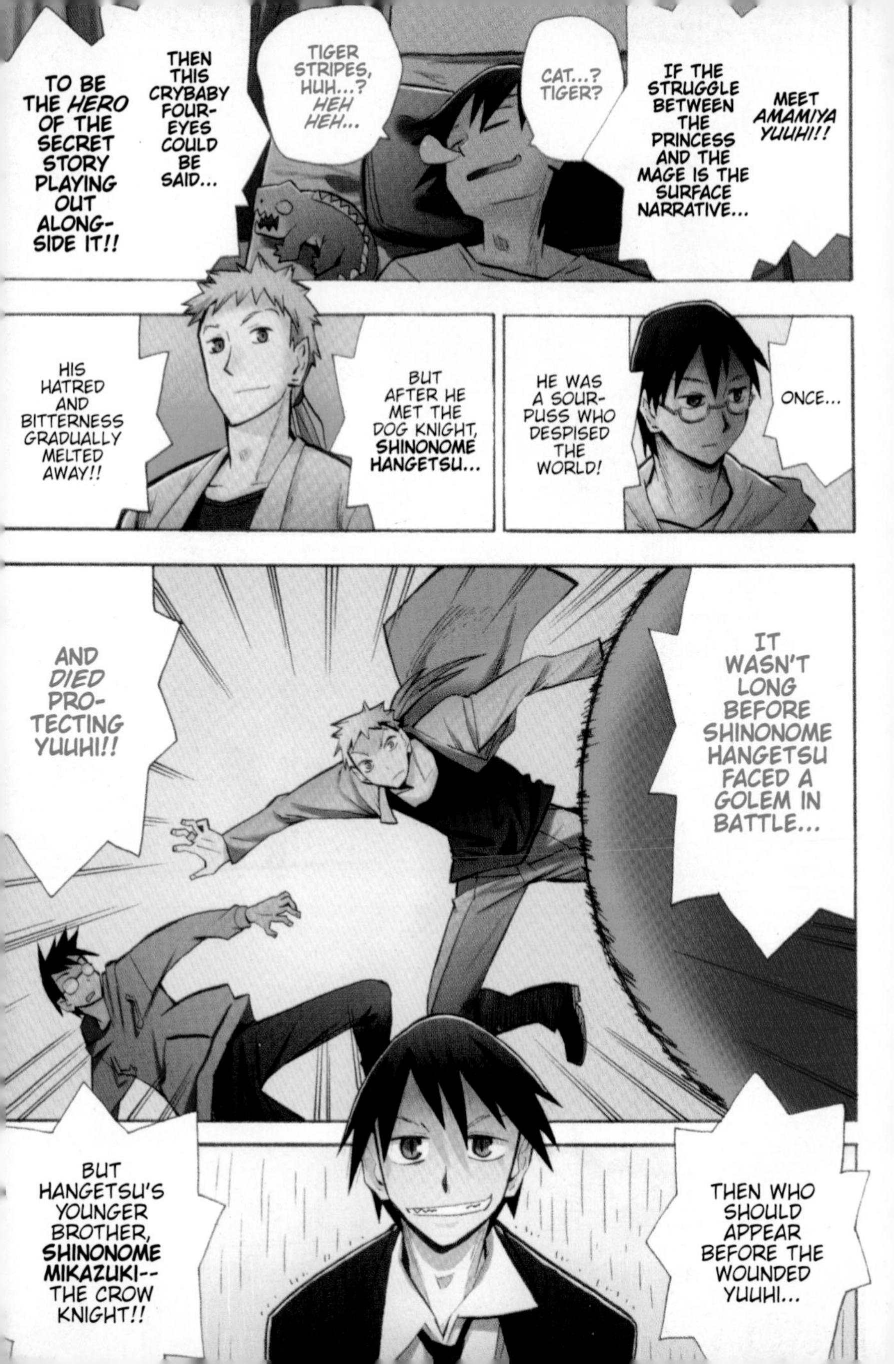
MEET AMAMIYA YUUHI!!
IF THE STRUGGLE BETWEEN THE PRINCESS AND THE MAGE IS THE SURFACE NARRATIVE...
CAT...? TIGER?
TIGER STRIPES, HUH...? HEH HEH...
THEN THIS CRYBABY FOUR-EYES COULD BE SAID...
TO BE THE HERO OF THE SECRET STORY PLAYING OUT ALONG-SIDE IT!!
ONCE...
HE WAS A SOUR-PUSS WHO DESPISED THE WORLD!
BUT AFTER HE MET THE DOG KNIGHT, SHINONOME HANGETSU...
HIS HATRED AND BITTERNESS GRADUALLY MELTED AWAY!!
IT WASN'T LONG BEFORE SHINONOME HANGETSU FACED A GOLEM IN BATTLE...
AND DIED PRO-TECTING YUUHI!!
THEN WHO SHOULD APPEAR BEFORE THE WOUNDED YUUHI...
BUT HANGETSU'S YOUNGER BROTHER, SHINONOME MIKAZUKI-- THE CROW KNIGHT!!

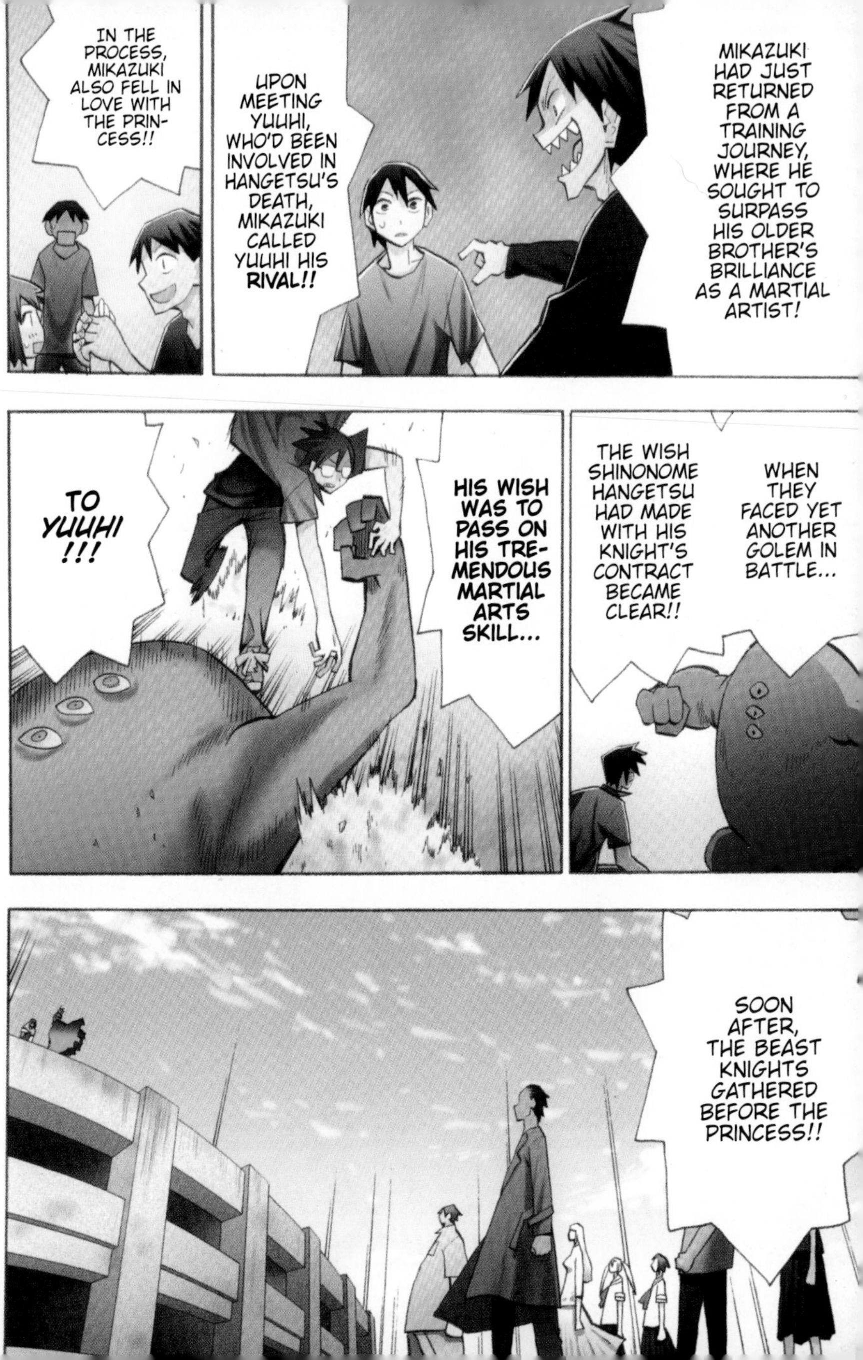
MIKAZUKI HAD JUST RETURNED FROM A TRAINING JOURNEY, WHERE HE SOUGHT TO SURPASS HIS OLDER BROTHER'S BRILLIANCE AS A MARTIAL ARTIST!
UPON MEETING YUUHI, WHO'D BEEN INVOLVED IN HANGETSU'S DEATH, MIKAZUKI CALLED YUUHI HIS RIVAL!!
IN THE PROCESS, MIKAZUKI ALSO FELL IN LOVE WITH THE PRINCESS!!
WHEN THEY FACED YET ANOTHER GOLEM IN BATTLE...
THE WISH SHINONOME HANGETSU HAD MADE WITH HIS KNIGHT'S CONTRACT BECAME CLEAR!!
HIS WISH WAS TO PASS ON HIS TREMENDOUS MARTIAL ARTS SKILL...
TO YUUHI!!!
SOON AFTER, THE BEAST KNIGHTS GATHERED BEFORE THE PRINCESS!!

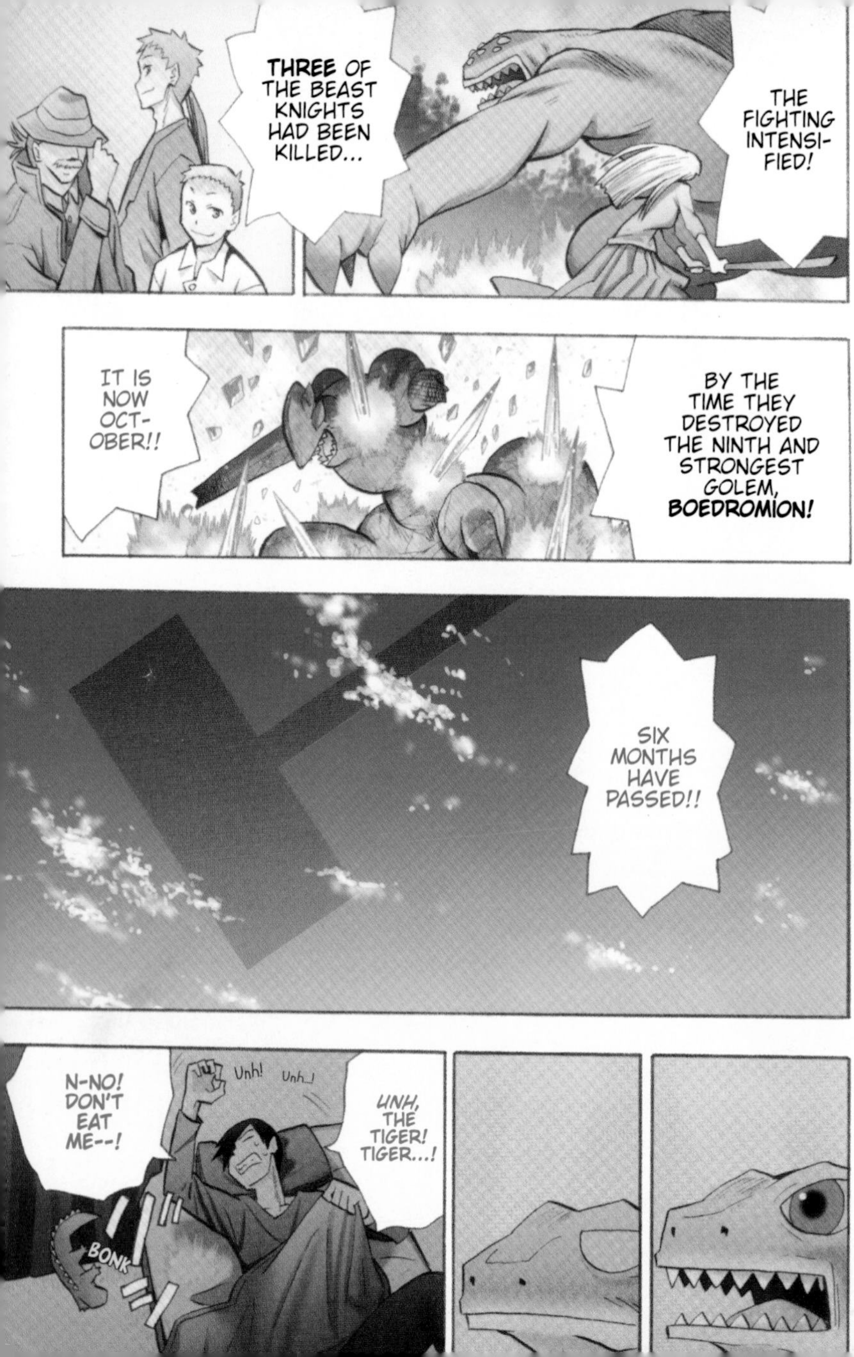
THE FIGHTING INTENSI-FIED!
THREE OF THE BEAST KNIGHTS HAD BEEN KILLED...
BY THE TIME THEY DESTROYED THE NINTH AND STRONGEST GOLEM, BOEDROMION!
IT IS NOW OCT-OBER!!
SIX MONTHS HAVE PASSED!!
UNH, THE TIGER! TIGER...!
Unh! Unh..!
N-NO! DON'T EAT ME--!
BONK

Chapter 42: Amamiya Yuuhi and the Shinonome Brothers (Part 2)

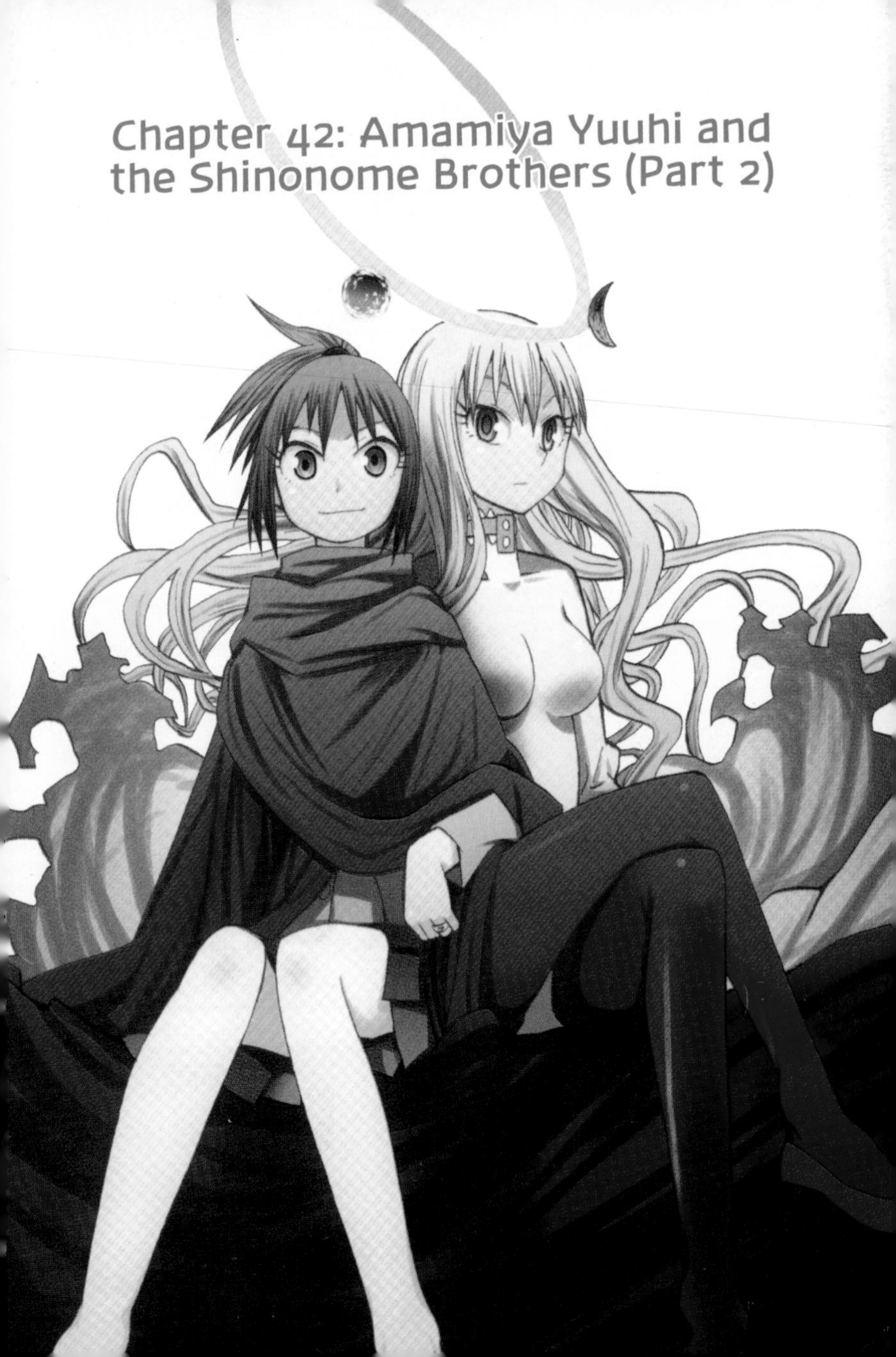

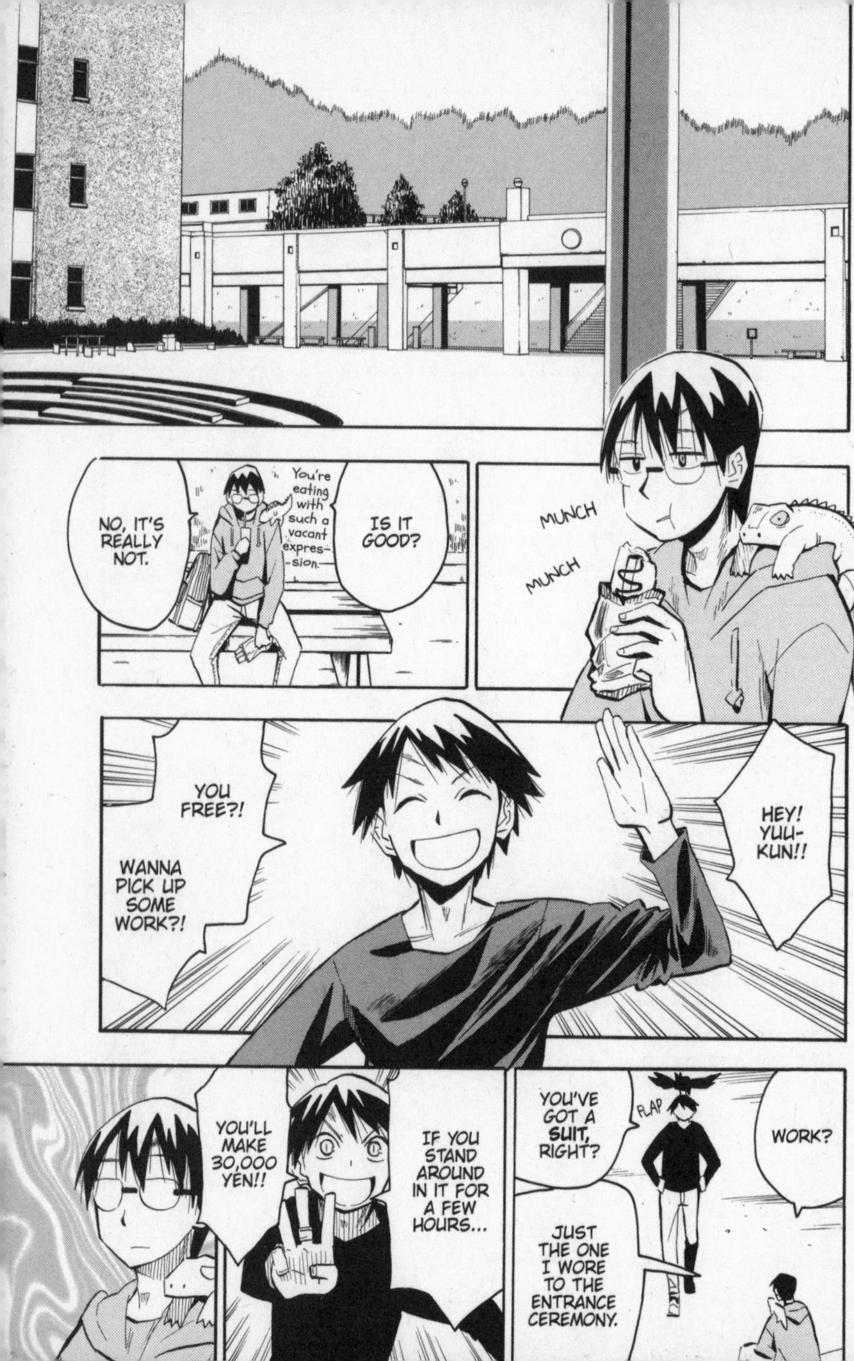
MUNCH
MUNCH
IS IT GOOD?
You're eating with such a vacant expres-sion.
NO, IT'S REALLY NOT.
HEY! YUU-KUN!!
YOU FREE?!
WANNA PICK UP SOME WORK?!
WORK?
FLAP
YOU'VE GOT A SUIT, RIGHT?
JUST THE ONE I WORE TO THE ENTRANCE CEREMONY.
IF YOU STAND AROUND IN IT FOR A FEW HOURS...
YOU'LL MAKE 30,000 YEN!!

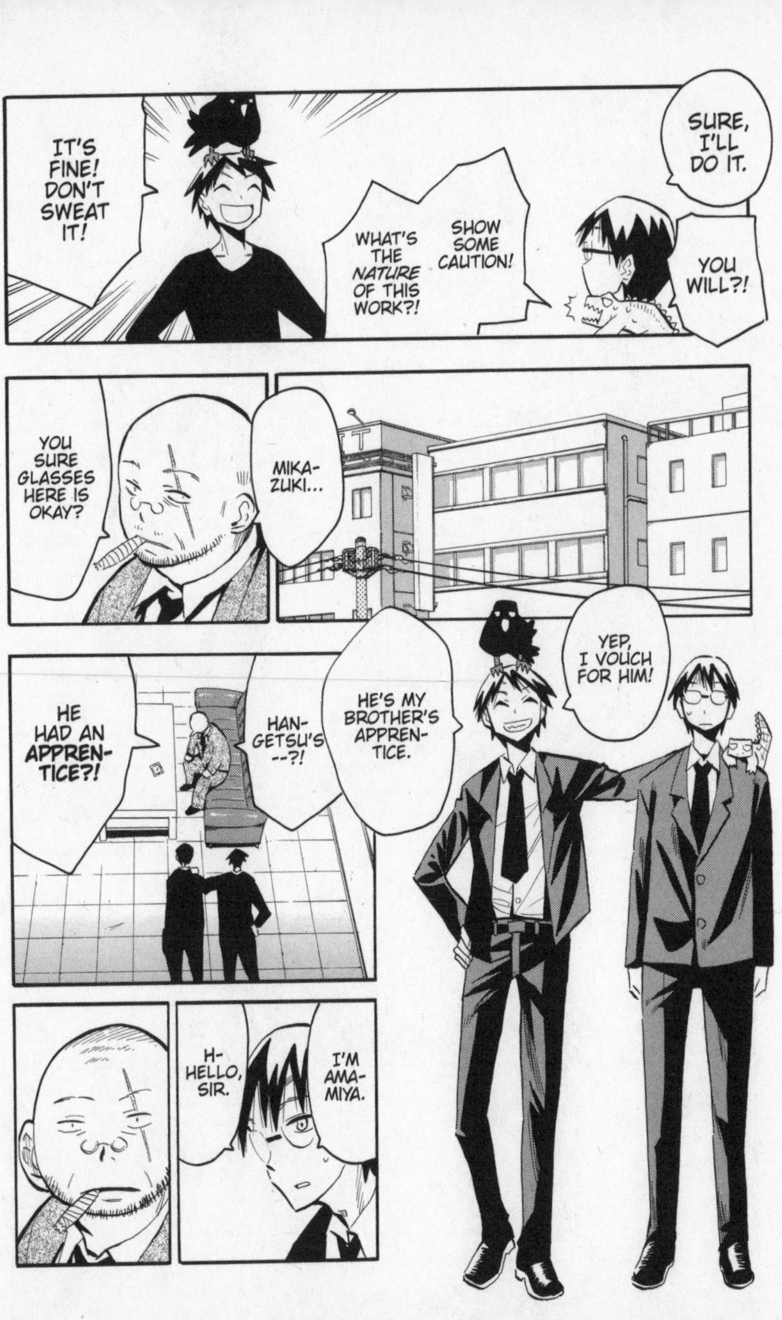
SURE, I'LL DO IT.
YOU WILL?!
SHOW SOME CAUTION!
WHAT'S THE *NATURE* OF THIS WORK?!
IT'S FINE! DON'T SWEAT IT!
MIKA-ZUKI...
YOU SURE GLASSES HERE IS OKAY?
YEP, I VOUCH FOR HIM!
HE'S MY BROTHER'S APPREN-TICE.
HAN-GETSU'S--?!
HE HAD AN **APPREN-TICE?!**
I'M AMA-MIYA.
H-HELLO, SIR.

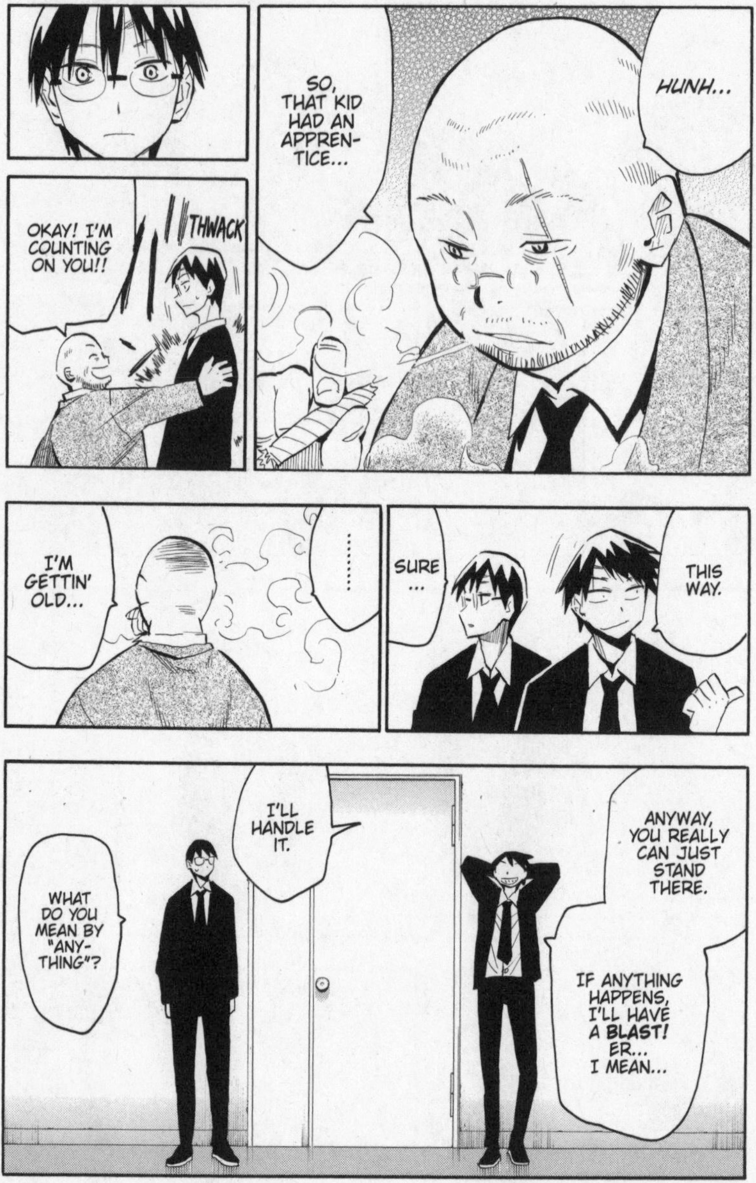
HUNH...
SO, THAT KID HAD AN APPREN-TICE...
THWACK
OKAY! I'M COUNTING ON YOU!!
THIS WAY.
SURE...
......
I'M GETTIN' OLD...
ANYWAY, YOU REALLY CAN JUST STAND THERE.
IF ANYTHING HAPPENS, I'LL HAVE A BLAST! ER... I MEAN...
I'LL HANDLE IT.
WHAT DO YOU MEAN BY "ANY-THING"?

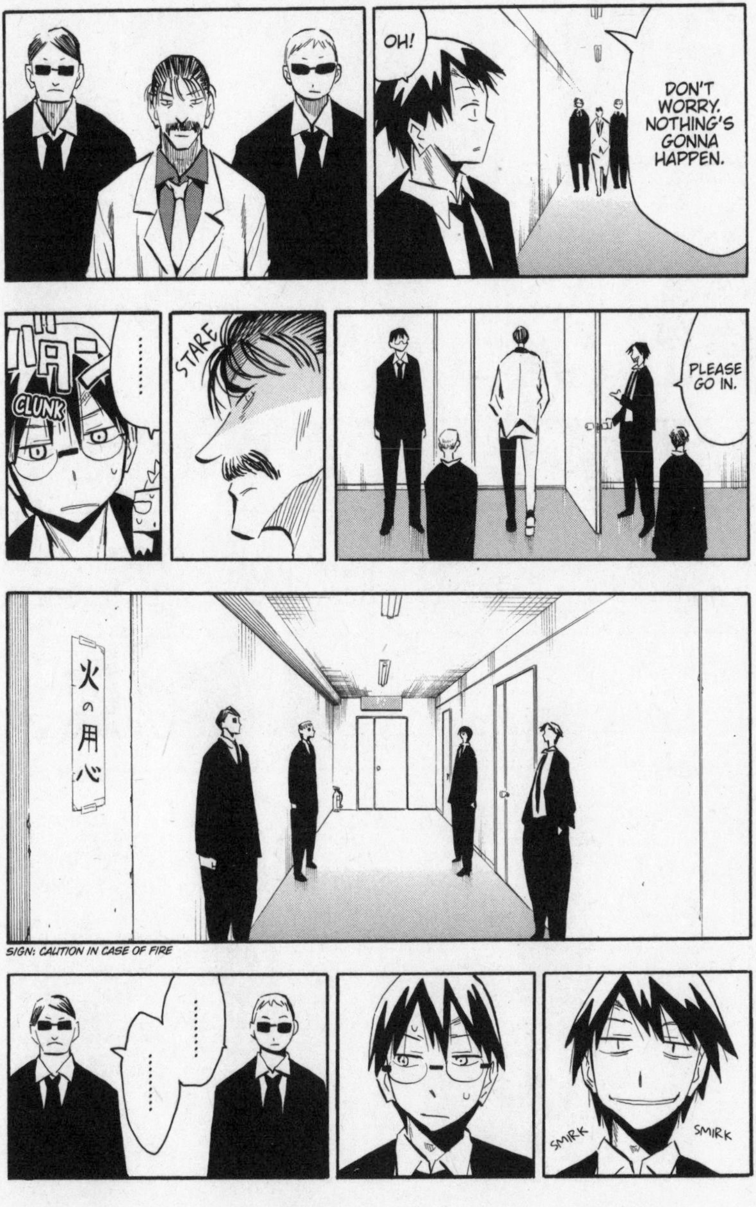
DON'T WORRY. NOTHING'S GONNA HAPPEN.
OH!
PLEASE GO IN.
STARE
……
CLUNK
火の用心
SIGN: CAUTION IN CASE OF FIRE
SMIRK
SMIRK
……
……

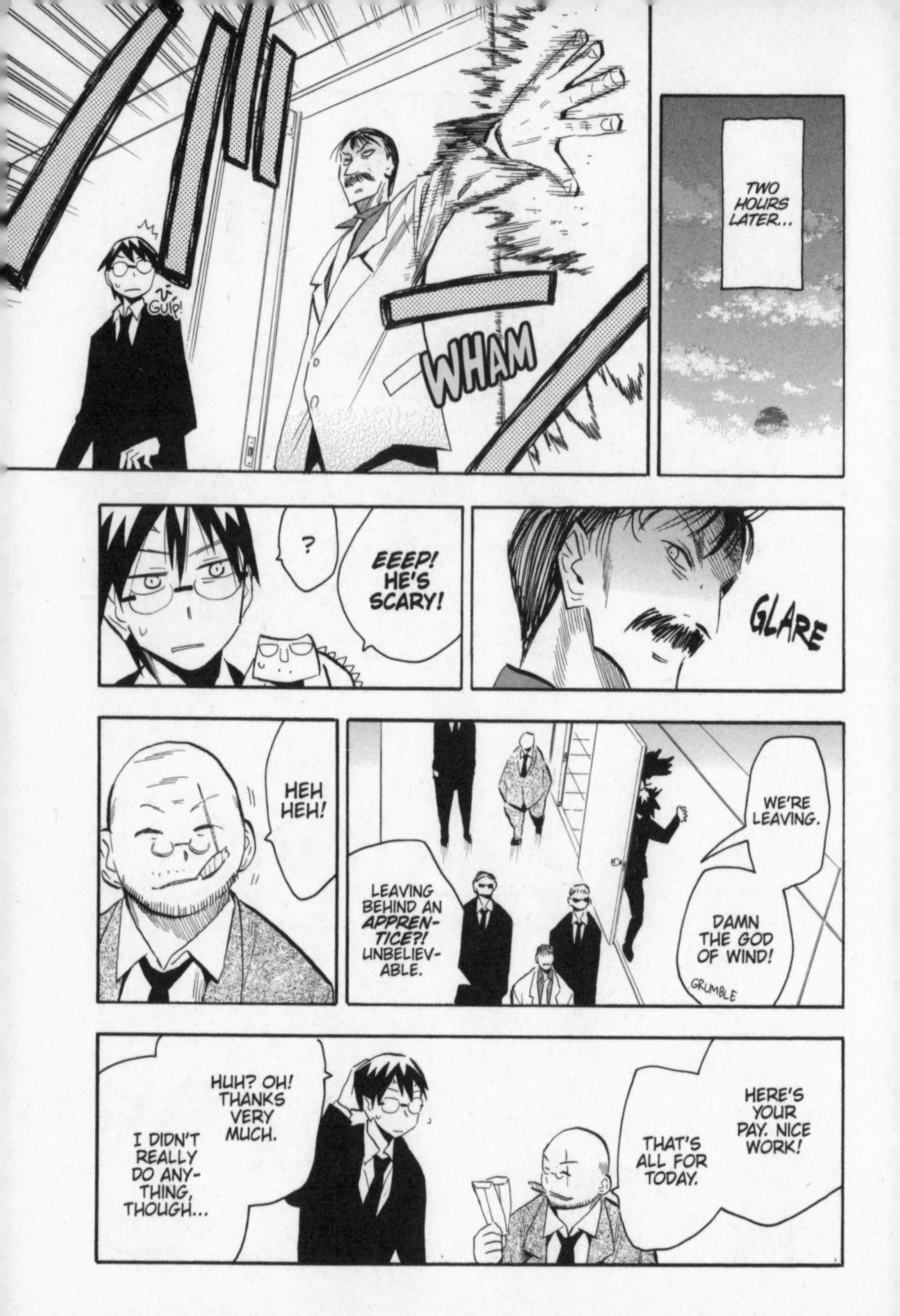
TWO HOURS LATER...
WHAM
GULP!
GLARE
EEEP! HE'S SCARY!
?
WE'RE LEAVING.
DAMN THE GOD OF WIND!
GRUMBLE
LEAVING BEHIND AN APPRENTICE?! UNBELIEVABLE.
HEH HEH!
HERE'S YOUR PAY. NICE WORK!
THAT'S ALL FOR TODAY.
HUH? OH! THANKS VERY MUCH.
I DIDN'T REALLY DO ANYTHING, THOUGH...

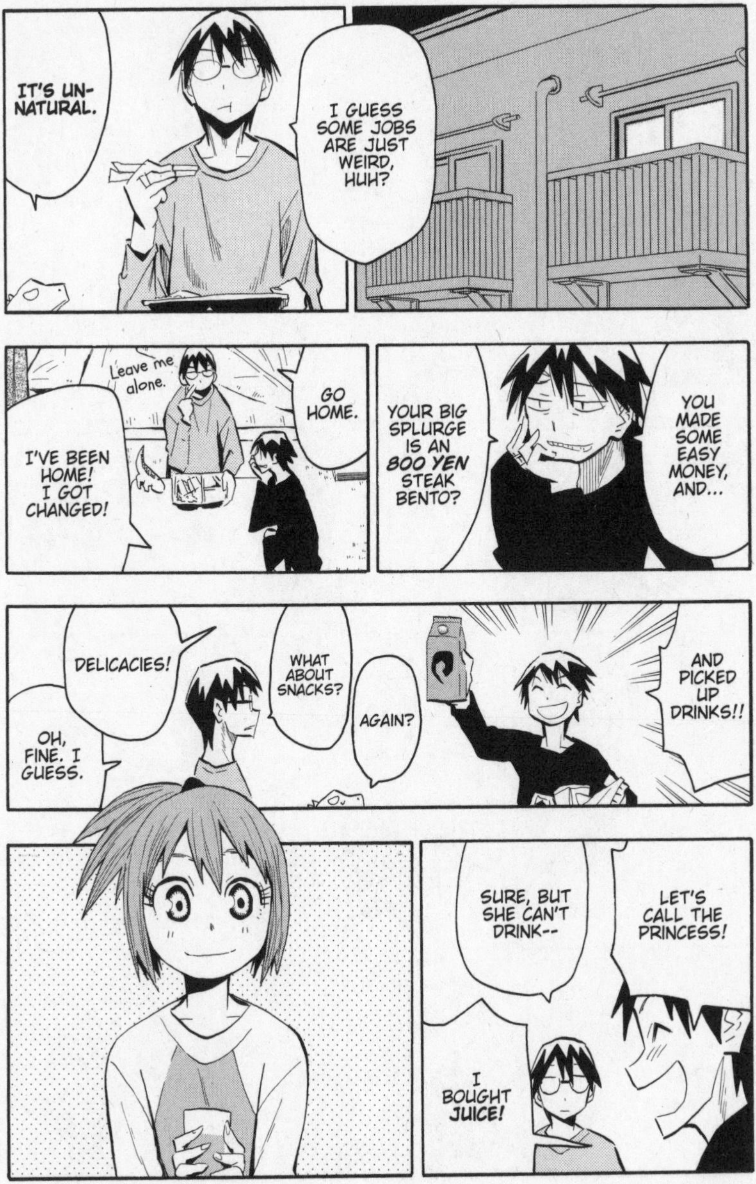
I GUESS SOME JOBS ARE JUST WEIRD, HUH?
IT'S UN-NATURAL.
YOU MADE SOME EASY MONEY, AND...
YOUR BIG SPLURGE IS AN 800 YEN STEAK BENTO?
GO HOME.
Leave me alone.
I'VE BEEN HOME! I GOT CHANGED!
AND PICKED UP DRINKS!!
AGAIN?
WHAT ABOUT SNACKS?
DELICACIES!
OH, FINE. I GUESS.
LET'S CALL THE PRINCESS!
SURE, BUT SHE CAN'T DRINK--
I BOUGHT JUICE!

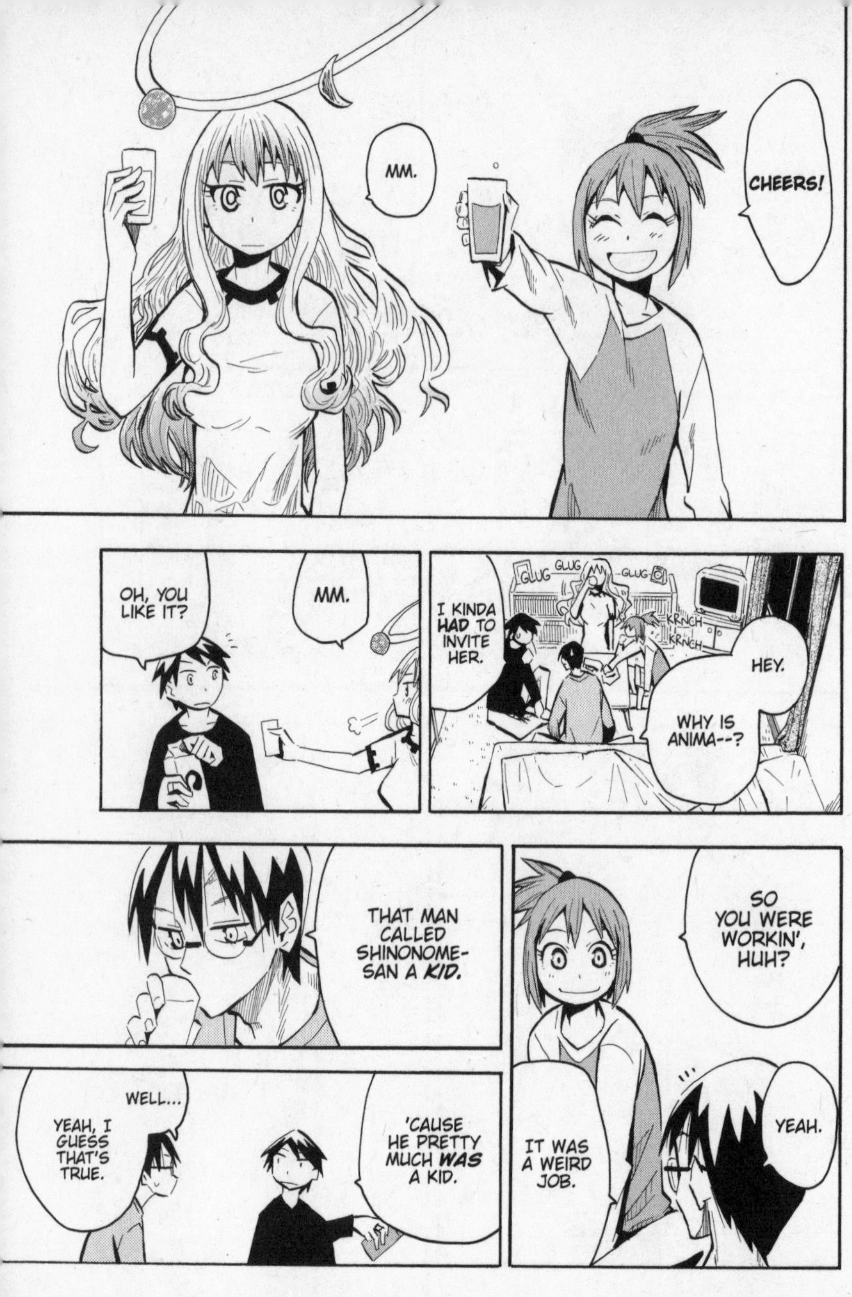
CHEERS!
MM.
GLUG GLUG GLUG
KRNCH KRNCH
HEY.
WHY IS ANIMA--?
I KINDA HAD TO INVITE HER.
OH, YOU LIKE IT?
MM.
SO YOU WERE WORKIN', HUH?
YEAH.
IT WAS A WEIRD JOB.
THAT MAN CALLED SHINONOME-SAN A KID.
'CAUSE HE PRETTY MUCH WAS A KID.
WELL...
YEAH, I GUESS THAT'S TRUE.

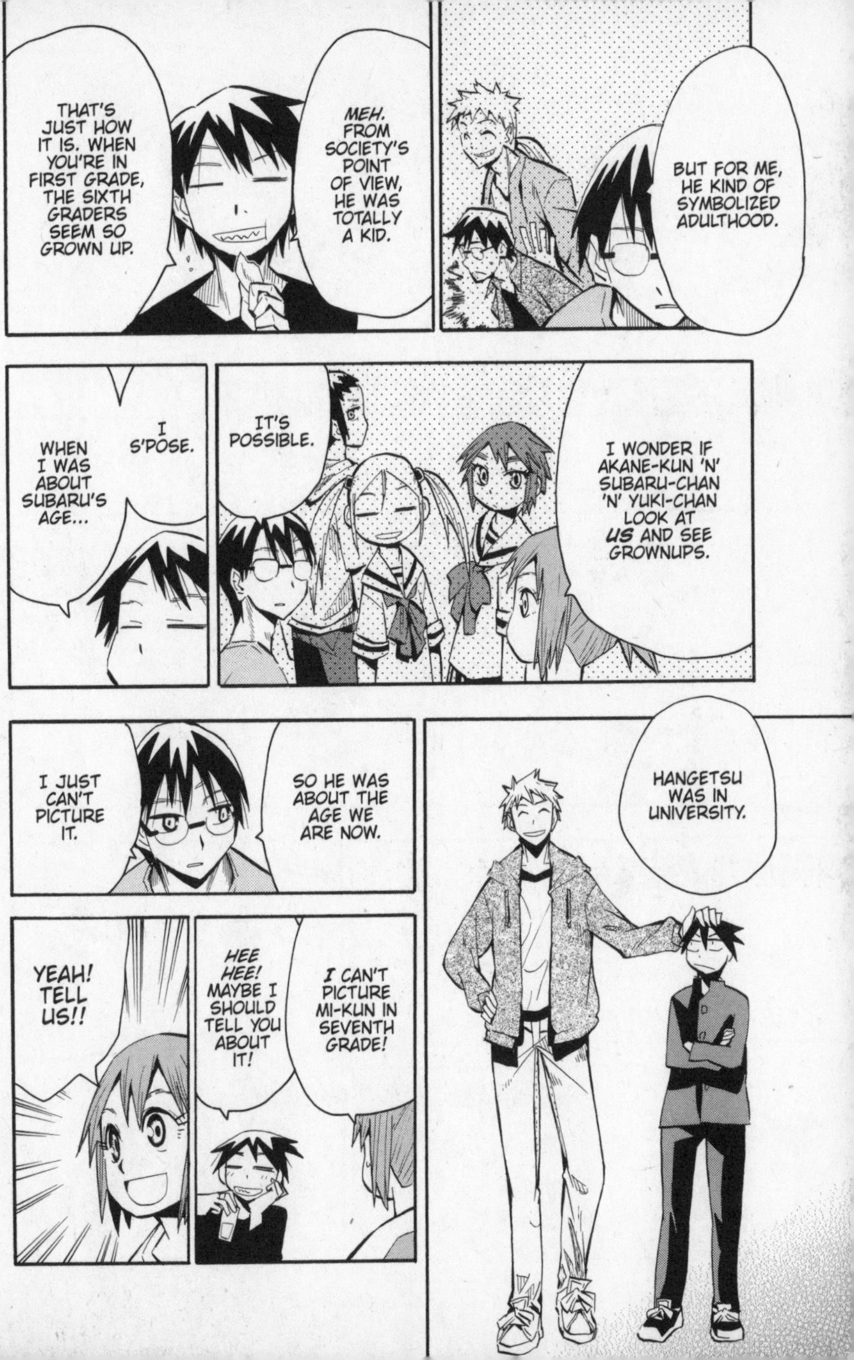
BUT FOR ME, HE KIND OF SYMBOLIZED ADULTHOOD.
MEH. FROM SOCIETY'S POINT OF VIEW, HE WAS TOTALLY A KID.
THAT'S JUST HOW IT IS. WHEN YOU'RE IN FIRST GRADE, THE SIXTH GRADERS SEEM SO GROWN UP.
I WONDER IF AKANE-KUN 'N' SUBARU-CHAN 'N' YUKI-CHAN LOOK AT *US* AND SEE GROWNUPS.
IT'S POSSIBLE.
I S'POSE.
WHEN I WAS ABOUT SUBARU'S AGE...
HANGETSU WAS IN UNIVERSITY.
SO HE WAS ABOUT THE AGE WE ARE NOW.
I JUST CAN'T PICTURE IT.
I CAN'T PICTURE MI-KUN IN SEVENTH GRADE!
HEE HEE! MAYBE I SHOULD TELL YOU ABOUT IT!
YEAH! TELL US!!

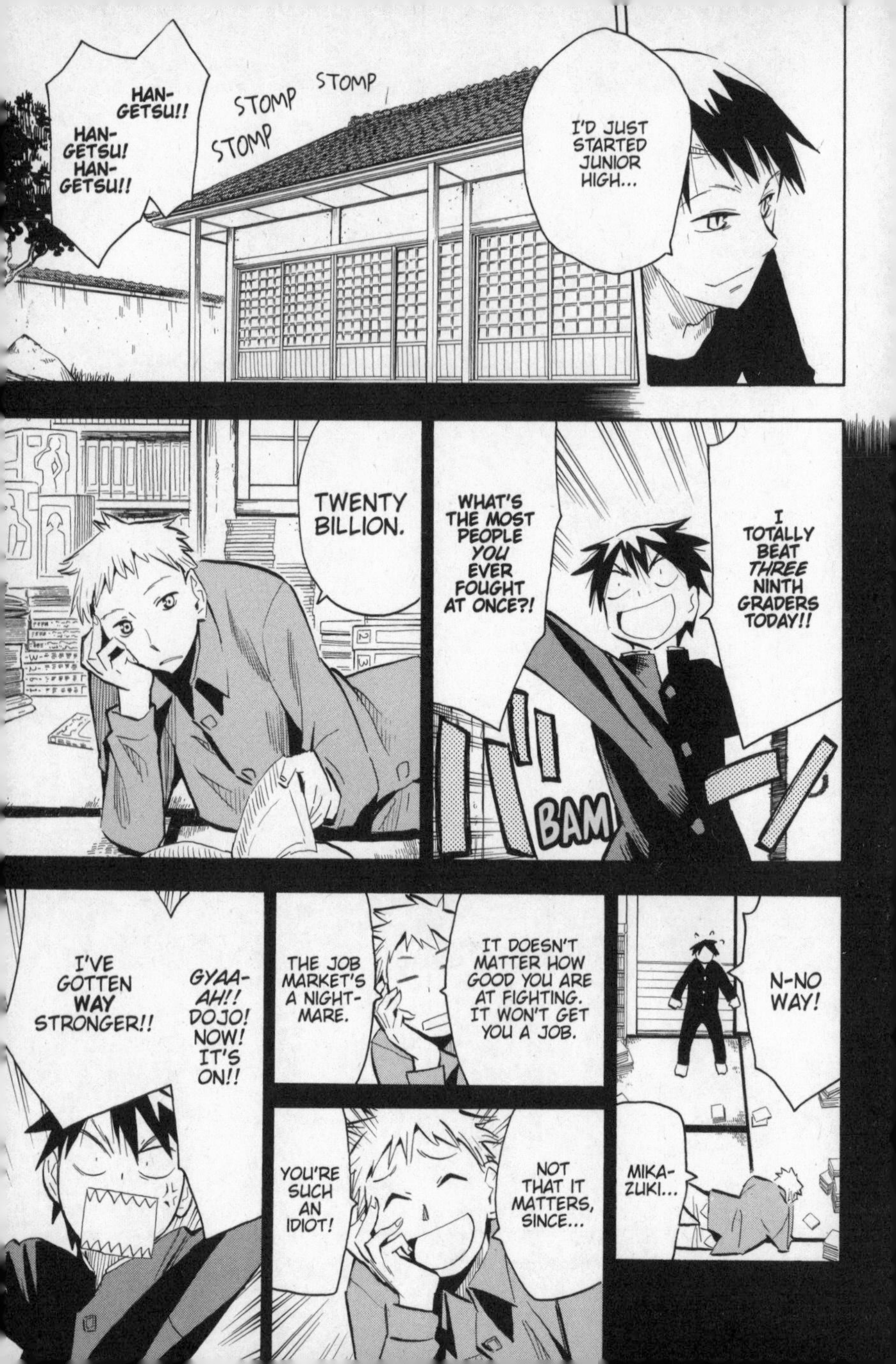
I'D JUST STARTED JUNIOR HIGH...
STOMP STOMP
STOMP
HAN-GETSU!! HAN-GETSU! HAN-GETSU!!
I TOTALLY BEAT *THREE* NINTH GRADERS TODAY!!
BAM
WHAT'S THE MOST PEOPLE *YOU* EVER FOUGHT AT ONCE?!
TWENTY BILLION.
N-NO WAY!
MIKA-ZUKI...
IT DOESN'T MATTER HOW GOOD YOU ARE AT FIGHTING. IT WON'T GET YOU A JOB.
THE JOB MARKET'S A NIGHT-MARE.
NOT THAT IT MATTERS, SINCE...
YOU'RE SUCH AN IDIOT!
GYAA-AH!! DOJO! NOW! IT'S ON!!
I'VE GOTTEN WAY STRONGER!!

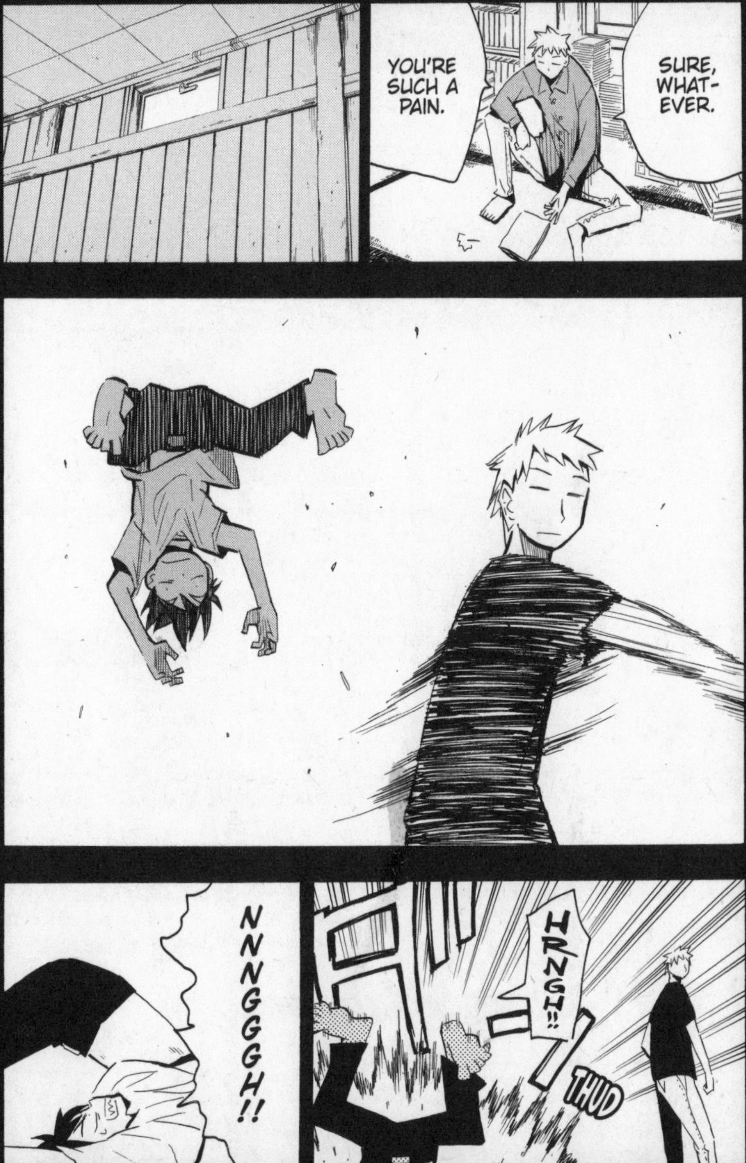
SURE, WHAT-EVER.
YOU'RE SUCH A PAIN.
HRNGH!!
THUD
NNNGGGH!!

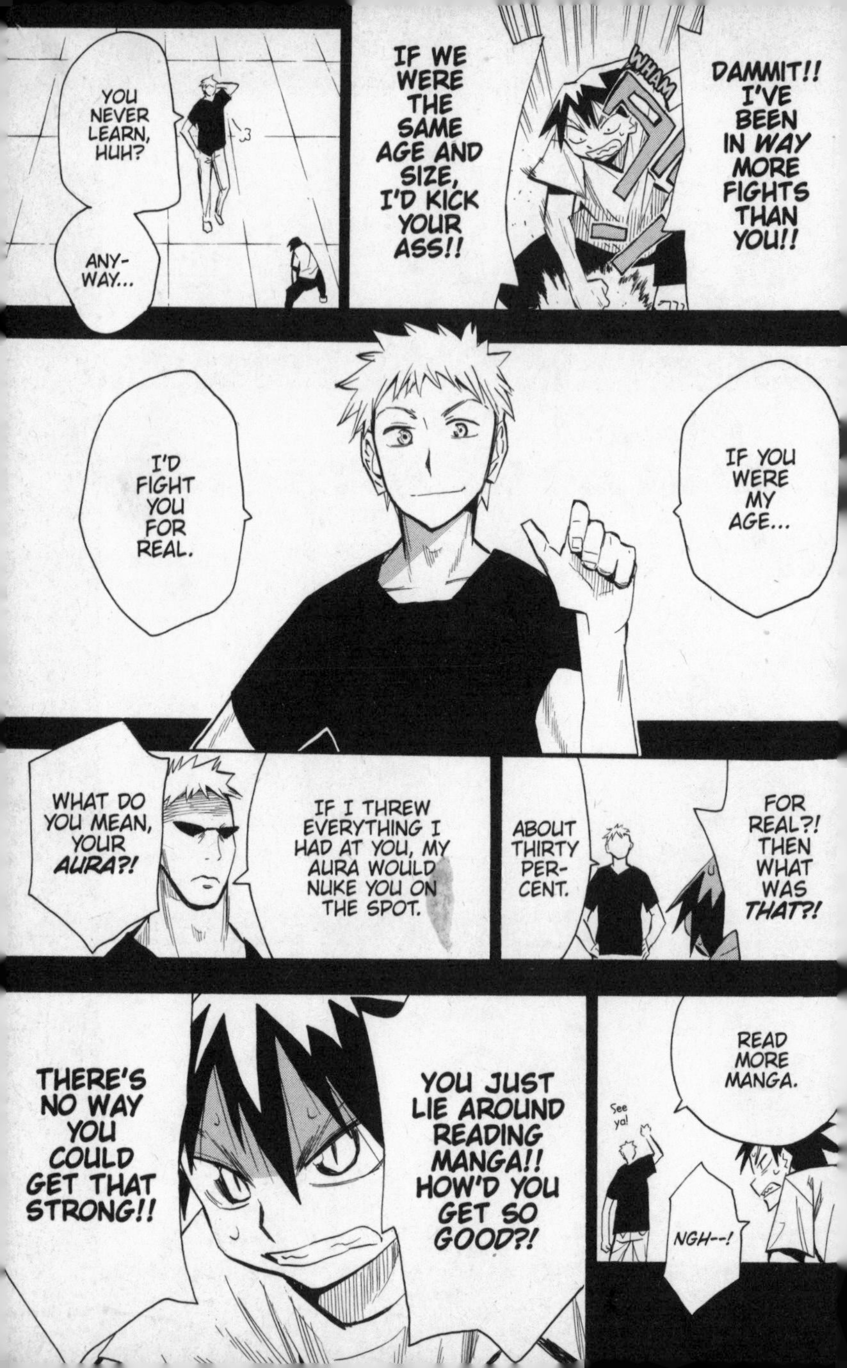
WHAM
DAMMIT!! I'VE BEEN IN WAY MORE FIGHTS THAN YOU!!
IF WE WERE THE SAME AGE AND SIZE, I'D KICK YOUR ASS!!
YOU NEVER LEARN, HUH?
ANY-WAY...
IF YOU WERE MY AGE...
I'D FIGHT YOU FOR REAL.
FOR REAL?! THEN WHAT WAS THAT?!
ABOUT THIRTY PER-CENT.
IF I THREW EVERYTHING I HAD AT YOU, MY AURA WOULD NUKE YOU ON THE SPOT.
WHAT DO YOU MEAN, YOUR AURA?!
READ MORE MANGA.
See ya!
NGH--!
YOU JUST LIE AROUND READING MANGA!! HOW'D YOU GET SO GOOD?!
THERE'S NO WAY YOU COULD GET THAT STRONG!!

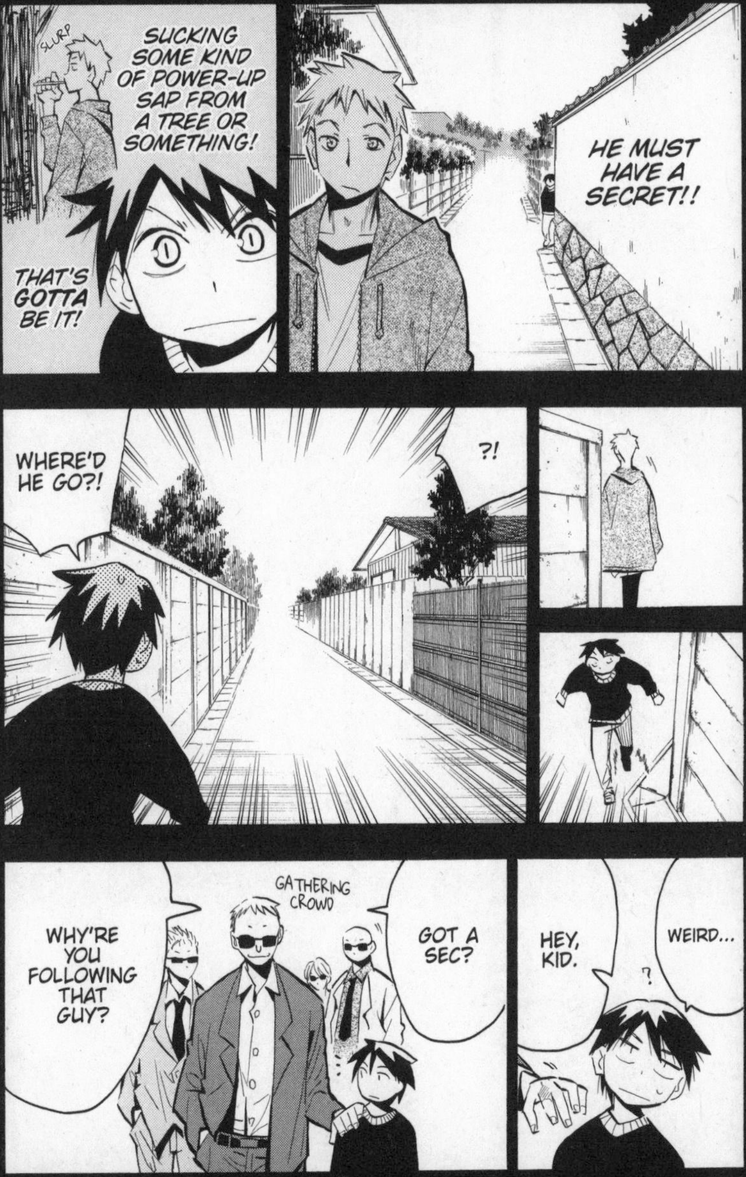
HE MUST HAVE A SECRET!!
SLURP
SUCKING SOME KIND OF POWER-UP SAP FROM A TREE OR SOMETHING!
THAT'S GOTTA BE IT!
?!
WHERE'D HE GO?!
WEIRD...
HEY, KID.
?
GOT A SEC?
GATHERING CROWD
WHY'RE YOU FOLLOWING THAT GUY?

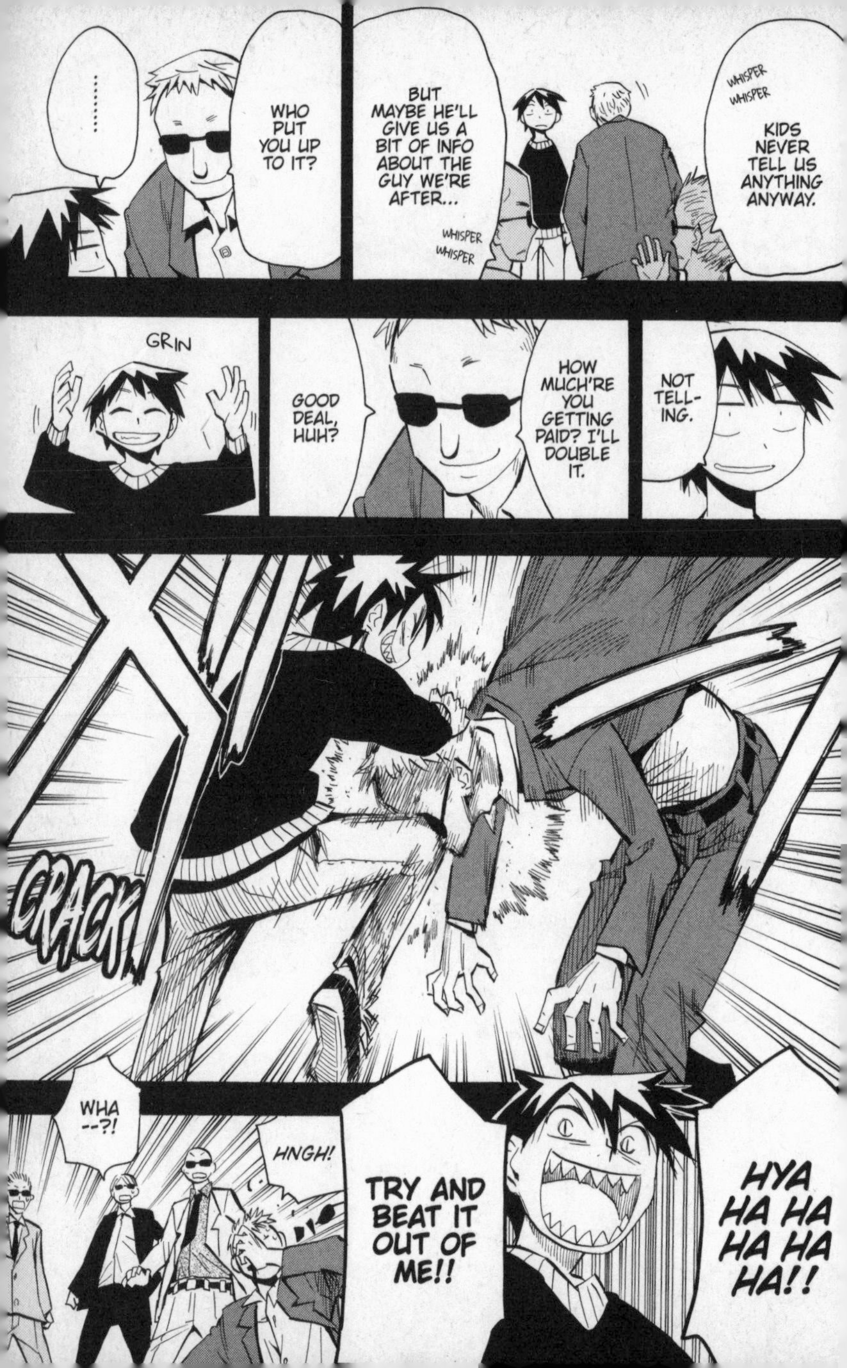
WHISPER WHISPER
KIDS NEVER TELL US ANYTHING ANYWAY.
BUT MAYBE HE'LL GIVE US A BIT OF INFO ABOUT THE GUY WE'RE AFTER...
WHISPER WHISPER
WHO PUT YOU UP TO IT?
......
NOT TELLING.
HOW MUCH'RE YOU GETTING PAID? I'LL DOUBLE IT.
GOOD DEAL, HUH?
GRIN
CRACK
HYA HA HA HA HA HA HA!!
TRY AND BEAT IT OUT OF ME!!
HNGH!
WHA--?!

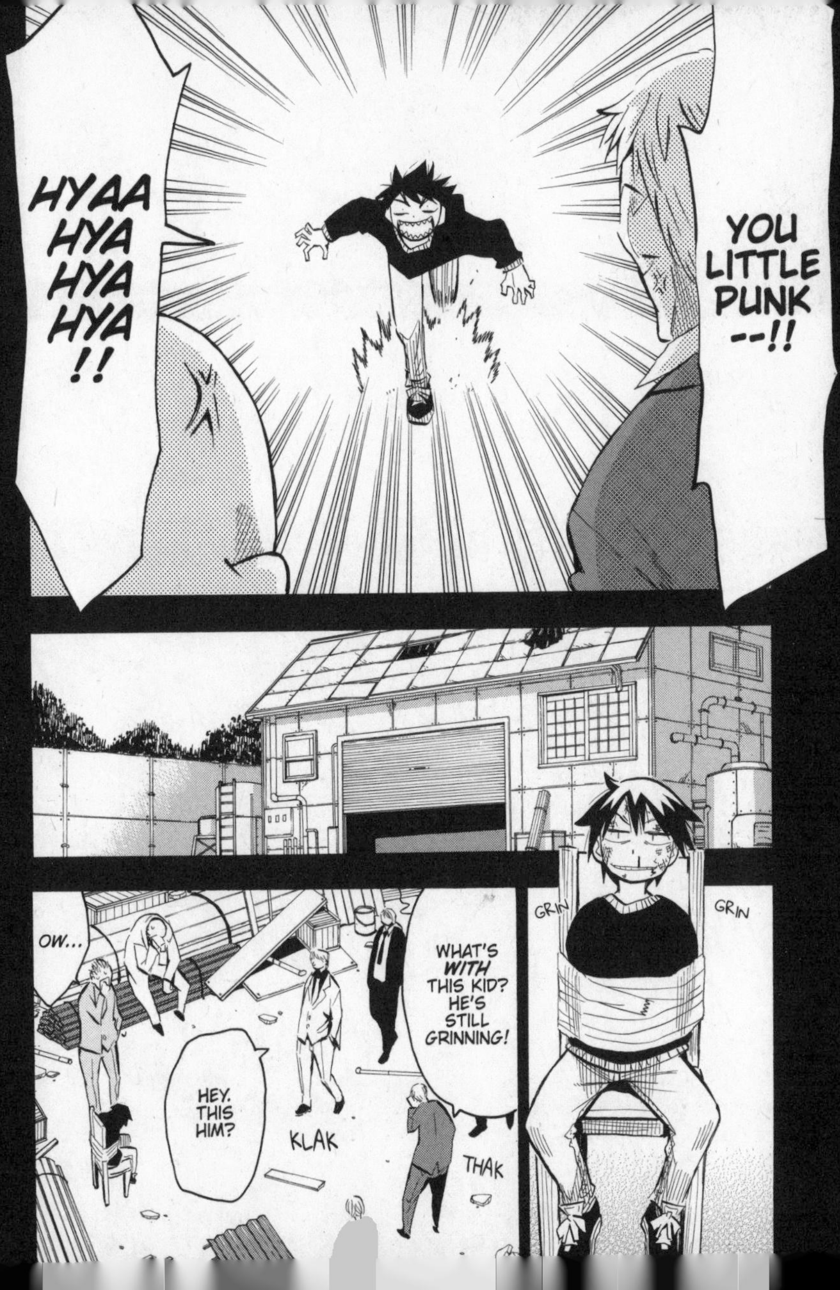
YOU LITTLE PUNK--!!
HYAA HYA HYA HYA!!
GRIN
GRIN
WHAT'S *WITH* THIS KID? HE'S STILL GRINNING!
OW...
HEY. THIS HIM?
KLAK
THAK

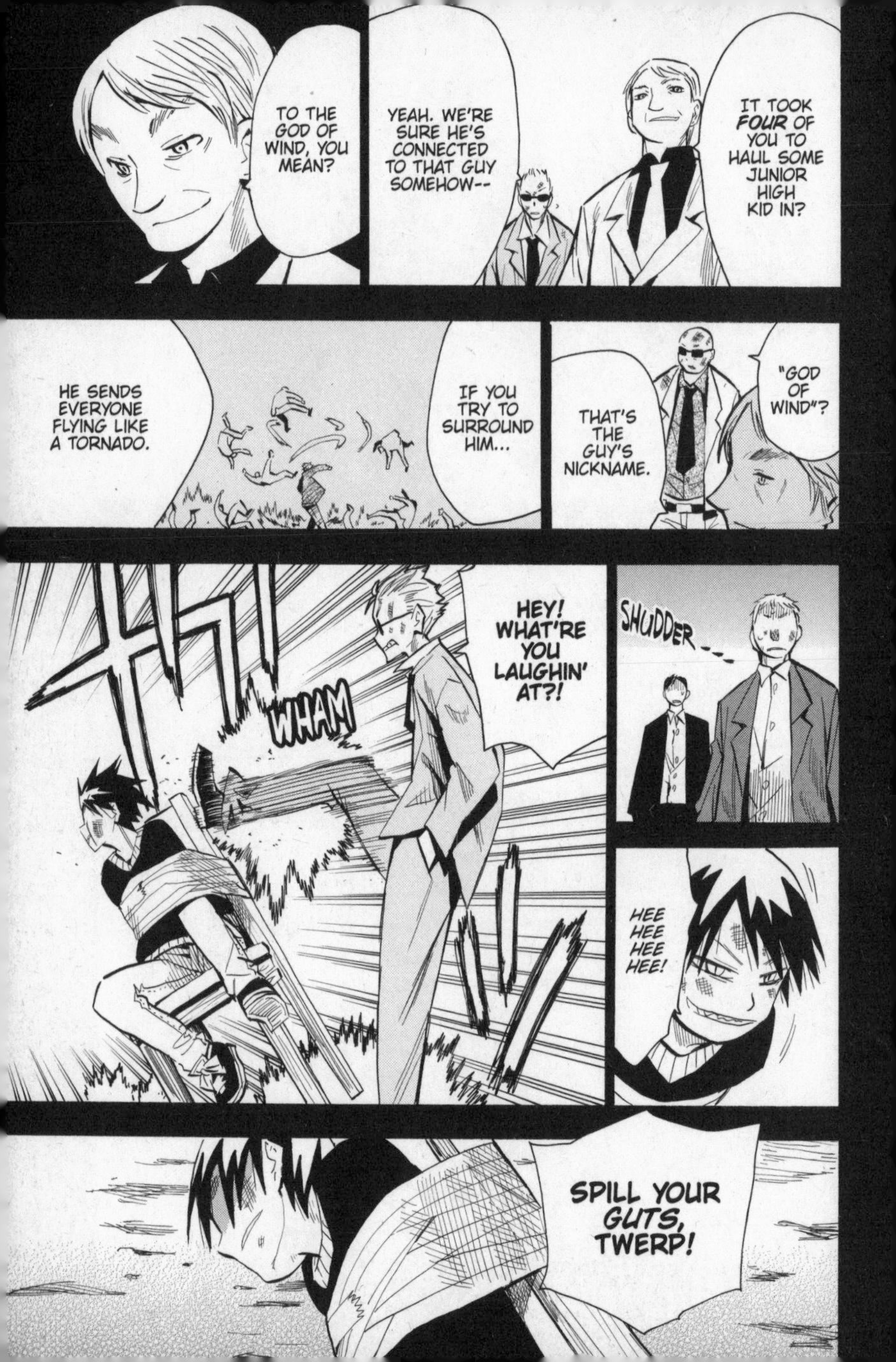
IT TOOK FOUR OF YOU TO HAUL SOME JUNIOR HIGH KID IN?
YEAH. WE'RE SURE HE'S CONNECTED TO THAT GUY SOMEHOW--
TO THE GOD OF WIND, YOU MEAN?
"GOD OF WIND"?
THAT'S THE GUY'S NICKNAME.
IF YOU TRY TO SURROUND HIM...
HE SENDS EVERYONE FLYING LIKE A TORNADO.
SHUDDER...
HEE HEE HEE HEE!
HEY! WHAT'RE YOU LAUGHIN' AT?!
WHAM
SPILL YOUR GUTS, TWERP!

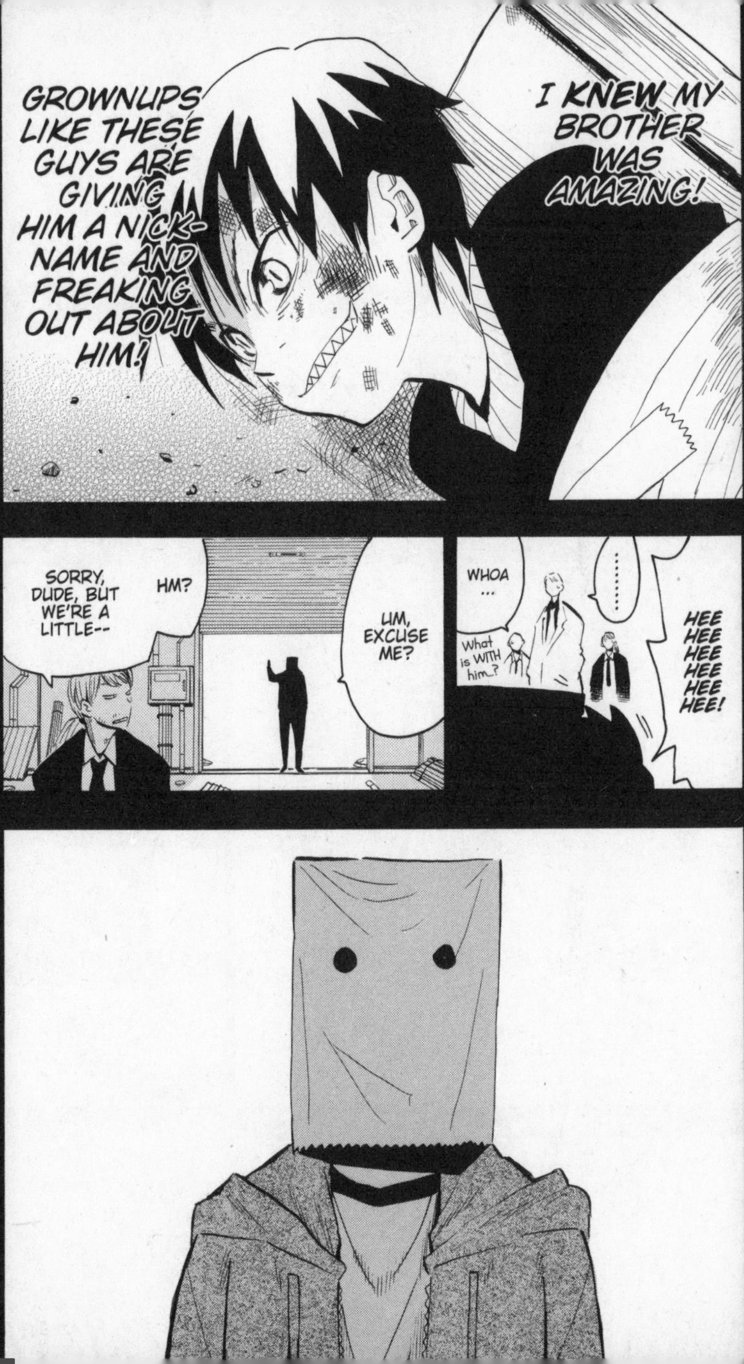
I KNEW MY BROTHER WAS AMAZING!
GROWNUPS LIKE THESE GUYS ARE GIVING HIM A NICK-NAME AND FREAKING OUT ABOUT HIM!
......
HEE HEE HEE HEE HEE HEE!
WHOA ...
What is WITH him...?
UM, EXCUSE ME?
HM?
SORRY, DUDE, BUT WE'RE A LITTLE--

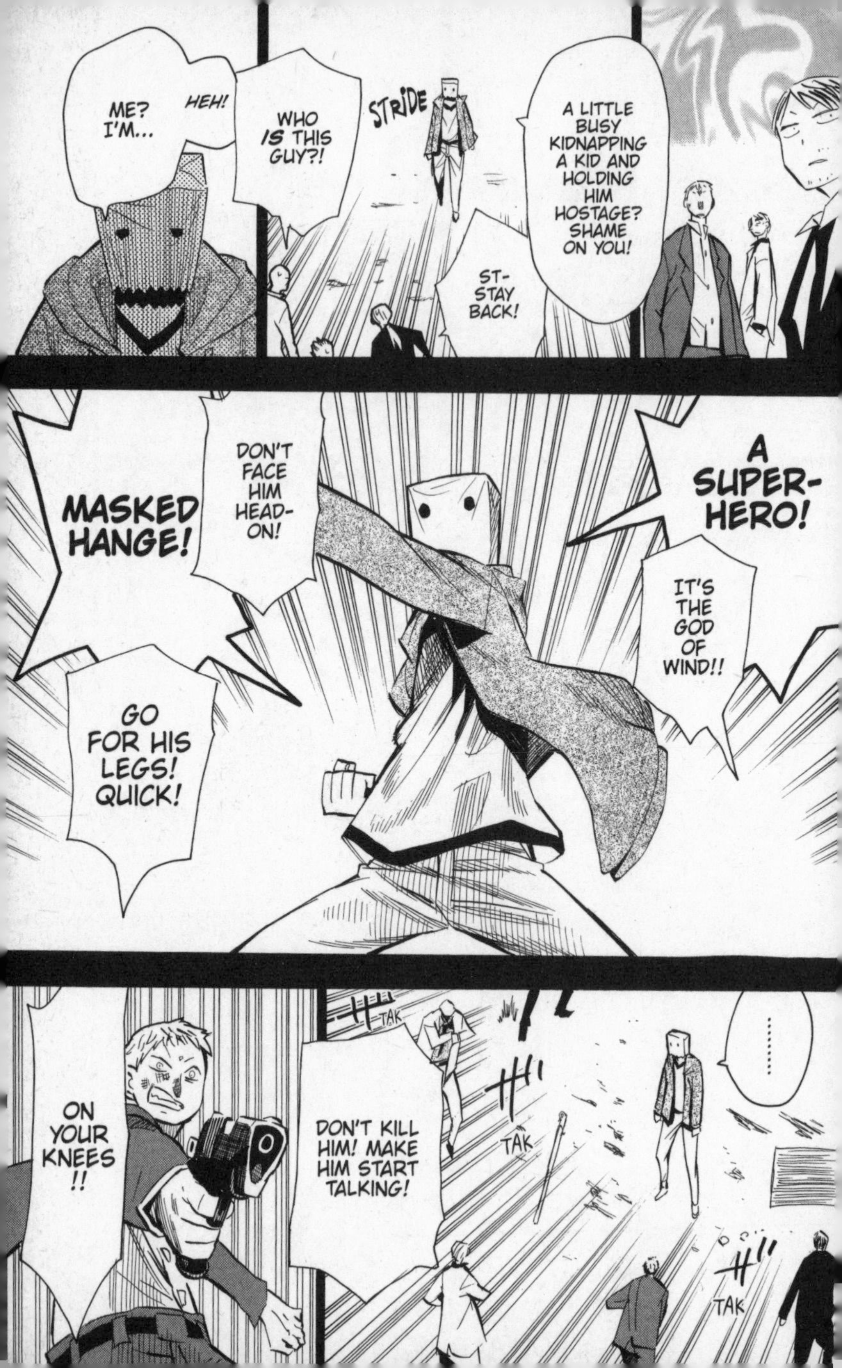
A LITTLE BUSY KIDNAPPING A KID AND HOLDING HIM HOSTAGE? SHAME ON YOU!
STRIDE
WHO IS THIS GUY?!
ST- STAY BACK!
HEH!
ME? I'M...
A SUPER-HERO!
IT'S THE GOD OF WIND!!
DON'T FACE HIM HEAD-ON!
MASKED HANGE!
GO FOR HIS LEGS! QUICK!
......
TAK
TAK
TAK
DON'T KILL HIM! MAKE HIM START TALKING!
ON YOUR KNEES!!

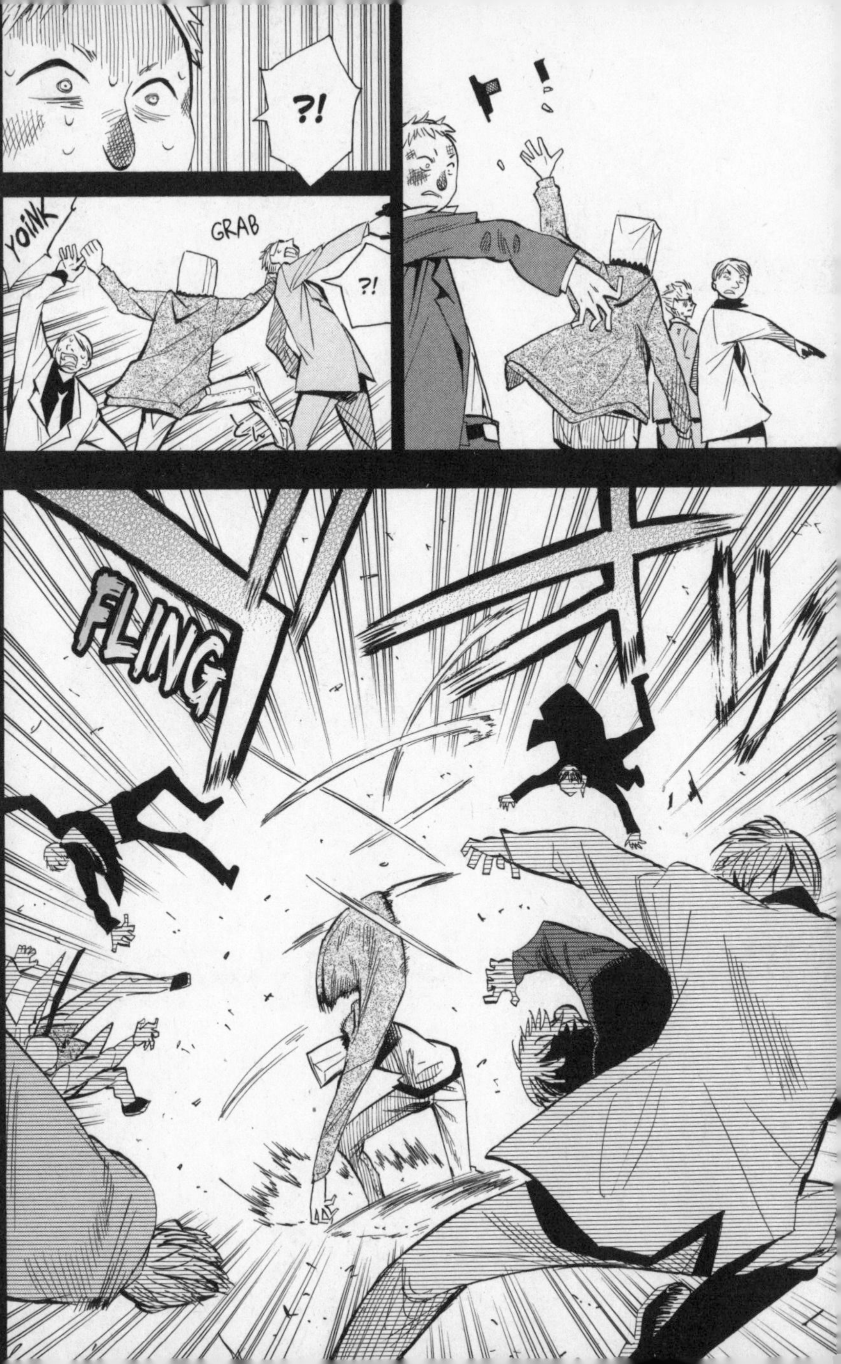
?!
?!
GRAB
YOINK
FLING

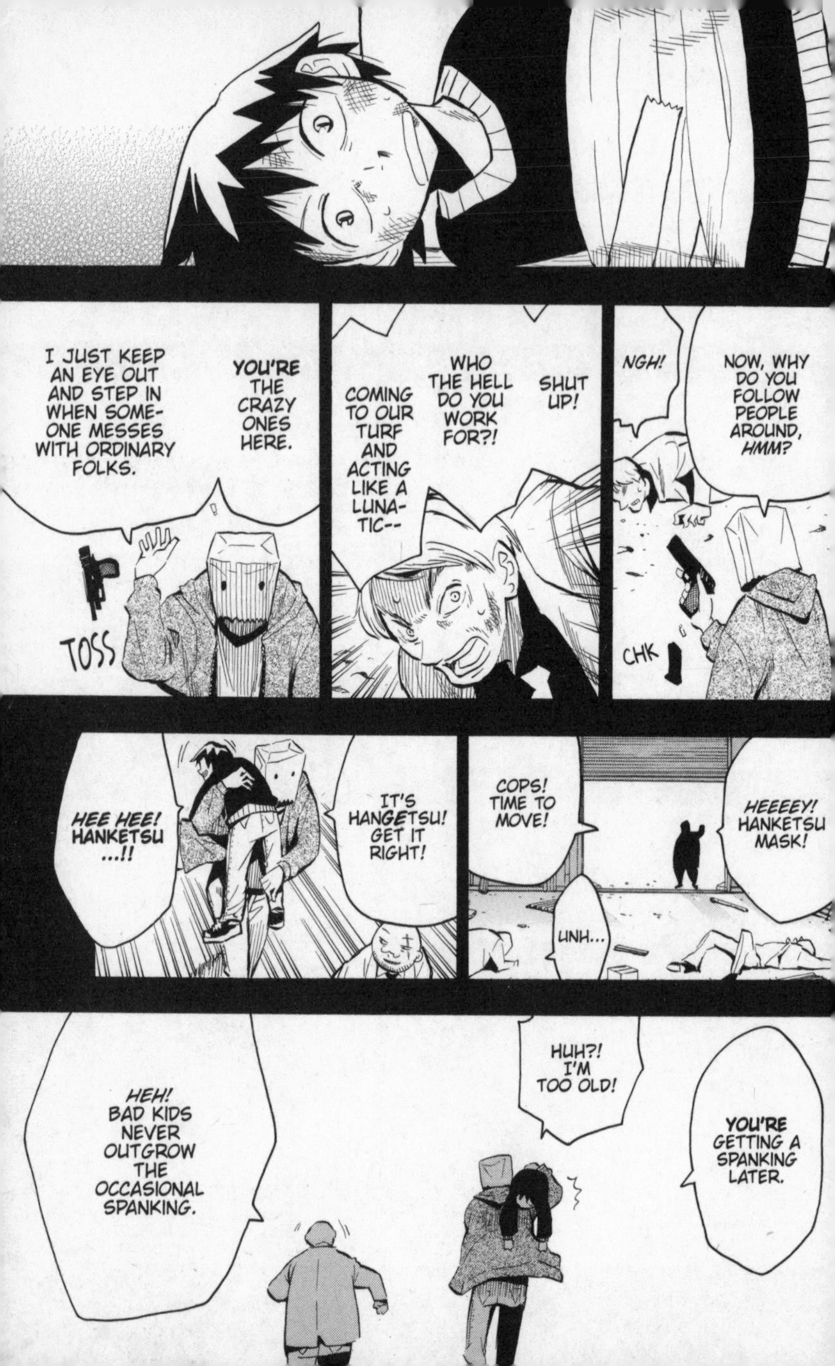
NOW, WHY DO YOU FOLLOW PEOPLE AROUND, HMM?
NGH!
CHK
SHUT UP!
WHO THE HELL DO YOU WORK FOR?!
COMING TO OUR TURF AND ACTING LIKE A LUNATIC--
YOU'RE THE CRAZY ONES HERE.
I JUST KEEP AN EYE OUT AND STEP IN WHEN SOME-ONE MESSES WITH ORDINARY FOLKS.
!
TOSS
HEEEEY! HANKETSU MASK!
COPS! TIME TO MOVE!
UNH...
IT'S HANGETSU! GET IT RIGHT!
HEE HEE! HANKETSU ...!!
YOU'RE GETTING A SPANKING LATER.
HUH?! I'M TOO OLD!
HEH! BAD KIDS NEVER OUTGROW THE OCCASIONAL SPANKING.

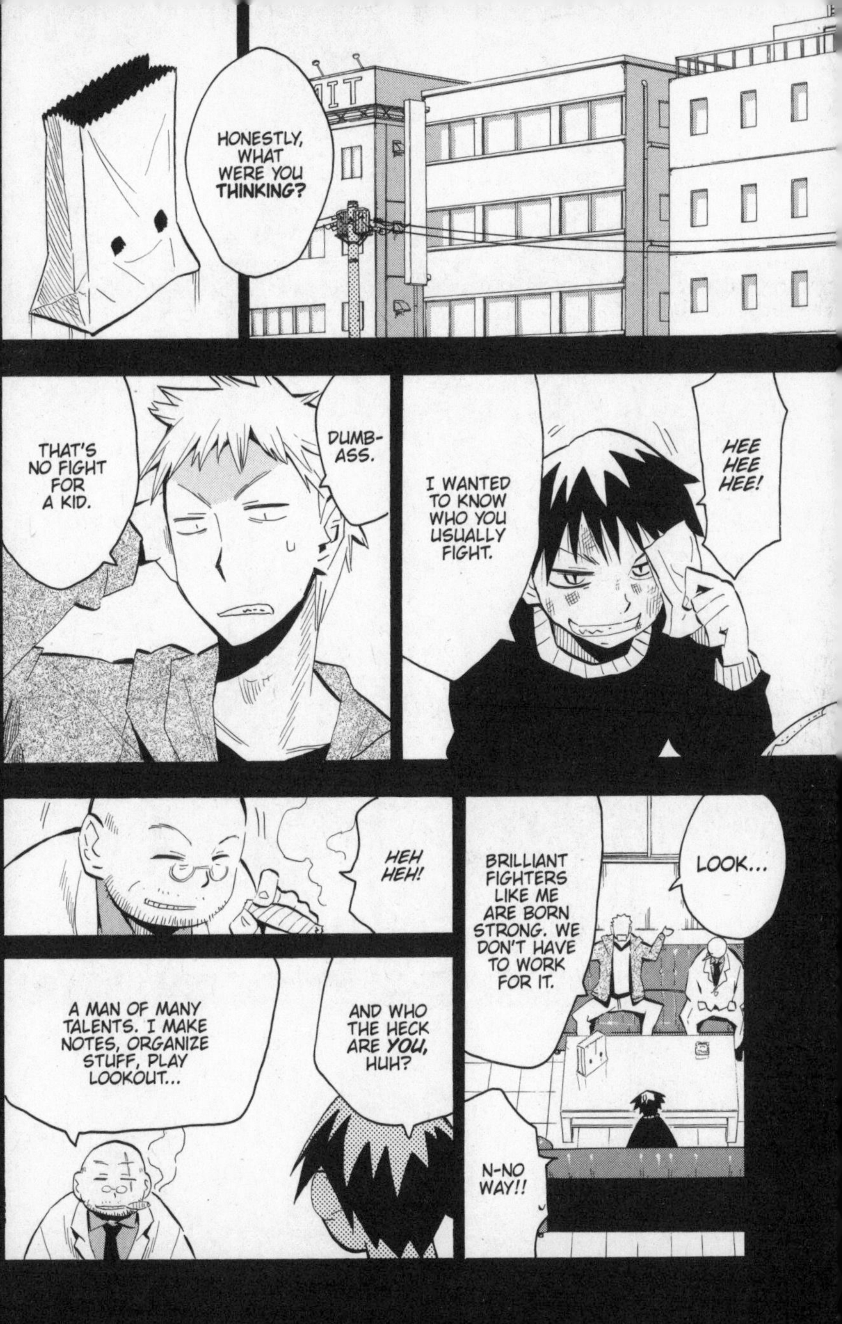
HONESTLY, WHAT WERE YOU THINKING?
HEE HEE HEE!
I WANTED TO KNOW WHO YOU USUALLY FIGHT.
DUMB-ASS.
THAT'S NO FIGHT FOR A KID.
LOOK...
BRILLIANT FIGHTERS LIKE ME ARE BORN STRONG. WE DON'T HAVE TO WORK FOR IT.
N-NO WAY!!
HEH HEH!
AND WHO THE HECK ARE YOU, HUH?
A MAN OF MANY TALENTS. I MAKE NOTES, ORGANIZE STUFF, PLAY LOOKOUT...

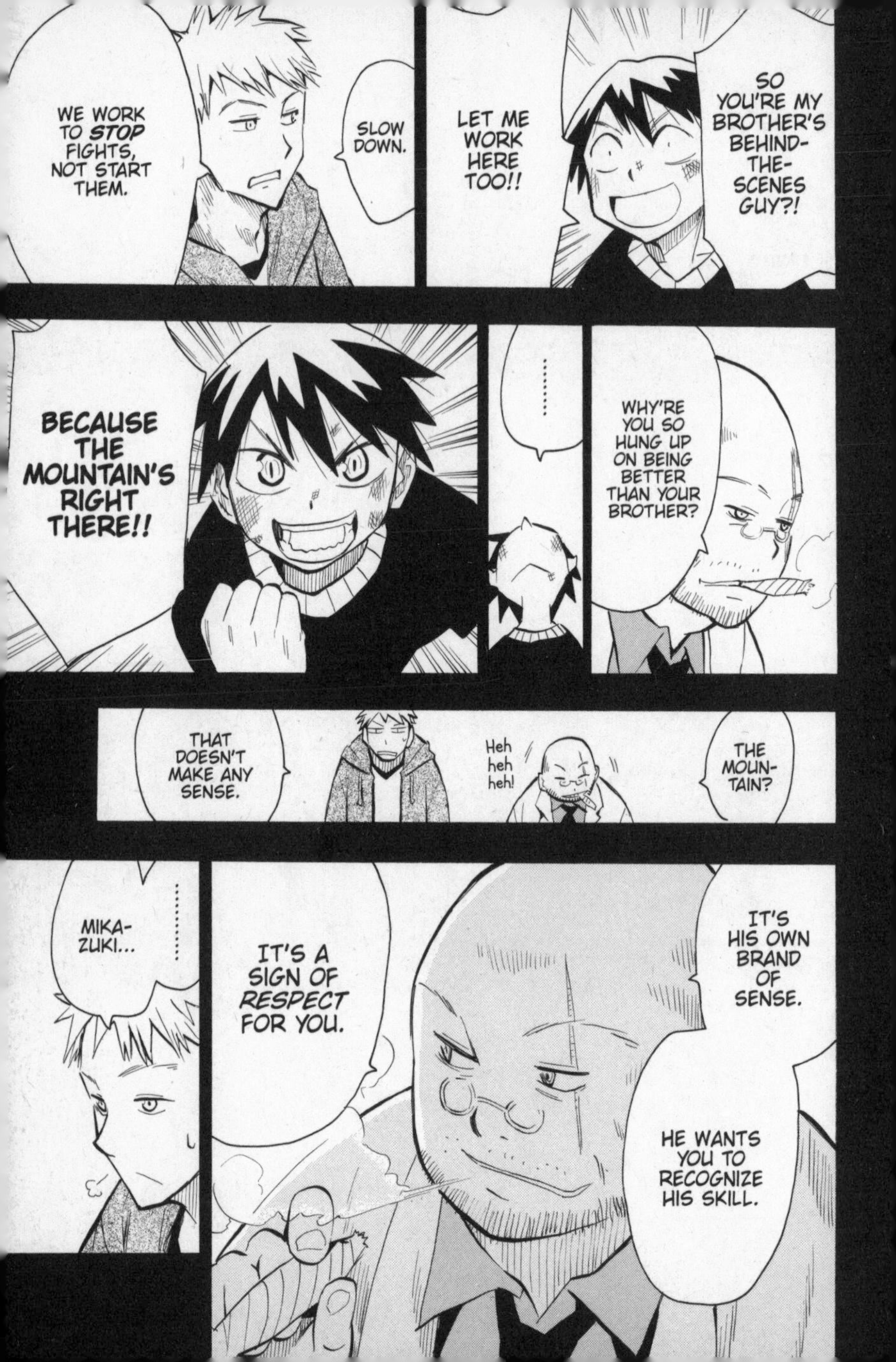
SO YOU'RE MY BROTHER'S BEHIND-THE-SCENES GUY?!
LET ME WORK HERE TOO!!
SLOW DOWN.
WE WORK TO *STOP* FIGHTS, NOT START THEM.
WHY'RE YOU SO HUNG UP ON BEING BETTER THAN YOUR BROTHER?
......
BECAUSE THE MOUNTAIN'S RIGHT THERE!!
THE MOUN-TAIN?
Heh heh heh!
THAT DOESN'T MAKE ANY SENSE.
IT'S HIS OWN BRAND OF SENSE.
HE WANTS YOU TO RECOGNIZE HIS SKILL.
IT'S A SIGN OF *RESPECT* FOR YOU.
......
MIKA-ZUKI...

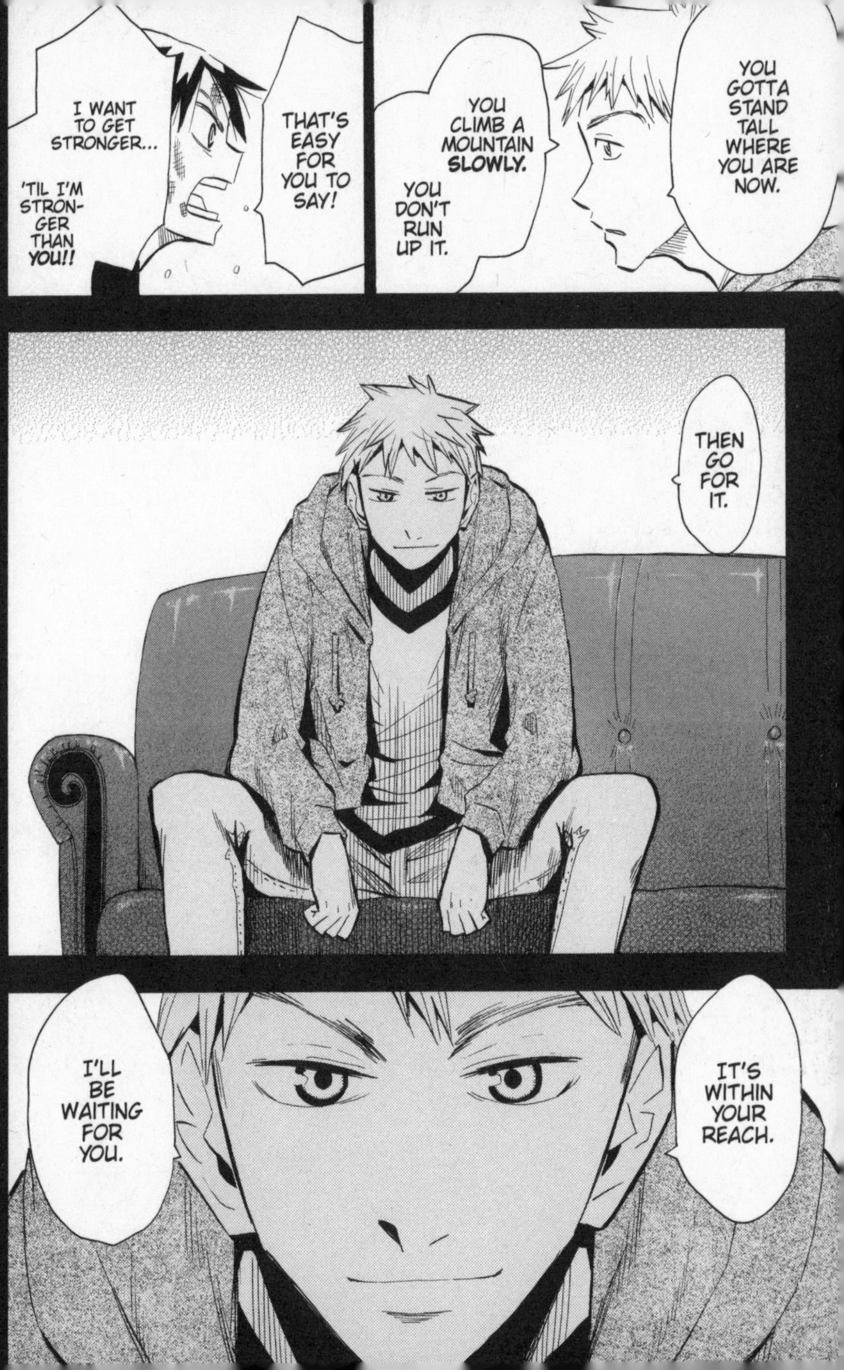
YOU GOTTA STAND TALL WHERE YOU ARE NOW.
YOU CLIMB A MOUNTAIN **SLOWLY.**
YOU DON'T RUN UP IT.
THAT'S EASY FOR YOU TO SAY!
I WANT TO GET STRONGER...
'TIL I'M STRONGER THAN *YOU!!*
THEN GO FOR IT.
IT'S WITHIN YOUR REACH.
I'LL BE WAITING FOR YOU.

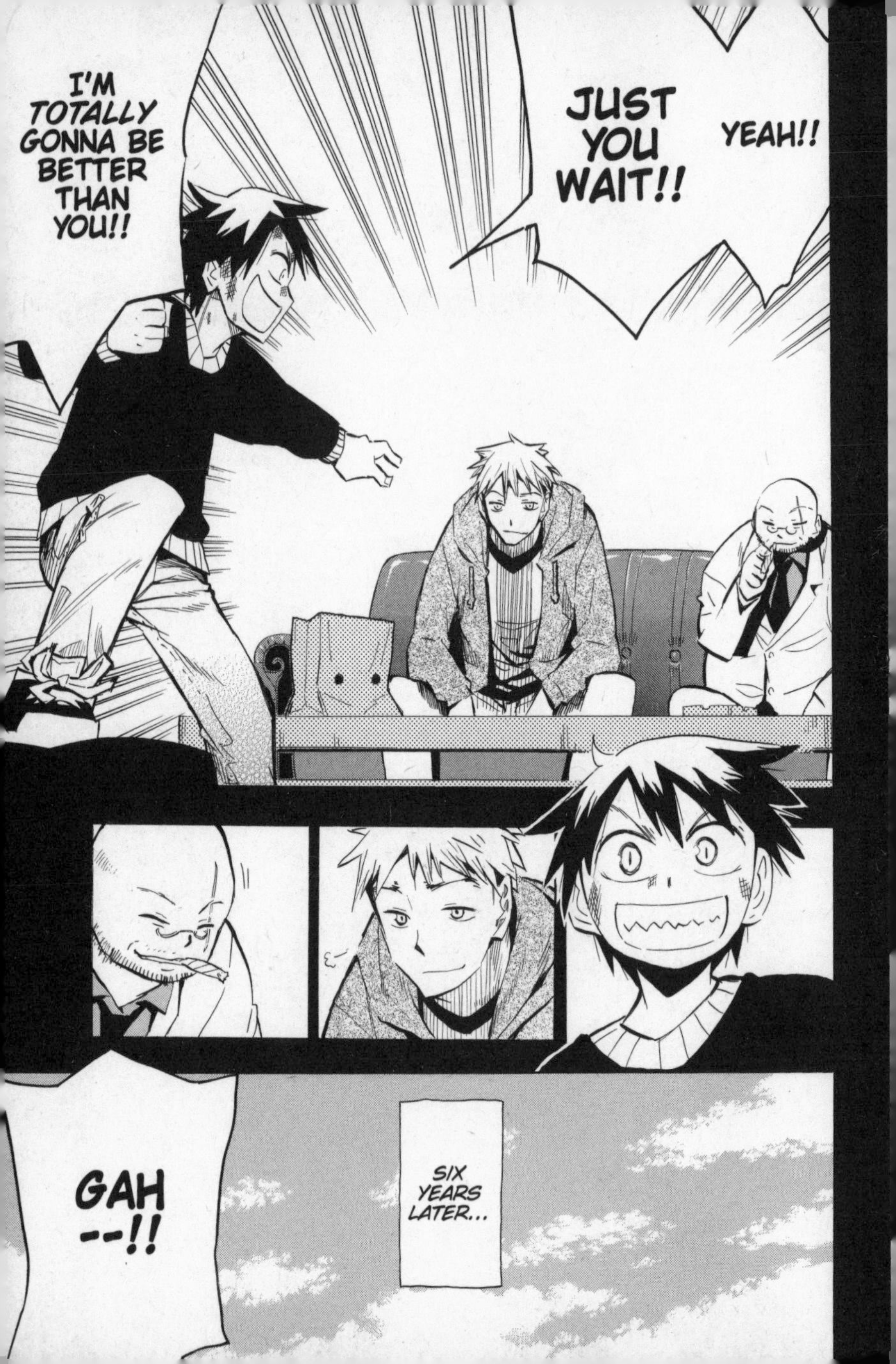
YEAH!!
JUST YOU WAIT!!
I'M TOTALLY GONNA BE BETTER THAN YOU!!
SIX YEARS LATER...
GAH --!!

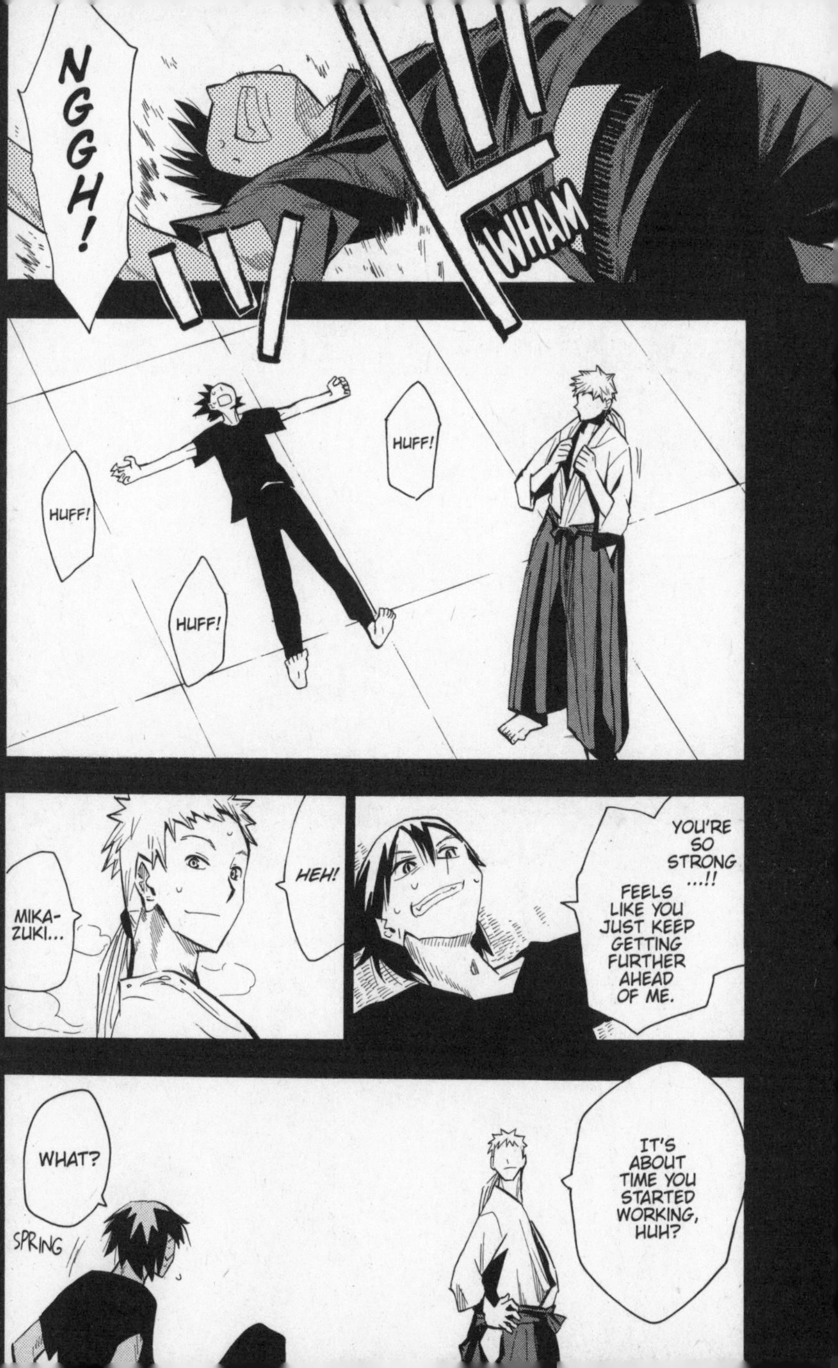
WHAM
NGGH!
HUFF!
HUFF!
HUFF!
YOU'RE SO STRONG ...!!
FEELS LIKE YOU JUST KEEP GETTING FURTHER AHEAD OF ME.
HEH!
MIKAZUKI...
IT'S ABOUT TIME YOU STARTED WORKING, HUH?
WHAT?
SPRING

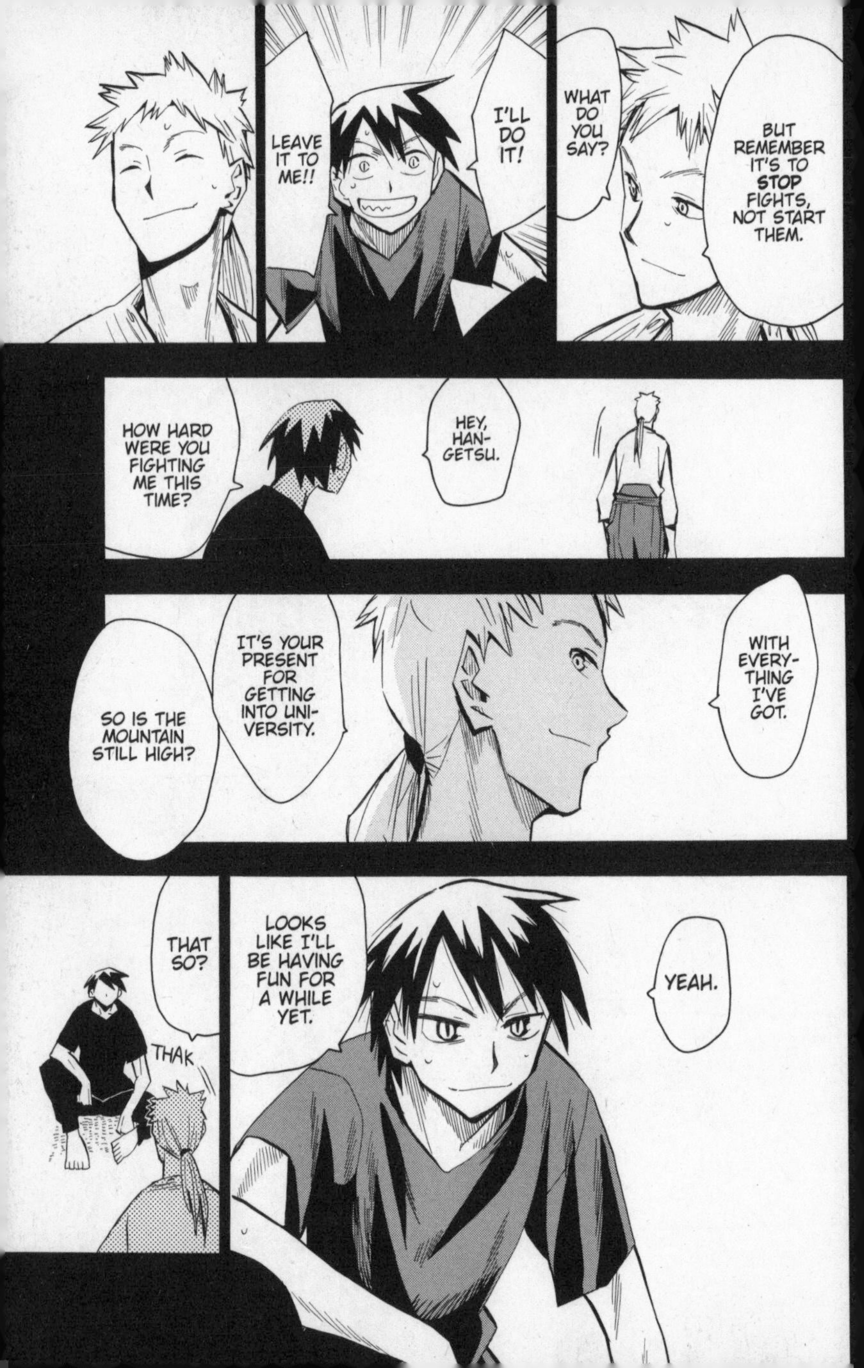
BUT REMEMBER IT'S TO STOP FIGHTS, NOT START THEM.
WHAT DO YOU SAY?
I'LL DO IT!
LEAVE IT TO ME!!
HEY, HAN-GETSU.
HOW HARD WERE YOU FIGHTING ME THIS TIME?
WITH EVERY-THING I'VE GOT.
IT'S YOUR PRESENT FOR GETTING INTO UNI-VERSITY.
SO IS THE MOUNTAIN STILL HIGH?
YEAH.
LOOKS LIKE I'LL BE HAVING FUN FOR A WHILE YET.
THAT SO?
THAK

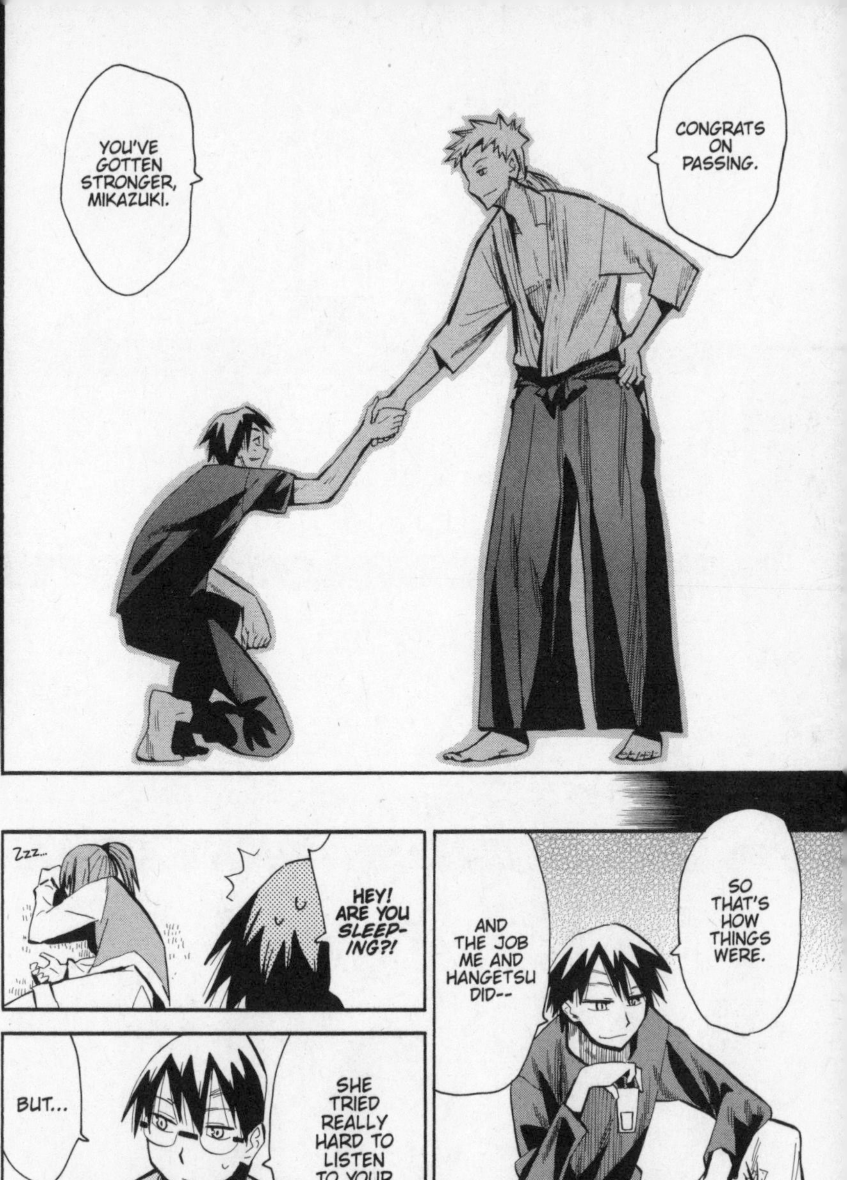
CONGRATS ON PASSING.
YOU'VE GOTTEN STRONGER, MIKAZUKI.
SO THAT'S HOW THINGS WERE.
AND THE JOB ME AND HANGETSU DID--
HEY! ARE YOU SLEEP-ING?!
Zzz...
SHE TRIED REALLY HARD TO LISTEN TO YOUR STORY...
BUT...

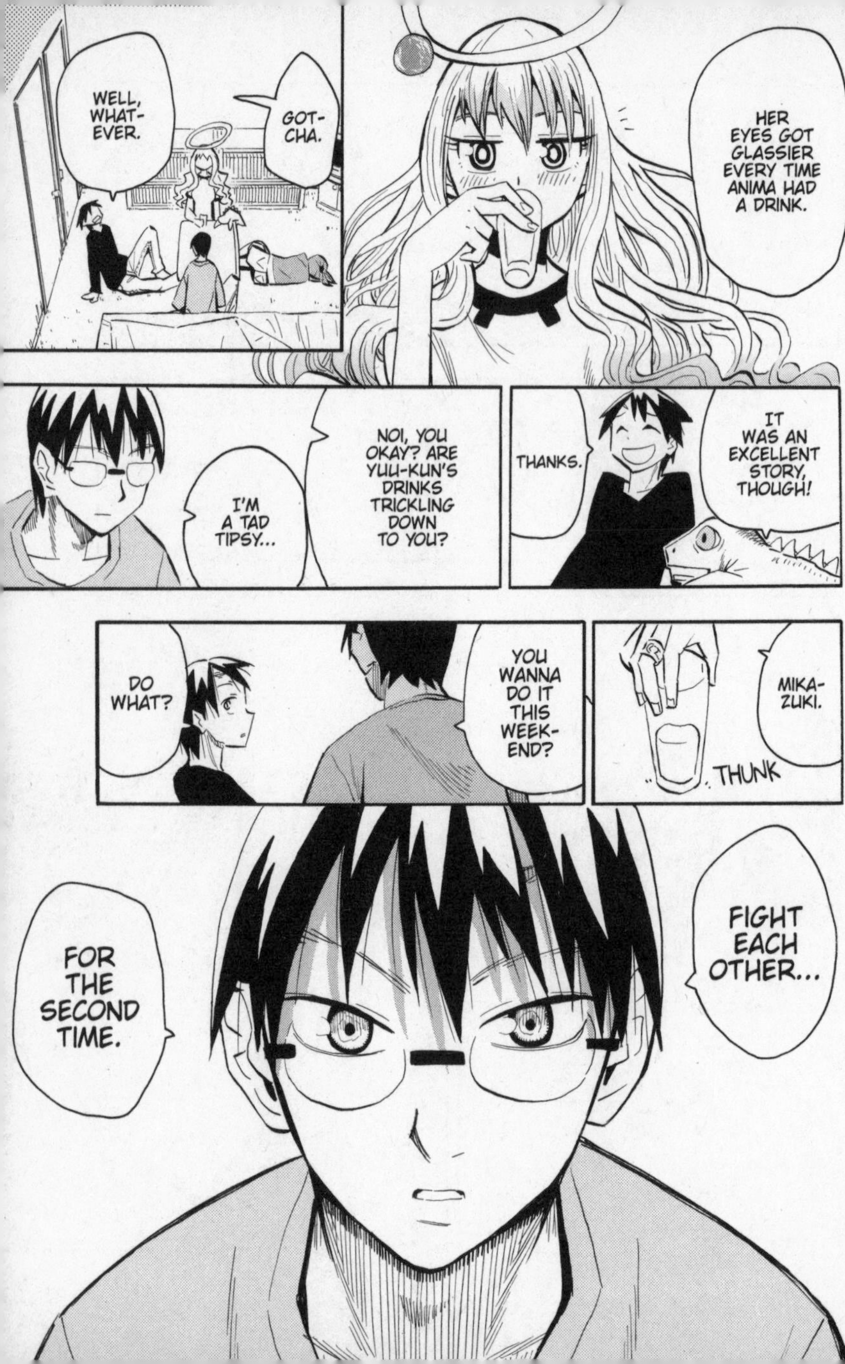
HER EYES GOT GLASSIER EVERY TIME ANIMA HAD A DRINK.
GOT-CHA.
WELL, WHAT-EVER.
IT WAS AN EXCELLENT STORY, THOUGH!
THANKS.
NOI, YOU OKAY? ARE YUU-KUN'S DRINKS TRICKLING DOWN TO YOU?
I'M A TAD TIPSY...
MIKA-ZUKI.
THUNK
YOU WANNA DO IT THIS WEEK-END?
DO WHAT?
FIGHT EACH OTHER...
FOR THE SECOND TIME.

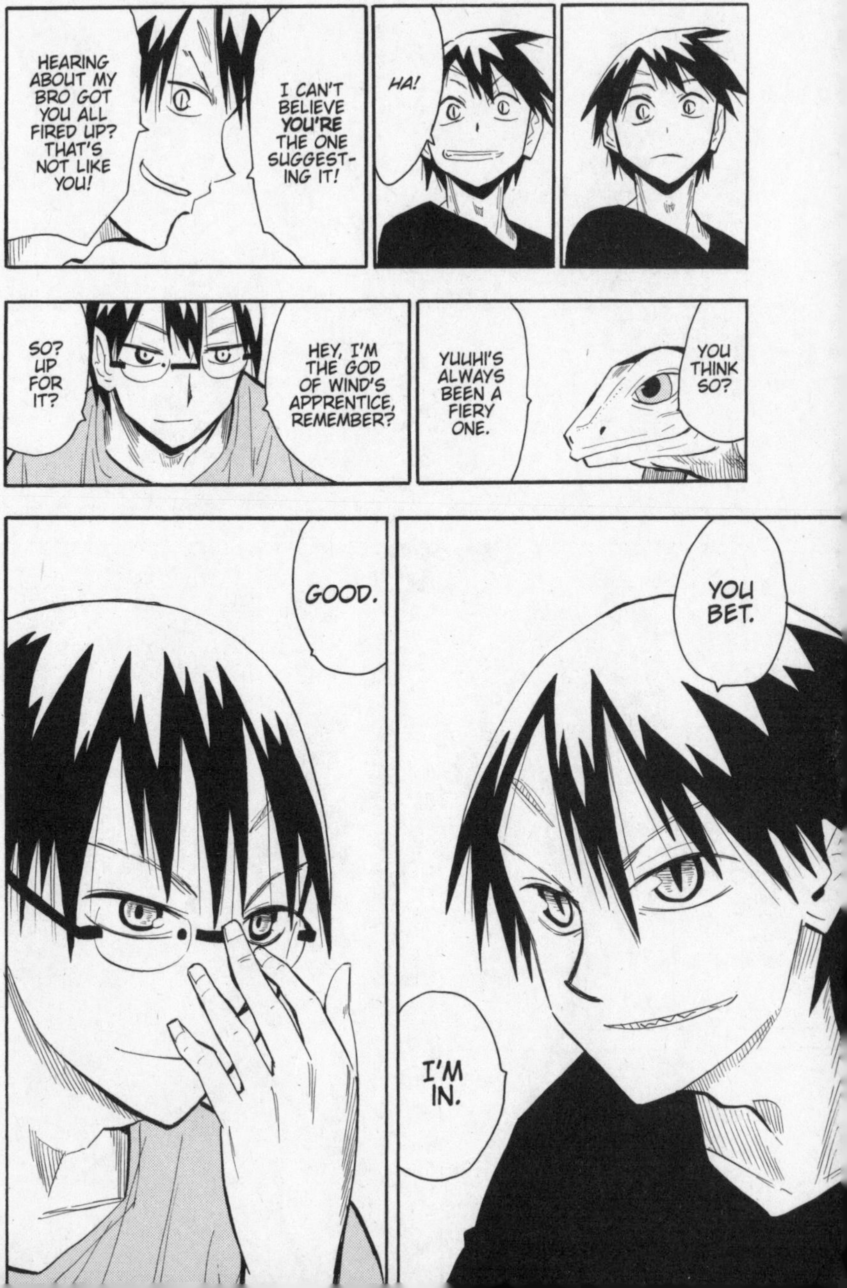
HA!
I CAN'T BELIEVE **YOU'RE** THE ONE SUGGEST-ING IT!
HEARING ABOUT MY BRO GOT YOU ALL FIRED UP? THAT'S NOT LIKE YOU!
YOU THINK SO?
YUUHI'S ALWAYS BEEN A FIERY ONE.
HEY, I'M THE GOD OF WIND'S APPRENTICE, REMEMBER?
SO? UP FOR IT?
YOU BET.
I'M IN.
GOOD.

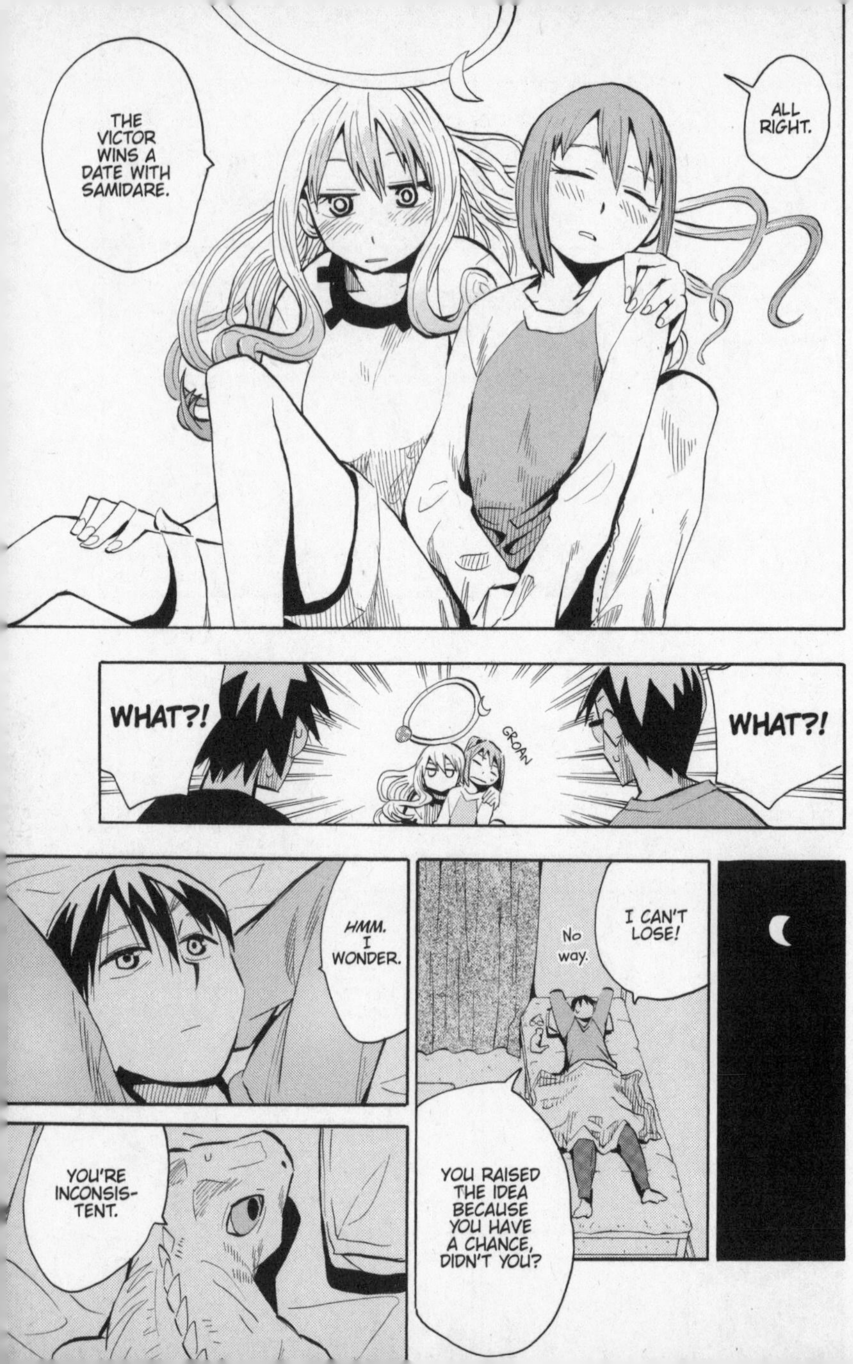
ALL RIGHT.
THE VICTOR WINS A DATE WITH SAMIDARE.
WHAT?!
GROAN
WHAT?!
I CAN'T LOSE!
No way.
YOU RAISED THE IDEA BECAUSE YOU HAVE A CHANCE, DIDN'T YOU?
HMM. I WONDER.
YOU'RE INCONSIS-TENT.

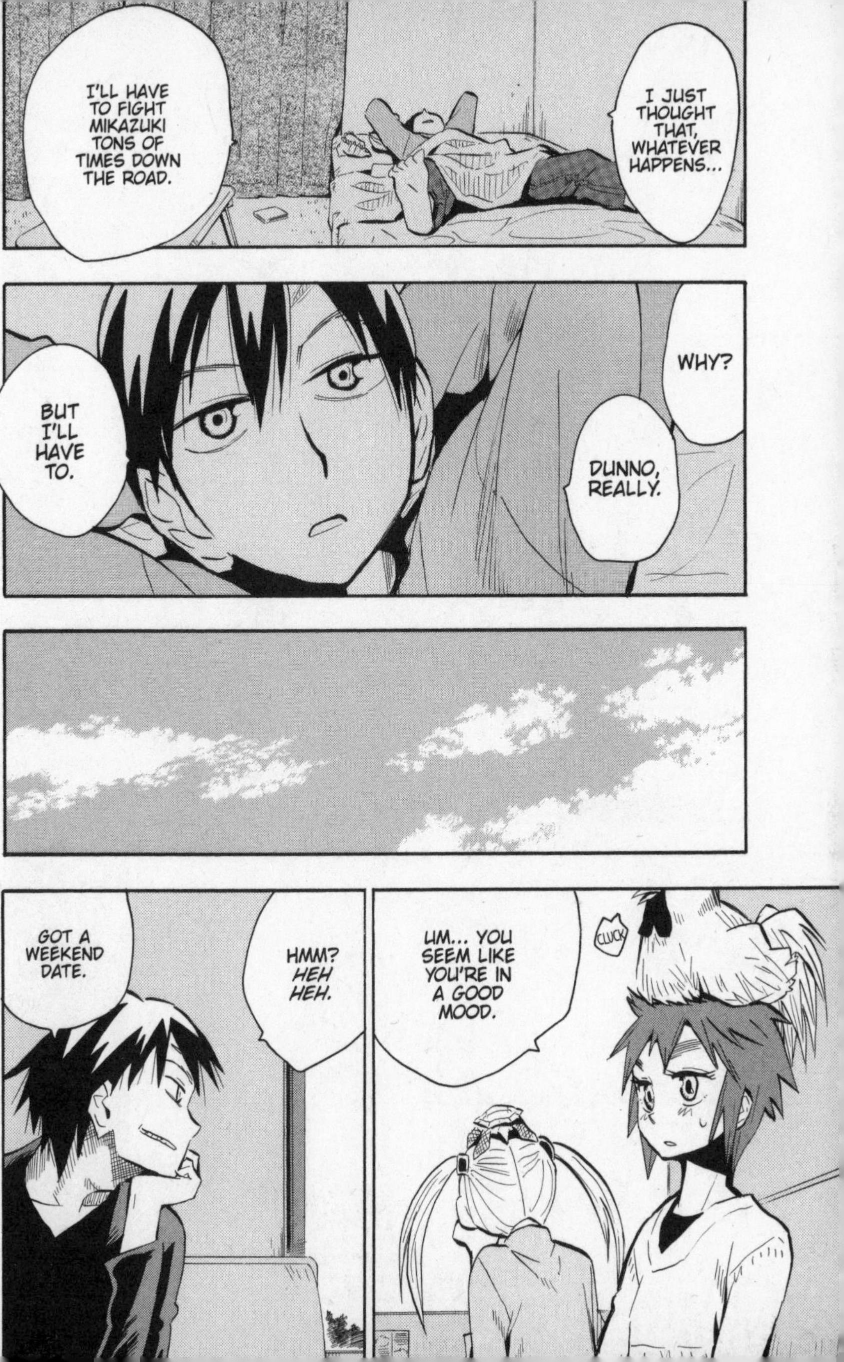
I JUST THOUGHT THAT, WHATEVER HAPPENS...
I'LL HAVE TO FIGHT MIKAZUKI TONS OF TIMES DOWN THE ROAD.
WHY?
DUNNO, REALLY.
BUT I'LL HAVE TO.
CLUCK
UM... YOU SEEM LIKE YOU'RE IN A GOOD MOOD.
HMM? *HEH HEH.*
GOT A WEEKEND DATE.

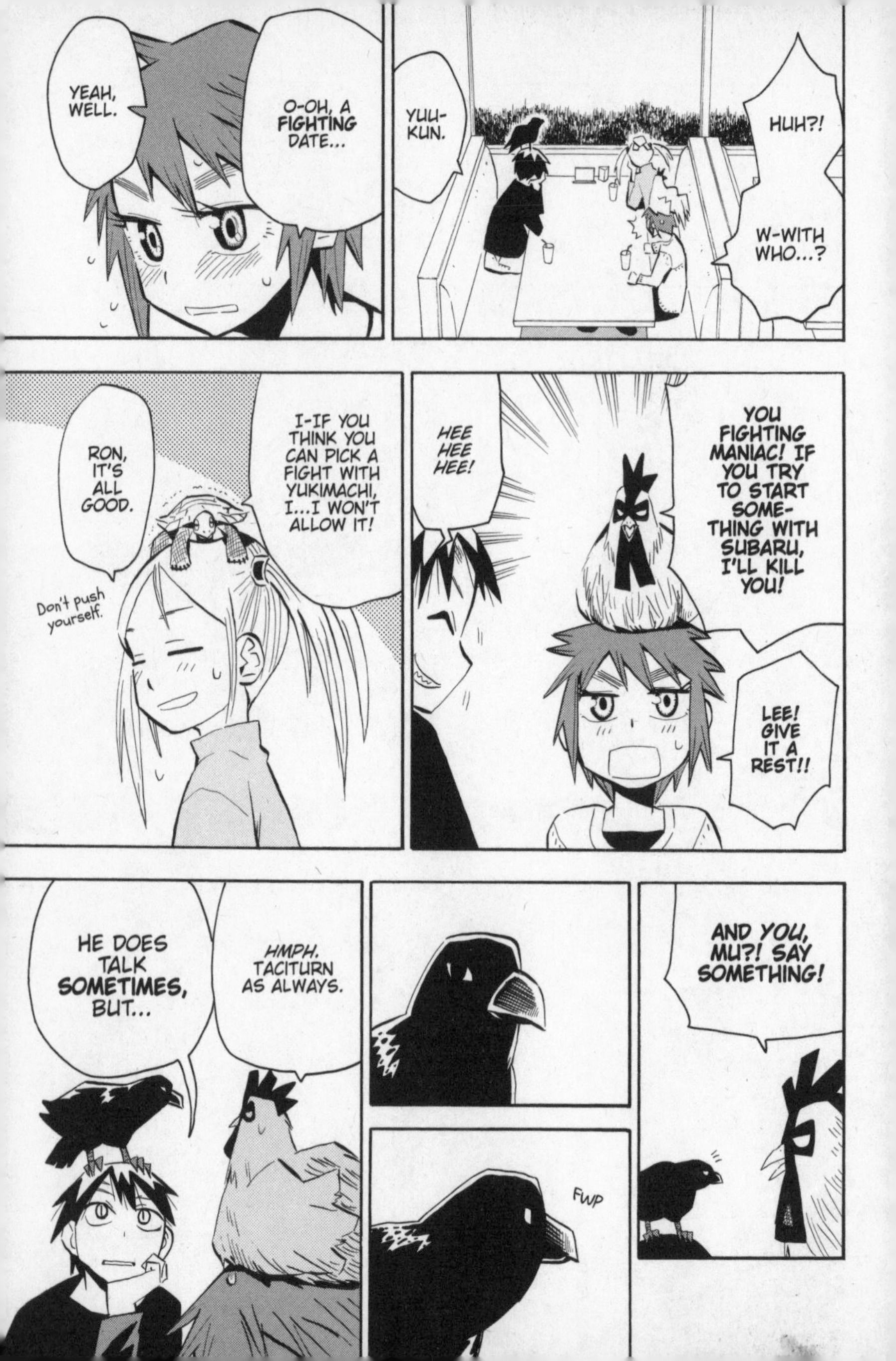
HUH?!
W-WITH WHO...?
YUU-KUN.
O-OH, A FIGHTING DATE...
YEAH, WELL.
YOU FIGHTING MANIAC! IF YOU TRY TO START SOME-THING WITH SUBARU, I'LL KILL YOU!
LEE! GIVE IT A REST!!
HEE HEE HEE!
I-IF YOU THINK YOU CAN PICK A FIGHT WITH YUKIMACHI, I...I WON'T ALLOW IT!
RON, IT'S ALL GOOD.
Don't push yourself.
AND YOU, MU?! SAY SOMETHING!
HMPH. TACITURN AS ALWAYS.
HE DOES TALK SOMETIMES, BUT...
FWP

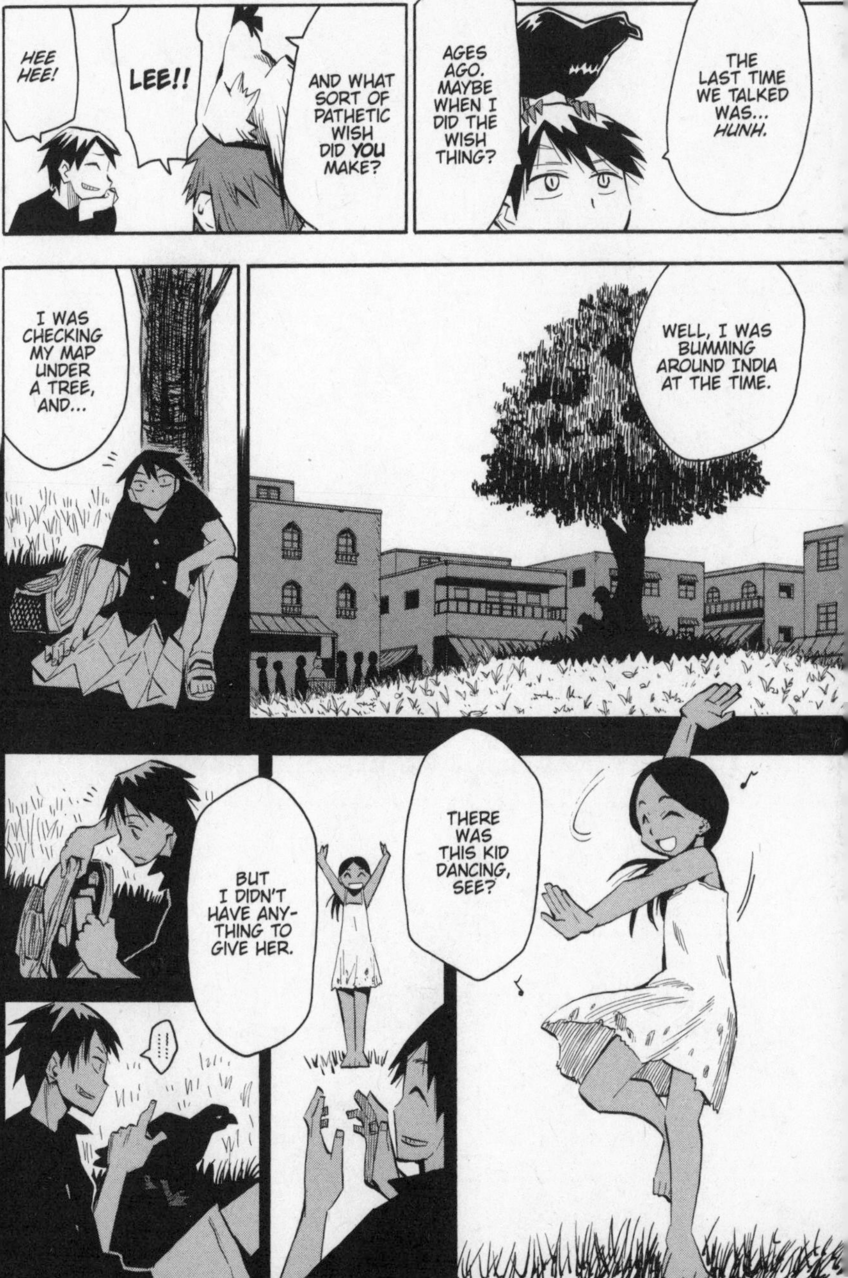
THE LAST TIME WE TALKED WAS... HUNH.
AGES AGO. MAYBE WHEN I DID THE WISH THING?
AND WHAT SORT OF PATHETIC WISH DID YOU MAKE?
LEE!!
HEE HEE!
WELL, I WAS BUMMING AROUND INDIA AT THE TIME.
I WAS CHECKING MY MAP UNDER A TREE, AND...
THERE WAS THIS KID DANCING, SEE?
BUT I DIDN'T HAVE ANYTHING TO GIVE HER.

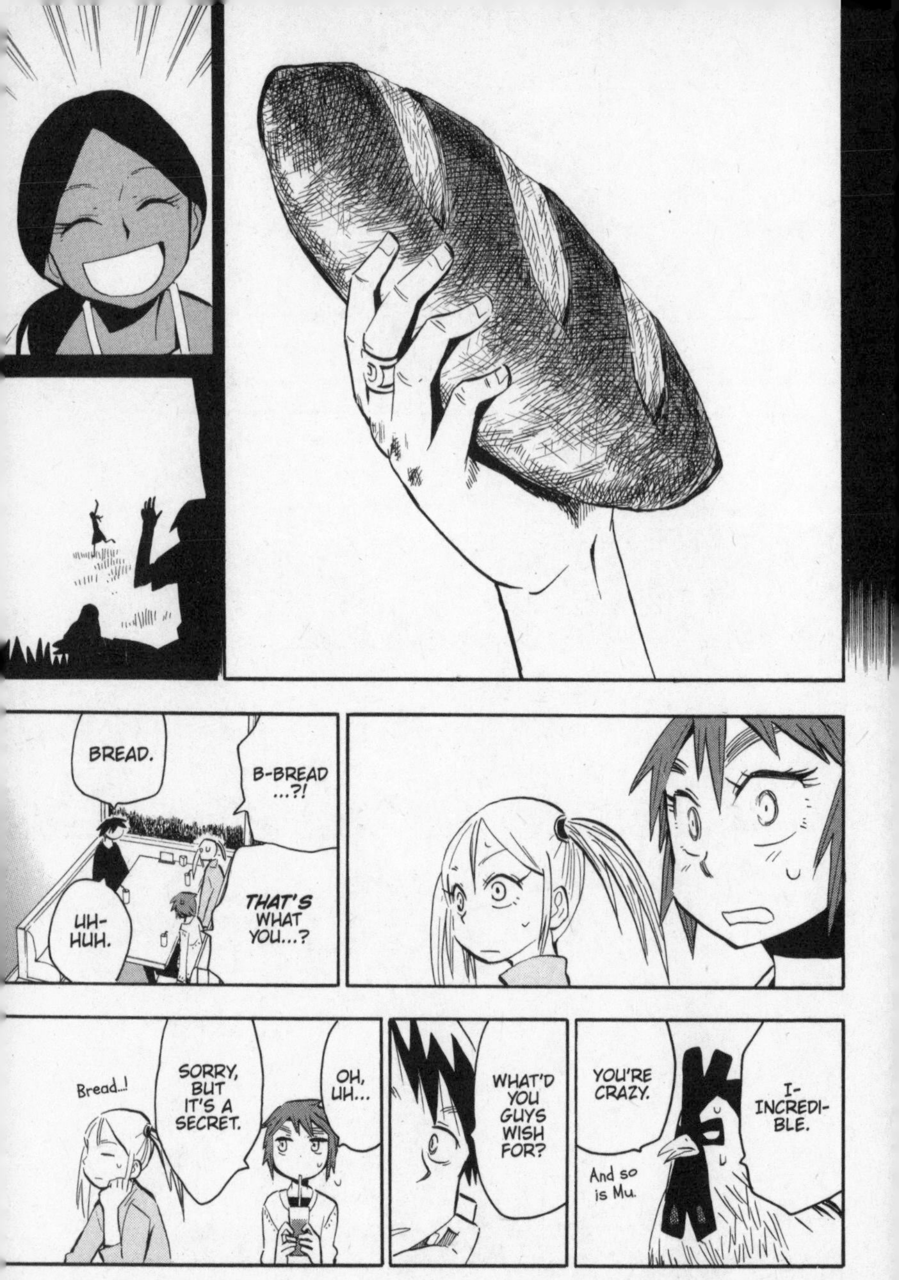
BREAD.
B-BREAD ...?!
THAT'S WHAT YOU...?
UH-HUH.
I-INCREDIBLE.
YOU'RE CRAZY.
And so is Mu.
WHAT'D YOU GUYS WISH FOR?
OH, UH...
SORRY, BUT IT'S A SECRET.
Bread...!

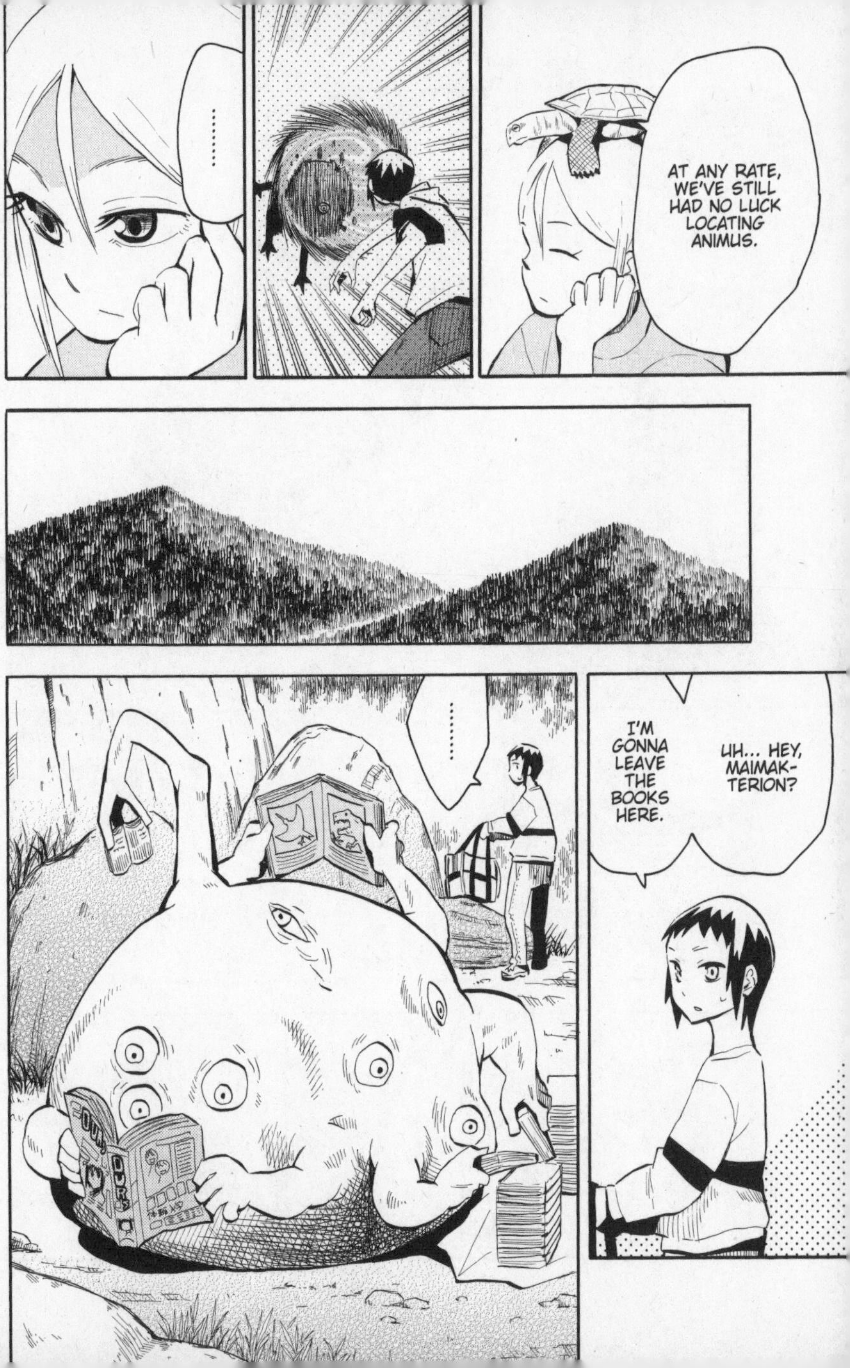
AT ANY RATE, WE'VE STILL HAD NO LUCK LOCATING ANIMUS.
......
UH... HEY, MAIMAK-TERION?
I'M GONNA LEAVE THE BOOKS HERE.
......

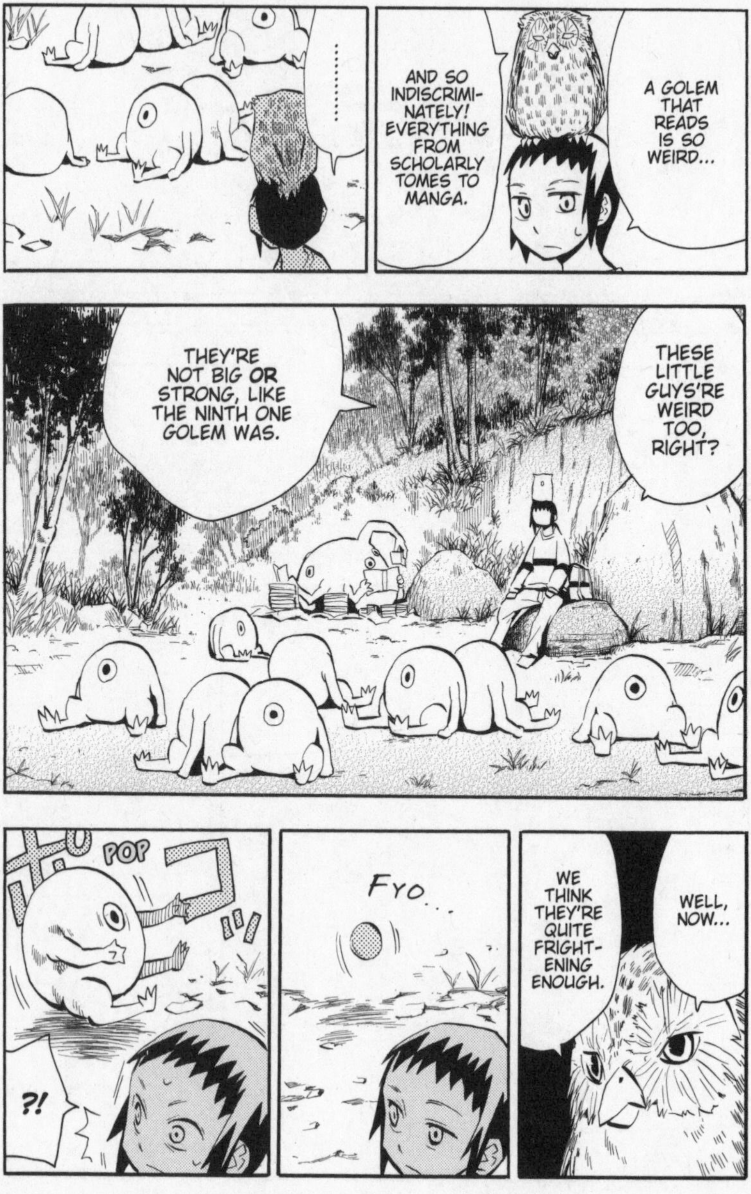
A GOLEM THAT READS IS SO WEIRD...
AND SO INDISCRIMINATELY! EVERYTHING FROM SCHOLARLY TOMES TO MANGA.
......
THESE LITTLE GUYS'RE WEIRD TOO, RIGHT?
THEY'RE NOT BIG OR STRONG, LIKE THE NINTH ONE GOLEM WAS.
WELL, NOW...
WE THINK THEY'RE QUITE FRIGHTENING ENOUGH.
FYO...
POP
?!

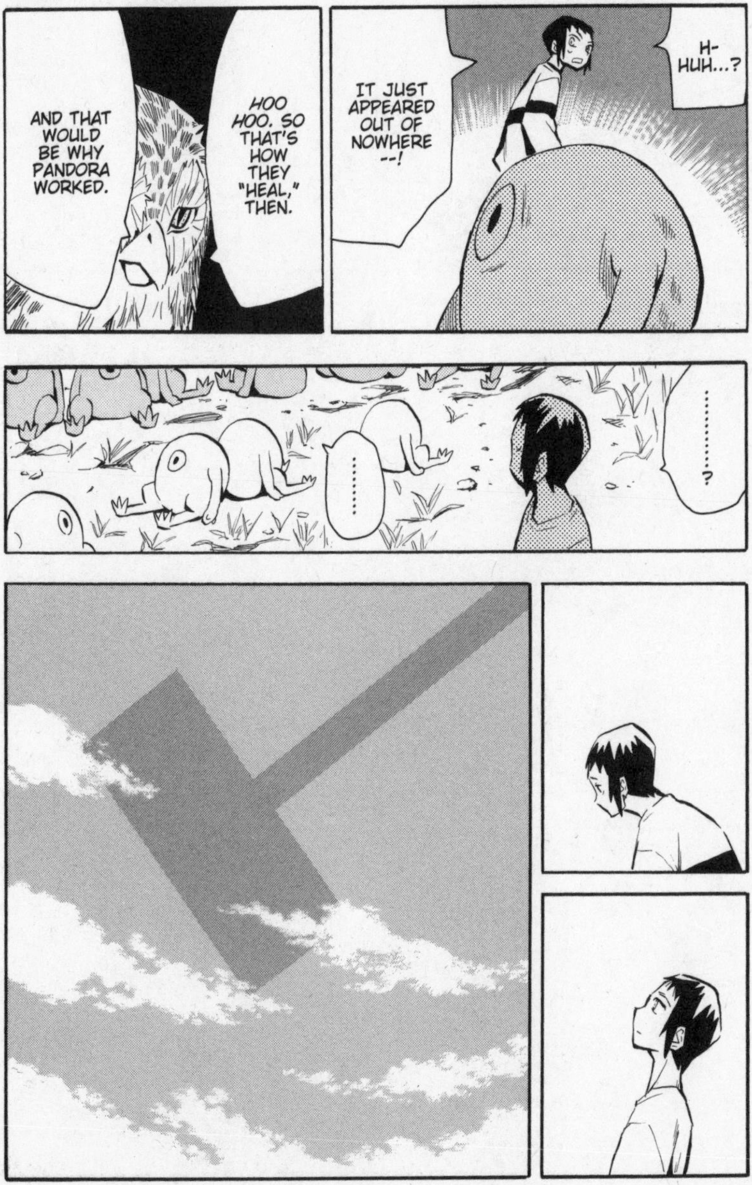
H-HUH...?
IT JUST APPEARED OUT OF NOWHERE--!
HOO HOO. SO THAT'S HOW THEY "HEAL," THEN.
AND THAT WOULD BE WHY PANDORA WORKED.
..........?
....

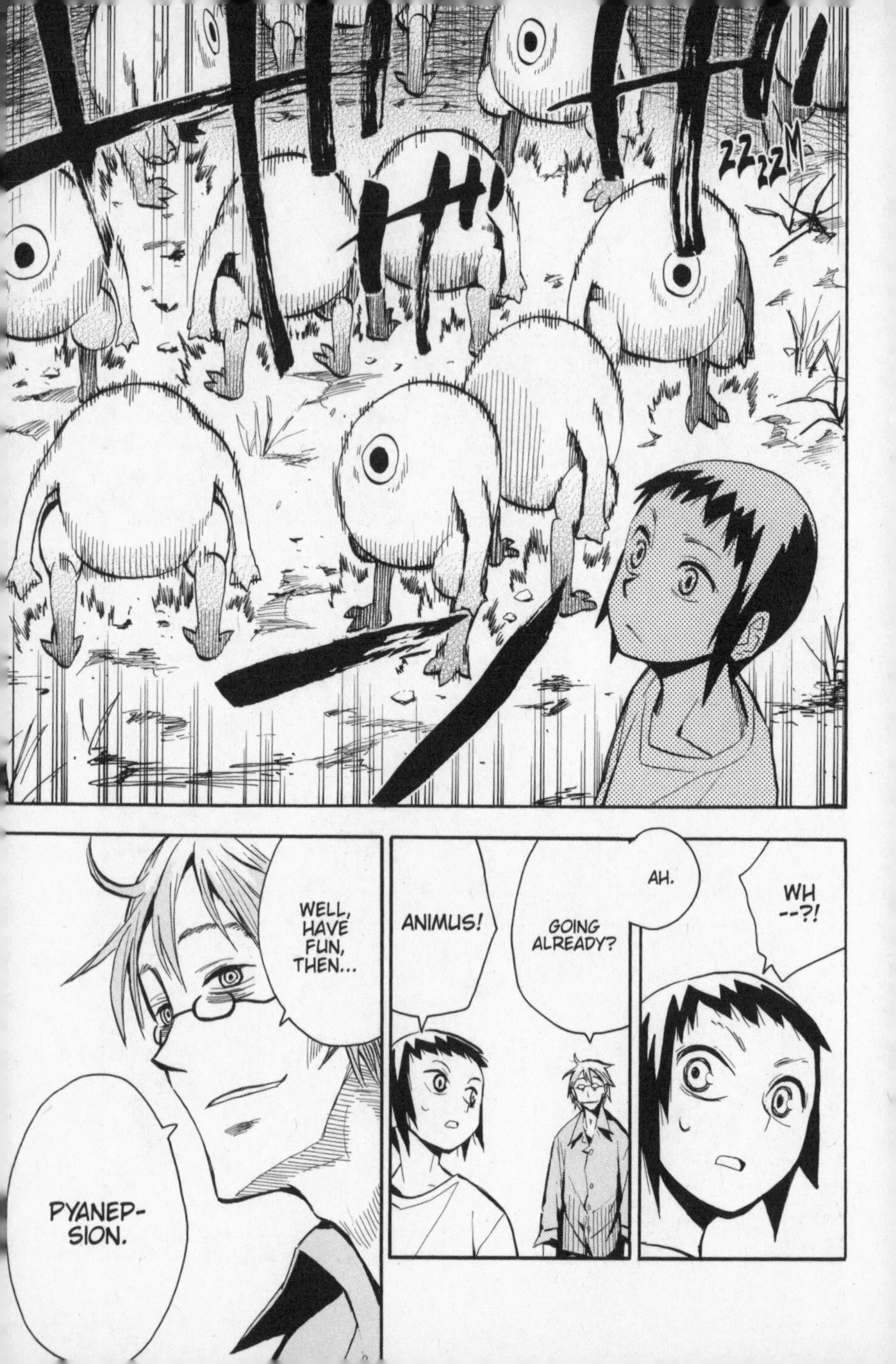
ZZZZM
WH --?!
AH.
GOING ALREADY?
ANIMUS!
WELL, HAVE FUN, THEN...
PYANEP-SION.

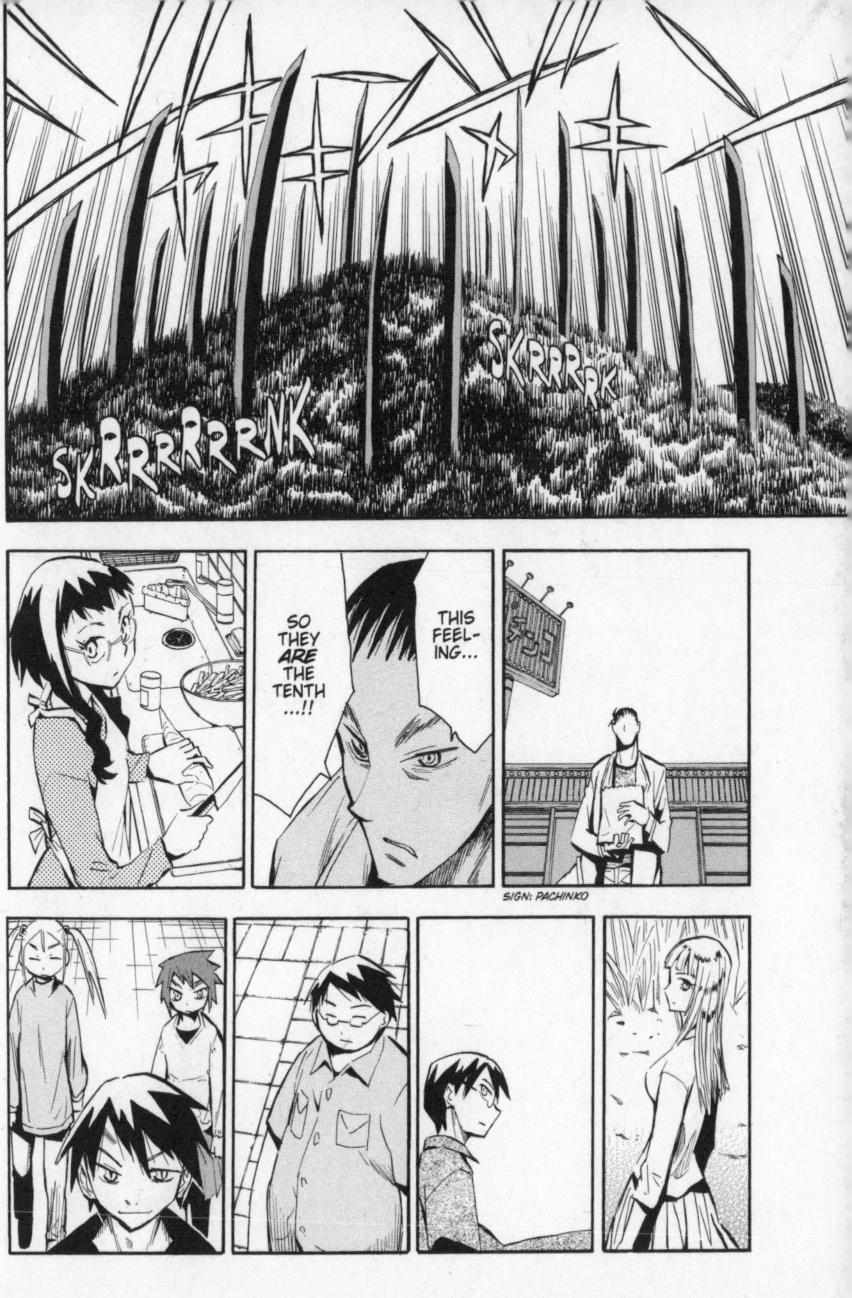
SKRRRRK
SKRRRRRRNK
THIS FEEL-ING...
SO THEY *ARE* THE TENTH ...!!
SIGN: PACHINKO

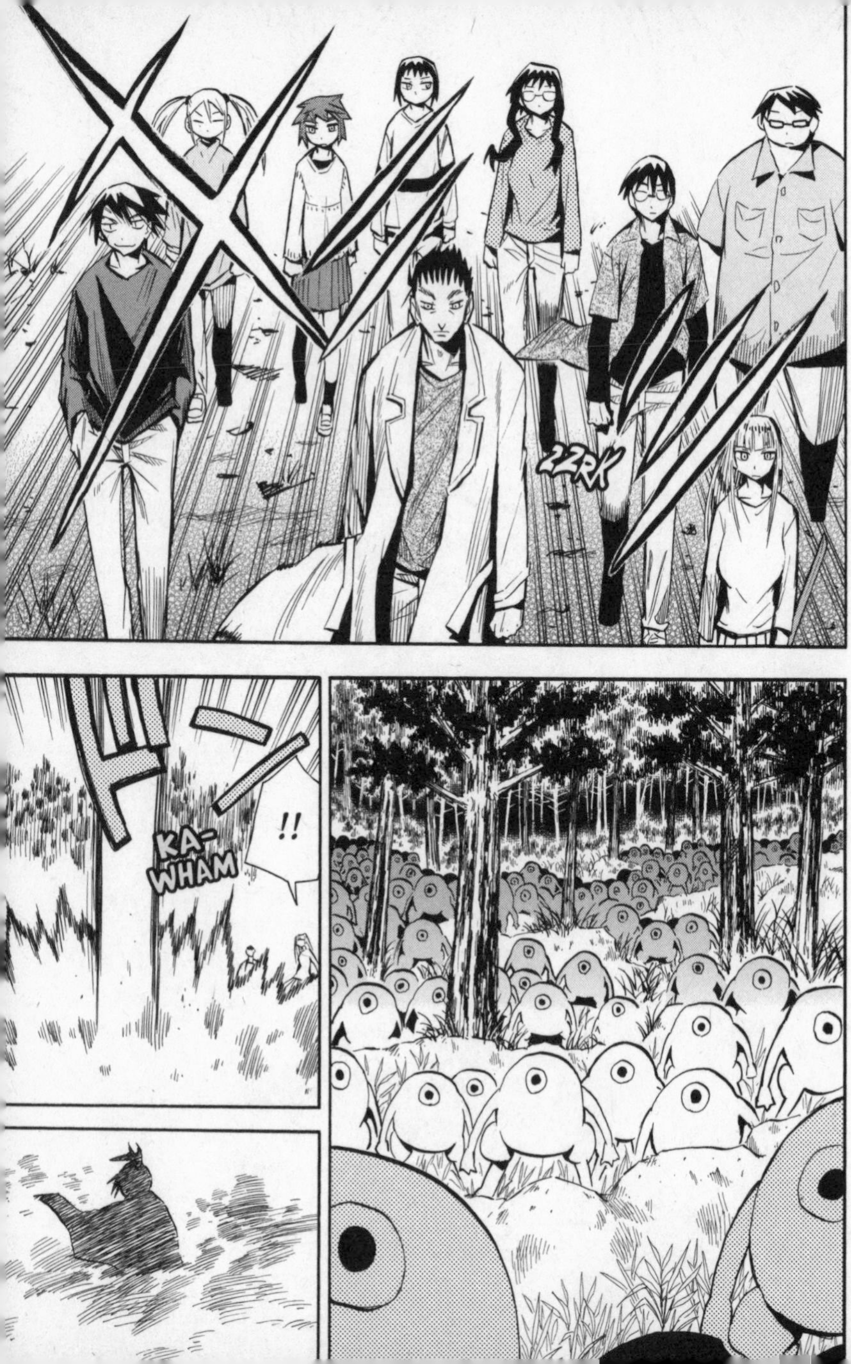
ZZRK
!!
KA-WHAM

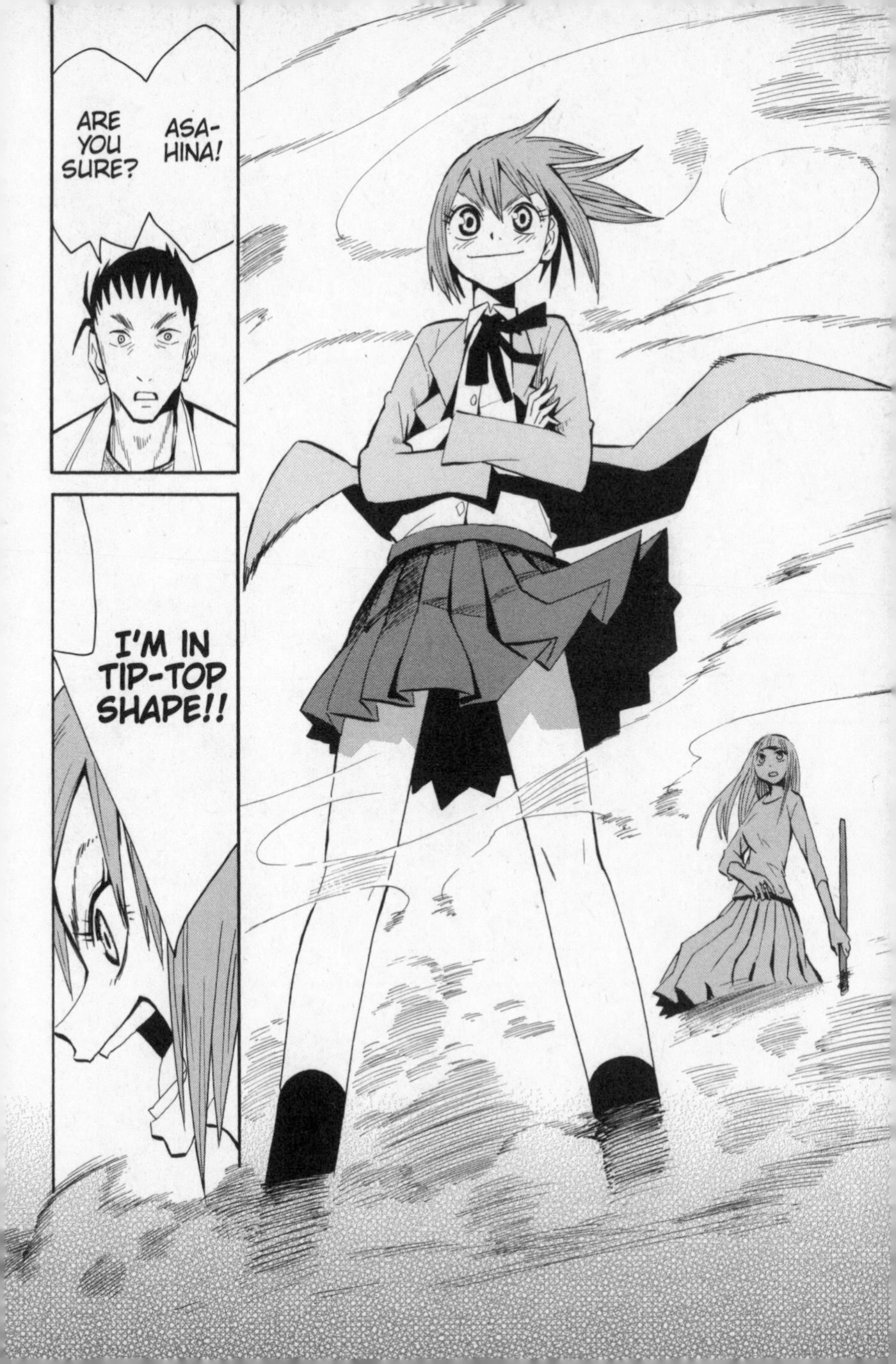
ASA-HINA!
ARE YOU SURE?
I'M IN TIP-TOP SHAPE!!

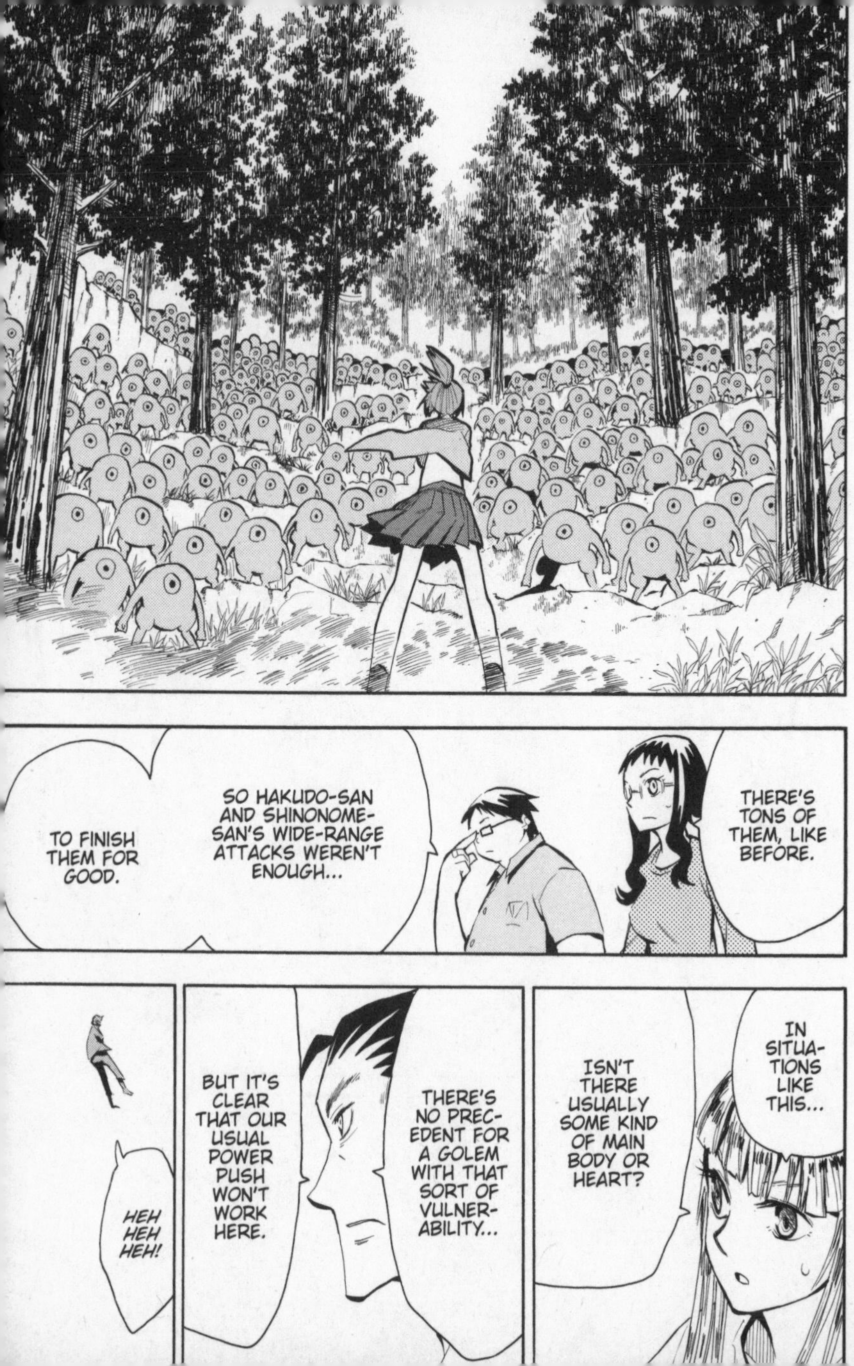
THERE'S TONS OF THEM, LIKE BEFORE.
SO HAKUDO-SAN AND SHINONOME-SAN'S WIDE-RANGE ATTACKS WEREN'T ENOUGH...
TO FINISH THEM FOR GOOD.
IN SITUATIONS LIKE THIS...
ISN'T THERE USUALLY SOME KIND OF MAIN BODY OR HEART?
THERE'S NO PRECEDENT FOR A GOLEM WITH THAT SORT OF VULNERABILITY...
BUT IT'S CLEAR THAT OUR USUAL POWER PUSH WON'T WORK HERE.
HEH HEH HEH!

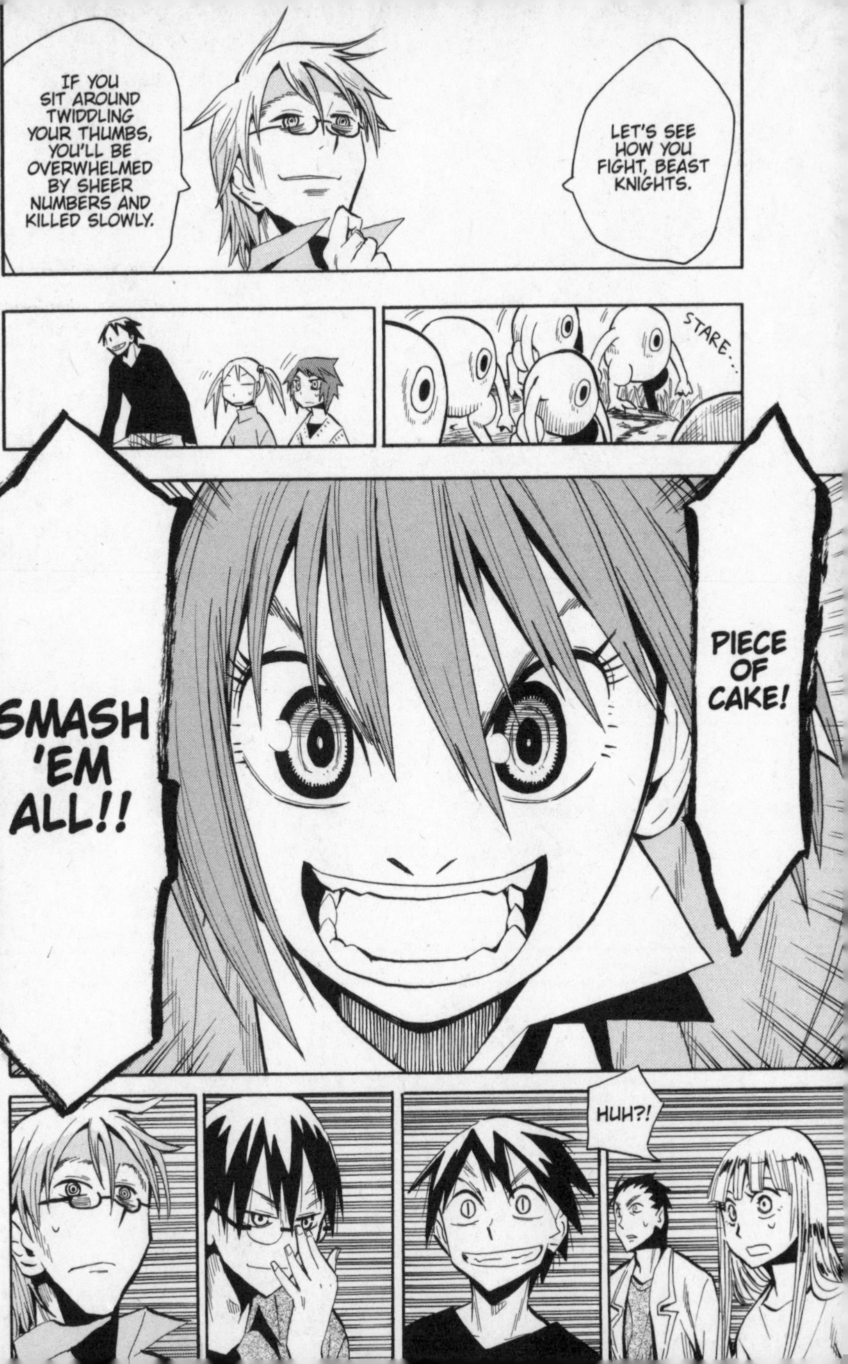
LET'S SEE HOW YOU FIGHT, BEAST KNIGHTS.
IF YOU SIT AROUND TWIDDLING YOUR THUMBS, YOU'LL BE OVERWHELMED BY SHEER NUMBERS AND KILLED SLOWLY.
STARE...
PIECE OF CAKE!
SMASH 'EM ALL!!
HUH?!

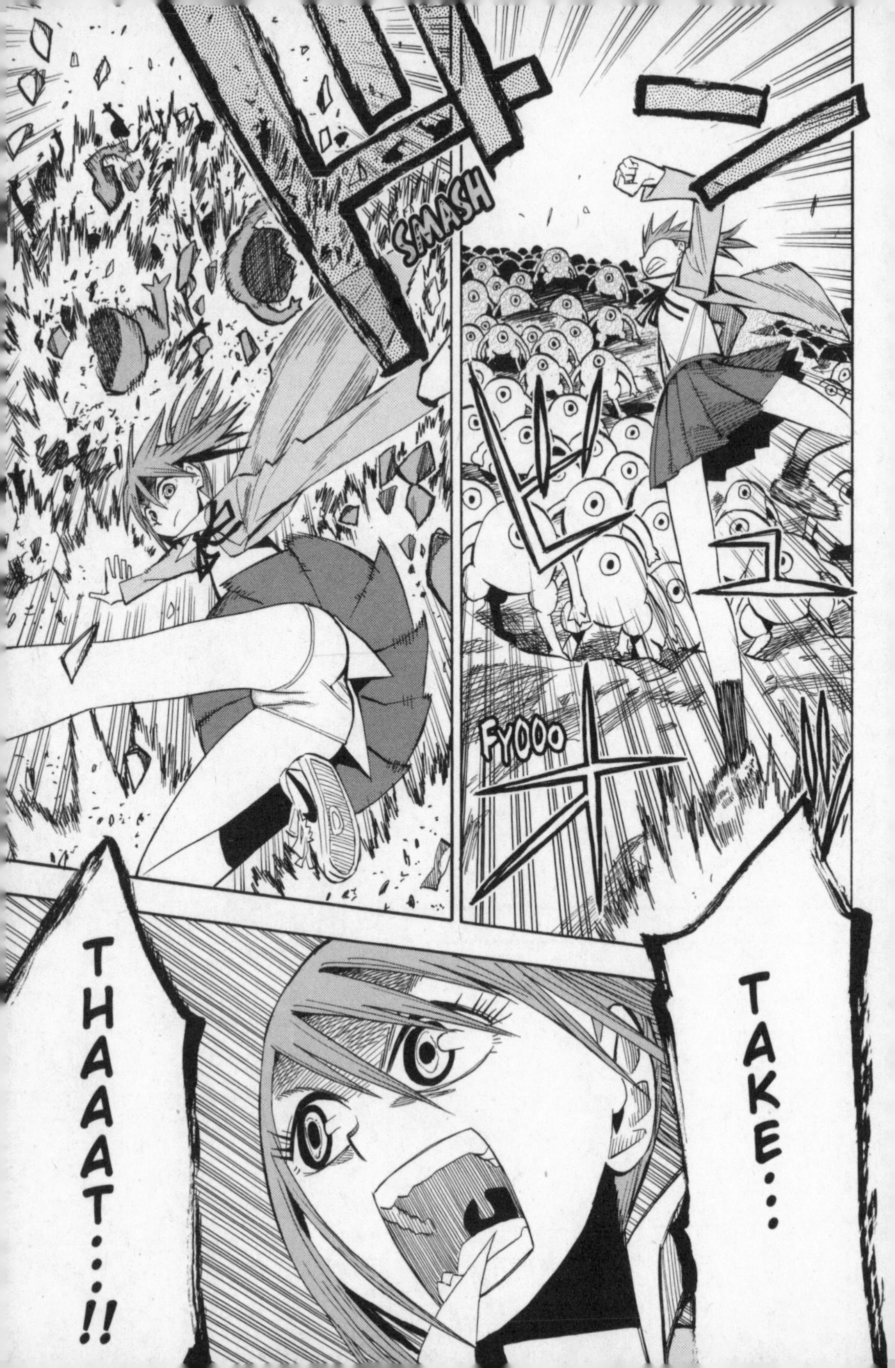
FYOOO
SMASH
TAKE...
THAAAT...!!

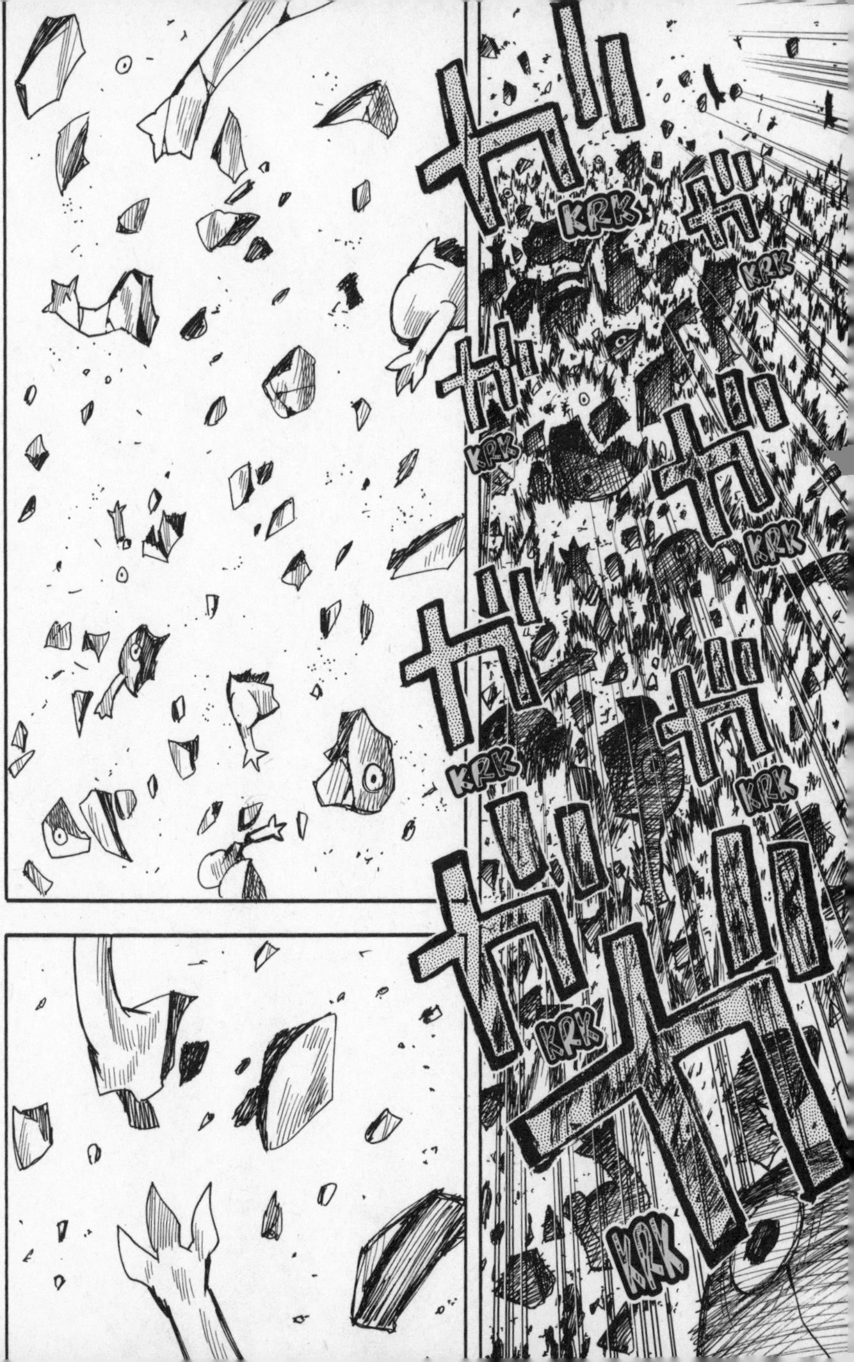
ガ
ガ
KRK
KRK
ガ
KRK
ガ
KRK
ガ
ガ
KRK
KRK
ガ
KRK
KRK

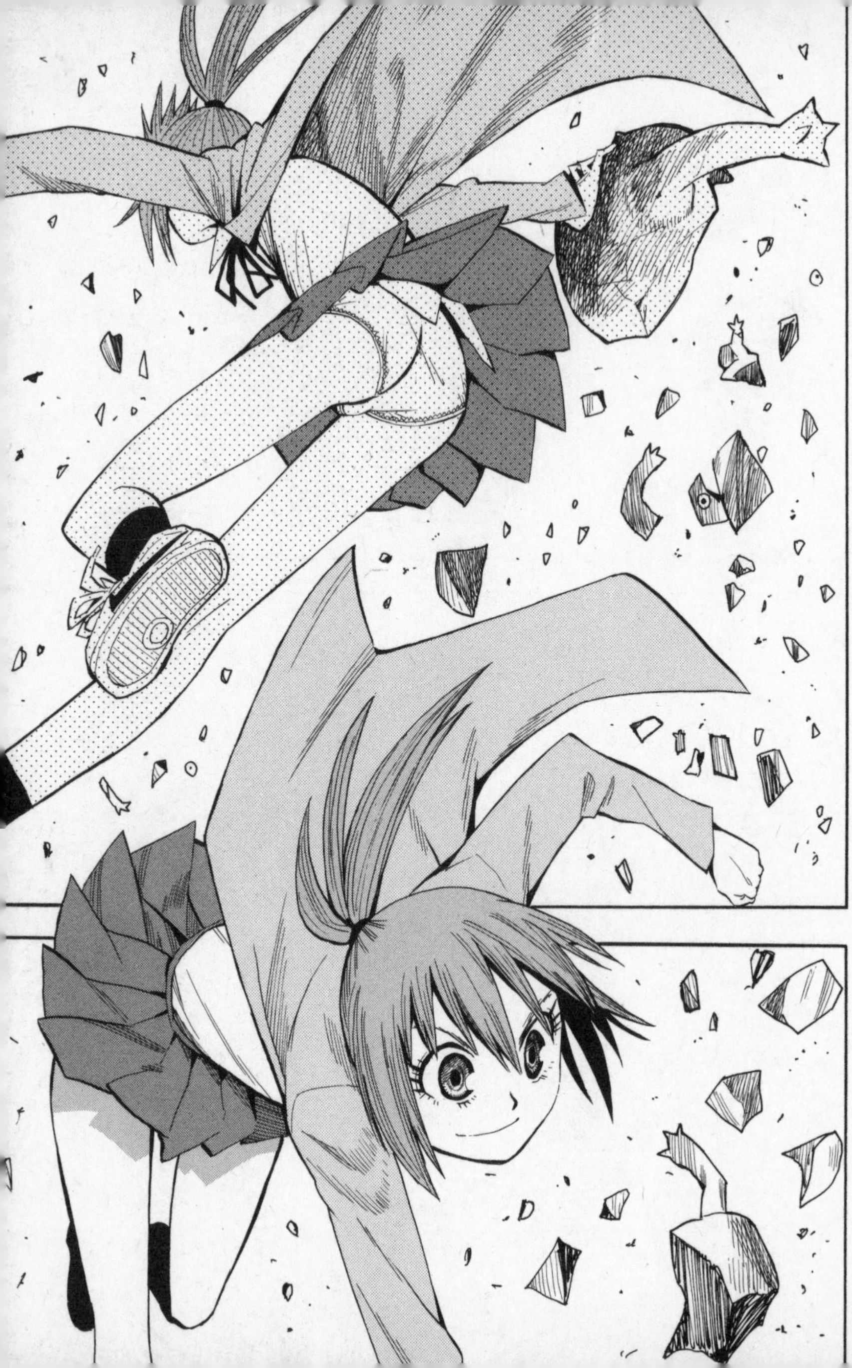

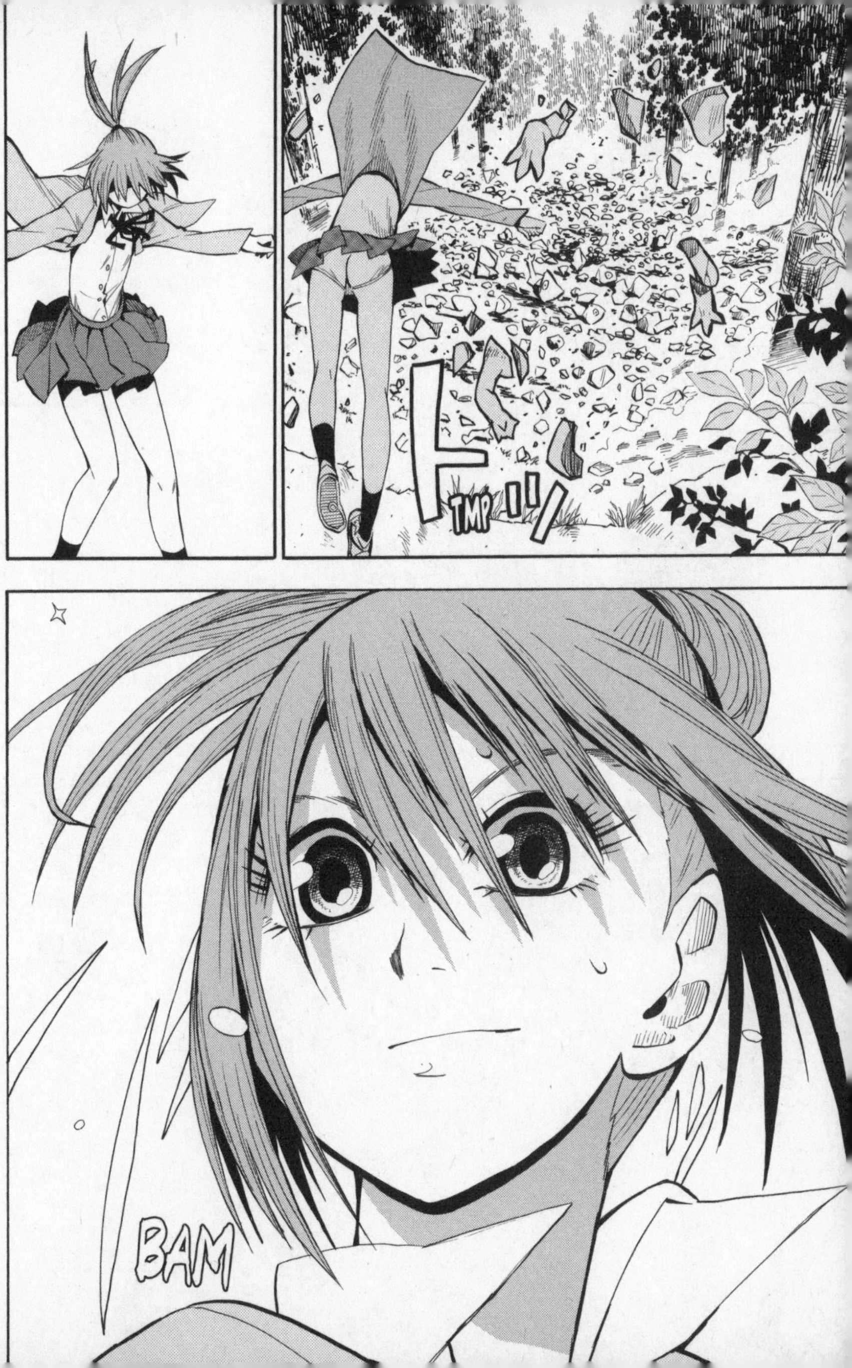
TMP
BAM

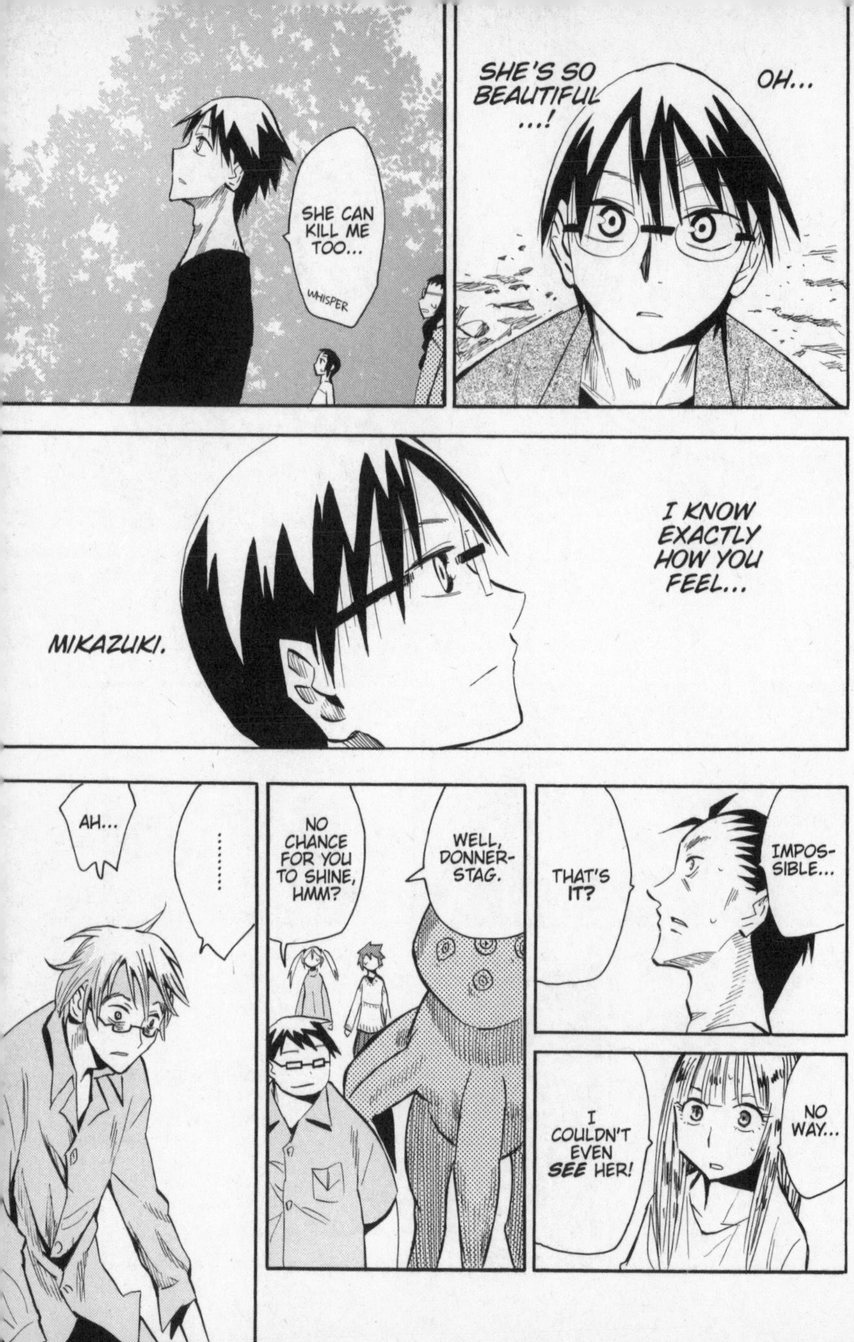
OH...
SHE'S SO BEAUTIFUL ...!
SHE CAN KILL ME TOO...
WHISPER
I KNOW EXACTLY HOW YOU FEEL...
MIKAZUKI.
IMPOS- SIBLE...
THAT'S IT?
NO WAY...
I COULDN'T EVEN SEE HER!
WELL, DONNER- STAG.
NO CHANCE FOR YOU TO SHINE, HMM?
......
AH...

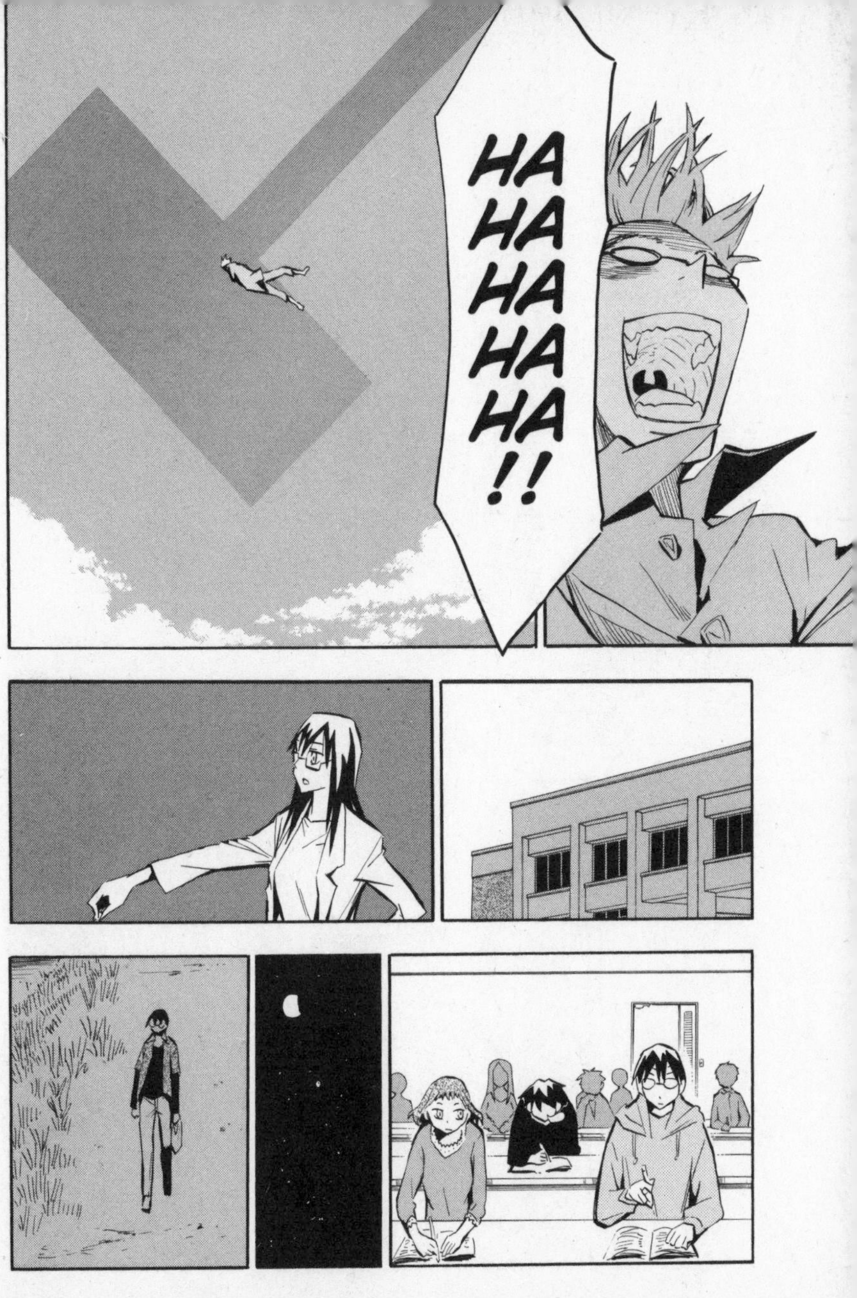
HA HA HA HA HA!!

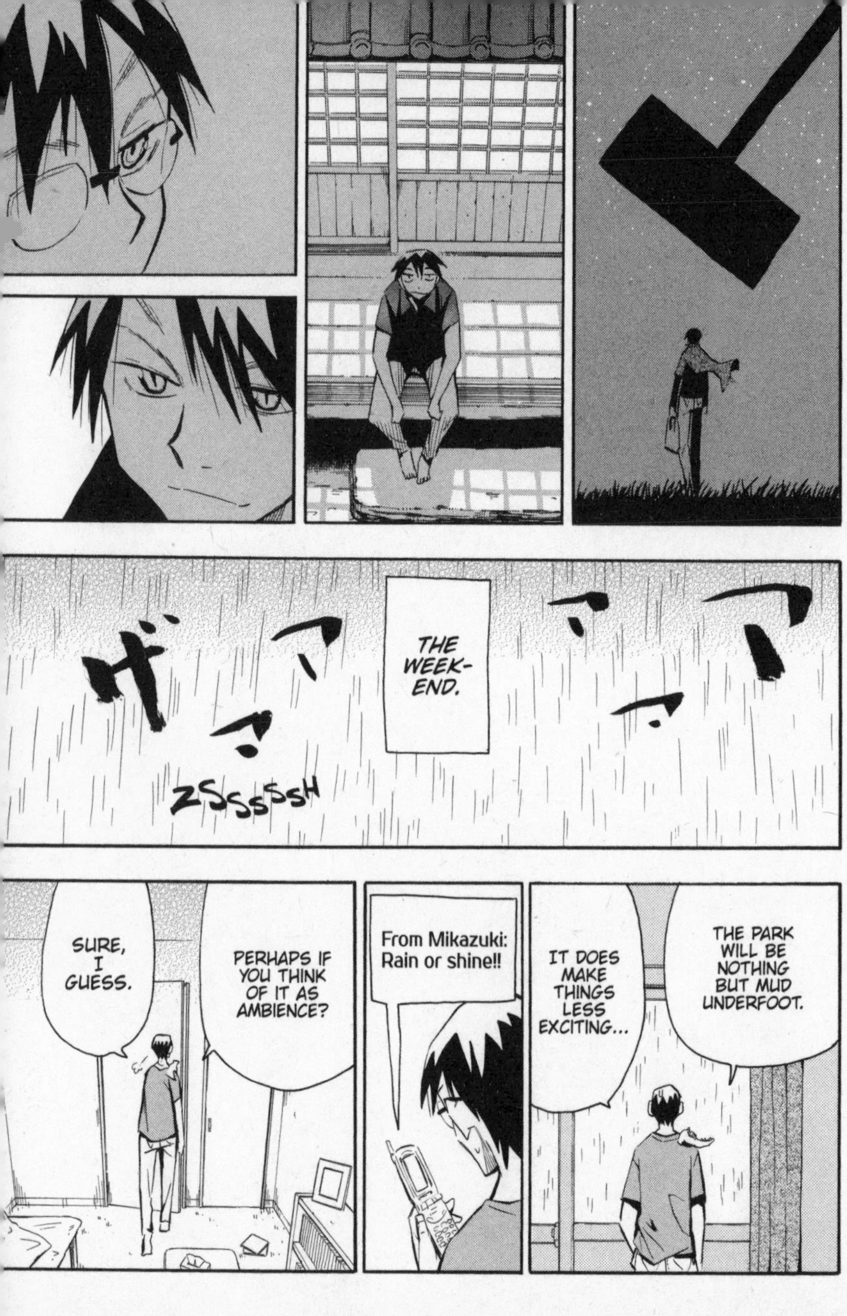
THE WEEK-END.
ZSSSSSH
THE PARK WILL BE NOTHING BUT MUD UNDERFOOT.
IT DOES MAKE THINGS LESS EXCITING...
From Mikazuki: Rain or shine!!
PERHAPS IF YOU THINK OF IT AS AMBIENCE?
SURE, I GUESS.

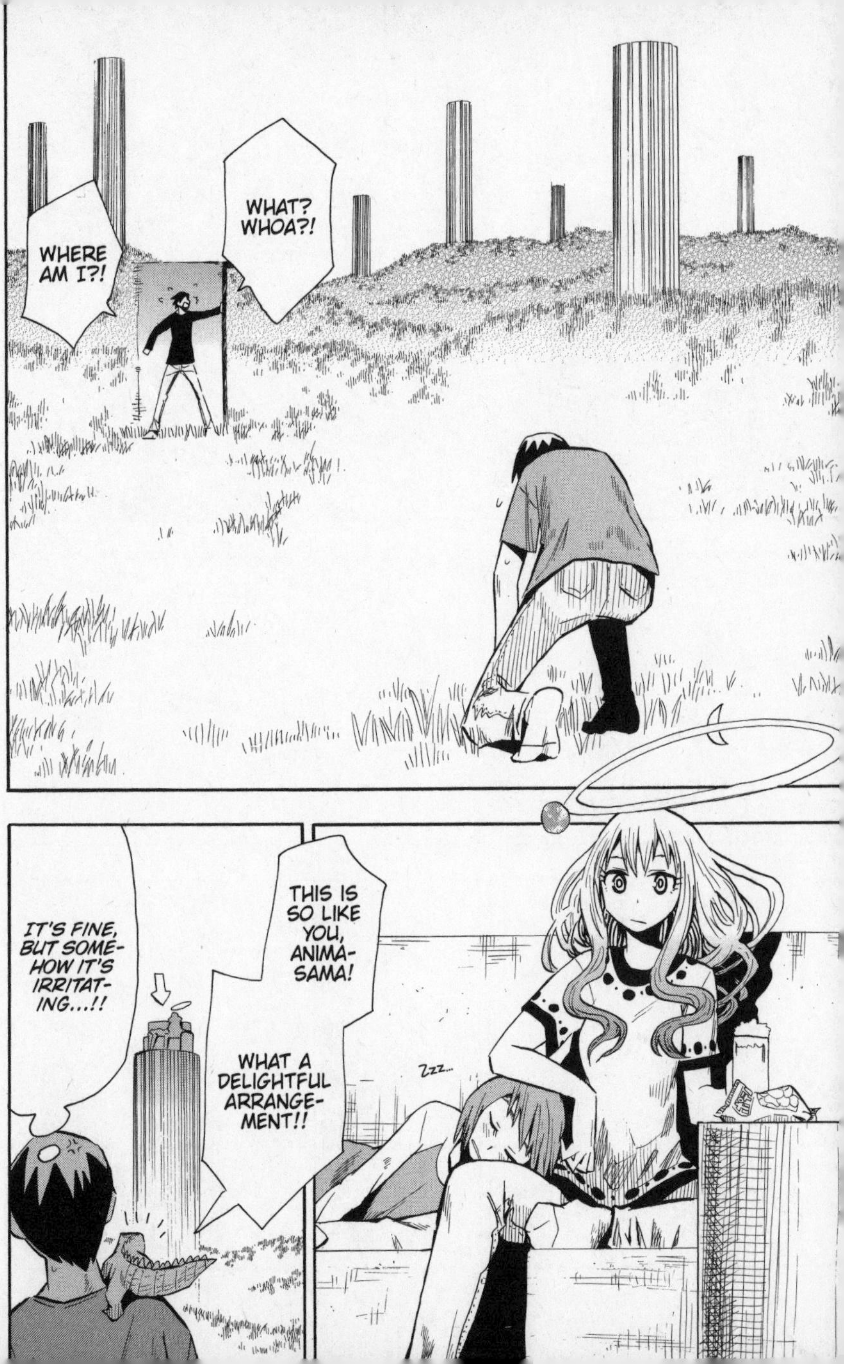
WHAT? WHOA?!
WHERE AM I?!
Zzz...
THIS IS SO LIKE YOU, ANIMA-SAMA!
WHAT A DELIGHTFUL ARRANGEMENT!!
IT'S FINE, BUT SOMEHOW IT'S IRRITATING...!!

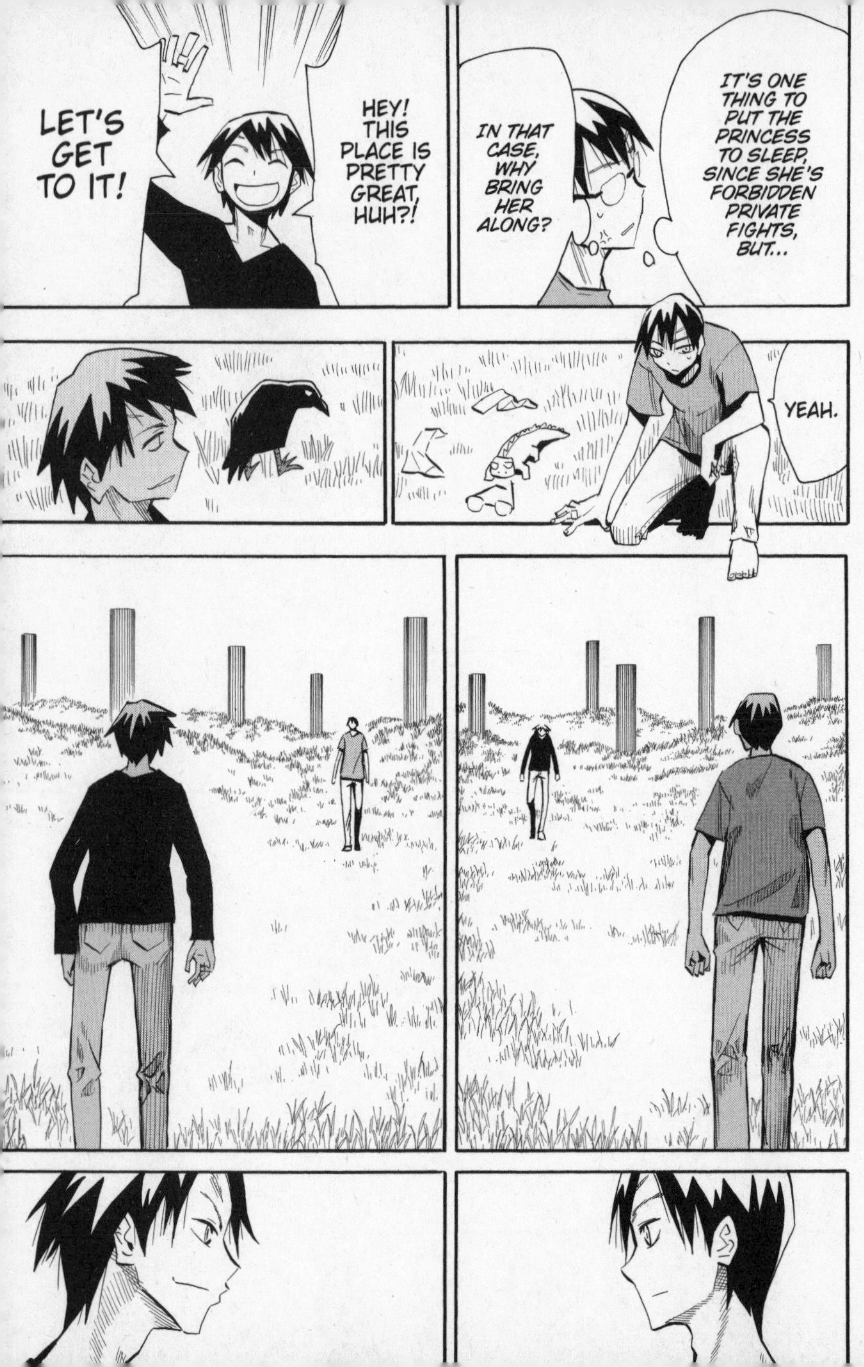
IT'S ONE THING TO PUT THE PRINCESS TO SLEEP, SINCE SHE'S FORBIDDEN PRIVATE FIGHTS, BUT...
IN THAT CASE, WHY BRING HER ALONG?
HEY! THIS PLACE IS PRETTY GREAT, HUH?!
LET'S GET TO IT!
YEAH.

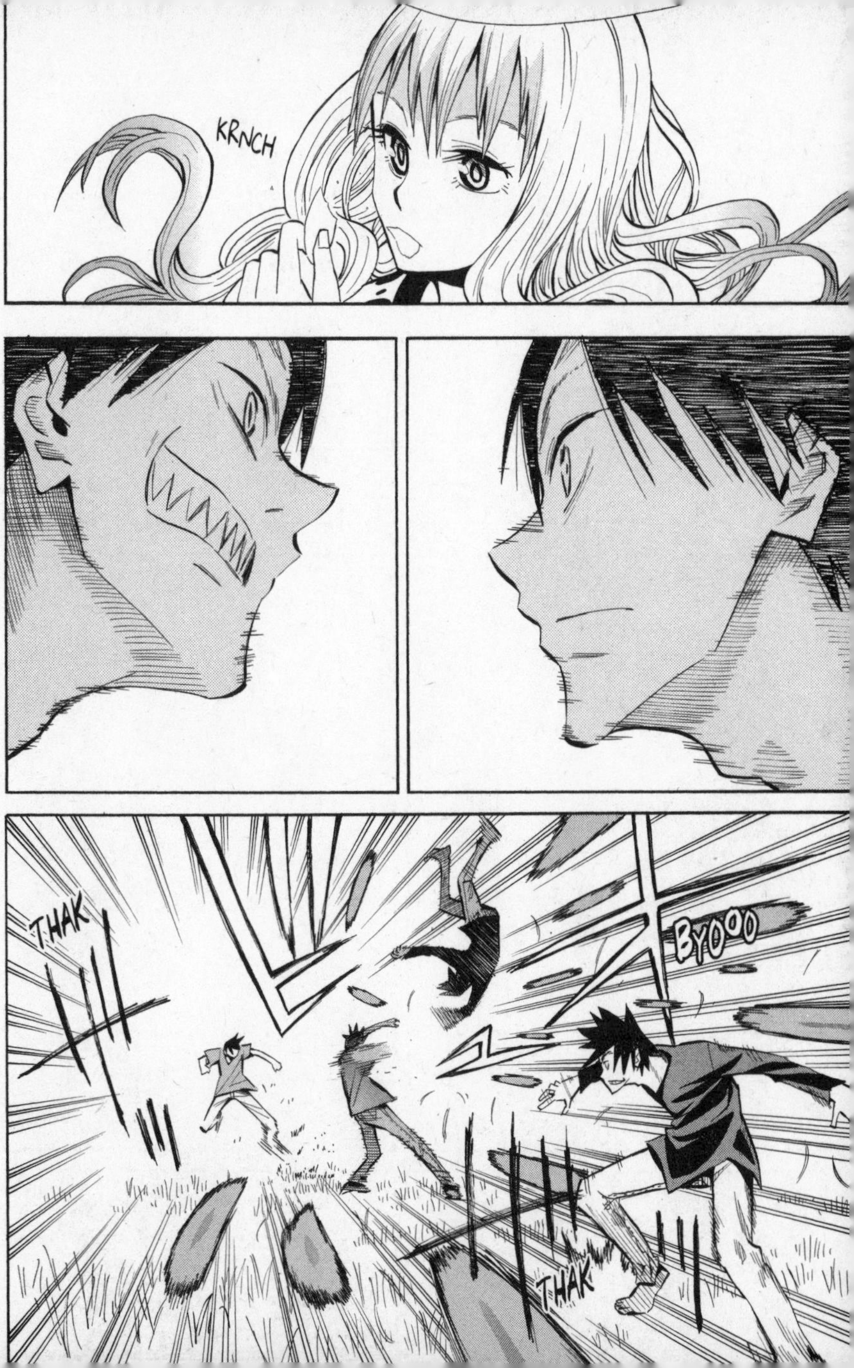
KRNCH
BYOOO
THAK
THAK

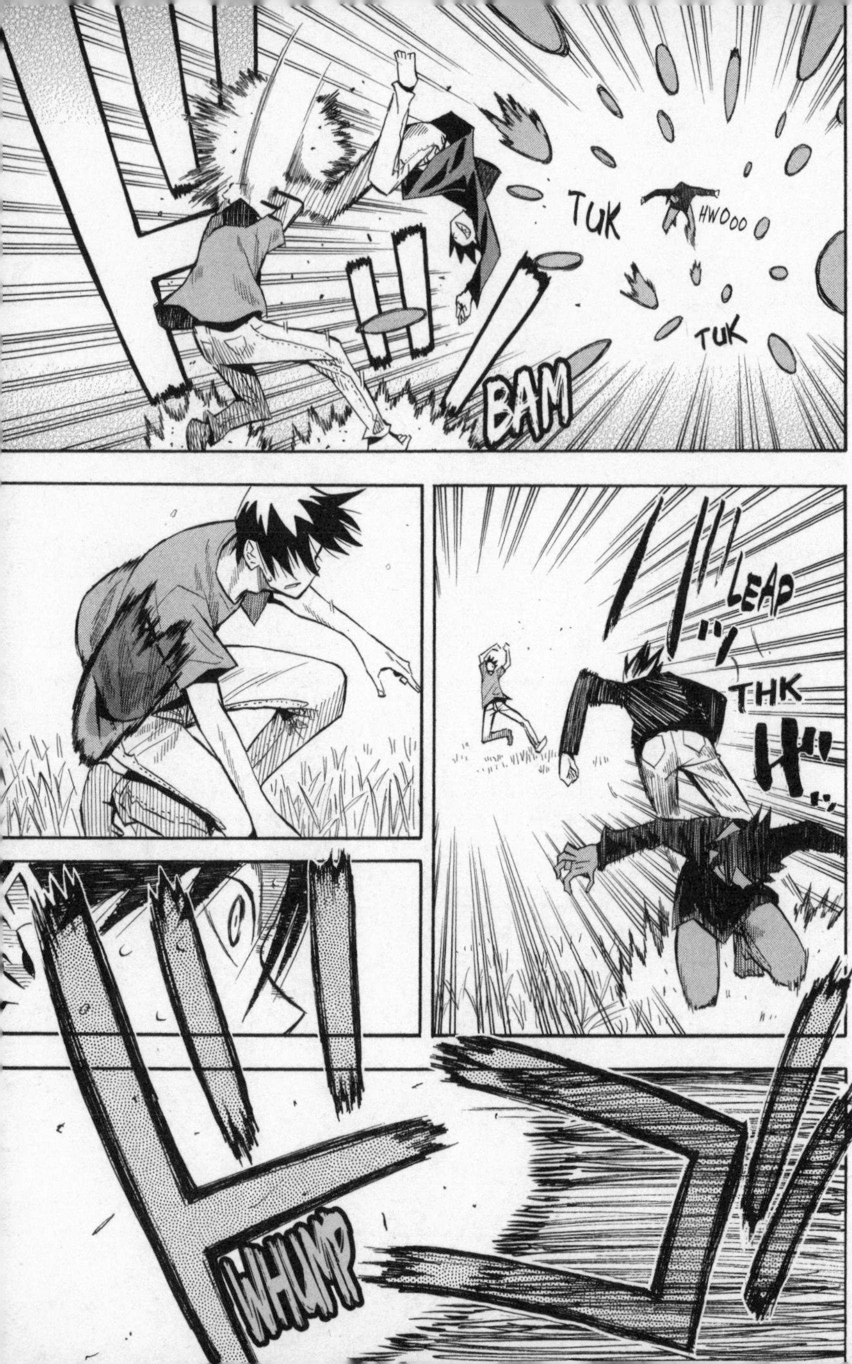
HWOOO
TUK
TUK
BAM
LEAP
THK
WHUMP

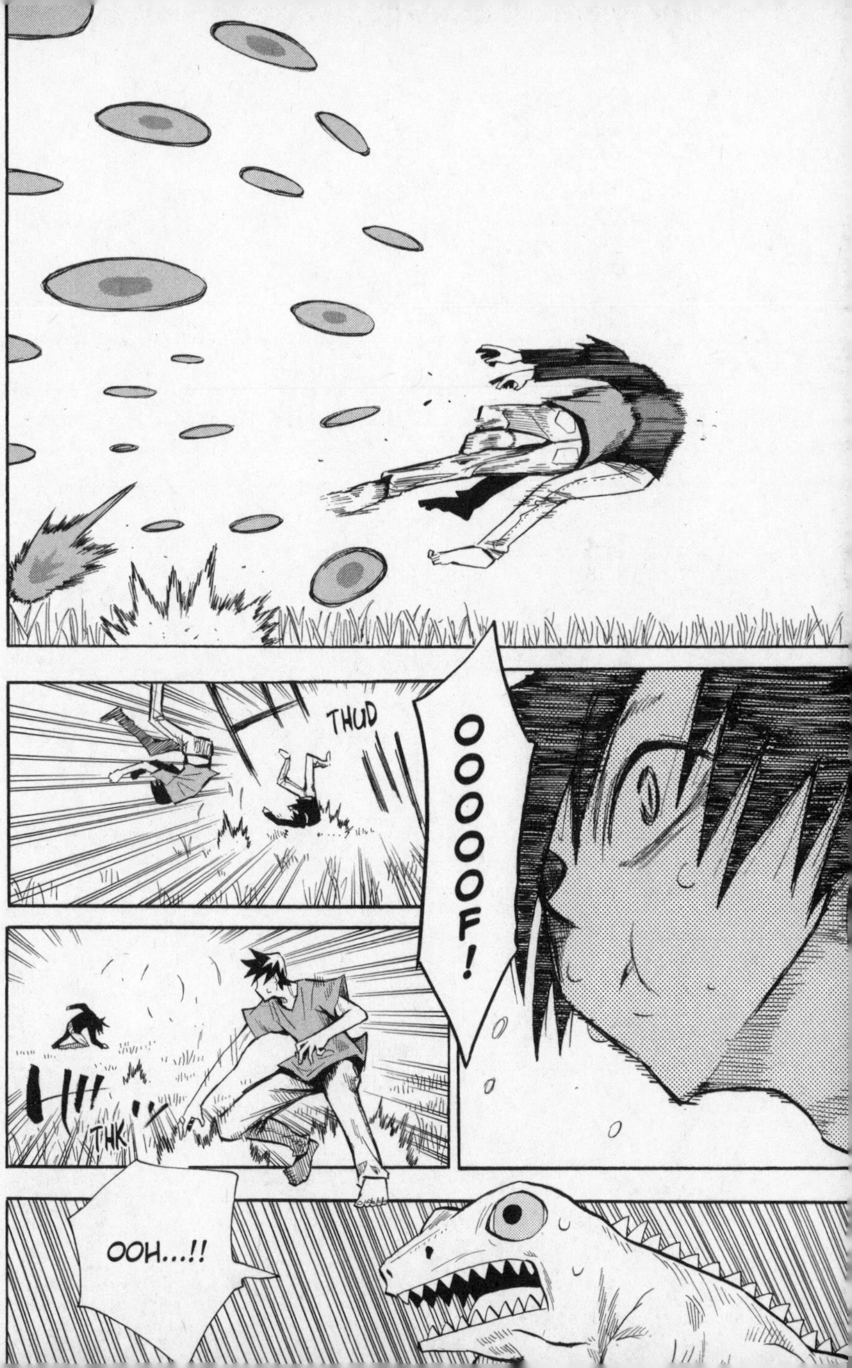
OOOOOOF!
THUD
THK
OOH...!!

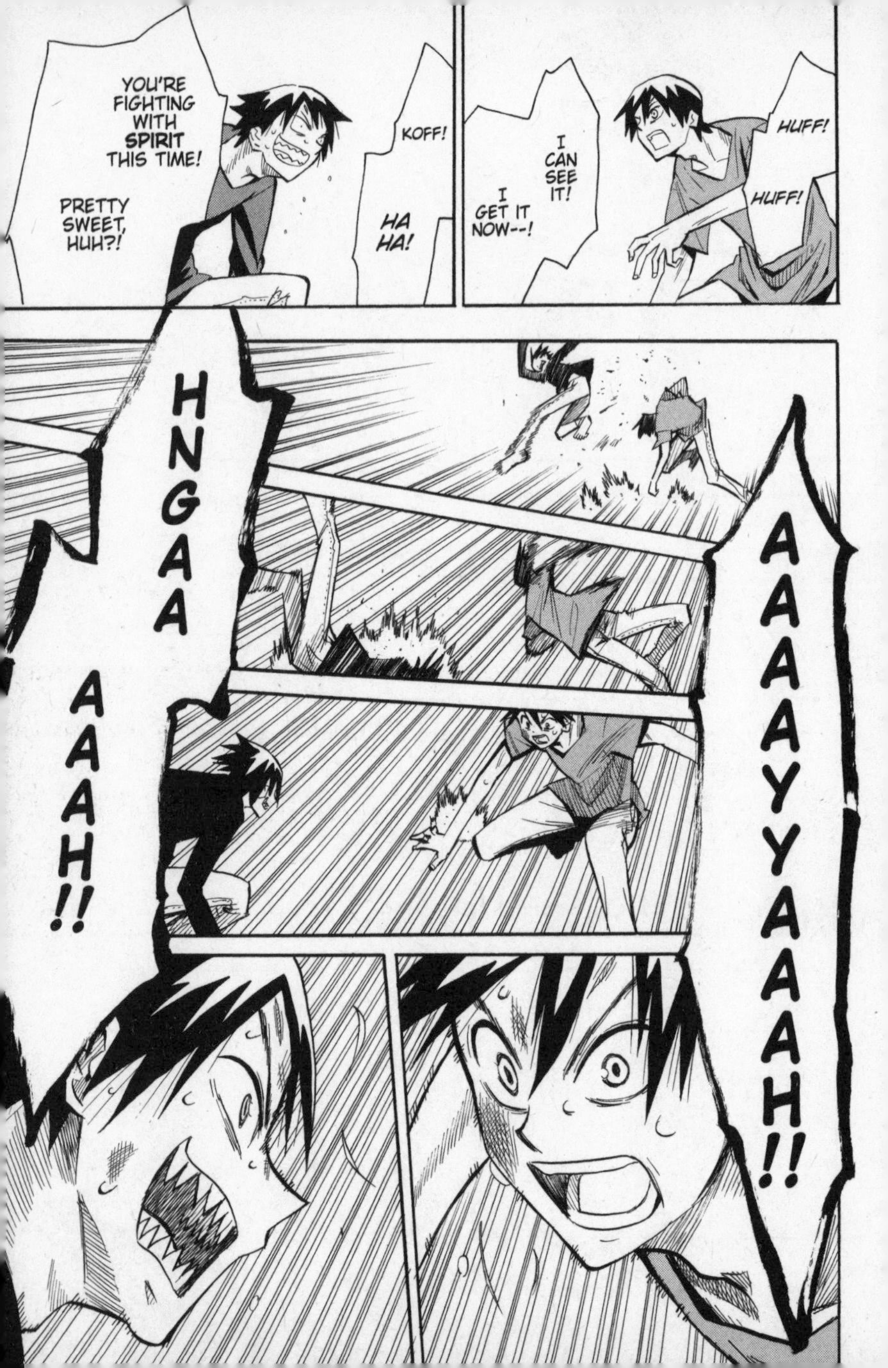

HUFF!
HUFF!
I CAN SEE IT!
I GET IT NOW--!
KOFF!
HA HA!
YOU'RE FIGHTING WITH **SPIRIT** THIS TIME!
PRETTY SWEET, HUH?!
AAAAYYAAAH!!
HNGAAAAAH!!

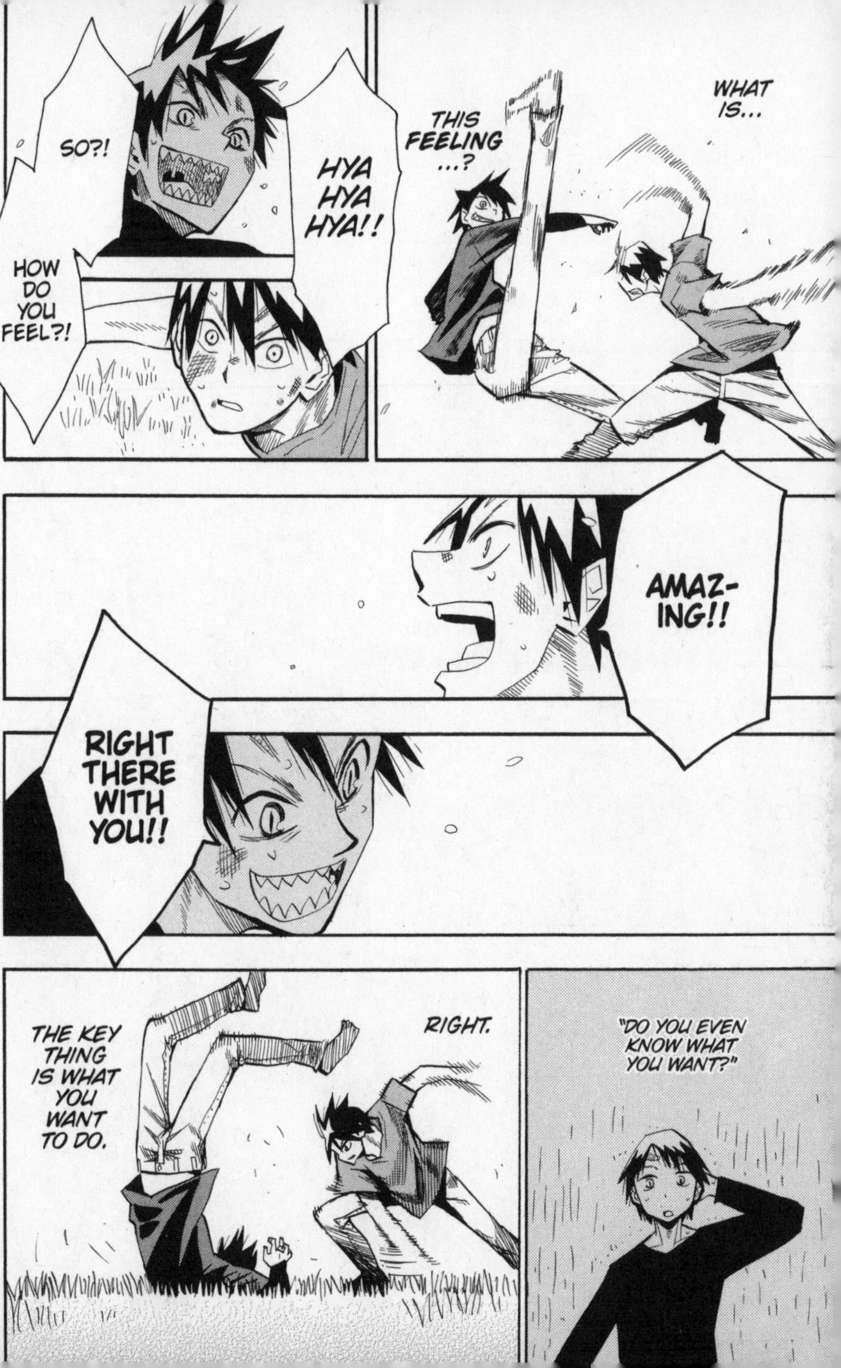
WHAT IS...
THIS FEELING ...?
HYA HYA HYA!!
SO?!
HOW DO YOU FEEL?!
AMAZ-ING!!
RIGHT THERE WITH YOU!!
"DO YOU EVEN KNOW WHAT YOU WANT?"
RIGHT.
THE KEY THING IS WHAT YOU WANT TO DO.

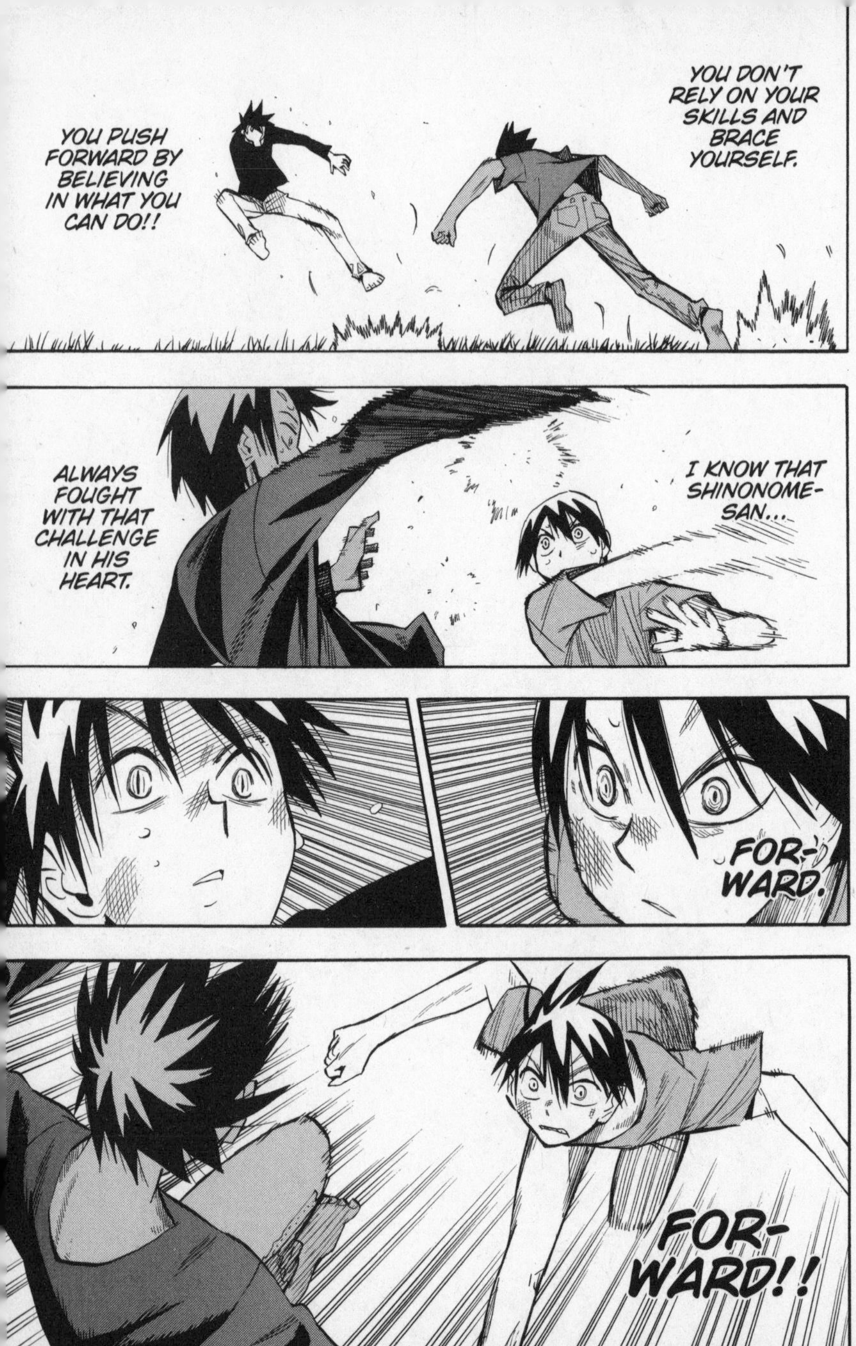
YOU DON'T RELY ON YOUR SKILLS AND BRACE YOURSELF.
YOU PUSH FORWARD BY BELIEVING IN WHAT YOU CAN DO!!
I KNOW THAT SHINONOME-SAN...
ALWAYS FOUGHT WITH THAT CHALLENGE IN HIS HEART.
FOR-WARD.
FOR-WARD!!

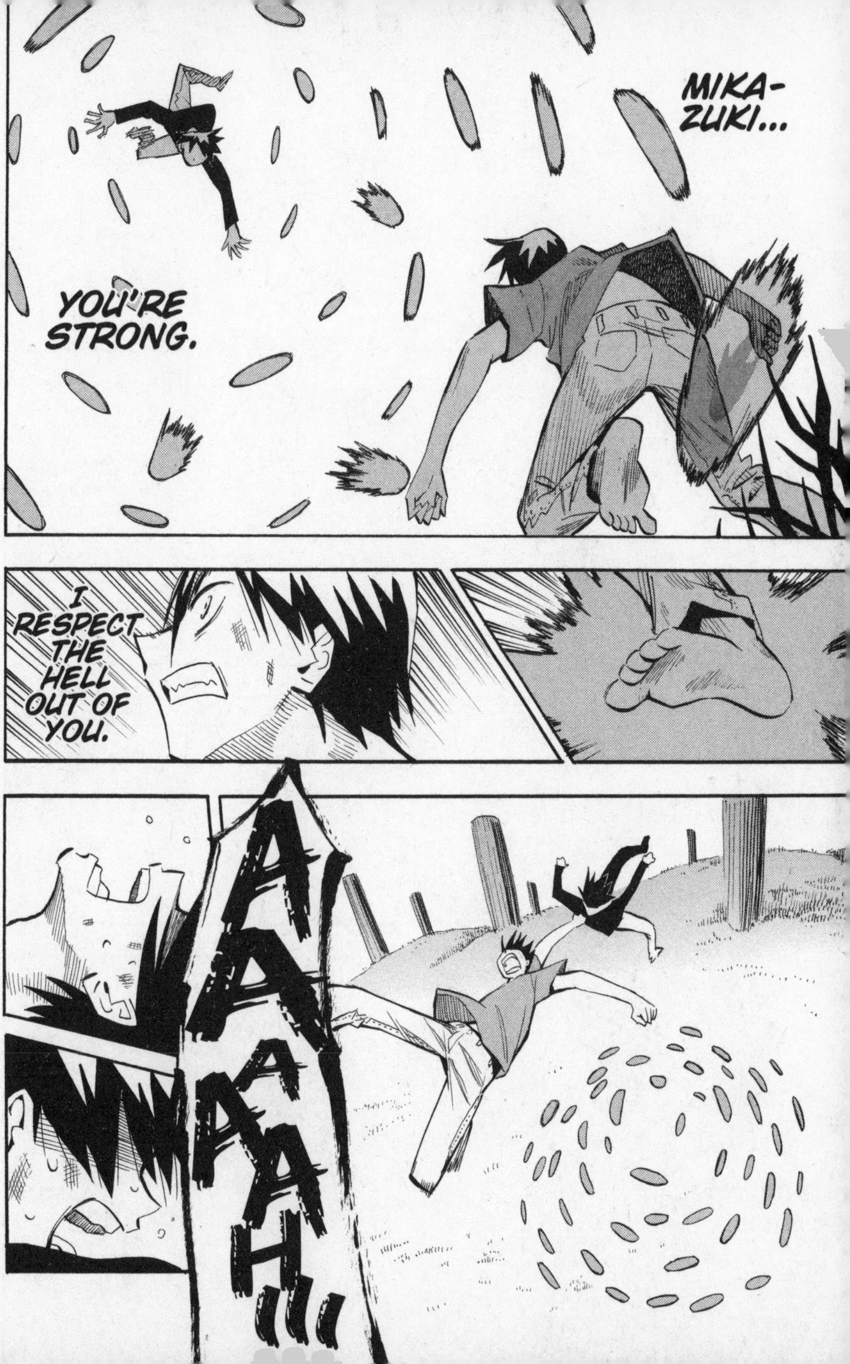
MIKA-ZUKI...
YOU'RE STRONG.
I RESPECT THE HELL OUT OF YOU.
AAAAAH!!!

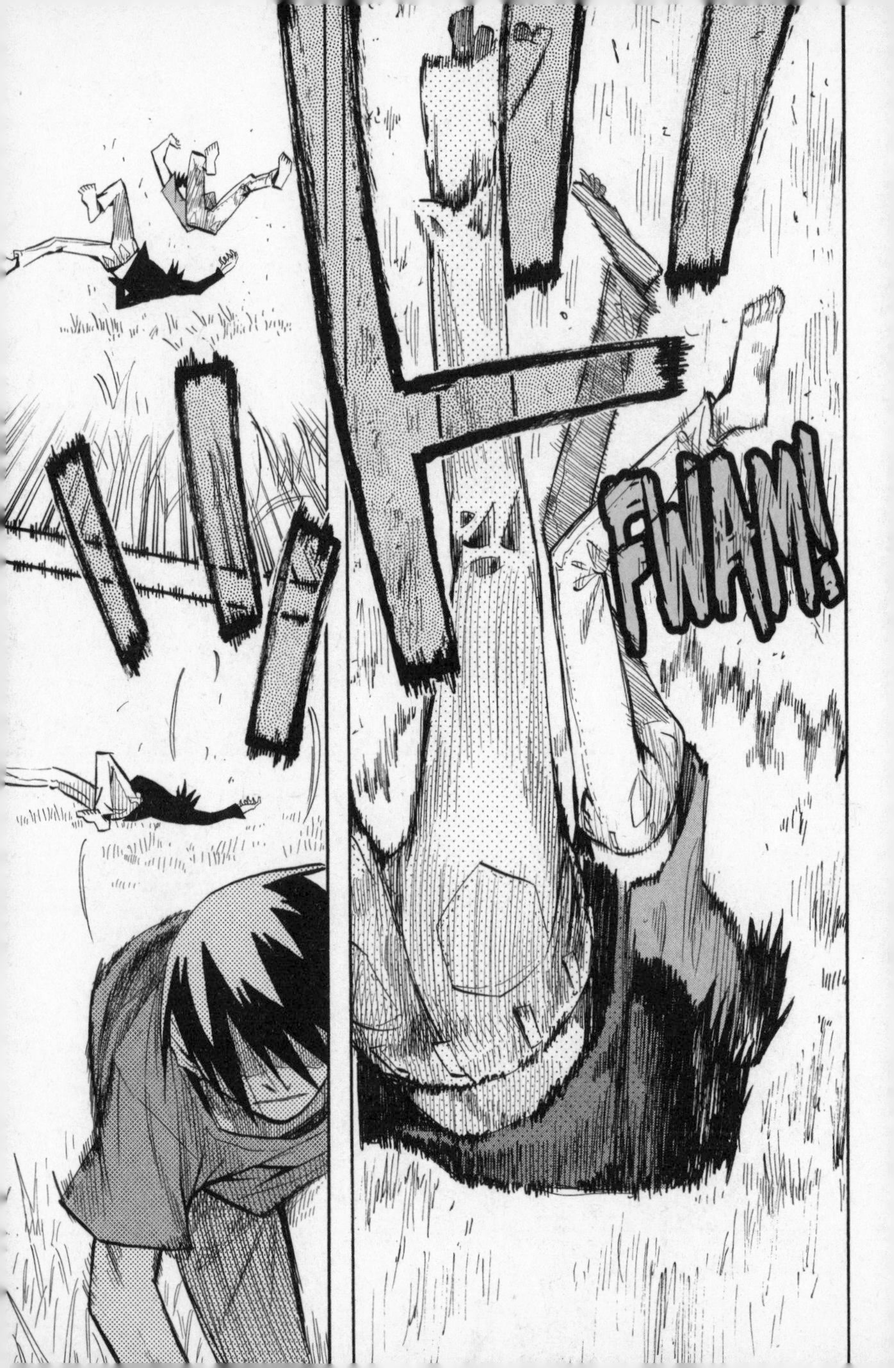
FWAM!

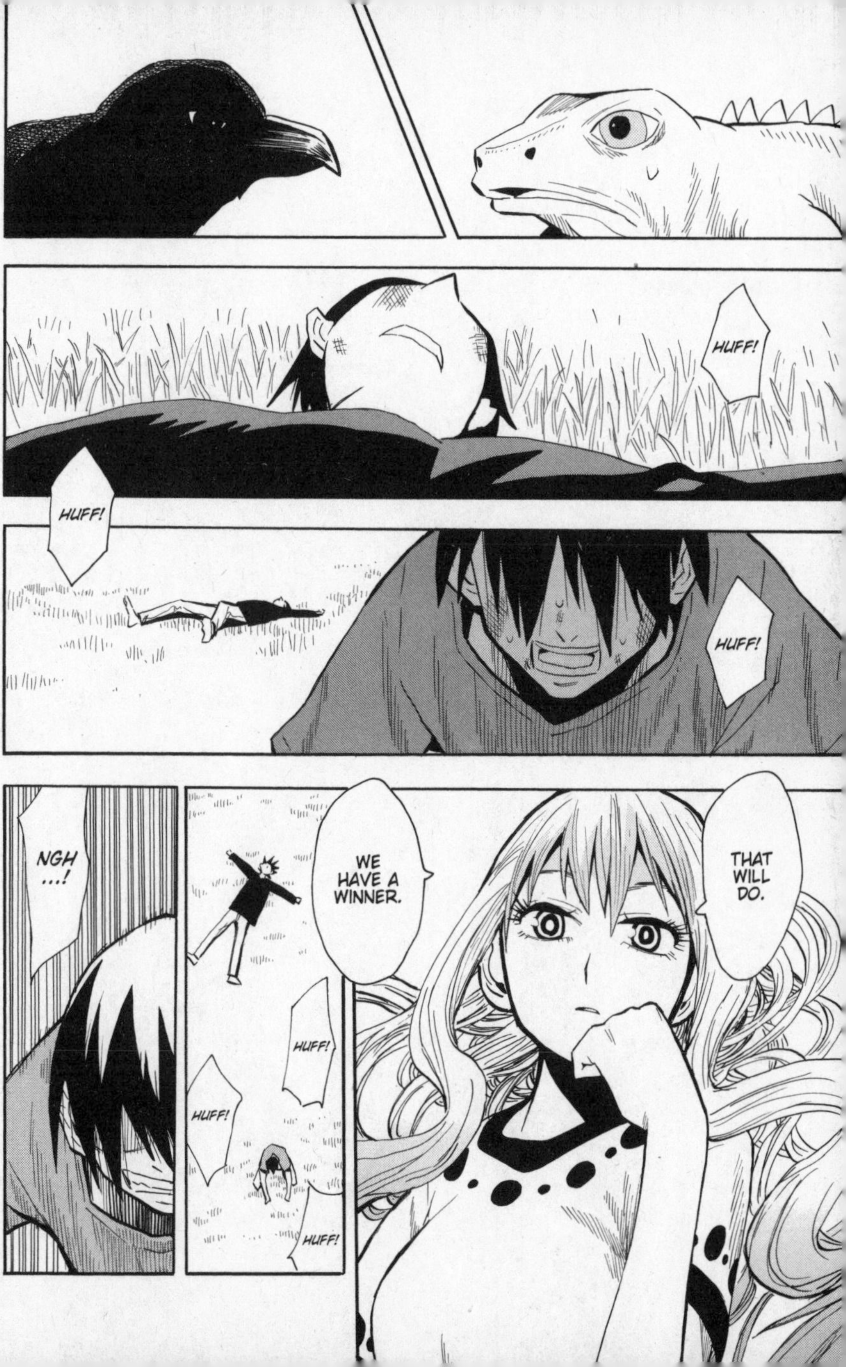
HUFF!
HUFF!
HUFF!
THAT WILL DO.
WE HAVE A WINNER.
HUFF!
HUFF!
HUFF!
NGH ...!

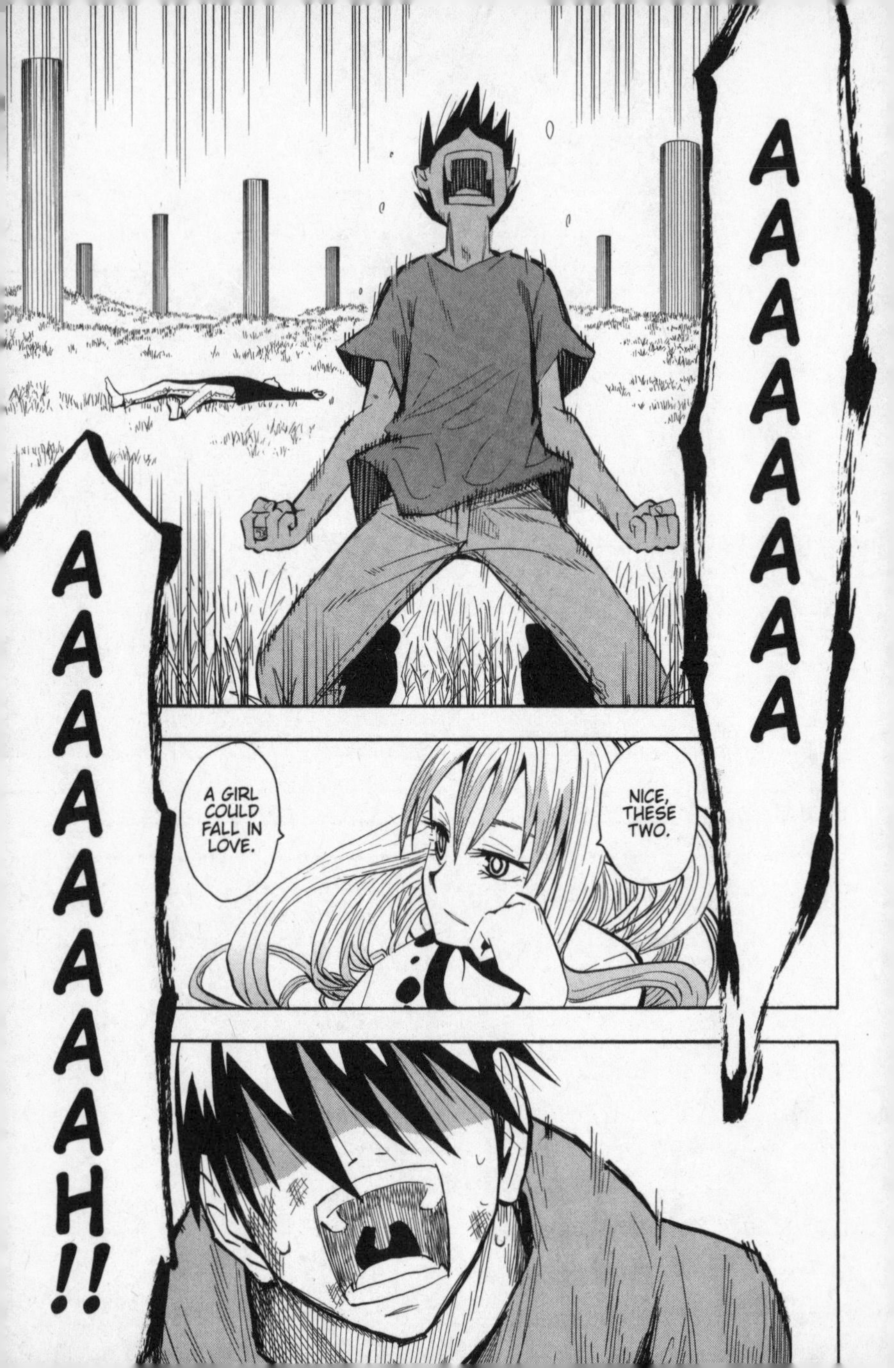
AAAAAAAA
NICE, THESE TWO.
A GIRL COULD FALL IN LOVE.
AAAAAAAAH!!

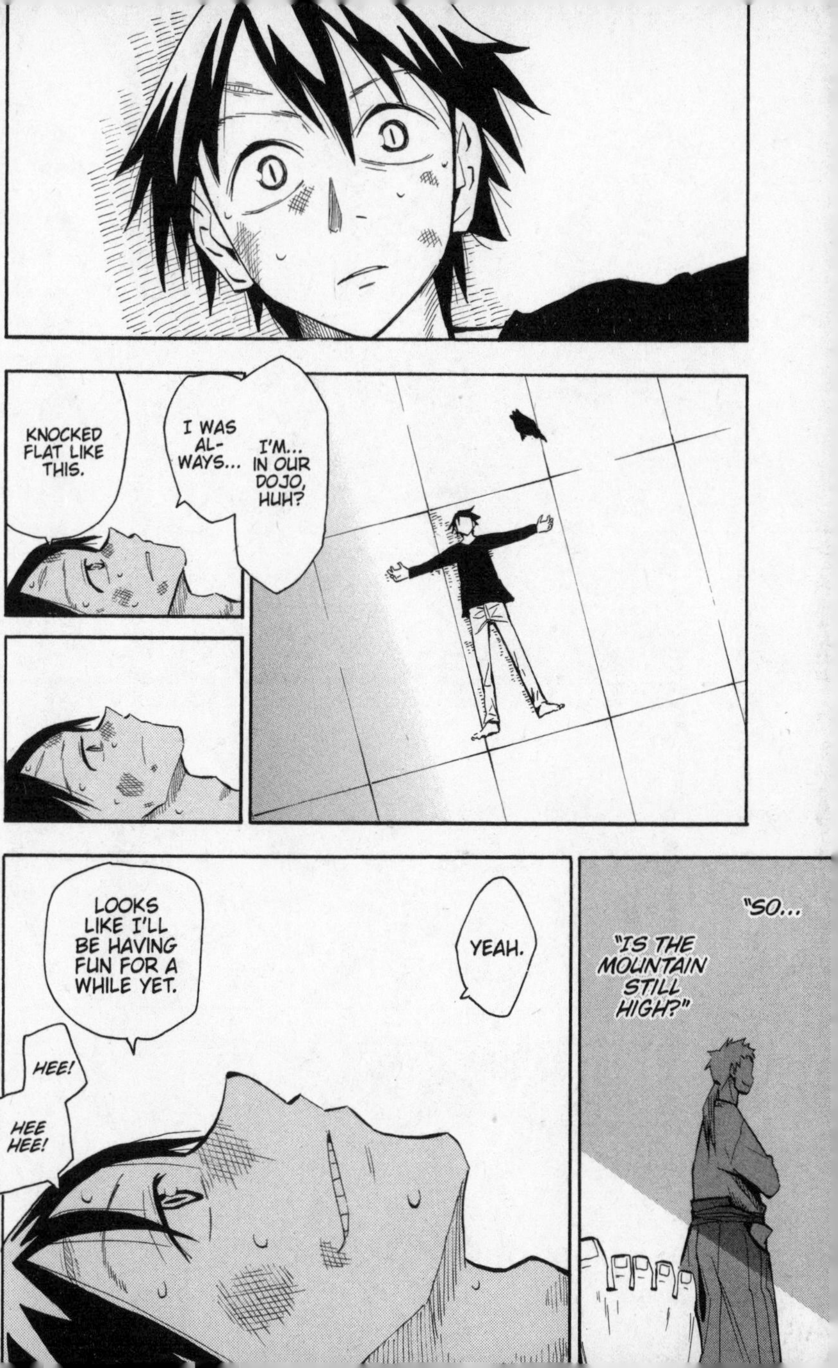
I'M... IN OUR DOJO, HUH?
I WAS AL-WAYS...
KNOCKED FLAT LIKE THIS.
"SO...
"IS THE MOUNTAIN STILL HIGH?"
YEAH.
LOOKS LIKE I'LL BE HAVING FUN FOR A WHILE YET.
HEE!
HEE HEE!

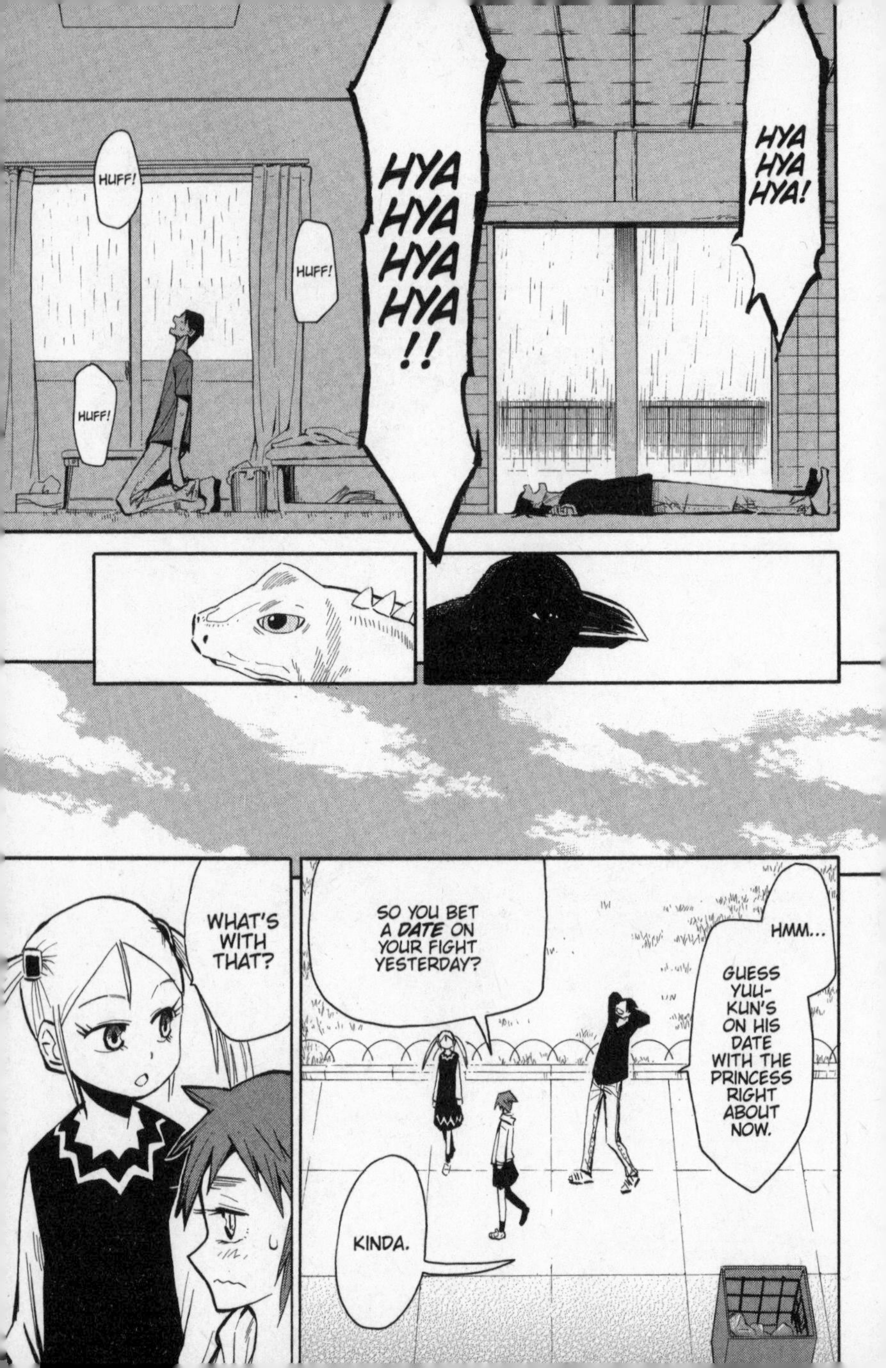
HYA HYA HYA!
HYA HYA HYA HYA!!
HUFF!
HUFF!
HUFF!
HMM...
GUESS YUU-KUN'S ON HIS DATE WITH THE PRINCESS RIGHT ABOUT NOW.
SO YOU BET A *DATE* ON YOUR FIGHT YESTERDAY?
KINDA.
WHAT'S WITH THAT?

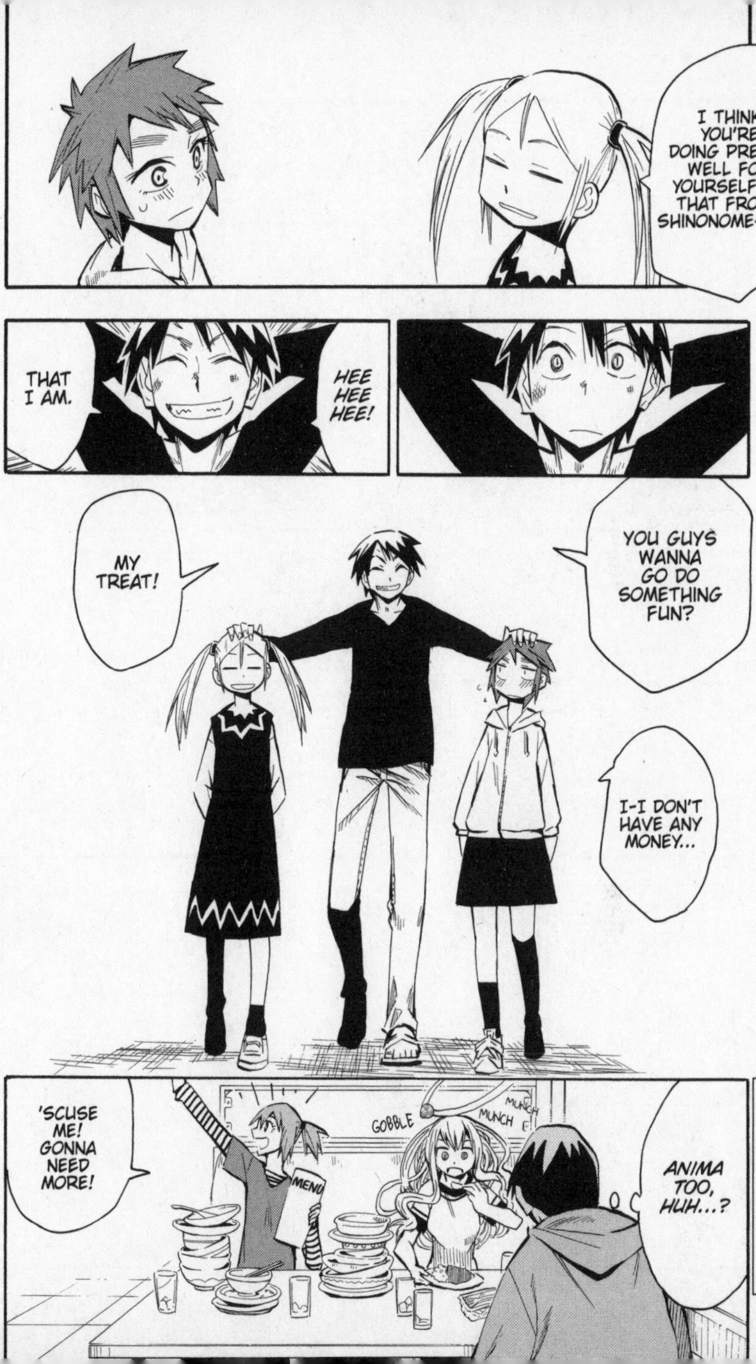
I THINK YOU'RE DOING PRETTY WELL FOR YOURSELF ON THAT FRONT, SHINONOME-SAN.
HEE HEE HEE!
THAT I AM.
YOU GUYS WANNA GO DO SOMETHING FUN?
MY TREAT!
I-I DON'T HAVE ANY MONEY...
Chapter 42/END
ANIMA TOO, HUH...?
MUNCH
MUNCH
GOBBLE
'SCUSE ME! GONNA NEED MORE!
MENU

Chapter 43

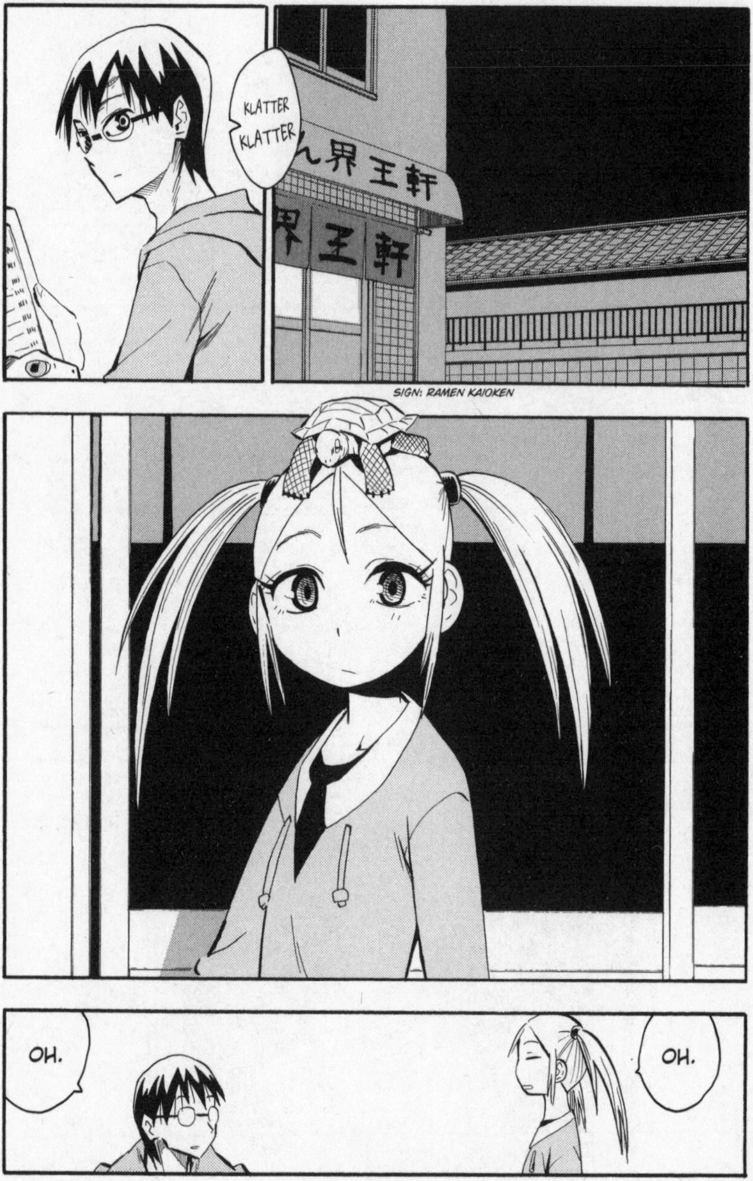
ん界王軒
界王軒
SIGN: RAMEN KAIOKEN
KLATTER KLATTER
OH.
OH.

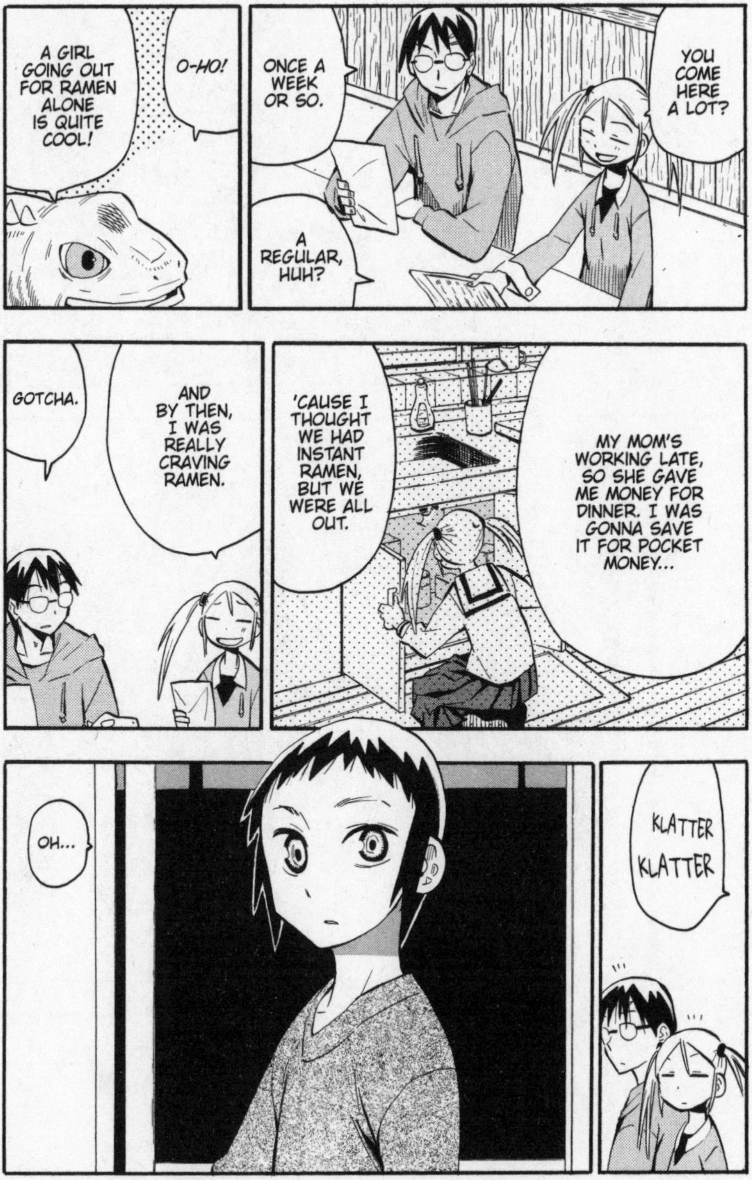
YOU COME HERE A LOT?
ONCE A WEEK OR SO.
A REGULAR, HUH?
O-HO!
A GIRL GOING OUT FOR RAMEN ALONE IS QUITE COOL!
MY MOM'S WORKING LATE, SO SHE GAVE ME MONEY FOR DINNER. I WAS GONNA SAVE IT FOR POCKET MONEY...
'CAUSE I THOUGHT WE HAD INSTANT RAMEN, BUT WE WERE ALL OUT.
AND BY THEN, I WAS REALLY CRAVING RAMEN.
GOTCHA.
KLATTER KLATTER
OH...

Chapter 43: Yukimachi and Subaru

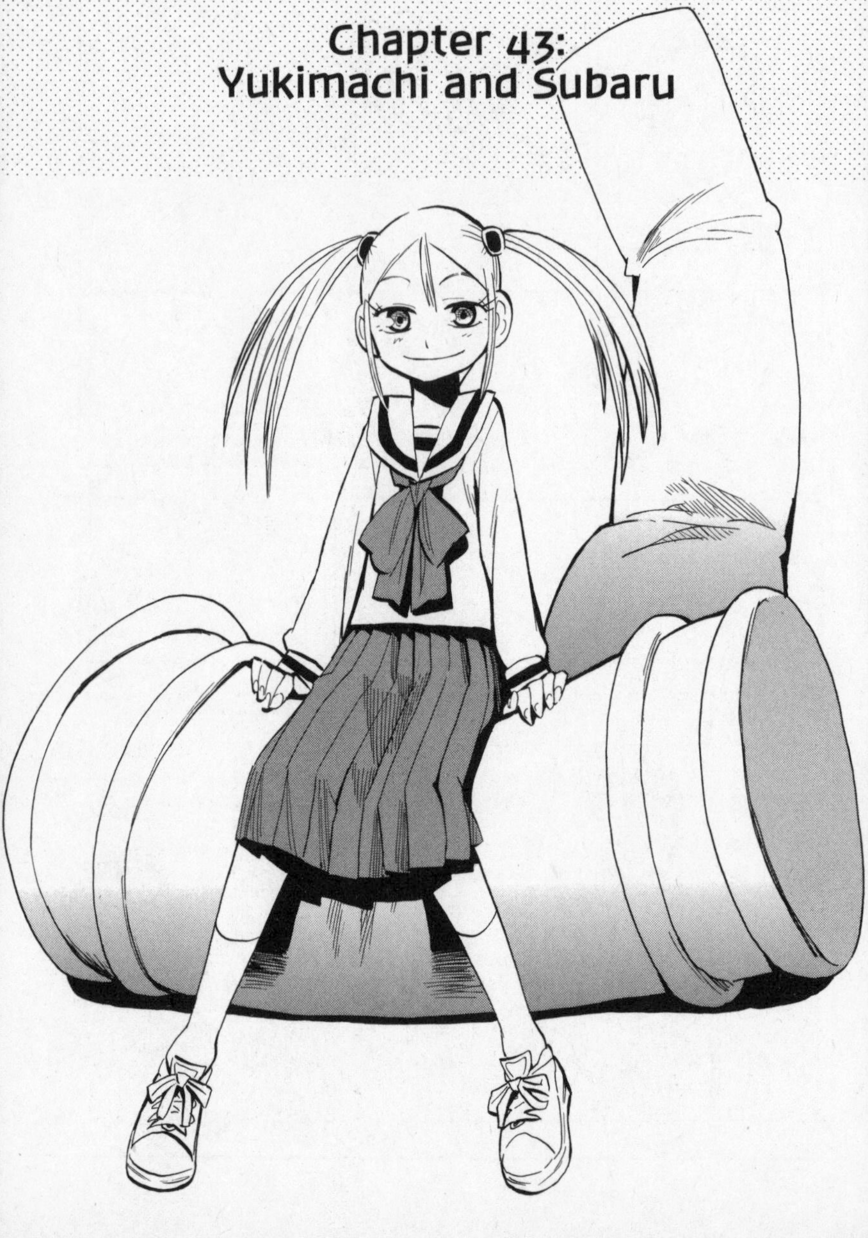

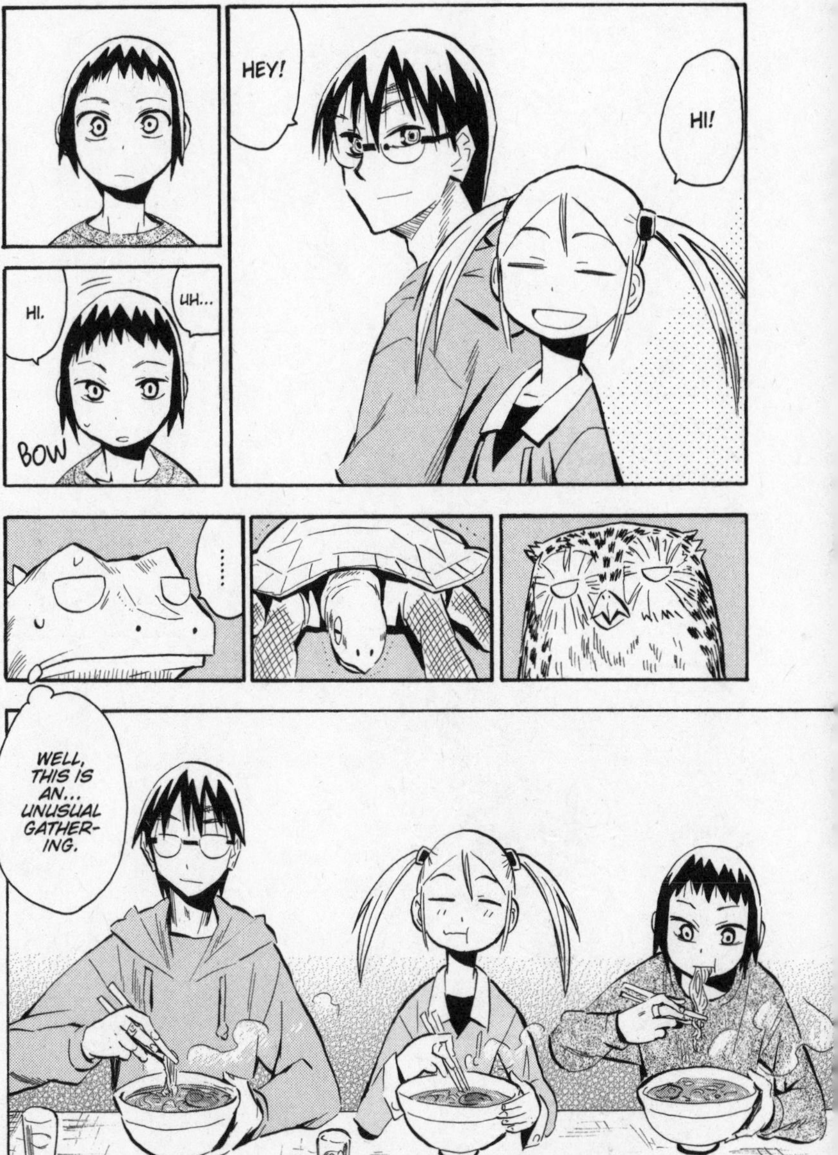
HI!
HEY!
UH...
HI.
BOW
......
WELL, THIS IS AN... UNUSUAL GATHER-ING.

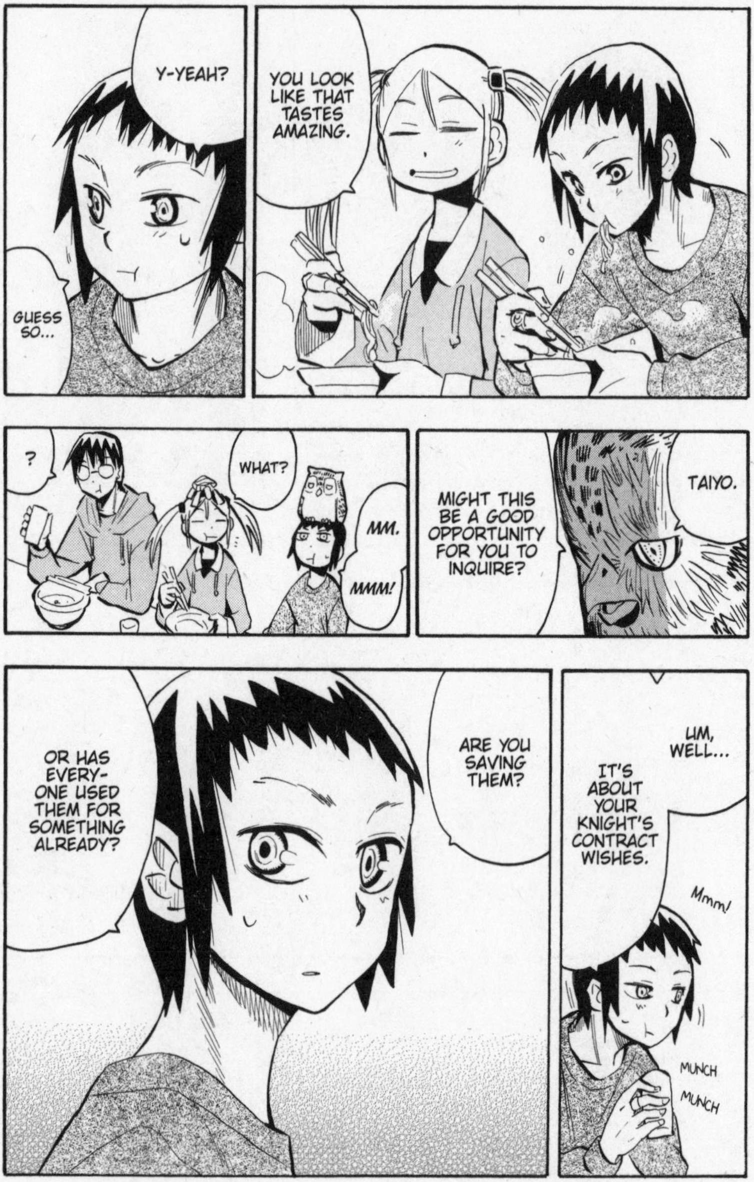
YOU LOOK LIKE THAT TASTES AMAZING.
Y-YEAH?
GUESS SO...
TAIYO.
MIGHT THIS BE A GOOD OPPORTUNITY FOR YOU TO INQUIRE?
MM.
MMM!
WHAT?
?
UM, WELL...
IT'S ABOUT YOUR KNIGHT'S CONTRACT WISHES.
Mmm!
MUNCH
MUNCH
ARE YOU SAVING THEM?
OR HAS EVERY-ONE USED THEM FOR SOMETHING ALREADY?

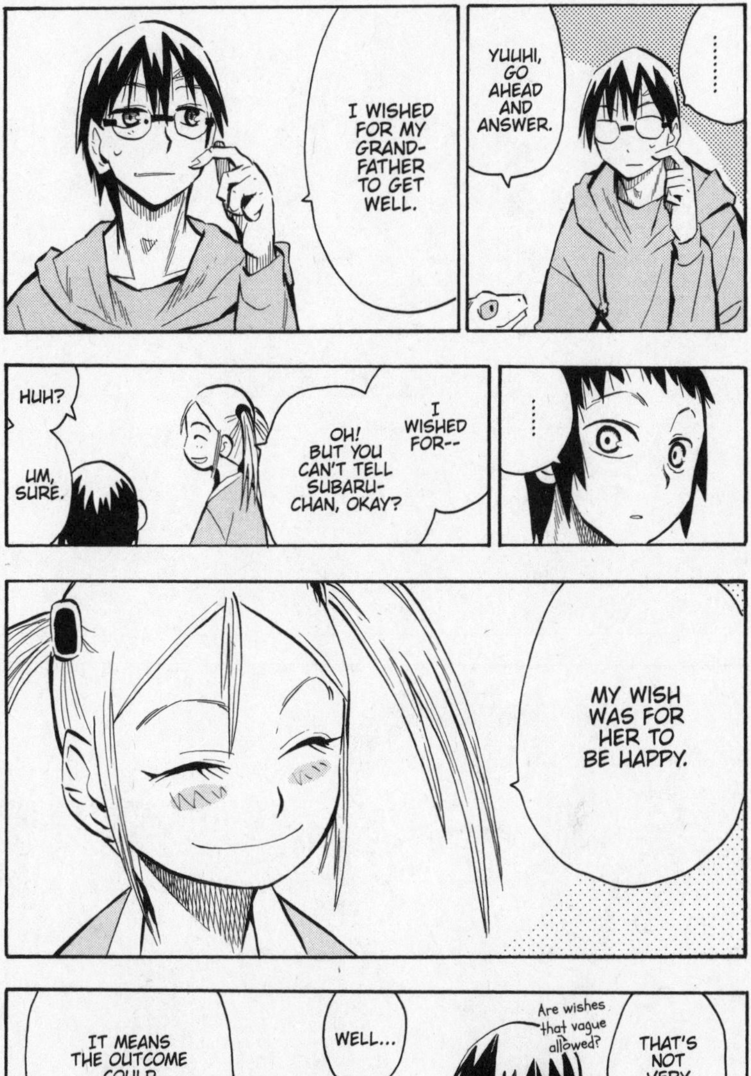
......
YUUHI, GO AHEAD AND ANSWER.
I WISHED FOR MY GRAND-FATHER TO GET WELL.
......
I WISHED FOR--
OH! BUT YOU CAN'T TELL SUBARU-CHAN, OKAY?
HUH?
UM, SURE.
MY WISH WAS FOR HER TO BE HAPPY.
THAT'S NOT VERY SPECIFIC.
Are wishes that vague allowed?
WELL...
IT MEANS THE OUTCOME COULD VARY A BIT.

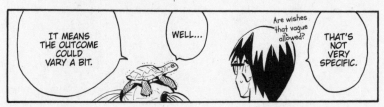

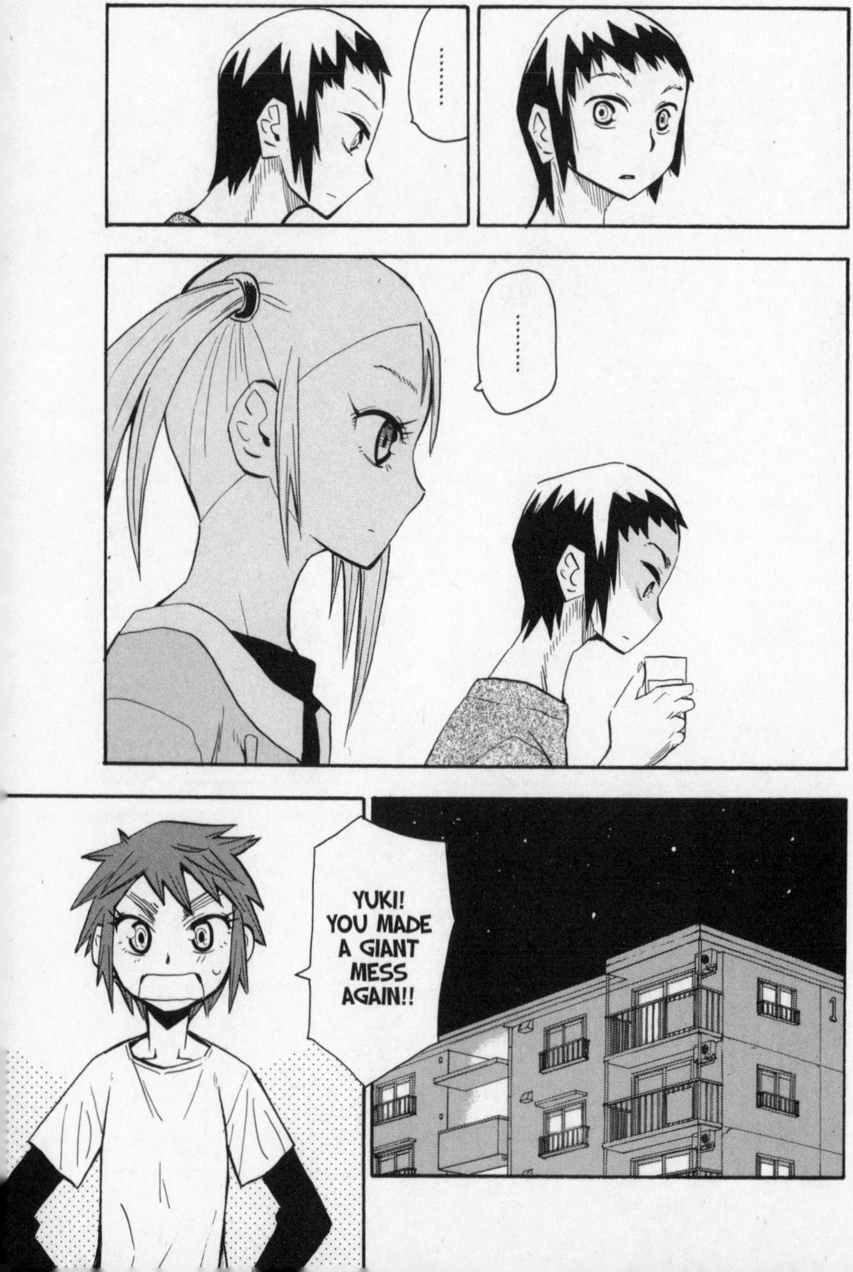
……
……
YUKI! YOU MADE A GIANT MESS AGAIN!!

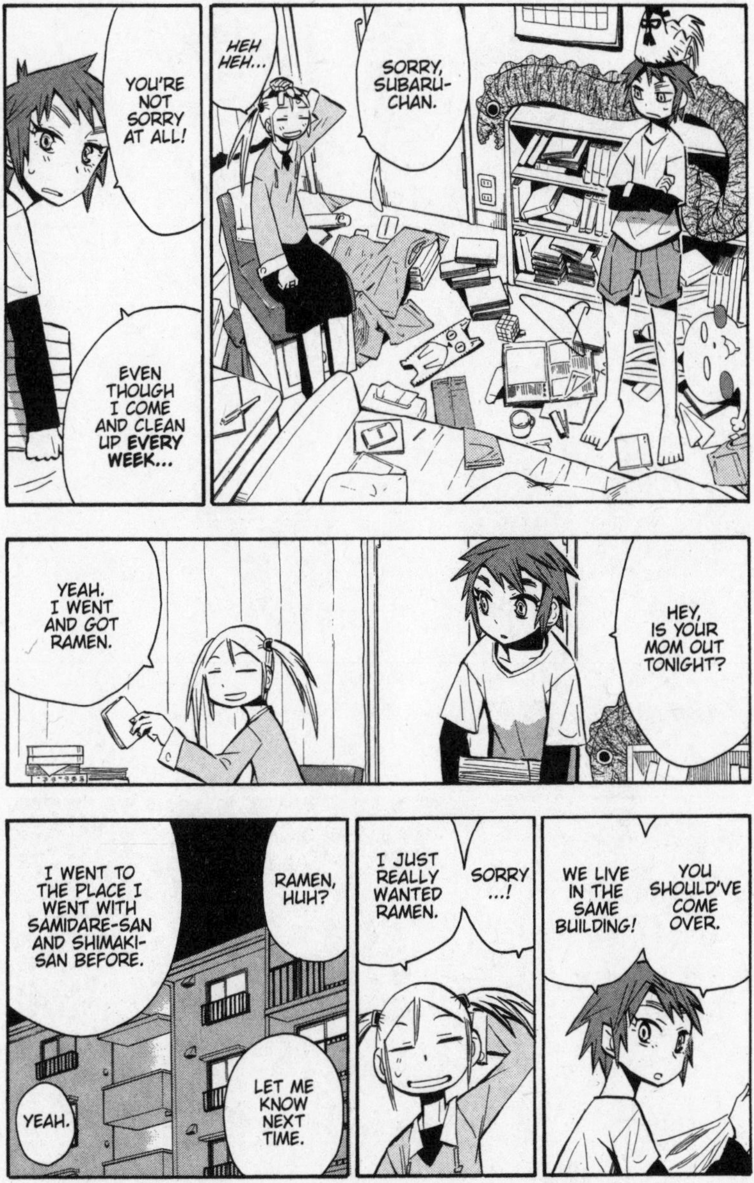
SORRY, SUBARU-CHAN.
HEH HEH...
YOU'RE NOT SORRY AT ALL!
EVEN THOUGH I COME AND CLEAN UP **EVERY WEEK...**
HEY, IS YOUR MOM OUT TONIGHT?
YEAH. I WENT AND GOT RAMEN.
YOU SHOULD'VE COME OVER.
WE LIVE IN THE SAME BUILDING!
SORRY ...!
I JUST REALLY WANTED RAMEN.
RAMEN, HUH?
I WENT TO THE PLACE I WENT WITH SAMIDARE-SAN AND SHIMAKI-SAN BEFORE.
LET ME KNOW NEXT TIME.
YEAH.

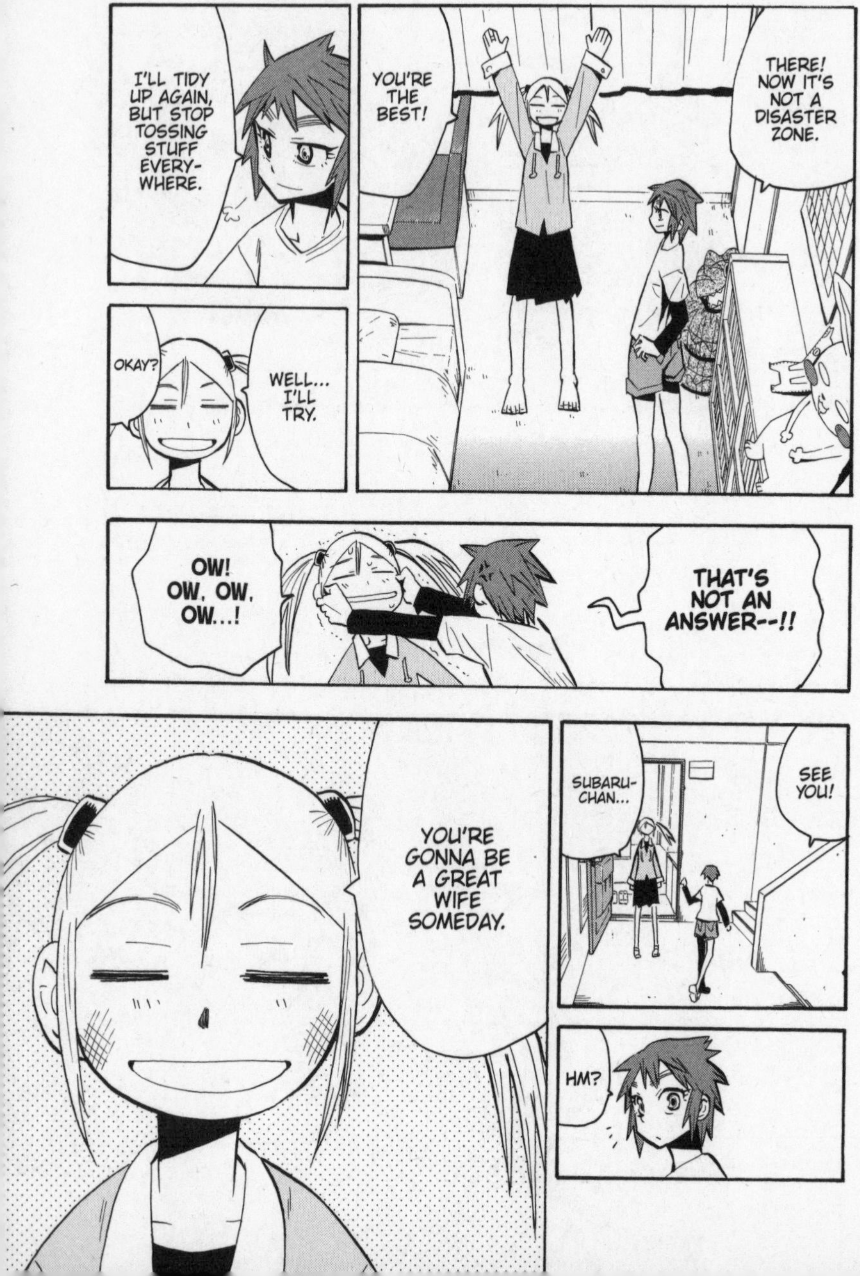
THERE! NOW IT'S NOT A DISASTER ZONE.
YOU'RE THE BEST!
I'LL TIDY UP AGAIN, BUT STOP TOSSING STUFF EVERY-WHERE.
WELL... I'LL TRY.
OKAY?
THAT'S NOT AN ANSWER--!!
OW! OW, OW, OW...!
SEE YOU!
SUBARU-CHAN...
HM?
YOU'RE GONNA BE A GREAT WIFE SOMEDAY.

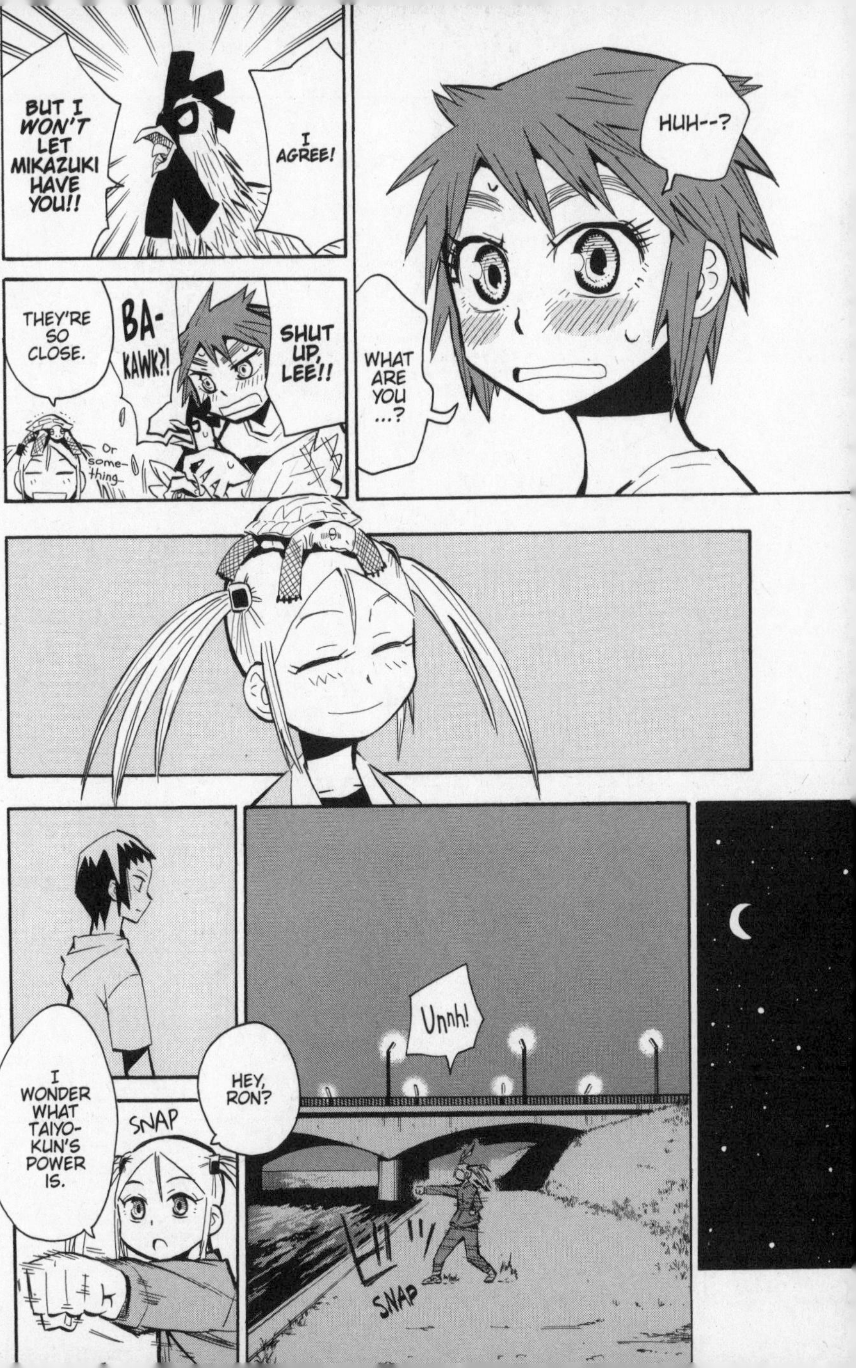
HUH--?
WHAT ARE YOU ...?
I AGREE!
BUT I WON'T LET MIKAZUKI HAVE YOU!!
SHUT UP, LEE!!
BA-KAWK?!
THEY'RE SO CLOSE.
Or some-thing...
Unnh!
SNAP
HEY, RON?
SNAP
I WONDER WHAT TAIYO-KUN'S POWER IS.

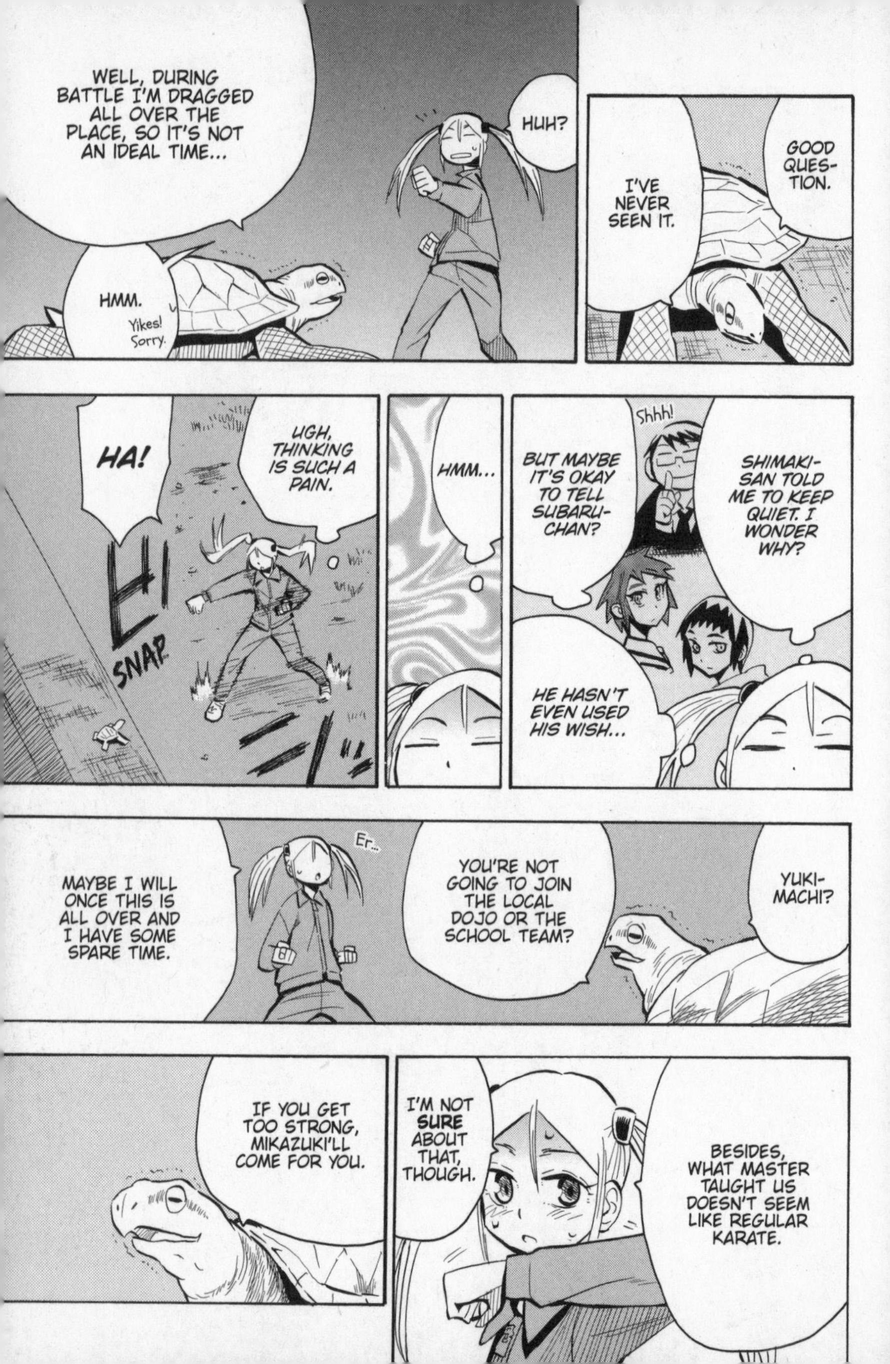
GOOD QUESTION.
I'VE NEVER SEEN IT.
HUH?
WELL, DURING BATTLE I'M DRAGGED ALL OVER THE PLACE, SO IT'S NOT AN IDEAL TIME...
HMM.
Yikes! Sorry.
SHIMAKI-SAN TOLD ME TO KEEP QUIET. I WONDER WHY?
Shhh!
BUT MAYBE IT'S OKAY TO TELL SUBARU-CHAN?
HE HASN'T EVEN USED HIS WISH...
HMM...
UGH, THINKING IS SUCH A PAIN.
HA!
SNAP
YUKI-MACHI?
YOU'RE NOT GOING TO JOIN THE LOCAL DOJO OR THE SCHOOL TEAM?
Er...
MAYBE I WILL ONCE THIS IS ALL OVER AND I HAVE SOME SPARE TIME.
BESIDES, WHAT MASTER TAUGHT US DOESN'T SEEM LIKE REGULAR KARATE.
I'M NOT **SURE** ABOUT THAT, THOUGH.
IF YOU GET TOO STRONG, MIKAZUKI'LL COME FOR YOU.

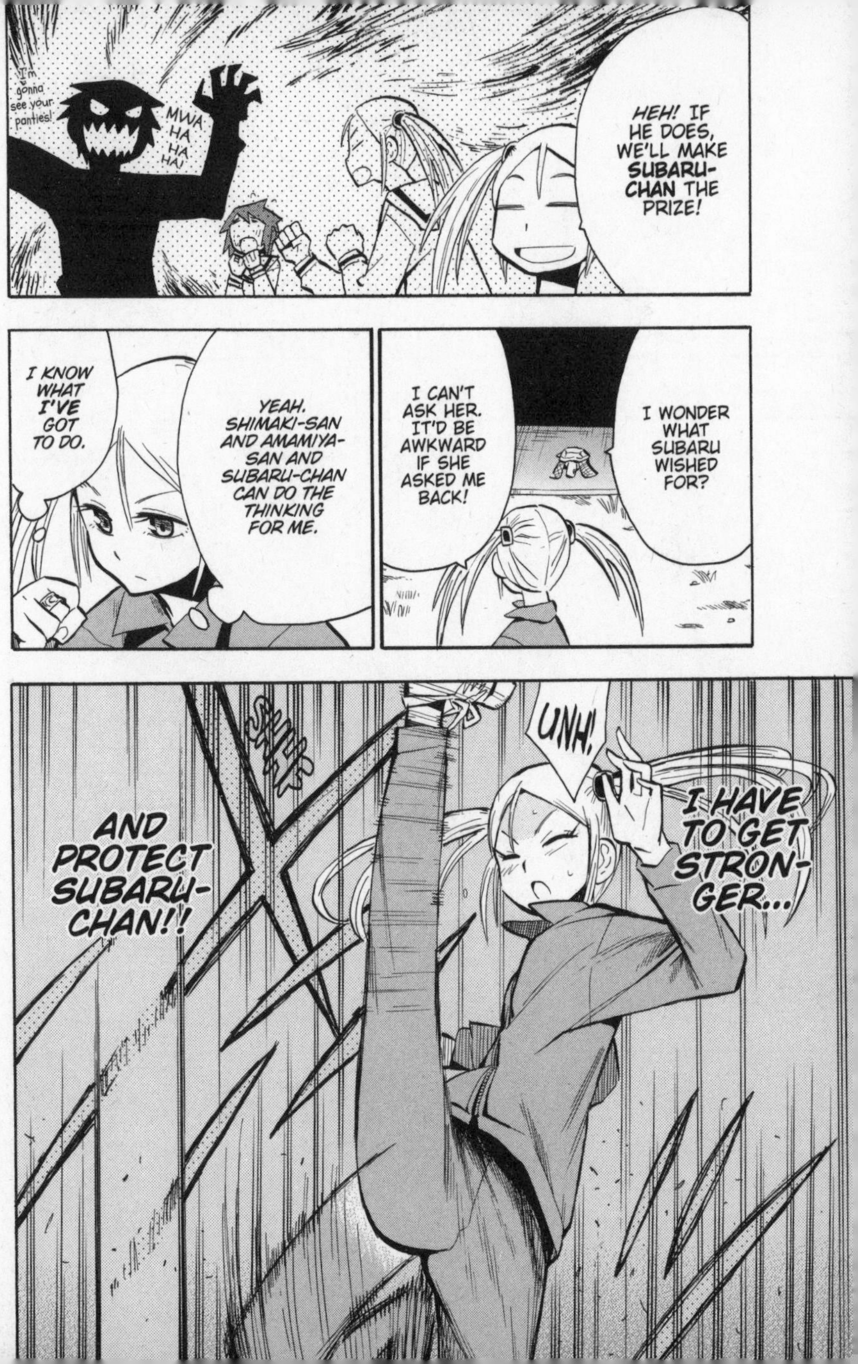
HEH! IF HE DOES, WE'LL MAKE SUBARU-CHAN THE PRIZE!
MWA HA HA HA!
I'm gonna see your panties!
I WONDER WHAT SUBARU WISHED FOR?
I CAN'T ASK HER. IT'D BE AWKWARD IF SHE ASKED ME BACK!
YEAH. SHIMAKI-SAN AND AMAMIYA-SAN AND SUBARU-CHAN CAN DO THE THINKING FOR ME.
I KNOW WHAT I'VE GOT TO DO.
UNH!
I HAVE TO GET STRONGER...
AND PROTECT SUBARU-CHAN!!

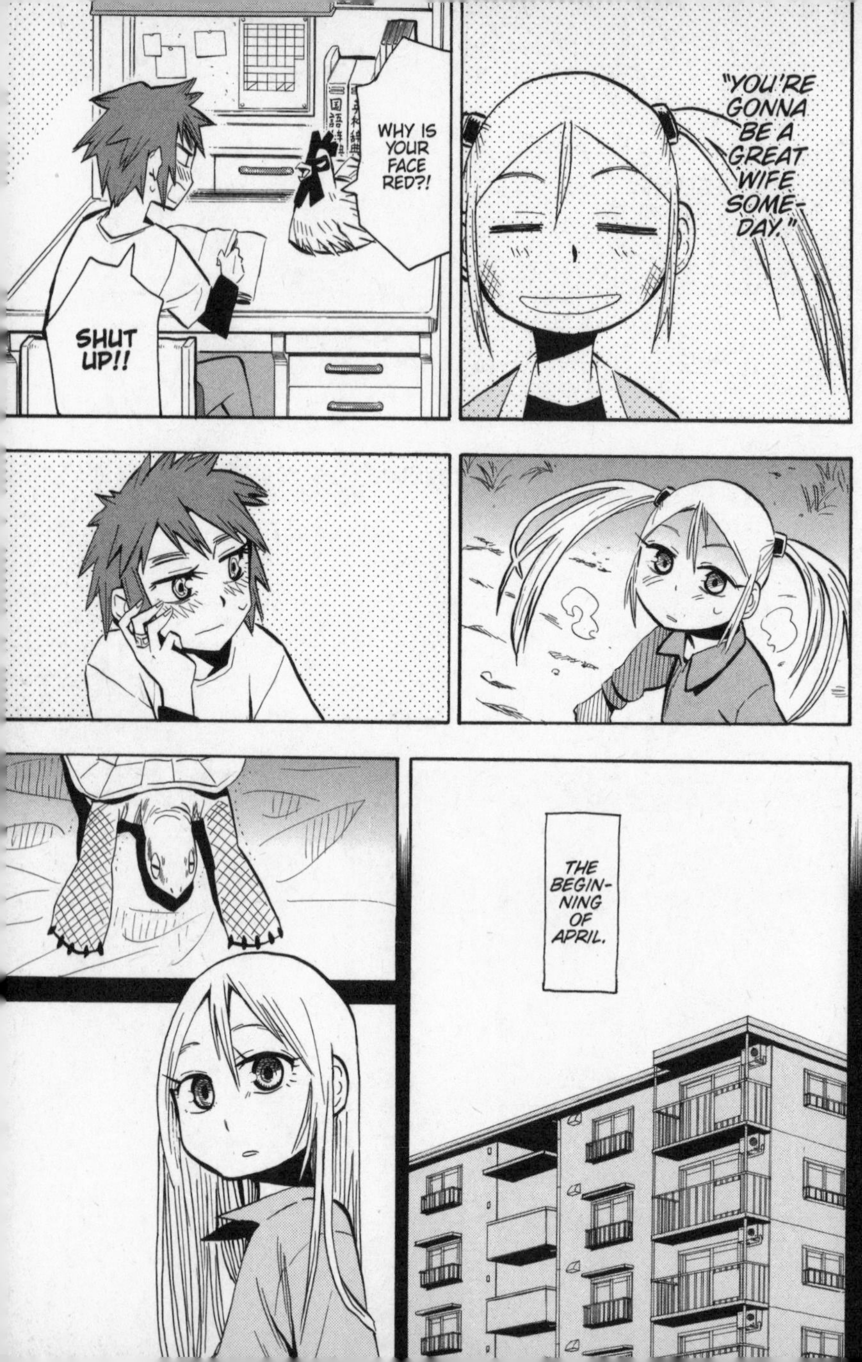
"YOU'RE GONNA BE A GREAT WIFE SOMEDAY."
WHY IS YOUR FACE RED?!
SHUT UP!!
THE BEGINNING OF APRIL.

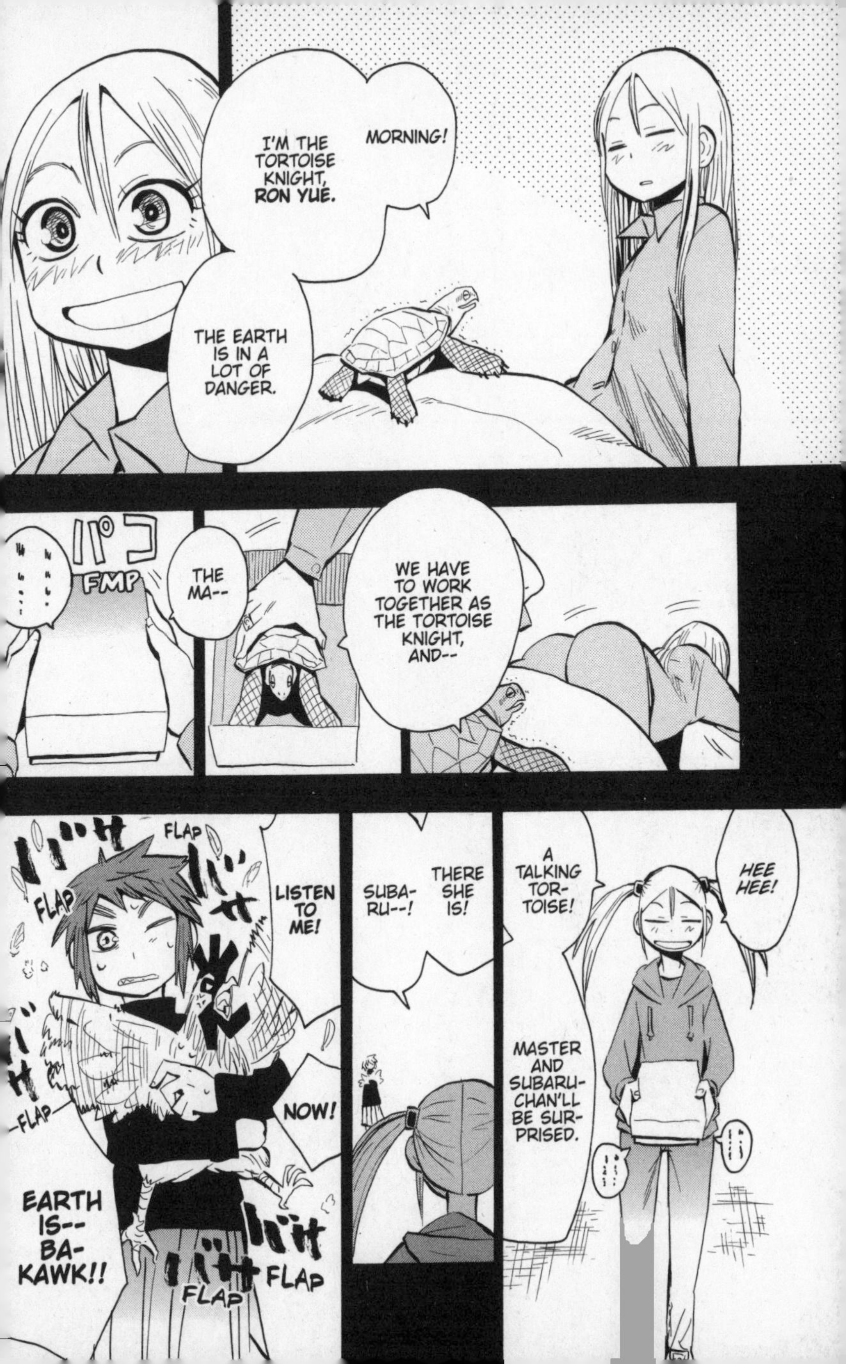
MORNING!
I'M THE TORTOISE KNIGHT, RON YUE.
THE EARTH IS IN A LOT OF DANGER.
WE HAVE TO WORK TOGETHER AS THE TORTOISE KNIGHT, AND--
THE MA--
パコ
FMP
HEE HEE!
A TALKING TOR-TOISE!
MASTER AND SUBARU-CHAN'LL BE SUR-PRISED.
THERE SHE IS!
SUBA-RU--!
LISTEN TO ME!
FLAP
FLAP
NOW!
FLAP
EARTH IS-- BA-KAWK!!
FLAP
FLAP

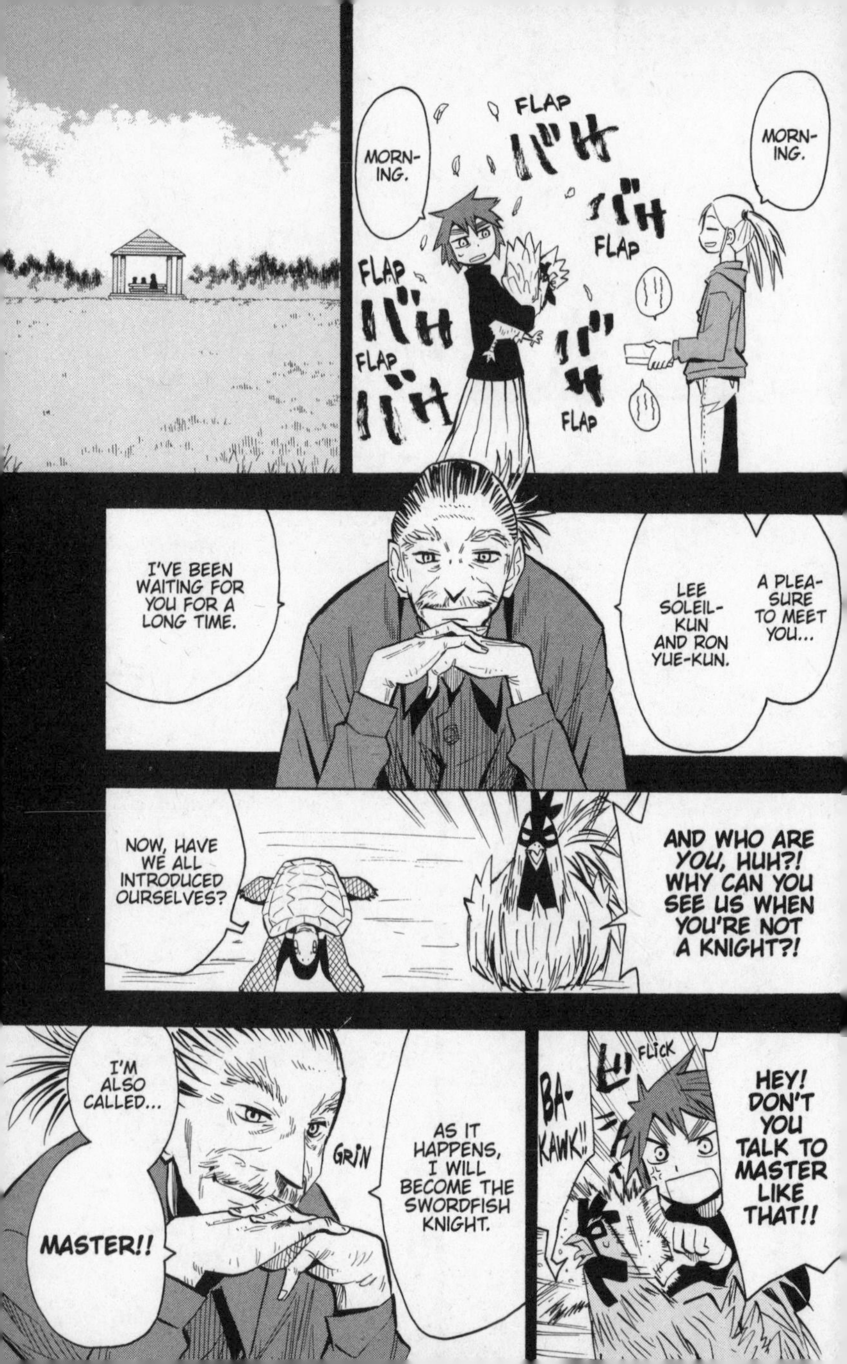
MORN-ING.
FLAP
MORN-ING.
FLAP
FLAP
FLAP
FLAP
FLAP
A PLEA-SURE TO MEET YOU...
LEE SOLEIL-KUN AND RON YUE-KUN.
I'VE BEEN WAITING FOR YOU FOR A LONG TIME.
AND WHO ARE YOU, HUH?! WHY CAN YOU SEE US WHEN YOU'RE NOT A KNIGHT?!
NOW, HAVE WE ALL INTRODUCED OURSELVES?
HEY! DON'T YOU TALK TO MASTER LIKE THAT!!
FLICK
BA-KAWK!!
AS IT HAPPENS, I WILL BECOME THE SWORDFISH KNIGHT.
GRIN
I'M ALSO CALLED...
MASTER!!

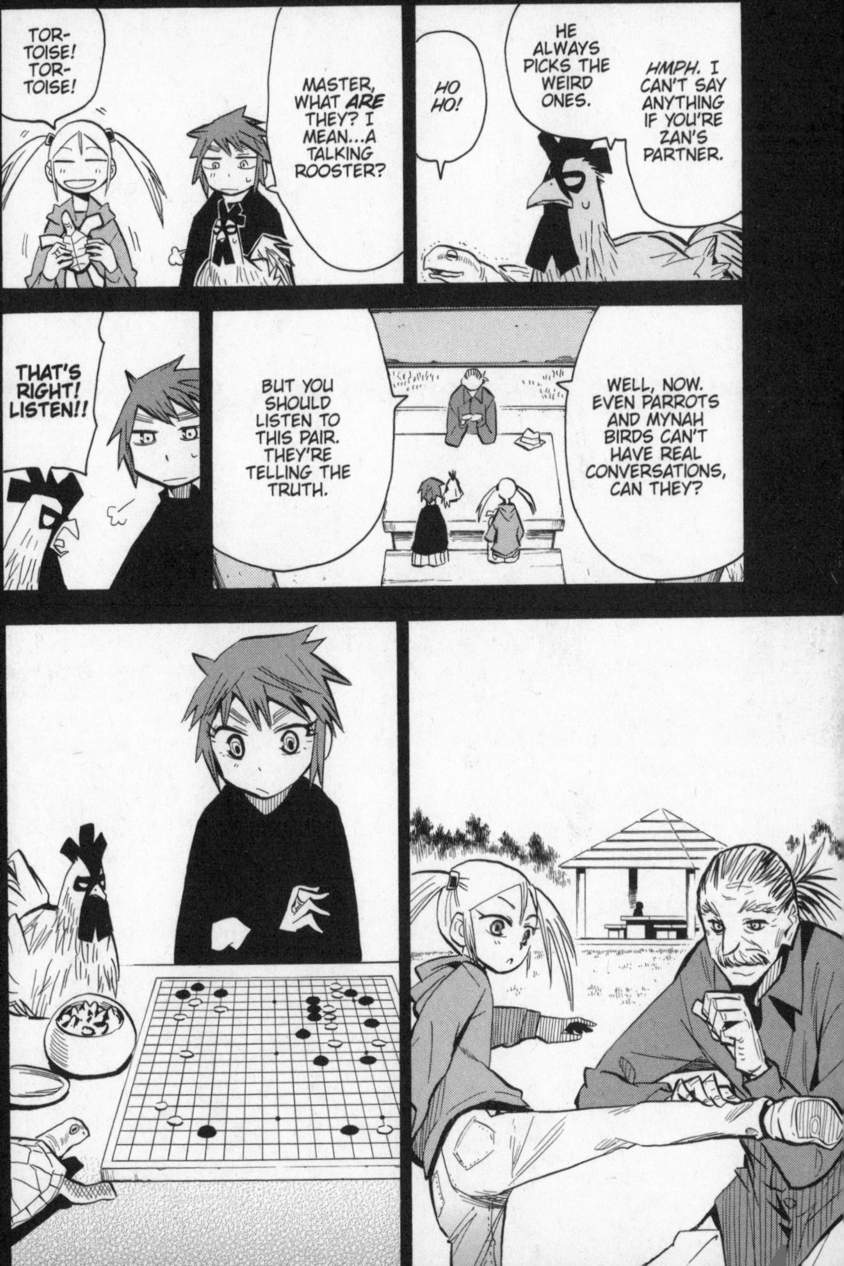

HMPH. I CAN'T SAY ANYTHING IF YOU'RE ZAN'S PARTNER.
HE ALWAYS PICKS THE WEIRD ONES.
HO HO!
MASTER, WHAT *ARE* THEY? I MEAN...A TALKING ROOSTER?
TOR-TOISE! TOR-TOISE!
WELL, NOW. EVEN PARROTS AND MYNAH BIRDS CAN'T HAVE REAL CONVERSATIONS, CAN THEY?
BUT YOU SHOULD LISTEN TO THIS PAIR. THEY'RE TELLING THE TRUTH.
THAT'S RIGHT! LISTEN!!

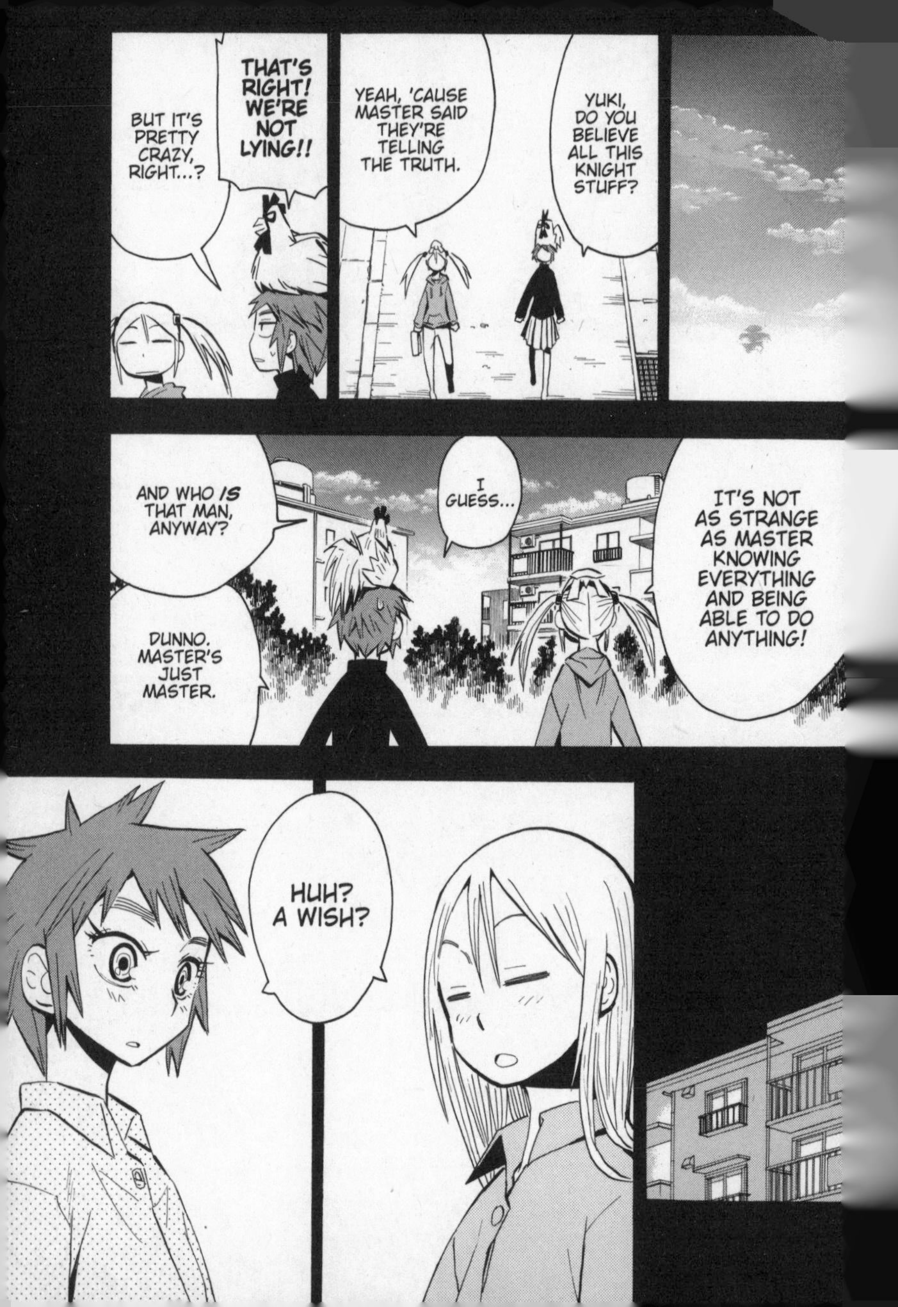
YUKI, DO YOU BELIEVE ALL THIS KNIGHT STUFF?
YEAH, 'CAUSE MASTER SAID THEY'RE TELLING THE TRUTH.
THAT'S RIGHT! WE'RE NOT LYING!!
BUT IT'S PRETTY CRAZY, RIGHT...?
IT'S NOT AS STRANGE AS MASTER KNOWING EVERYTHING AND BEING ABLE TO DO ANYTHING!
I GUESS...
AND WHO *IS* THAT MAN, ANYWAY?
DUNNO. MASTER'S JUST MASTER.
HUH? A WISH?

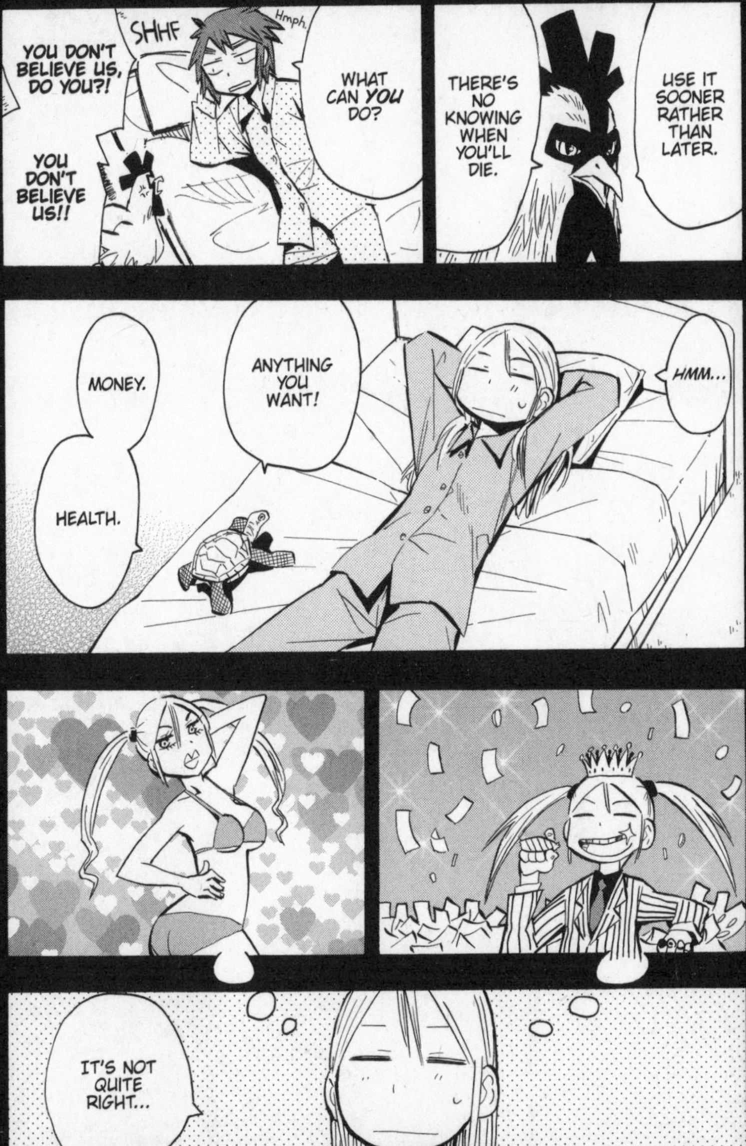
USE IT SOONER RATHER THAN LATER.
THERE'S NO KNOWING WHEN YOU'LL DIE.
WHAT CAN *YOU* DO?
Hmph,
SHHF
YOU DON'T BELIEVE US, DO YOU?!
YOU DON'T BELIEVE US!!
HMM...
ANYTHING YOU WANT!
MONEY.
HEALTH.
IT'S NOT QUITE RIGHT...

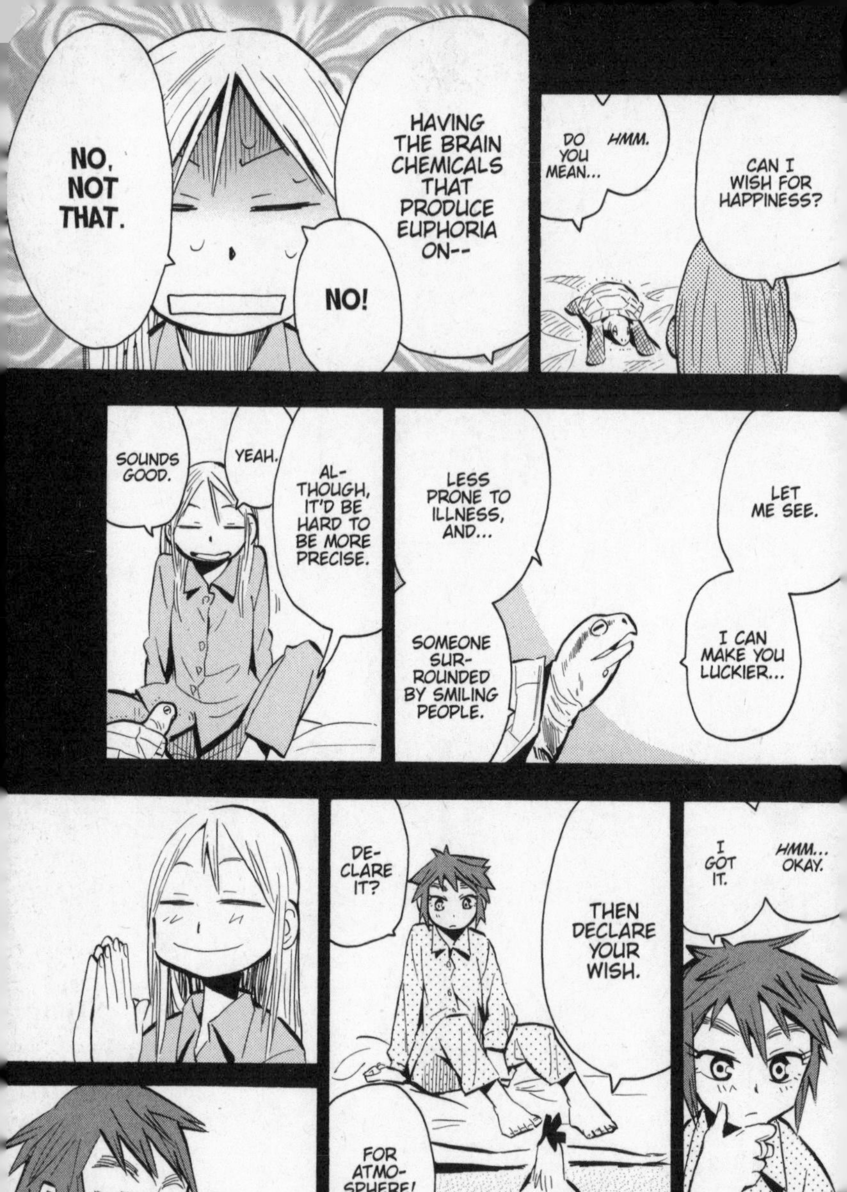
CAN I WISH FOR HAPPINESS?
HMM.
DO YOU MEAN...
HAVING THE BRAIN CHEMICALS THAT PRODUCE EUPHORIA ON--
NO!
NO, NOT THAT.
LET ME SEE.
I CAN MAKE YOU LUCKIER...
LESS PRONE TO ILLNESS, AND...
SOMEONE SUR-ROUNDED BY SMILING PEOPLE.
AL-THOUGH, IT'D BE HARD TO BE MORE PRECISE.
YEAH.
SOUNDS GOOD.
HMM... OKAY.
I GOT IT.
THEN DECLARE YOUR WISH.
DE-CLARE IT?
FOR ATMO-SPHERE!

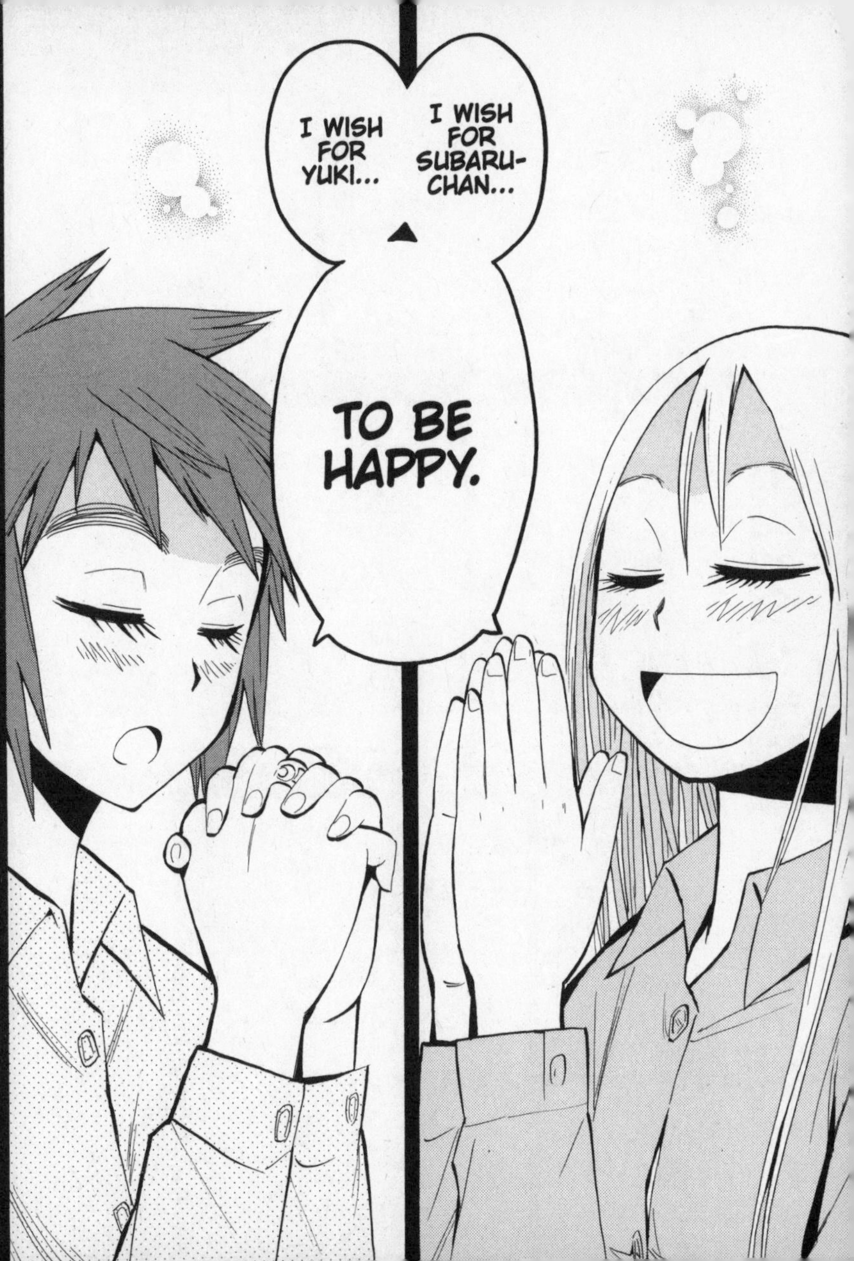
I WISH FOR SUBARU-CHAN...
I WISH FOR YUKI...
TO BE HAPPY.

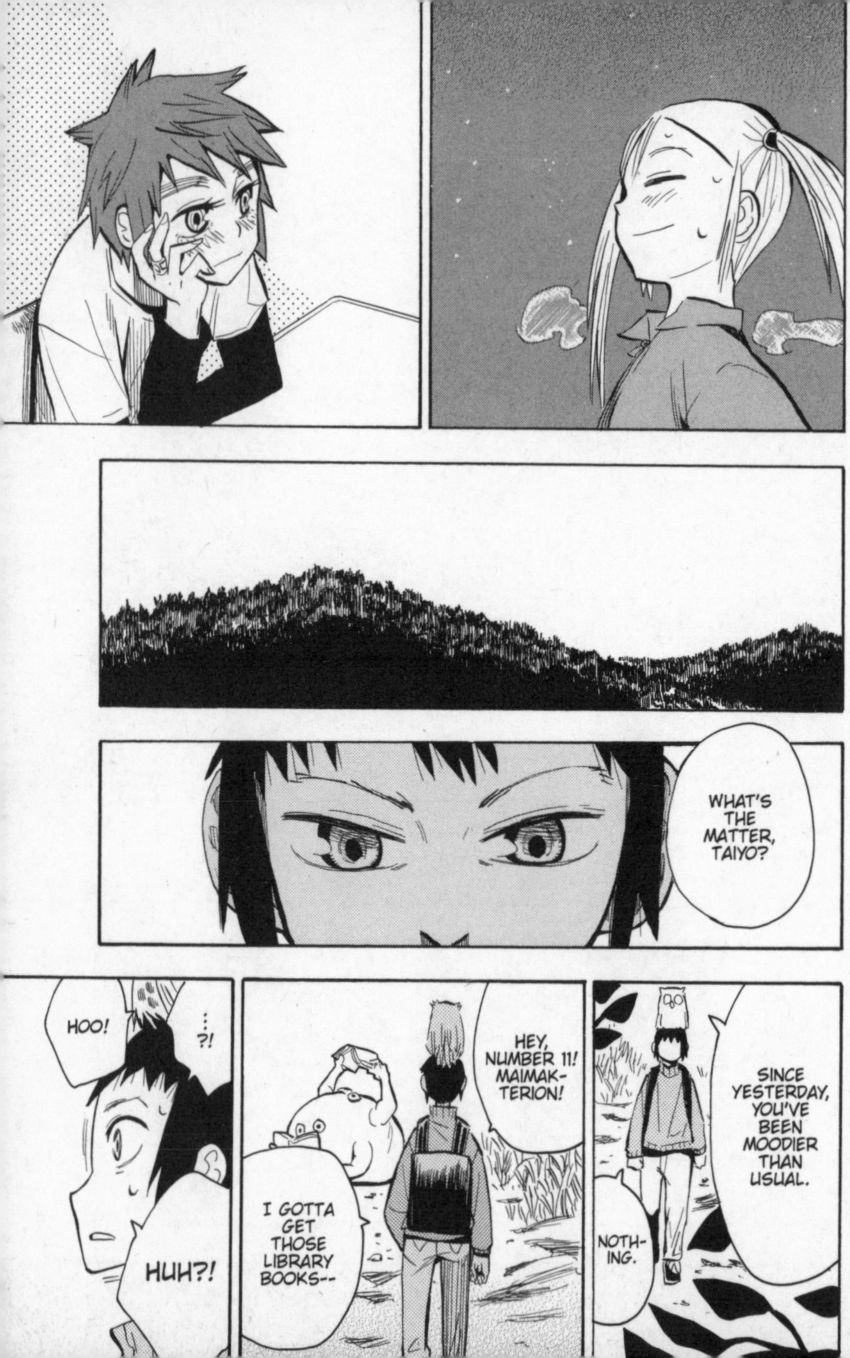
WHAT'S THE MATTER, TAIYO?
SINCE YESTERDAY, YOU'VE BEEN MOODIER THAN USUAL.
NOTH-ING.
HEY, NUMBER 11! MAIMAK-TERION!
I GOTTA GET THOSE LIBRARY BOOKS--
...?!
HOO!
HUH?!

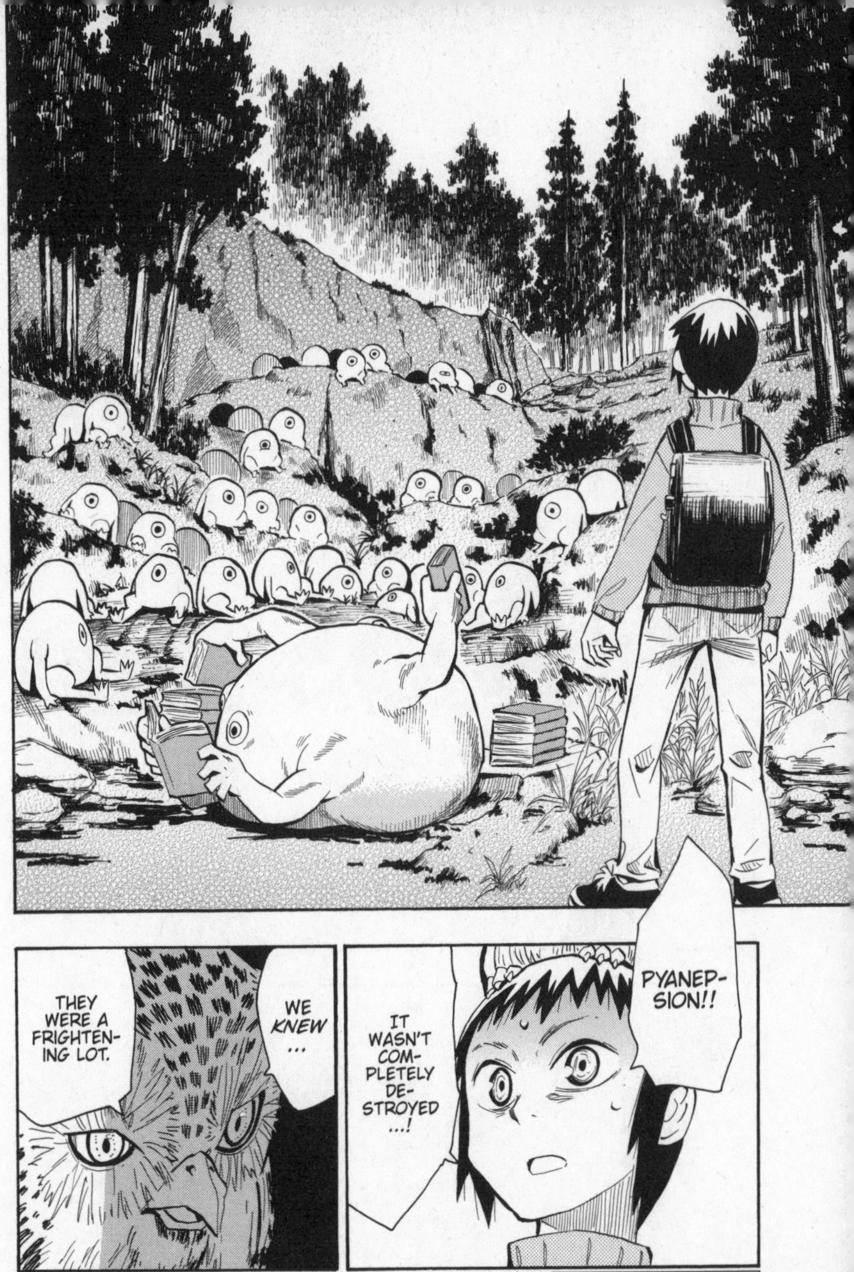
PYANEP-SION!!
IT WASN'T COM-PLETELY DE-STROYED ...!
WE KNEW ...
THEY WERE A FRIGHTEN-ING LOT.

Chapter 43/END

Chapter 44: Taiyo and the Golems

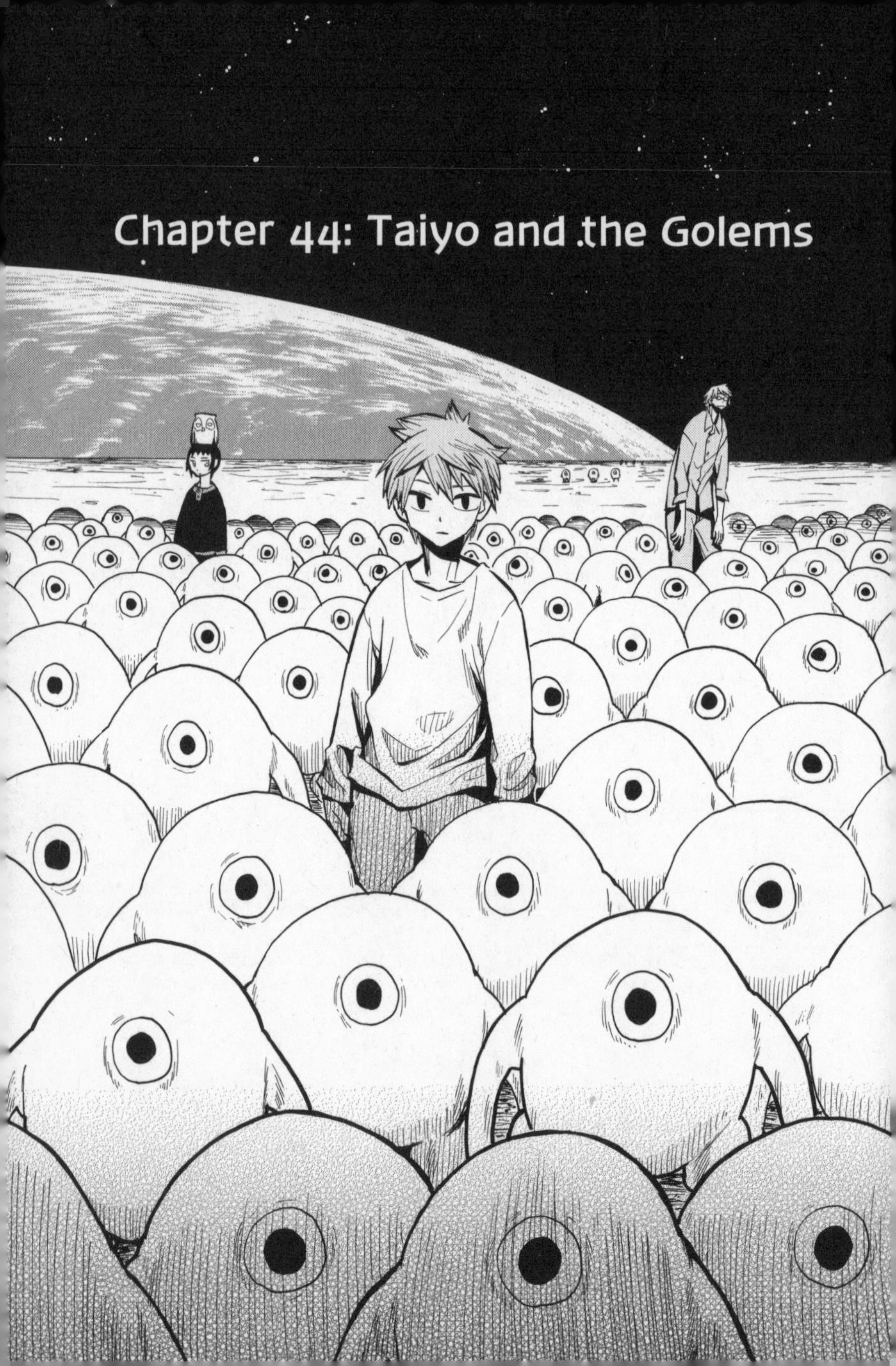

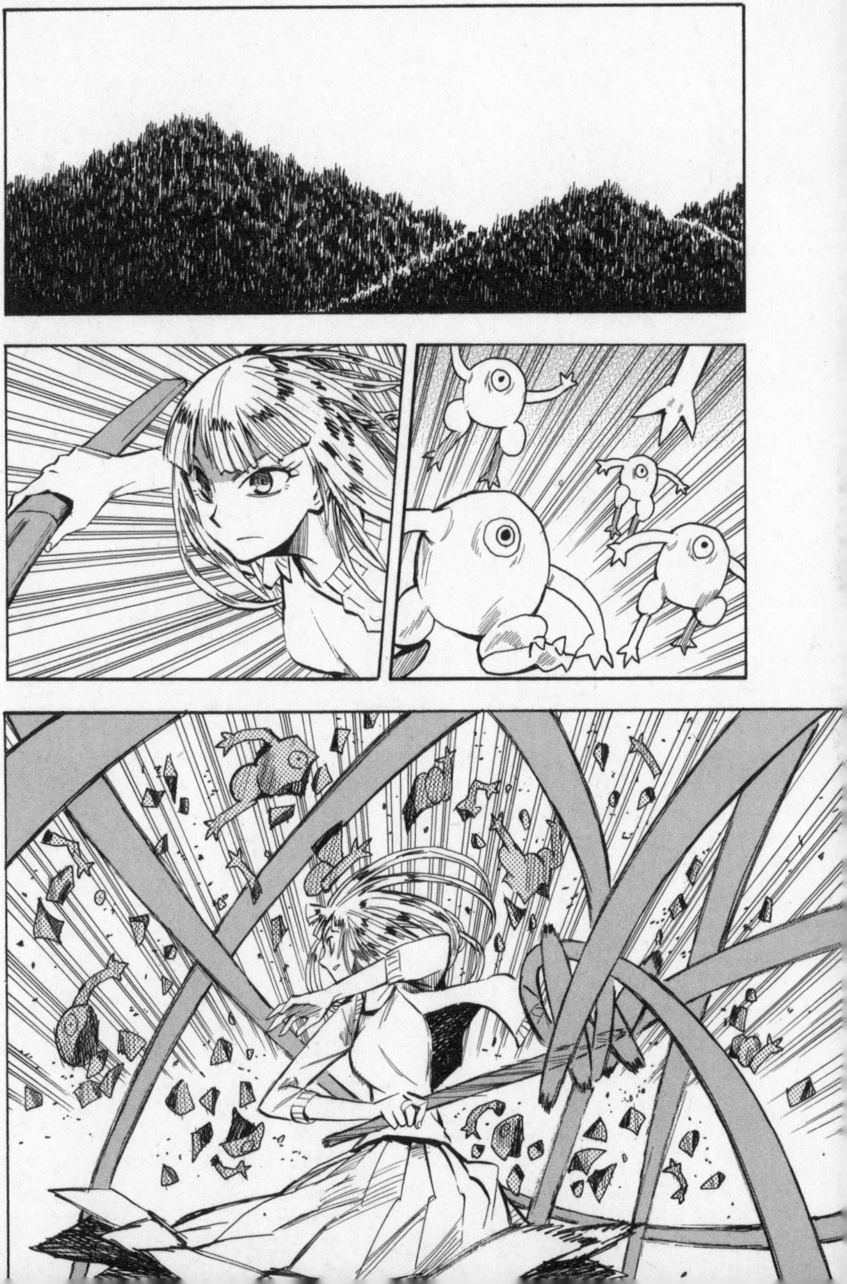

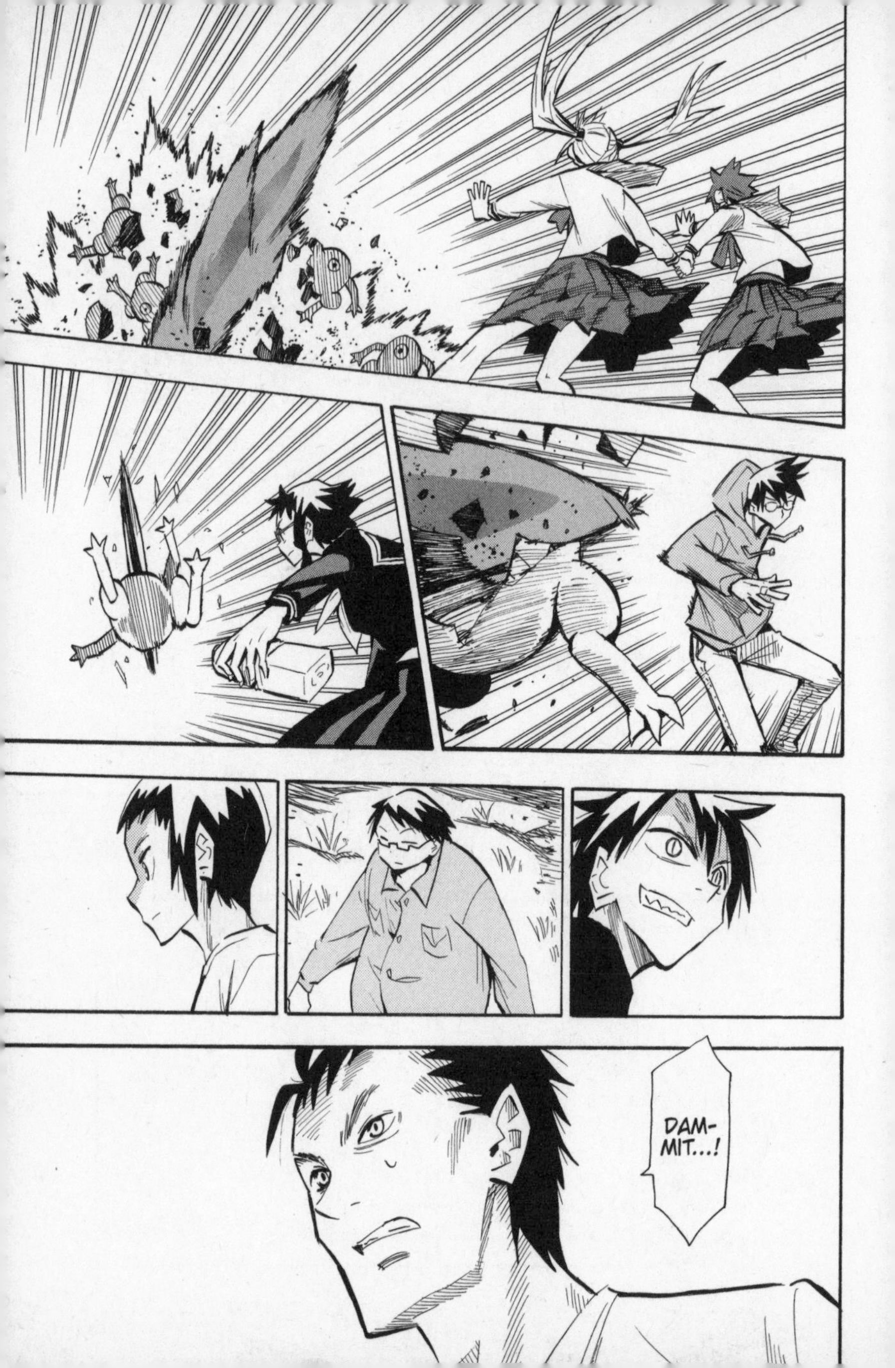
DAM-
MIT...!

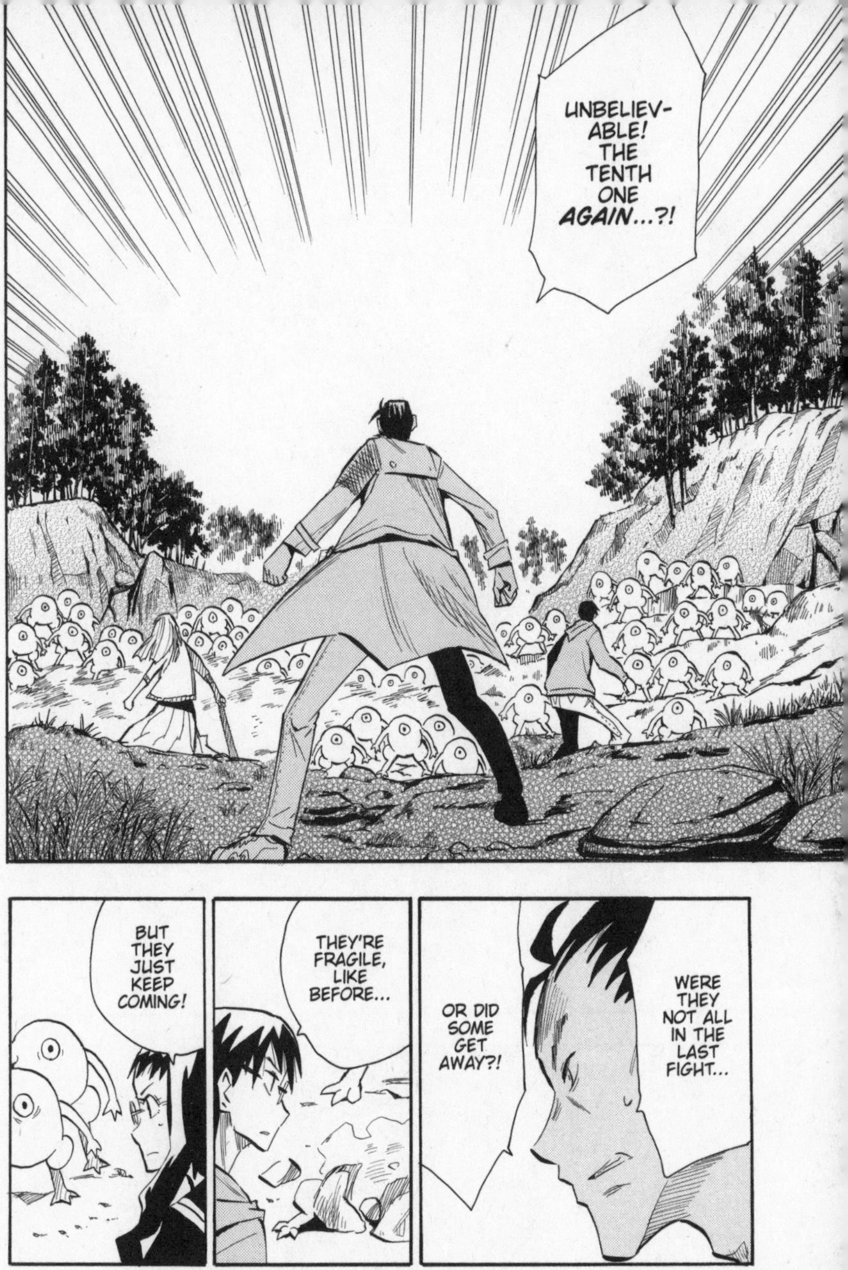
UNBELIEV-ABLE! THE TENTH ONE AGAIN...?!
WERE THEY NOT ALL IN THE LAST FIGHT...
OR DID SOME GET AWAY?!
THEY'RE FRAGILE, LIKE BEFORE...
BUT THEY JUST KEEP COMING!

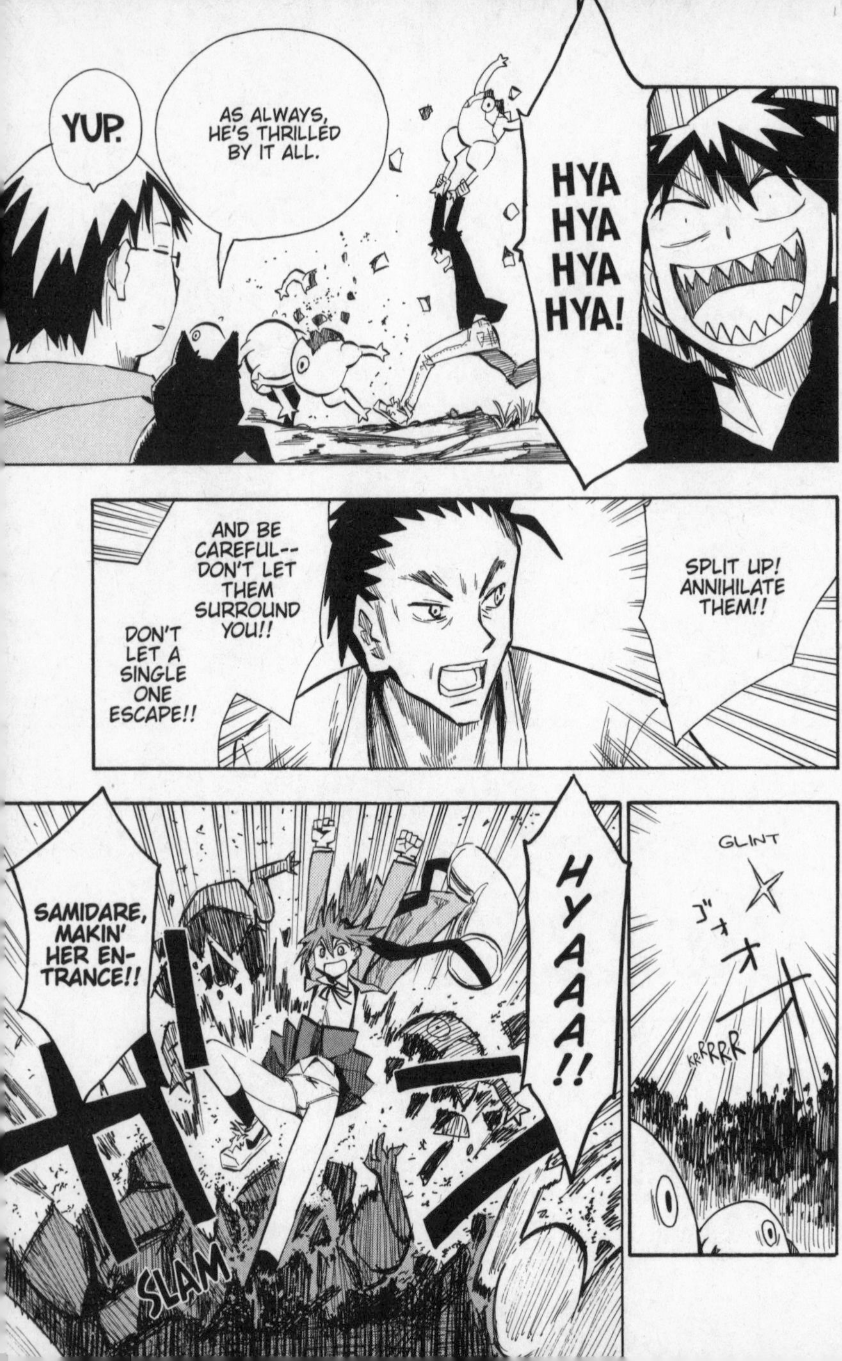
HYA HYA HYA HYA!
AS ALWAYS, HE'S THRILLED BY IT ALL.
YUP.
SPLIT UP! ANNIHILATE THEM!!
AND BE CAREFUL-- DON'T LET THEM SURROUND YOU!!
DON'T LET A SINGLE ONE ESCAPE!!
GLINT
ゴォオ
KRRRRR
HYAAAA!!
SAMIDARE, MAKIN' HER EN-TRANCE!!
SLAM

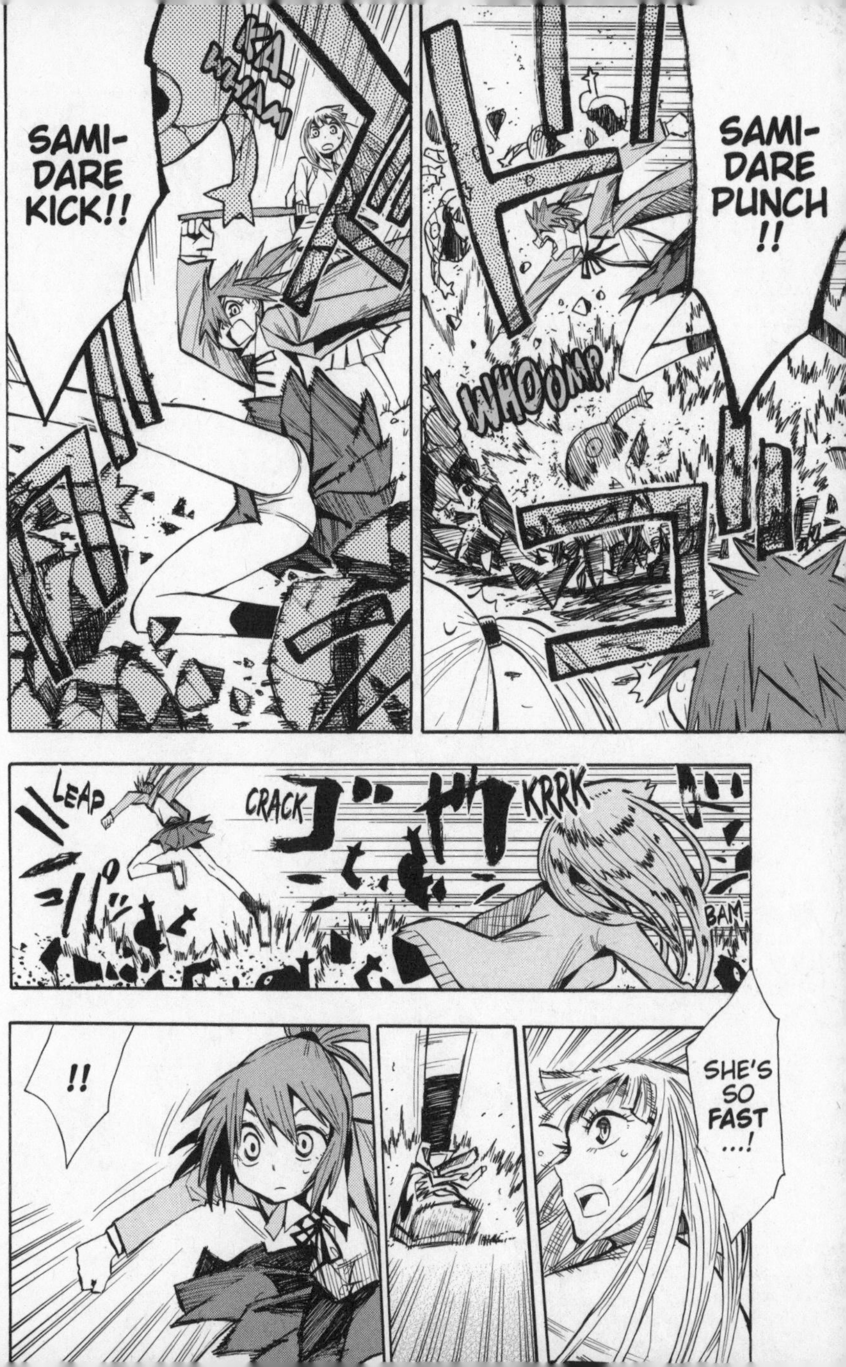
SAMI-DARE PUNCH !!
WHOOMP
SAMI-DARE KICK!!
KA-WHAM
BAM
KRRK
CRACK
LEAP
SHE'S SO FAST ...!
!!

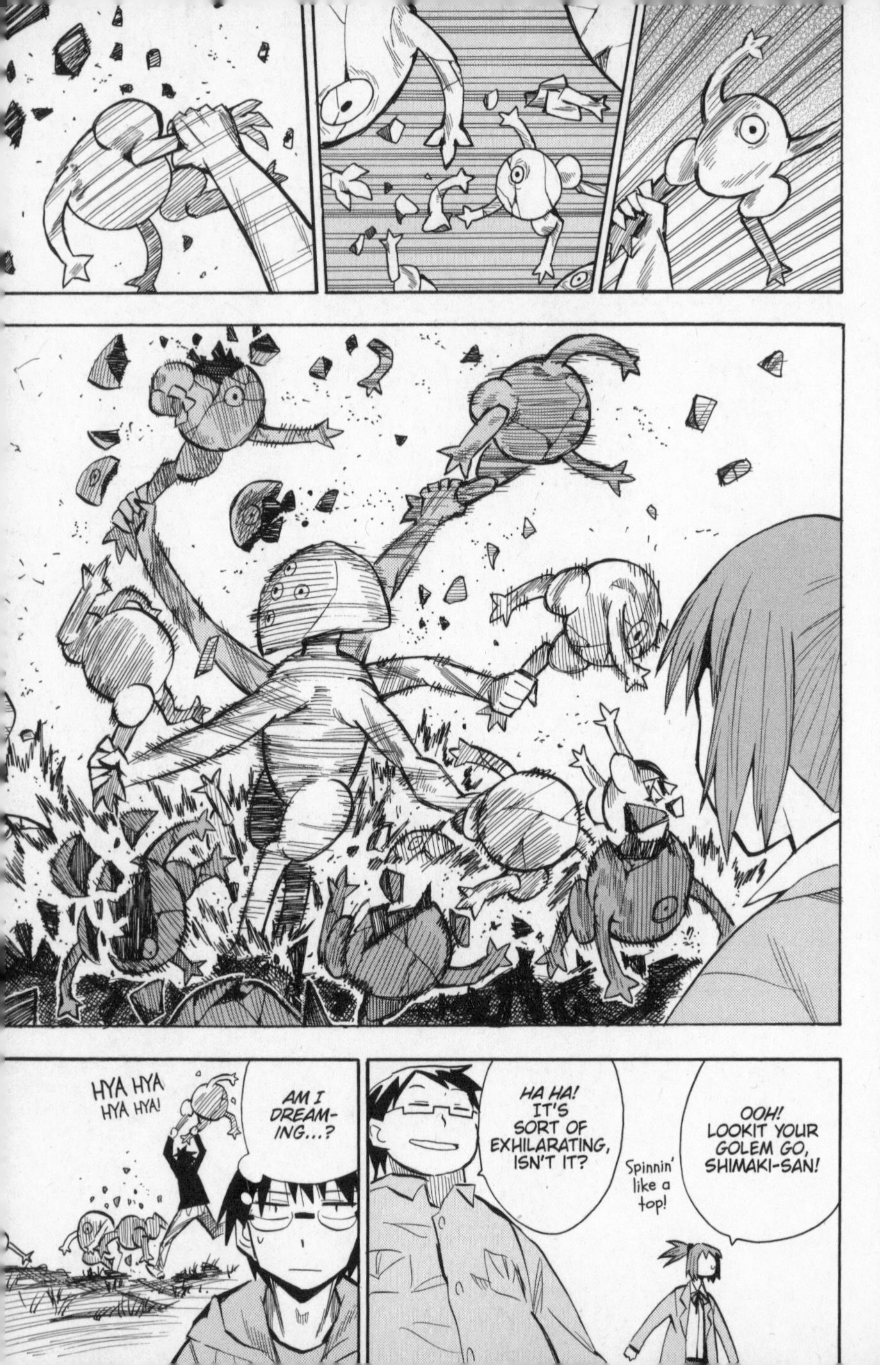
OOH! LOOKIT YOUR GOLEM GO, SHIMAKI-SAN!
Spinnin' like a top!
HA HA! IT'S SORT OF EXHILARATING, ISN'T IT?
AM I DREAMING...?
HYA HYA HYA HYA!

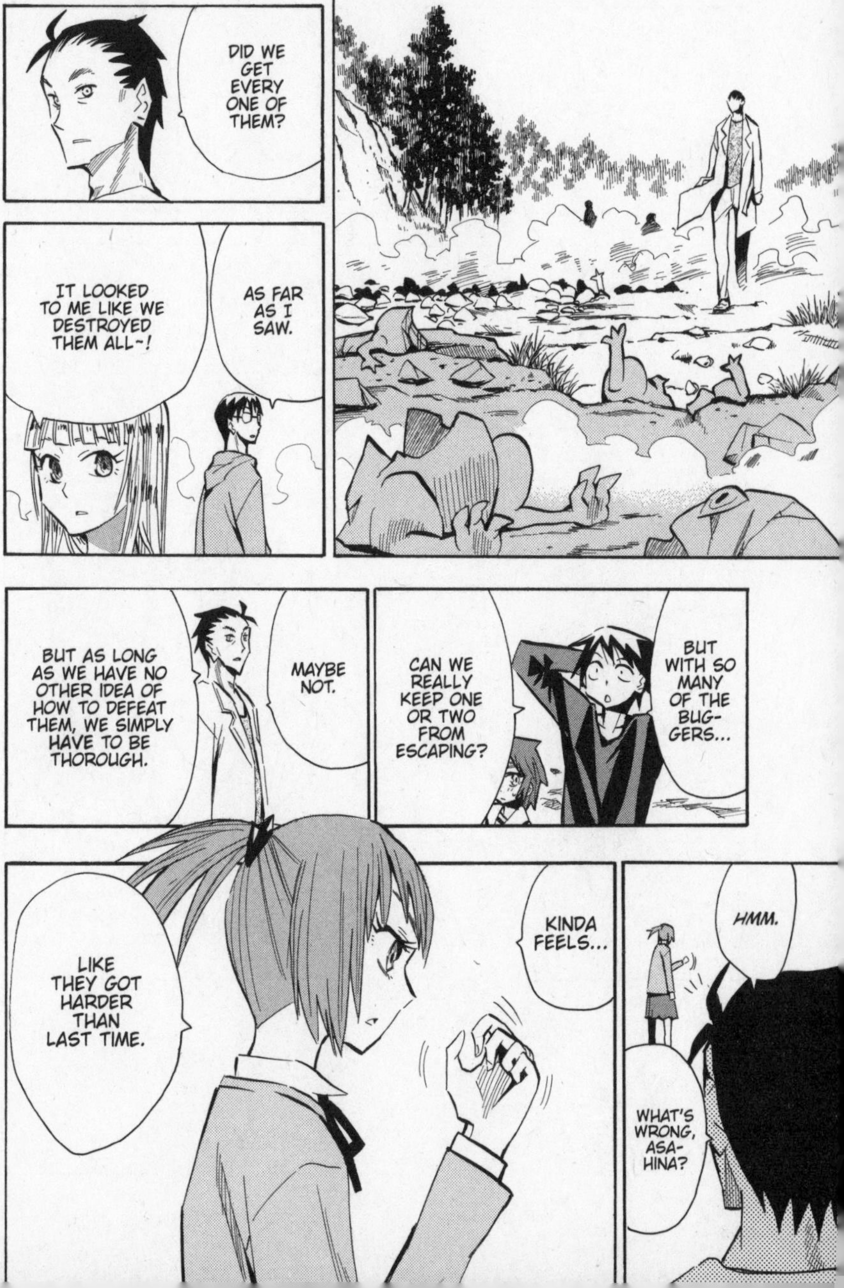
DID WE GET EVERY ONE OF THEM?
AS FAR AS I SAW.
IT LOOKED TO ME LIKE WE DESTROYED THEM ALL~!
BUT WITH SO MANY OF THE BUG-GERS...
CAN WE REALLY KEEP ONE OR TWO FROM ESCAPING?
MAYBE NOT.
BUT AS LONG AS WE HAVE NO OTHER IDEA OF HOW TO DEFEAT THEM, WE SIMPLY HAVE TO BE THOROUGH.
HMM.
WHAT'S WRONG, ASA-HINA?
KINDA FEELS...
LIKE THEY GOT HARDER THAN LAST TIME.

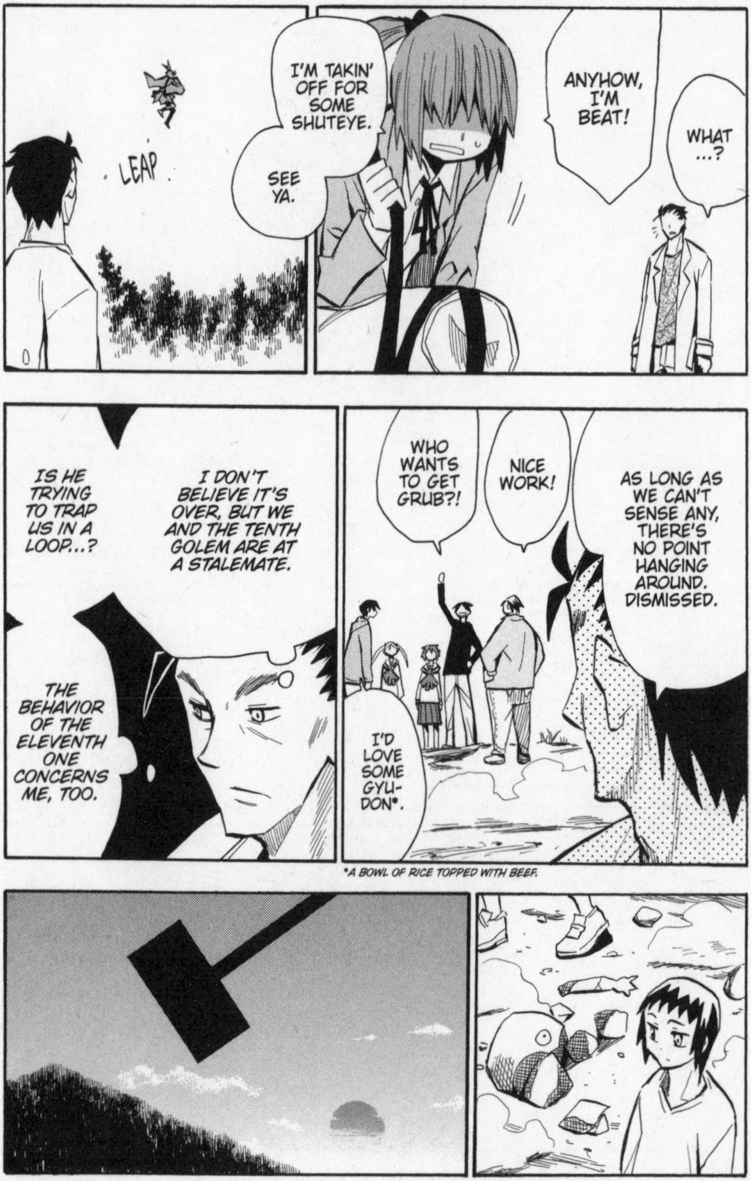
ANYHOW, I'M BEAT!
WHAT ...?
I'M TAKIN' OFF FOR SOME SHUTEYE.
SEE YA.
LEAP
AS LONG AS WE CAN'T SENSE ANY, THERE'S NO POINT HANGING AROUND. DISMISSED.
NICE WORK!
WHO WANTS TO GET GRUB?!
I'D LOVE SOME GYU-DON*.
I DON'T BELIEVE IT'S OVER, BUT WE AND THE TENTH GOLEM ARE AT A STALEMATE.
IS HE TRYING TO TRAP US IN A LOOP...?
THE BEHAVIOR OF THE ELEVENTH ONE CONCERNS ME, TOO.
*A BOWL OF RICE TOPPED WITH BEEF.

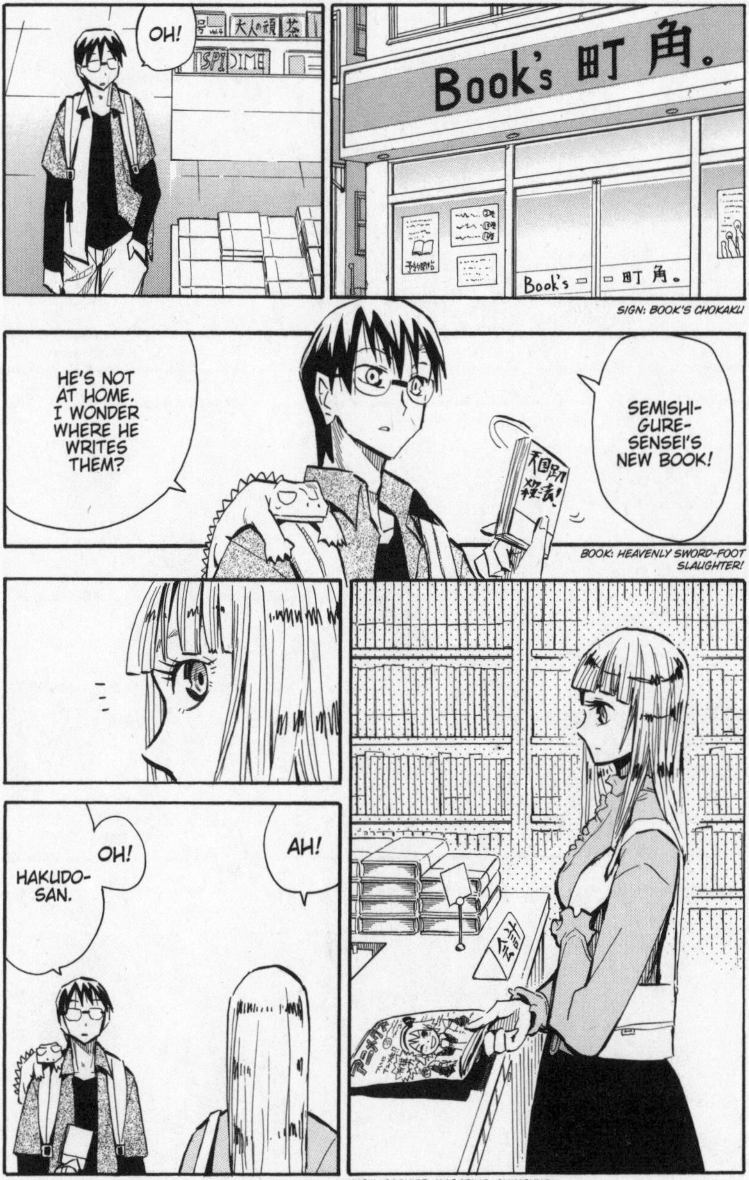
Book's 町角。
OH!
SIGN: BOOK'S CHOKAKU
SEMISHIGURE-SENSEI'S NEW BOOK!
HE'S NOT AT HOME. I WONDER WHERE HE WRITES THEM?
BOOK: HEAVENLY SWORD-FOOT SLAUGHTER!
...
AH!
OH! HAKUDO-SAN.
SIGN: CASHIER, MAGAZINE: ANIMEKUS

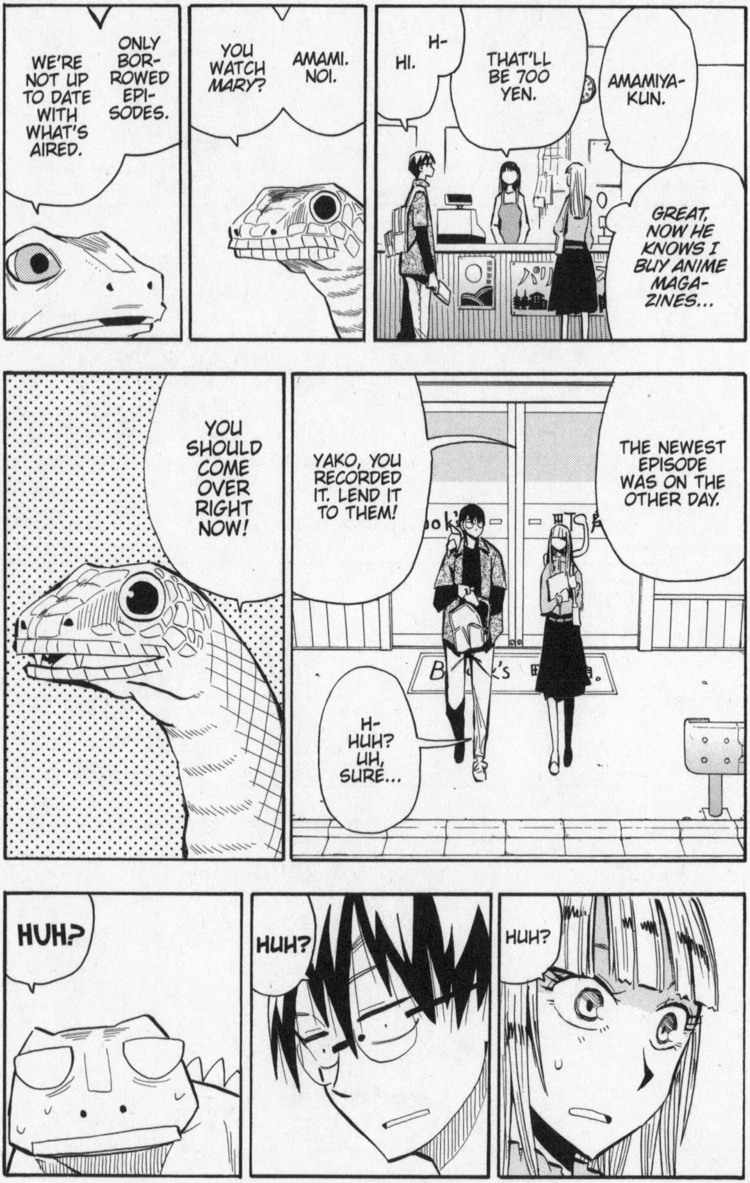
AMAMIYA-KUN.
THAT'LL BE 700 YEN.
H- HI.
GREAT, NOW HE KNOWS I BUY ANIME MAGAZINES...
AMAMI. NOI.
YOU WATCH MARY?
ONLY BORROWED EPISODES.
WE'RE NOT UP TO DATE WITH WHAT'S AIRED.
THE NEWEST EPISODE WAS ON THE OTHER DAY.
YAKO, YOU RECORDED IT. LEND IT TO THEM!
H-HUH? UH, SURE...
YOU SHOULD COME OVER RIGHT NOW!
HUH?
HUH?
HUH?

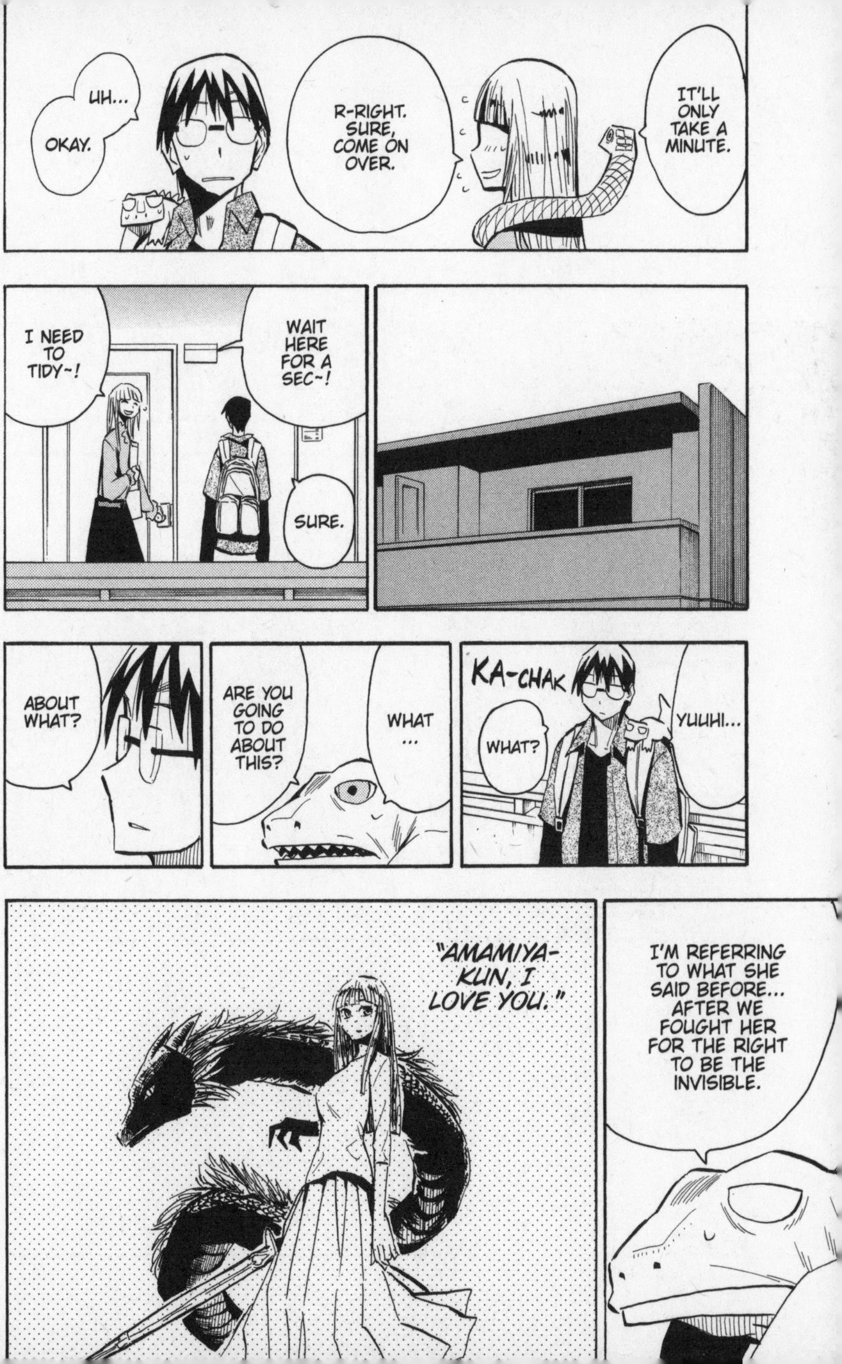
IT'LL ONLY TAKE A MINUTE.
R-RIGHT. SURE, COME ON OVER.
UH... OKAY.
WAIT HERE FOR A SEC~!
I NEED TO TIDY~!
SURE.
YUUHI...
KA-CHAK
WHAT?
WHAT ...
ARE YOU GOING TO DO ABOUT THIS?
ABOUT WHAT?
I'M REFERRING TO WHAT SHE SAID BEFORE... AFTER WE FOUGHT HER FOR THE RIGHT TO BE THE INVISIBLE.
"AMAMIYA-KUN, I LOVE YOU."

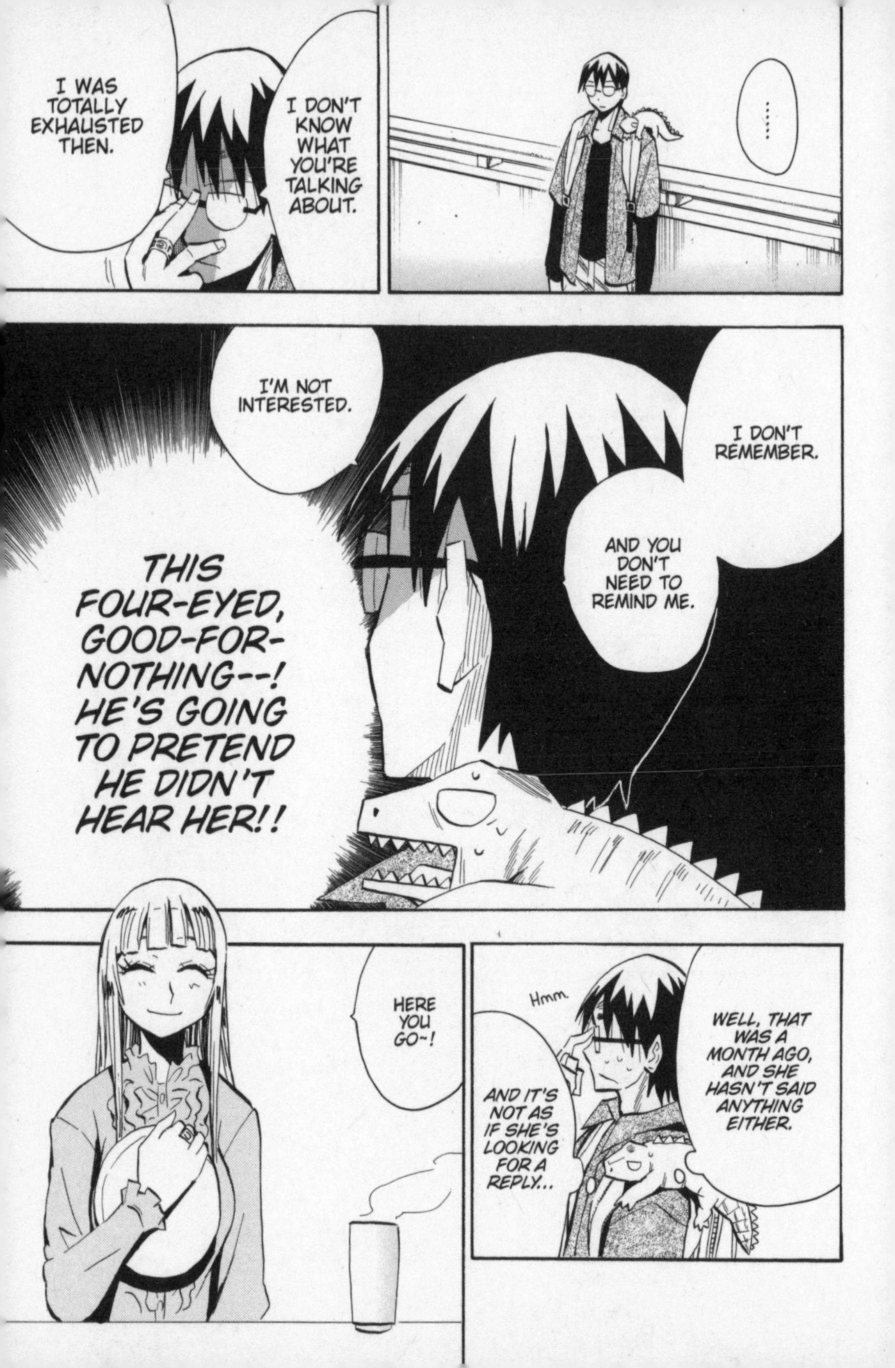
......
I DON'T KNOW WHAT YOU'RE TALKING ABOUT.
I WAS TOTALLY EXHAUSTED THEN.
I DON'T REMEMBER.
I'M NOT INTERESTED.
AND YOU DON'T NEED TO REMIND ME.
THIS FOUR-EYED, GOOD-FOR-NOTHING--! HE'S GOING TO PRETEND HE DIDN'T HEAR HER!!
WELL, THAT WAS A MONTH AGO, AND SHE HASN'T SAID ANYTHING EITHER.
Hmm.
AND IT'S NOT AS IF SHE'S LOOKING FOR A REPLY...
HERE YOU GO~!

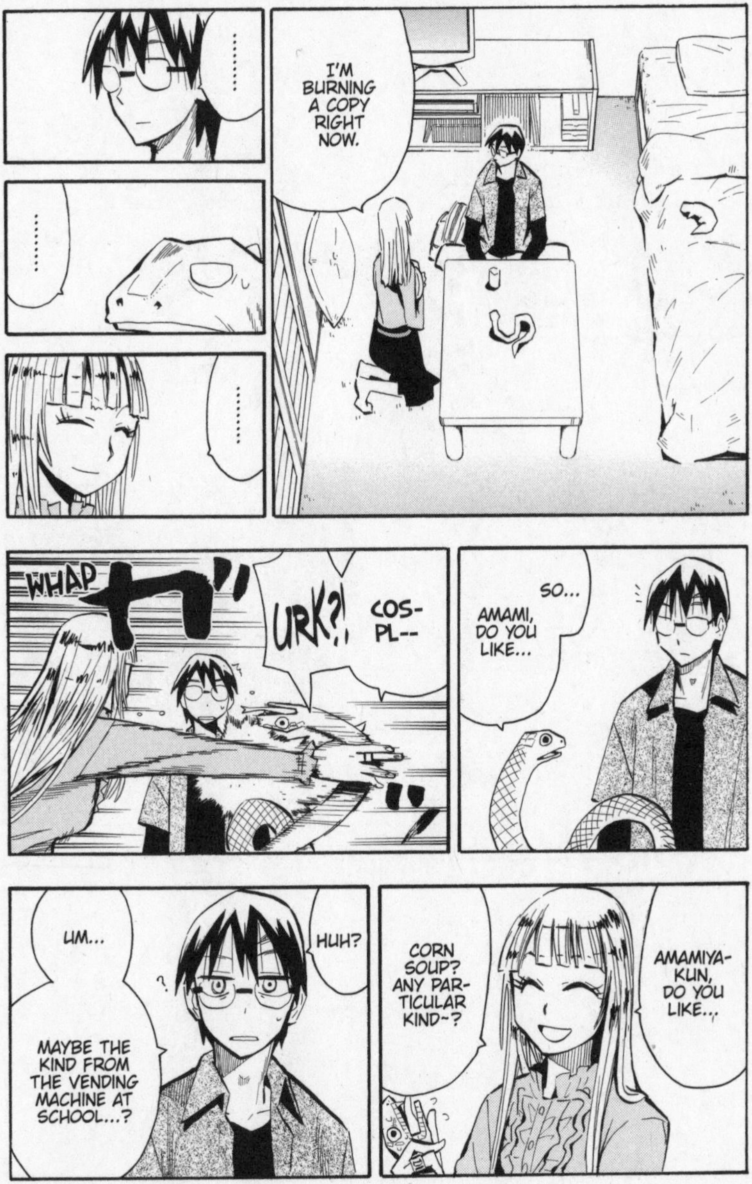
I'M BURNING A COPY RIGHT NOW.
......
......
......
SO...
AMAMI, DO YOU LIKE...
COS-PL--
URK?!
WHAP
AMAMIYA-KUN, DO YOU LIKE...
CORN SOUP? ANY PARTICULAR KIND~?
HUH?
UM...
MAYBE THE KIND FROM THE VENDING MACHINE AT SCHOOL...?

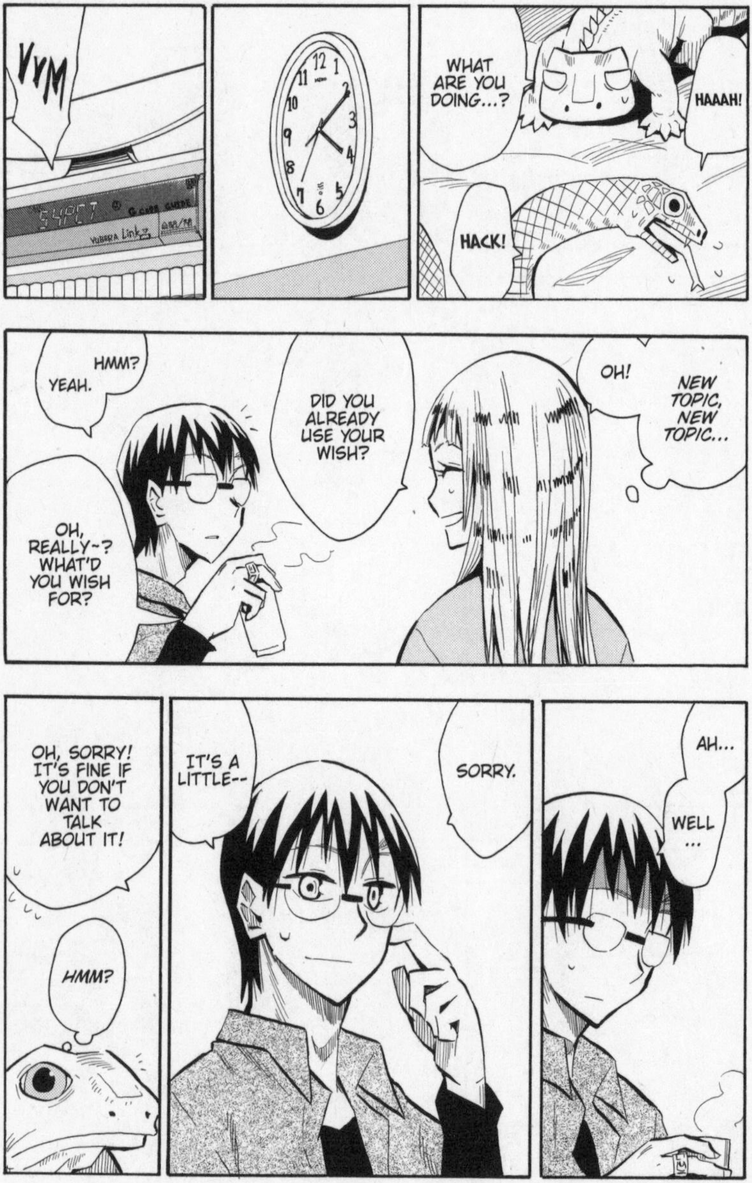
WHAT ARE YOU DOING...?
HAAAH!
HACK!
VVM
OH!
NEW TOPIC, NEW TOPIC...
DID YOU ALREADY USE YOUR WISH?
HMM? YEAH.
OH, REALLY~? WHAT'D YOU WISH FOR?
AH...
WELL...
SORRY.
IT'S A LITTLE--
OH, SORRY! IT'S FINE IF YOU DON'T WANT TO TALK ABOUT IT!
HMM?

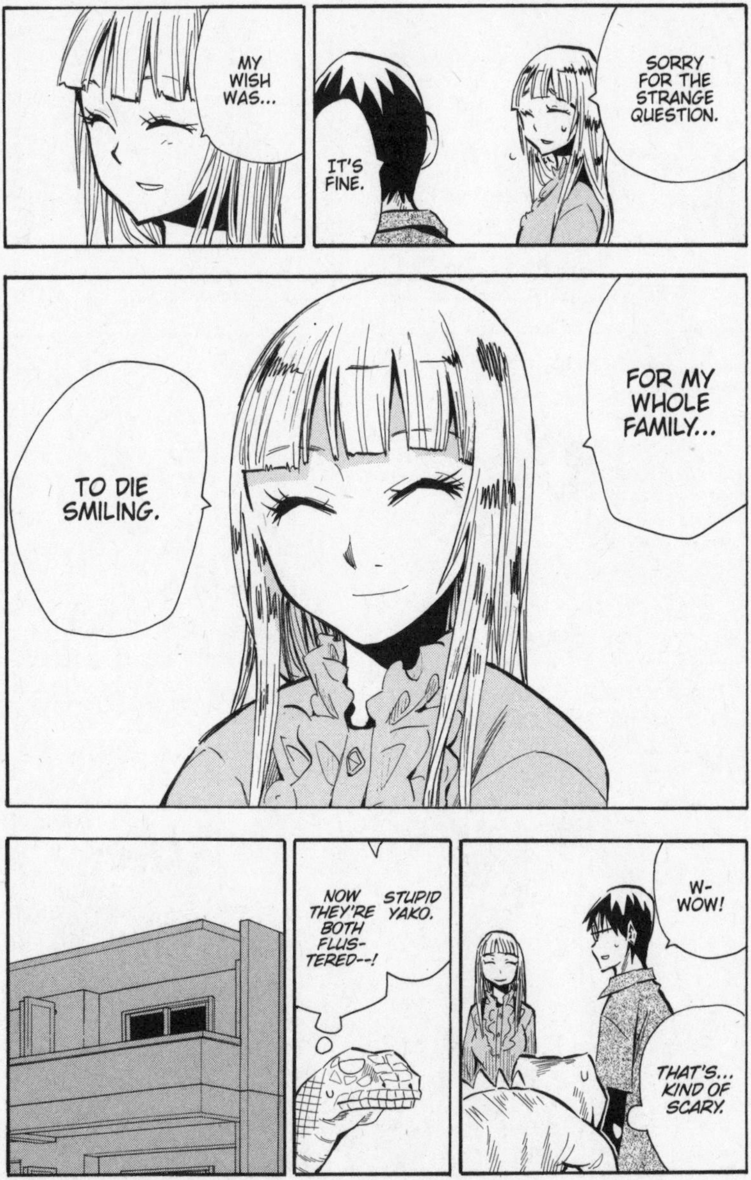
SORRY FOR THE STRANGE QUESTION.
IT'S FINE.
MY WISH WAS...
FOR MY WHOLE FAMILY...
TO DIE SMILING.
W-WOW!
THAT'S... KIND OF SCARY.
STUPID YAKO.
NOW THEY'RE BOTH FLUS-TERED--!

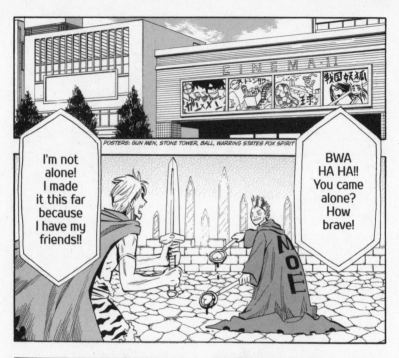

CINEMA 11
戦国妖狐
球
POSTERS: GUN MEN, STONE TOWER, BALL, WARRING STATES FOX SPIRIT
BWA HA HA!! You came alone? How brave!
I'm not alone! I made it this far because I have my friends!!
But the end of the world is nigh!!
What can YOU do?!
Aaaah! I'm going to stop you!!
GAAAA-AH--!!

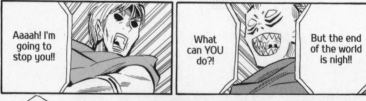

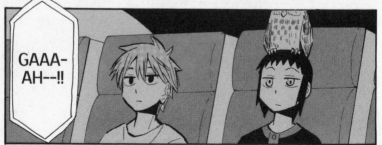

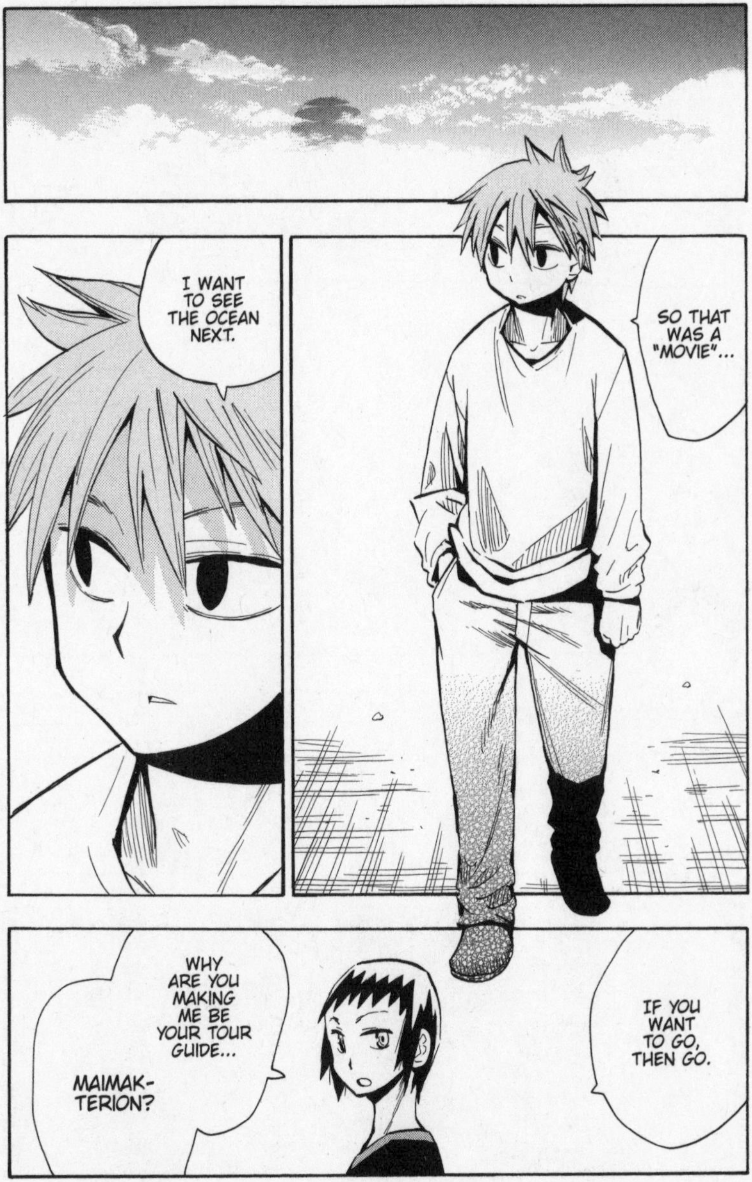
SO THAT WAS A "MOVIE"...
I WANT TO SEE THE OCEAN NEXT.
IF YOU WANT TO GO, THEN GO.
WHY ARE YOU MAKING ME BE YOUR TOUR GUIDE...
MAIMAK-TERION?

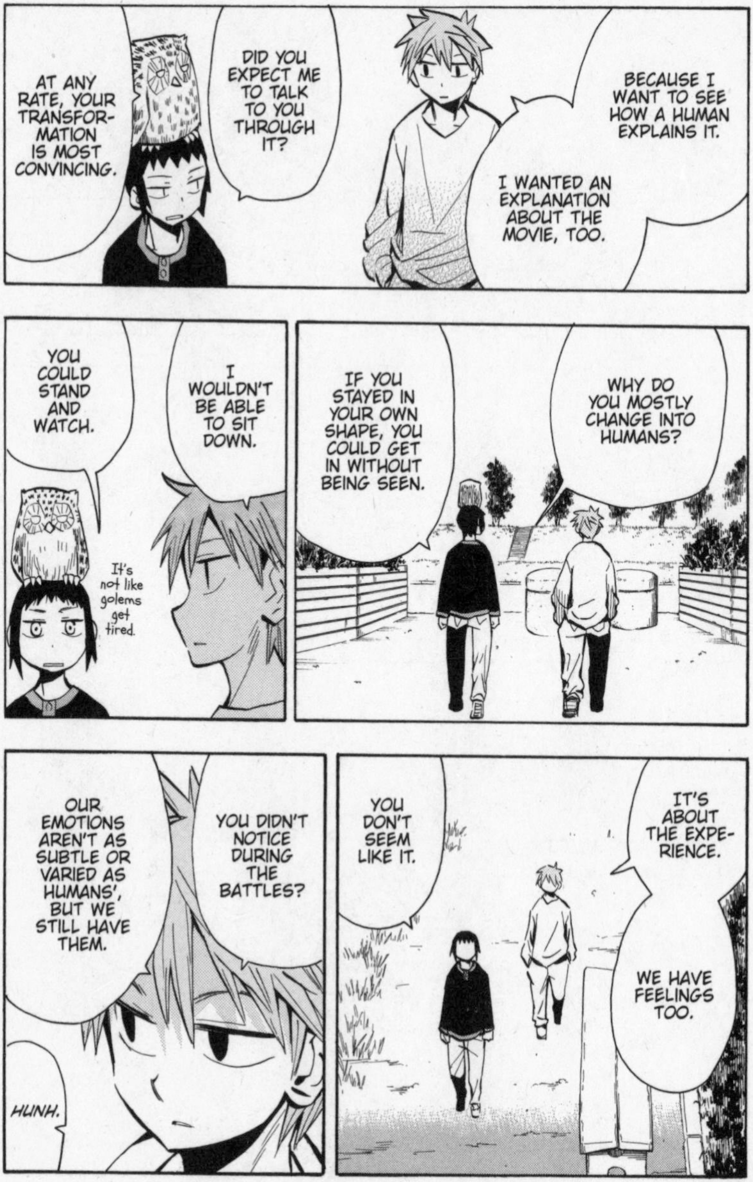
BECAUSE I WANT TO SEE HOW A HUMAN EXPLAINS IT.
I WANTED AN EXPLANATION ABOUT THE MOVIE, TOO.
DID YOU EXPECT ME TO TALK TO YOU THROUGH IT?
AT ANY RATE, YOUR TRANSFORMATION IS MOST CONVINCING.
WHY DO YOU MOSTLY CHANGE INTO HUMANS?
IF YOU STAYED IN YOUR OWN SHAPE, YOU COULD GET IN WITHOUT BEING SEEN.
I WOULDN'T BE ABLE TO SIT DOWN.
YOU COULD STAND AND WATCH.
It's not like golems get tired.
IT'S ABOUT THE EXPERIENCE.
YOU DON'T SEEM LIKE IT.
WE HAVE FEELINGS TOO.
YOU DIDN'T NOTICE DURING THE BATTLES?
OUR EMOTIONS AREN'T AS SUBTLE OR VARIED AS HUMANS', BUT WE STILL HAVE THEM.
HUNH.

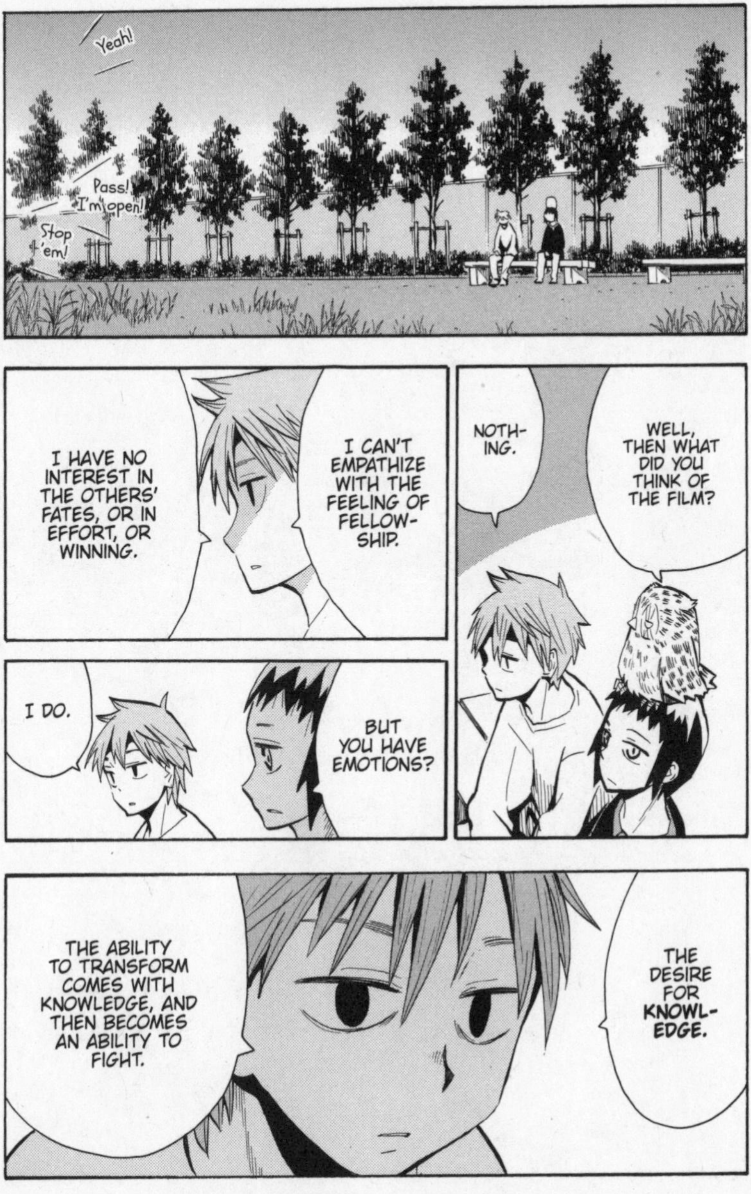
Yeah!
Pass! I'm open!
Stop 'em!
WELL, THEN WHAT DID YOU THINK OF THE FILM?
NOTHING.
I CAN'T EMPATHIZE WITH THE FEELING OF FELLOWSHIP.
I HAVE NO INTEREST IN THE OTHERS' FATES, OR IN EFFORT, OR WINNING.
BUT YOU HAVE EMOTIONS?
I DO.
THE DESIRE FOR KNOWLEDGE.
THE ABILITY TO TRANSFORM COMES WITH KNOWLEDGE, AND THEN BECOMES AN ABILITY TO FIGHT.

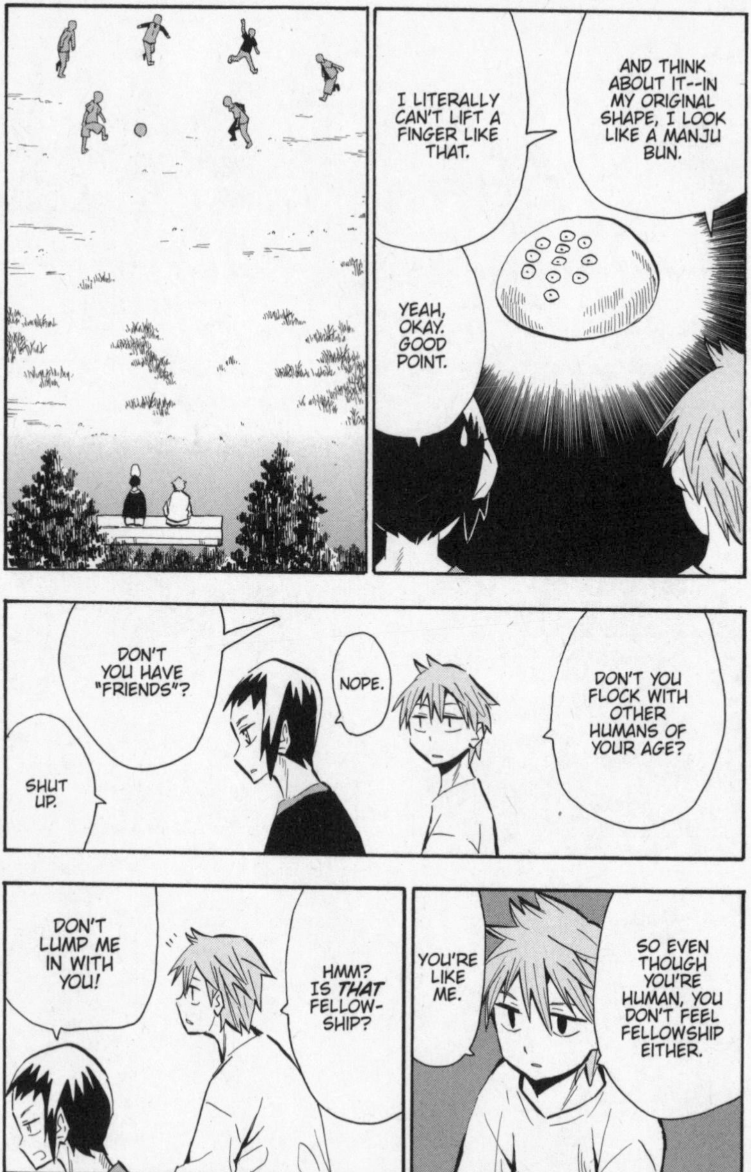
AND THINK ABOUT IT--IN MY ORIGINAL SHAPE, I LOOK LIKE A MANJU BUN.
I LITERALLY CAN'T LIFT A FINGER LIKE THAT.
YEAH, OKAY. GOOD POINT.
DON'T YOU FLOCK WITH OTHER HUMANS OF YOUR AGE?
NOPE.
DON'T YOU HAVE "FRIENDS"?
SHUT UP.
SO EVEN THOUGH YOU'RE HUMAN, YOU DON'T FEEL FELLOWSHIP EITHER.
YOU'RE LIKE ME.
HMM? IS *THAT* FELLOWSHIP?
DON'T LUMP ME IN WITH YOU!

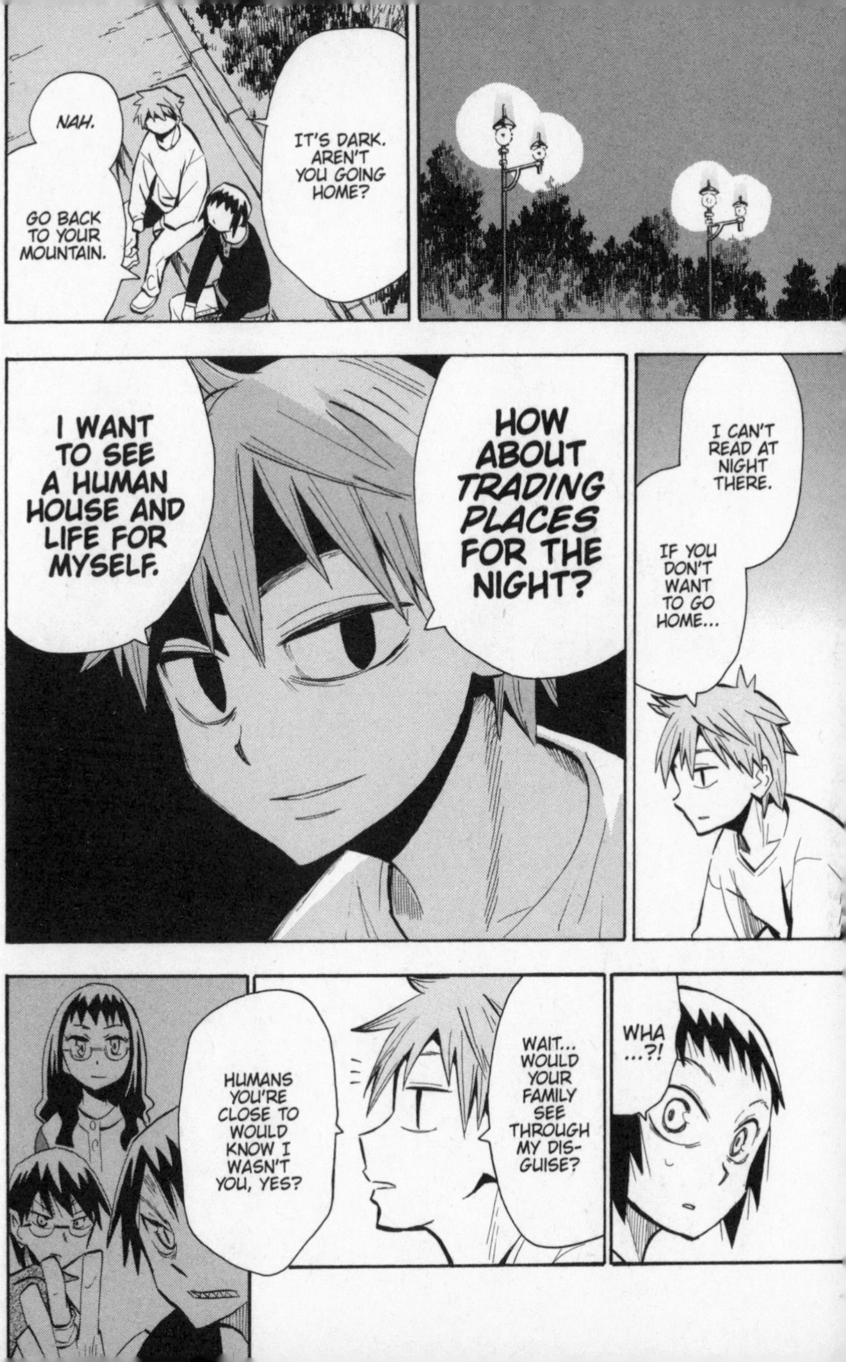
IT'S DARK. AREN'T YOU GOING HOME?
NAH.
GO BACK TO YOUR MOUNTAIN.
I CAN'T READ AT NIGHT THERE.
IF YOU DON'T WANT TO GO HOME...
HOW ABOUT *TRADING PLACES* FOR THE NIGHT?
I WANT TO SEE A HUMAN HOUSE AND LIFE FOR MYSELF.
WHA ...?!
WAIT... WOULD YOUR FAMILY SEE THROUGH MY DIS-GUISE?
HUMANS YOU'RE CLOSE TO WOULD KNOW I WASN'T YOU, YES?

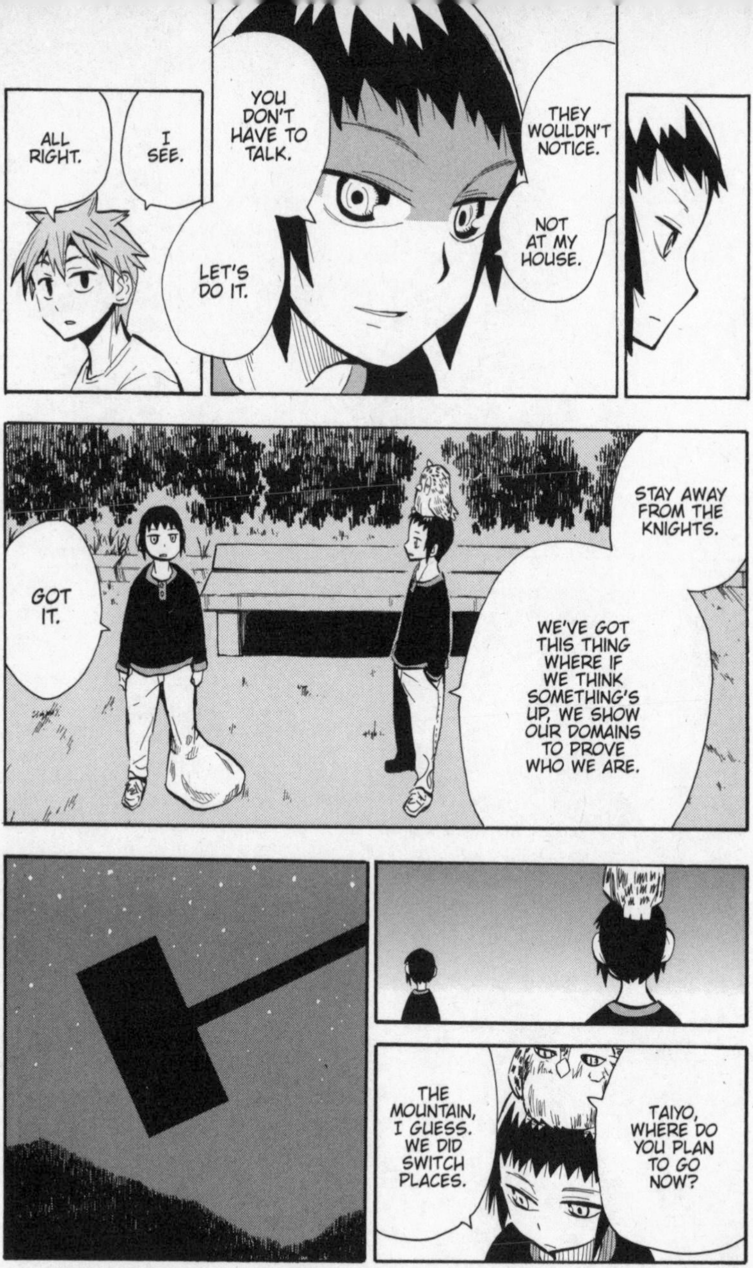
THEY WOULDN'T NOTICE.
NOT AT MY HOUSE.
YOU DON'T HAVE TO TALK.
LET'S DO IT.
I SEE.
ALL RIGHT.
STAY AWAY FROM THE KNIGHTS.
WE'VE GOT THIS THING WHERE IF WE THINK SOMETHING'S UP, WE SHOW OUR DOMAINS TO PROVE WHO WE ARE.
GOT IT.
TAIYO, WHERE DO YOU PLAN TO GO NOW?
THE MOUNTAIN, I GUESS. WE DID SWITCH PLACES.

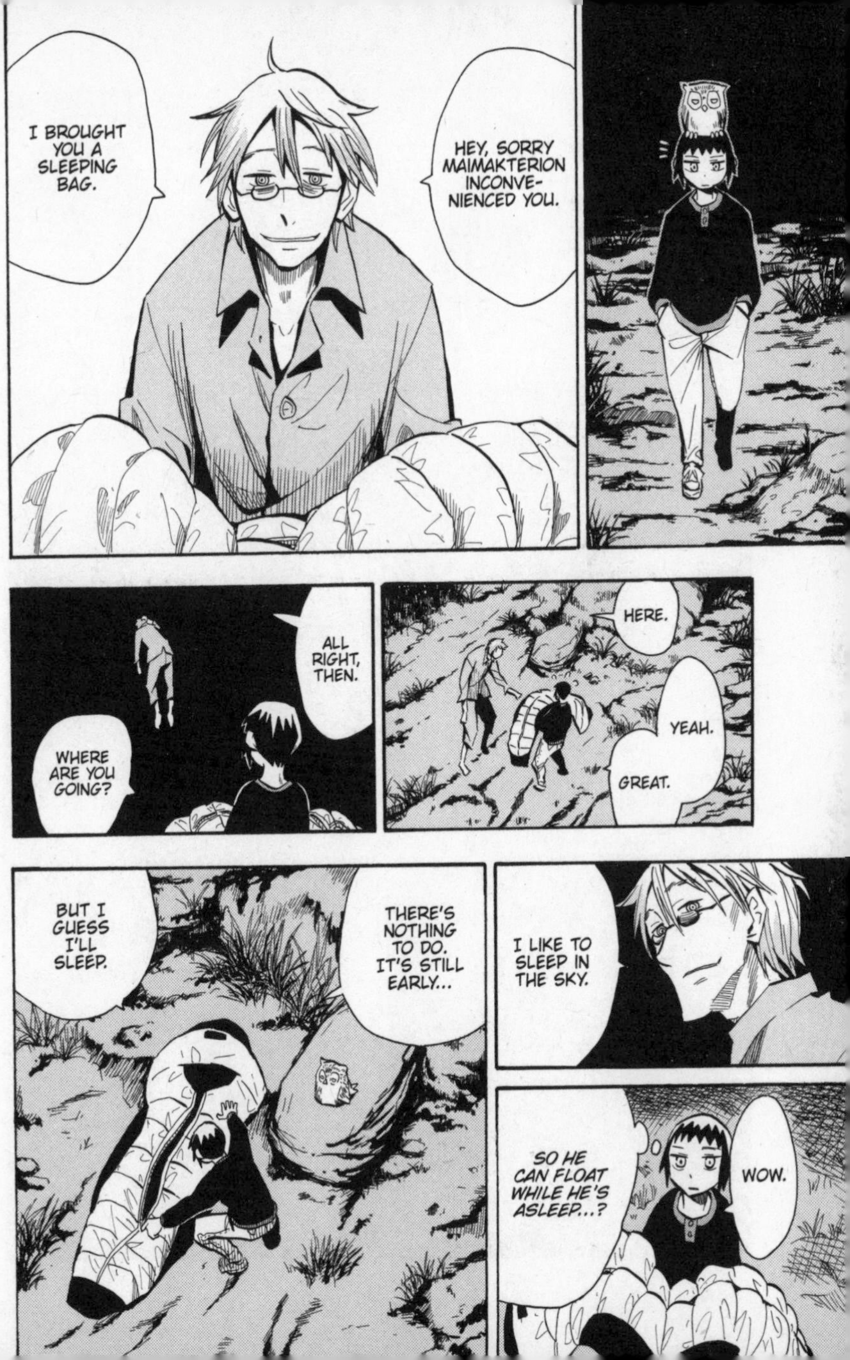
HEY, SORRY MAIMAKTERION INCONVE-NIENCED YOU.
I BROUGHT YOU A SLEEPING BAG.
HERE.
YEAH.
GREAT.
ALL RIGHT, THEN.
WHERE ARE YOU GOING?
I LIKE TO SLEEP IN THE SKY.
WOW.
SO HE CAN FLOAT WHILE HE'S ASLEEP...?
THERE'S NOTHING TO DO. IT'S STILL EARLY...
BUT I GUESS I'LL SLEEP.

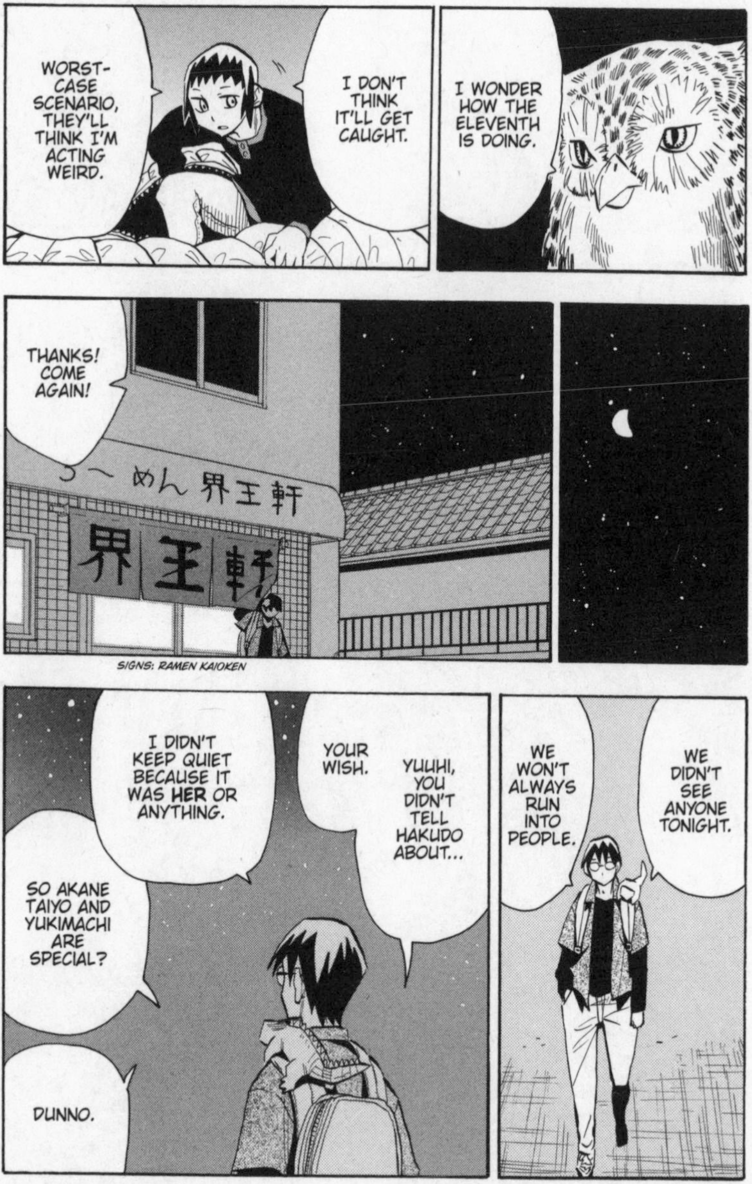
I WONDER HOW THE ELEVENTH IS DOING.
I DON'T THINK IT'LL GET CAUGHT.
WORST-CASE SCENARIO, THEY'LL THINK I'M ACTING WEIRD.
THANKS! COME AGAIN!
界王軒
界王軒
SIGNS: RAMEN KAIOKEN
WE DIDN'T SEE ANYONE TONIGHT.
WE WON'T ALWAYS RUN INTO PEOPLE.
YUUHI, YOU DIDN'T TELL HAKUDO ABOUT...
YOUR WISH.
I DIDN'T KEEP QUIET BECAUSE IT WAS HER OR ANYTHING.
SO AKANE TAIYO AND YUKIMACHI ARE SPECIAL?
DUNNO.

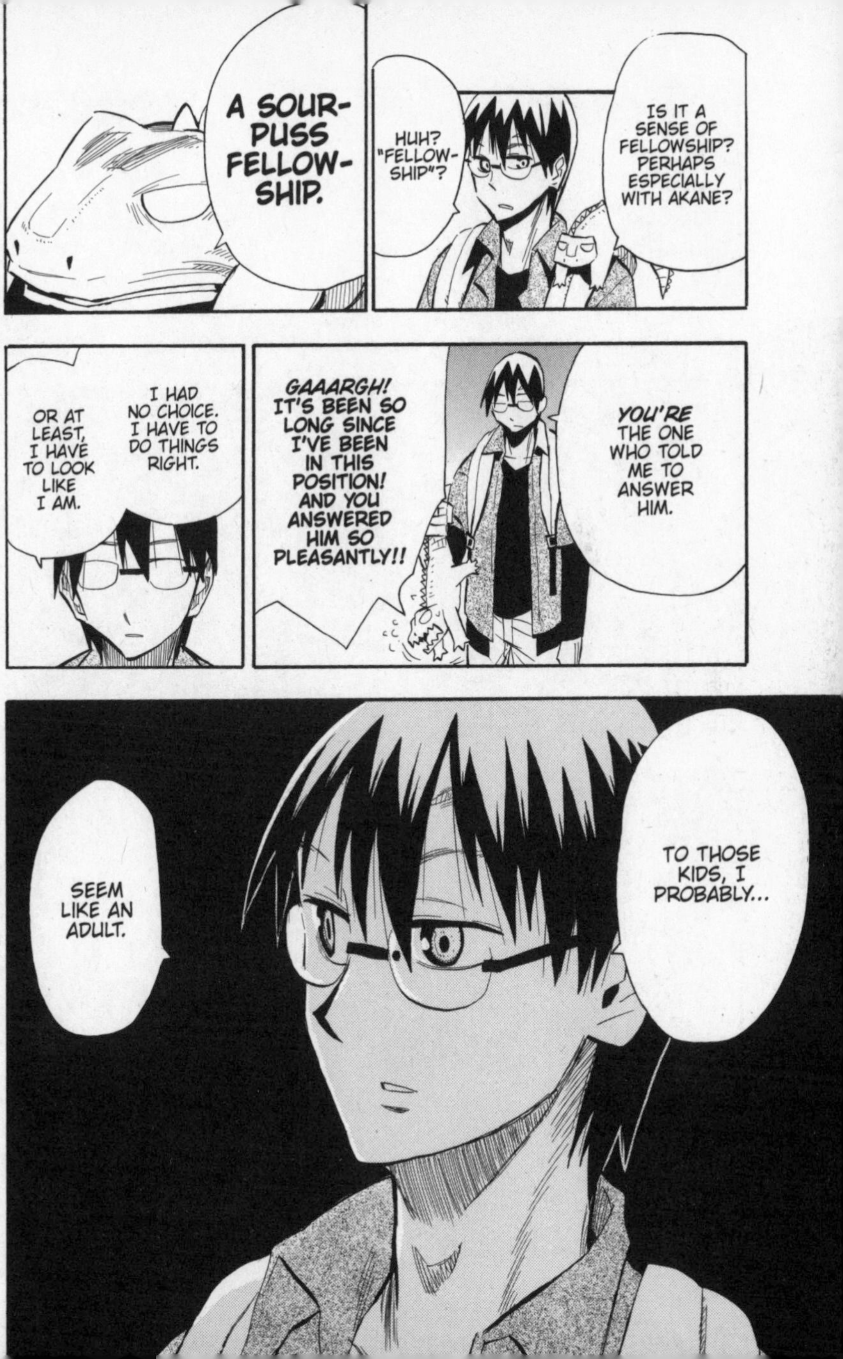

IS IT A SENSE OF FELLOWSHIP? PERHAPS ESPECIALLY WITH AKANE?
HUH? "FELLOW-SHIP"?
A SOUR-PUSS FELLOW-SHIP.
YOU'RE THE ONE WHO TOLD ME TO ANSWER HIM.
GAAARGH! IT'S BEEN SO LONG SINCE I'VE BEEN IN THIS POSITION! AND YOU ANSWERED HIM SO PLEASANTLY!!
I HAD NO CHOICE. I HAVE TO DO THINGS RIGHT.
OR AT LEAST, I HAVE TO LOOK LIKE I AM.
TO THOSE KIDS, I PROBABLY...
SEEM LIKE AN ADULT.

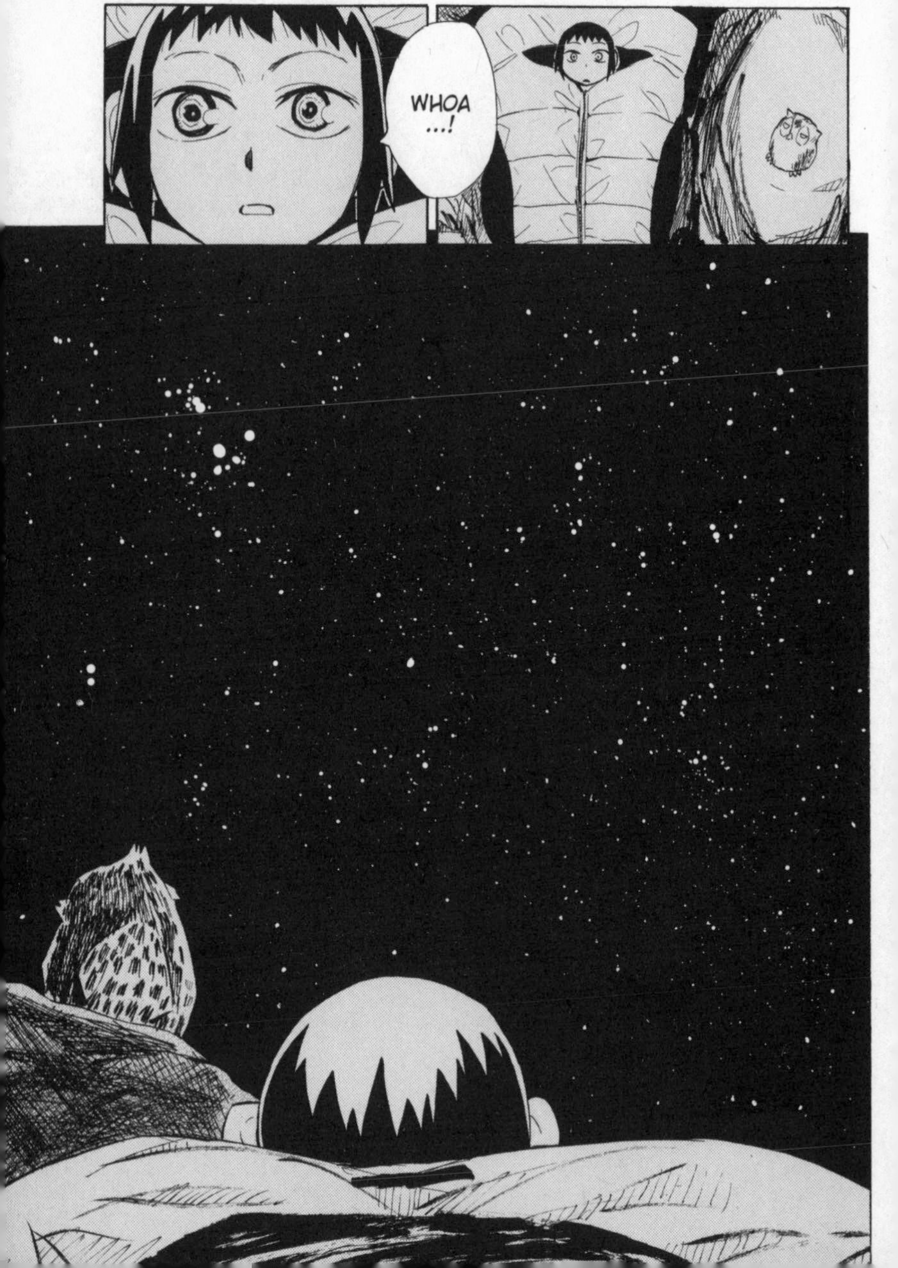
WHOA ...!

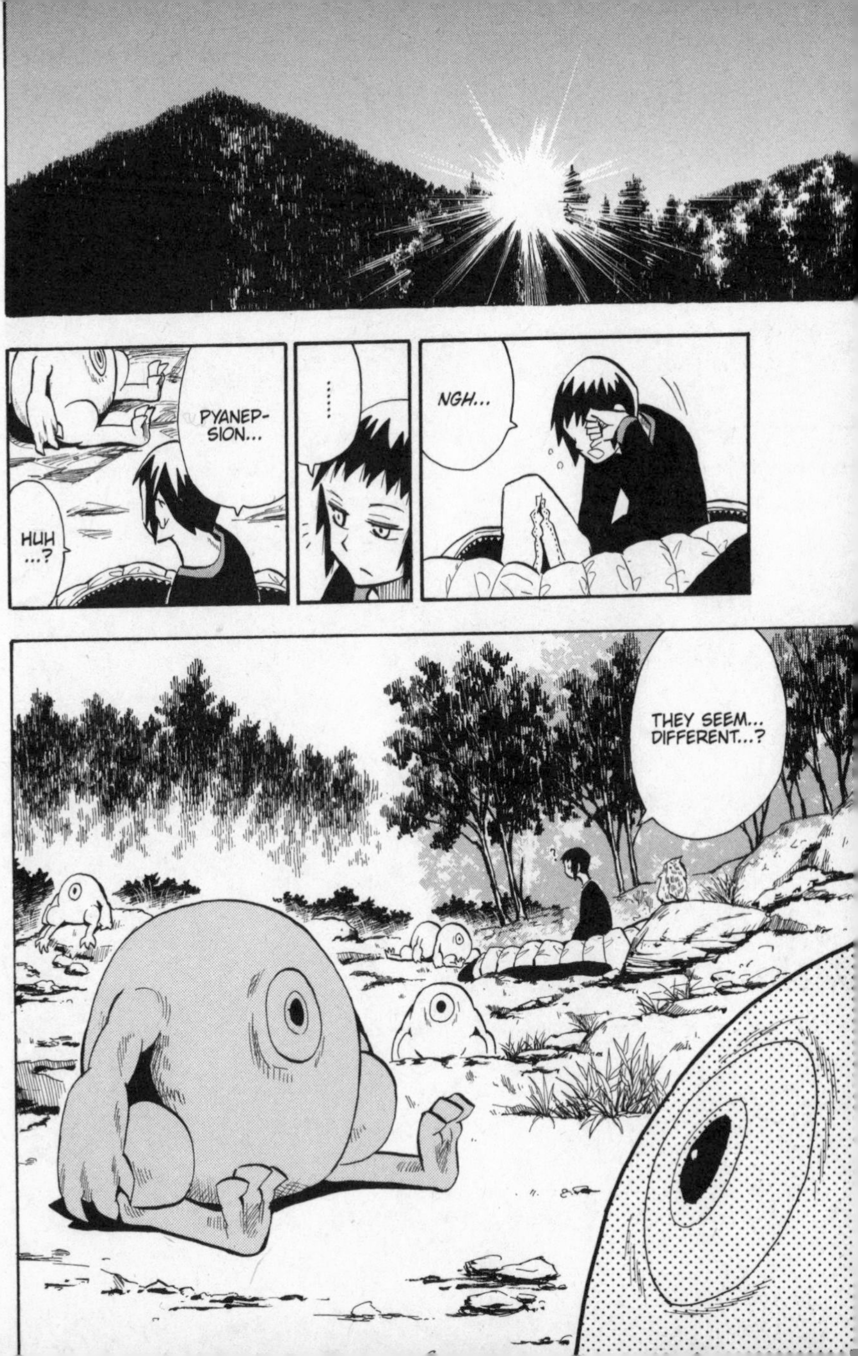
NGH...
......
PYANEP-SION...
HUH ...?
THEY SEEM... DIFFERENT...?

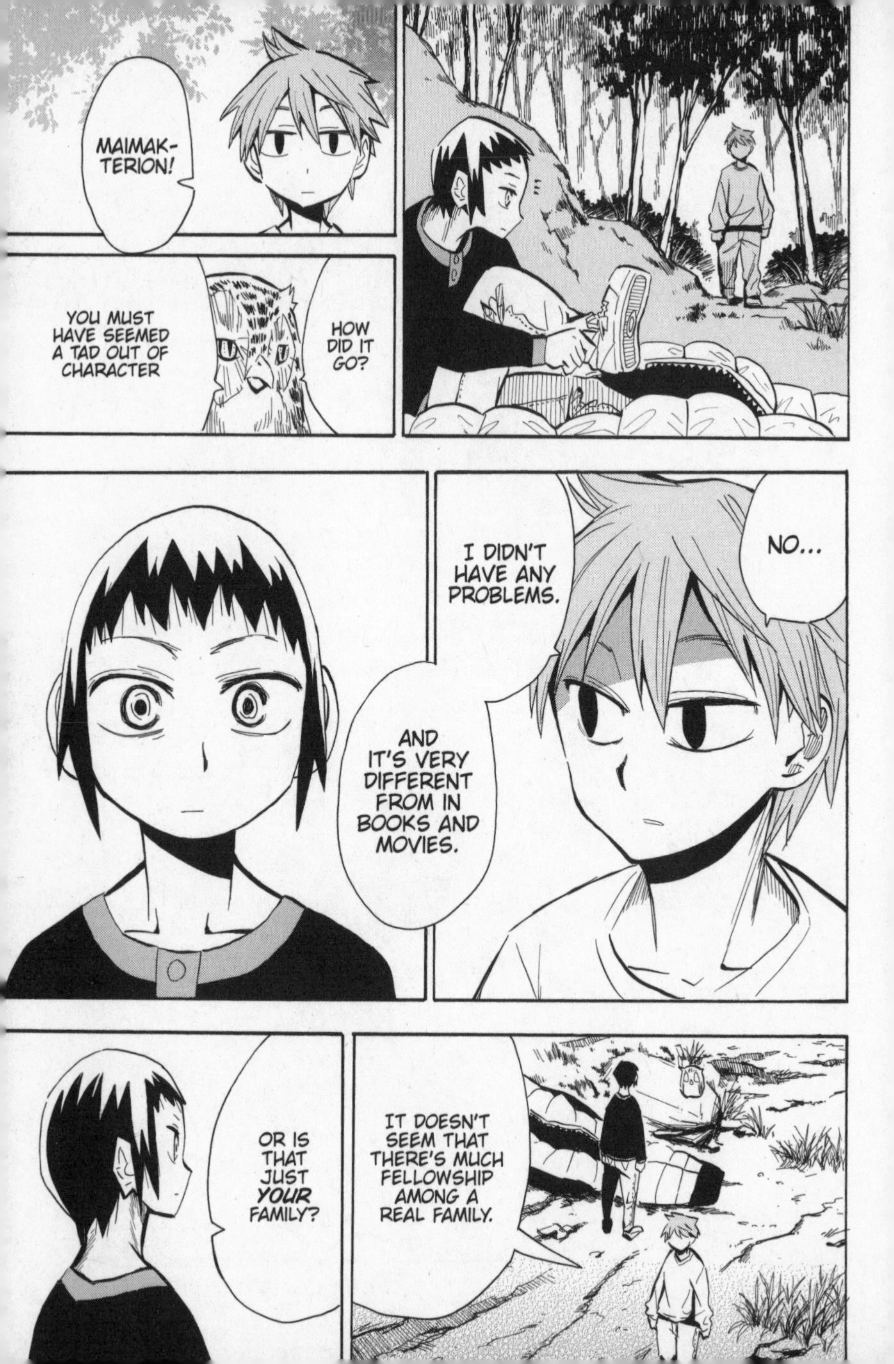
MAIMAK-TERION!
HOW DID IT GO?
YOU MUST HAVE SEEMED A TAD OUT OF CHARACTER
NO...
I DIDN'T HAVE ANY PROBLEMS.
AND IT'S VERY DIFFERENT FROM IN BOOKS AND MOVIES.
IT DOESN'T SEEM THAT THERE'S MUCH FELLOWSHIP AMONG A REAL FAMILY.
OR IS THAT JUST *YOUR* FAMILY?

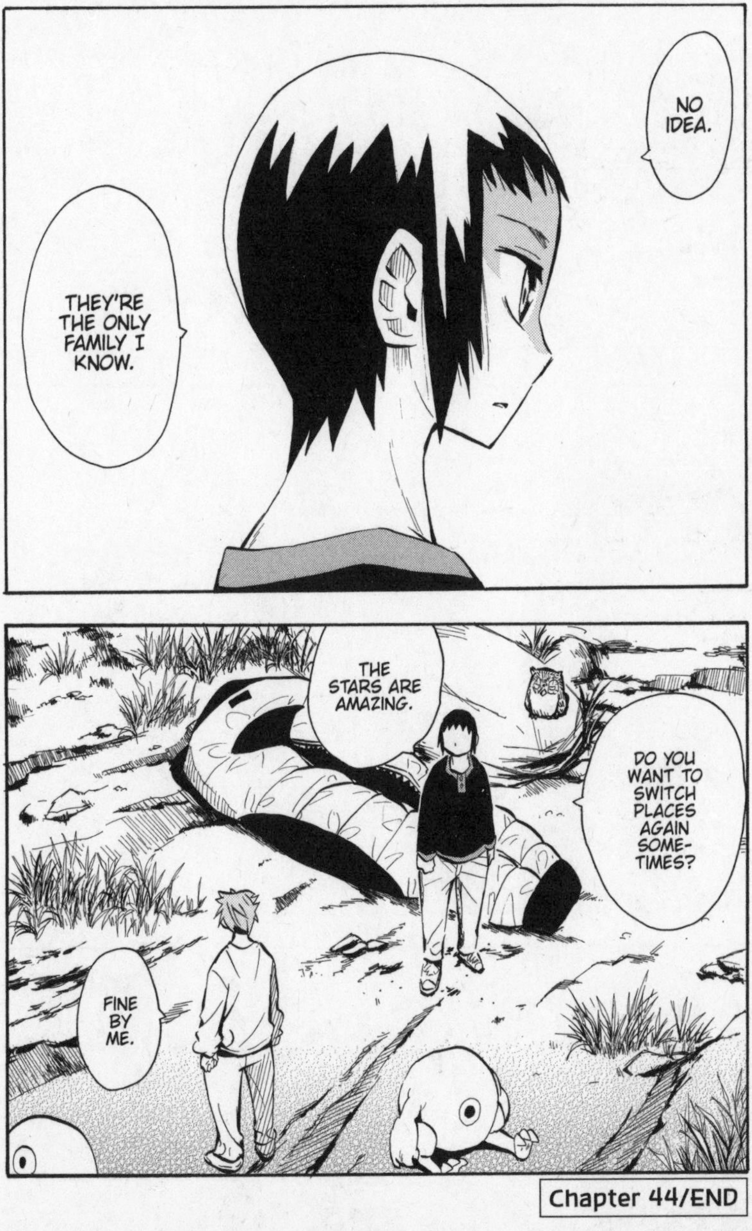
NO IDEA.
THEY'RE THE ONLY FAMILY I KNOW.
THE STARS ARE AMAZING.
DO YOU WANT TO SWITCH PLACES AGAIN SOMETIMES?
FINE BY ME.

Chapter 44/END

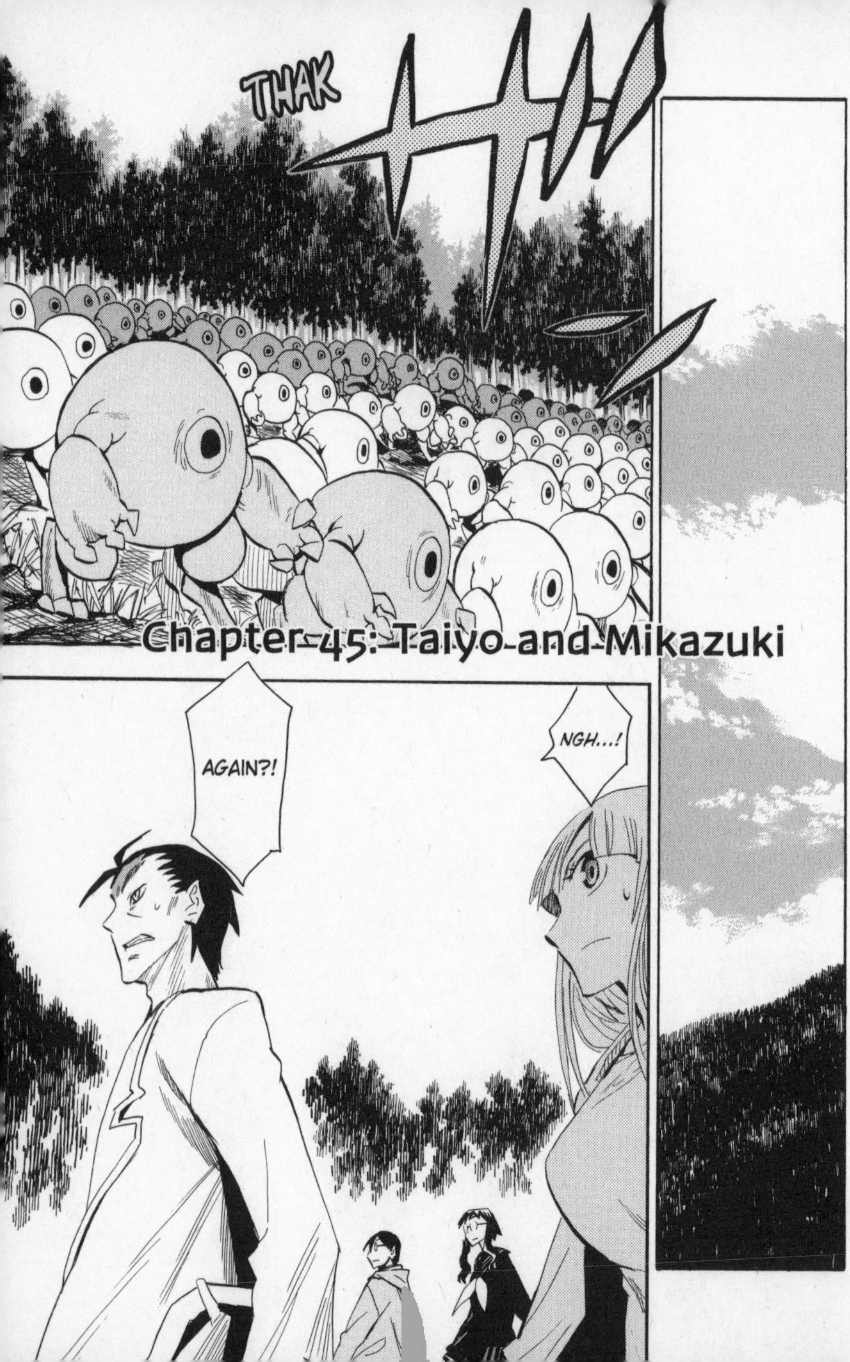
THAK
Chapter 45: Taiyo and Mikazuki
NGH...!
AGAIN?!

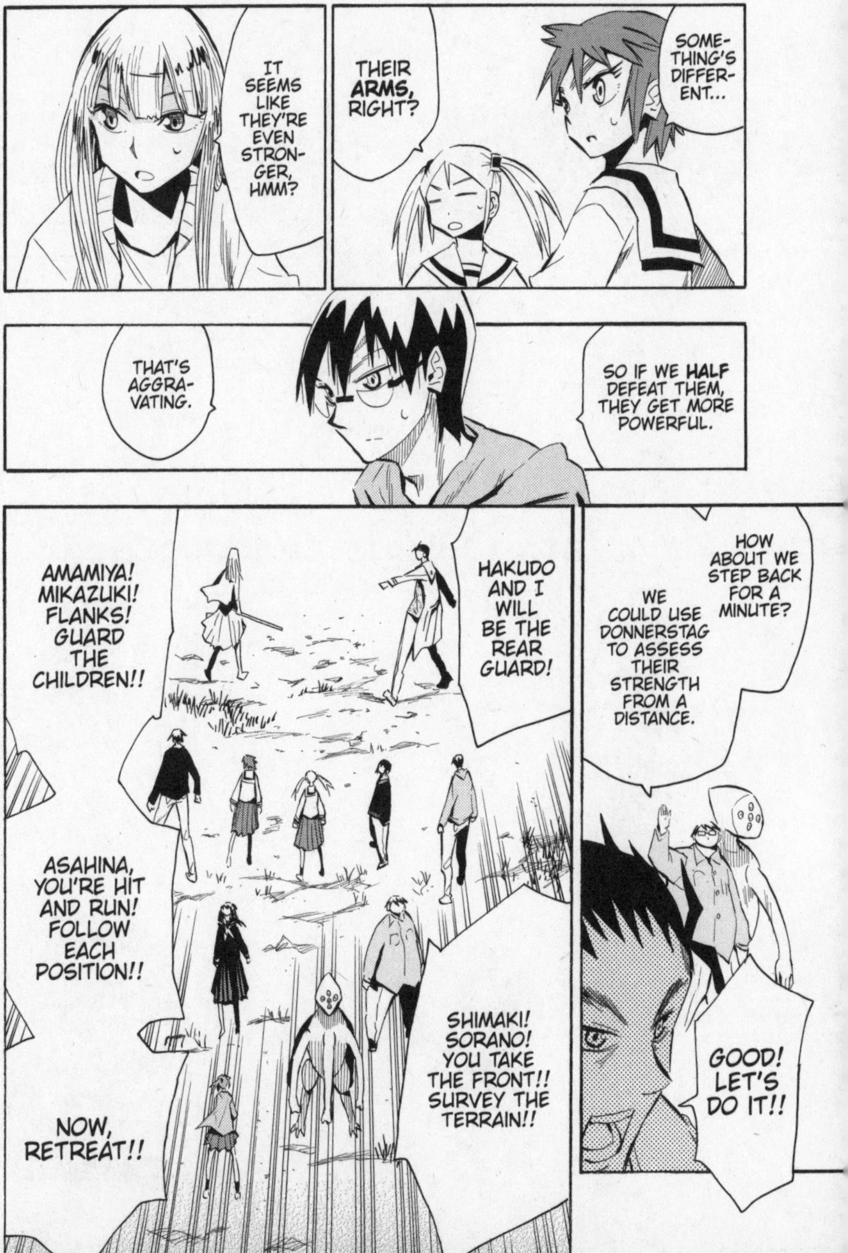
SOME-THING'S DIFFER-ENT...
THEIR **ARMS,** RIGHT?
IT SEEMS LIKE THEY'RE EVEN STRON-GER, HMM?
SO IF WE **HALF** DEFEAT THEM, THEY GET MORE POWERFUL.
THAT'S AGGRA-VATING.
HOW ABOUT WE STEP BACK FOR A MINUTE?
WE COULD USE DONNERSTAG TO ASSESS THEIR STRENGTH FROM A DISTANCE.
GOOD! LET'S DO IT!!
HAKUDO AND I WILL BE THE REAR GUARD!
AMAMIYA! MIKAZUKI! FLANKS! GUARD THE CHILDREN!!
SHIMAKI! SORANO! YOU TAKE THE FRONT!! SURVEY THE TERRAIN!!
ASAHINA, YOU'RE HIT AND RUN! FOLLOW EACH POSITION!!
NOW, RETREAT!!

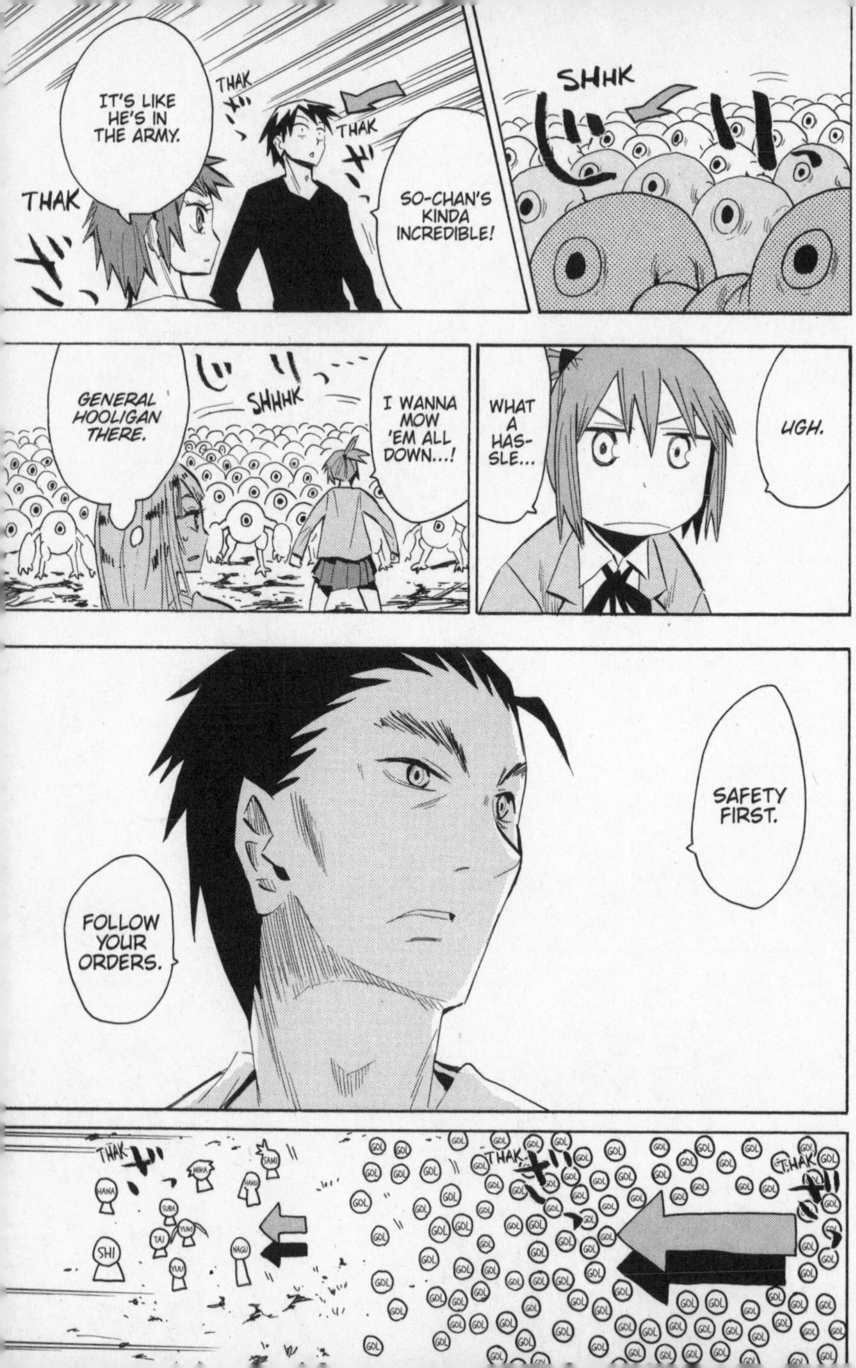
SHHK
SO-CHAN'S KINDA INCREDIBLE!
THAK
THAK
IT'S LIKE HE'S IN THE ARMY.
THAK
UGH.
WHAT A HAS-SLE...
I WANNA MOW 'EM ALL DOWN...!
SHHHK
GENERAL HOOLIGAN THERE.
SAFETY FIRST.
FOLLOW YOUR ORDERS.
T.HAK
THAK
THAK

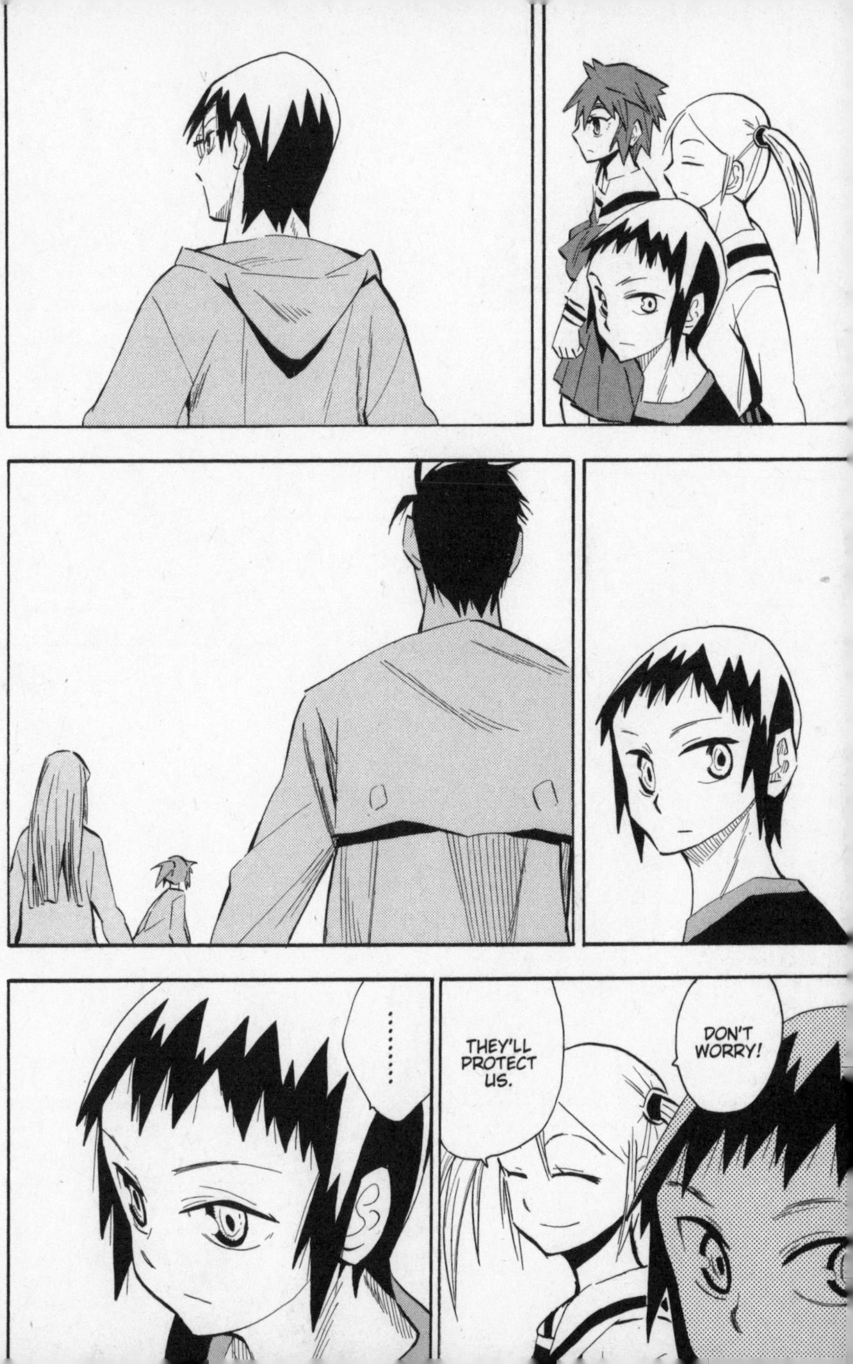
DON'T WORRY!
THEY'LL PROTECT US.
......

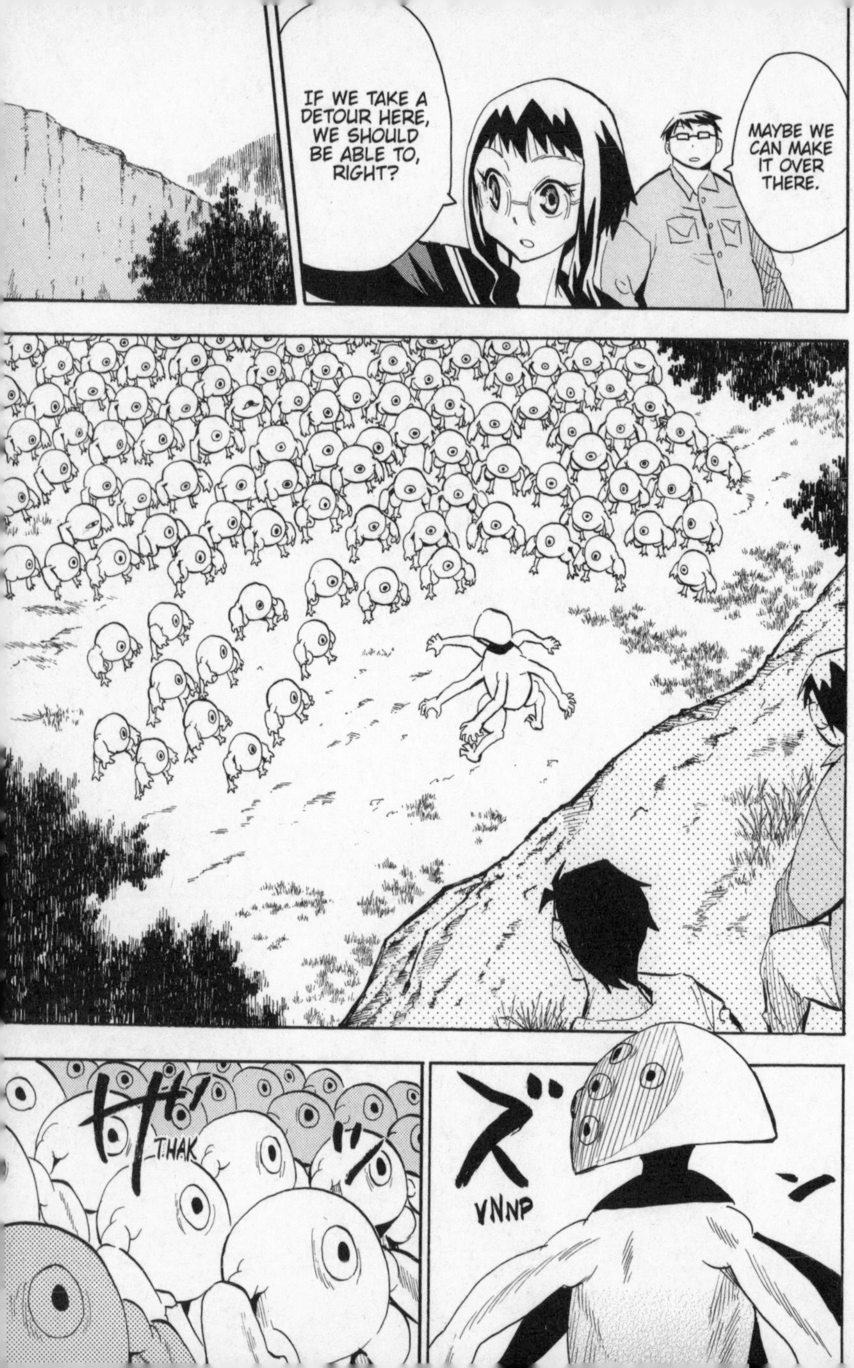
MAYBE WE CAN MAKE IT OVER THERE.
IF WE TAKE A DETOUR HERE, WE SHOULD BE ABLE TO, RIGHT?
VNNP
T.HAK

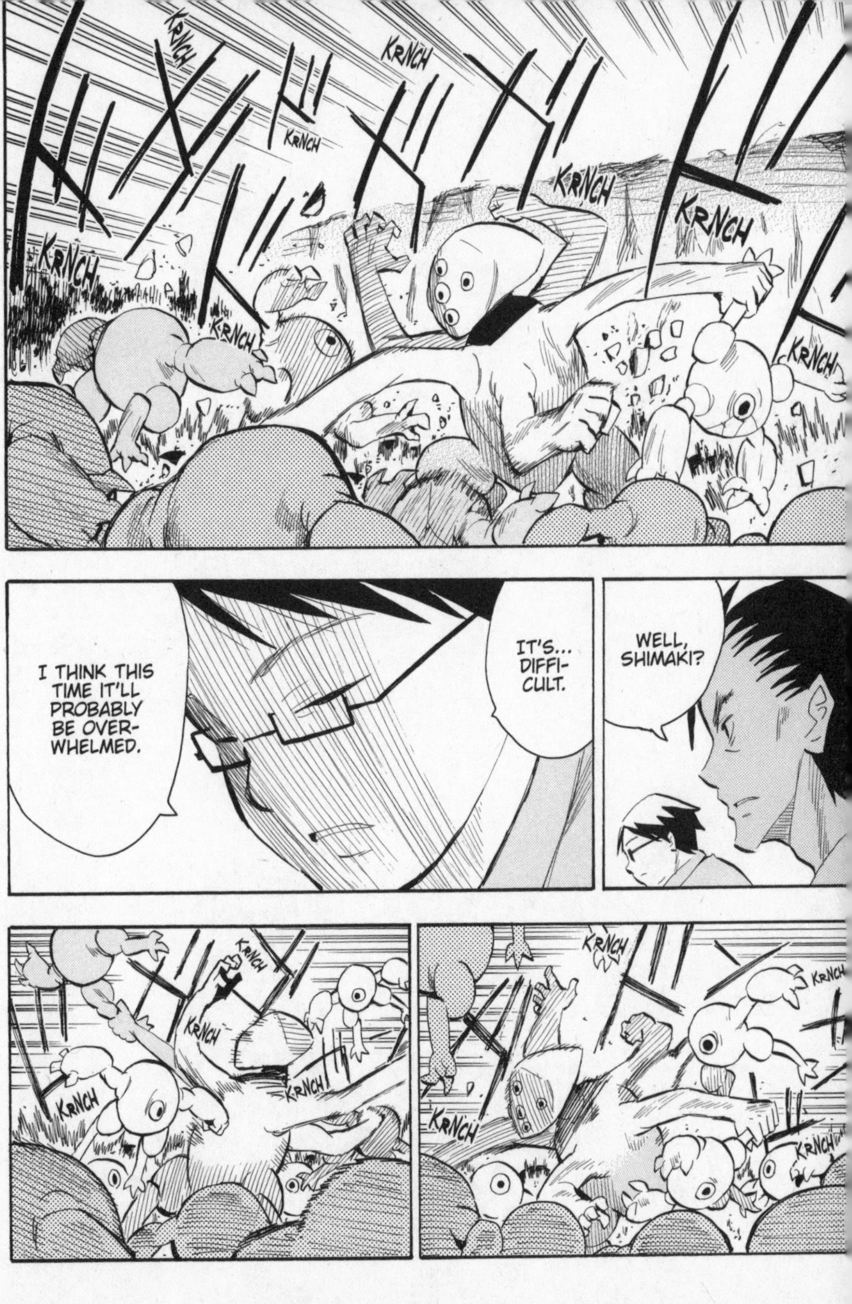
KRNCH
KRNCH
KRNCH
KRNCH
KRNCH
KRNCH
KRNCH
KRNCH
WELL, SHIMAKI?
IT'S... DIFFI-CULT.
I THINK THIS TIME IT'LL PROBABLY BE OVER-WHELMED.
KRNCH
KRNCH
KRNCH
KRNCH
KRNCH
KRNCH
KRNCH
KRNCH

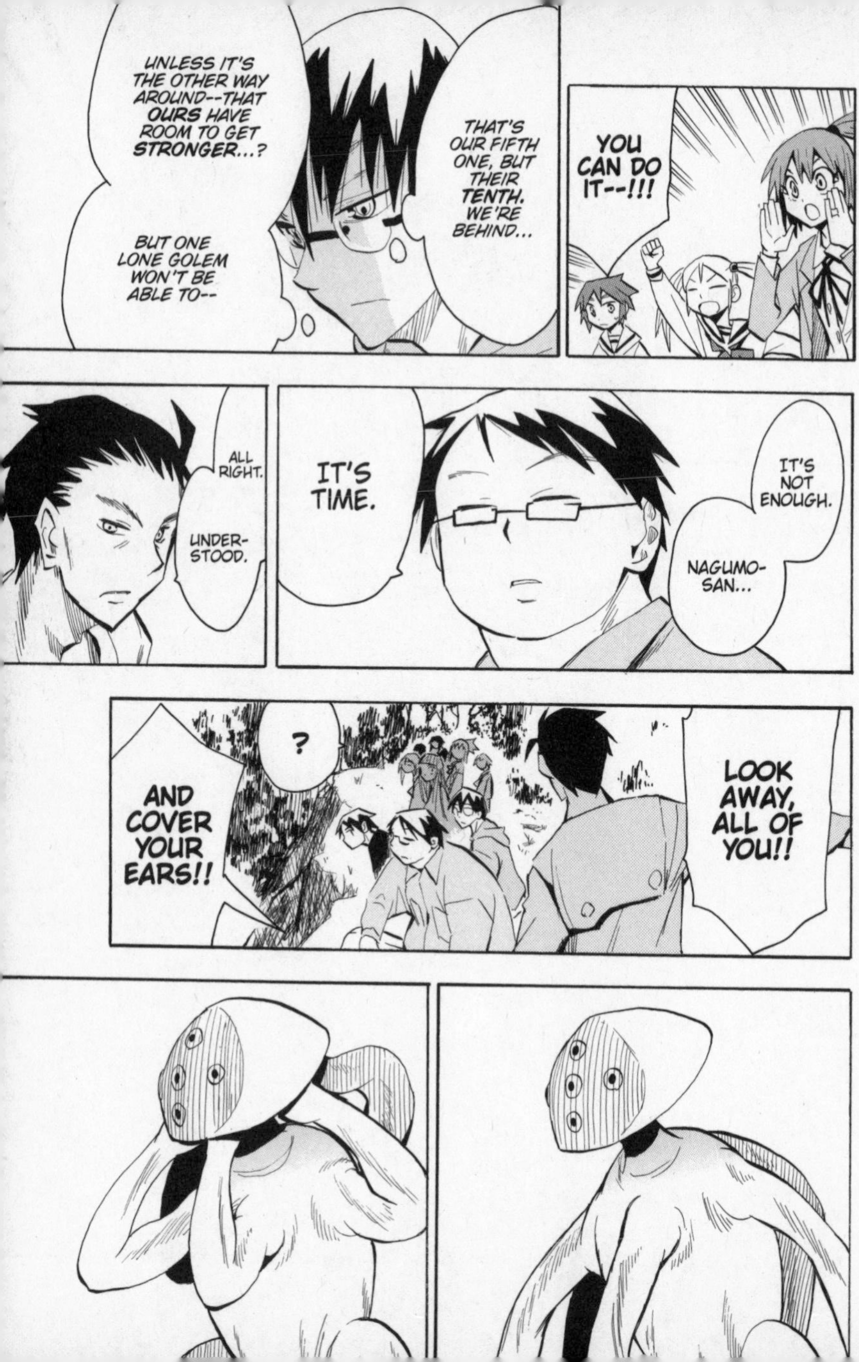
YOU CAN DO IT--!!!
THAT'S OUR FIFTH ONE, BUT THEIR TENTH. WE'RE BEHIND...
UNLESS IT'S THE OTHER WAY AROUND--THAT OURS HAVE ROOM TO GET STRONGER...?
BUT ONE LONE GOLEM WON'T BE ABLE TO--
IT'S NOT ENOUGH.
NAGUMO-SAN...
IT'S TIME.
ALL RIGHT.
UNDER-STOOD.
LOOK AWAY, ALL OF YOU!!
?
AND COVER YOUR EARS!!

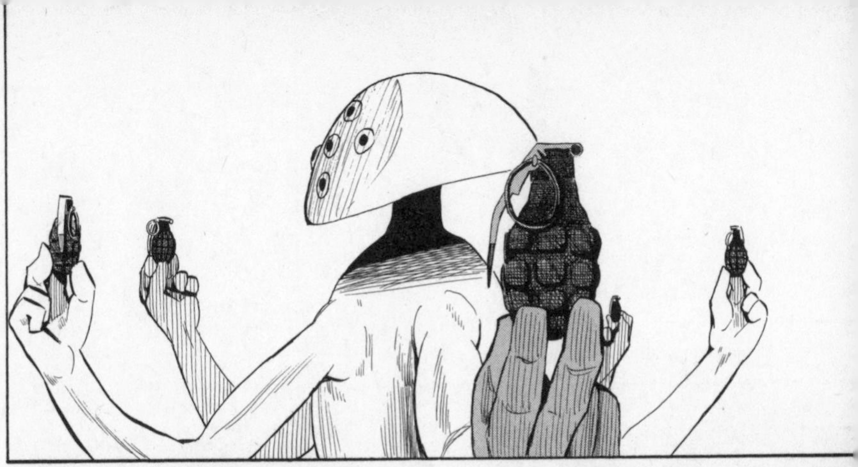

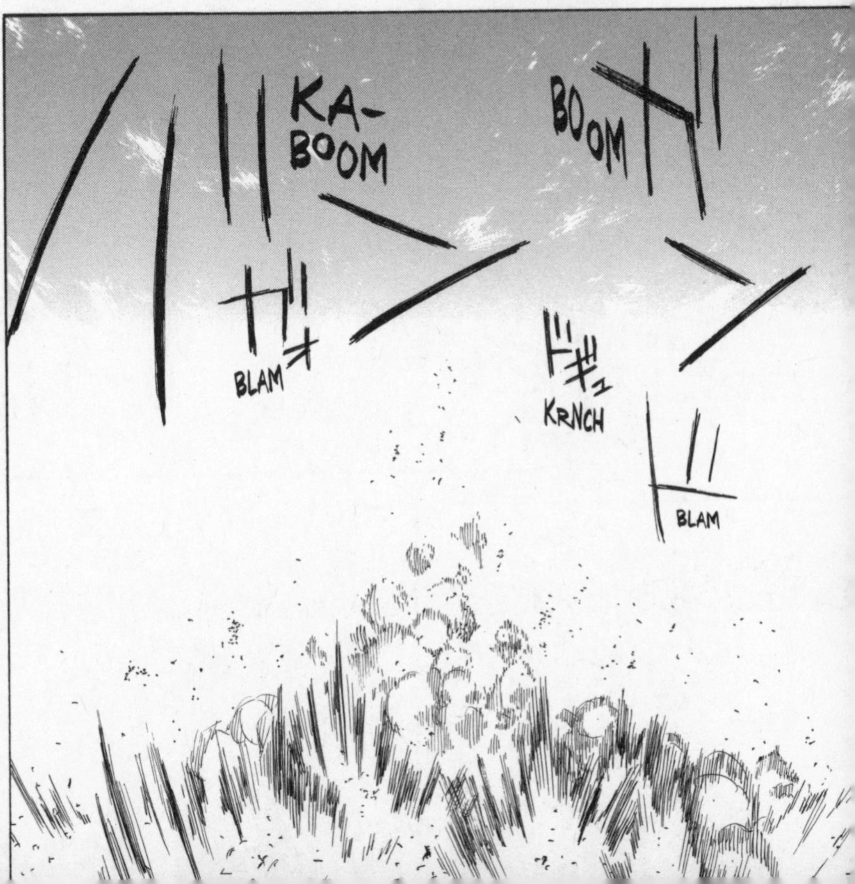
BOOM
KA-
BOOM
ドギュ
KRNCH
ガッ
BLAM
BLAM

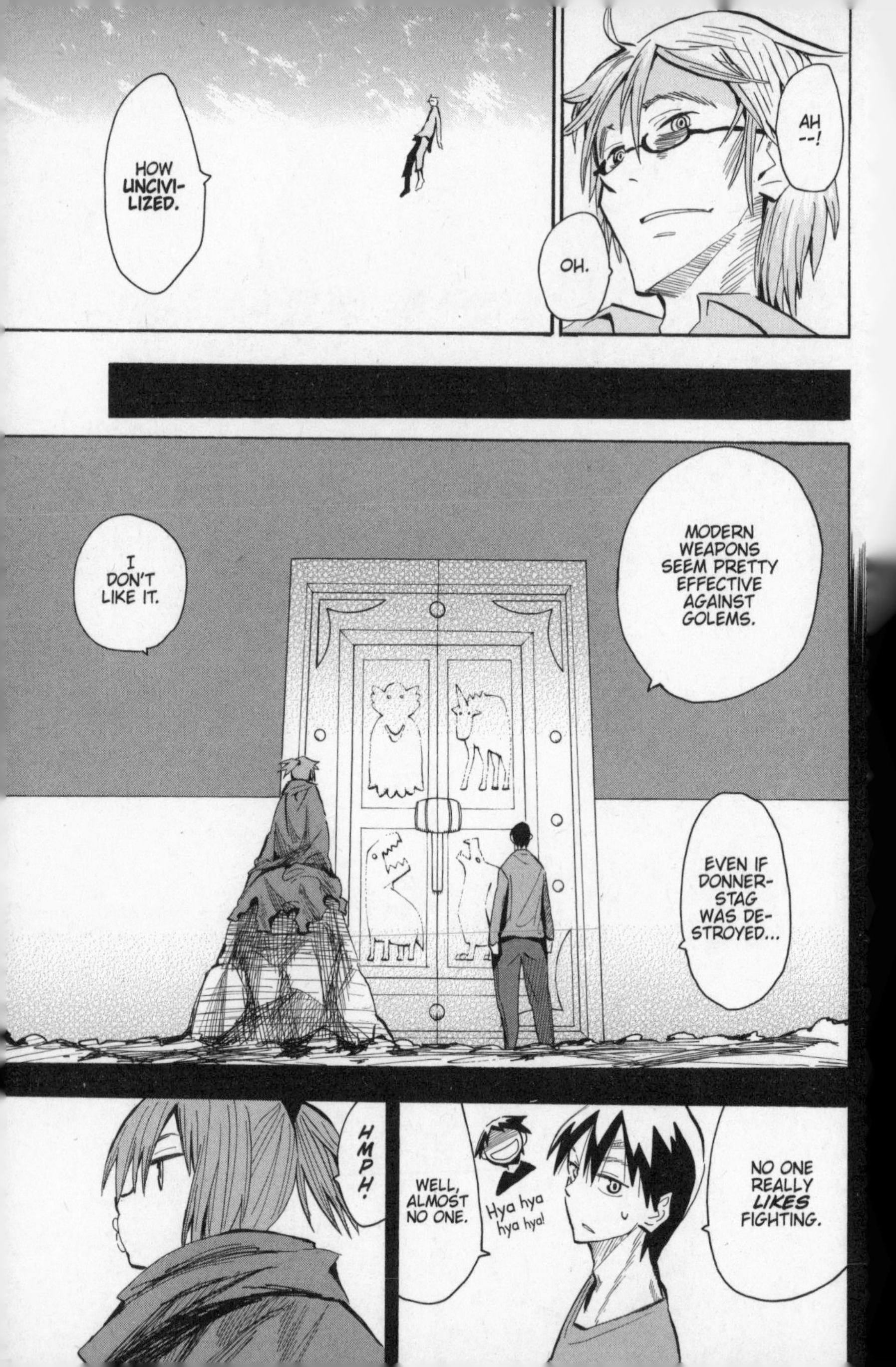
AH --!
OH.
HOW UNCIVILIZED.
MODERN WEAPONS SEEM PRETTY EFFECTIVE AGAINST GOLEMS.
EVEN IF DONNERSTAG WAS DESTROYED...
I DON'T LIKE IT.
NO ONE REALLY *LIKES* FIGHTING.
Hya hya hya hya!
WELL, ALMOST NO ONE.
HMPH!

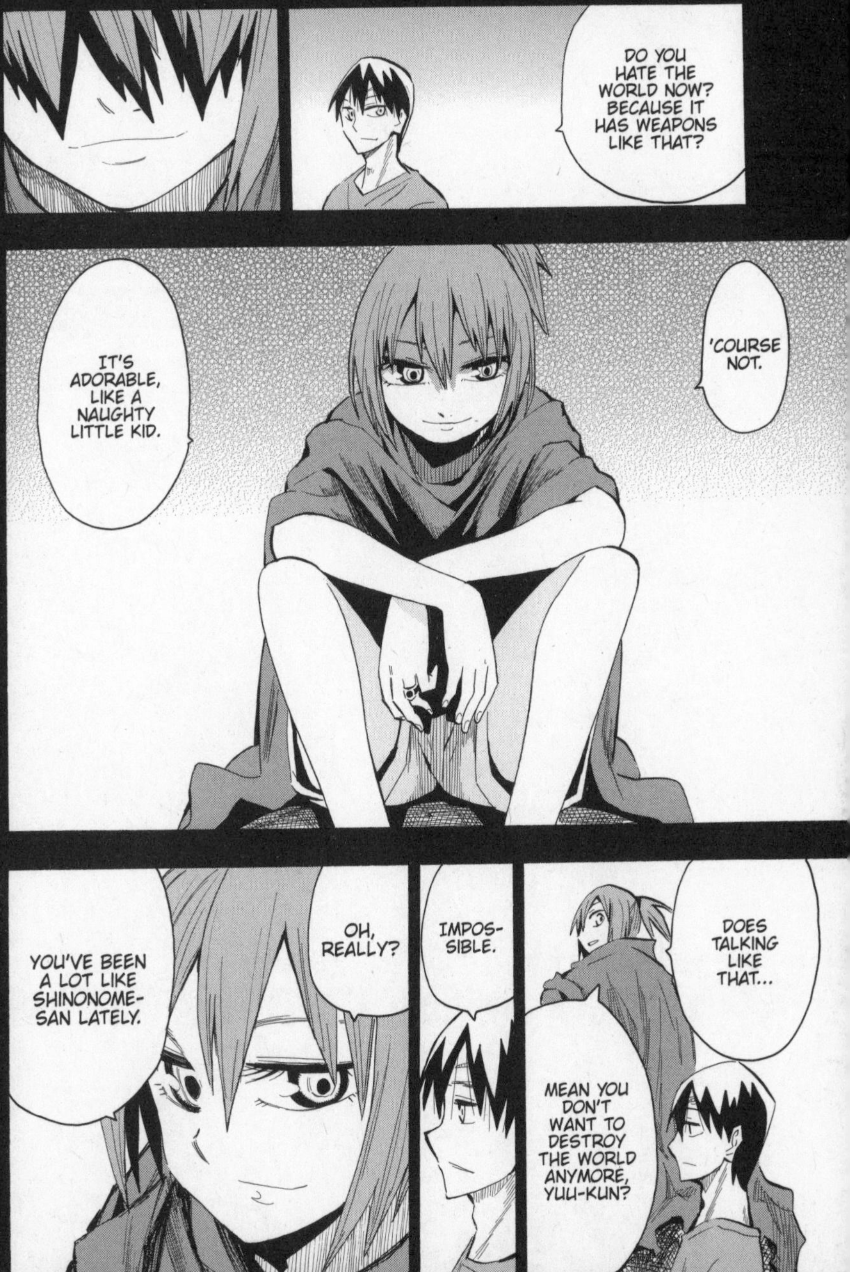
DO YOU HATE THE WORLD NOW? BECAUSE IT HAS WEAPONS LIKE THAT?
'COURSE NOT.
IT'S ADORABLE, LIKE A NAUGHTY LITTLE KID.
DOES TALKING LIKE THAT...
MEAN YOU DON'T WANT TO DESTROY THE WORLD ANYMORE, YUU-KUN?
IMPOS-SIBLE.
OH, REALLY?
YOU'VE BEEN A LOT LIKE SHINONOME-SAN LATELY.

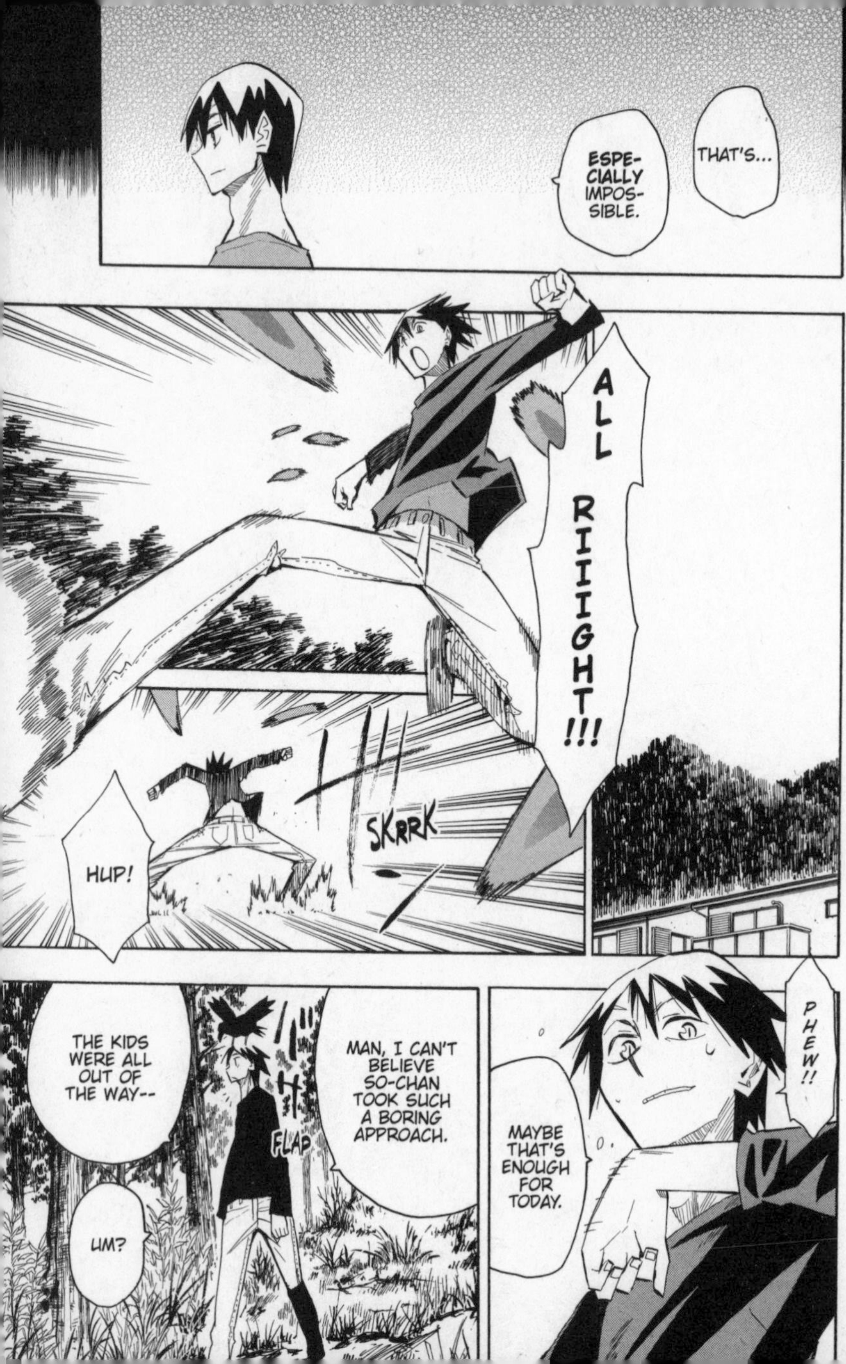
THAT'S...
ESPE-CIALLY IMPOS-SIBLE.
ALL RIIIGHT!!!
SKRRK
HUP!
PHEW!!
MAYBE THAT'S ENOUGH FOR TODAY.
MAN, I CAN'T BELIEVE SO-CHAN TOOK SUCH A BORING APPROACH.
THE KIDS WERE ALL OUT OF THE WAY--
FLAP
UM?

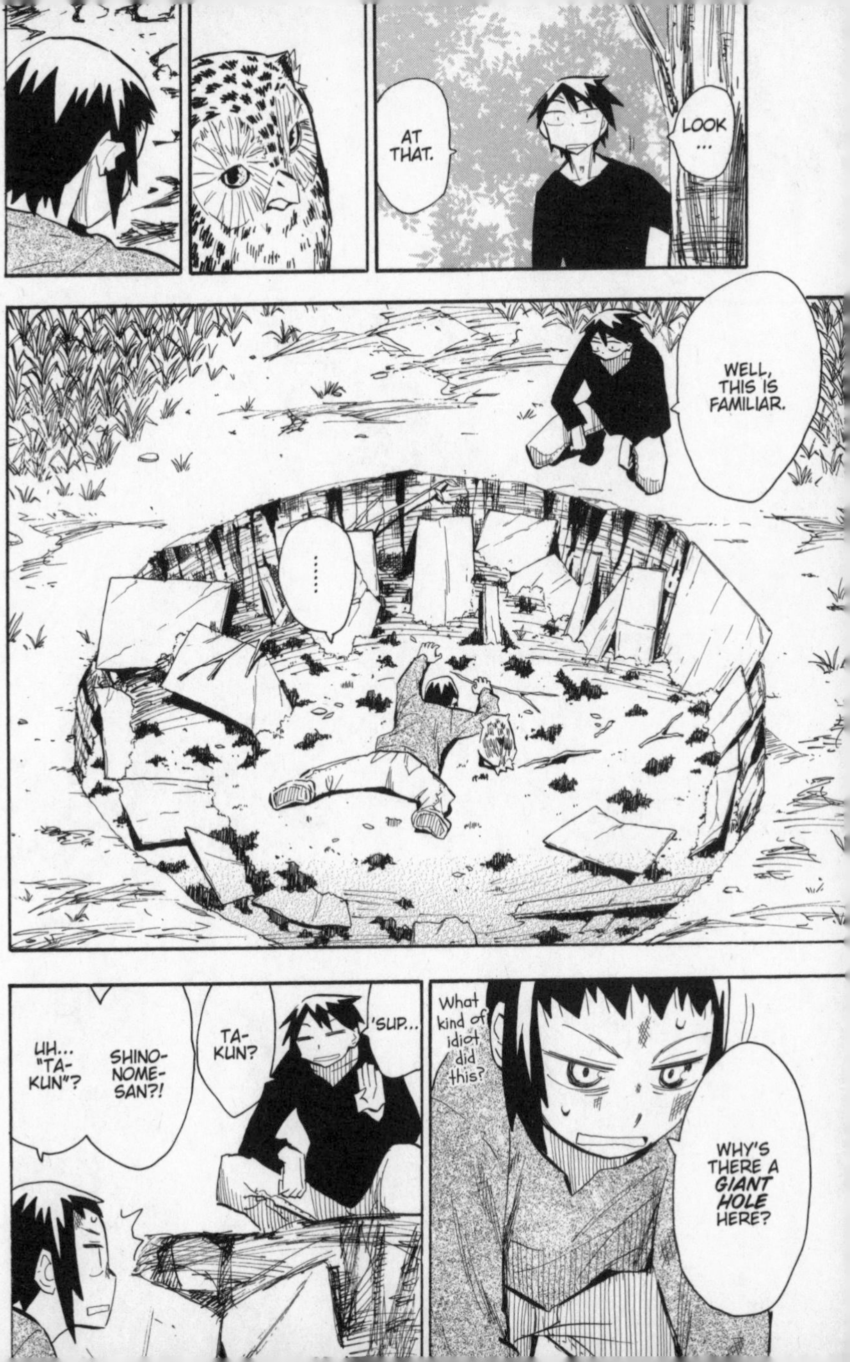

LOOK ...
AT THAT.
WELL, THIS IS FAMILIAR.
......
WHY'S THERE A GIANT HOLE HERE?
What kind of idiot did this?
'SUP...
TA-KUN?
SHINO-NOME-SAN?!
UH... "TA-KUN"?

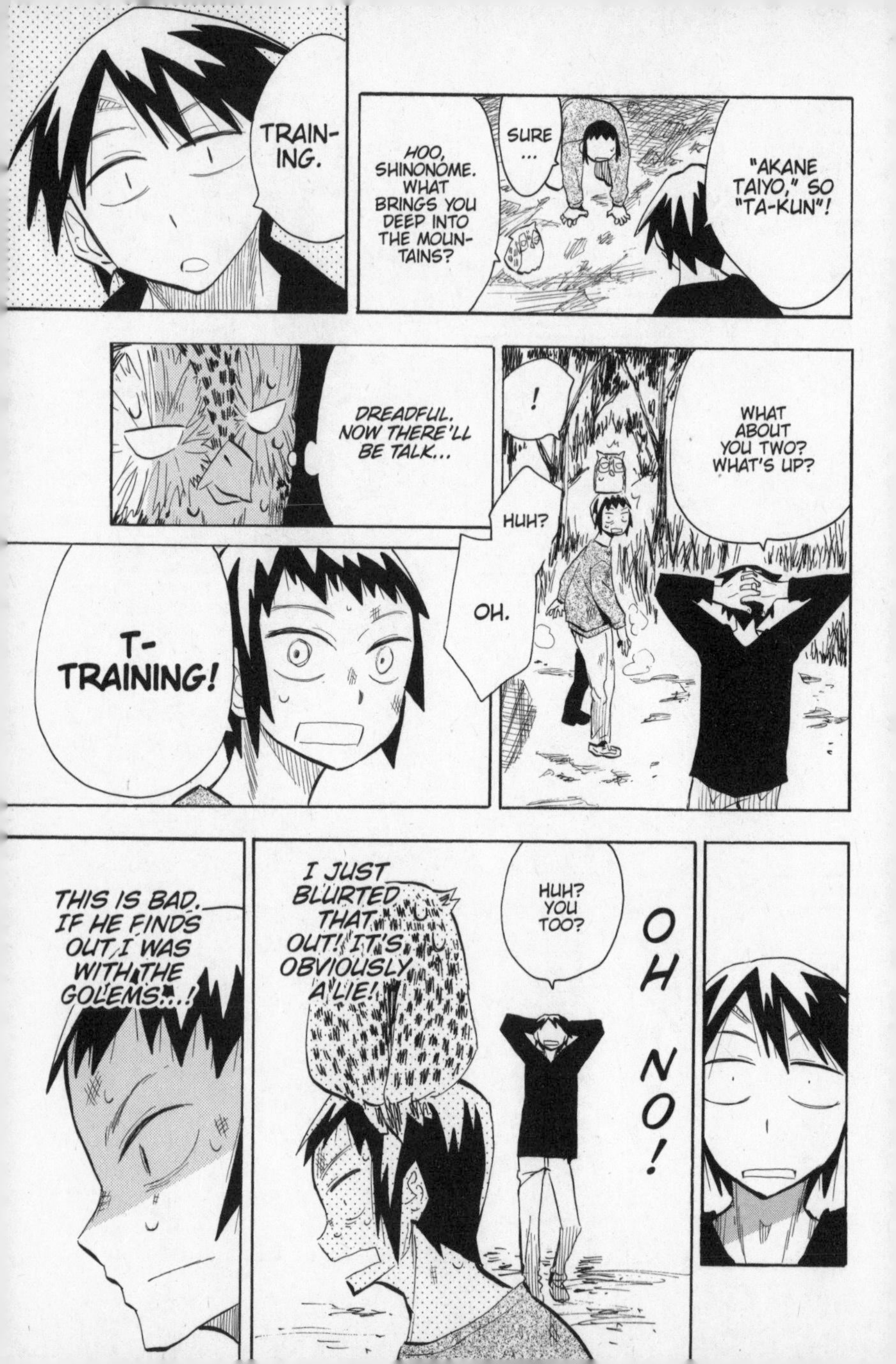
"AKANE TAIYO," SO "TA-KUN"!
SURE ...
HOO, SHINONOME. WHAT BRINGS YOU DEEP INTO THE MOUNTAINS?
TRAINING.
WHAT ABOUT YOU TWO? WHAT'S UP?
!
HUH?
OH.
DREADFUL. NOW THERE'LL BE TALK...
T-TRAINING!
OH NO!
HUH? YOU TOO?
I JUST BLURTED THAT OUT! IT'S OBVIOUSLY A LIE!
THIS IS BAD. IF HE FINDS OUT I WAS WITH THE GOLEMS...!

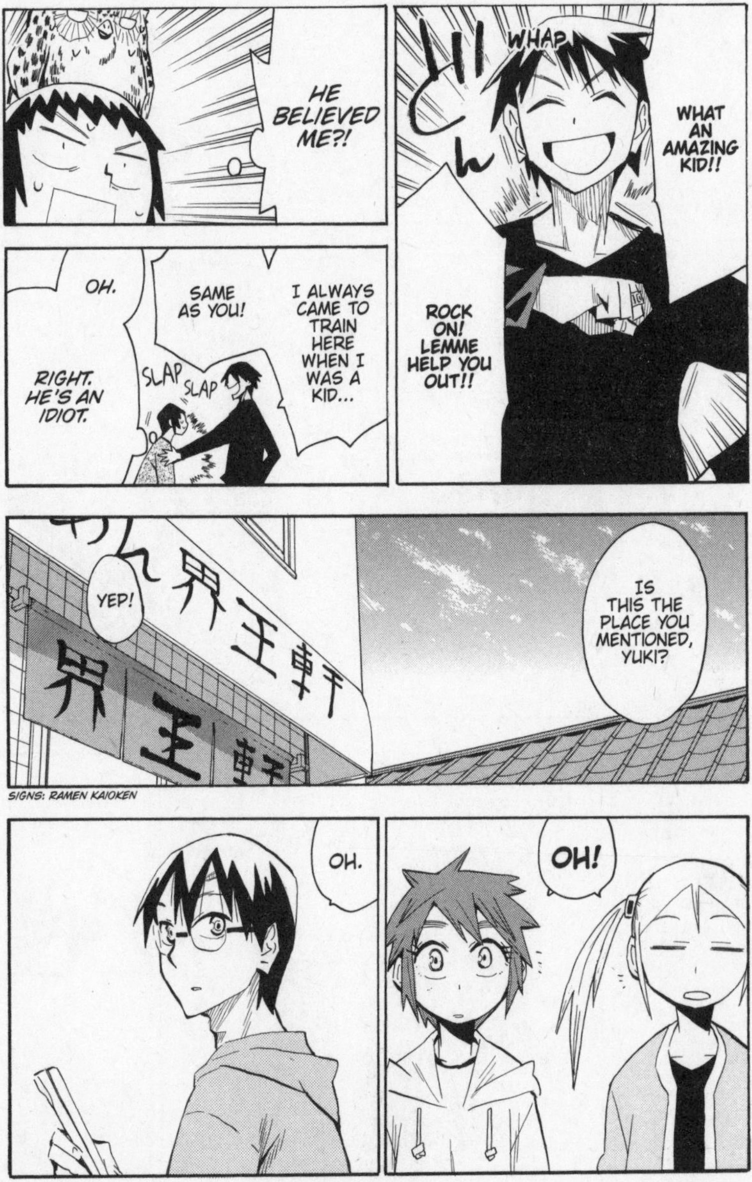
WHAP
WHAT AN AMAZING KID!!
ROCK ON! LEMME HELP YOU OUT!!
HE BELIEVED ME?!
I ALWAYS CAME TO TRAIN HERE WHEN I WAS A KID...
SAME AS YOU!
SLAP
SLAP
OH.
RIGHT. HE'S AN IDIOT.
IS THIS THE PLACE YOU MENTIONED, YUKI?
YEP!
OH!
OH.
SIGNS: RAMEN KAIOKEN

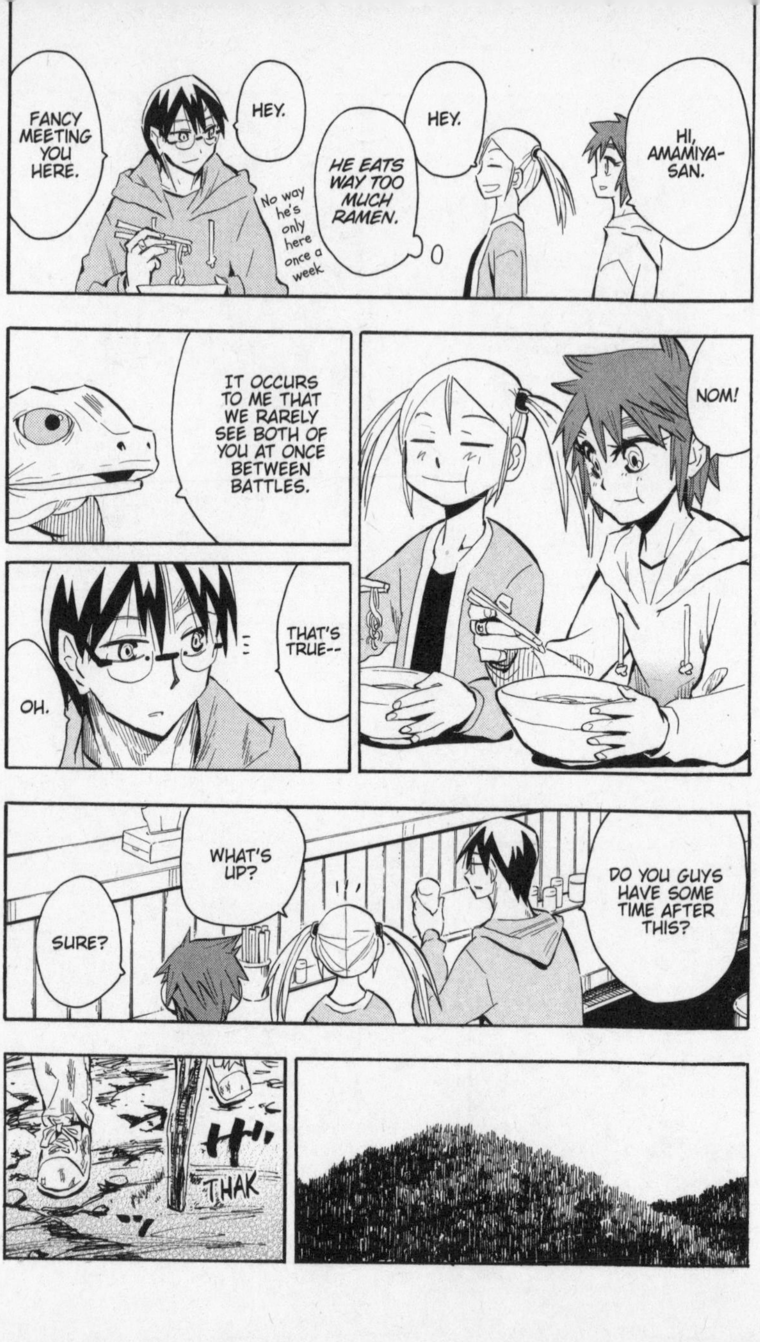
HI, AMAMIYA-SAN.
HEY.
HE EATS WAY TOO MUCH RAMEN.
HEY.
No way he's only here once a week
FANCY MEETING YOU HERE.
NOM!
IT OCCURS TO ME THAT WE RARELY SEE BOTH OF YOU AT ONCE BETWEEN BATTLES.
THAT'S TRUE--
OH.
DO YOU GUYS HAVE SOME TIME AFTER THIS?
WHAT'S UP?
SURE?
THAK

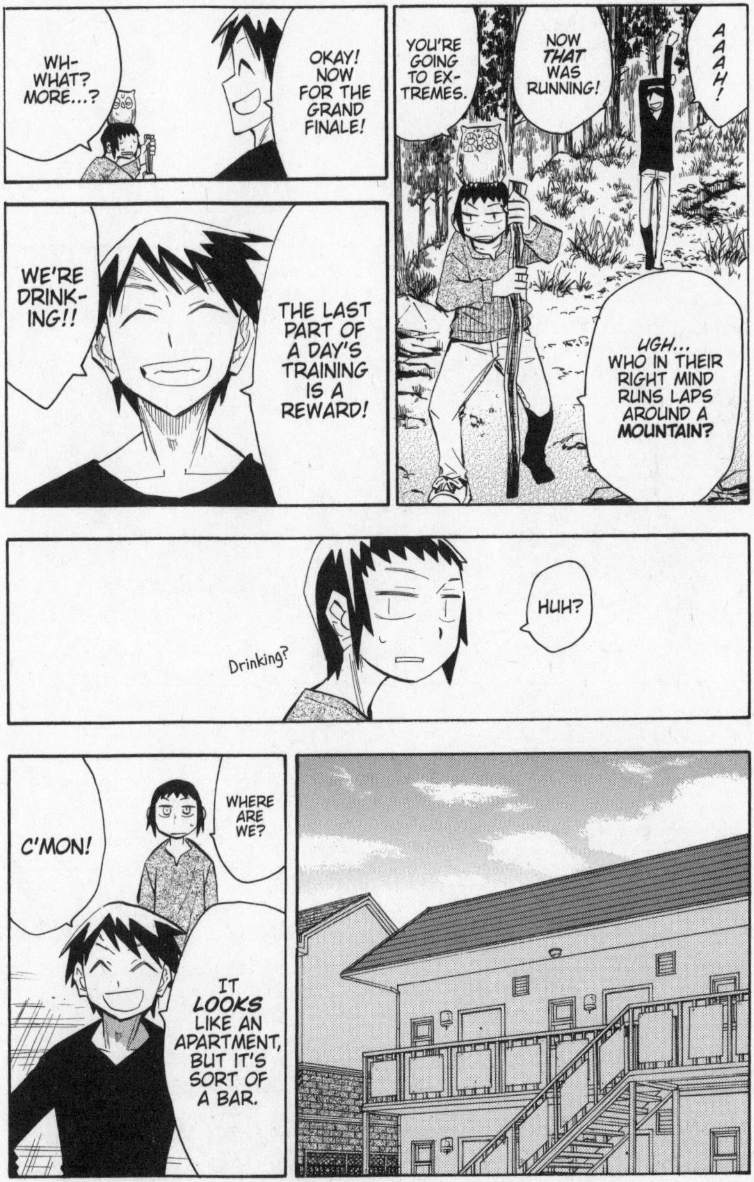
AAAAH!
NOW THAT WAS RUNNING!
YOU'RE GOING TO EXTREMES.
UGH... WHO IN THEIR RIGHT MIND RUNS LAPS AROUND A MOUNTAIN?
OKAY! NOW FOR THE GRAND FINALE!
WH-WHAT? MORE...?
THE LAST PART OF A DAY'S TRAINING IS A REWARD!
WE'RE DRINKING!!
HUH?
Drinking?
WHERE ARE WE?
C'MON!
IT LOOKS LIKE AN APARTMENT, BUT IT'S SORT OF A BAR.

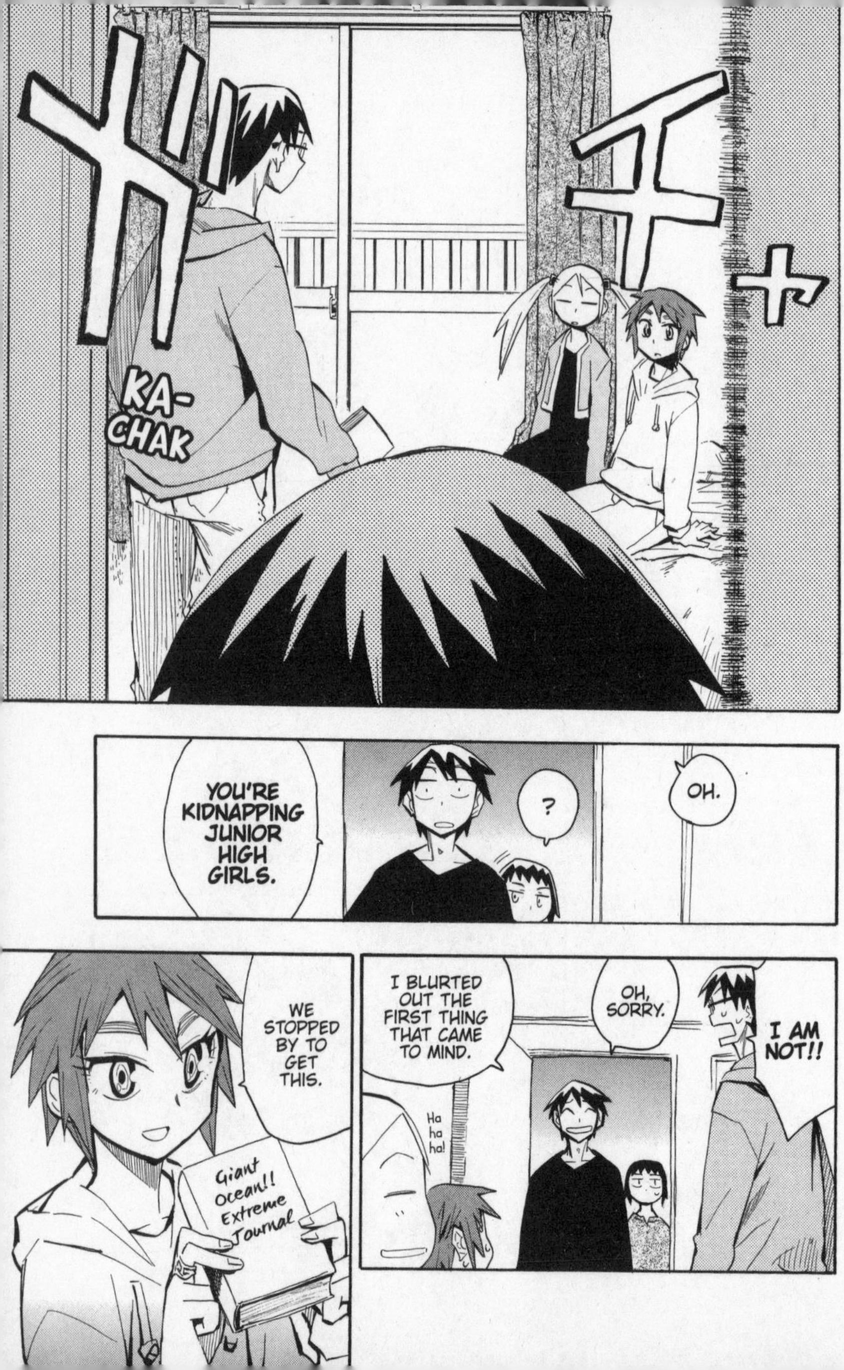
KA-CHAK
OH.
?
YOU'RE KIDNAPPING JUNIOR HIGH GIRLS.
I AM NOT!!
OH, SORRY.
I BLURTED OUT THE FIRST THING THAT CAME TO MIND.
Ha ha ha!
WE STOPPED BY TO GET THIS.
Giant Ocean!! Extreme Journal

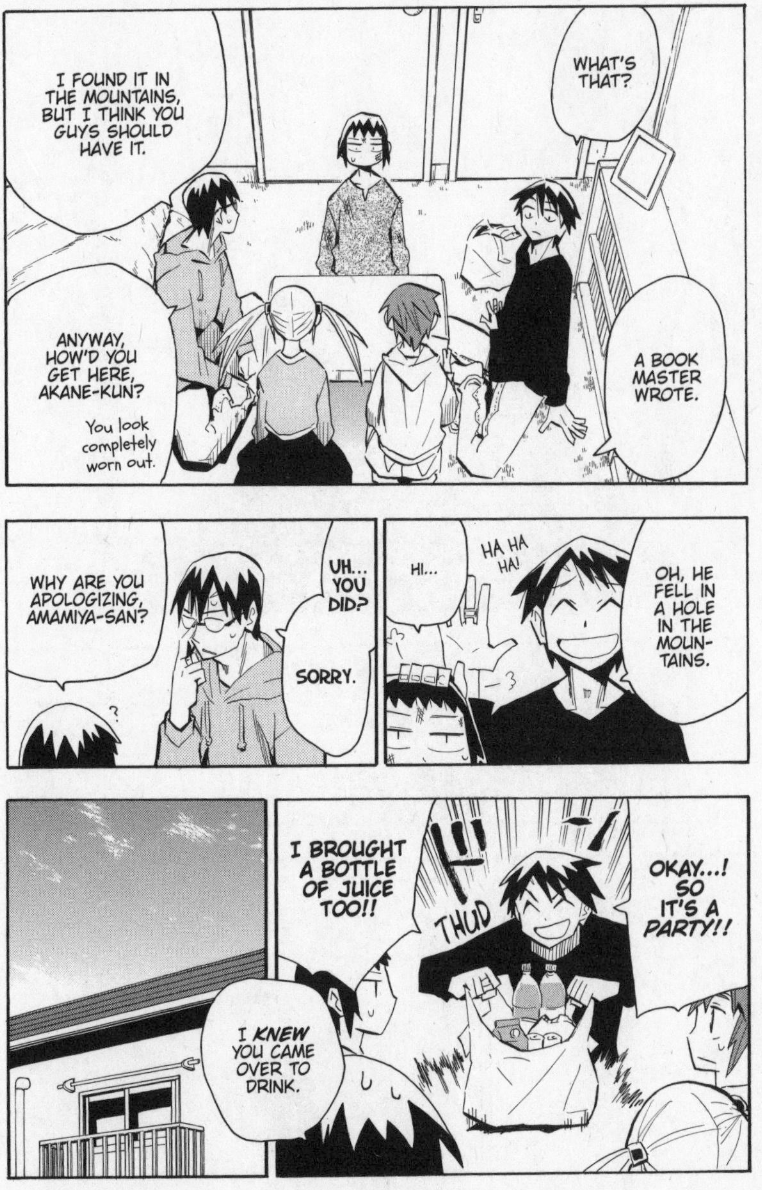
WHAT'S THAT?
A BOOK MASTER WROTE.
I FOUND IT IN THE MOUNTAINS, BUT I THINK YOU GUYS SHOULD HAVE IT.
ANYWAY, HOW'D YOU GET HERE, AKANE-KUN?
You look completely worn out.
OH, HE FELL IN A HOLE IN THE MOUNTAINS.
HA HA HA!
HI...
UH... YOU DID?
SORRY.
WHY ARE YOU APOLOGIZING, AMAMIYA-SAN?
OKAY...! SO IT'S A *PARTY*!!
I BROUGHT A BOTTLE OF JUICE TOO!!
THUD
I *KNEW* YOU CAME OVER TO DRINK.

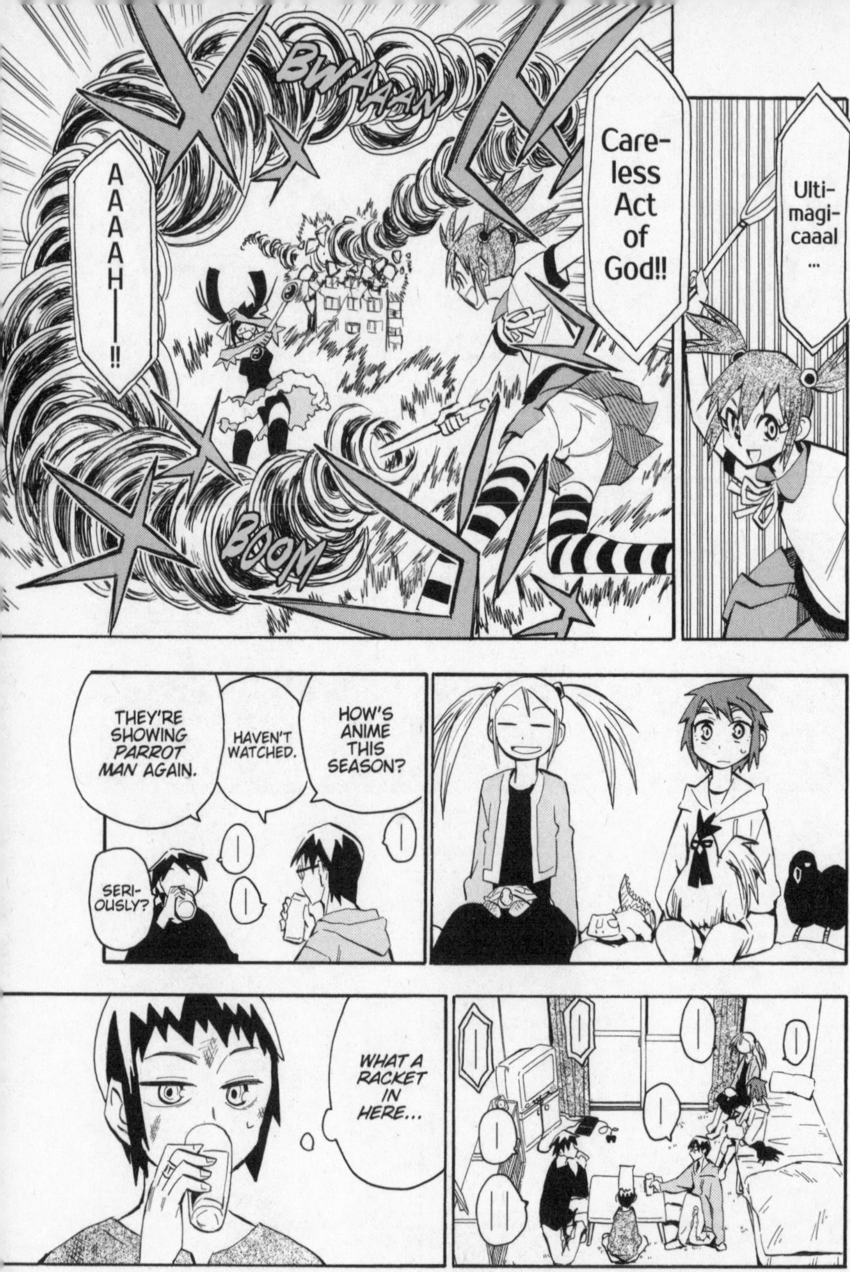
Ulti-magi-caaal...
Care-less Act of God!!
BWAAAN
AAAAAH!!
BOOM
HOW'S ANIME THIS SEASON?
HAVEN'T WATCHED.
THEY'RE SHOWING PARROT MAN AGAIN.
SERI-OUSLY?
WHAT A RACKET IN HERE...

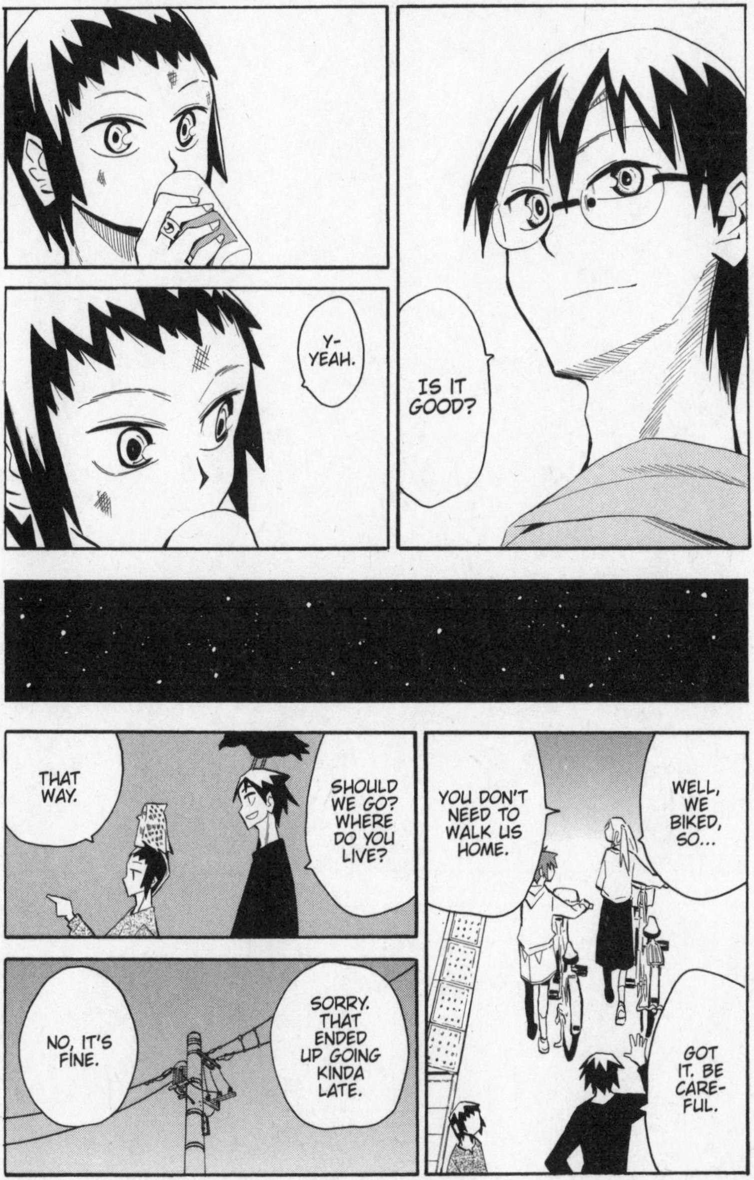
IS IT GOOD?
Y-YEAH.
WELL, WE BIKED, SO...
YOU DON'T NEED TO WALK US HOME.
GOT IT. BE CARE-FUL.
SHOULD WE GO? WHERE DO YOU LIVE?
THAT WAY.
SORRY. THAT ENDED UP GOING KINDA LATE.
NO, IT'S FINE.

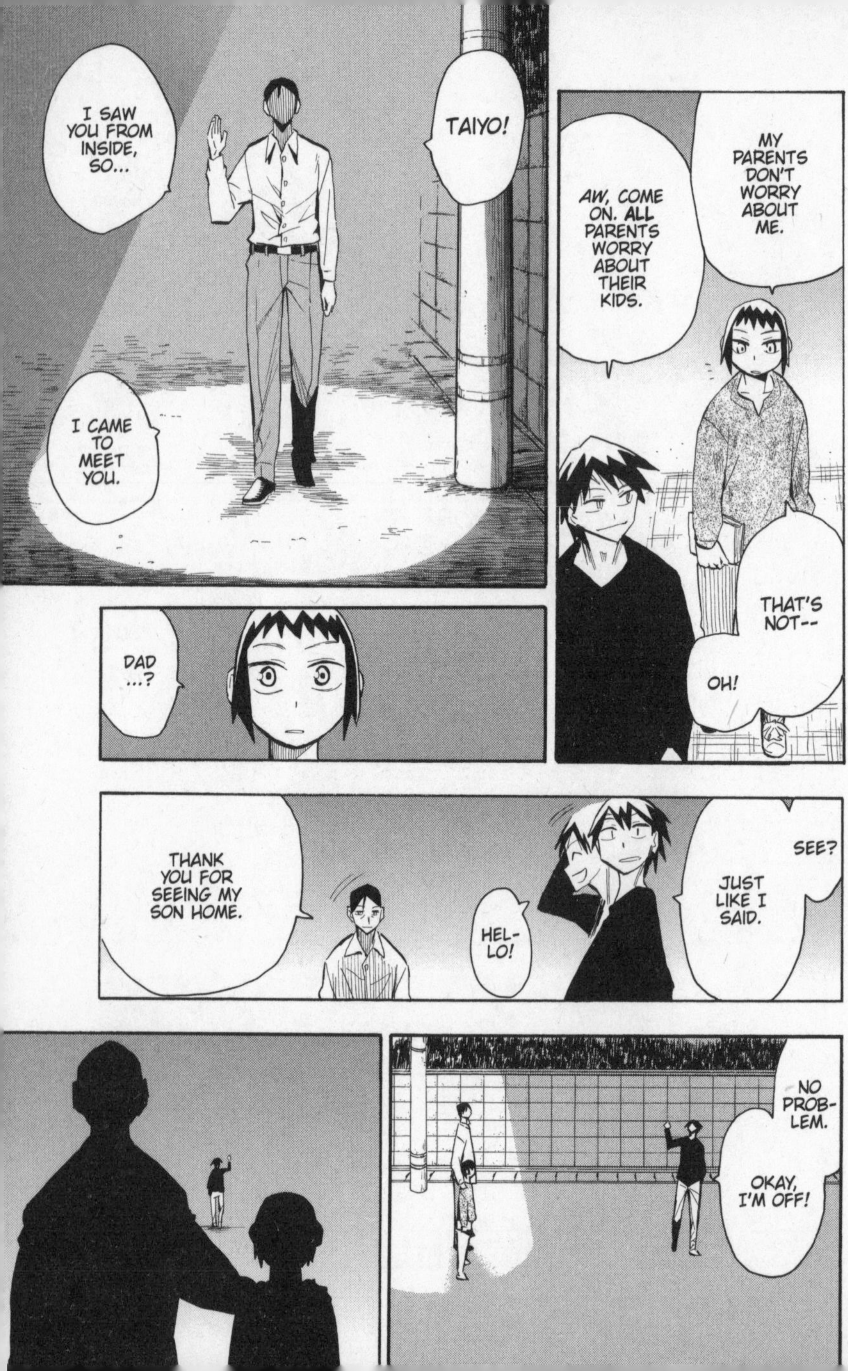
MY PARENTS DON'T WORRY ABOUT ME.
AW, COME ON. ALL PARENTS WORRY ABOUT THEIR KIDS.
THAT'S NOT--
OH!
TAIYO!
I SAW YOU FROM INSIDE, SO...
I CAME TO MEET YOU.
DAD ...?
SEE?
JUST LIKE I SAID.
HEL-LO!
THANK YOU FOR SEEING MY SON HOME.
NO PROB-LEM.
OKAY, I'M OFF!

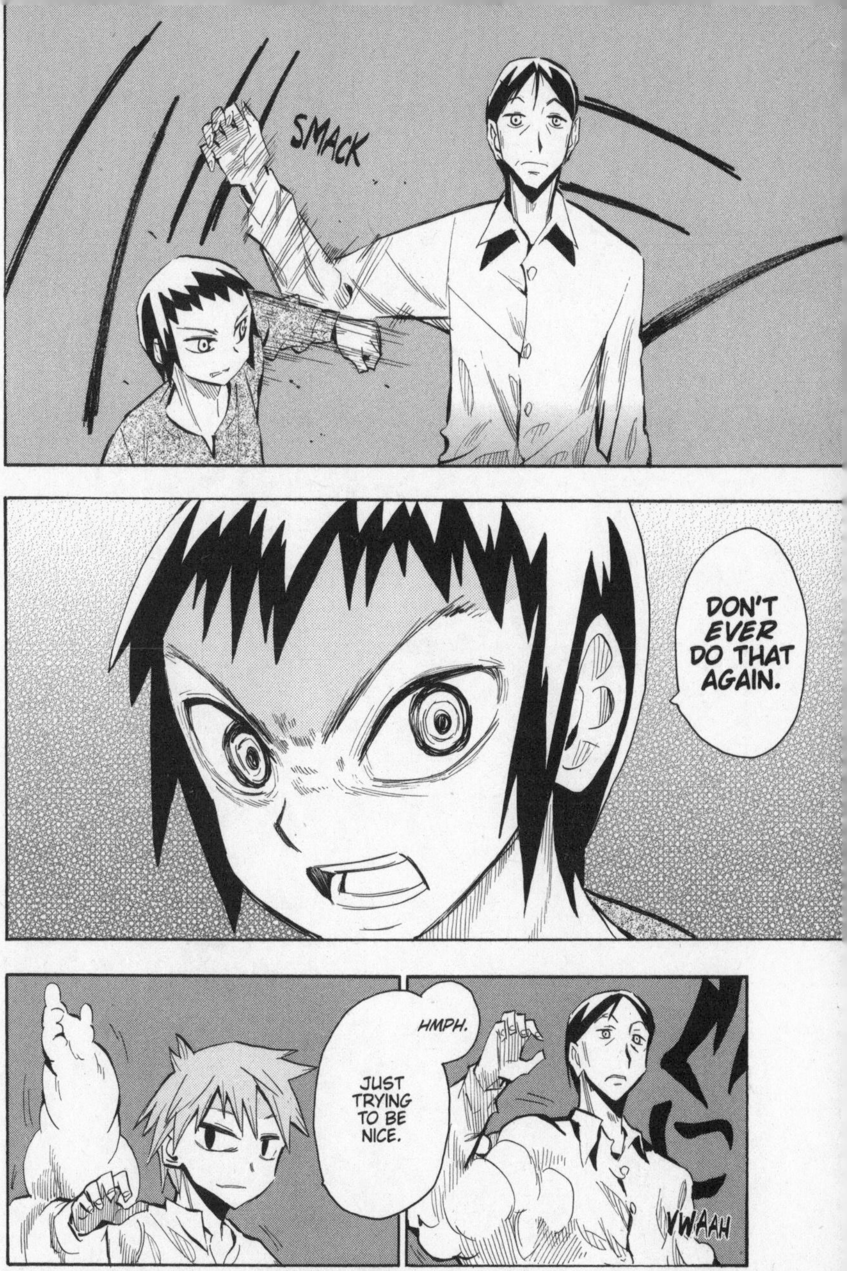
SMACK
DON'T EVER DO THAT AGAIN.
VWAAH
HMPH.
JUST TRYING TO BE NICE.

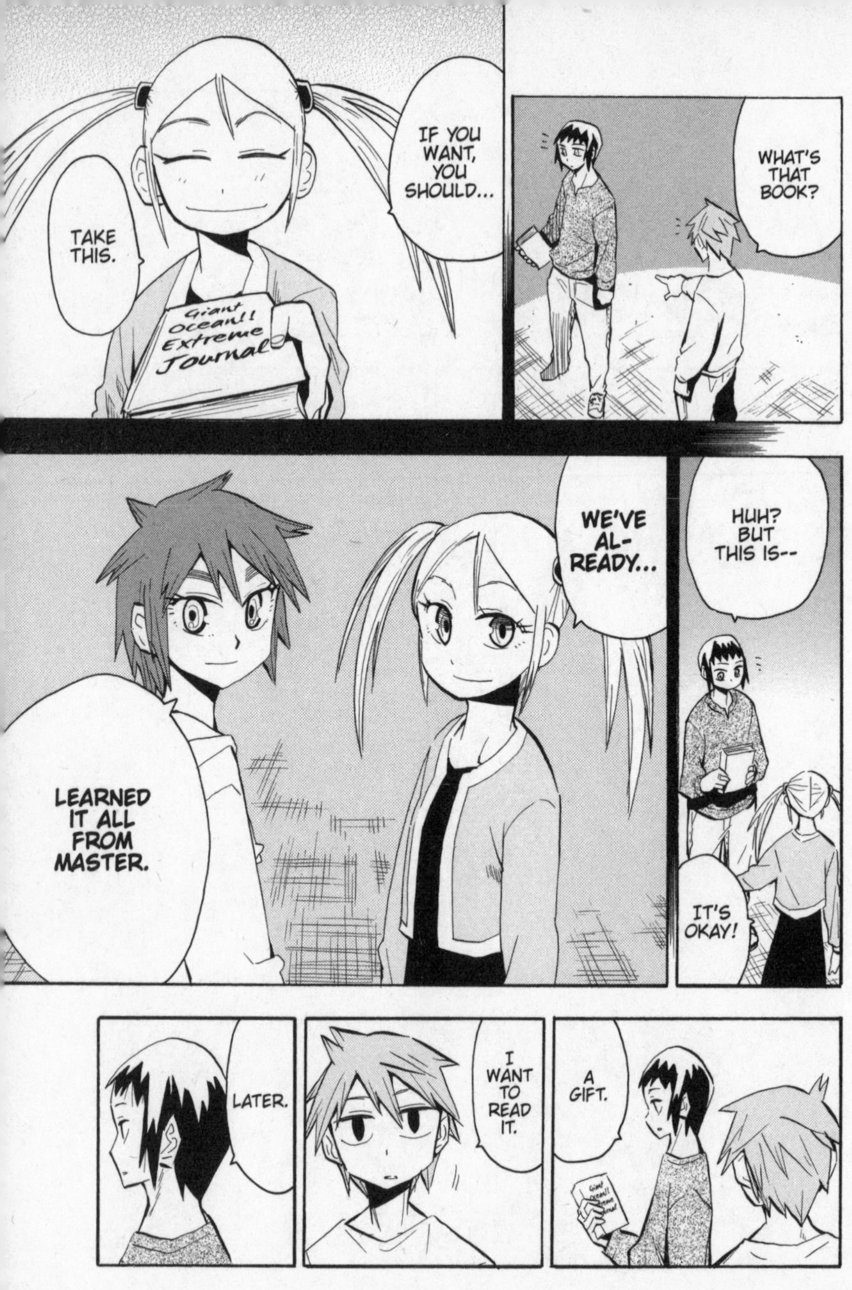
WHAT'S THAT BOOK?
IF YOU WANT, YOU SHOULD...
TAKE THIS.
Giant Ocean!! Extreme Journal
HUH? BUT THIS IS--
IT'S OKAY!
WE'VE AL-READY...
LEARNED IT ALL FROM MASTER.
A GIFT.
I WANT TO READ IT.
LATER.

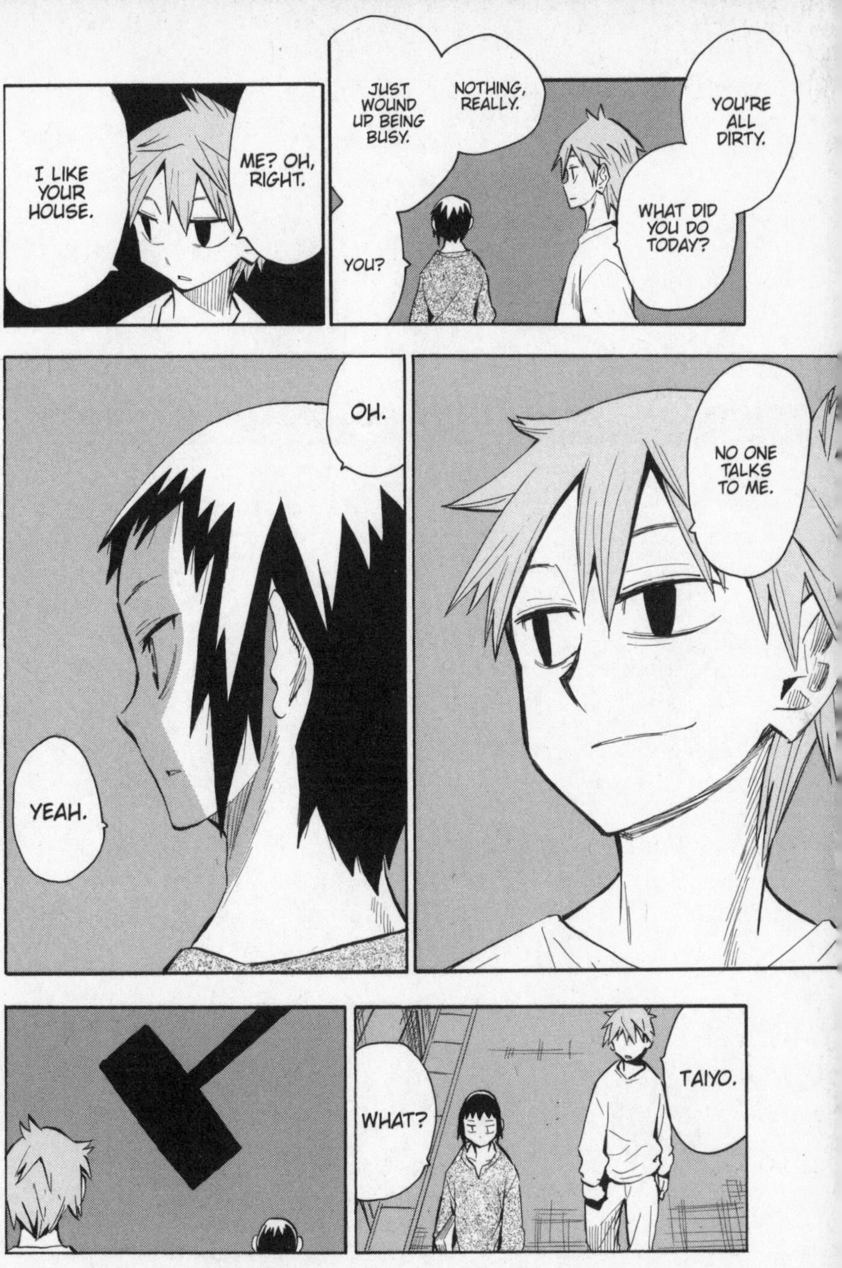
YOU'RE ALL DIRTY.
WHAT DID YOU DO TODAY?
NOTHING, REALLY.
JUST WOUND UP BEING BUSY.
YOU?
ME? OH, RIGHT.
I LIKE YOUR HOUSE.
NO ONE TALKS TO ME.
OH.
YEAH.
TAIYO.
WHAT?

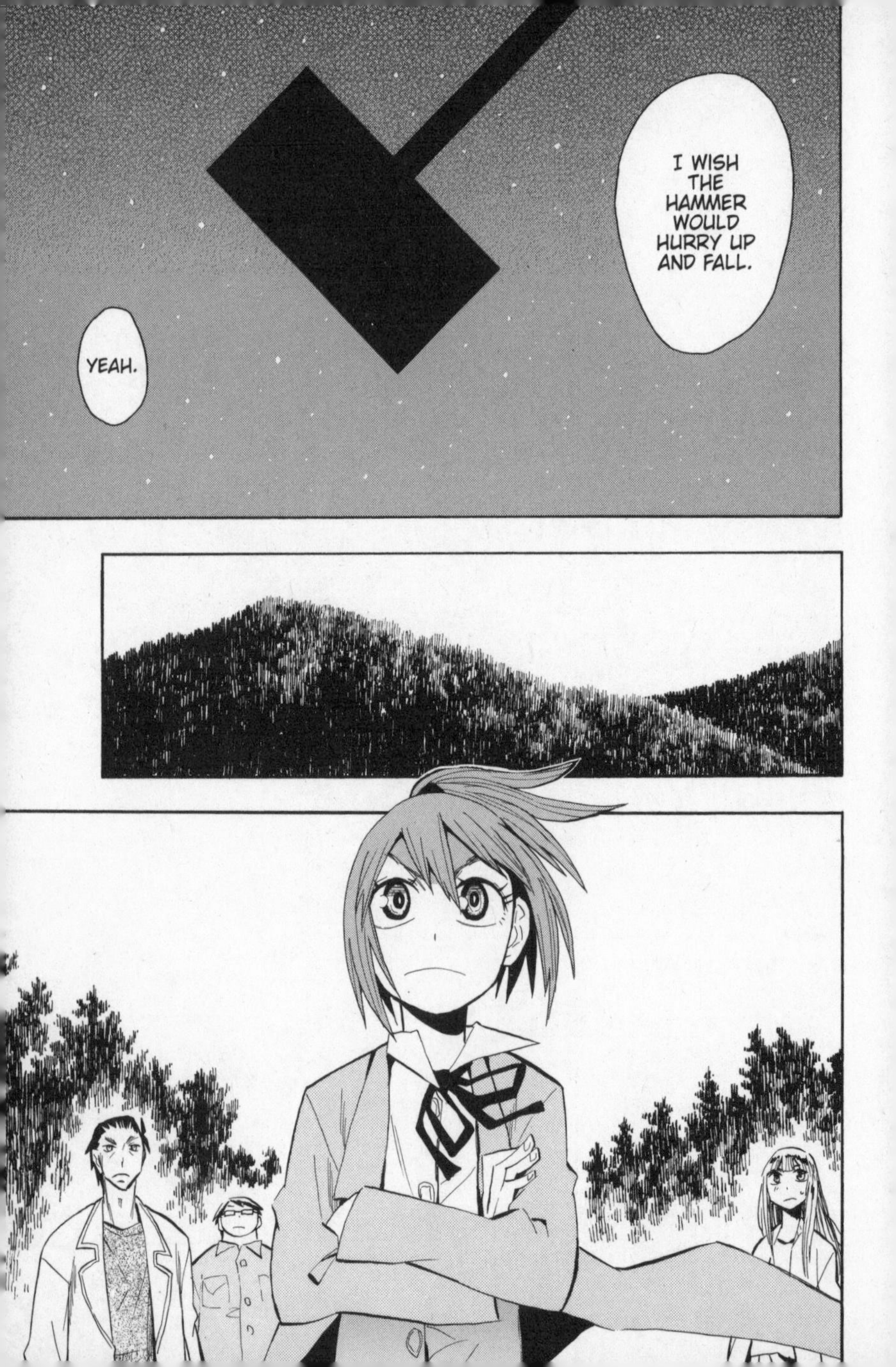
I WISH THE HAMMER WOULD HURRY UP AND FALL.
YEAH.

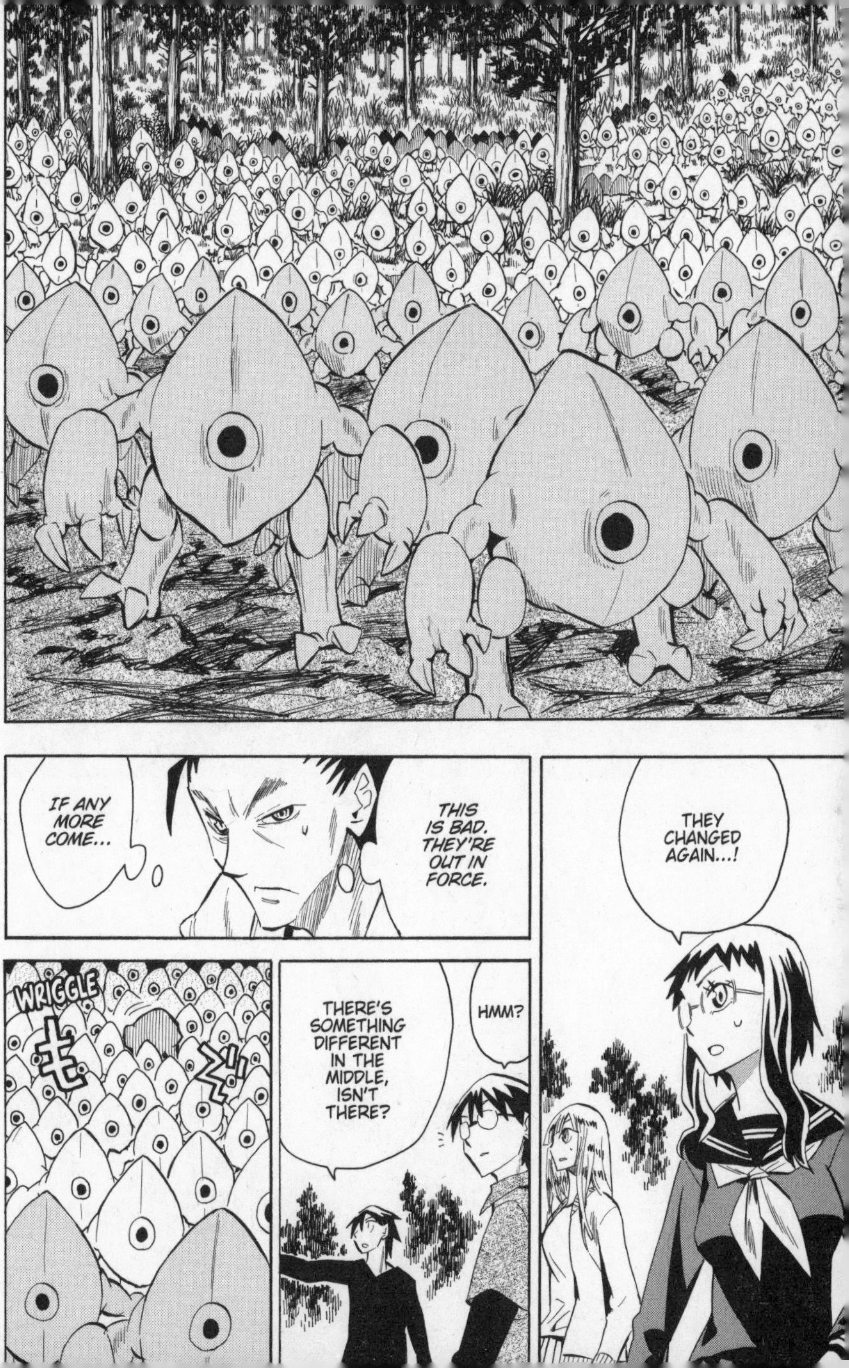
THEY CHANGED AGAIN...!
THIS IS BAD. THEY'RE OUT IN FORCE.
IF ANY MORE COME...
HMM?
THERE'S SOMETHING DIFFERENT IN THE MIDDLE, ISN'T THERE?
WRIGGLE

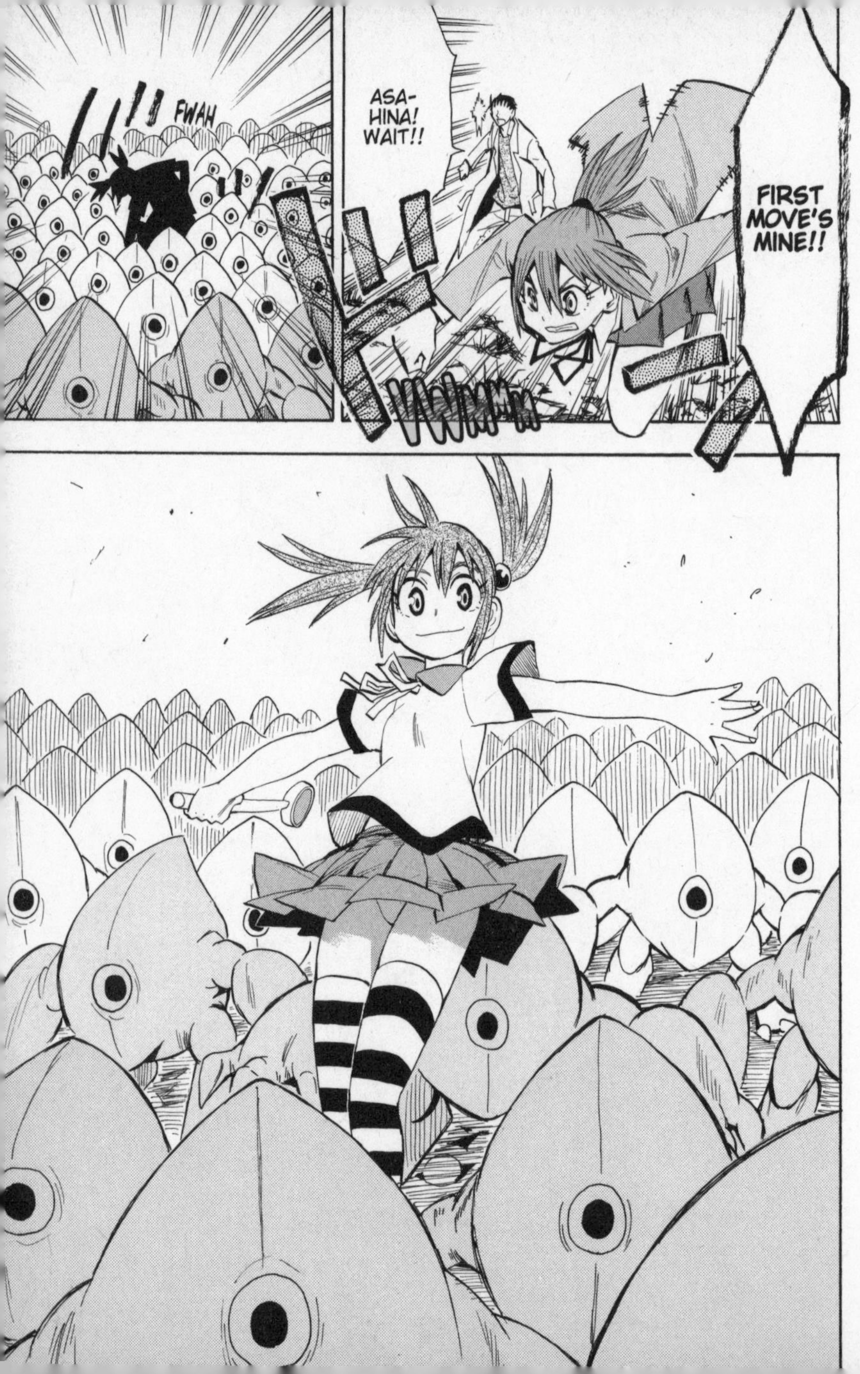
FIRST MOVE'S MINE!!
ASA-HINA! WAIT!!
FWAH

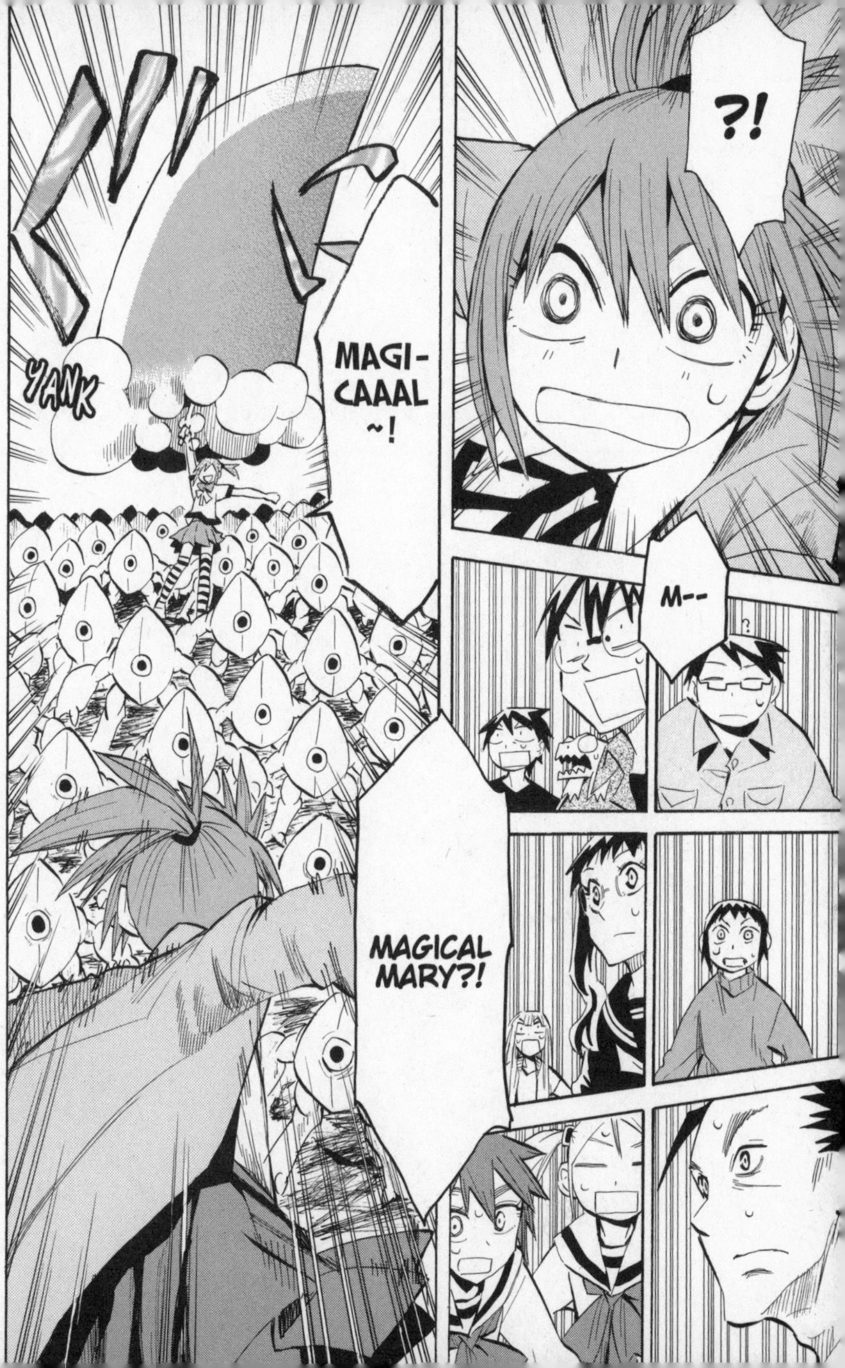
?!
M--
MAGICAL MARY?!
MAGI-CAAAL ~!
YANK

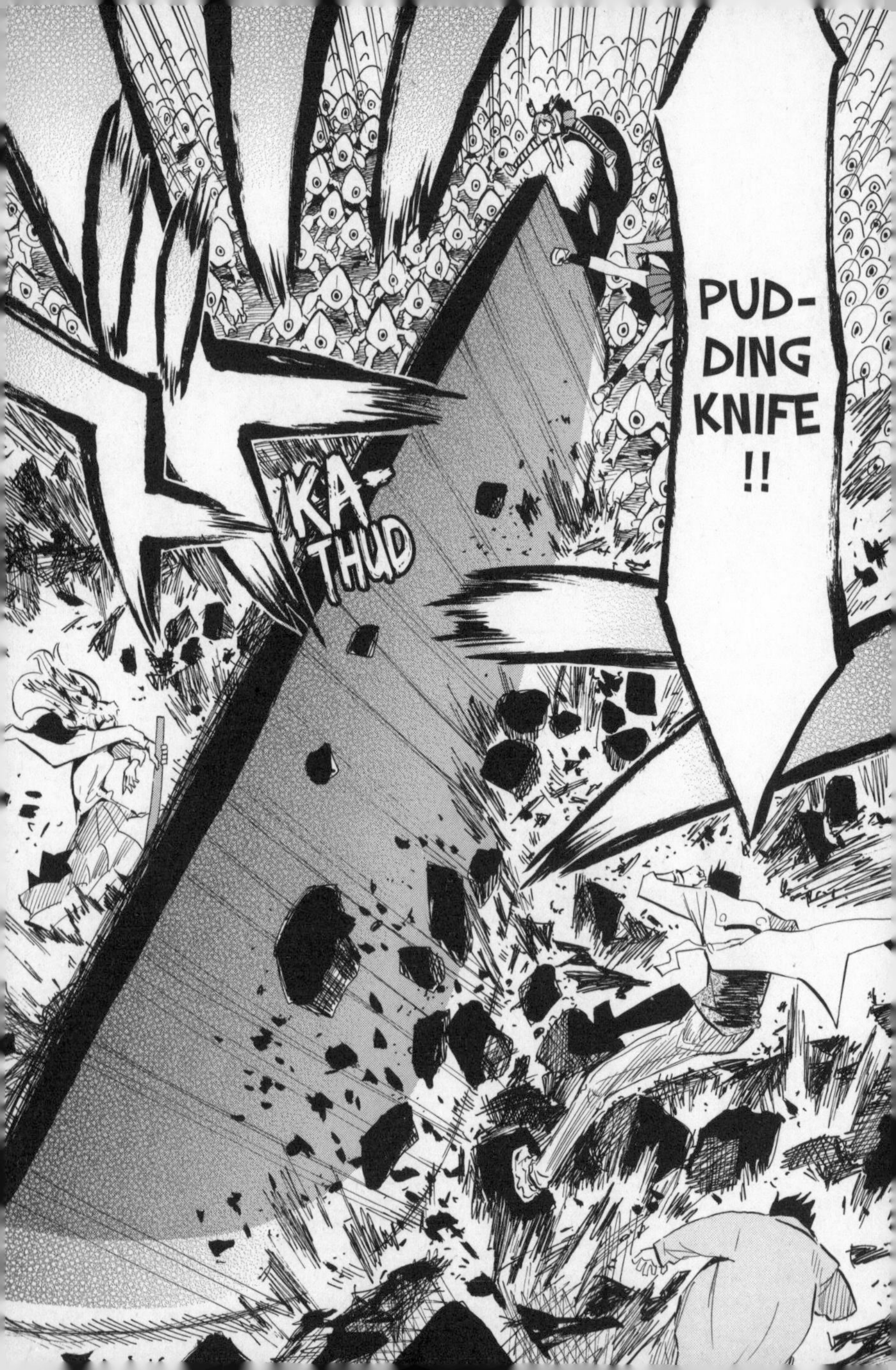
PUD-
DING
KNIFE
!!
KA
THUD

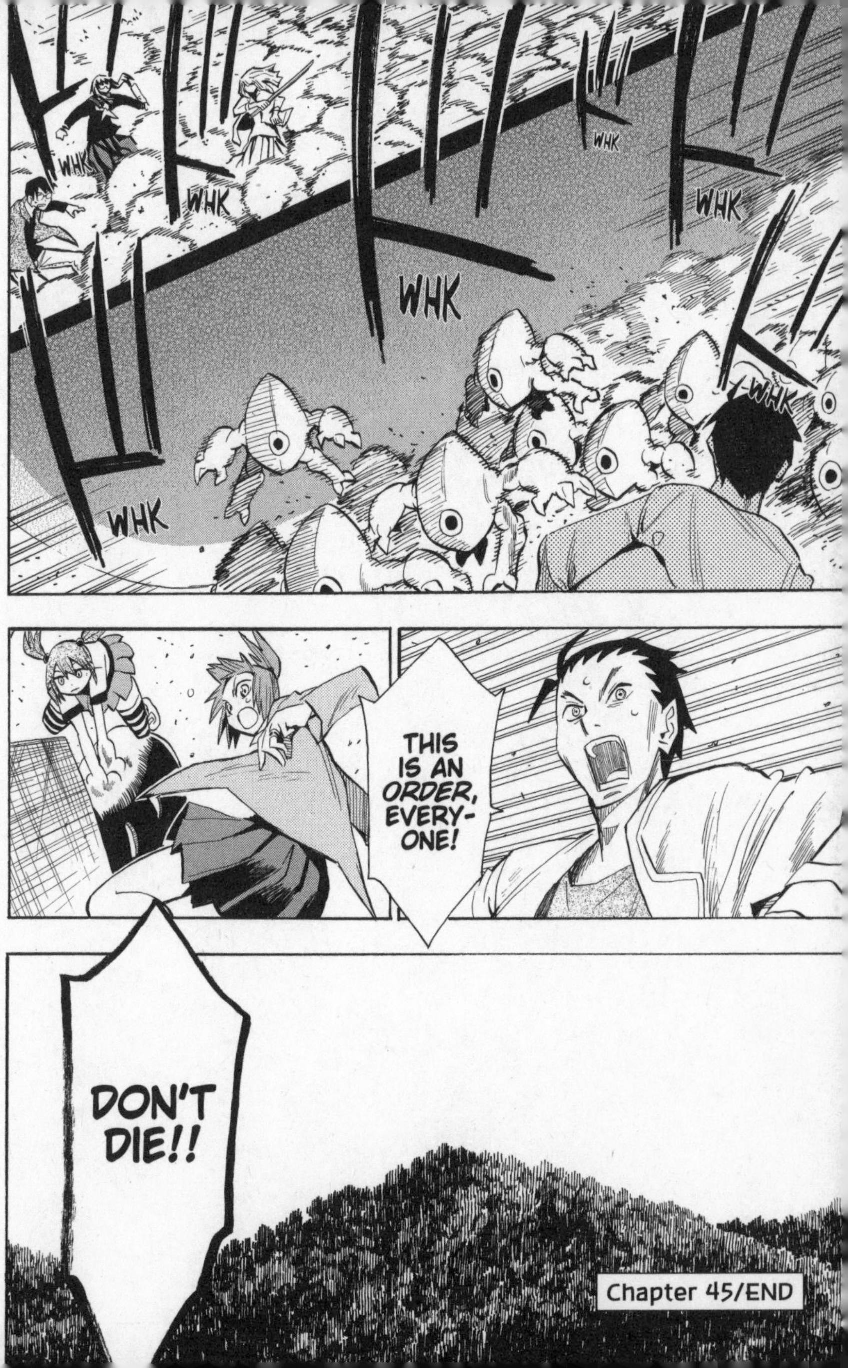
WHK
WHK
WHK
WHK
WHK
WHK
WHK
THIS IS AN ORDER, EVERY-ONE!
DON'T DIE!!
Chapter 45/END

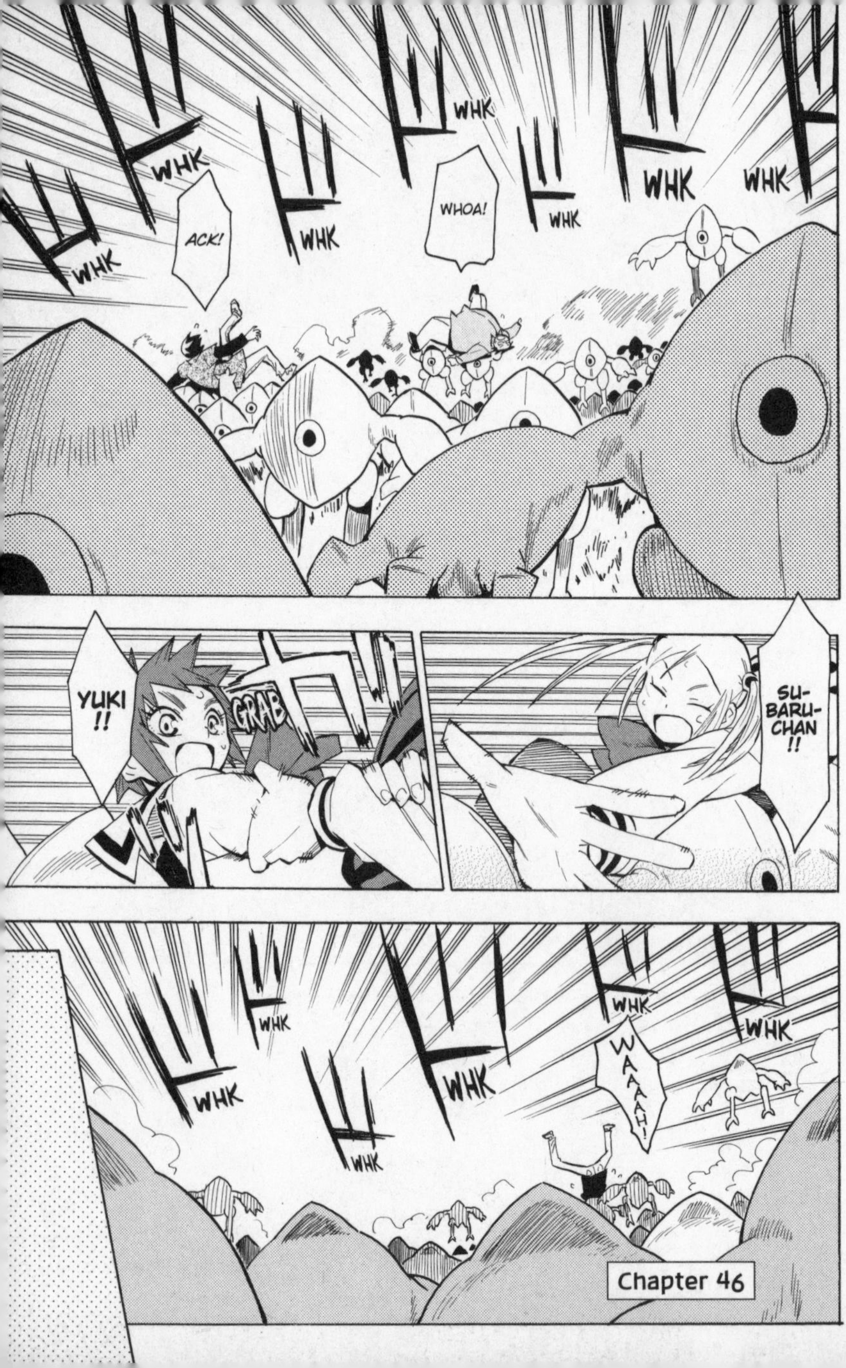
WHK
WHK
WHK
WHOA!
WHK
WHK
ACK!
WHK
WHK
SU-BARU-CHAN!!
GRAB
YUKI!!
WHK
WHK
WAAAAAH!
WHK
WHK
WHK
WHK
Chapter 46

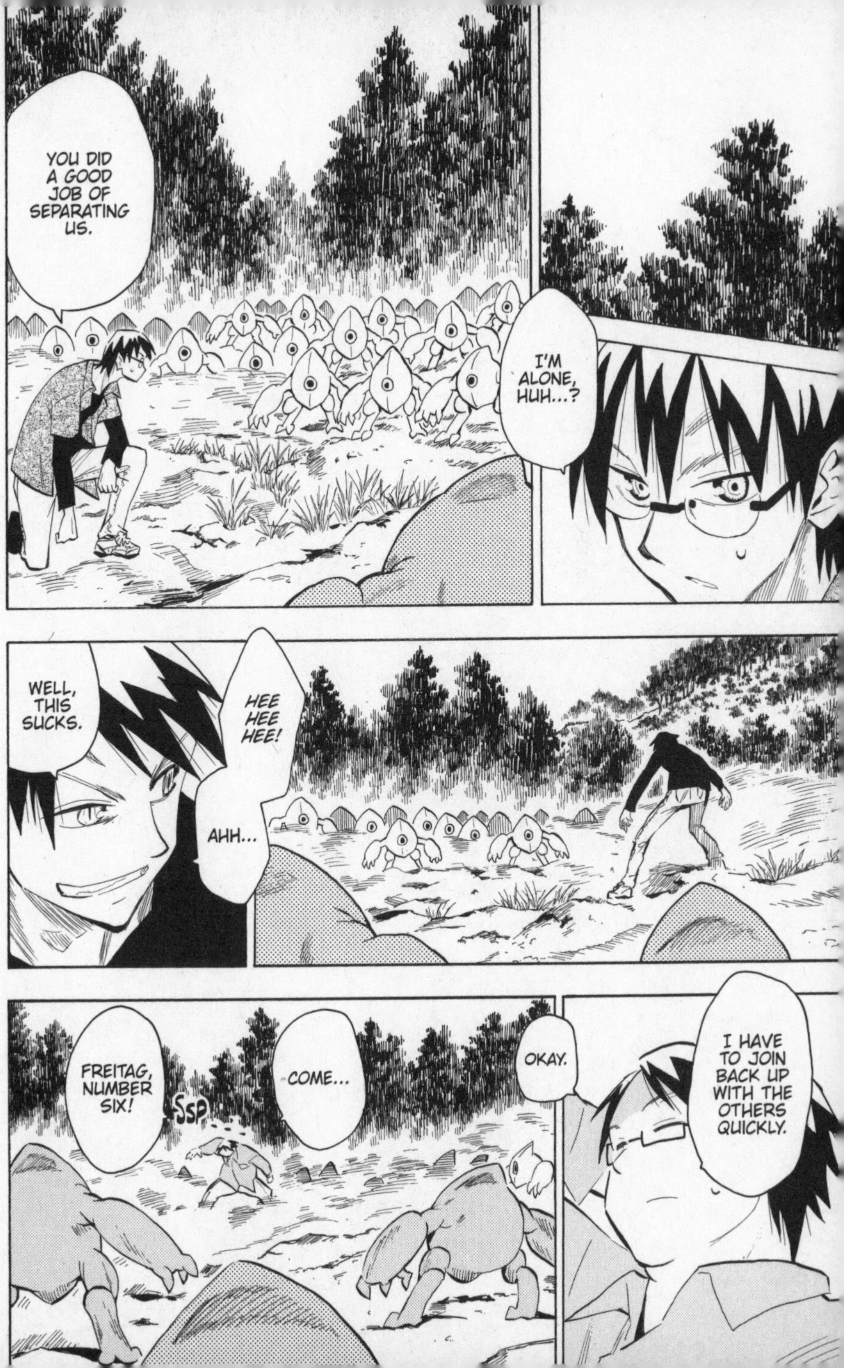
I'M ALONE, HUH...?
YOU DID A GOOD JOB OF SEPARATING US.
HEE HEE HEE!
AHH...
WELL, THIS SUCKS.
I HAVE TO JOIN BACK UP WITH THE OTHERS QUICKLY.
OKAY.
COME...
SSP
FREITAG, NUMBER SIX!

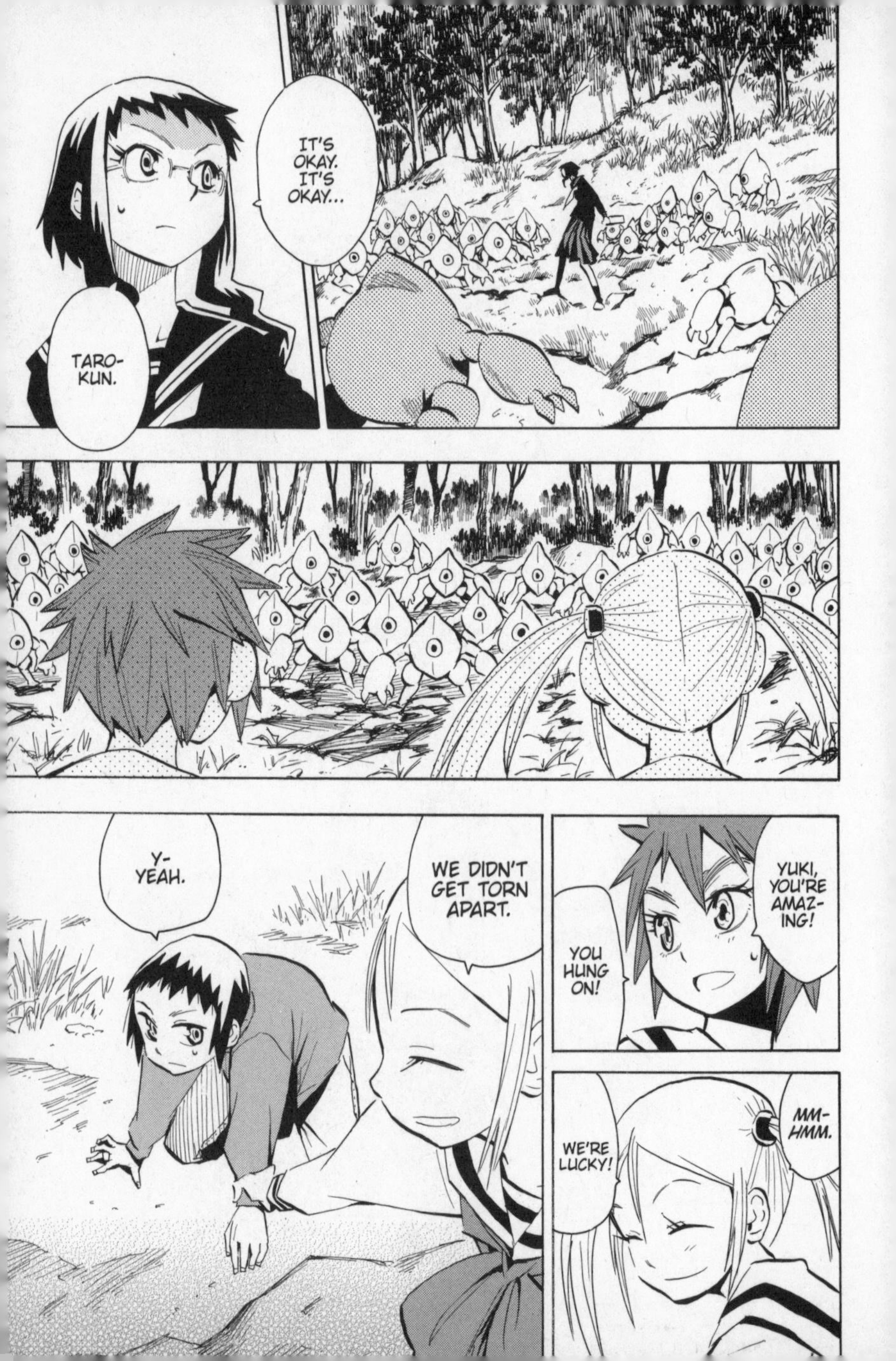
IT'S OKAY. IT'S OKAY...
TARO-KUN.
YUKI, YOU'RE AMAZ-ING!
YOU HUNG ON!
MM-HMM.
WE'RE LUCKY!
WE DIDN'T GET TORN APART.
Y-YEAH.

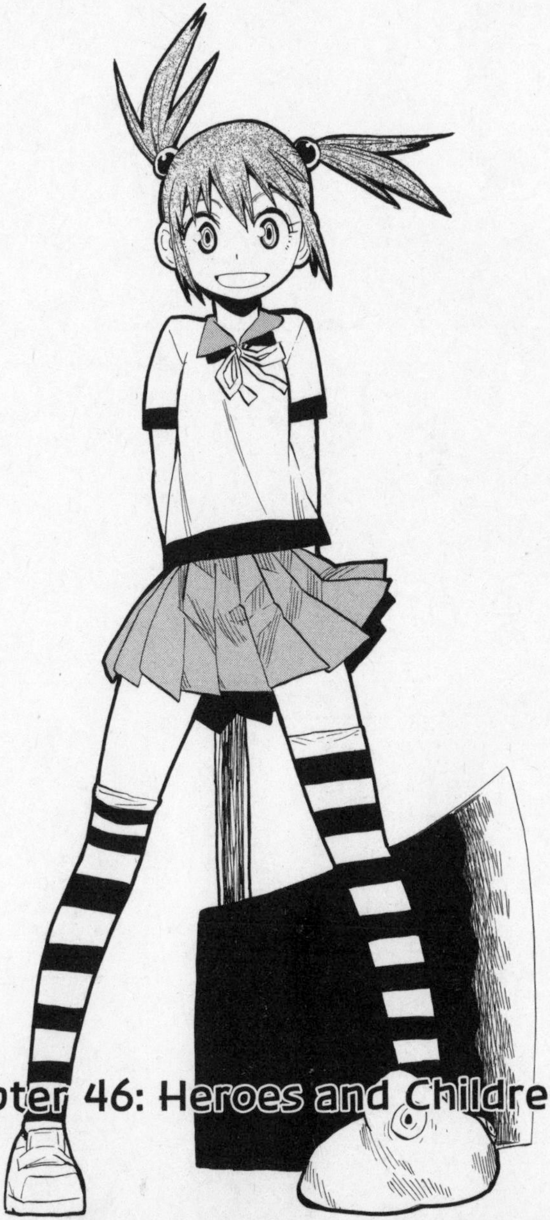

Chapter 46: Heroes and Children

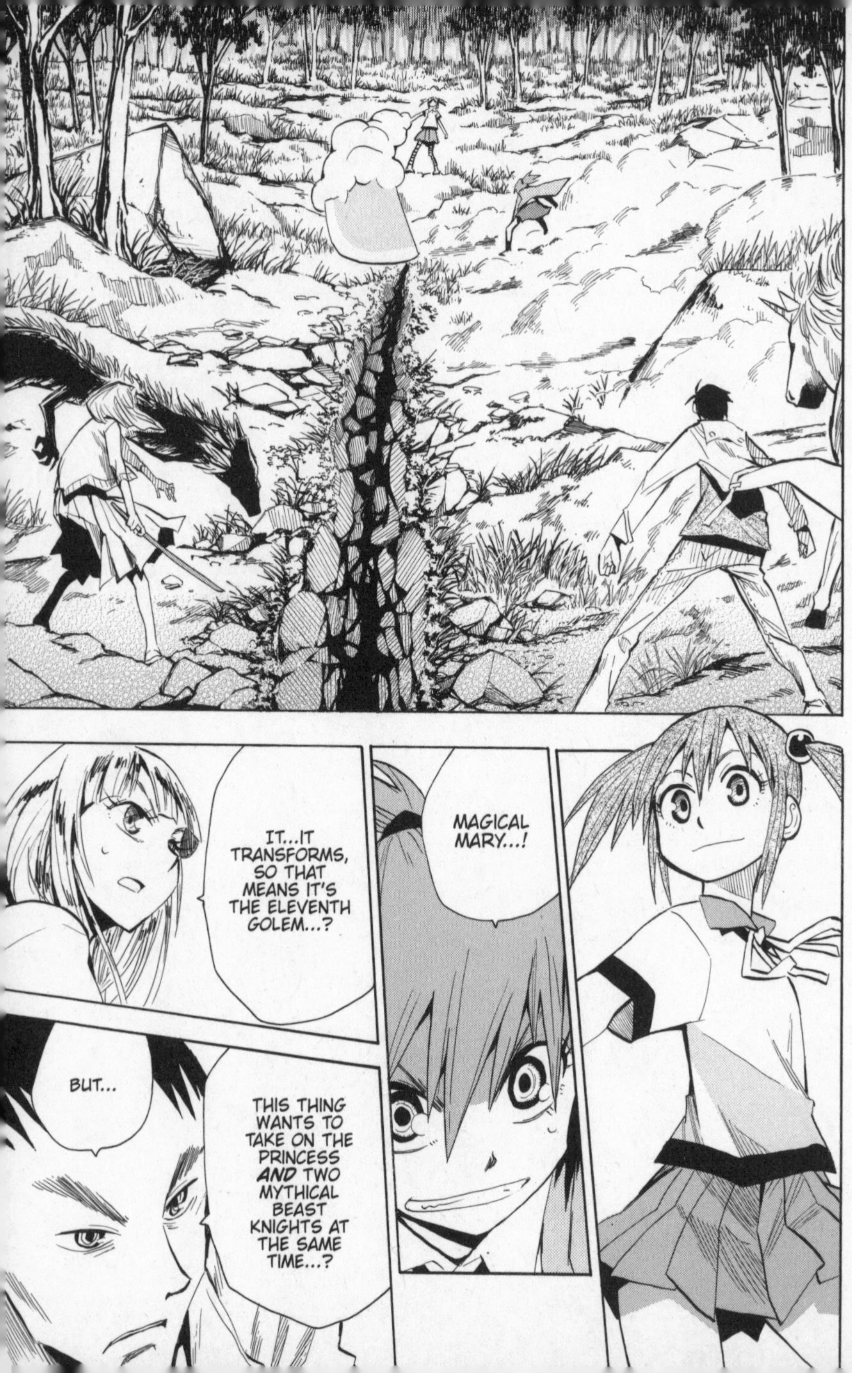
MAGICAL MARY...!
IT...IT TRANSFORMS, SO THAT MEANS IT'S THE ELEVENTH GOLEM...?
BUT...
THIS THING WANTS TO TAKE ON THE PRINCESS *AND* TWO MYTHICAL BEAST KNIGHTS AT THE SAME TIME...?

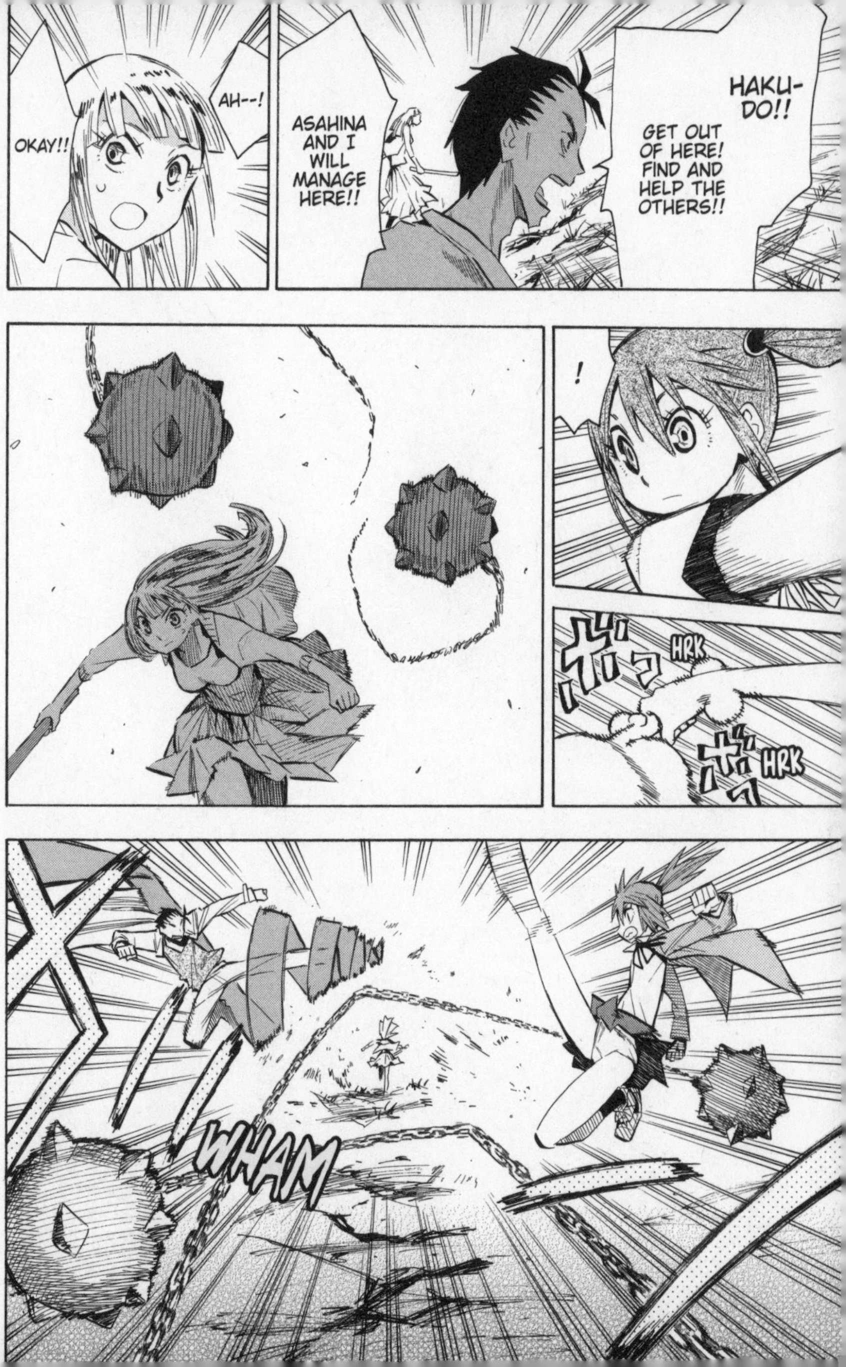
HAKU-DO!!
GET OUT OF HERE! FIND AND HELP THE OTHERS!!
ASAHINA AND I WILL MANAGE HERE!!
AH--!
OKAY!!
!
ガッ HRK
ガッ HRK
WHAM

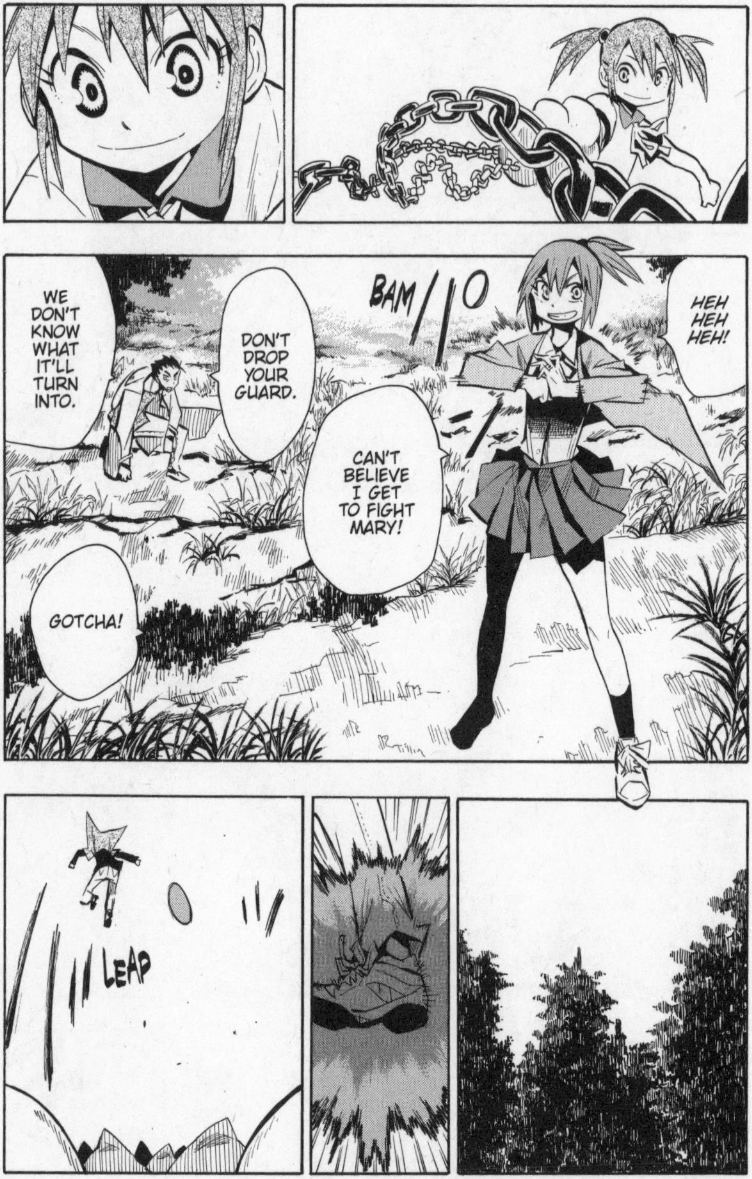

HEH HEH HEH!
BAM
CAN'T BELIEVE I GET TO FIGHT MARY!
DON'T DROP YOUR GUARD.
WE DON'T KNOW WHAT IT'LL TURN INTO.
GOTCHA!
LEAP

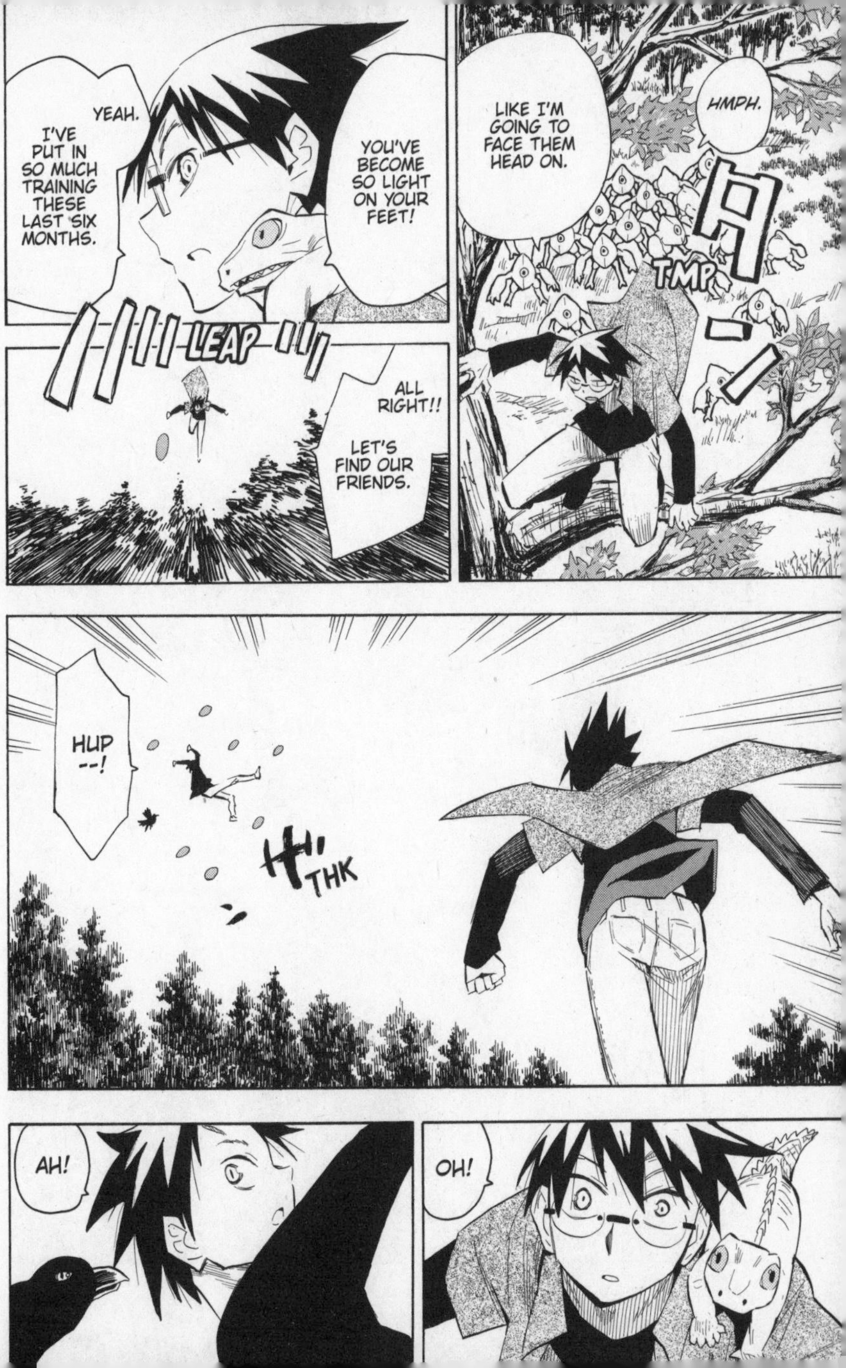
HMPH.
LIKE I'M GOING TO FACE THEM HEAD ON.
TMP
YOU'VE BECOME SO LIGHT ON YOUR FEET!
YEAH.
I'VE PUT IN SO MUCH TRAINING THESE LAST SIX MONTHS.
LEAP
ALL RIGHT!!
LET'S FIND OUR FRIENDS.
HUP --!
THK
OH!
AH!

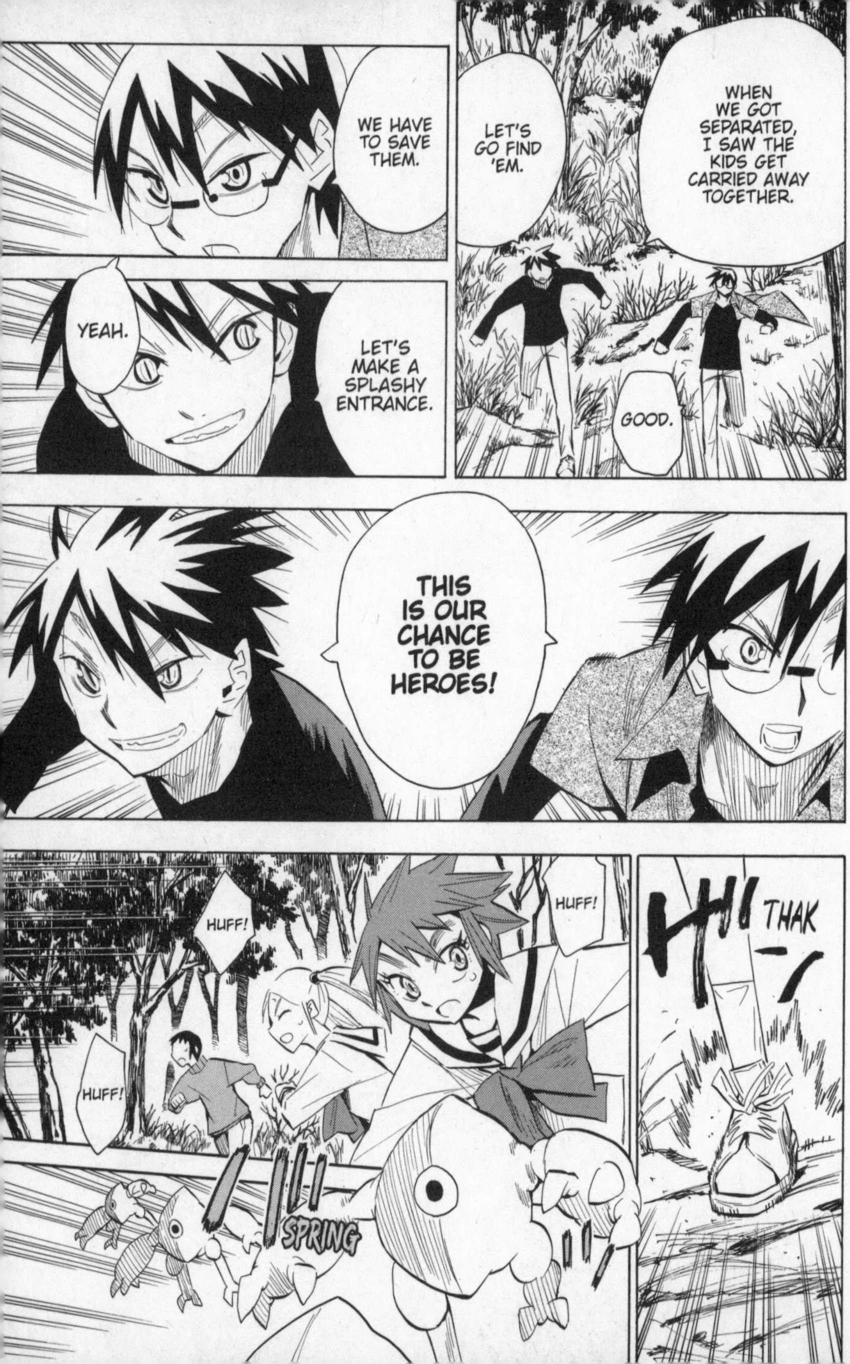
WHEN WE GOT SEPARATED, I SAW THE KIDS GET CARRIED AWAY TOGETHER.
LET'S GO FIND 'EM.
GOOD.
WE HAVE TO SAVE THEM.
LET'S MAKE A SPLASHY ENTRANCE.
YEAH.
THIS IS OUR CHANCE TO BE HEROES!
THAK
HUFF!
HUFF!
HUFF!
SPRING

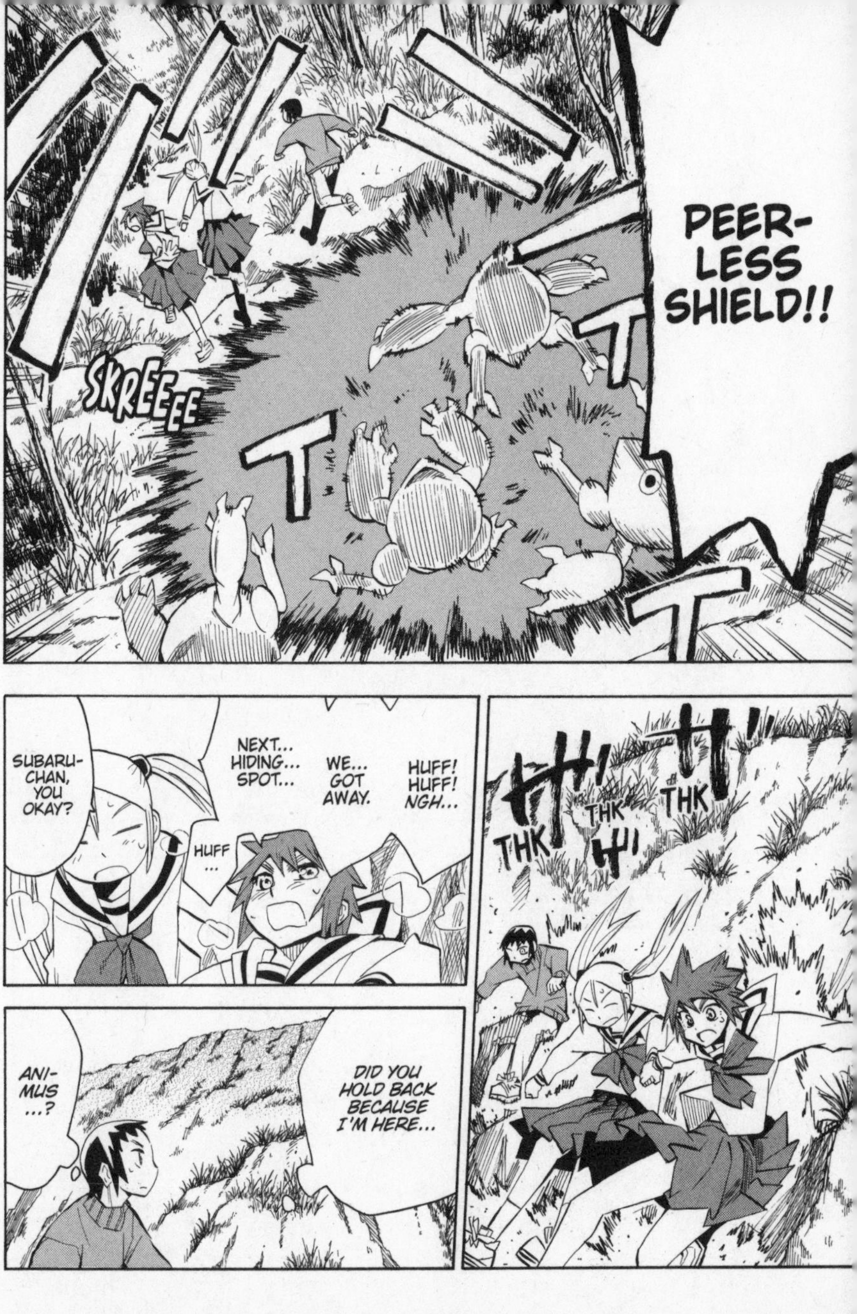
PEER-LESS SHIELD!!
SKREEEEE
THK
THK
THK
HUFF! HUFF! NGH...
WE... GOT AWAY.
NEXT... HIDING... SPOT...
HUFF ...
SUBARU-CHAN, YOU OKAY?
DID YOU HOLD BACK BECAUSE I'M HERE...
ANI-MUS ...?

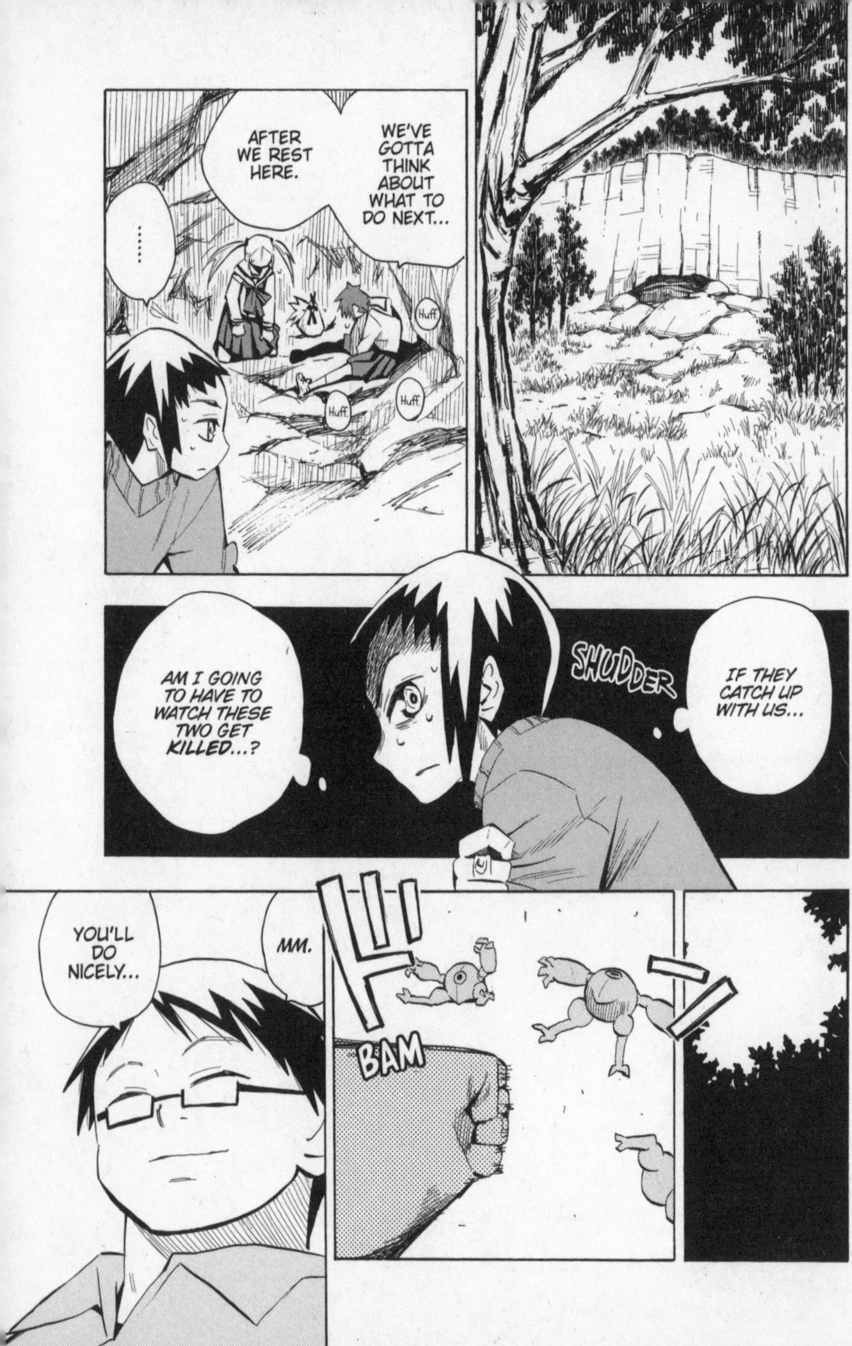
WE'VE GOTTA THINK ABOUT WHAT TO DO NEXT...
AFTER WE REST HERE.
......
Huff.
Huff.
Huff.
IF THEY CATCH UP WITH US...
SHUDDER
AM I GOING TO HAVE TO WATCH THESE TWO GET *KILLED*...?
BAM
MM.
YOU'LL DO NICELY...

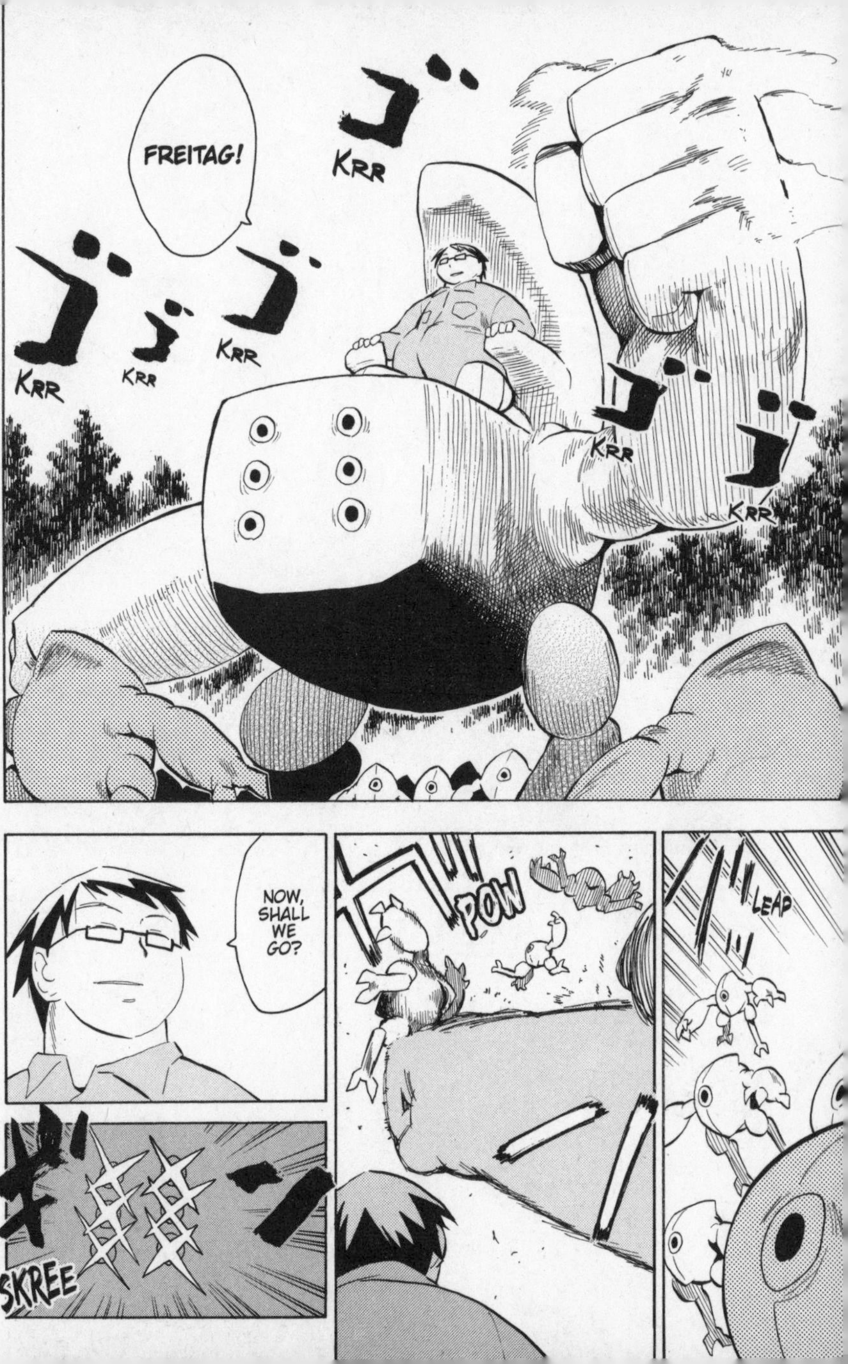
KRR
KRR
KRR
FREITAG!
KRR
KRR
KRR
LEAP
POW
NOW, SHALL WE GO?
SKREE

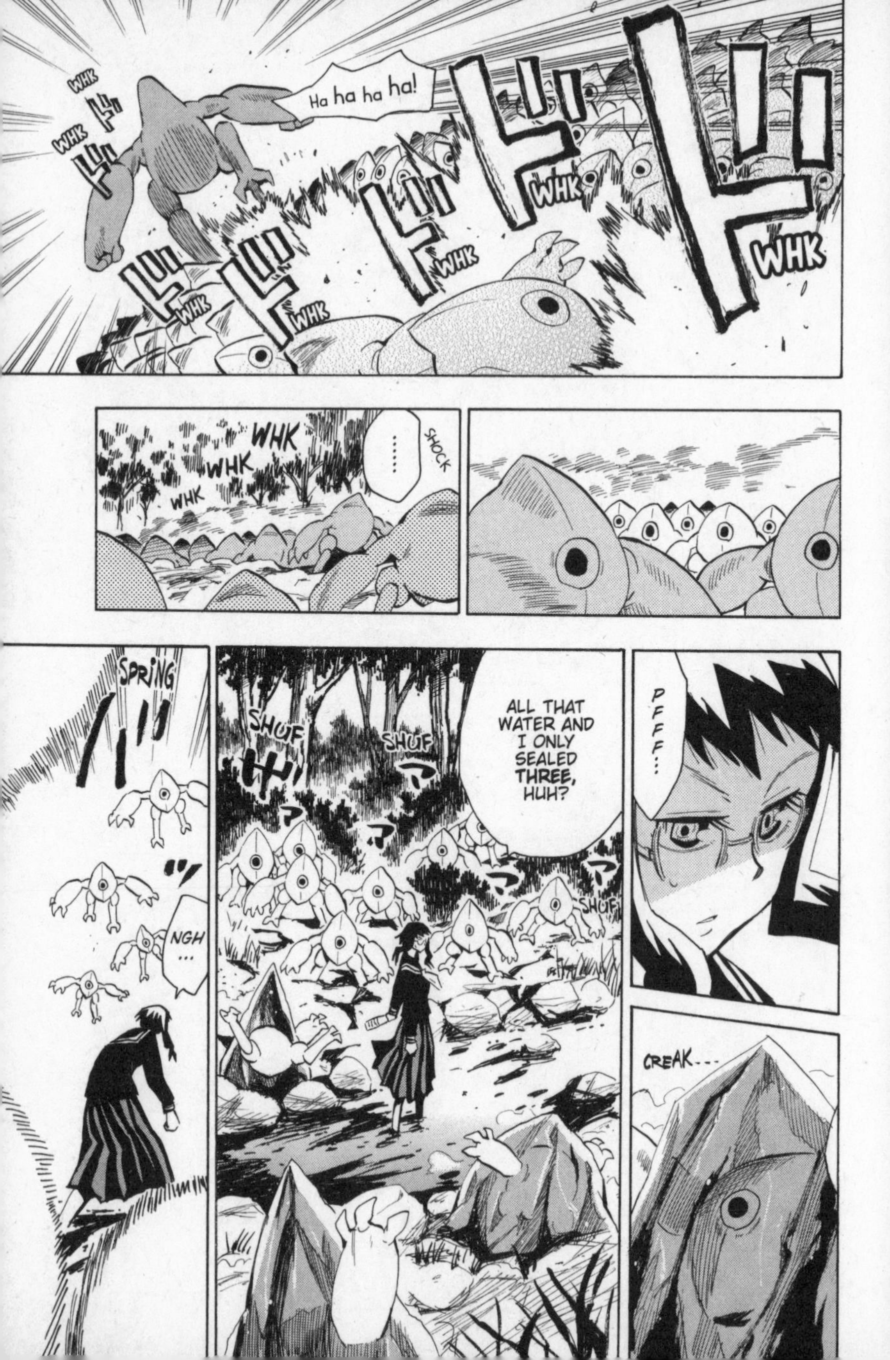
WHK
WHK
WHK
WHK
WHK
WHK
Ha ha ha ha!
WHK
WHK
......
SHOCK
WHK
WHK
WHK
PFFF...
CREAK...
ALL THAT WATER AND I ONLY SEALED THREE, HUH?
SHUF
SHUF
SHUF
SPRING
NGH...

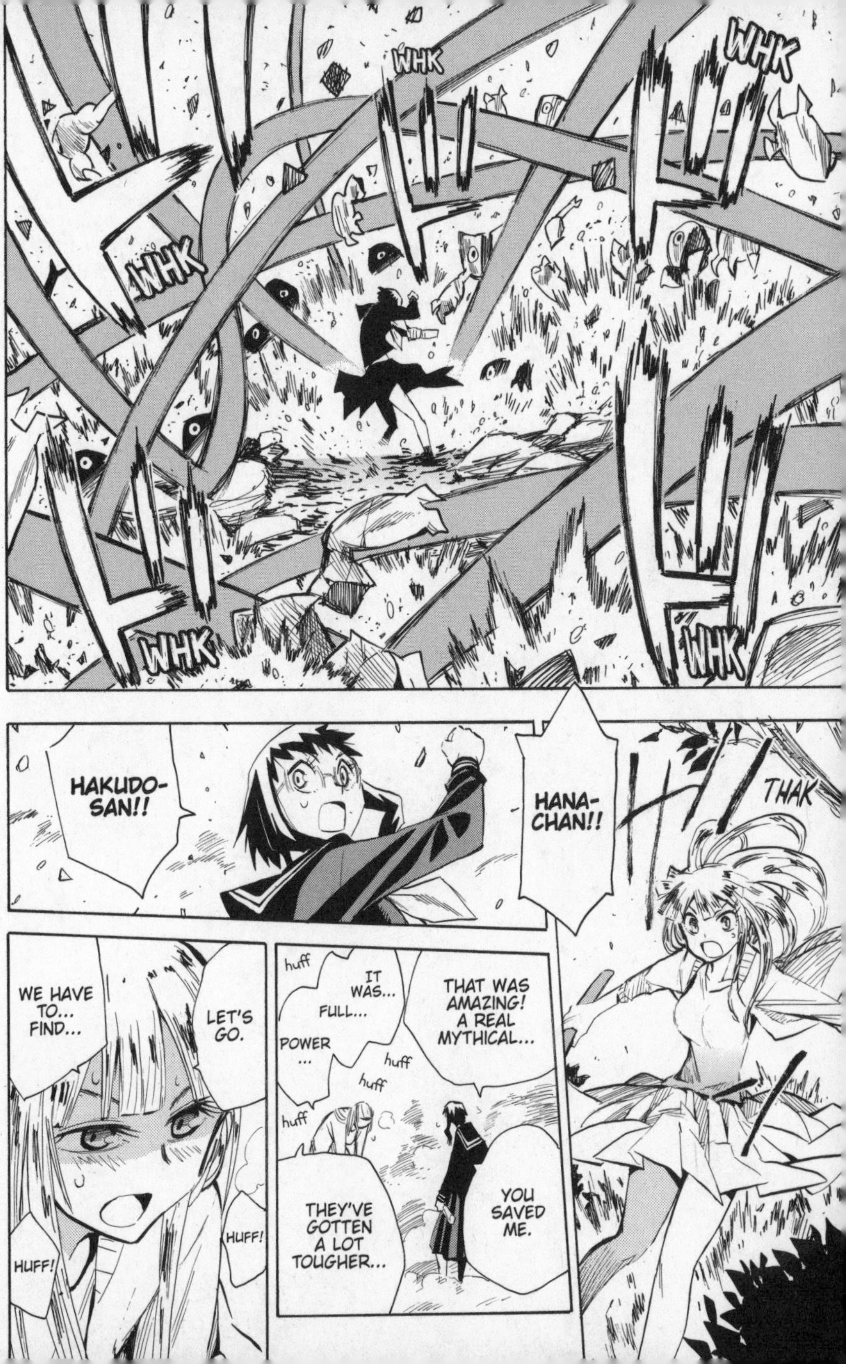
WHK
WHK
WHK
WHK
WHK
THAK
HANA-CHAN!!
HAKUDO-SAN!!
THAT WAS AMAZING! A REAL MYTHICAL...
IT WAS... FULL... POWER...
huff
huff
huff
huff
YOU SAVED ME.
THEY'VE GOTTEN A LOT TOUGHER...
LET'S GO.
WE HAVE TO... FIND...
HUFF!
HUFF!

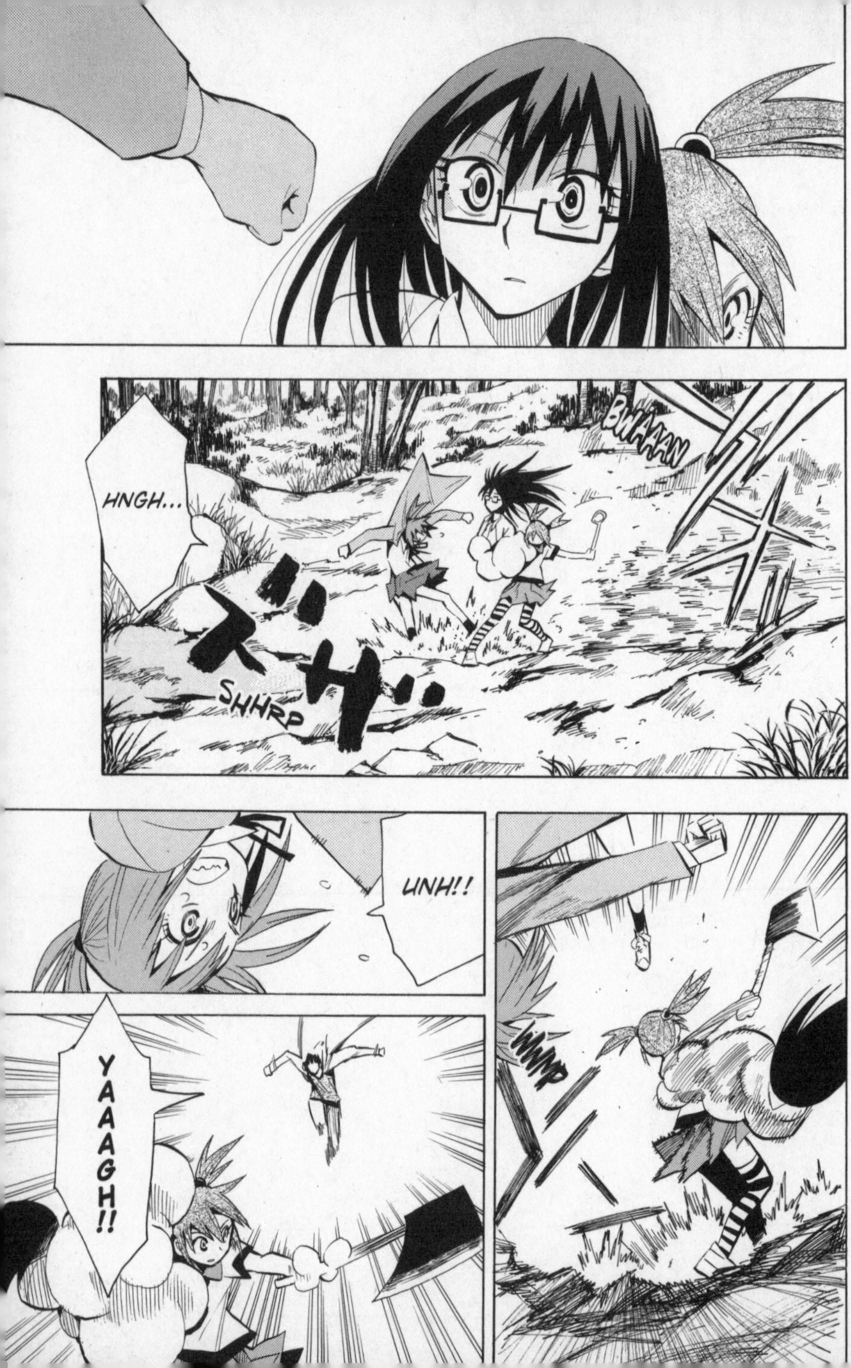
BWAAAN
HNGH...
ズザッ
SHHRP
WMMP
UNH!!
YAAAAGH!!

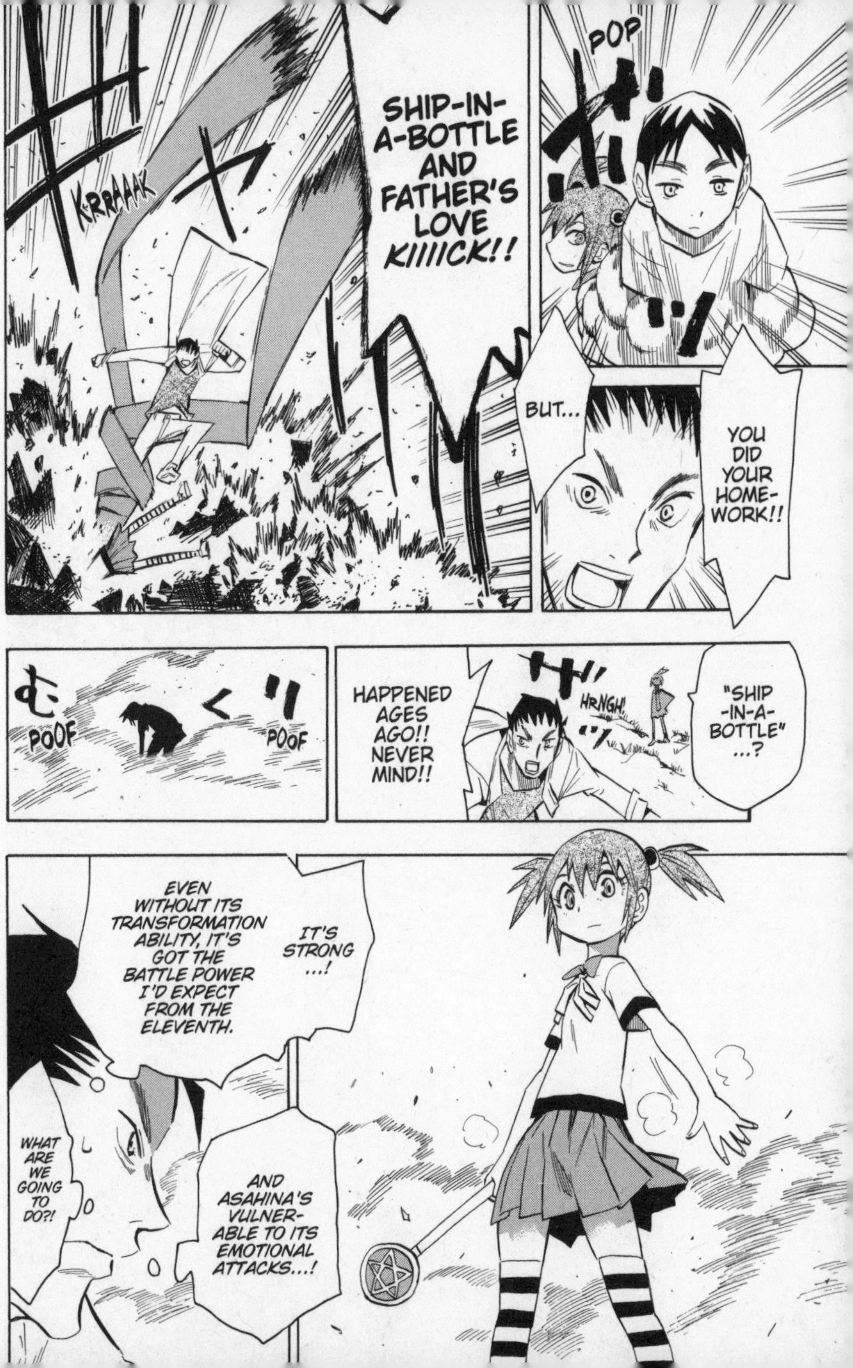
POP
YOU DID YOUR HOME-WORK!!
BUT...
SHIP-IN-A-BOTTLE AND FATHER'S LOVE KIIIICK!!
K-RRAAAK
"SHIP-IN-A-BOTTLE"...?
HRNGH!
HAPPENED AGES AGO!! NEVER MIND!!
POOF
POOF
IT'S STRONG...!
EVEN WITHOUT ITS TRANSFORMATION ABILITY, IT'S GOT THE BATTLE POWER I'D EXPECT FROM THE ELEVENTH.
AND ASAHINA'S VULNER-ABLE TO ITS EMOTIONAL ATTACKS...!
WHAT ARE WE GOING TO DO?!

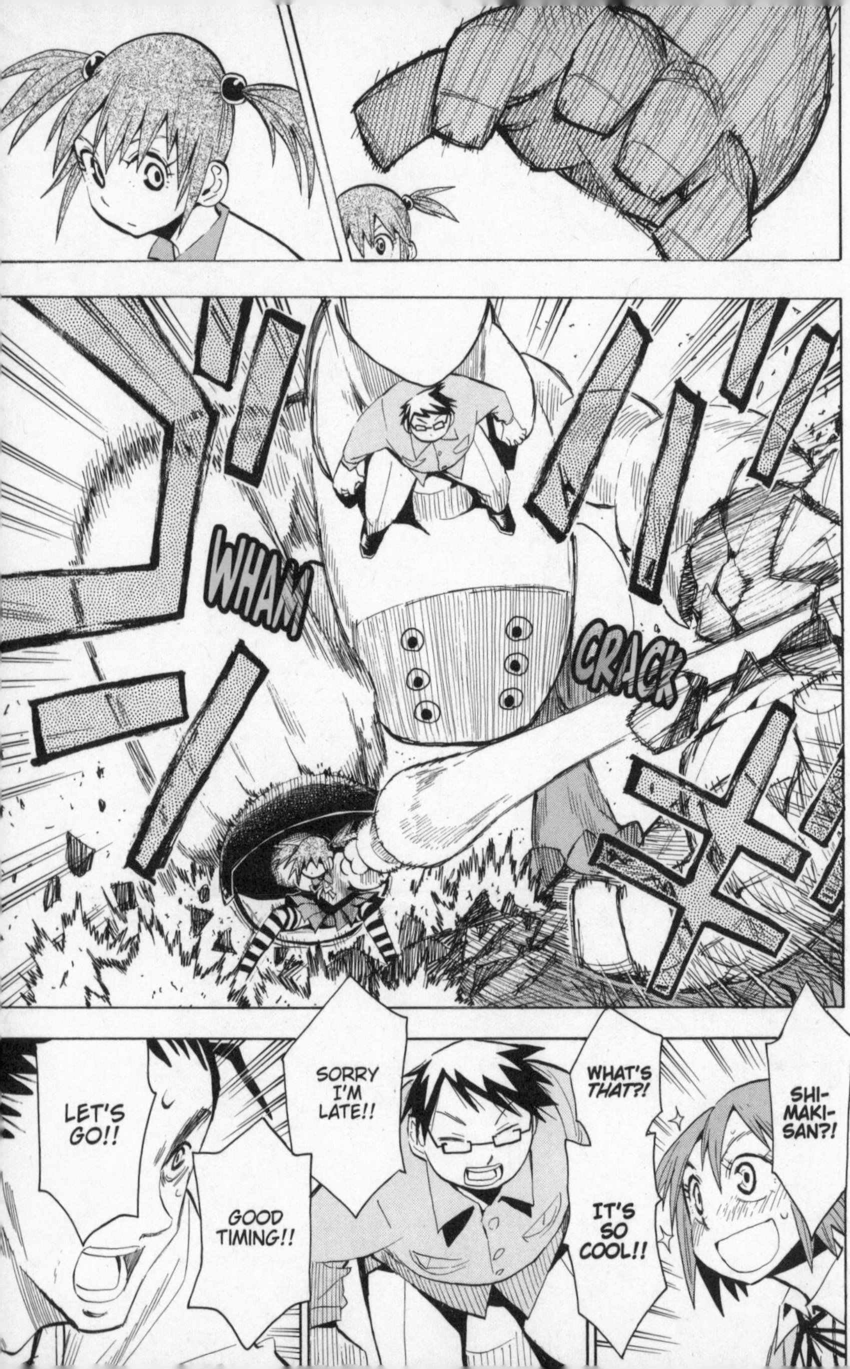
WHAM
CRACK
SHI-MAKI-SAN?!
WHAT'S THAT?!
IT'S SO COOL!!
SORRY I'M LATE!!
GOOD TIMING!!
LET'S GO!!

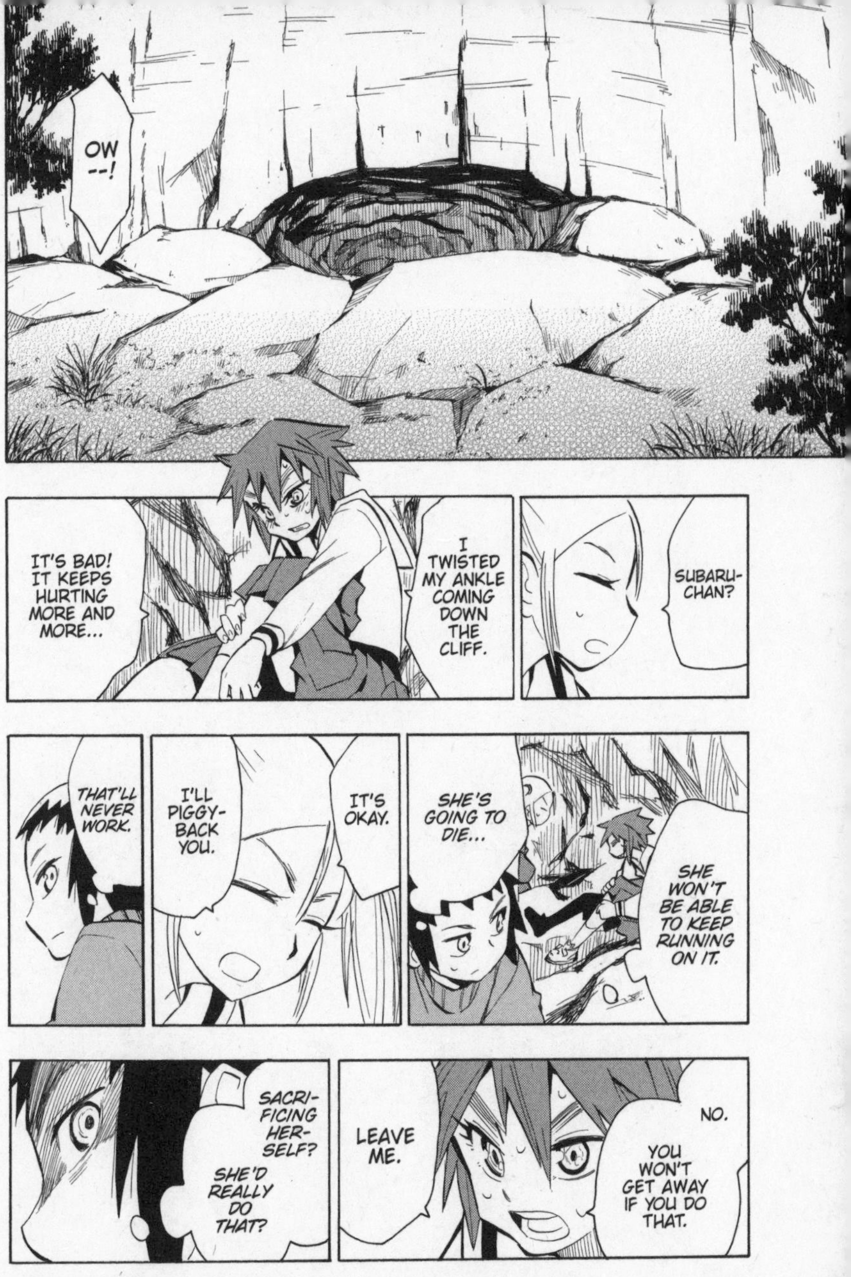
OW --!
SUBARU-CHAN?
I TWISTED MY ANKLE COMING DOWN THE CLIFF.
IT'S BAD! IT KEEPS HURTING MORE AND MORE...
SHE WON'T BE ABLE TO KEEP RUNNING ON IT.
SHE'S GOING TO DIE...
IT'S OKAY.
I'LL PIGGY-BACK YOU.
THAT'LL NEVER WORK.
NO.
YOU WON'T GET AWAY IF YOU DO THAT.
LEAVE ME.
SACRI-FICING HER-SELF?
SHE'D REALLY DO THAT?

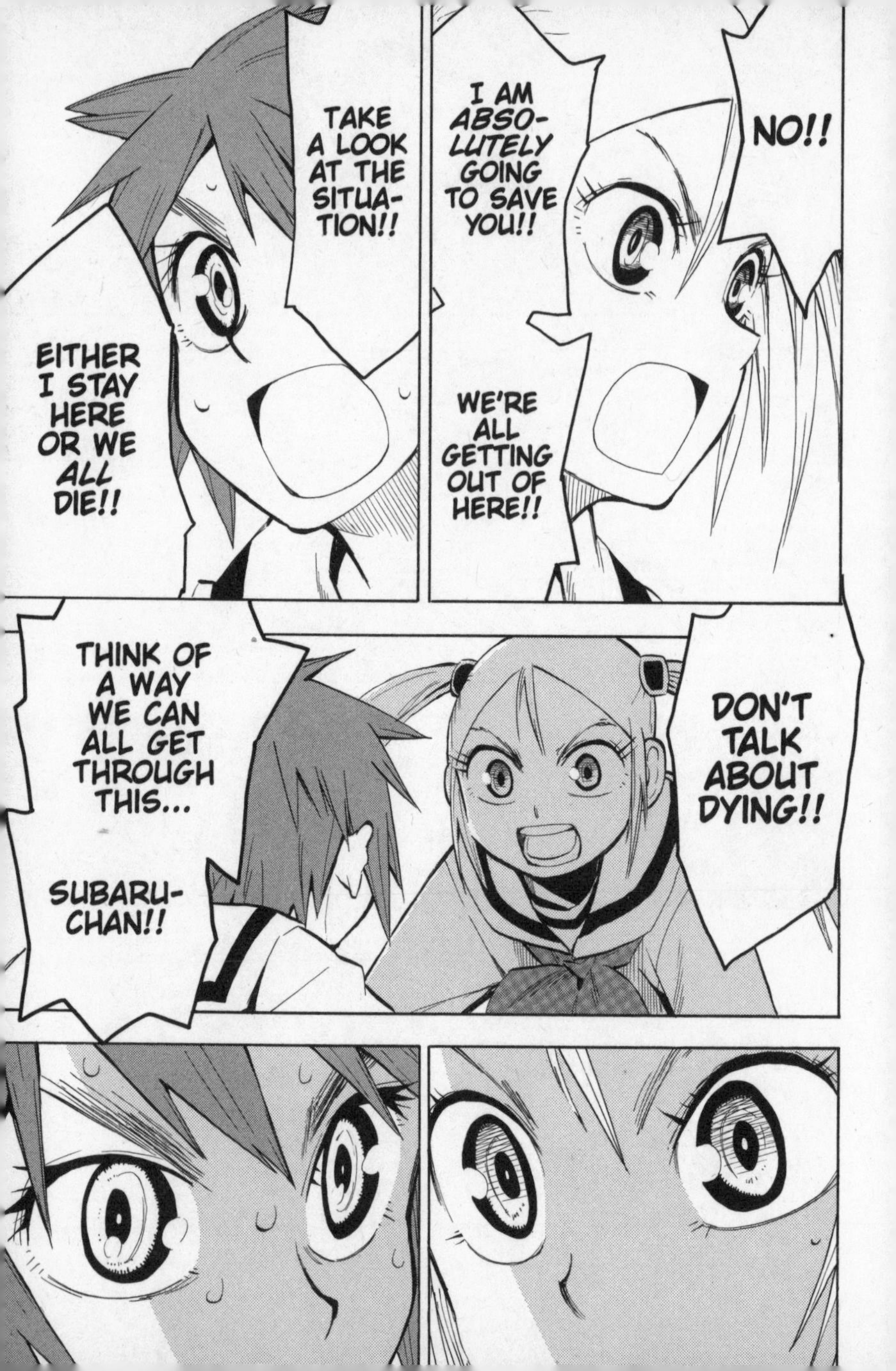
NO!!
I AM ABSO-LUTELY GOING TO SAVE YOU!!
WE'RE ALL GETTING OUT OF HERE!!
TAKE A LOOK AT THE SITUA-TION!!
EITHER I STAY HERE OR WE ALL DIE!!
DON'T TALK ABOUT DYING!!
THINK OF A WAY WE CAN ALL GET THROUGH THIS...
SUBARU-CHAN!!

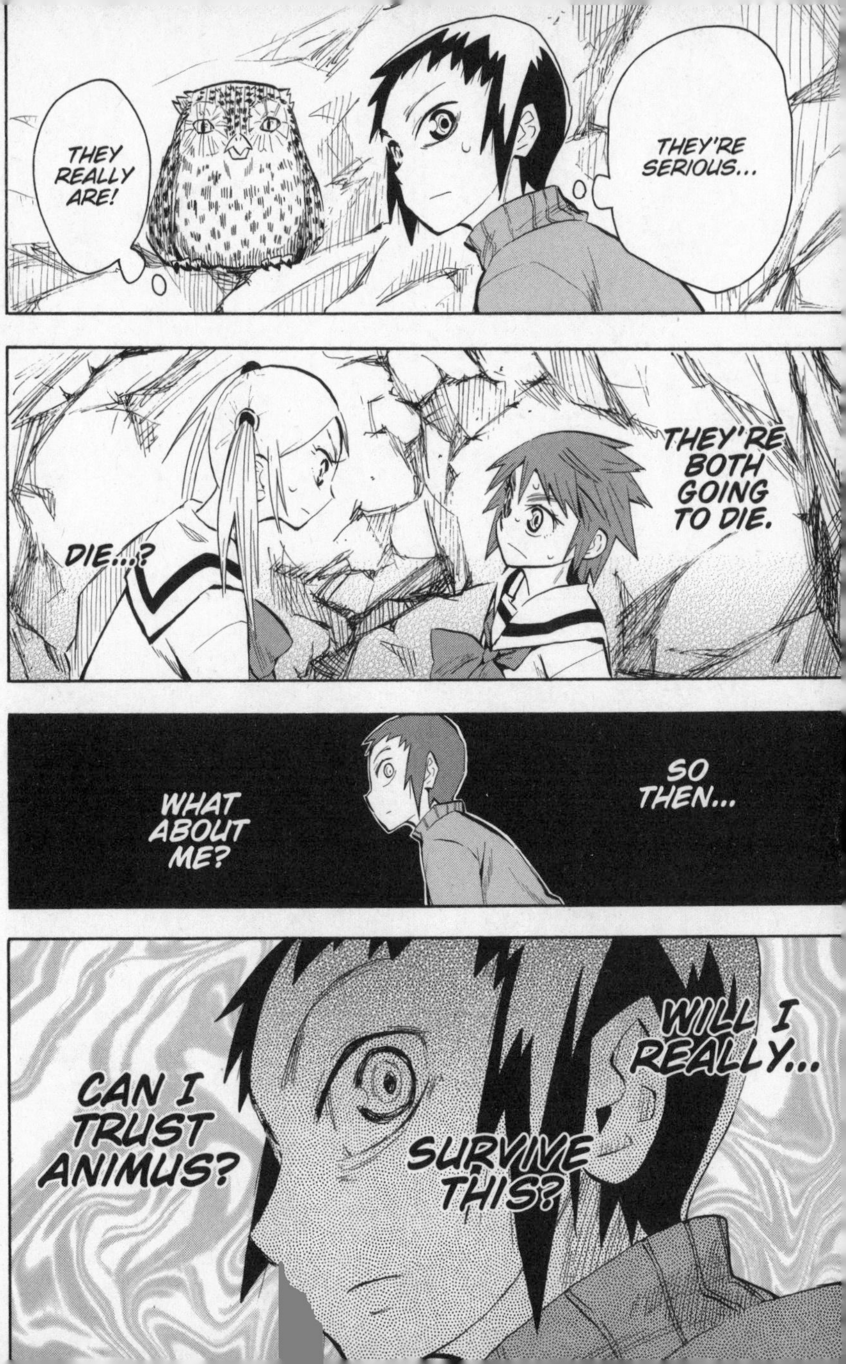
THEY'RE SERIOUS...
THEY REALLY ARE!
THEY'RE BOTH GOING TO DIE.
DIE...?
SO THEN...
WHAT ABOUT ME?
WILL I REALLY...
SURVIVE THIS?
CAN I TRUST ANIMUS?

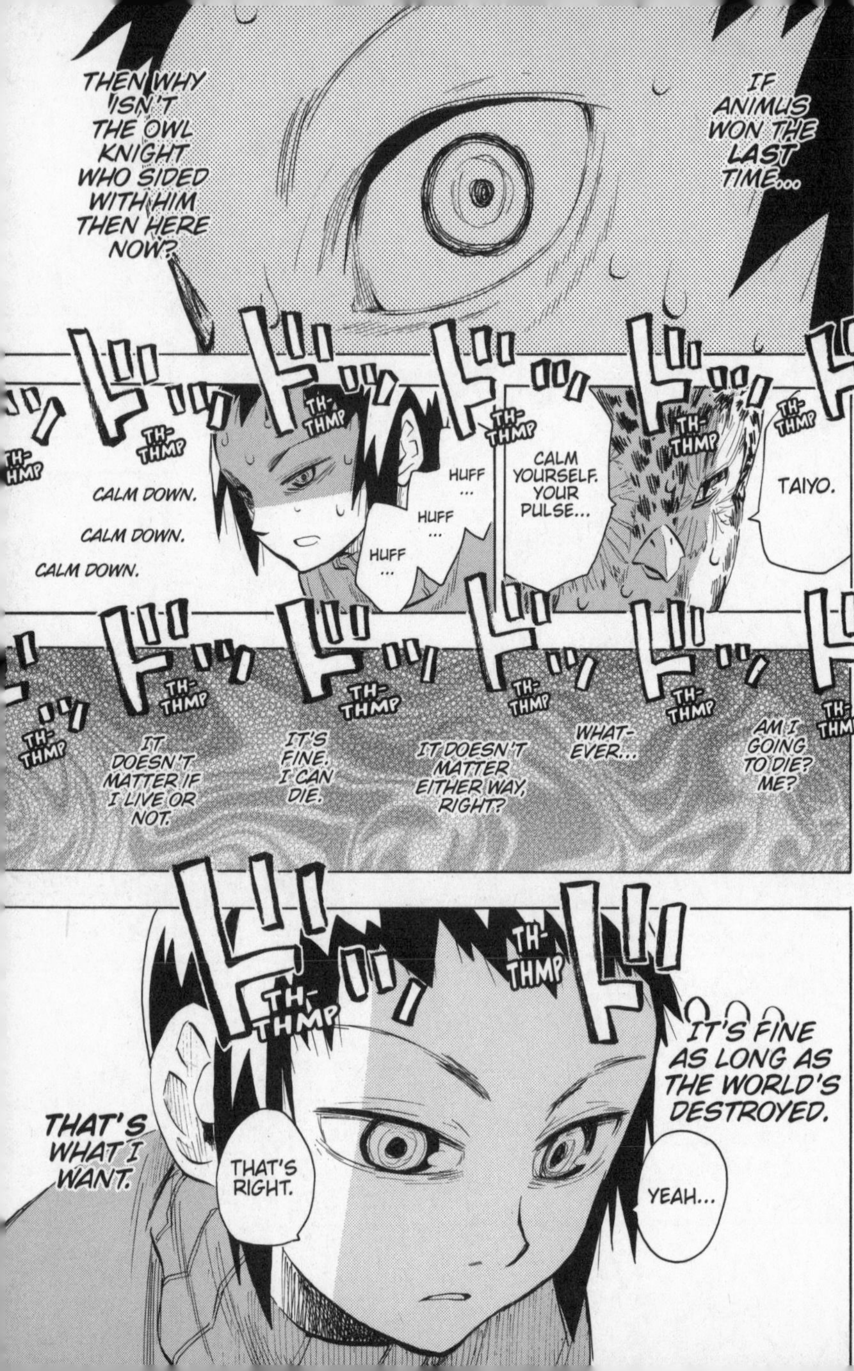
IF ANIMUS WON THE LAST TIME...
THEN WHY ISN'T THE OWL KNIGHT WHO SIDED WITH HIM THEN HERE NOW?
TH-THMP
TAIYO.
TH-THMP
CALM YOURSELF. YOUR PULSE...
TH-THMP
TH-THMP
HUFF...
HUFF...
HUFF...
TH-THMP
CALM DOWN.
CALM DOWN.
CALM DOWN.
TH-THMP
TH-THMP
AM I GOING TO DIE? ME?
TH-THMP
WHAT-EVER...
TH-THMP
IT DOESN'T MATTER EITHER WAY, RIGHT?
TH-THMP
IT'S FINE. I CAN DIE.
TH-THMP
IT DOESN'T MATTER IF I LIVE OR NOT.
TH-THMP
TH-THMP
TH-THMP
IT'S FINE AS LONG AS THE WORLD'S DESTROYED.
YEAH...
THAT'S RIGHT.
THAT'S WHAT I WANT.

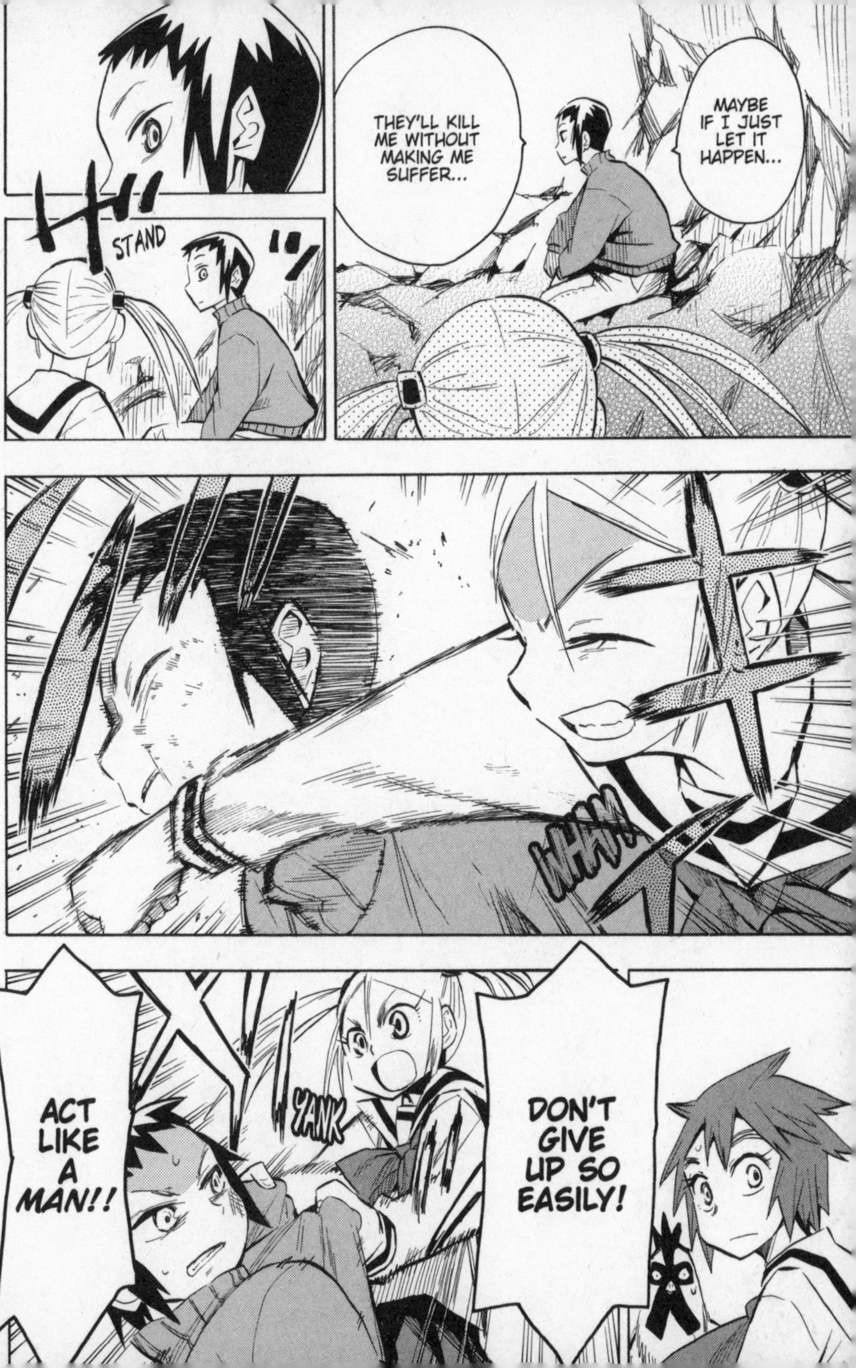
MAYBE IF I JUST LET IT HAPPEN...
THEY'LL KILL ME WITHOUT MAKING ME SUFFER...
STAND
WHAM
DON'T GIVE UP SO EASILY!
YANK
ACT LIKE A MAN!!

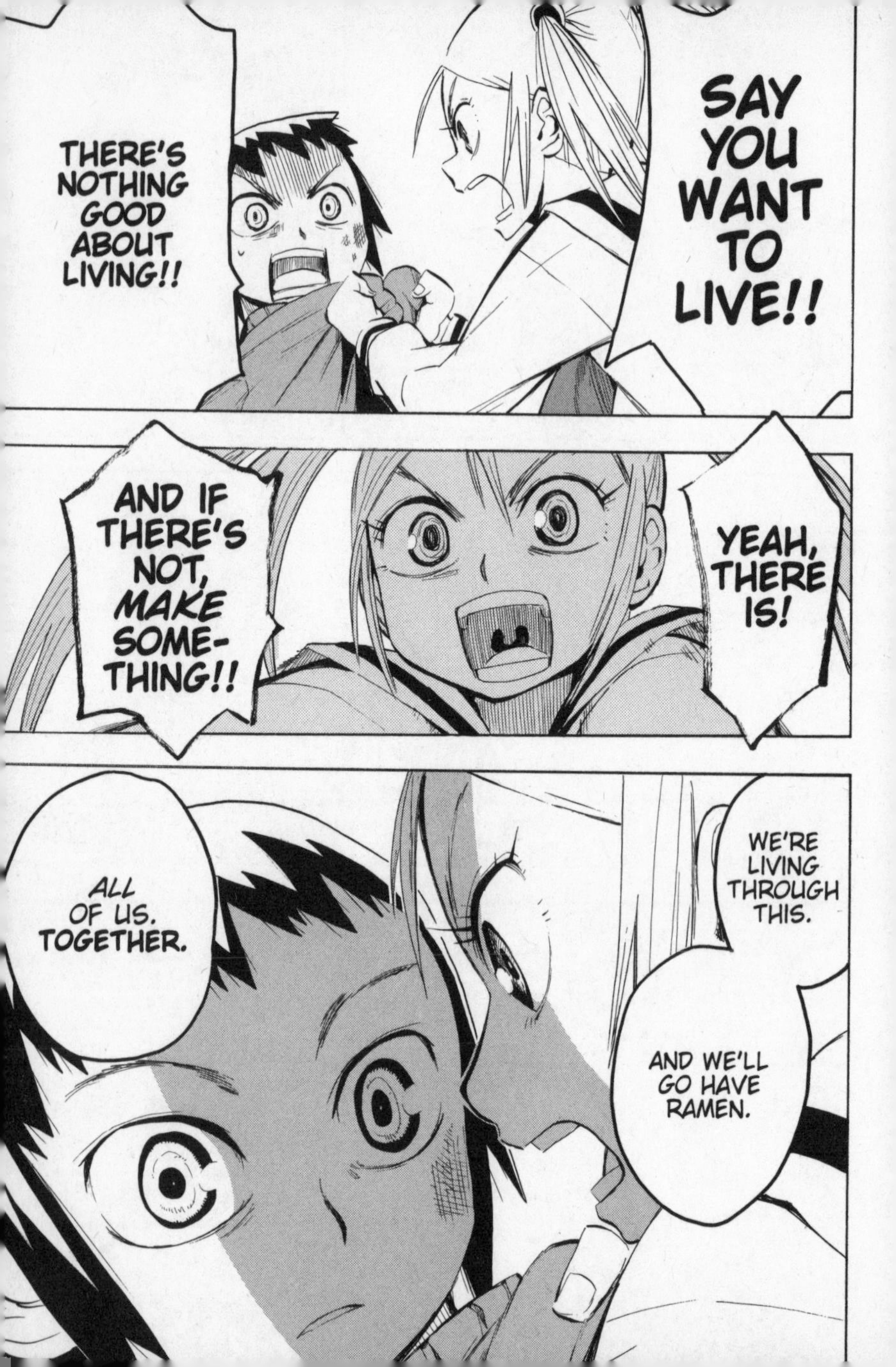
SAY YOU WANT TO LIVE!!
THERE'S NOTHING GOOD ABOUT LIVING!!
YEAH, THERE IS!
AND IF THERE'S NOT, *MAKE* SOMETHING!!
WE'RE LIVING THROUGH THIS.
ALL OF US. TOGETHER.
AND WE'LL GO HAVE RAMEN.

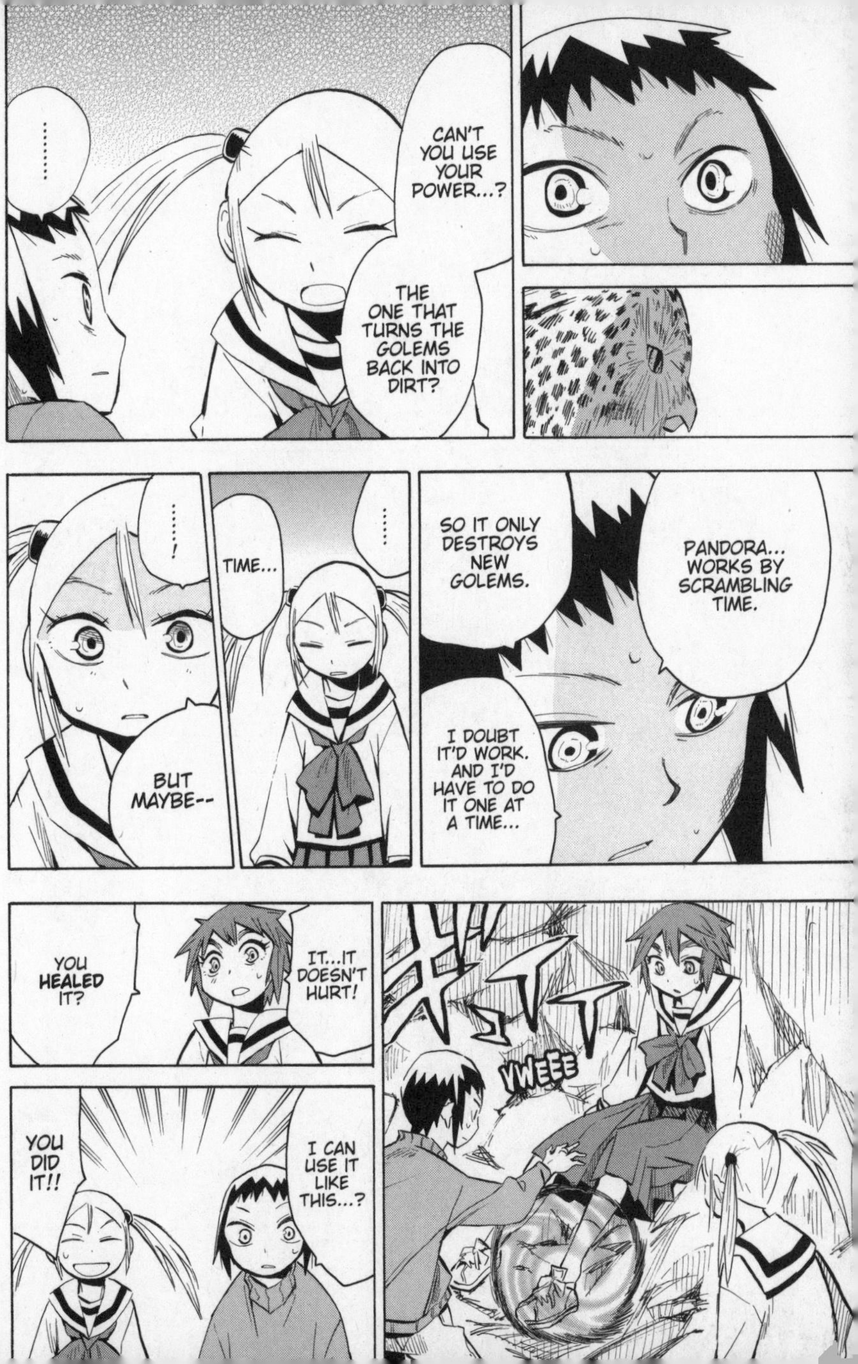
CAN'T YOU USE YOUR POWER...?
THE ONE THAT TURNS THE GOLEMS BACK INTO DIRT?
......
PANDORA... WORKS BY SCRAMBLING TIME.
SO IT ONLY DESTROYS NEW GOLEMS.
I DOUBT IT'D WORK. AND I'D HAVE TO DO IT ONE AT A TIME...
......
TIME...
......!
BUT MAYBE--
YWEEE
IT...IT DOESN'T HURT!
YOU HEALED IT?
I CAN USE IT LIKE THIS...?
YOU DID IT!!

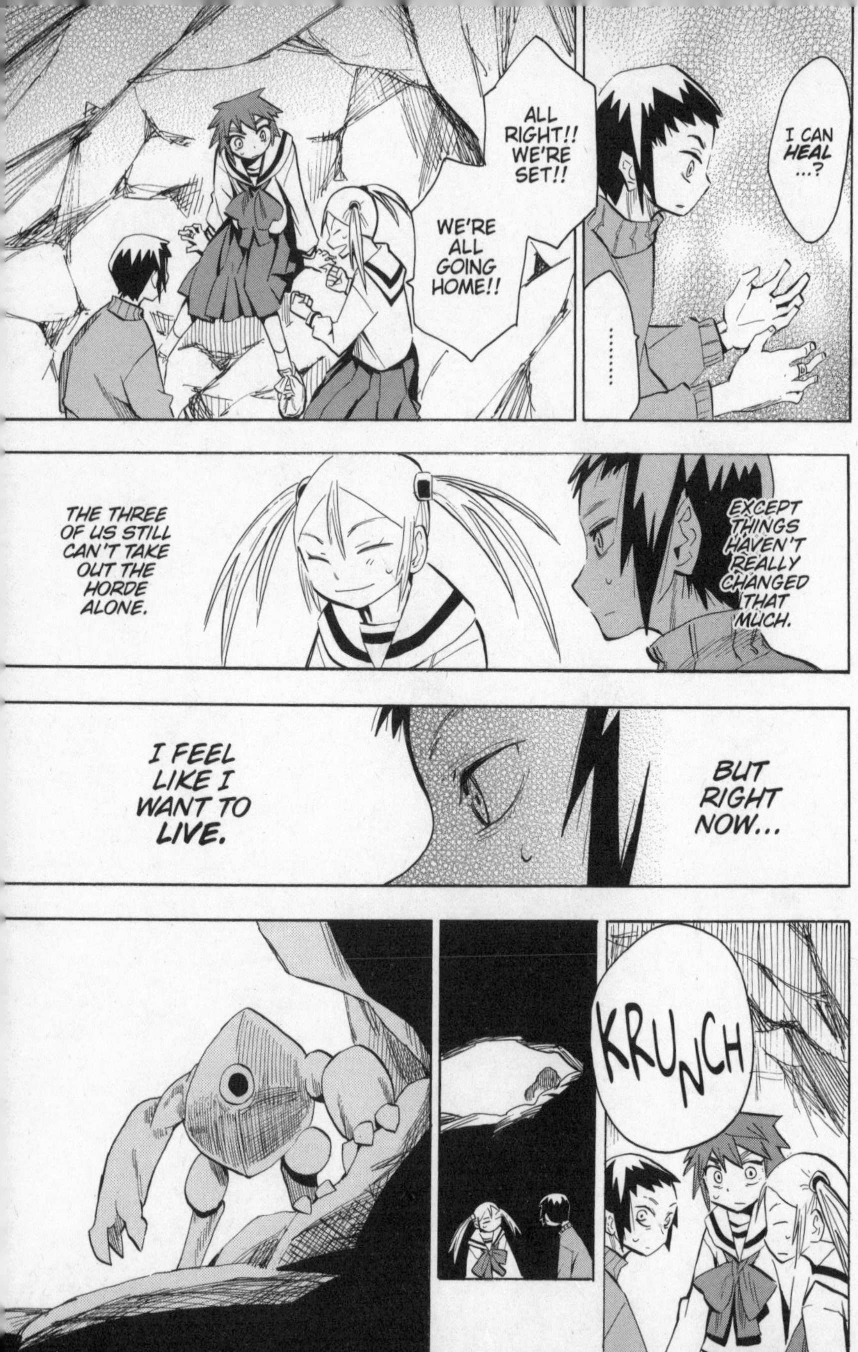
I CAN HEAL ...?
......
ALL RIGHT!! WE'RE SET!!
WE'RE ALL GOING HOME!!
EXCEPT THINGS HAVEN'T REALLY CHANGED THAT MUCH.
THE THREE OF US STILL CAN'T TAKE OUT THE HORDE ALONE.
BUT RIGHT NOW...
I FEEL LIKE I WANT TO LIVE.
KRUNCH

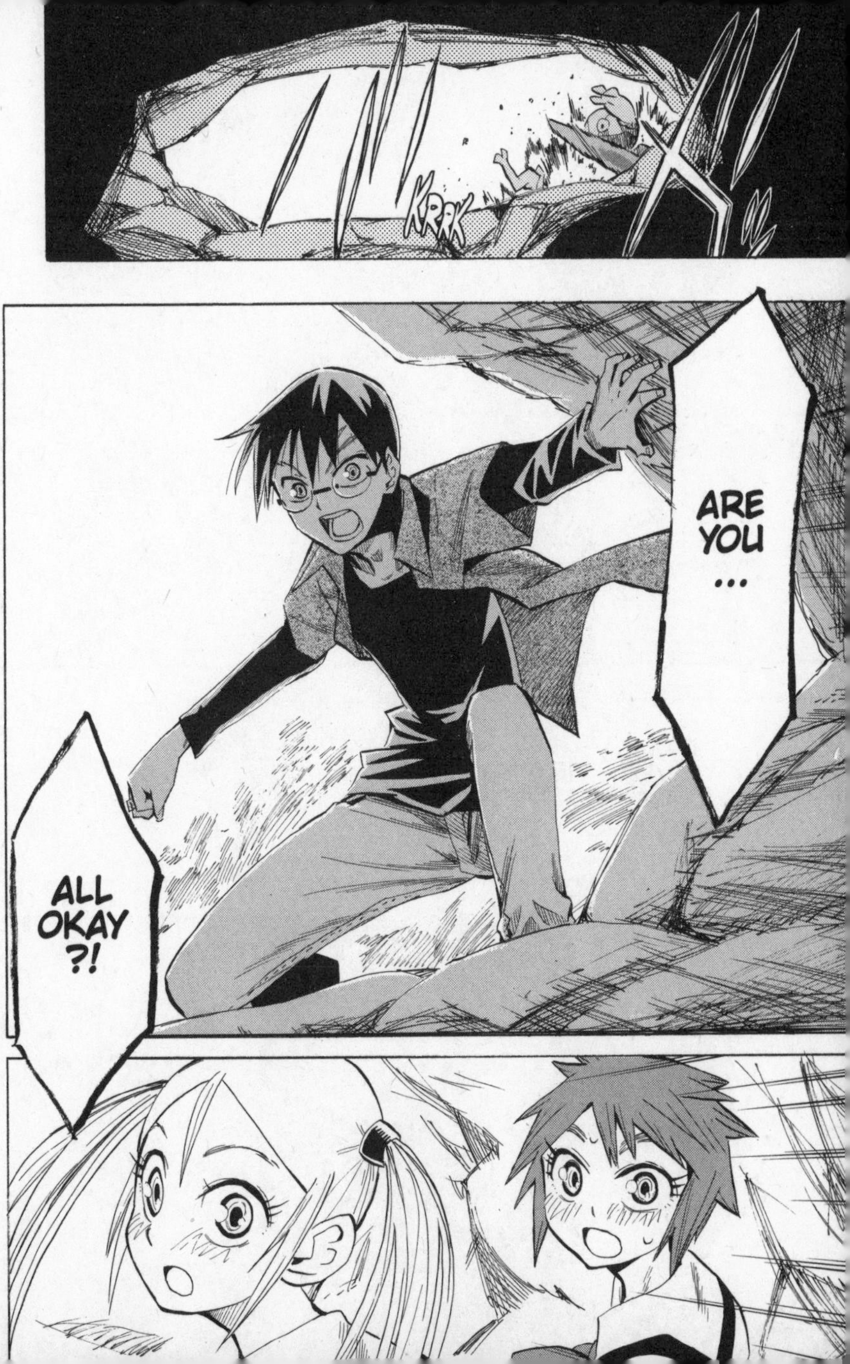
KRRK
ARE YOU ...
ALL OKAY ?!

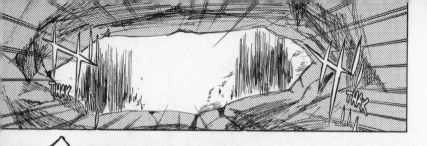

SORRY FOR THE WAIT, KIDS!

WE CAME TO SAVE YOU!!

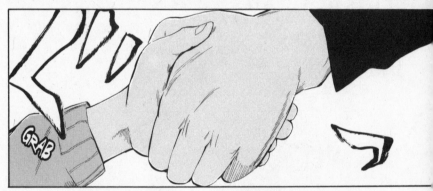

GRAB

YOU DID GREAT.

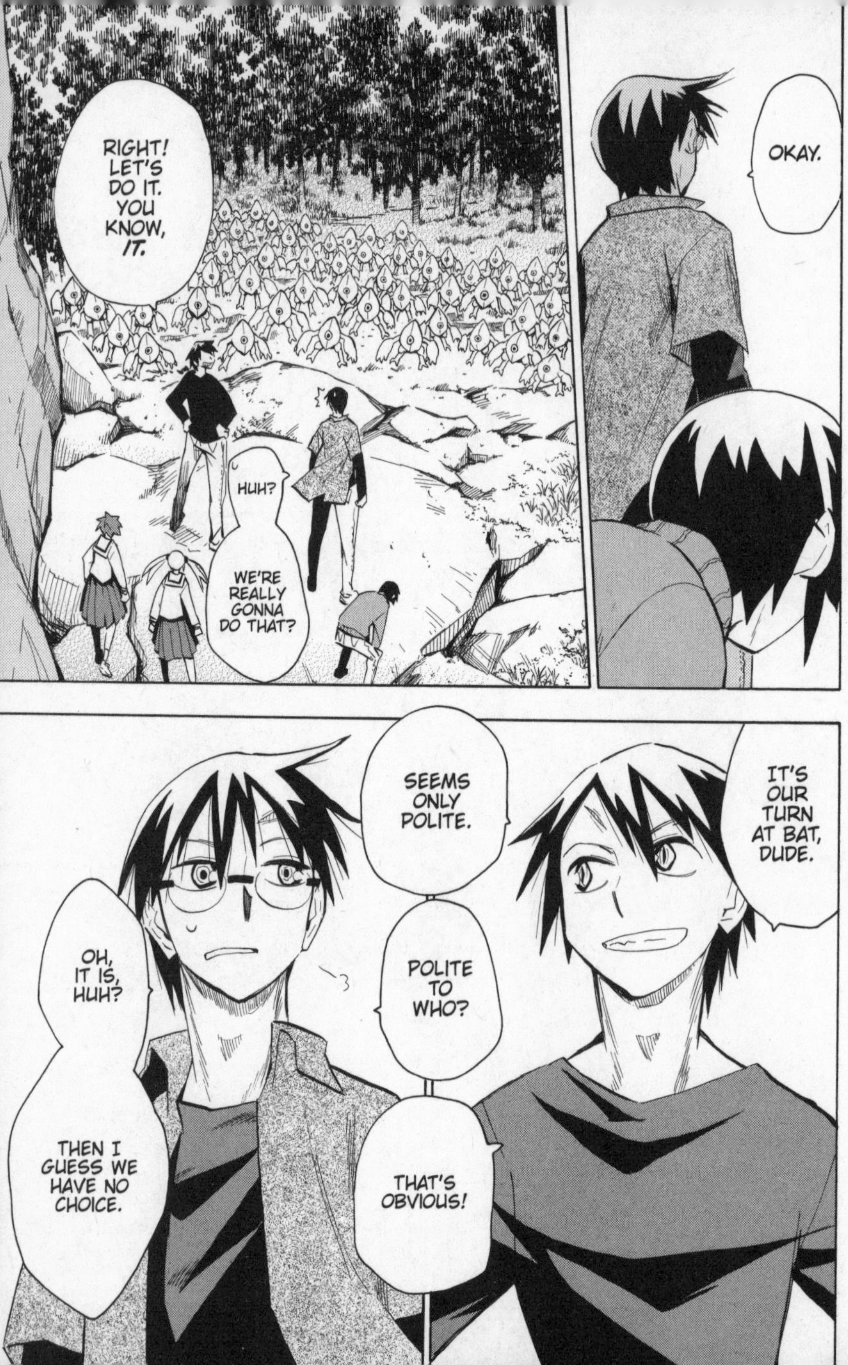
OKAY.
RIGHT! LET'S DO IT. YOU KNOW, *IT.*
HUH?
WE'RE REALLY GONNA DO THAT?
IT'S OUR TURN AT BAT, DUDE.
SEEMS ONLY POLITE.
POLITE TO WHO?
THAT'S OBVIOUS!
OH, IT IS, HUH?
THEN I GUESS WE HAVE NO CHOICE.

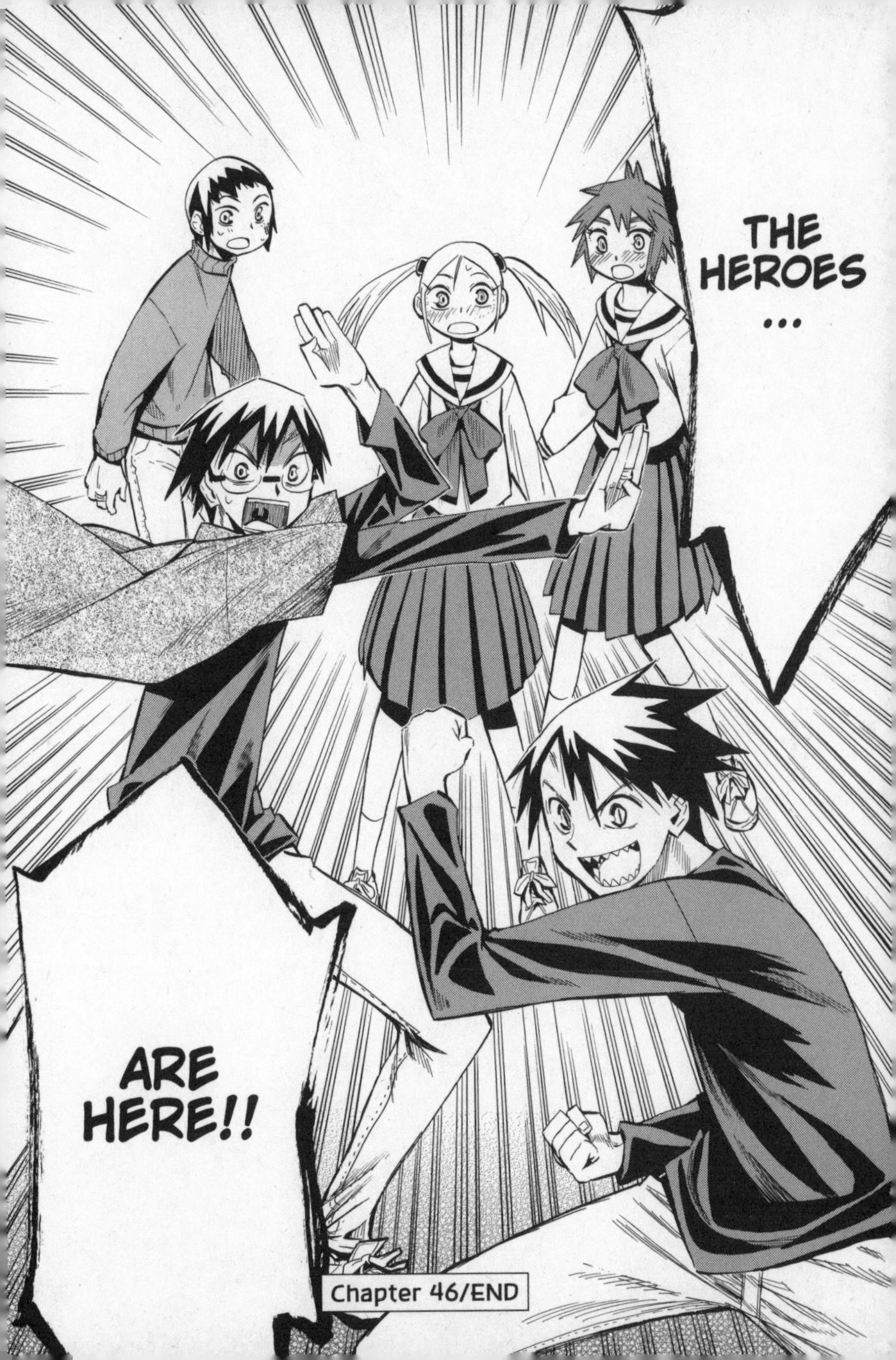
THE HEROES
...
ARE HERE!!
Chapter 46/END

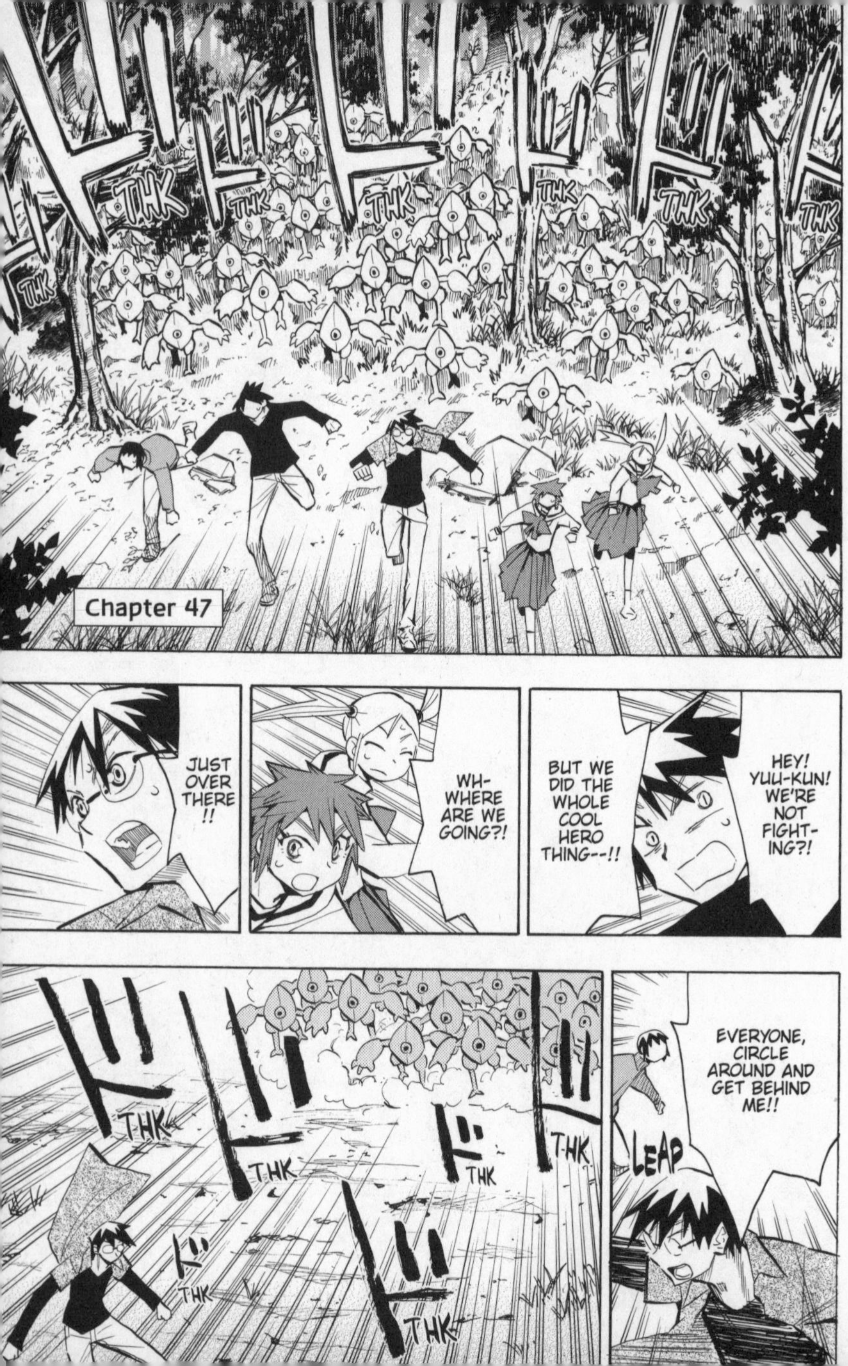
THK
THK
THK
THK
THK
THK
THK
Chapter 47
HEY! YUU-KUN! WE'RE NOT FIGHT-ING?!
BUT WE DID THE WHOLE COOL HERO THING--!!
WH-WHERE ARE WE GOING?!
JUST OVER THERE!!
EVERYONE, CIRCLE AROUND AND GET BEHIND ME!!
LEAP
THK
THK
THK
THK
THK
THK

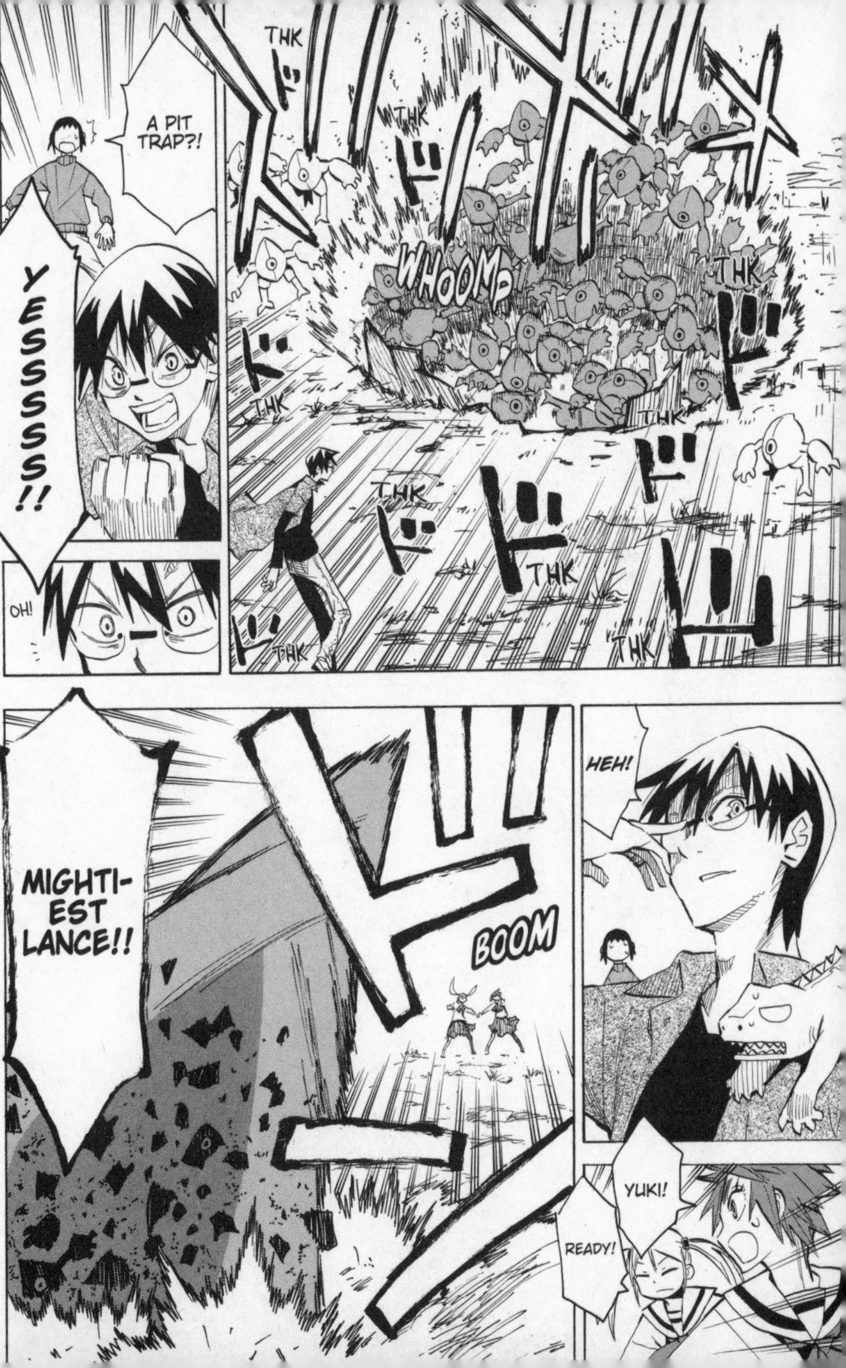
THK
THK
WHOOMP
THK
THK
THK
THK
THK
THK
A PIT TRAP?!
YESSSSSS!!
OH!
HEH!
YUKI!
READY!
MIGHTI-EST LANCE!!
BOOM

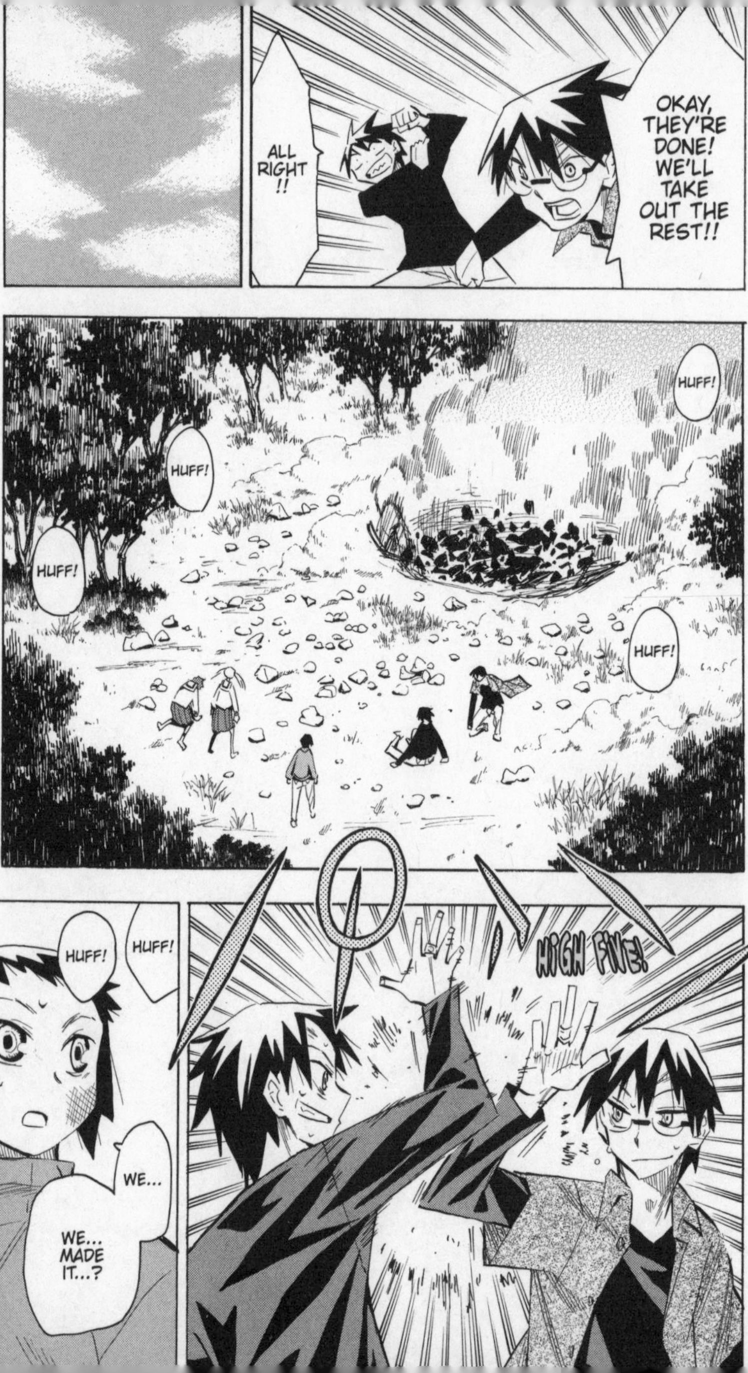

OKAY, THEY'RE DONE! WE'LL TAKE OUT THE REST!!
ALL RIGHT!!
HUFF!
HUFF!
HUFF!
HUFF!
HIGH FIVE!
HUFF!
HUFF!
WE...
WE... MADE IT...?

Chapter 47: The Boy Akane Taiyo

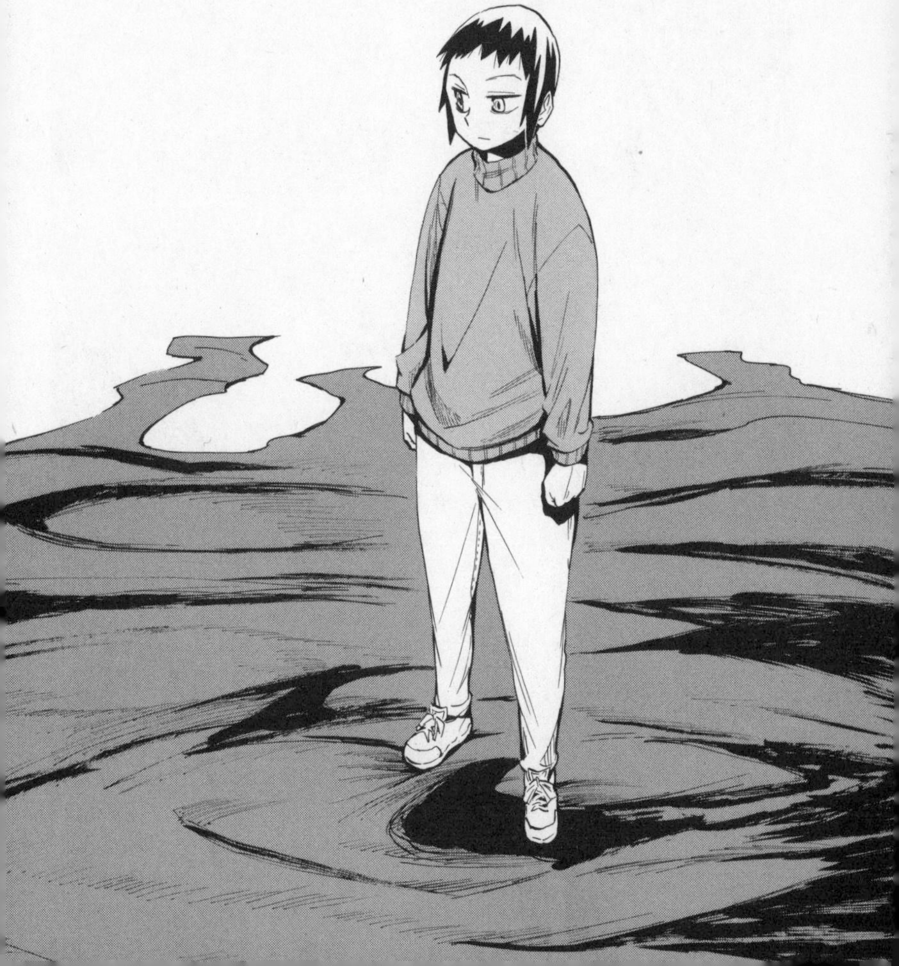

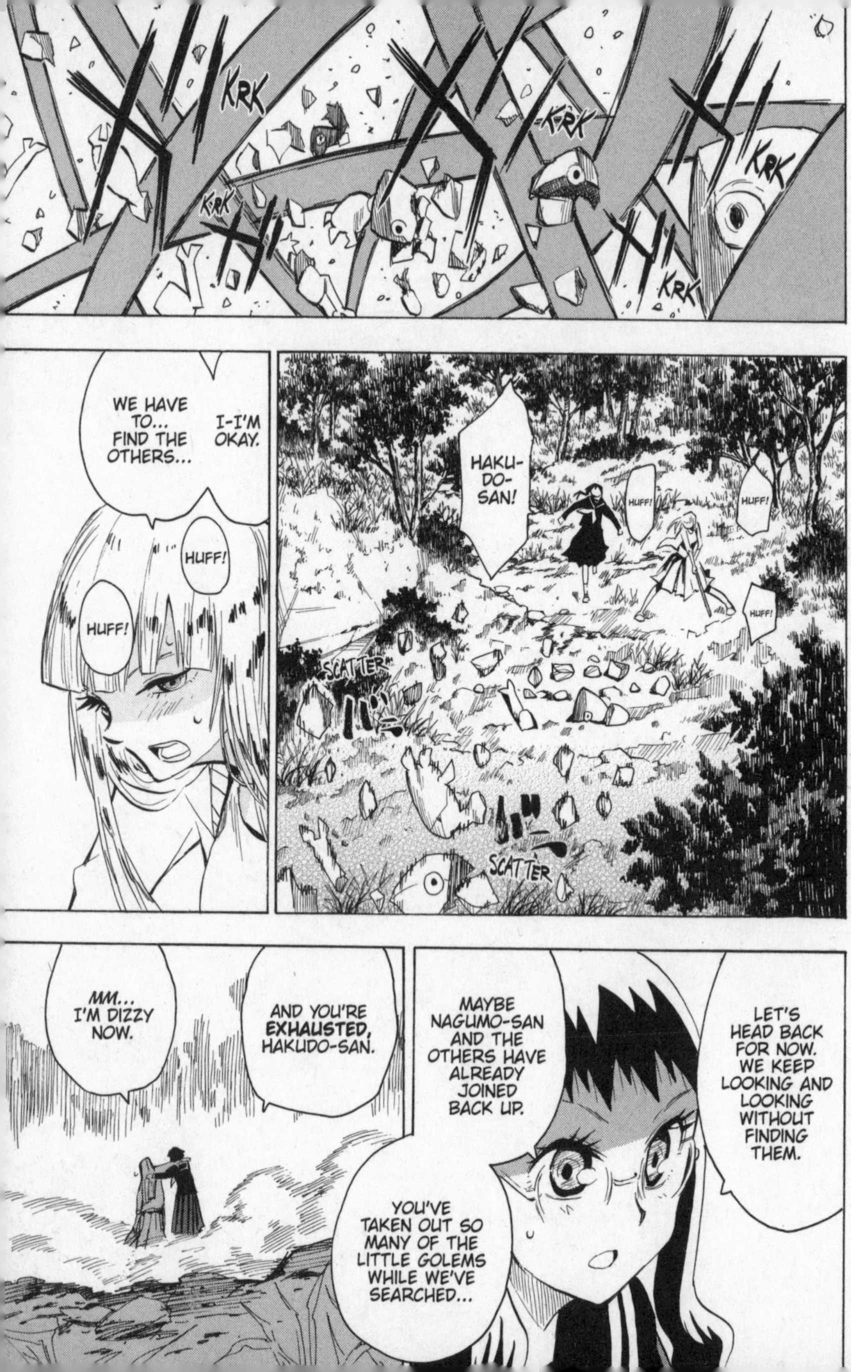
KRK
-K-RK
KRK
KRK
K-RK
KRK
HAKU-DO-SAN!
HUFF!
HUFF!
HUFF!
SCATTER
SCATTER
I-I'M OKAY.
WE HAVE TO... FIND THE OTHERS...
HUFF!
HUFF!
LET'S HEAD BACK FOR NOW. WE KEEP LOOKING AND LOOKING WITHOUT FINDING THEM.
MAYBE NAGUMO-SAN AND THE OTHERS HAVE ALREADY JOINED BACK UP.
YOU'VE TAKEN OUT SO MANY OF THE LITTLE GOLEMS WHILE WE'VE SEARCHED...
AND YOU'RE EXHAUSTED, HAKUDO-SAN.
MM... I'M DIZZY NOW.

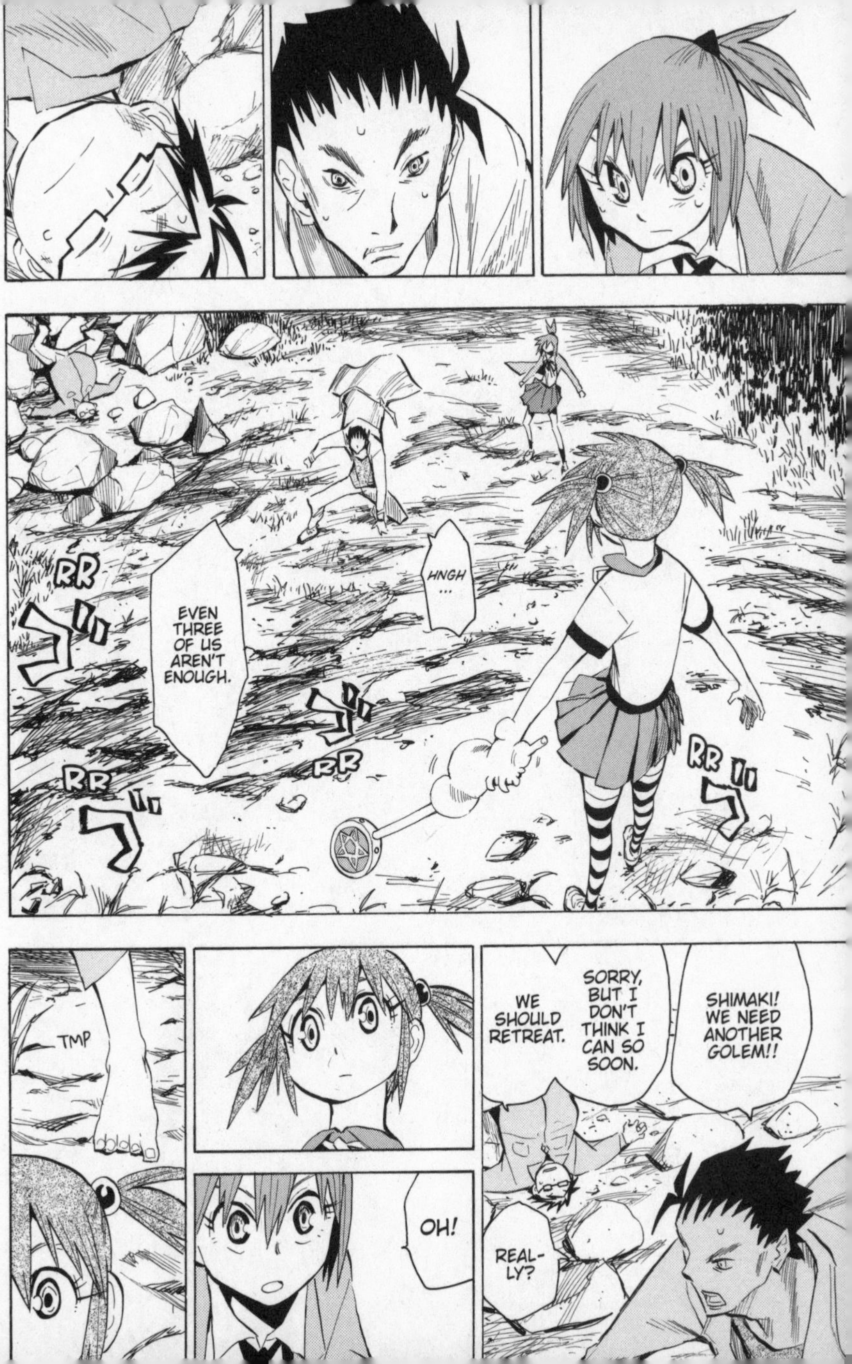
RR
HNGH...
EVEN THREE OF US AREN'T ENOUGH.
RR
RR
RR
SHIMAKI! WE NEED ANOTHER GOLEM!!
SORRY, BUT I DON'T THINK I CAN SO SOON.
WE SHOULD RETREAT.
REAL-LY?
TMP
OH!

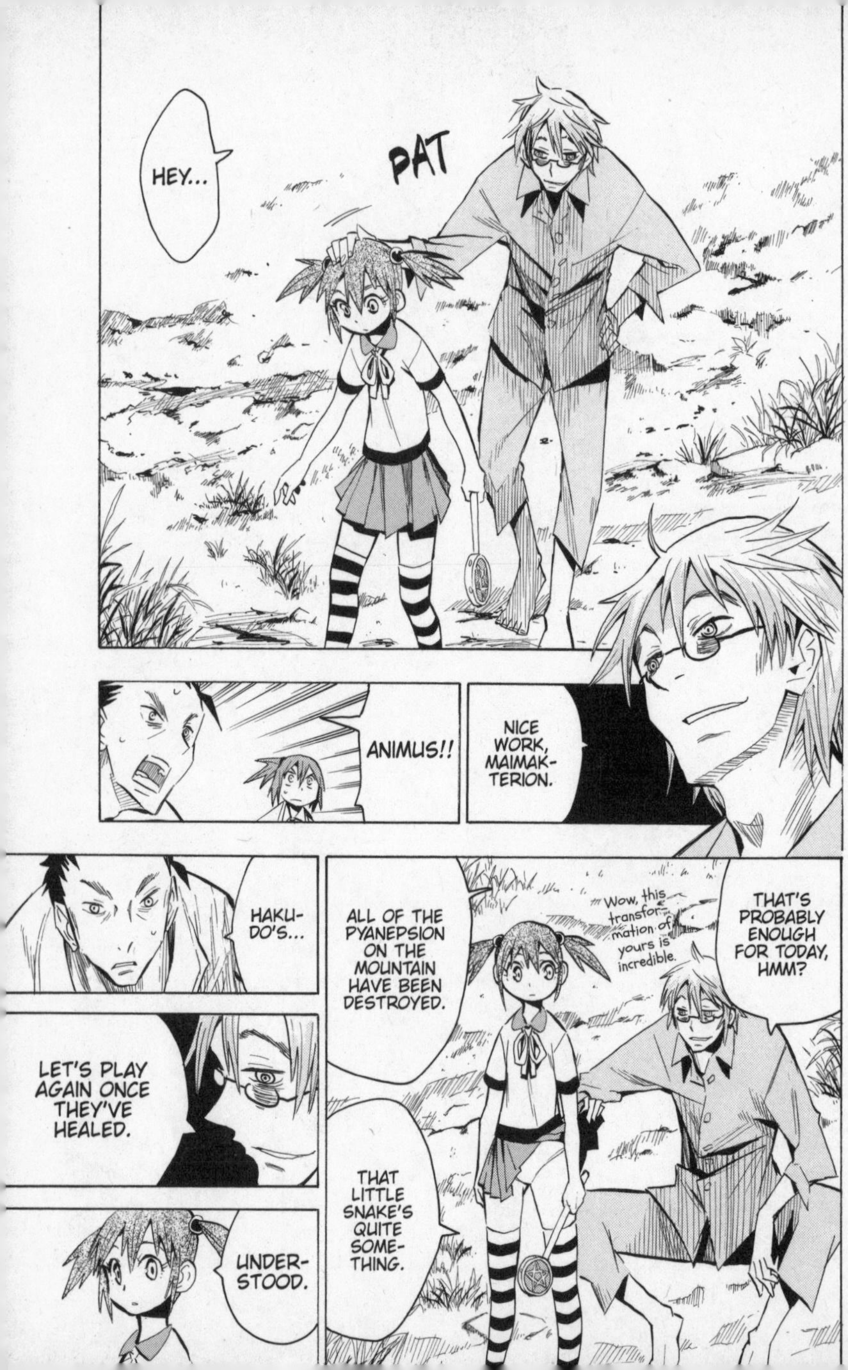
PAT
HEY...
NICE WORK, MAIMAK-TERION.
ANIMUS!!
THAT'S PROBABLY ENOUGH FOR TODAY, HMM?
Wow, this transformation of yours is incredible.
ALL OF THE PYANEPSION ON THE MOUNTAIN HAVE BEEN DESTROYED.
THAT LITTLE SNAKE'S QUITE SOME-THING.
HAKU-DO'S...
LET'S PLAY AGAIN ONCE THEY'VE HEALED.
UNDER-STOOD.

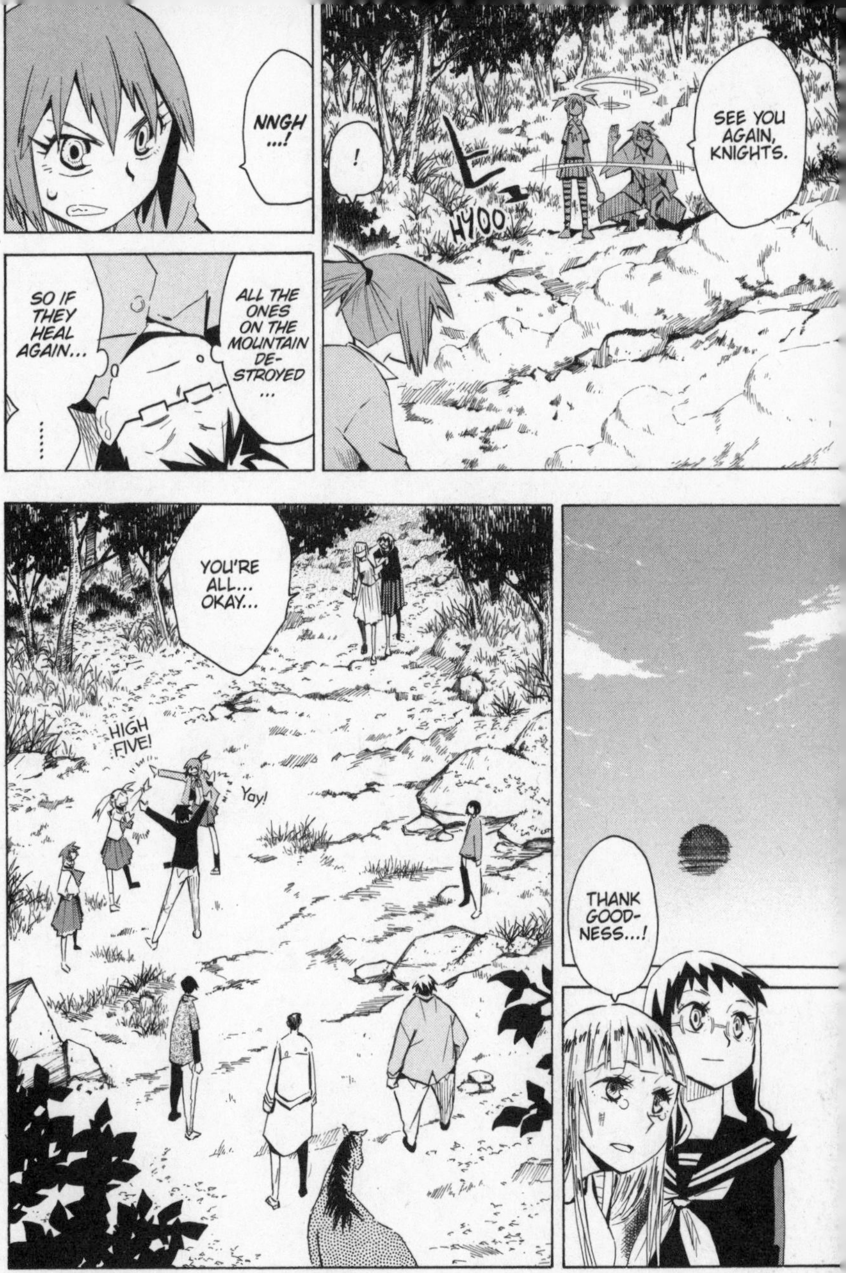
SEE YOU AGAIN, KNIGHTS.
!
HYOO
NNGH ...!
ALL THE ONES ON THE MOUNTAIN DE- STROYED ...
SO IF THEY HEAL AGAIN...
......
THANK GOOD- NESS...!
YOU'RE ALL... OKAY...
HIGH FIVE!
Yay!

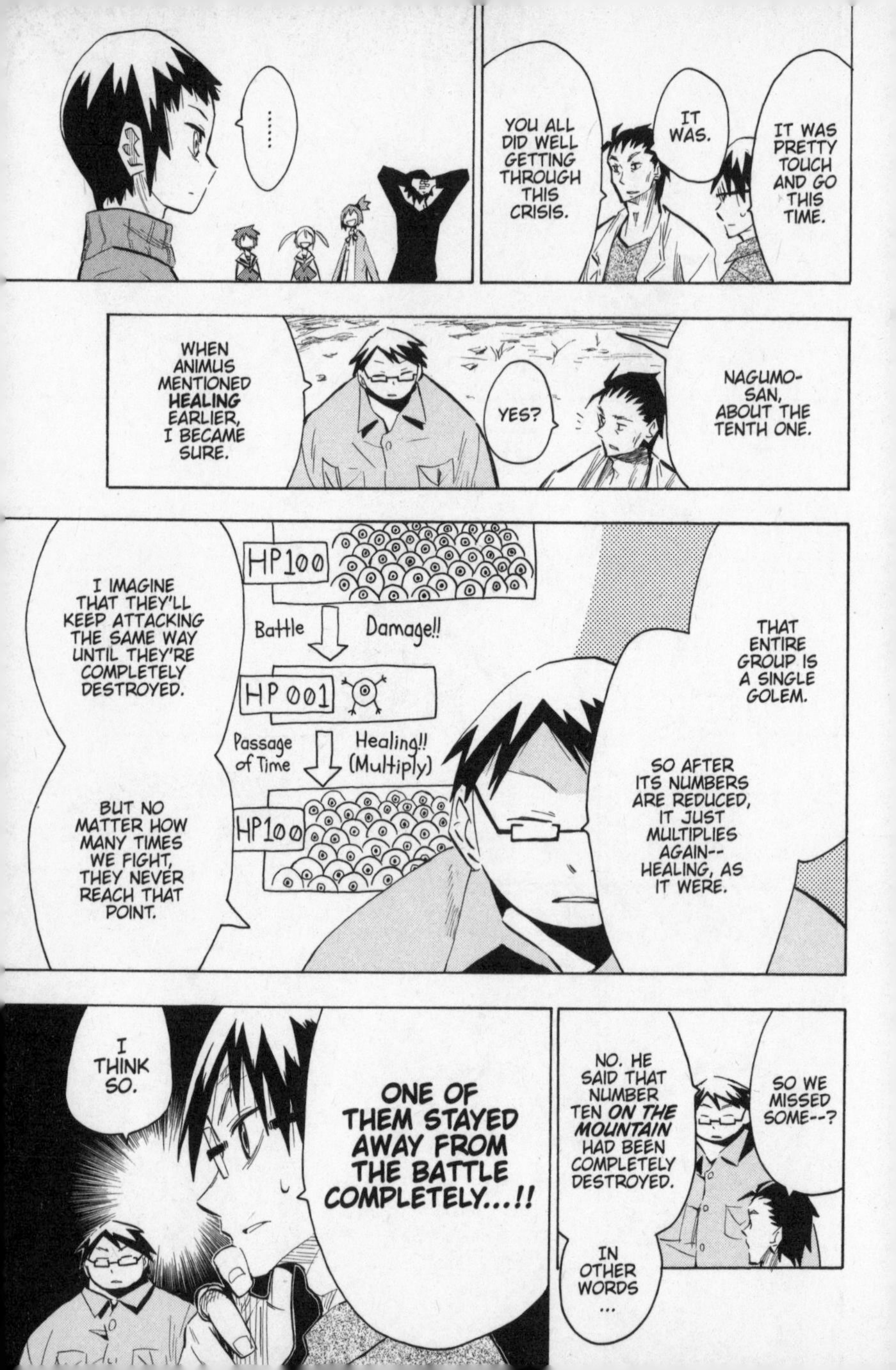
IT WAS PRETTY TOUCH AND GO THIS TIME.
IT WAS.
YOU ALL DID WELL GETTING THROUGH THIS CRISIS.
......
NAGUMO-SAN, ABOUT THE TENTH ONE.
YES?
WHEN ANIMUS MENTIONED HEALING EARLIER, I BECAME SURE.
THAT ENTIRE GROUP IS A SINGLE GOLEM.
SO AFTER ITS NUMBERS ARE REDUCED, IT JUST MULTIPLIES AGAIN--HEALING, AS IT WERE.
HP100
Battle
Damage!!
HP 001
Passage of Time
Healing!! (Multiply)
HP100
I IMAGINE THAT THEY'LL KEEP ATTACKING THE SAME WAY UNTIL THEY'RE COMPLETELY DESTROYED.
BUT NO MATTER HOW MANY TIMES WE FIGHT, THEY NEVER REACH THAT POINT.
SO WE MISSED SOME--?
NO. HE SAID THAT NUMBER TEN ON THE MOUNTAIN HAD BEEN COMPLETELY DESTROYED.
IN OTHER WORDS...
ONE OF THEM STAYED AWAY FROM THE BATTLE COMPLETELY...!!
I THINK SO.

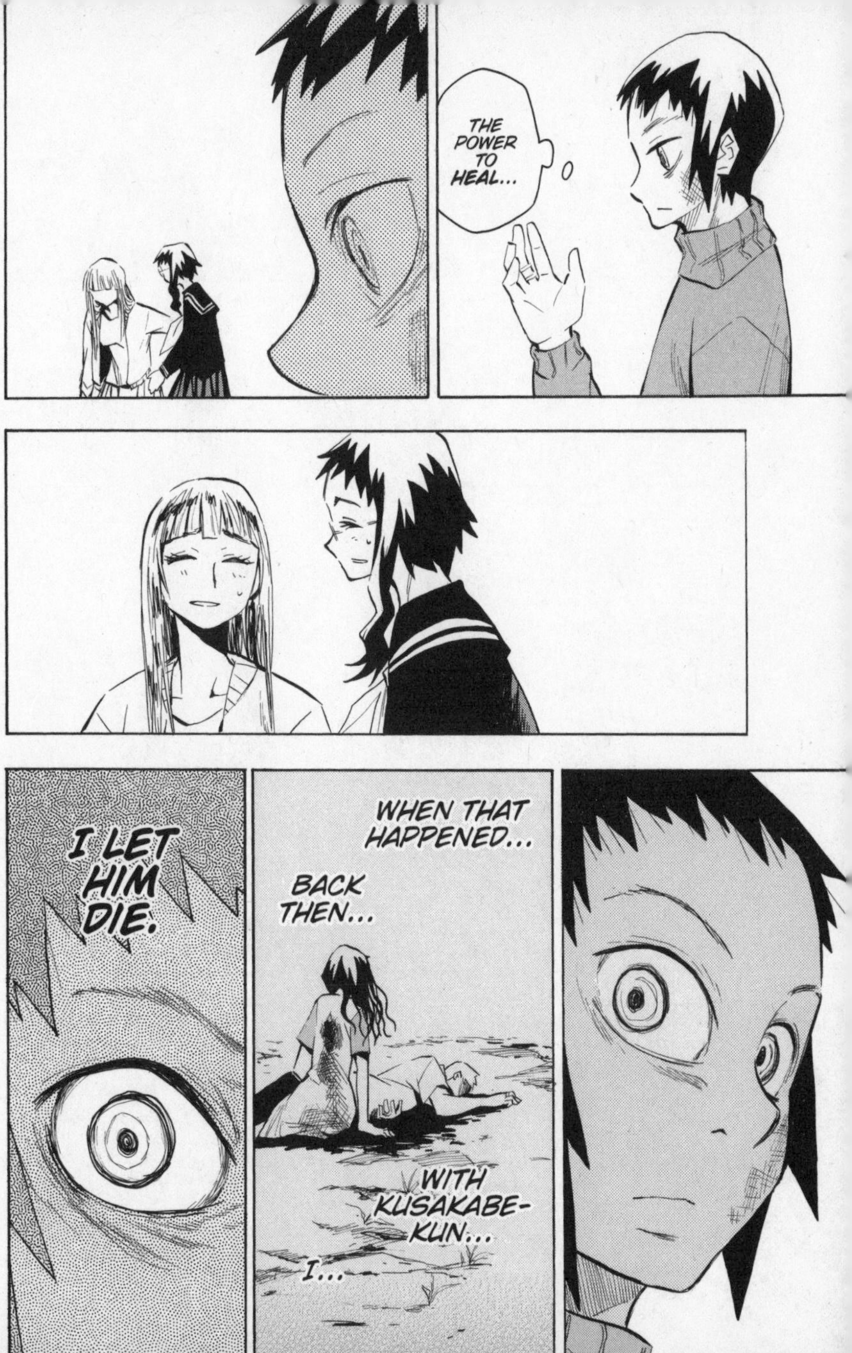
THE POWER TO HEAL...
WHEN THAT HAPPENED...
BACK THEN...
WITH KUSAKABE-KUN...
I...
I LET HIM DIE.

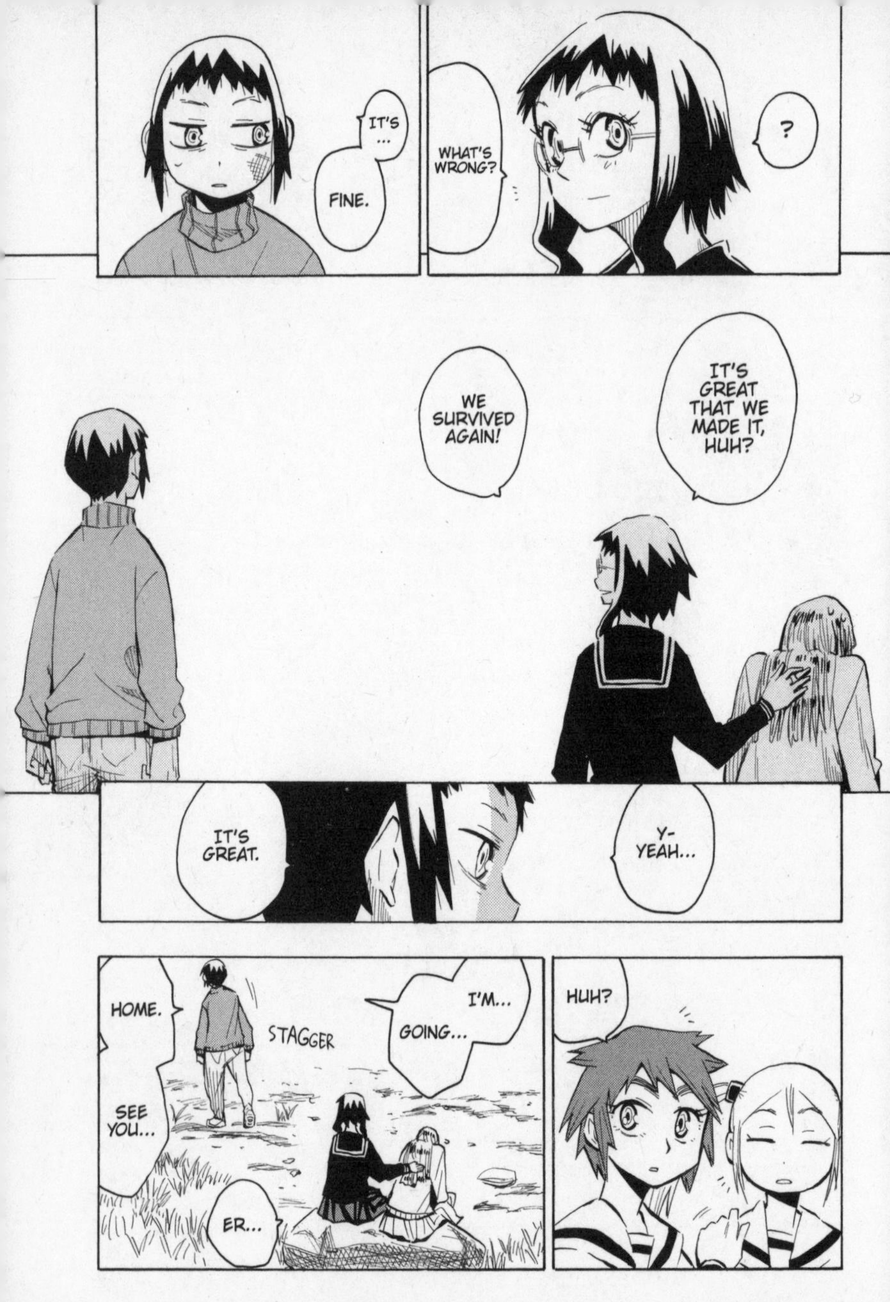
?
WHAT'S WRONG?
IT'S ...
FINE.
IT'S GREAT THAT WE MADE IT, HUH?
WE SURVIVED AGAIN!
Y-YEAH...
IT'S GREAT.
HUH?
I'M...
GOING...
HOME.
STAGGER
SEE YOU...
ER...

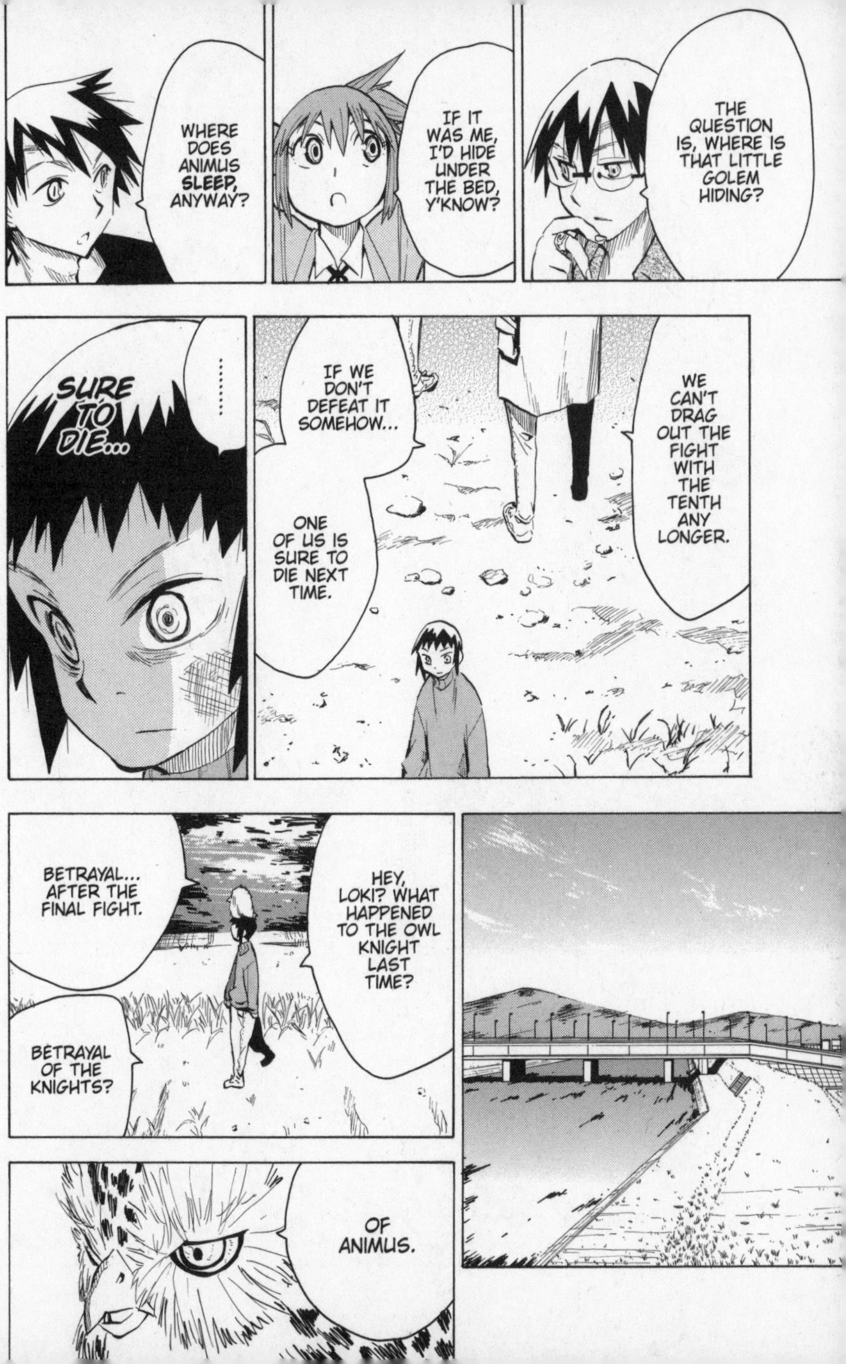
THE QUESTION IS, WHERE IS THAT LITTLE GOLEM HIDING?
IF IT WAS ME, I'D HIDE UNDER THE BED, Y'KNOW?
WHERE DOES ANIMUS SLEEP, ANYWAY?
WE CAN'T DRAG OUT THE FIGHT WITH THE TENTH ANY LONGER.
IF WE DON'T DEFEAT IT SOMEHOW...
ONE OF US IS SURE TO DIE NEXT TIME.
......
SURE TO DIE...
HEY, LOKI? WHAT HAPPENED TO THE OWL KNIGHT LAST TIME?
BETRAYAL... AFTER THE FINAL FIGHT.
BETRAYAL OF THE KNIGHTS?
OF ANIMUS.

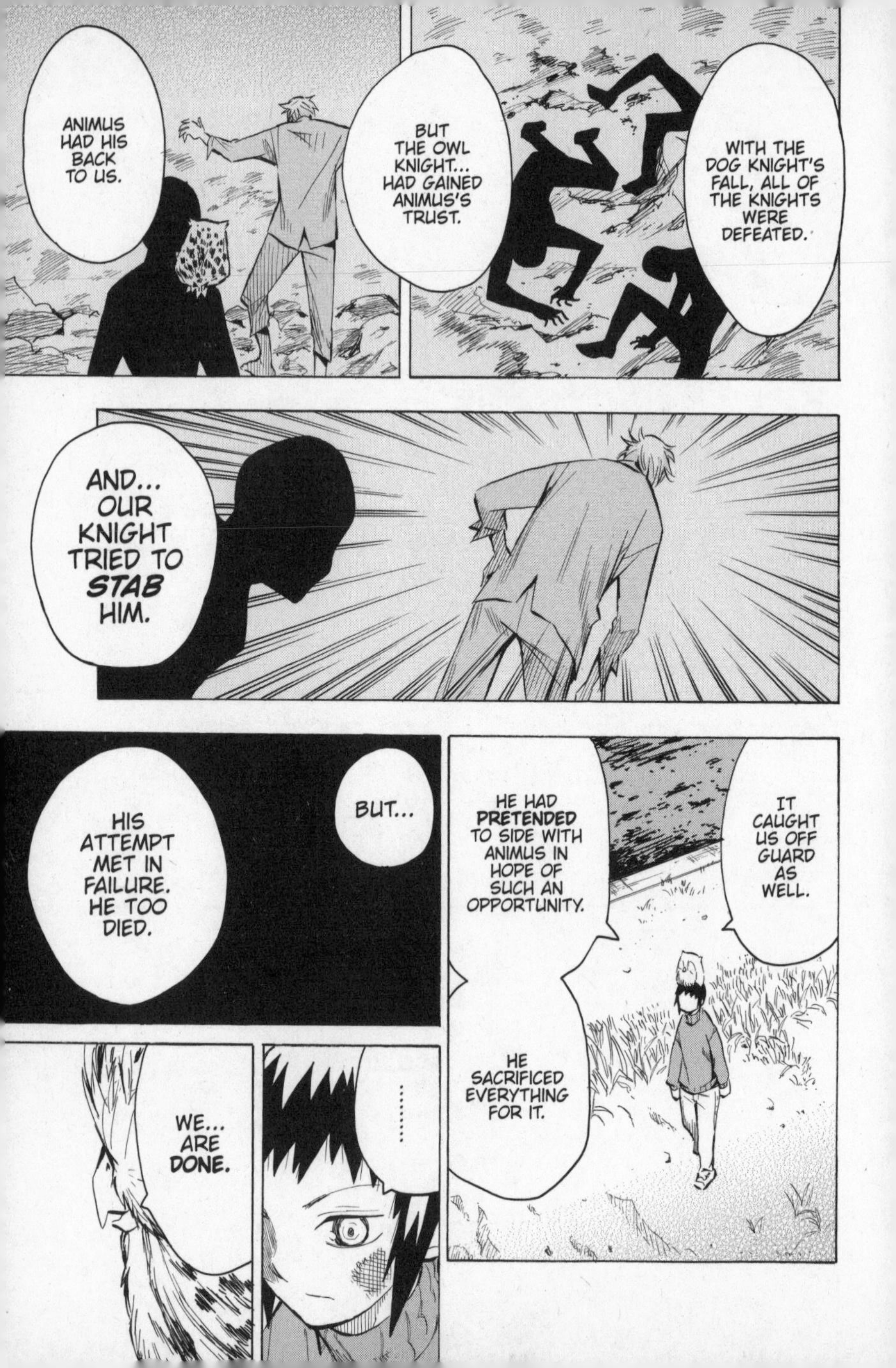
WITH THE DOG KNIGHT'S FALL, ALL OF THE KNIGHTS WERE DEFEATED.
BUT THE OWL KNIGHT... HAD GAINED ANIMUS'S TRUST.
ANIMUS HAD HIS BACK TO US.
AND... OUR KNIGHT TRIED TO **STAB** HIM.
IT CAUGHT US OFF GUARD AS WELL.
HE HAD **PRETENDED** TO SIDE WITH ANIMUS IN HOPE OF SUCH AN OPPORTUNITY.
HE SACRIFICED EVERYTHING FOR IT.
BUT...
HIS ATTEMPT MET IN FAILURE. HE TOO DIED.
......
WE... ARE **DONE**.

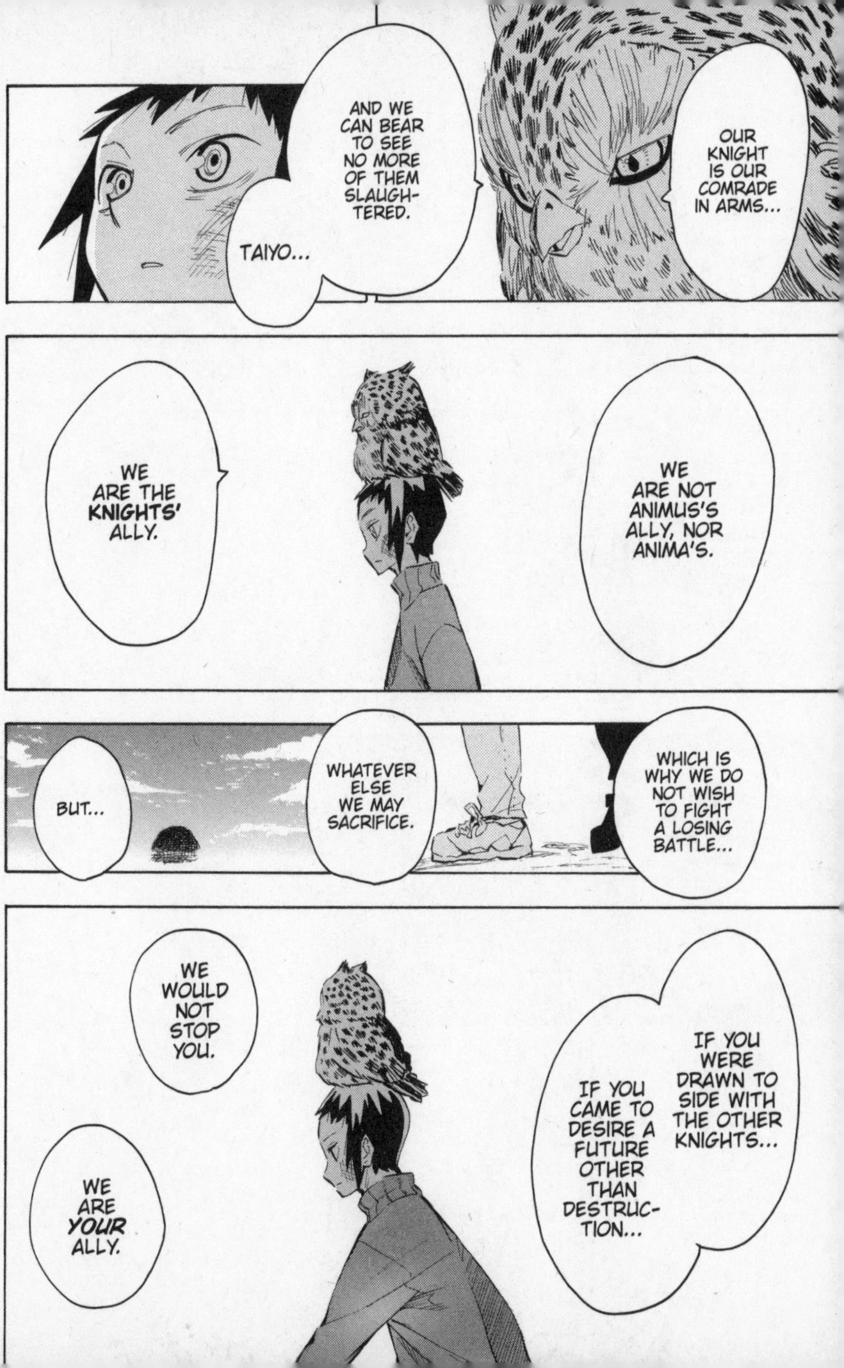

OUR KNIGHT IS OUR COMRADE IN ARMS...
AND WE CAN BEAR TO SEE NO MORE OF THEM SLAUGHTERED.
TAIYO...
WE ARE NOT ANIMUS'S ALLY, NOR ANIMA'S.
WE ARE THE KNIGHTS' ALLY.
WHICH IS WHY WE DO NOT WISH TO FIGHT A LOSING BATTLE...
WHATEVER ELSE WE MAY SACRIFICE.
BUT...
IF YOU WERE DRAWN TO SIDE WITH THE OTHER KNIGHTS...
IF YOU CAME TO DESIRE A FUTURE OTHER THAN DESTRUCTION...
WE WOULD NOT STOP YOU.
WE ARE YOUR ALLY.

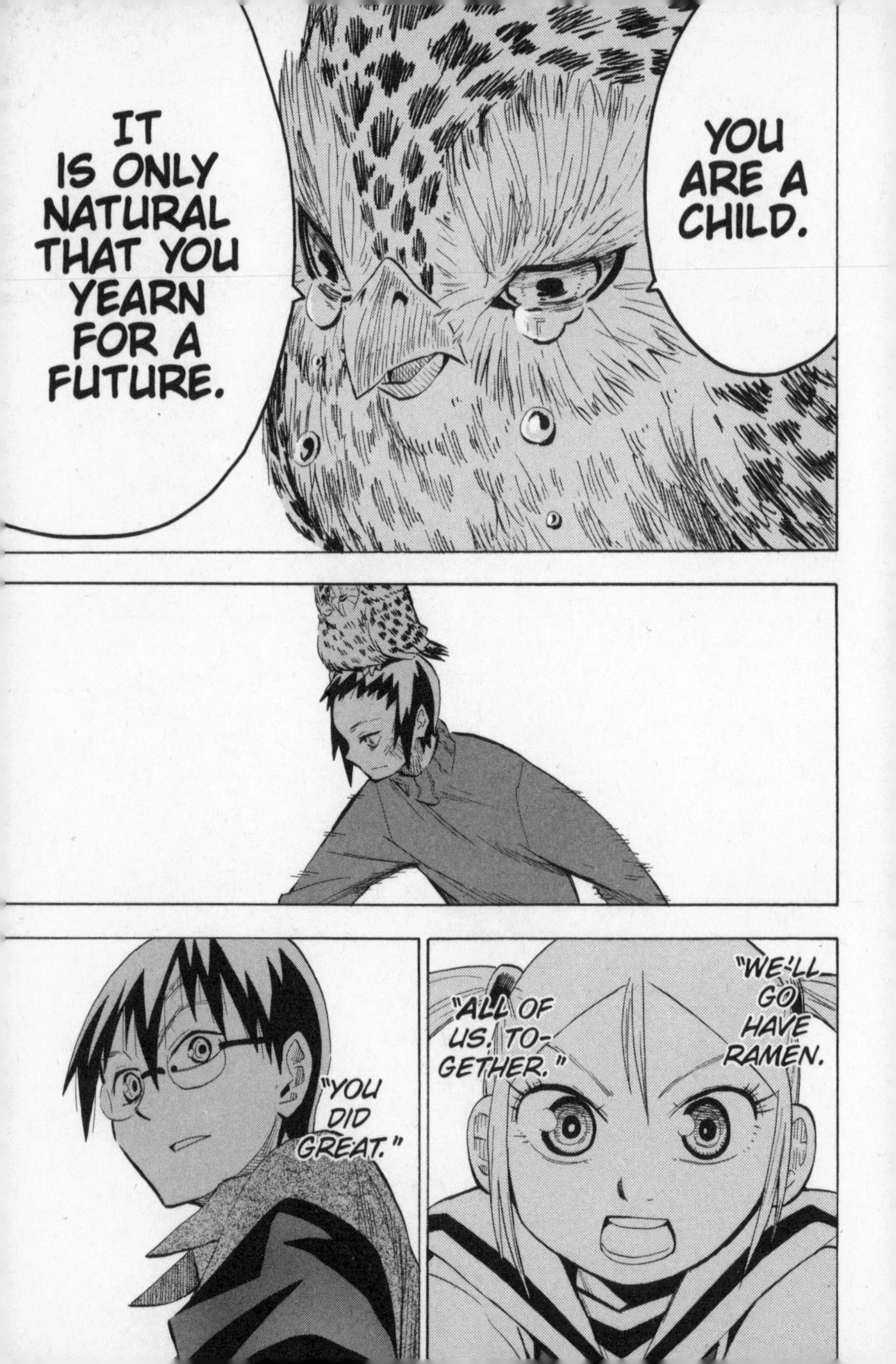
YOU ARE A CHILD.
IT IS ONLY NATURAL THAT YOU YEARN FOR A FUTURE.
"WE'LL GO HAVE RAMEN.
"ALL OF US. TO-GETHER."
"YOU DID GREAT."

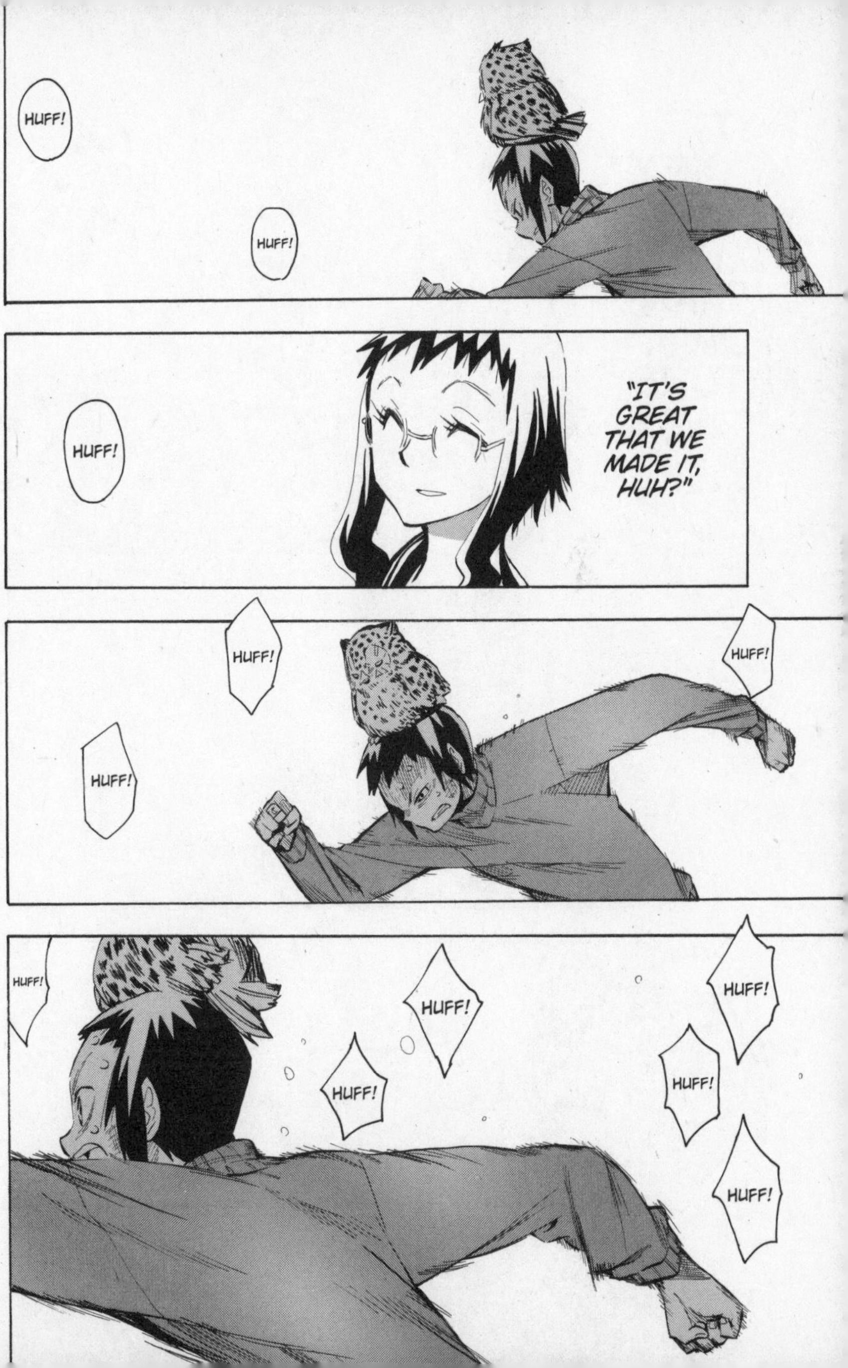
HUFF!
HUFF!
"IT'S GREAT THAT WE MADE IT, HUH?"
HUFF!
HUFF!
HUFF!
HUFF!
HUFF!
HUFF!
HUFF!
HUFF!
HUFF!
HUFF!
HUFF!

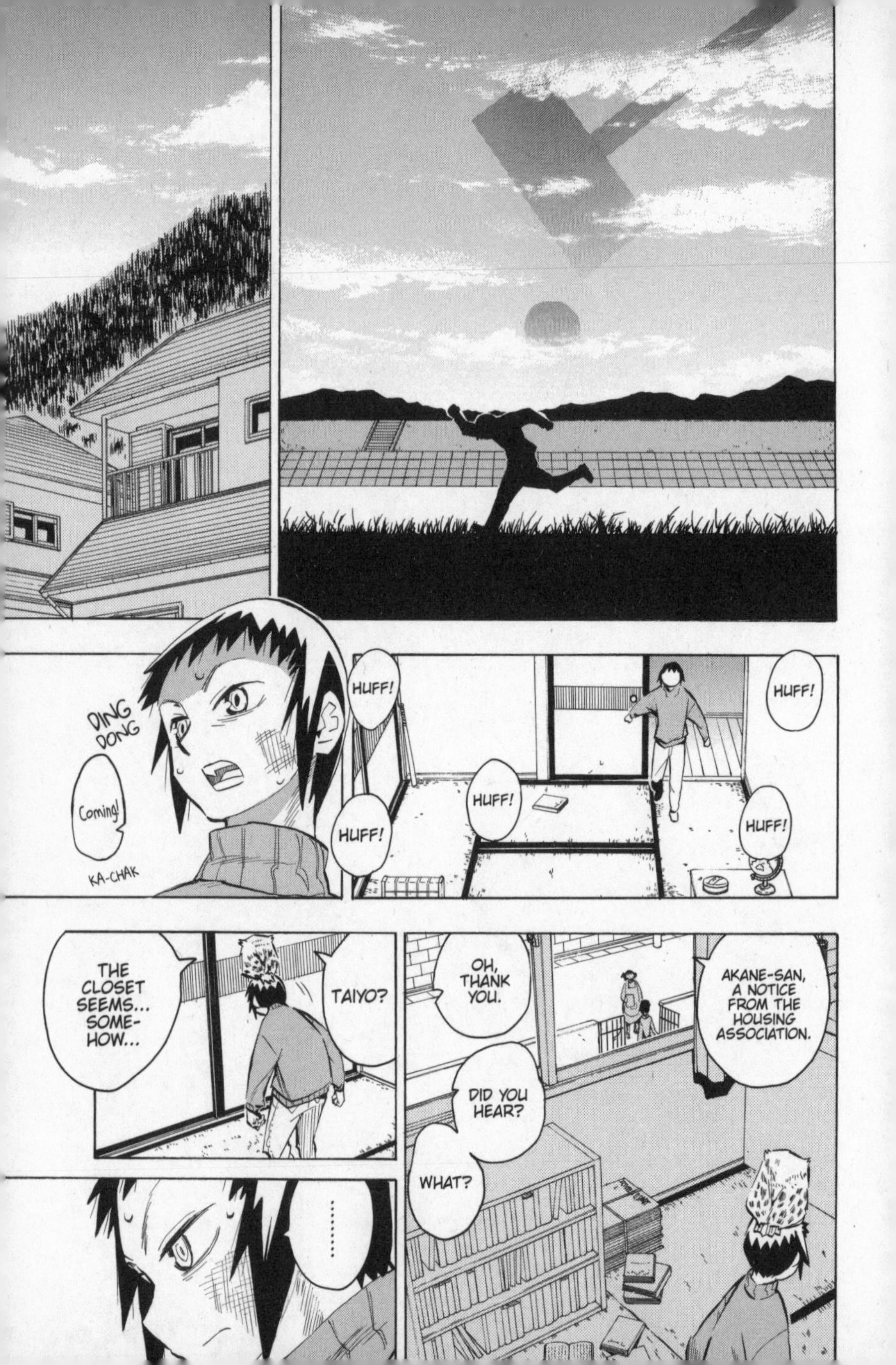
HUFF!
HUFF!
HUFF!
HUFF!
HUFF!
DING DONG
Coming!
KA-CHAK
AKANE-SAN, A NOTICE FROM THE HOUSING ASSOCIATION.
OH, THANK YOU.
DID YOU HEAR?
WHAT?
TAIYO?
THE CLOSET SEEMS... SOME-HOW...
......

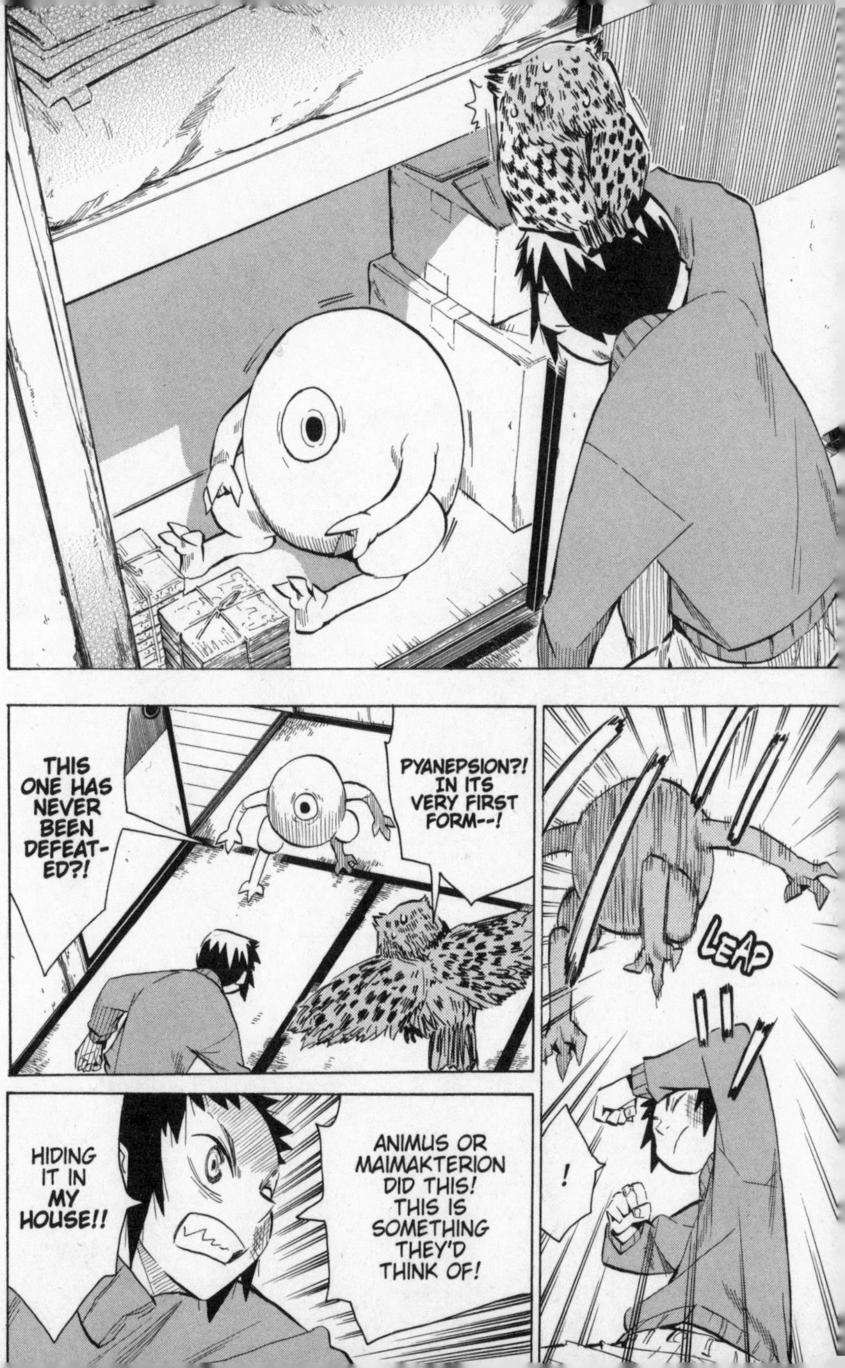
LEAP
!
PYANEPSION?! IN ITS VERY FIRST FORM--!
THIS ONE HAS NEVER BEEN DEFEAT-ED?!
ANIMUS OR MAIMAKTERION DID THIS! THIS IS SOMETHING THEY'D THINK OF!
HIDING IT IN MY HOUSE!!

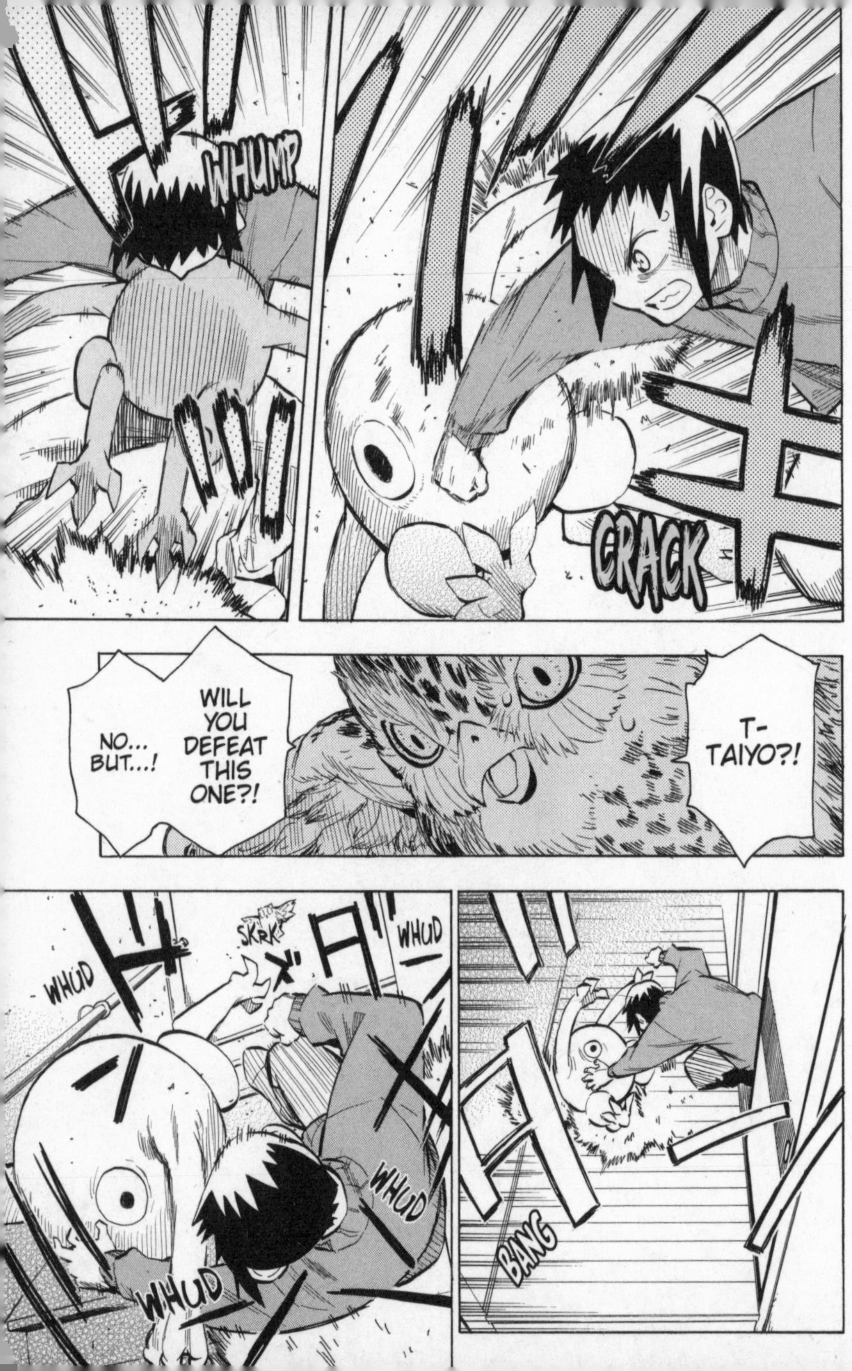
CRACK
WHUMP
T-TAIYO?!
WILL YOU DEFEAT THIS ONE?!
NO... BUT...!
BANG
WHUD
SKRK
WHUD
WHUD
WHUD

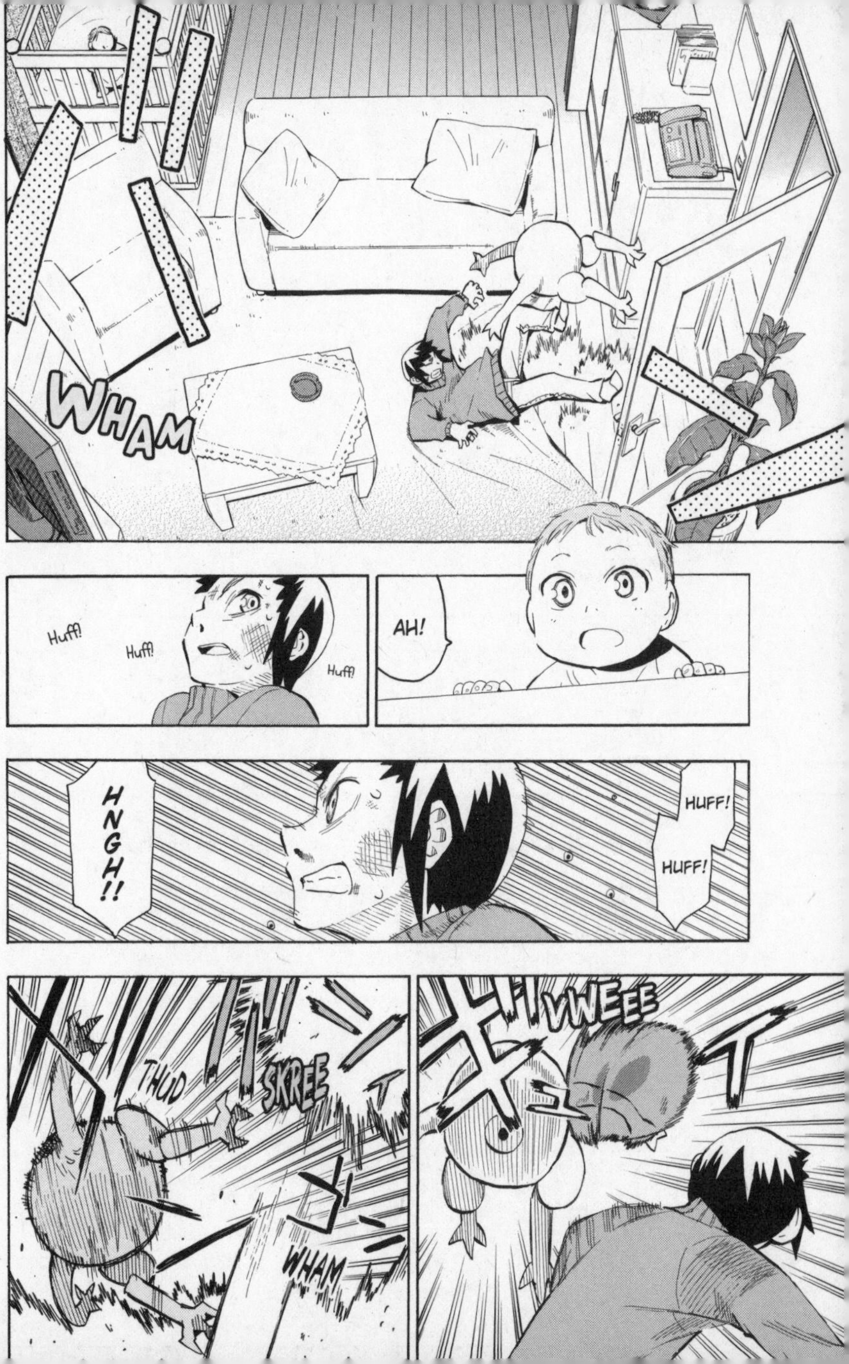
WHAM
AH!
Huff!
Huff!
Huff!
HUFF!
HUFF!
HNGH!!
VWEEE
SKREE
THUD
WHAM

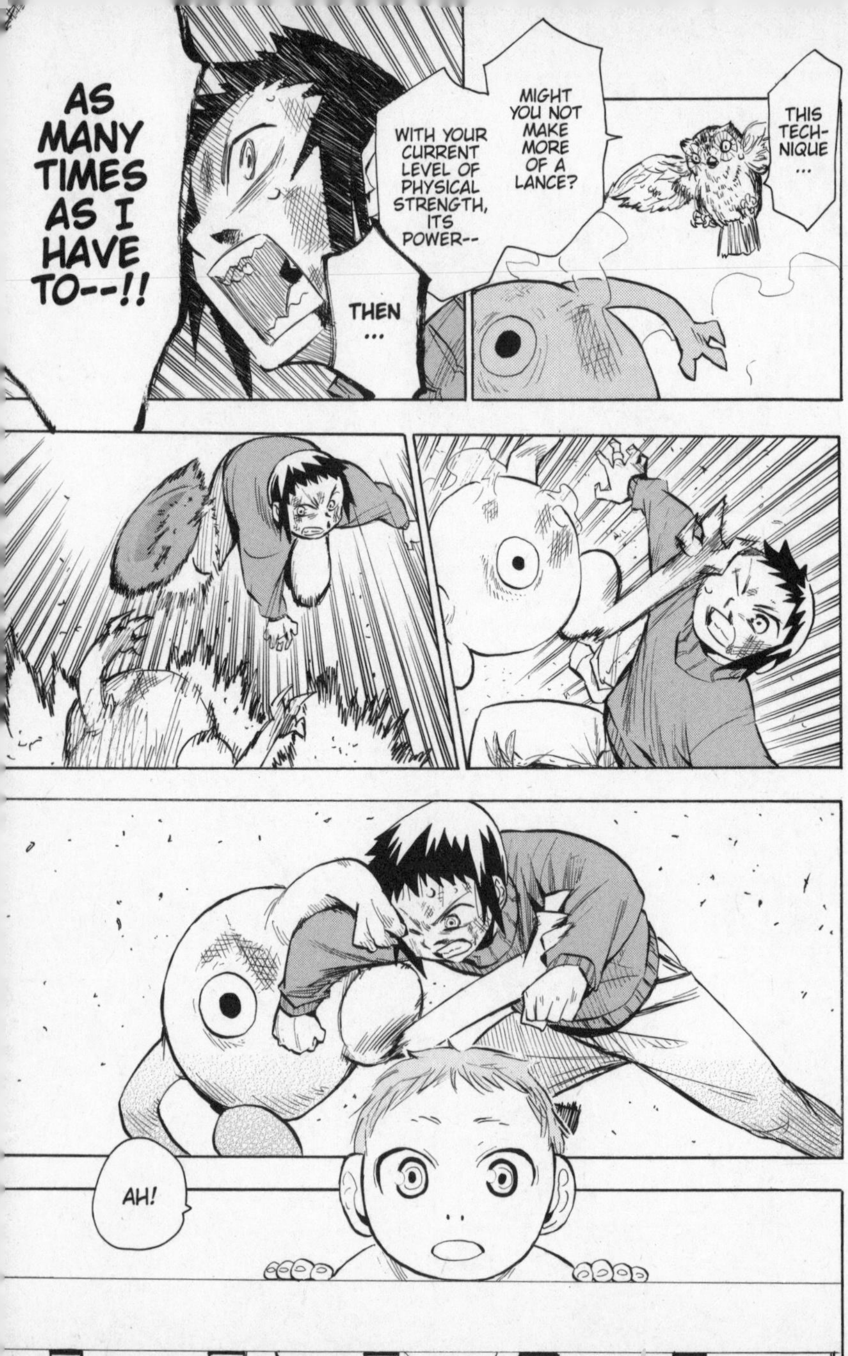
THIS TECH-NIQUE ...
MIGHT YOU NOT MAKE MORE OF A LANCE?
WITH YOUR CURRENT LEVEL OF PHYSICAL STRENGTH, ITS POWER--
THEN ...
AS MANY TIMES AS I HAVE TO--!!
AH!

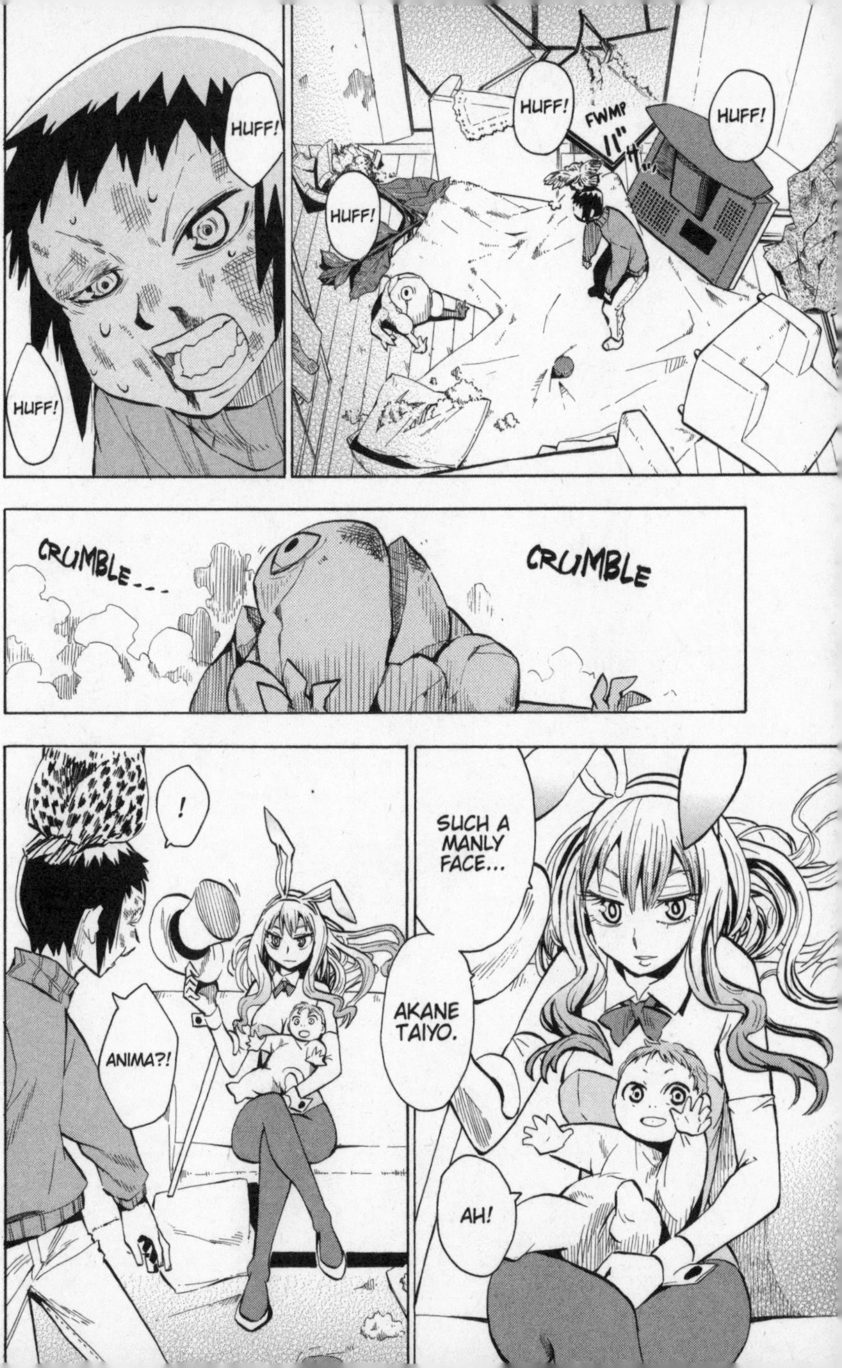
HUFF!
HUFF!
FWMP
HUFF!
HUFF!
HUFF!
CRUMBLE
CRUMBLE...
SUCH A MANLY FACE...
AKANE TAIYO.
AH!
!
ANIMA?!

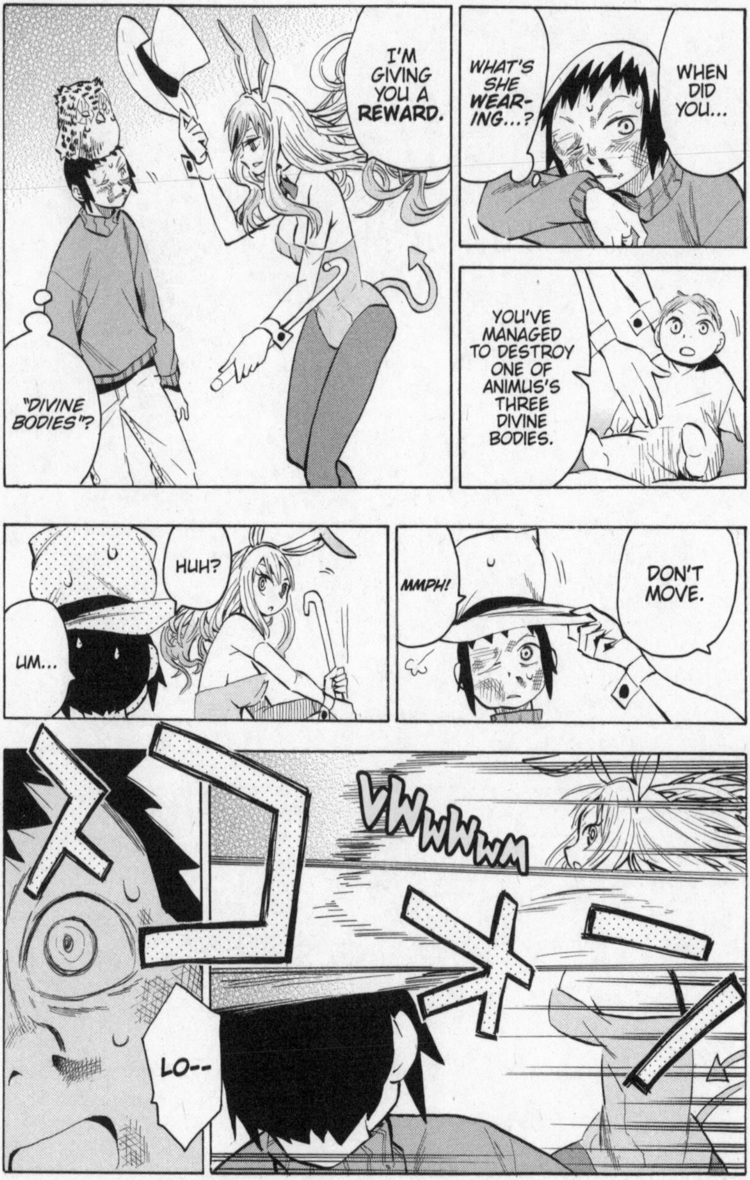
WHEN DID YOU...
WHAT'S SHE WEARING...?
YOU'VE MANAGED TO DESTROY ONE OF ANIMUS'S THREE DIVINE BODIES.
I'M GIVING YOU A **REWARD.**
"DIVINE BODIES"?
DON'T MOVE.
MMPH!
HUH?
UM...
VWWWWWM
LO--

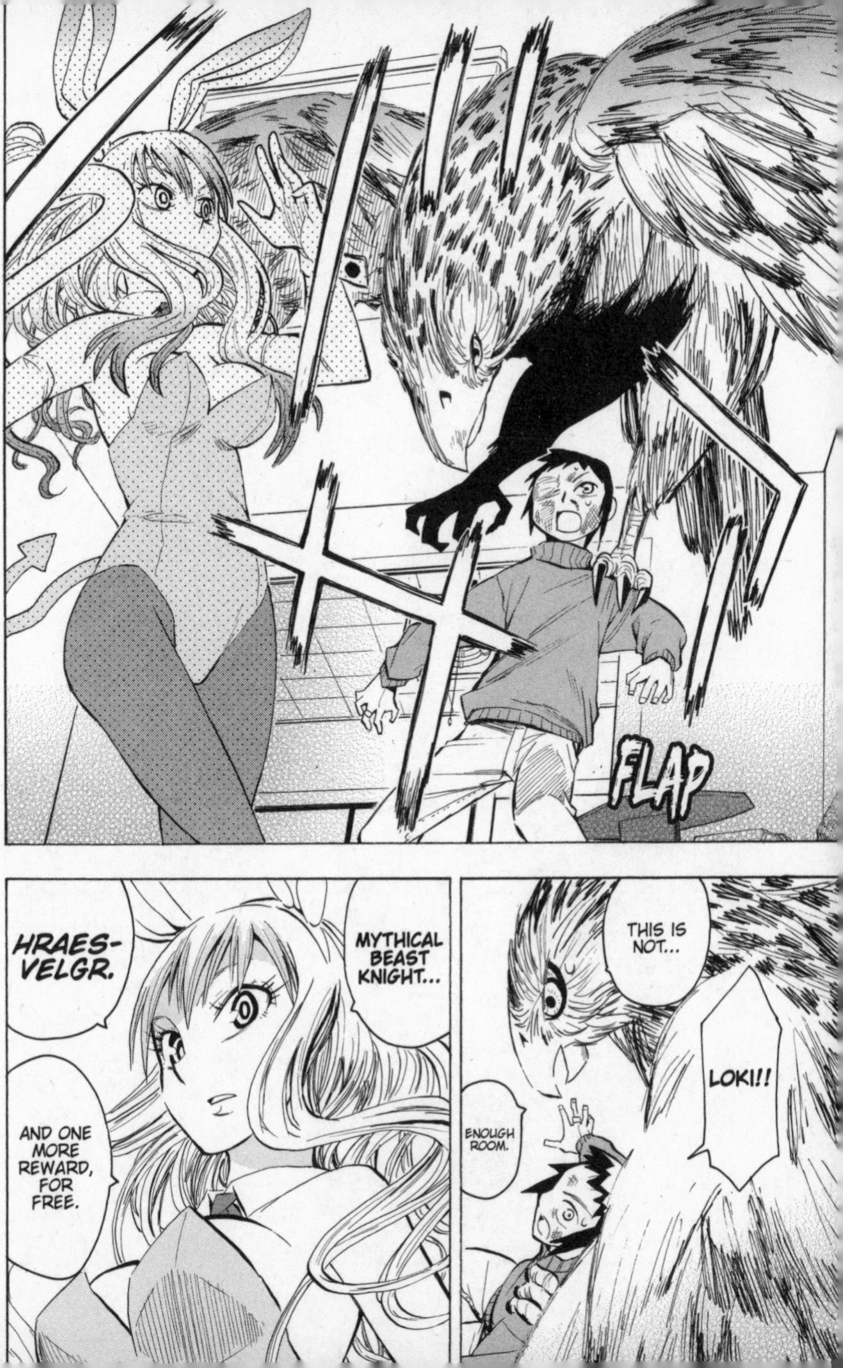
FLAP
THIS IS NOT...
LOKI!!
ENOUGH ROOM.
MYTHICAL BEAST KNIGHT...
HRAES-VELGR.
AND ONE MORE REWARD, FOR FREE.

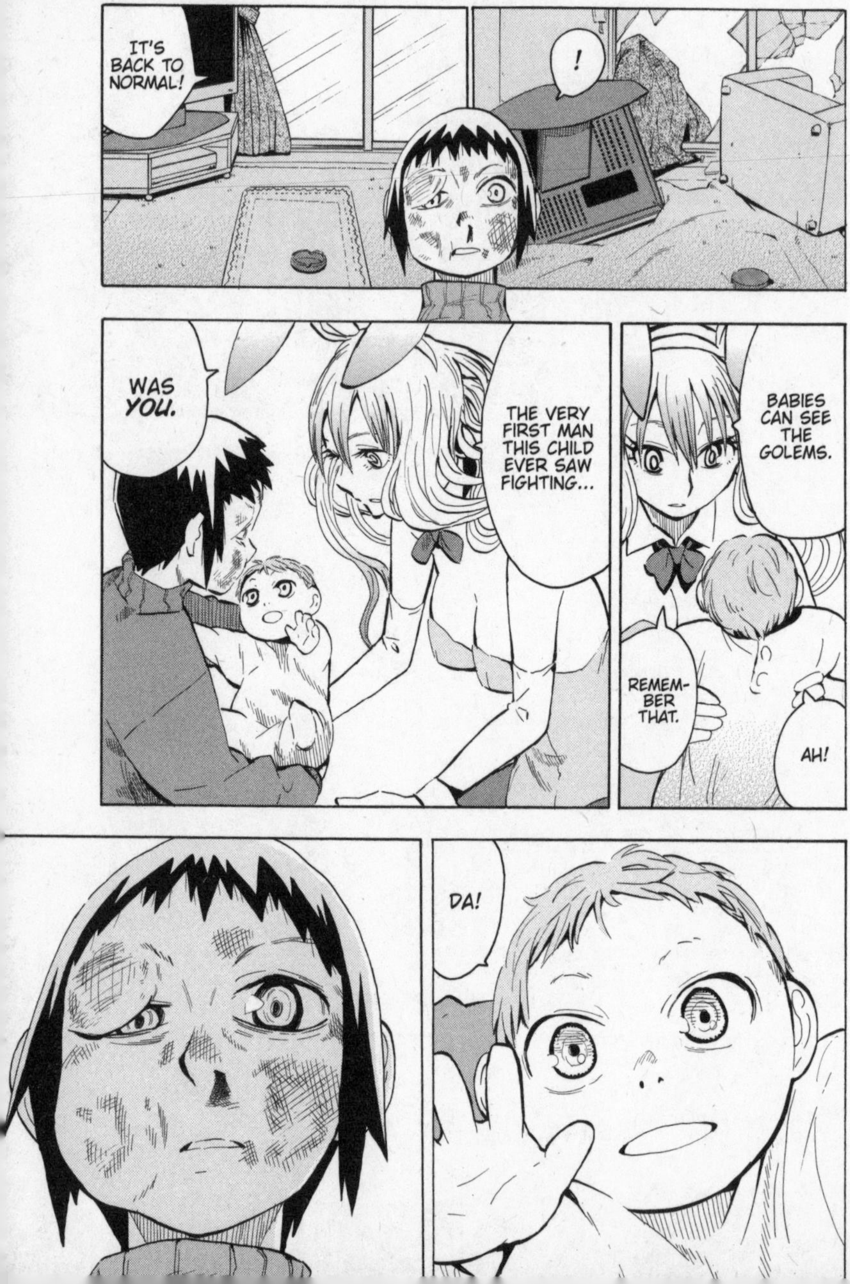
!
IT'S BACK TO NORMAL!
BABIES CAN SEE THE GOLEMS.
REMEMBER THAT.
AH!
THE VERY FIRST MAN THIS CHILD EVER SAW FIGHTING...
WAS *YOU.*
DA!

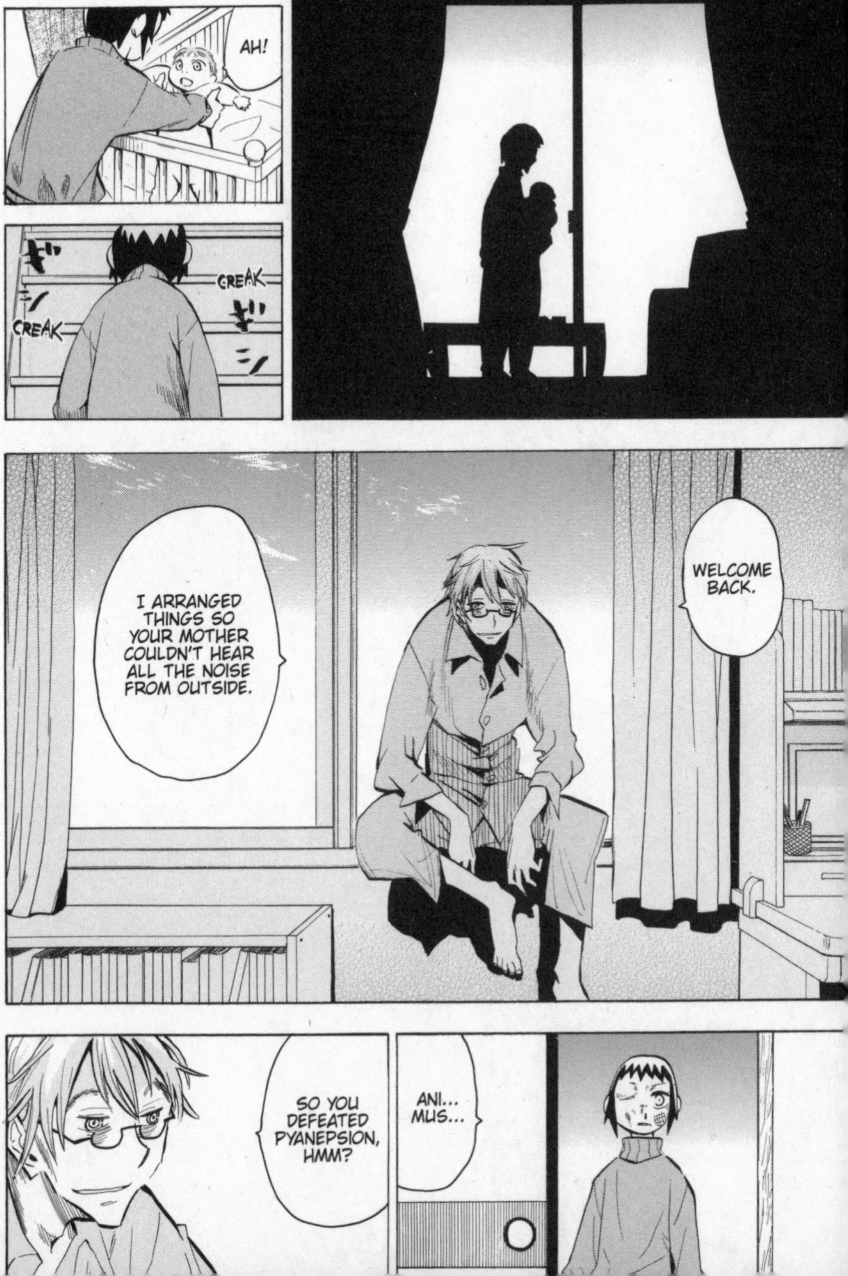
AH!
CREAK
CREAK
WELCOME BACK.
I ARRANGED THINGS SO YOUR MOTHER COULDN'T HEAR ALL THE NOISE FROM OUTSIDE.
ANI... MUS...
SO YOU DEFEATED PYANEPSION, HMM?

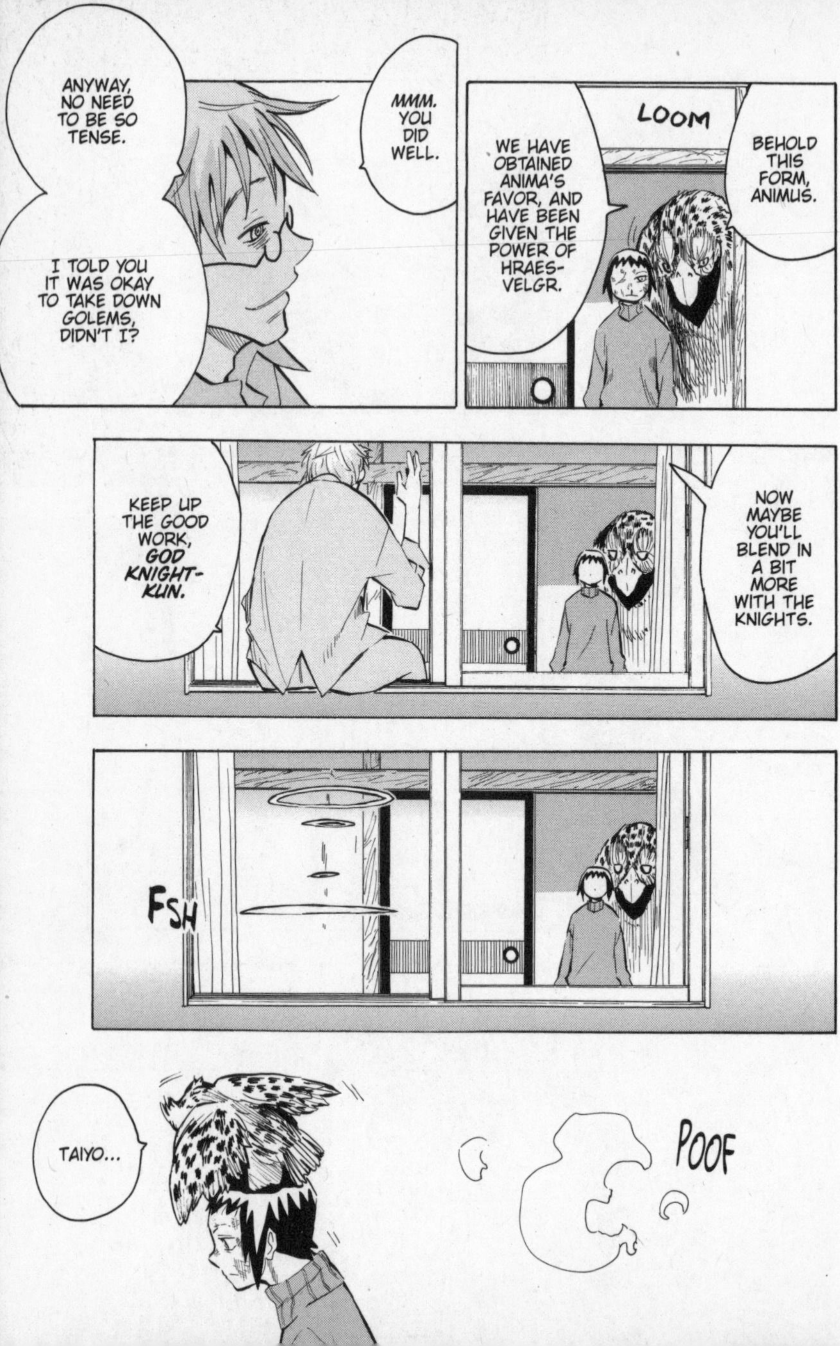
BEHOLD THIS FORM, ANIMUS.
LOOM
WE HAVE OBTAINED ANIMA'S FAVOR, AND HAVE BEEN GIVEN THE POWER OF HRAES-VELGR.
MMM. YOU DID WELL.
ANYWAY, NO NEED TO BE SO TENSE.
I TOLD YOU IT WAS OKAY TO TAKE DOWN GOLEMS, DIDN'T I?
NOW MAYBE YOU'LL BLEND IN A BIT MORE WITH THE KNIGHTS.
KEEP UP THE GOOD WORK, GOD KNIGHT-KUN.
FSH
POOF
TAIYO...

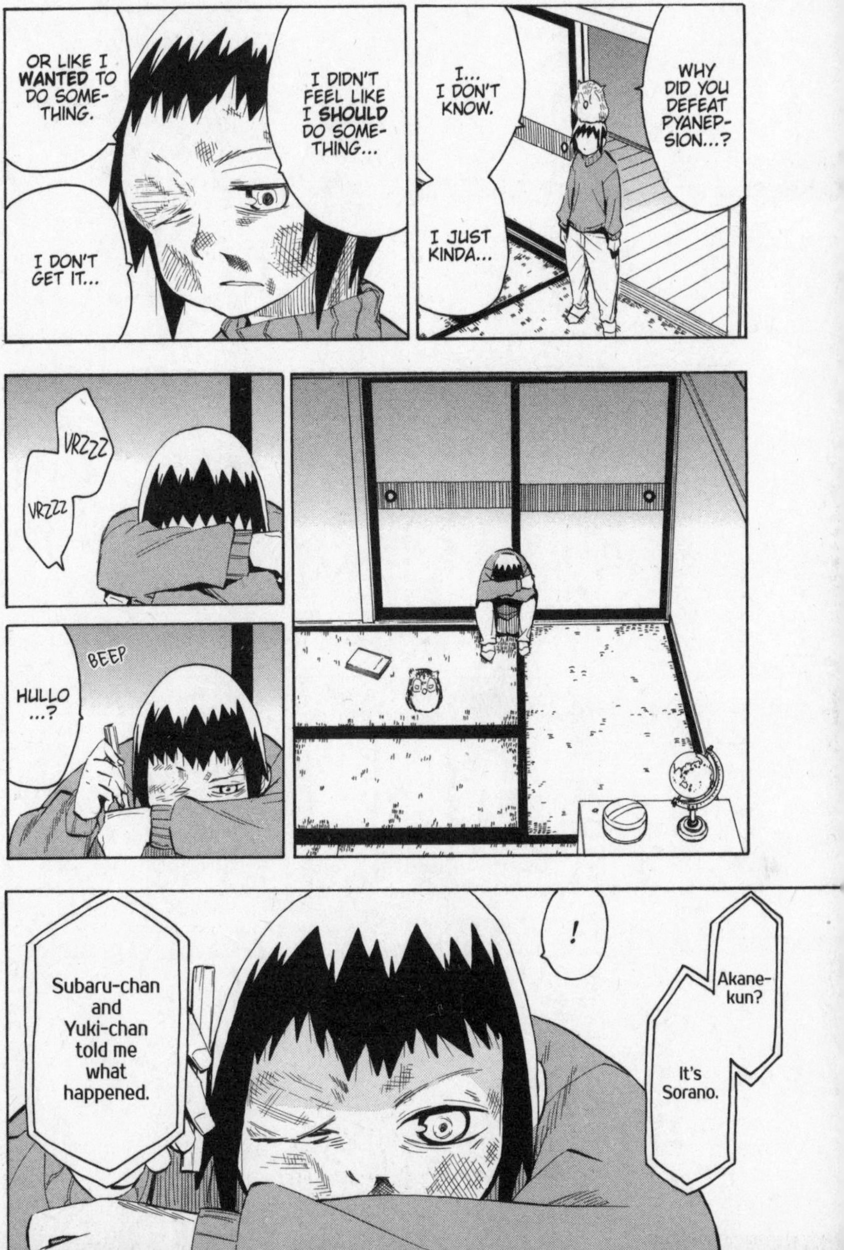
WHY DID YOU DEFEAT PYANEPSION...?
I... I DON'T KNOW.
I JUST KINDA...
I DIDN'T FEEL LIKE I **SHOULD** DO SOMETHING...
OR LIKE I **WANTED** TO DO SOMETHING.
I DON'T GET IT...
VRZZZ
VRZZZ
BEEP
HULLO ...?
!
Akane-kun?
It's Sorano.
Subaru-chan and Yuki-chan told me what happened.

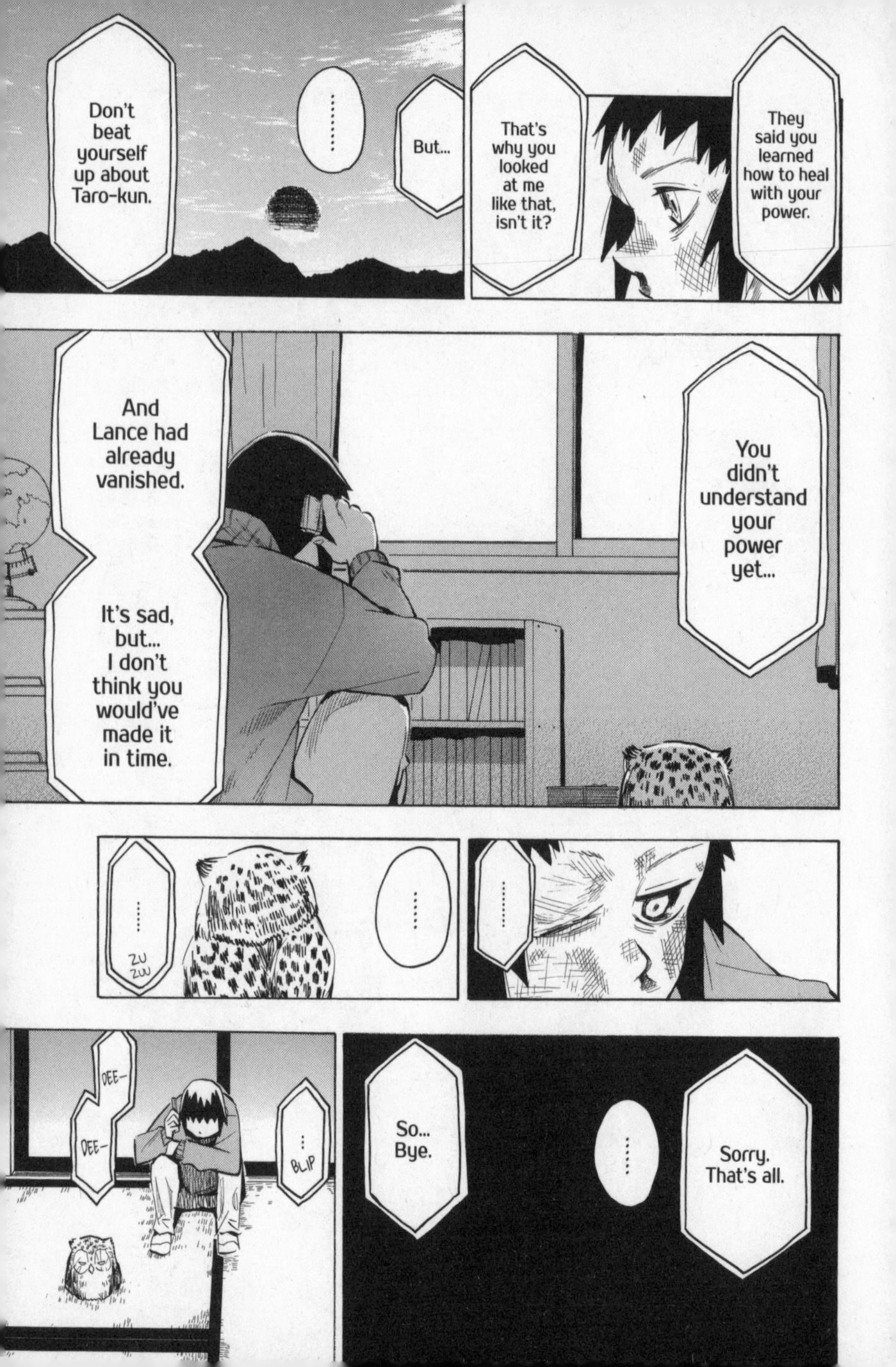
They said you learned how to heal with your power.
That's why you looked at me like that, isn't it?
But...
......
Don't beat yourself up about Taro-kun.
You didn't understand your power yet...
And Lance had already vanished.
It's sad, but... I don't think you would've made it in time.
......
......
......
ZU ZUU
Sorry. That's all.
......
So... Bye.
...
BLIP
DEE-
DEE-

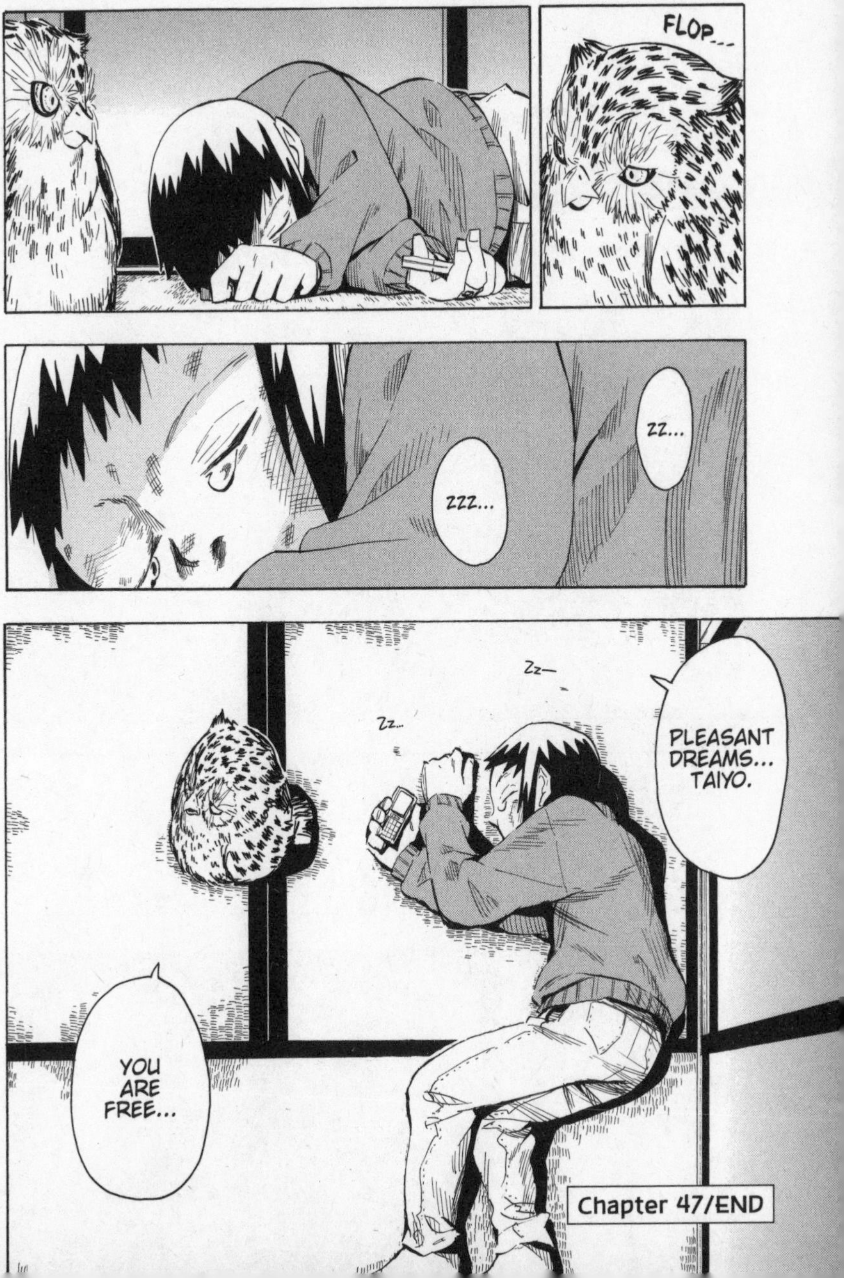
FLOP...
ZZ...
ZZZ...
PLEASANT DREAMS... TAIYO.
Zz—
Zz...
YOU ARE FREE...
Chapter 47/END

Lucifer and the Biscuit Hammer
Volume 7
"Children"

Production staff
  Tonpuku Tanabe
  Daria Asahina
  Abeshi Kobayashi
  Kenta Ishizaka
  Jueru Choden

Japanese logo/Cover design
  Eiichi Hagiwara (big body)

Supervising editor
  Ami Adachi

VOLUME 7
AFTERWORD

NORMALLY, I PUT SOME FORETHOUGHT
INTO WHAT I'M GOING TO WRITE ABOUT
IN THIS KIND OF SPACE, BUT THEN WHEN
I ACTUALLY GET TO WRITING, EITHER I
DON'T HAVE TIME OR I'M WRITING DURING
A BREAK FROM SOME OTHER WORK, SO
I DON'T REMEMBER WHAT I WANTED
TO WRITE ABOUT SO BADLY. OR IF I DO
REMEMBER, I CAN'T MANAGE TO CONVEY
IT VERY WELL. I THINK IT'S BEST TO WRITE
ABOUT RECENT EVENTS OR SOMETHING,
BUT ALL I DO IS DRAW MANGA ALL DAY,
AND THERE'S NOTHING INTERESTING TO
SAY ABOUT THAT. FOR THE PAST YEAR OR
SO, I'VE BEEN PRACTICING OUT-OF-BODY
EXPERIENCES, BUT THAT'S SORT OF
HARD TO EXPLAIN...

OH, THAT REMINDS ME! RECENTLY,
I'VE ACQUIRED AROUND 30 MILLION YEN
IN DEBT.
OOPS! OUT OF TIME.
BYE.

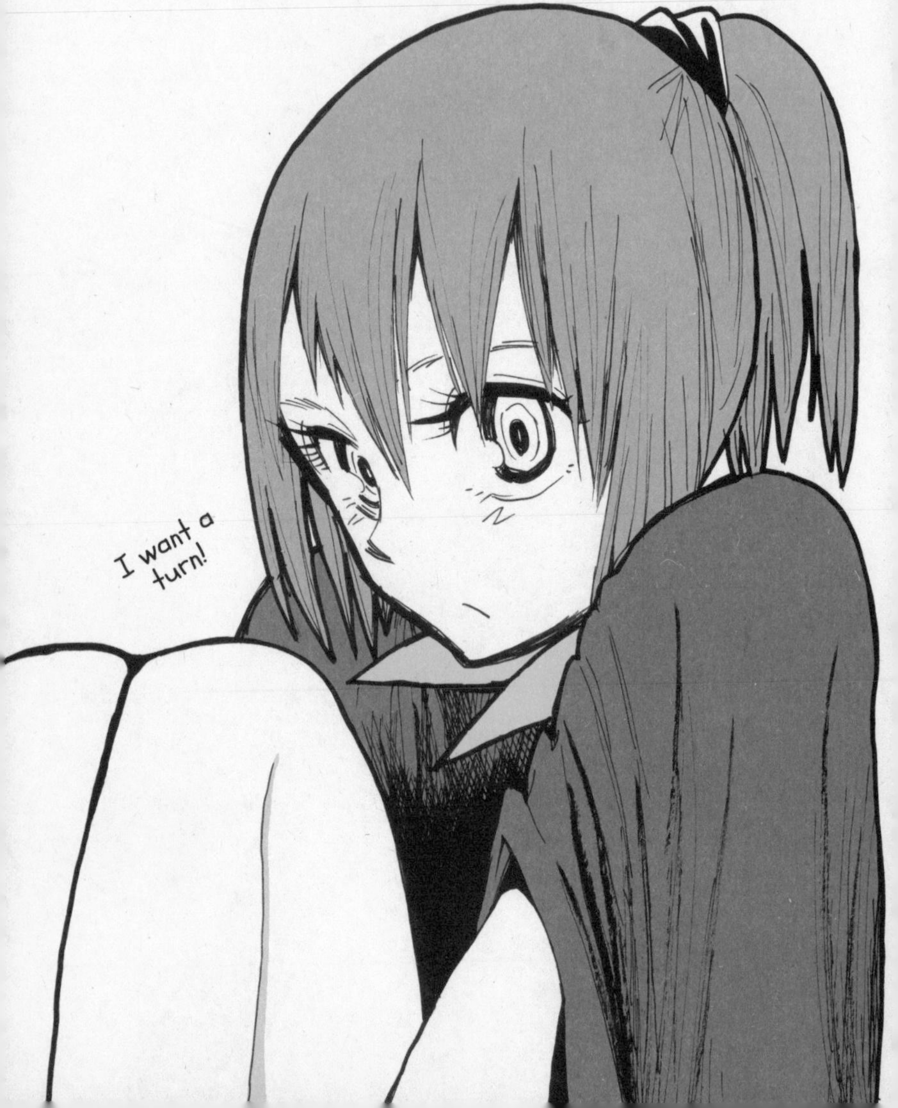
I want a turn!

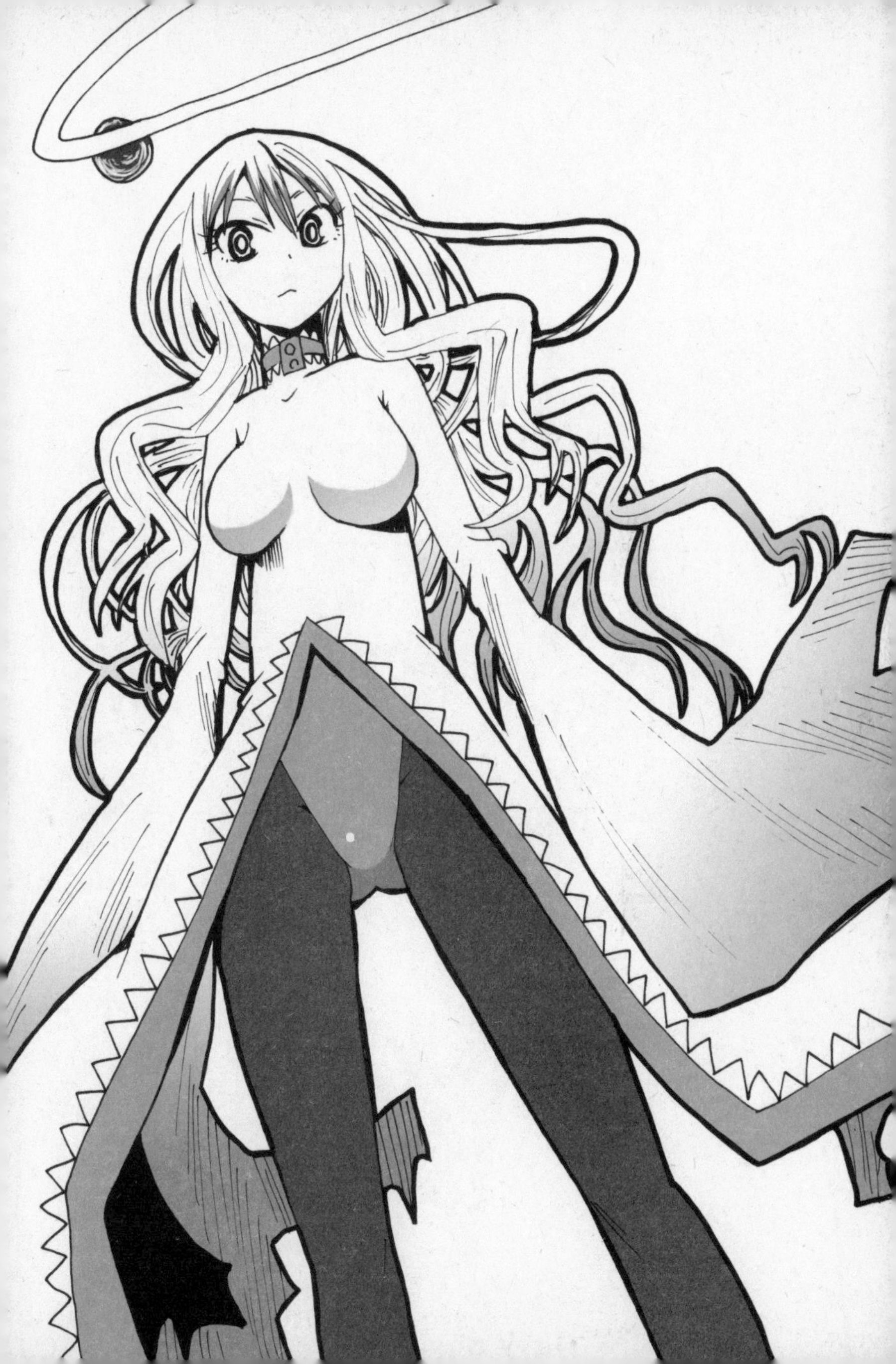

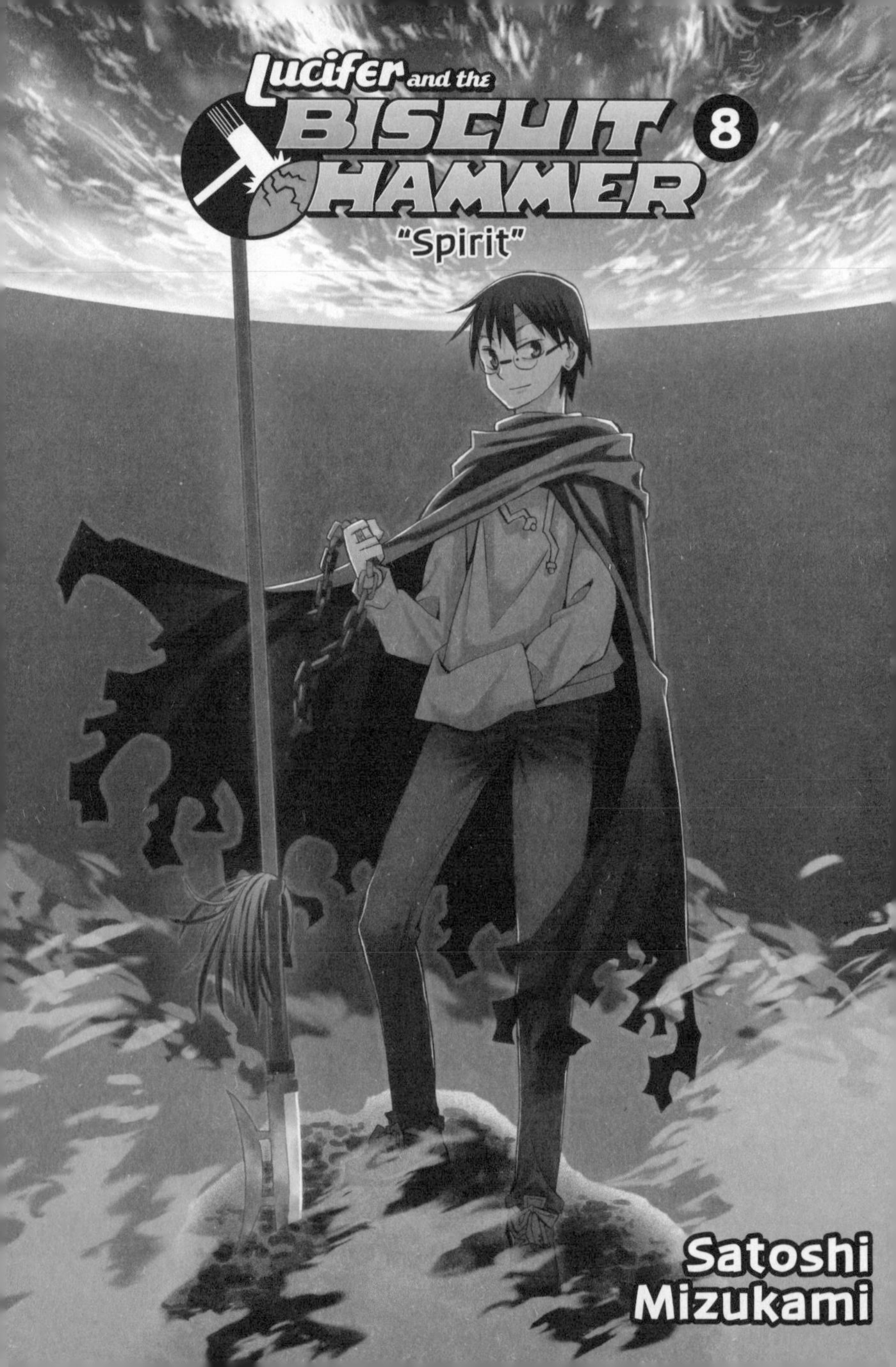
Lucifer and the
BISCUIT HAMMER
8
"Spirit"
Satoshi
Mizukami

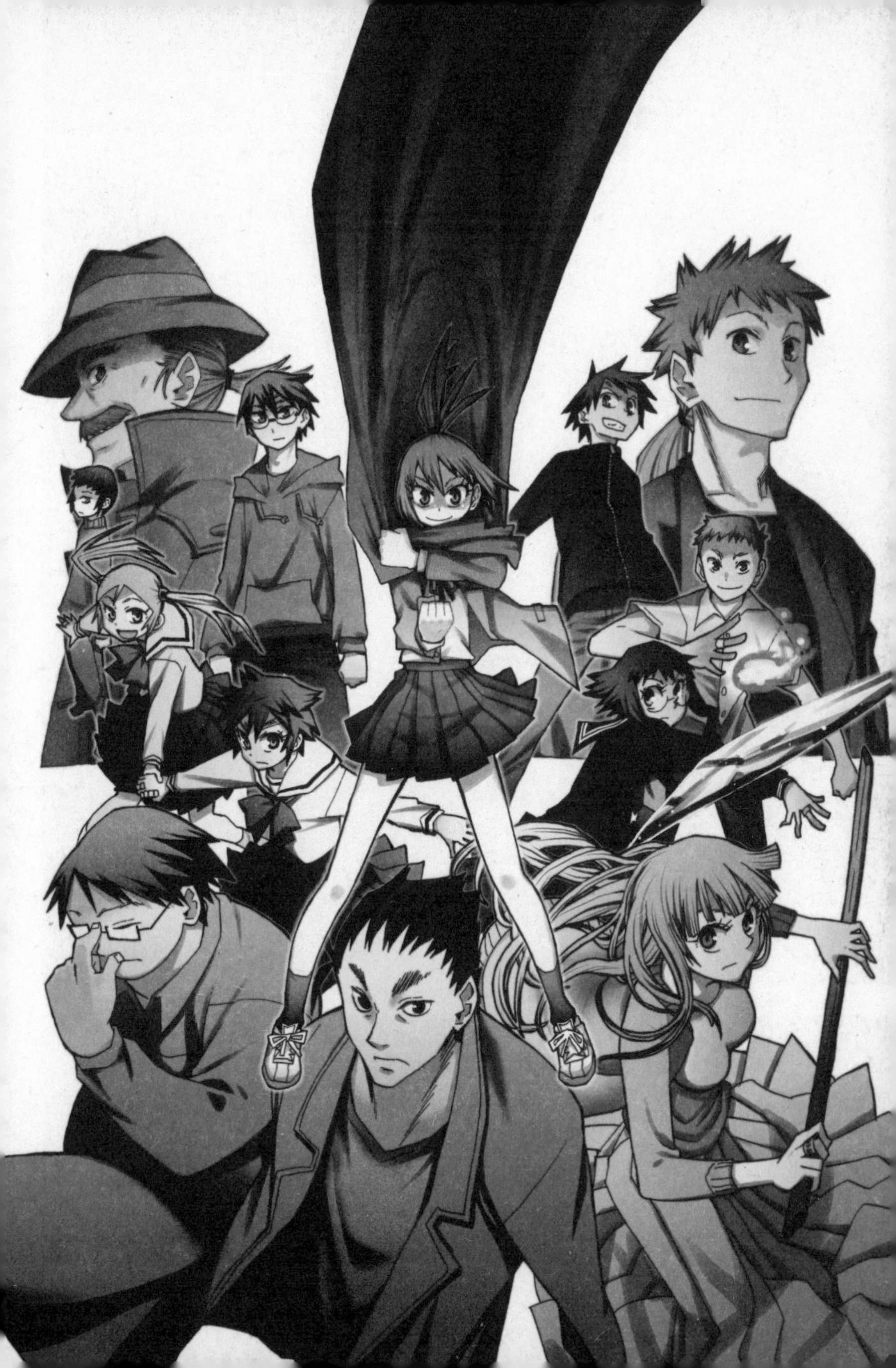

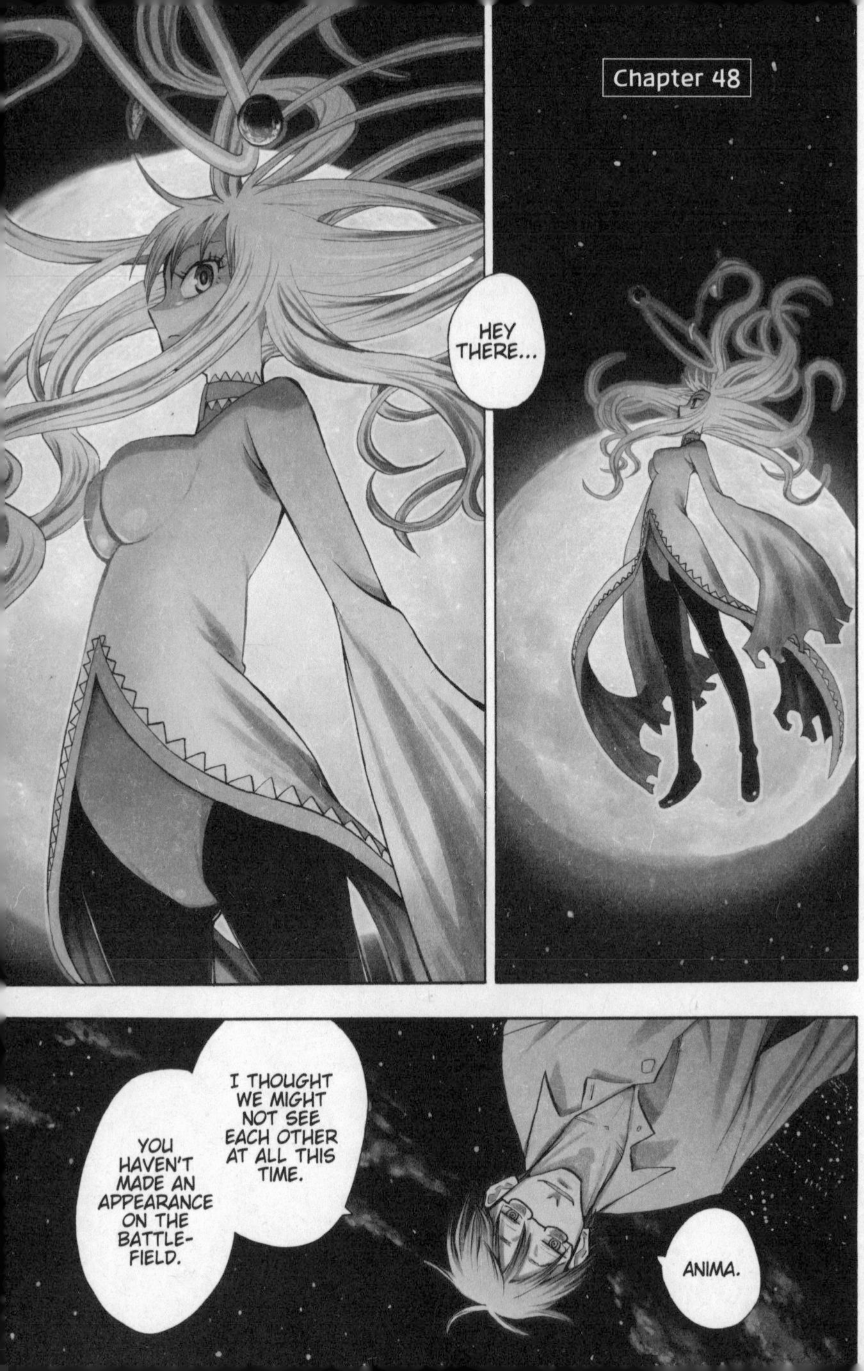
Chapter 48
HEY THERE...
ANIMA.
I THOUGHT WE MIGHT NOT SEE EACH OTHER AT ALL THIS TIME.
YOU HAVEN'T MADE AN APPEARANCE ON THE BATTLE-FIELD.

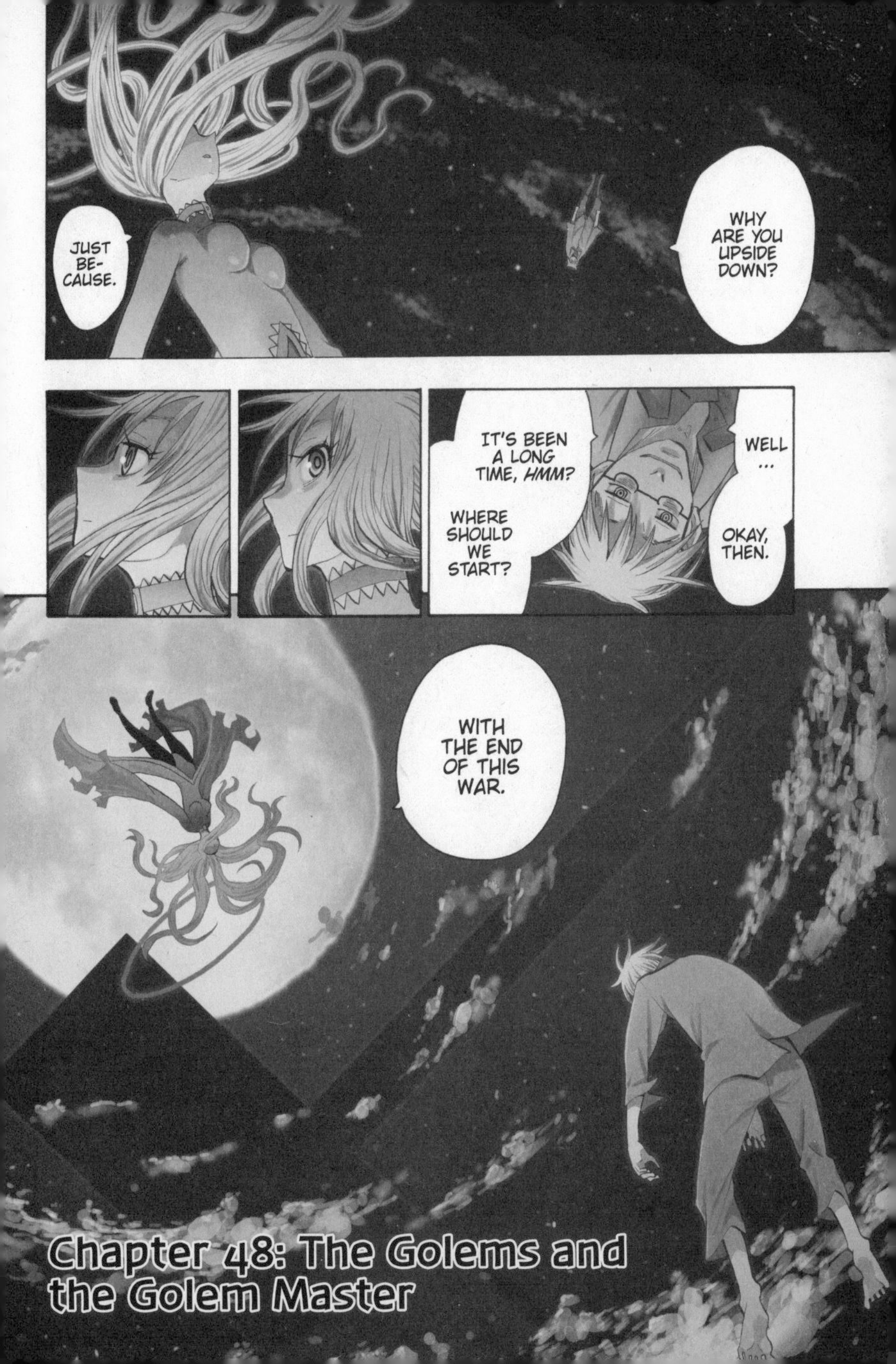
WHY ARE YOU UPSIDE DOWN?
JUST BE-CAUSE.
WELL ... OKAY, THEN.
IT'S BEEN A LONG TIME, *HMM*? WHERE SHOULD WE START?
WITH THE END OF THIS WAR.

Chapter 48: The Golems and the Golem Master

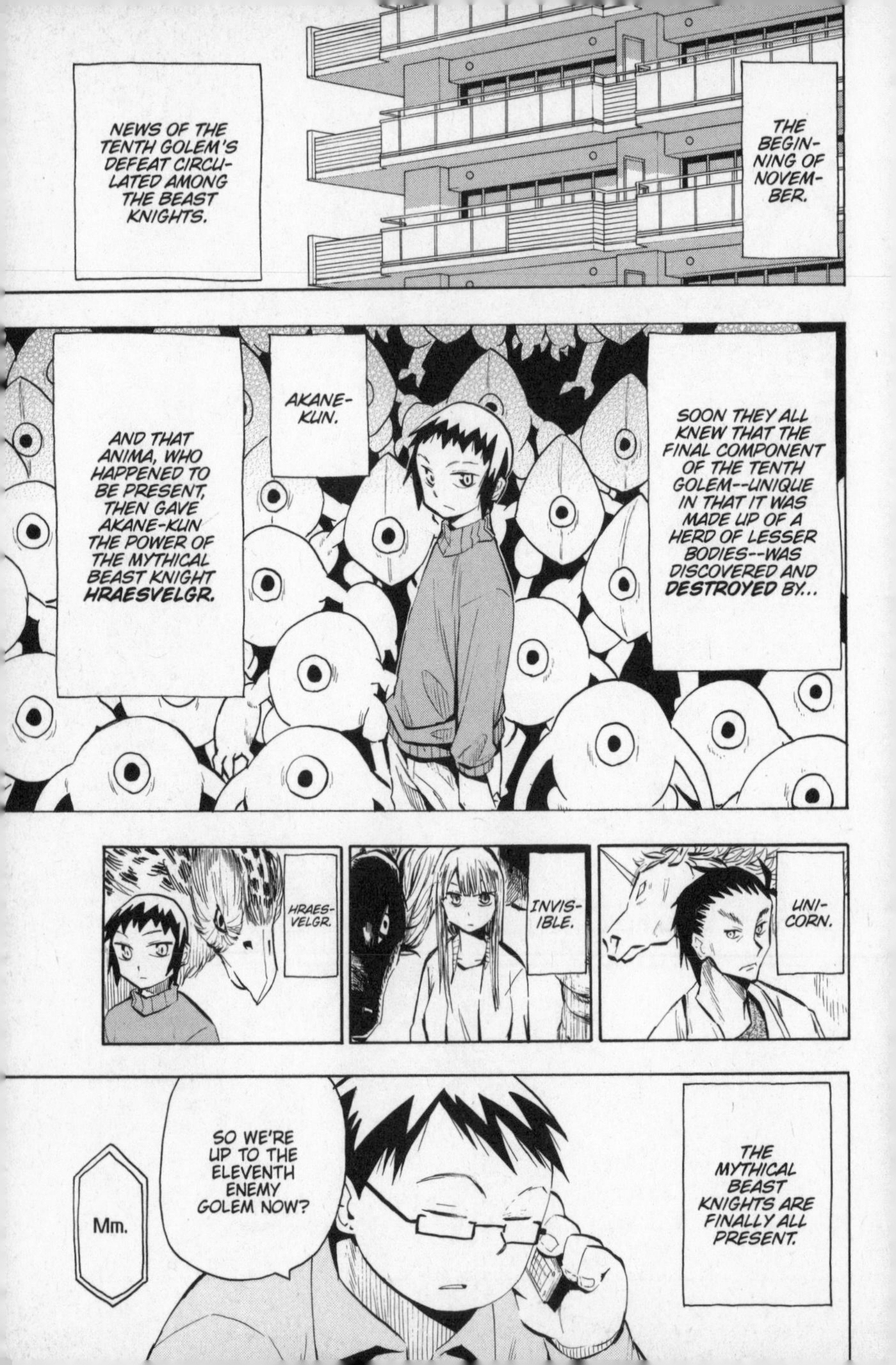

THE BEGINNING OF NOVEMBER.
NEWS OF THE TENTH GOLEM'S DEFEAT CIRCULATED AMONG THE BEAST KNIGHTS.
SOON THEY ALL KNEW THAT THE FINAL COMPONENT OF THE TENTH GOLEM--UNIQUE IN THAT IT WAS MADE UP OF A HERD OF LESSER BODIES--WAS DISCOVERED AND DESTROYED BY...
AKANE-KUN.
AND THAT ANIMA, WHO HAPPENED TO BE PRESENT, THEN GAVE AKANE-KUN THE POWER OF THE MYTHICAL BEAST KNIGHT HRAESVELGR.
UNICORN.
INVISIBLE.
HRAESVELGR.
THE MYTHICAL BEAST KNIGHTS ARE FINALLY ALL PRESENT.
SO WE'RE UP TO THE ELEVENTH ENEMY GOLEM NOW?
Mm.

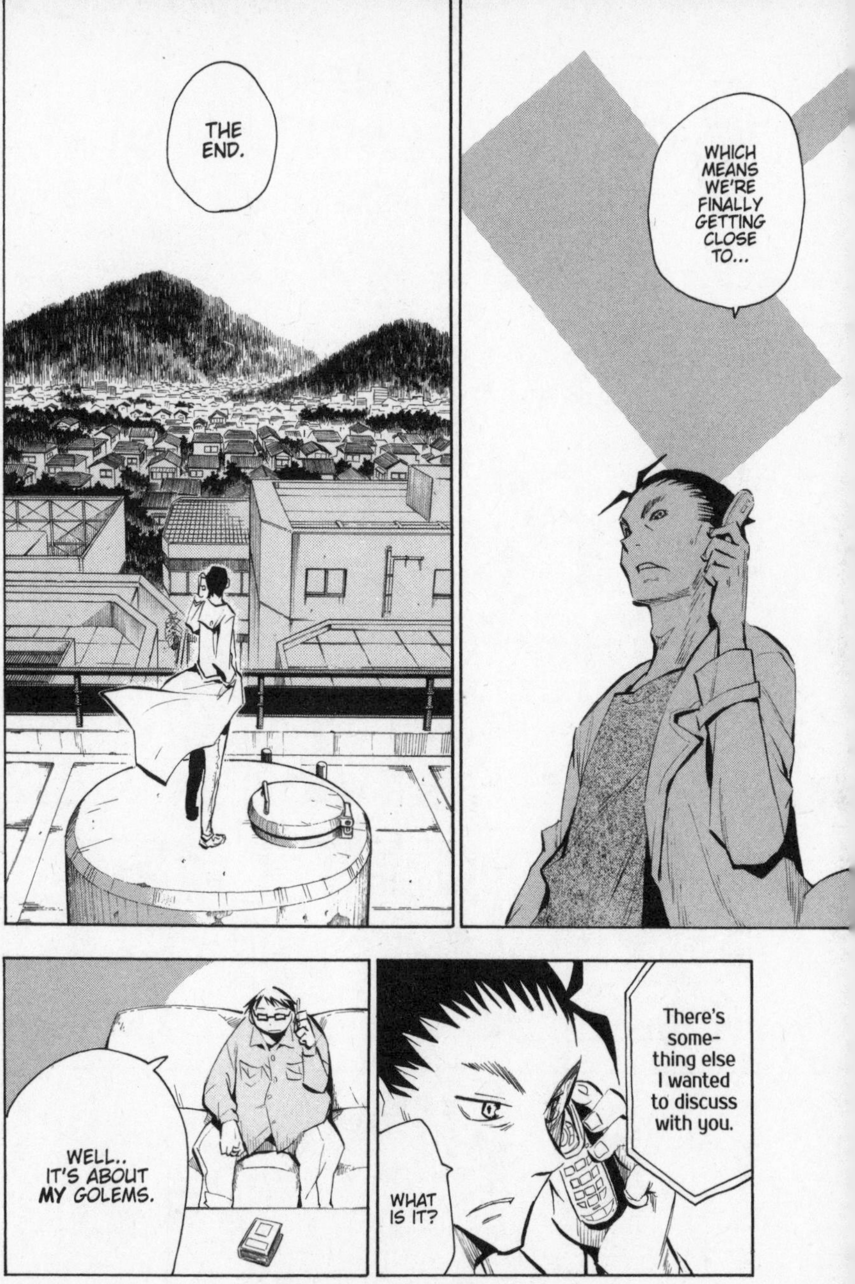
WHICH MEANS WE'RE FINALLY GETTING CLOSE TO...
THE END.
There's something else I wanted to discuss with you.
WHAT IS IT?
WELL.. IT'S ABOUT MY GOLEMS.

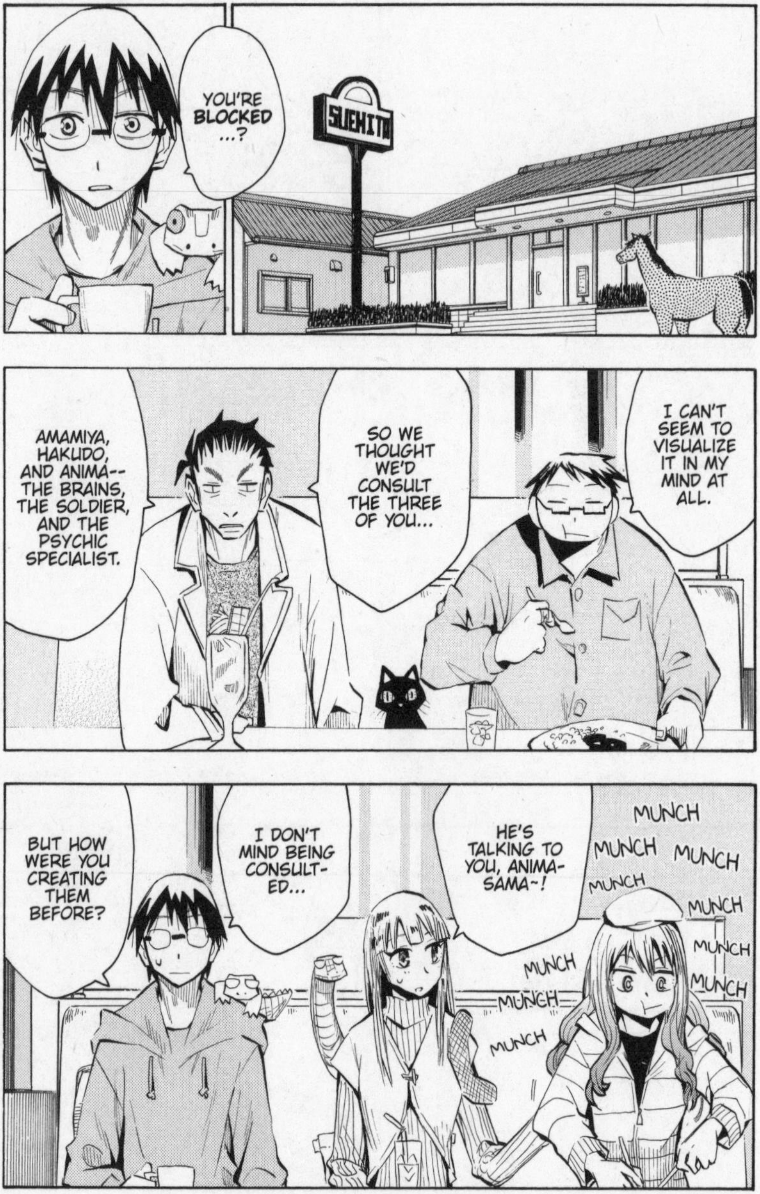
SUEHITO
YOU'RE BLOCKED ...?
I CAN'T SEEM TO VISUALIZE IT IN MY MIND AT ALL.
SO WE THOUGHT WE'D CONSULT THE THREE OF YOU...
AMAMIYA, HAKUDO, AND ANIMA-- THE BRAINS, THE SOLDIER, AND THE PSYCHIC SPECIALIST.
MUNCH MUNCH MUNCH MUNCH MUNCH MUNCH MUNCH MUNCH MUNCH MUNCH
HE'S TALKING TO YOU, ANIMA-SAMA~!
I DON'T MIND BEING CONSULT-ED...
BUT HOW WERE YOU CREATING THEM BEFORE?

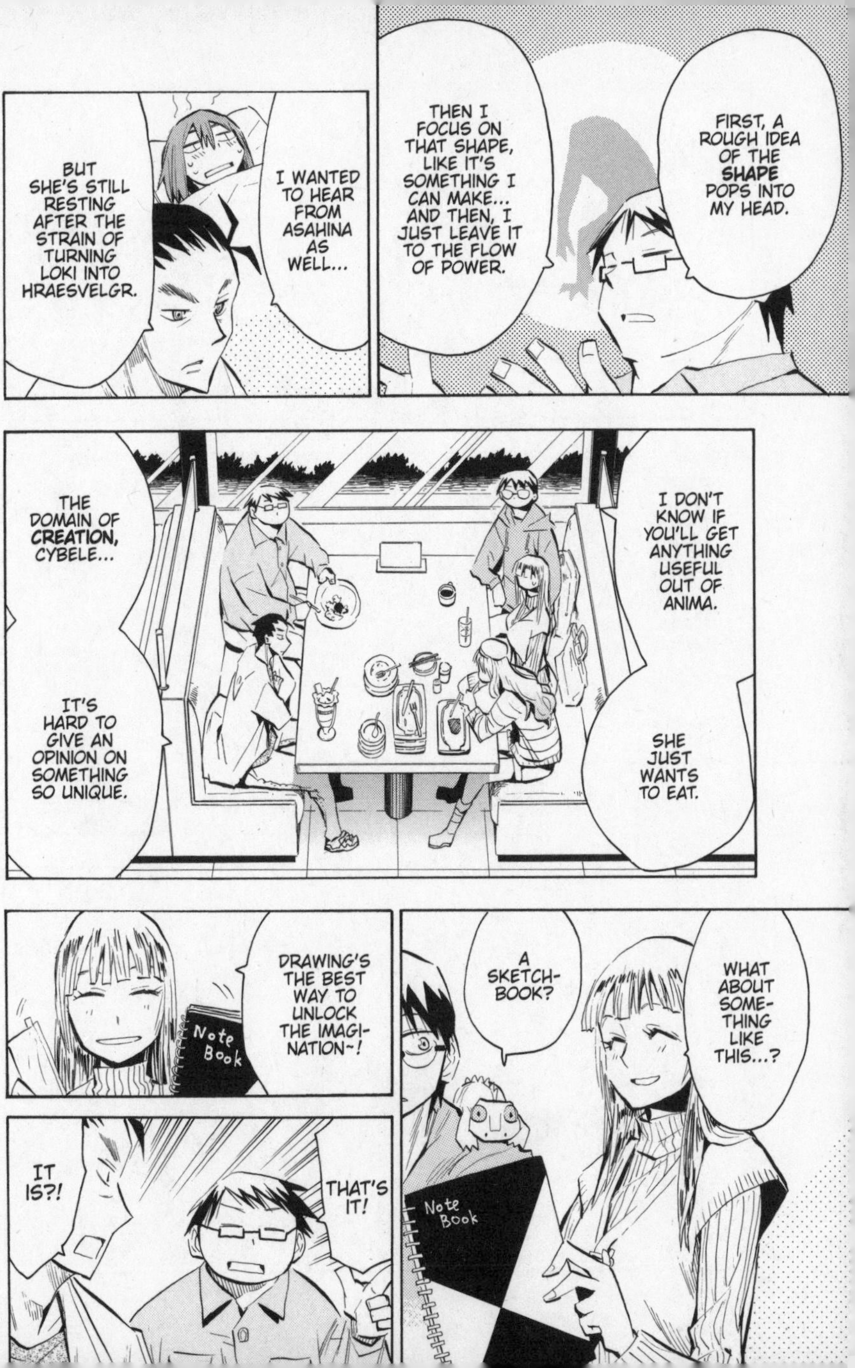

FIRST, A ROUGH IDEA OF THE **SHAPE** POPS INTO MY HEAD.
THEN I FOCUS ON THAT SHAPE, LIKE IT'S SOMETHING I CAN MAKE... AND THEN, I JUST LEAVE IT TO THE FLOW OF POWER.
I WANTED TO HEAR FROM ASAHINA AS WELL...
BUT SHE'S STILL RESTING AFTER THE STRAIN OF TURNING LOKI INTO HRAESVELGR.
I DON'T KNOW IF YOU'LL GET ANYTHING USEFUL OUT OF ANIMA.
SHE JUST WANTS TO EAT.
THE DOMAIN OF **CREATION,** CYBELE...
IT'S HARD TO GIVE AN OPINION ON SOMETHING SO UNIQUE.
WHAT ABOUT SOMETHING LIKE THIS...?
A SKETCH-BOOK?
Note Book
DRAWING'S THE BEST WAY TO UNLOCK THE IMAGI-NATION~!
Note Book
THAT'S IT!
IT IS?!

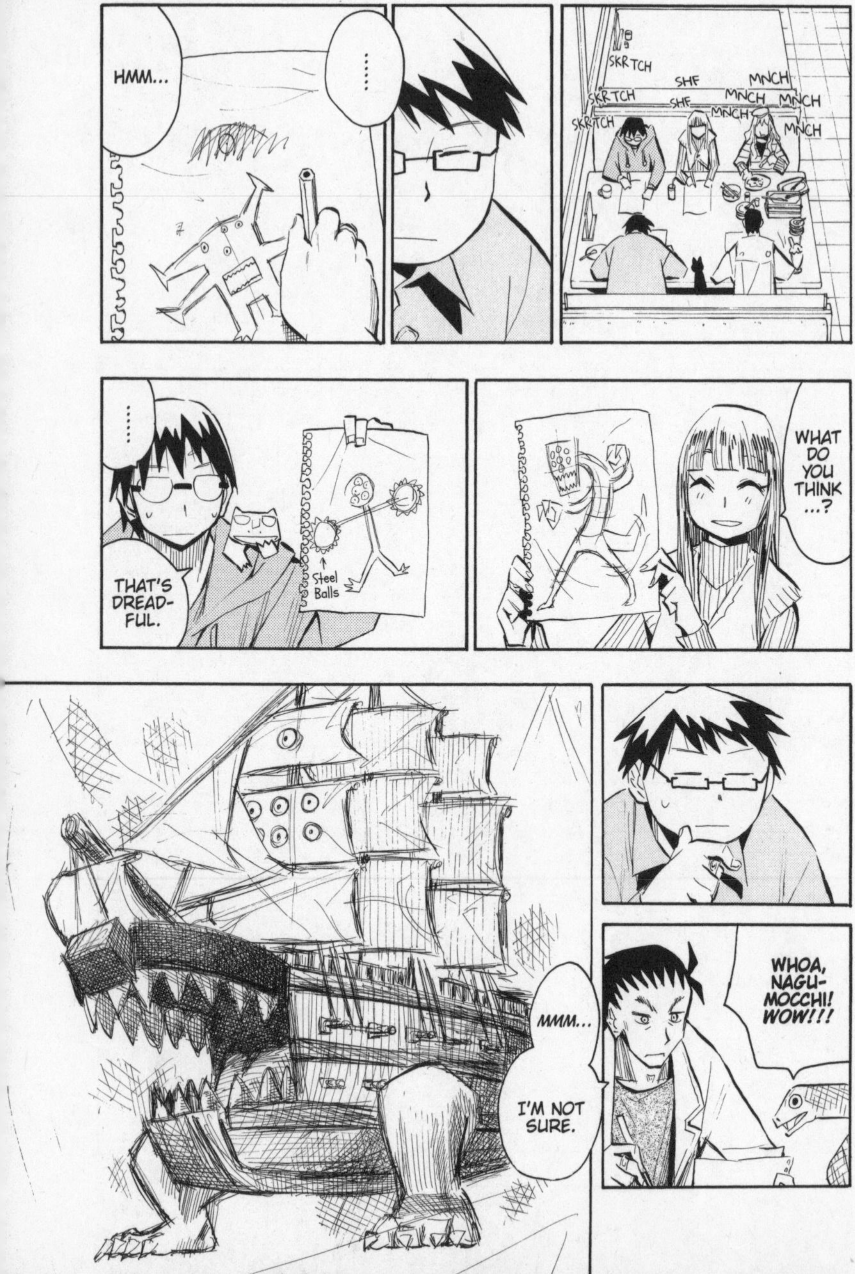

SKRTCH
SKRTCH
SKRTCH
SHF
SHF
MNCH
MNCH
MNCH
MNCH
MNCH
......
HMM...
WHAT DO YOU THINK ...?
......
Steel Balls
THAT'S DREAD-FUL.
WHOA, NAGU-MOCCHI! WOW!!!
MMM...
I'M NOT SURE.

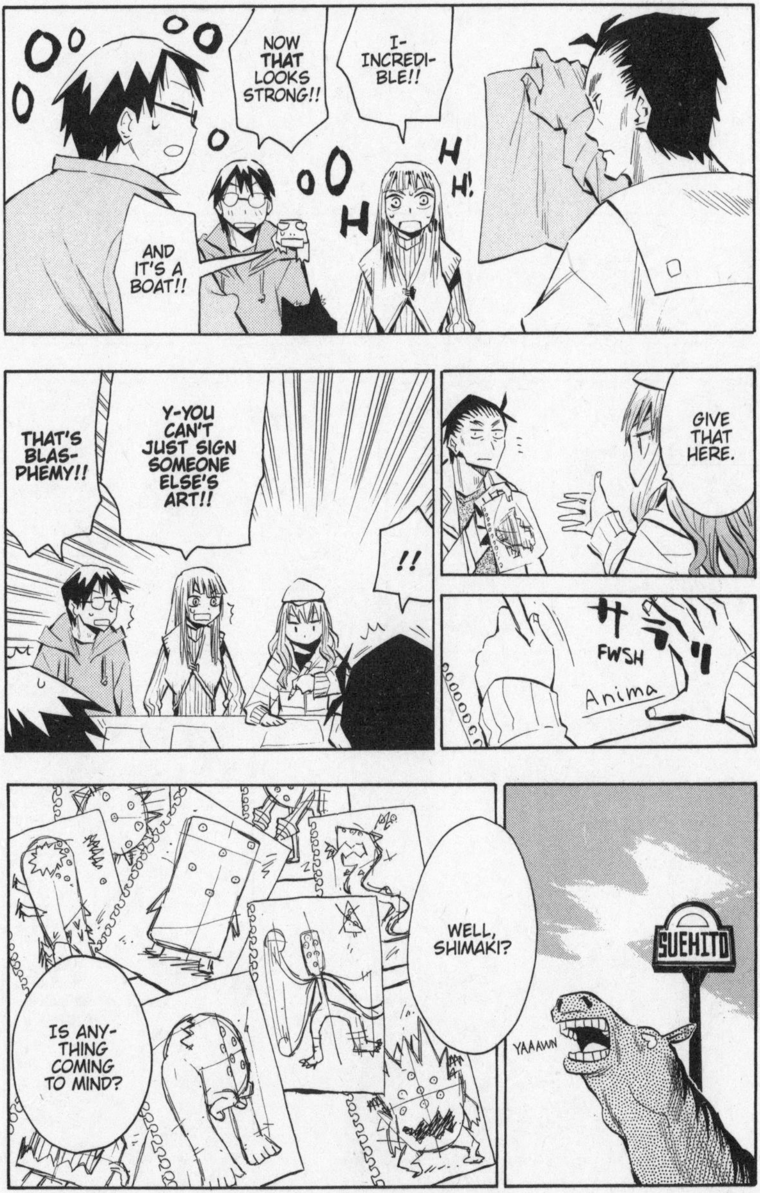
I- INCREDIBLE!!
NOW THAT LOOKS STRONG!!
AND IT'S A BOAT!!
GIVE THAT HERE.
サラッ
FWSH
Anima
!!
Y-YOU CAN'T JUST SIGN SOMEONE ELSE'S ART!!
THAT'S BLASPHEMY!!
SUEHITO
YAAAWN
WELL, SHIMAKI?
IS ANYTHING COMING TO MIND?

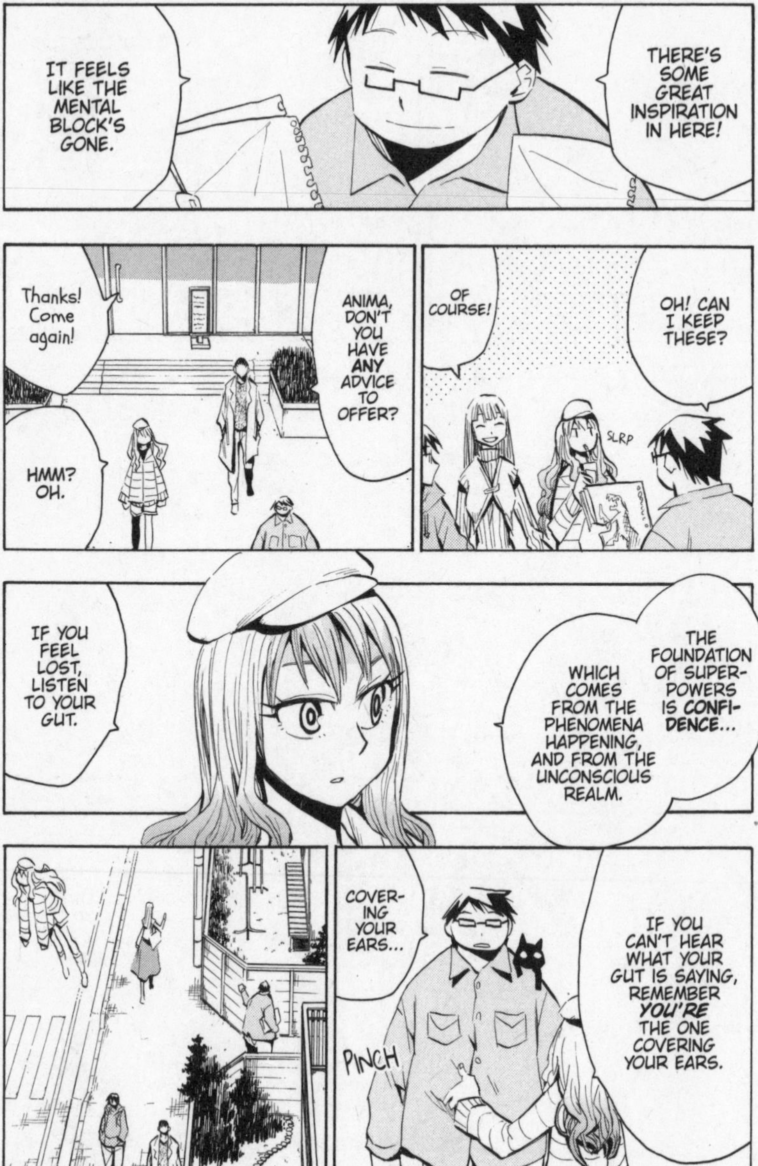
THERE'S SOME GREAT INSPIRATION IN HERE!
IT FEELS LIKE THE MENTAL BLOCK'S GONE.
OH! CAN I KEEP THESE?
OF COURSE!
SLRP
ANIMA, DON'T YOU HAVE ANY ADVICE TO OFFER?
Thanks! Come again!
HMM? OH.
THE FOUNDATION OF SUPER-POWERS IS CONFIDENCE...
WHICH COMES FROM THE PHENOMENA HAPPENING, AND FROM THE UNCONSCIOUS REALM.
IF YOU FEEL LOST, LISTEN TO YOUR GUT.
IF YOU CAN'T HEAR WHAT YOUR GUT IS SAYING, REMEMBER YOU'RE THE ONE COVERING YOUR EARS.
COVERING YOUR EARS...
PINCH

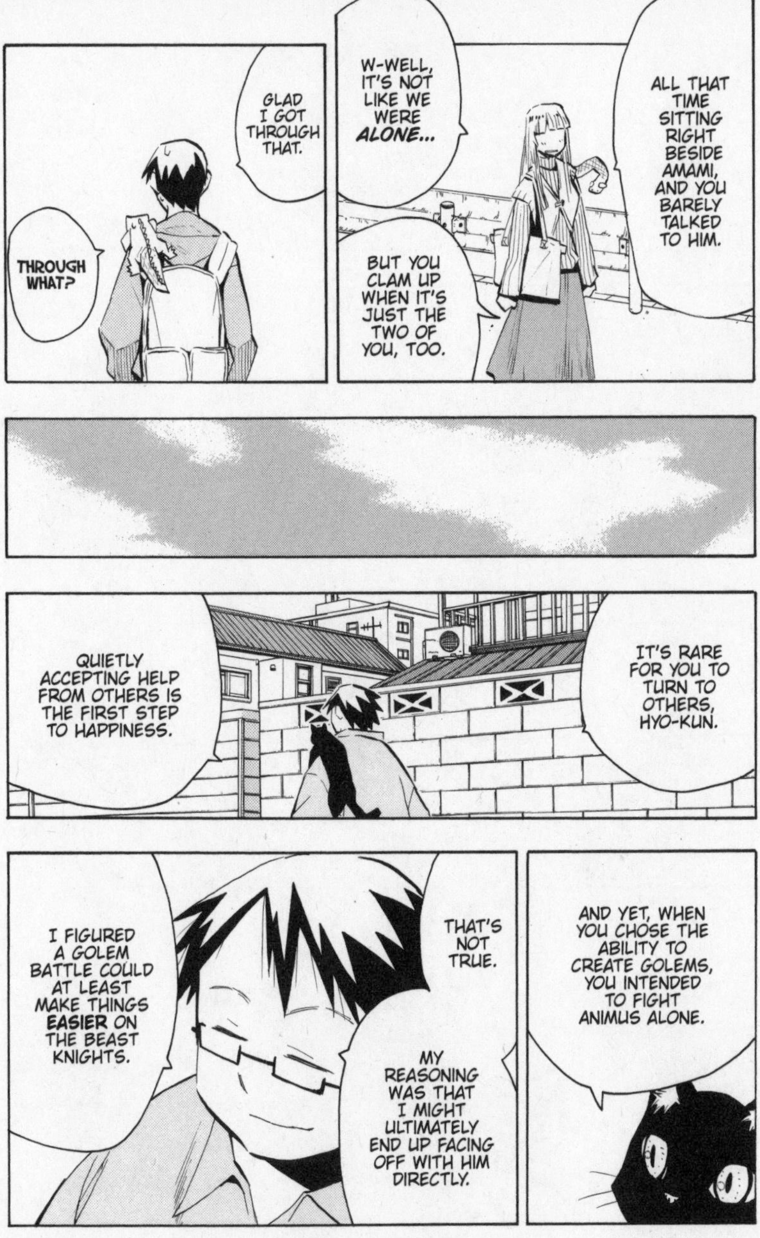
ALL THAT TIME SITTING RIGHT BESIDE AMAMI, AND YOU BARELY TALKED TO HIM.
W-WELL, IT'S NOT LIKE WE WERE **ALONE...**
BUT YOU CLAM UP WHEN IT'S JUST THE TWO OF YOU, TOO.
GLAD I GOT THROUGH THAT.
THROUGH WHAT?
IT'S RARE FOR YOU TO TURN TO OTHERS, HYO-KUN.
QUIETLY ACCEPTING HELP FROM OTHERS IS THE FIRST STEP TO HAPPINESS.
AND YET, WHEN YOU CHOSE THE ABILITY TO CREATE GOLEMS, YOU INTENDED TO FIGHT ANIMUS ALONE.
THAT'S NOT TRUE.
I FIGURED A GOLEM BATTLE COULD AT LEAST MAKE THINGS **EASIER** ON THE BEAST KNIGHTS.
MY REASONING WAS THAT I MIGHT ULTIMATELY END UP FACING OFF WITH HIM DIRECTLY.

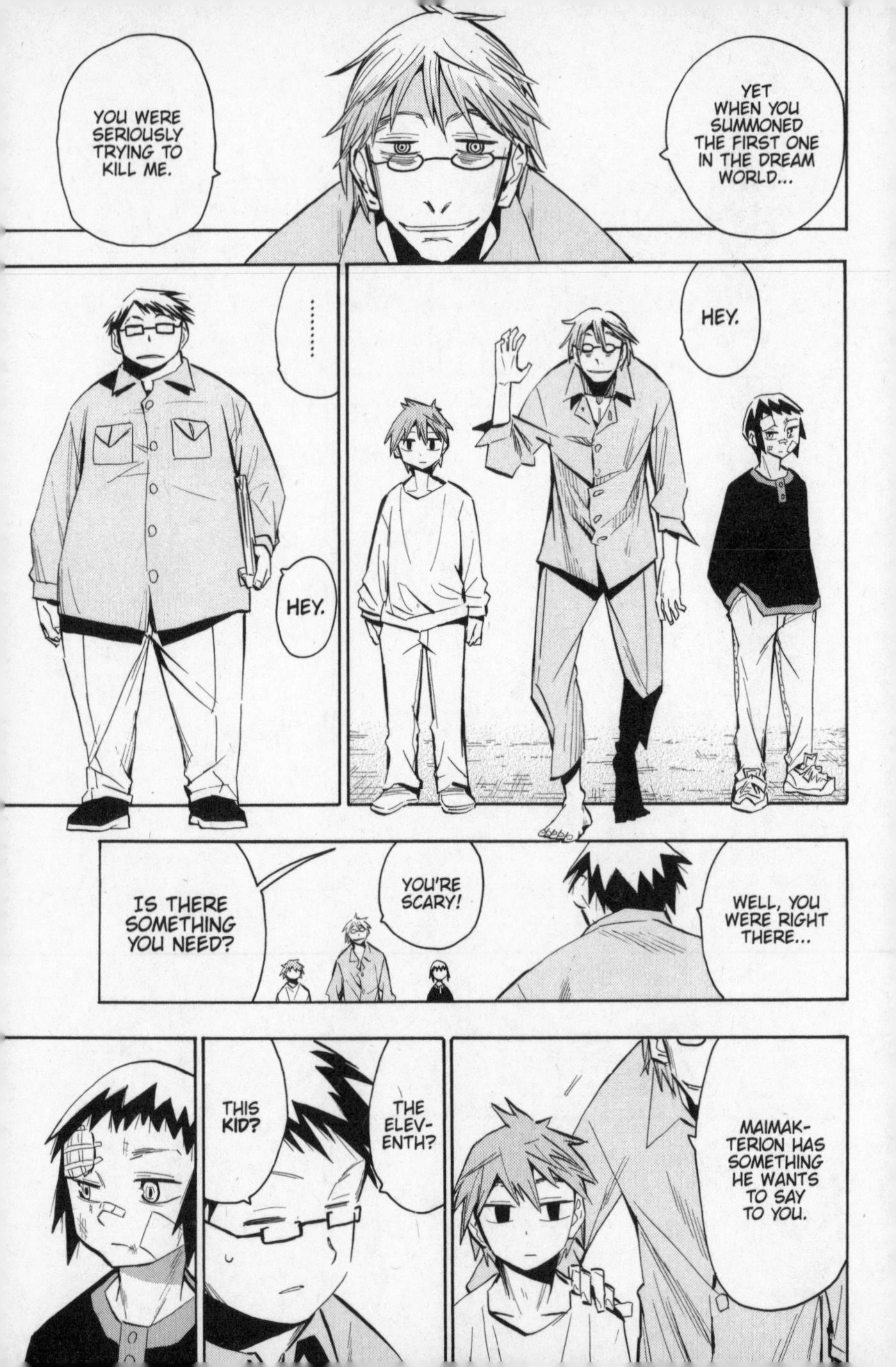
YET WHEN YOU SUMMONED THE FIRST ONE IN THE DREAM WORLD...
YOU WERE SERIOUSLY TRYING TO KILL ME.
HEY.
......
HEY.
WELL, YOU WERE RIGHT THERE...
YOU'RE SCARY!
IS THERE SOMETHING YOU NEED?
MAIMAKTERION HAS SOMETHING HE WANTS TO SAY TO YOU.
THE ELEVENTH?
THIS KID?

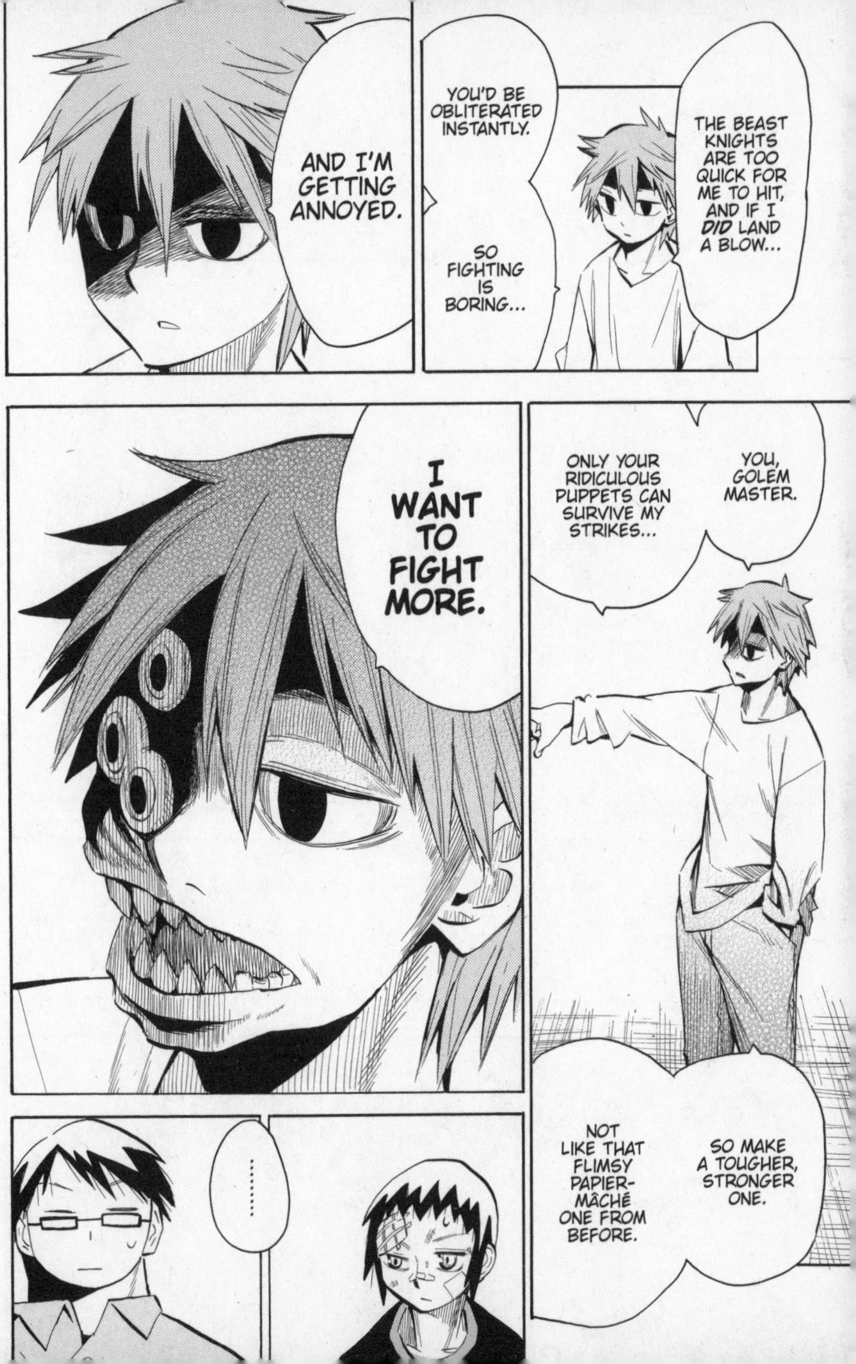

THE BEAST KNIGHTS ARE TOO QUICK FOR ME TO HIT, AND IF I *DID* LAND A BLOW...
YOU'D BE OBLITERATED INSTANTLY.
SO FIGHTING IS BORING...
AND I'M GETTING ANNOYED.
YOU, GOLEM MASTER.
ONLY YOUR RIDICULOUS PUPPETS CAN SURVIVE MY STRIKES...
SO MAKE A TOUGHER, STRONGER ONE.
NOT LIKE THAT FLIMSY PAPIER-MÂCHÉ ONE FROM BEFORE.
I WANT TO FIGHT MORE.
....

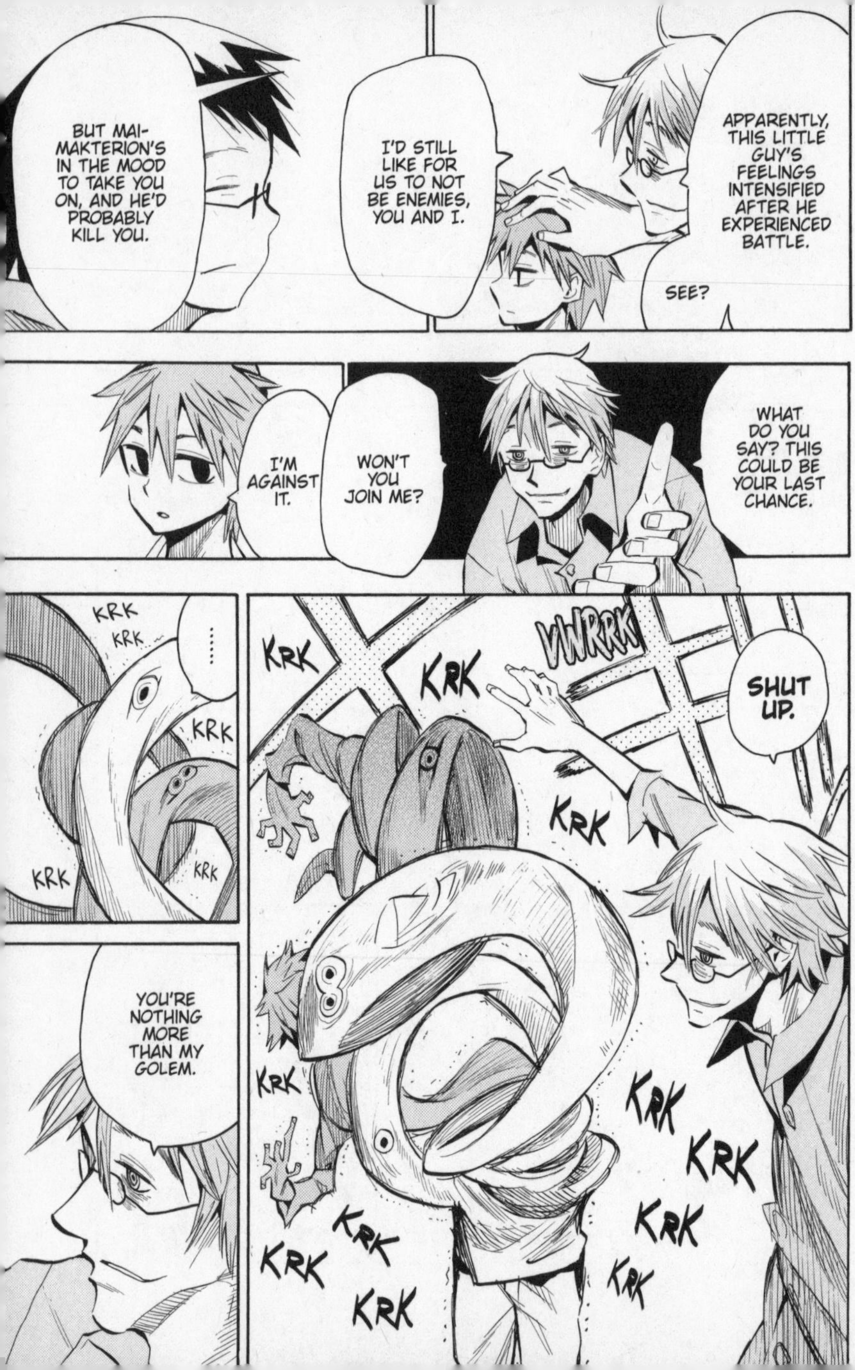
APPARENTLY, THIS LITTLE GUY'S FEELINGS INTENSIFIED AFTER HE EXPERIENCED BATTLE.
SEE?
I'D STILL LIKE FOR US TO NOT BE ENEMIES, YOU AND I.
BUT MAI-MAKTERION'S IN THE MOOD TO TAKE YOU ON, AND HE'D PROBABLY KILL YOU.
WHAT DO YOU SAY? THIS COULD BE YOUR LAST CHANCE.
WON'T YOU JOIN ME?
I'M AGAINST IT.
VWRRK
SHUT UP.
KRK
KRK
KRK
KRK
KRK
KRK
KRK
KRK
KRK
KRK
KRK
......
KRK
KRK
KRK
KRK
KRK
YOU'RE NOTHING MORE THAN MY GOLEM.

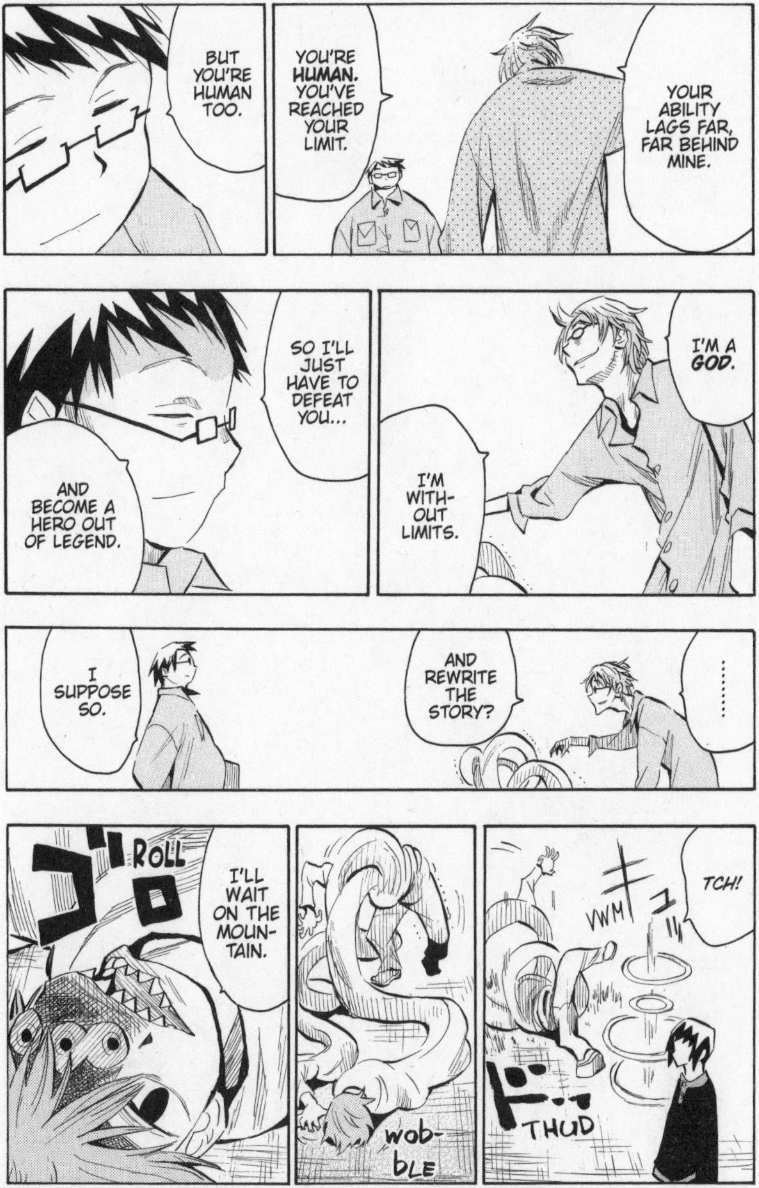
YOUR ABILITY LAGS FAR, FAR BEHIND MINE.
YOU'RE **HUMAN.** YOU'VE REACHED YOUR LIMIT.
BUT YOU'RE HUMAN TOO.
I'M A ***GOD.***
I'M WITH-OUT LIMITS.
SO I'LL JUST HAVE TO DEFEAT YOU...
AND BECOME A HERO OUT OF LEGEND.
......
AND REWRITE THE STORY?
I SUPPOSE SO.
TCH!
VWM
THUD
wob-bLE
I'LL WAIT ON THE MOUN-TAIN.
ROLL

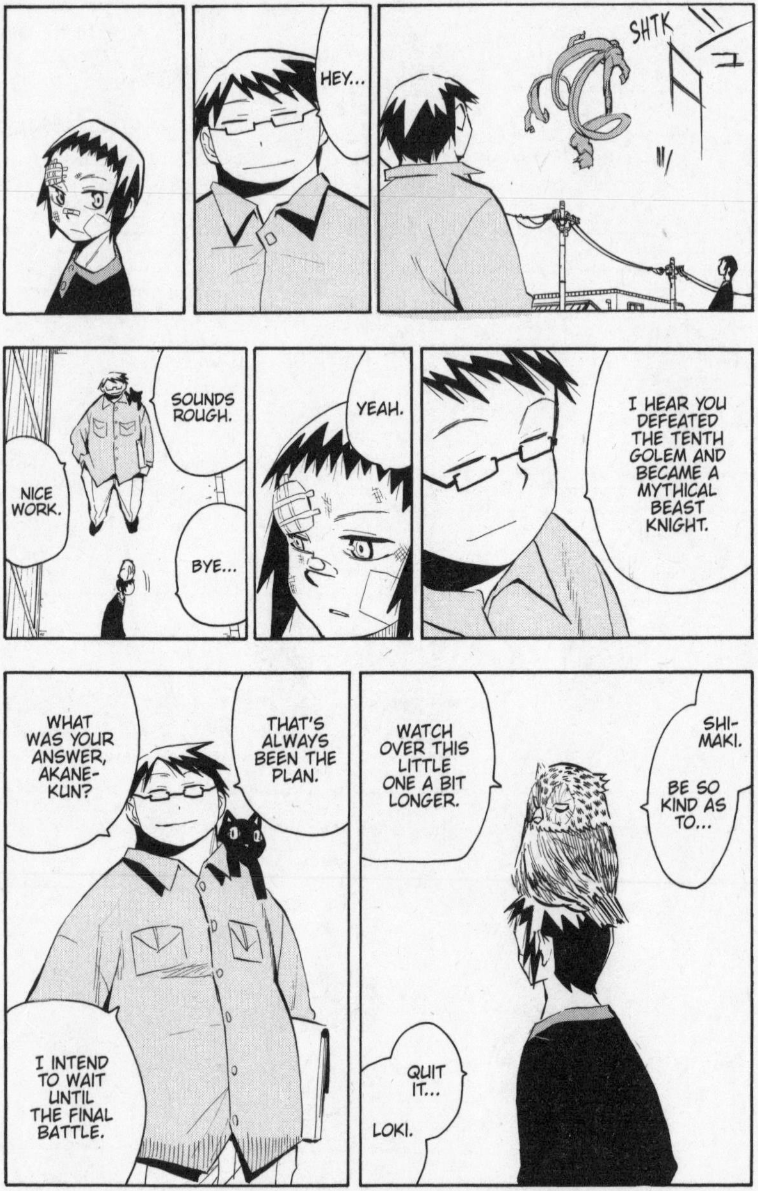
SHTK
HEY...
I HEAR YOU DEFEATED THE TENTH GOLEM AND BECAME A MYTHICAL BEAST KNIGHT.
YEAH.
SOUNDS ROUGH.
NICE WORK.
BYE...
SHI-MAKI.
BE SO KIND AS TO...
WATCH OVER THIS LITTLE ONE A BIT LONGER.
QUIT IT...
LOKI.
THAT'S ALWAYS BEEN THE PLAN.
WHAT WAS YOUR ANSWER, AKANE-KUN?
I INTEND TO WAIT UNTIL THE FINAL BATTLE.

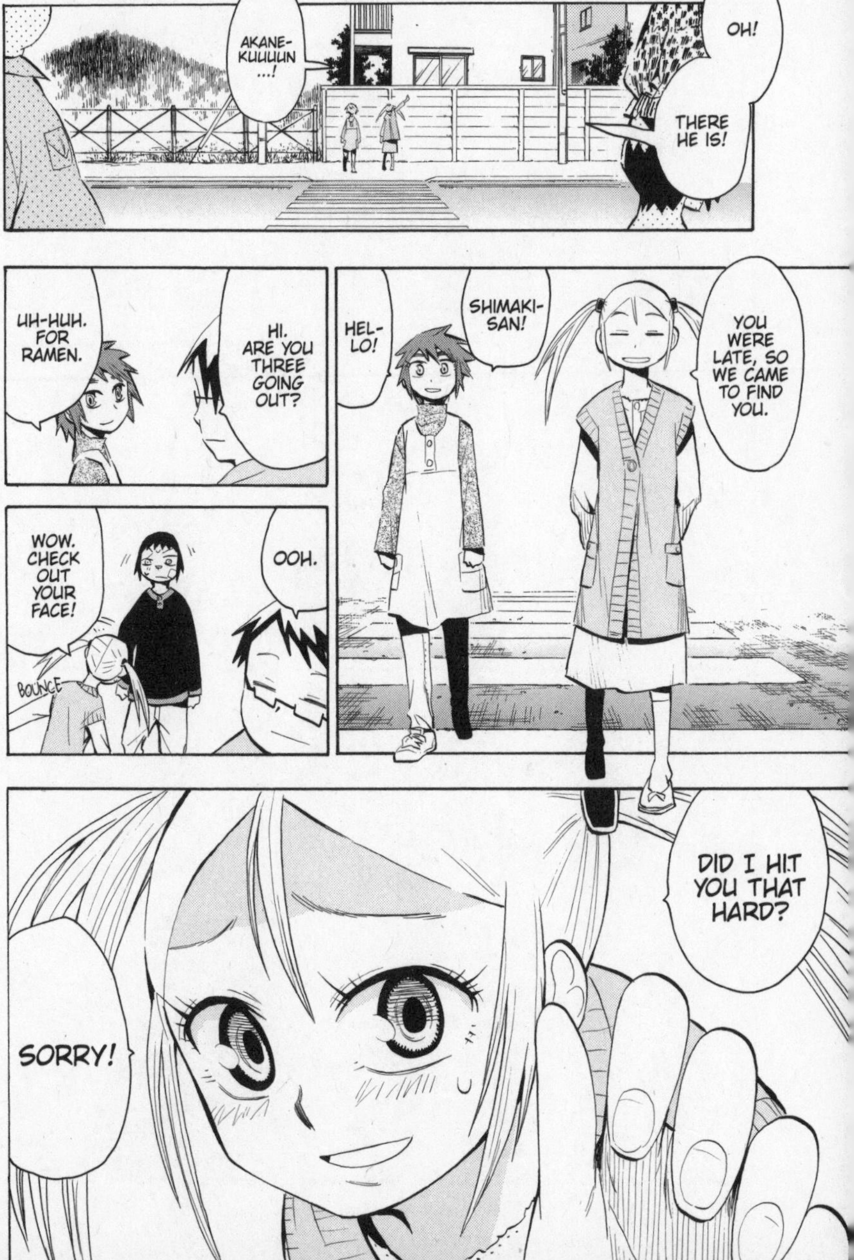
OH!
THERE HE IS!
AKANE-KUUUUN...!
YOU WERE LATE, SO WE CAME TO FIND YOU.
SHIMAKI-SAN!
HEL-LO!
HI. ARE YOU THREE GOING OUT?
UH-HUH. FOR RAMEN.
OOH.
WOW. CHECK OUT YOUR FACE!
BOUNCE
DID I HIT YOU THAT HARD?
SORRY!

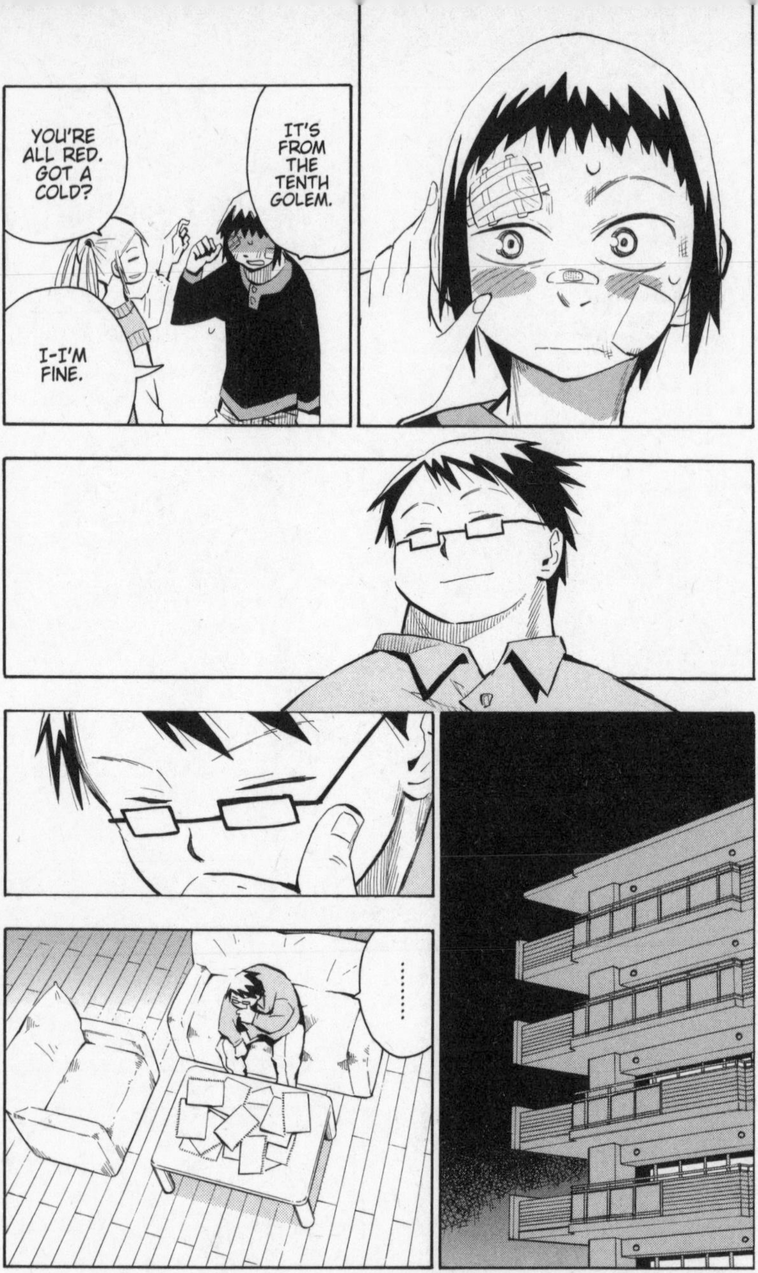
IT'S FROM THE TENTH GOLEM.
YOU'RE ALL RED. GOT A COLD?
I-I'M FINE.
......

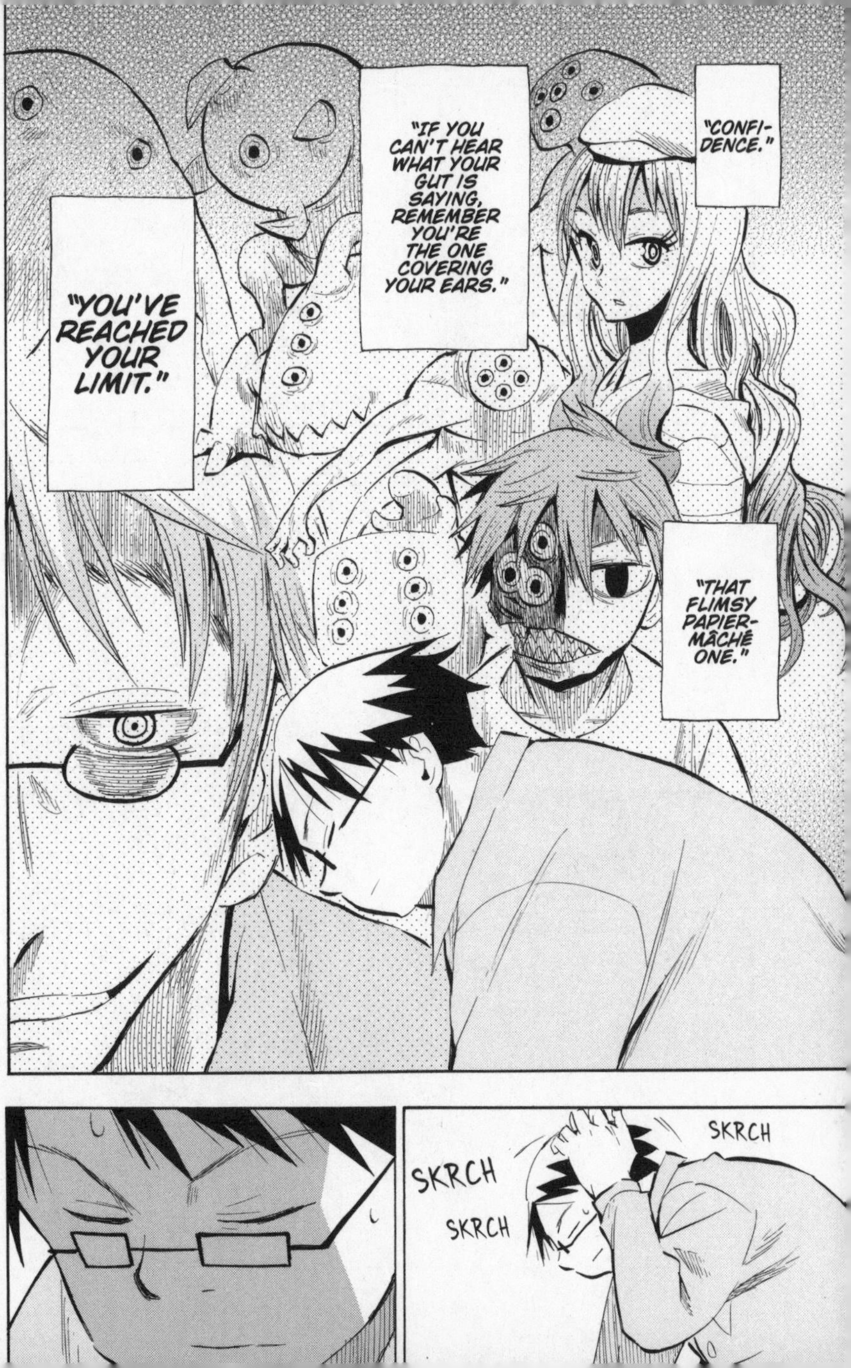
"CONFI-DENCE."
"IF YOU CAN'T HEAR WHAT YOUR GUT IS SAYING, REMEMBER YOU'RE THE ONE COVERING YOUR EARS."
"YOU'VE REACHED YOUR LIMIT."
"THAT FLIMSY PAPIER-MÂCHÉ ONE."
SKRCH
SKRCH
SKRCH

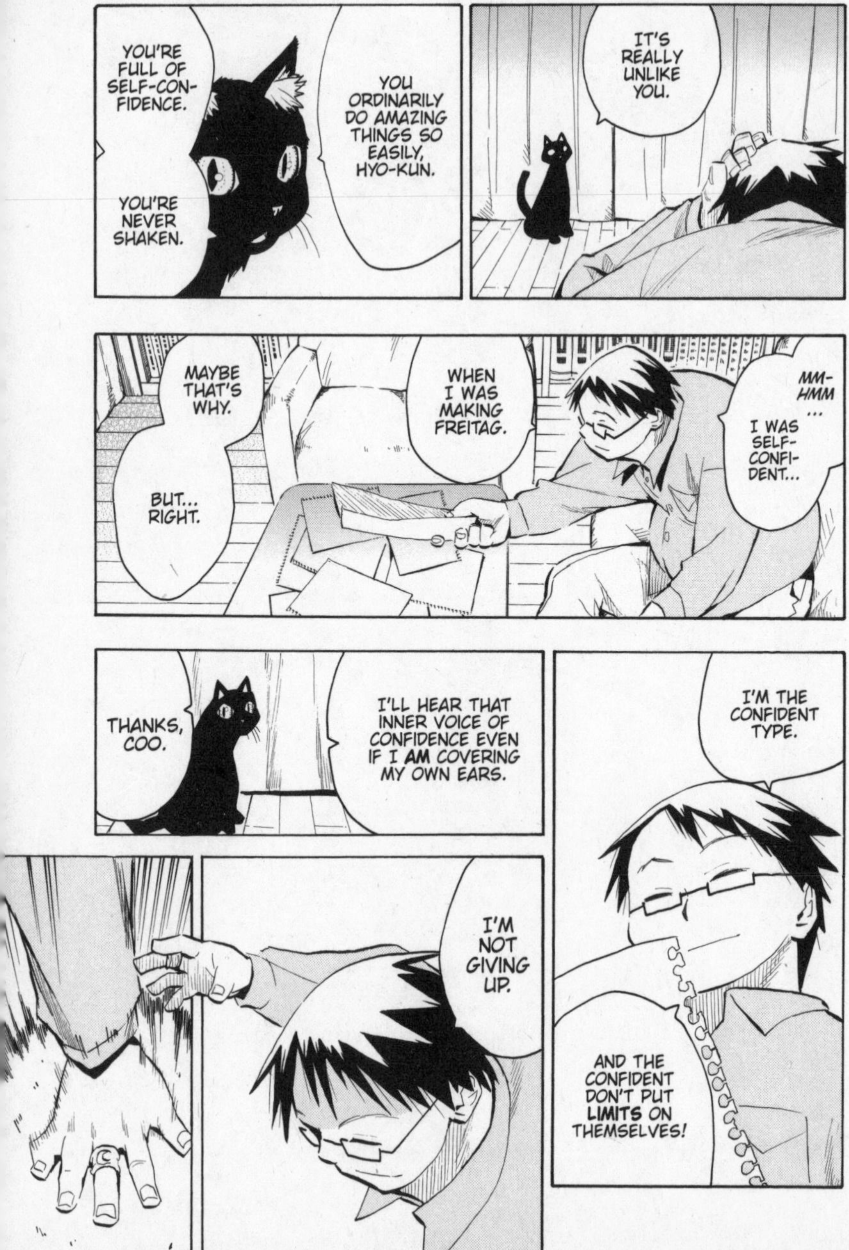
IT'S REALLY UNLIKE YOU.
YOU ORDINARILY DO AMAZING THINGS SO EASILY, HYO-KUN.
YOU'RE FULL OF SELF-CONFIDENCE.
YOU'RE NEVER SHAKEN.
MM-HMM... I WAS SELF-CONFIDENT...
WHEN I WAS MAKING FREITAG.
MAYBE THAT'S WHY.
BUT... RIGHT.
I'M THE CONFIDENT TYPE.
AND THE CONFIDENT DON'T PUT LIMITS ON THEMSELVES!
I'LL HEAR THAT INNER VOICE OF CONFIDENCE EVEN IF I AM COVERING MY OWN EARS.
THANKS, COO.
I'M NOT GIVING UP.

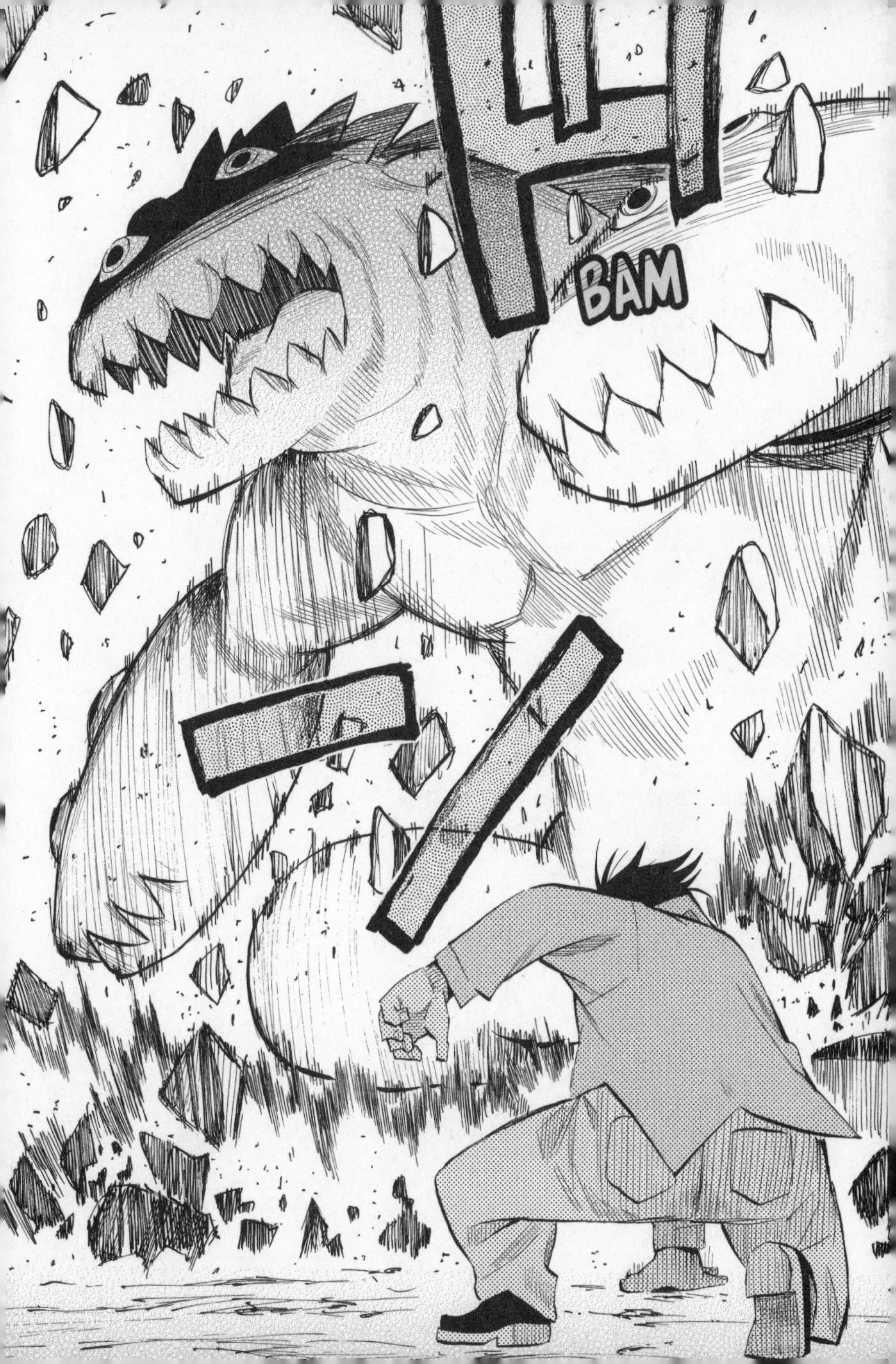
BAM

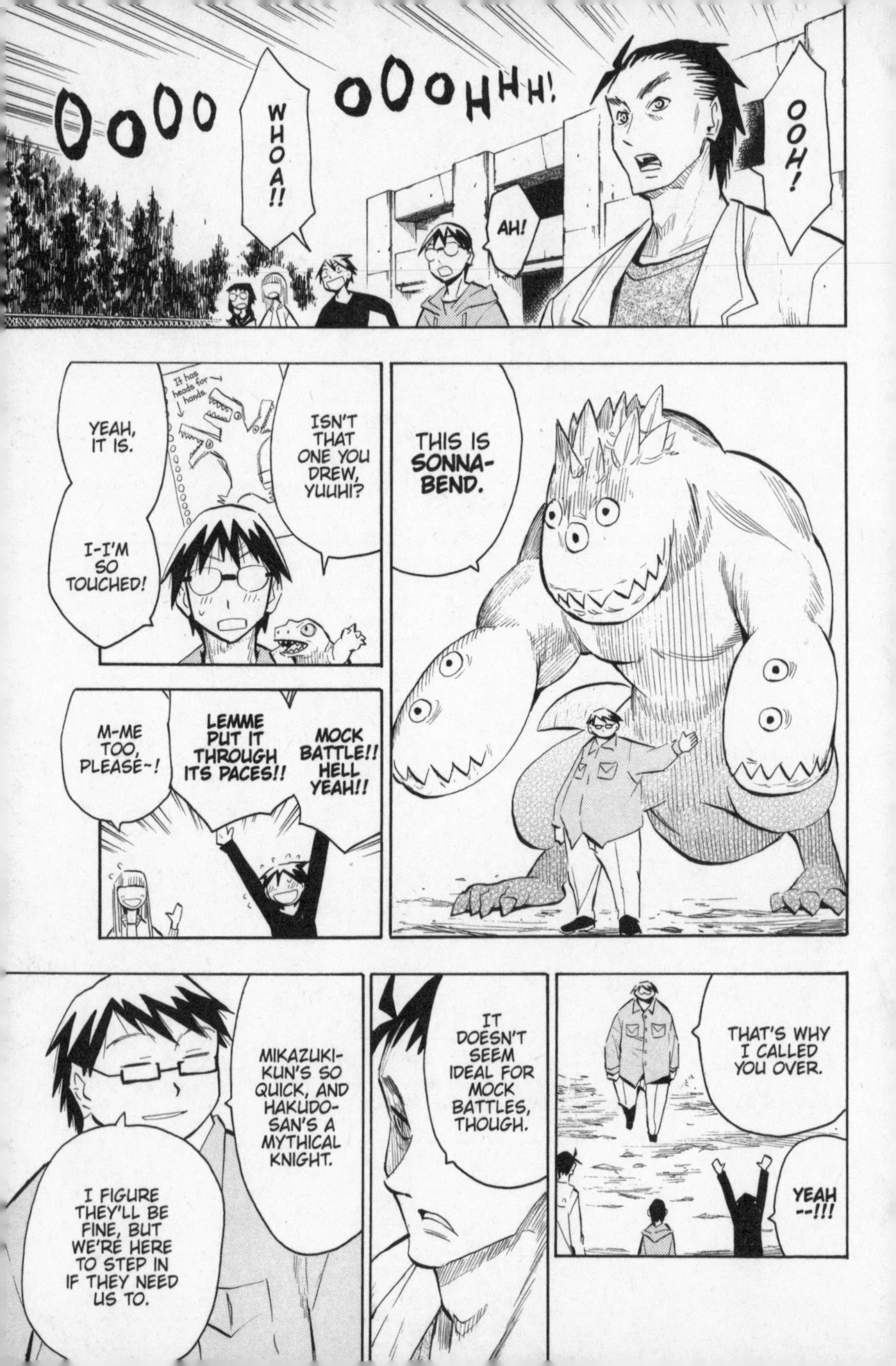
OOOO OOOOHHHH!
OOH!
AH!
WHOA!!
THIS IS SONNA-BEND.
ISN'T THAT ONE YOU DREW, YUUHI?
YEAH, IT IS.
It has heads for hands.
I-I'M SO TOUCHED!
MOCK BATTLE!! HELL YEAH!!
LEMME PUT IT THROUGH ITS PACES!!
M-ME TOO, PLEASE~!
THAT'S WHY I CALLED YOU OVER.
YEAH--!!!
IT DOESN'T SEEM IDEAL FOR MOCK BATTLES, THOUGH.
MIKAZUKI-KUN'S SO QUICK, AND HAKUDO-SAN'S A MYTHICAL KNIGHT.
I FIGURE THEY'LL BE FINE, BUT WE'RE HERE TO STEP IN IF THEY NEED US TO.

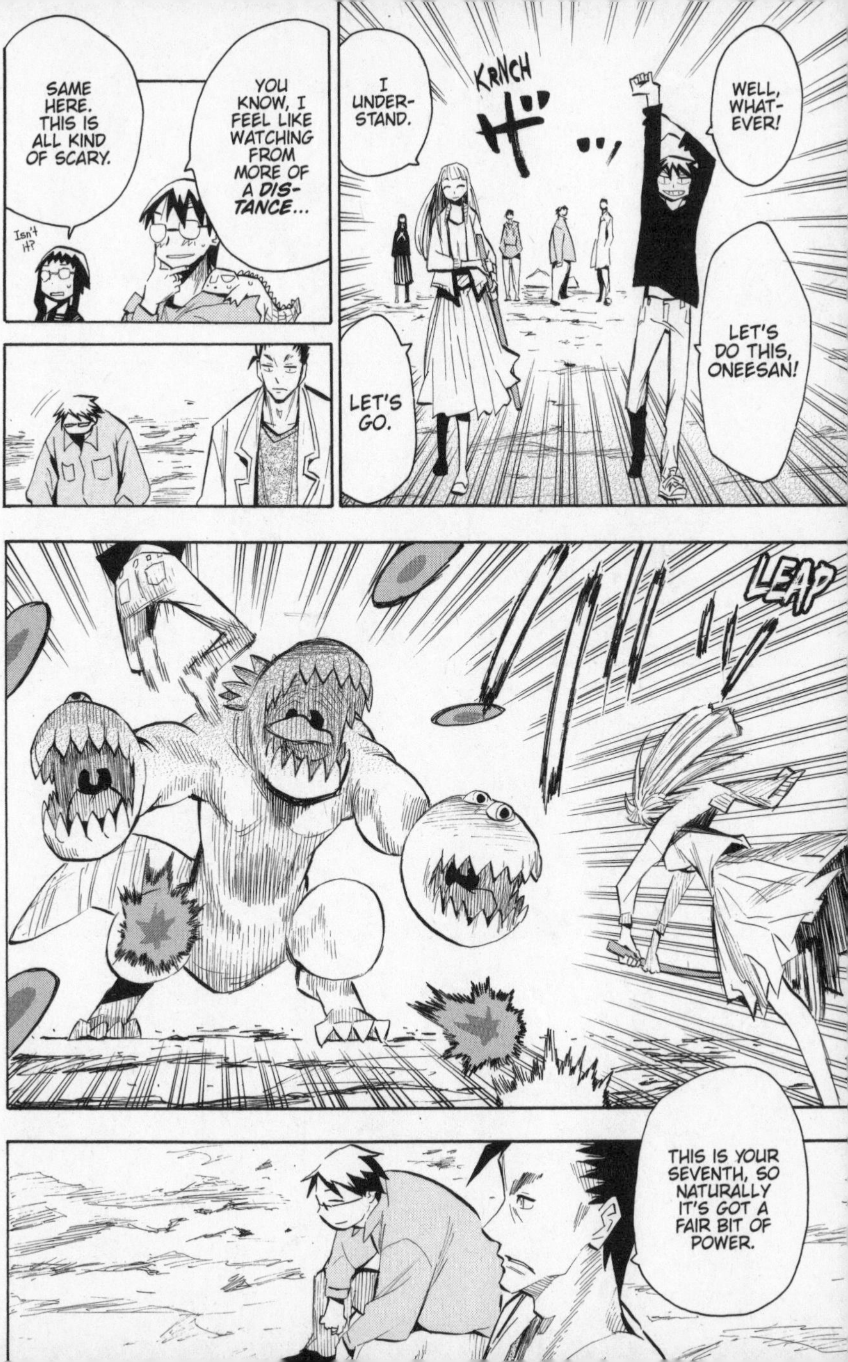
WELL, WHAT-EVER!
KRNCH
LET'S DO THIS, ONEESAN!
I UNDER-STAND.
LET'S GO.
YOU KNOW, I FEEL LIKE WATCHING FROM MORE OF A DIS-TANCE...
SAME HERE. THIS IS ALL KIND OF SCARY.
Isn't it?
LEAP
THIS IS YOUR SEVENTH, SO NATURALLY IT'S GOT A FAIR BIT OF POWER.

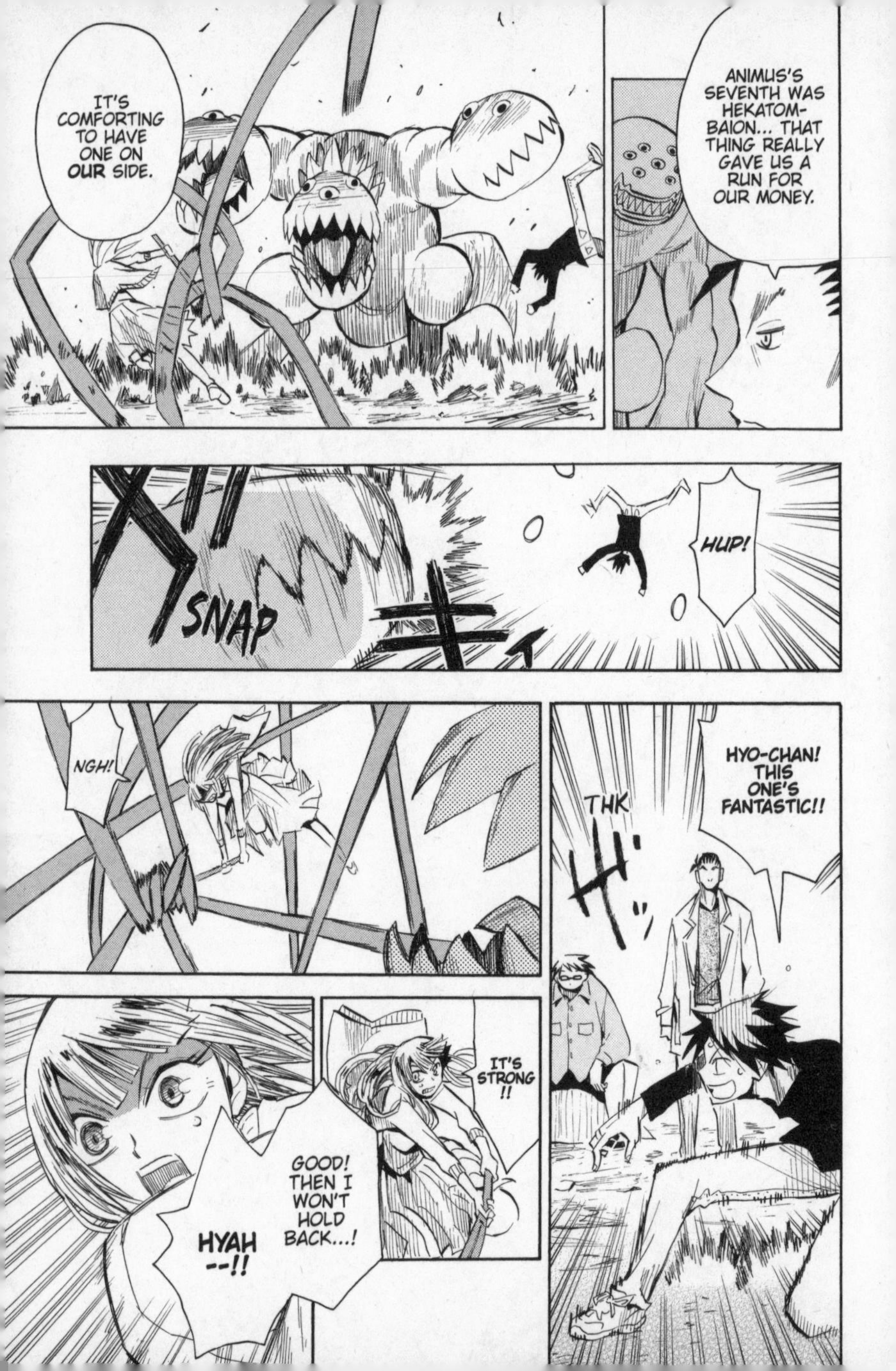
ANIMUS'S SEVENTH WAS HEKATOM-BAION... THAT THING REALLY GAVE US A RUN FOR OUR MONEY.
IT'S COMFORTING TO HAVE ONE ON **OUR** SIDE.
HUP!
SNAP
HYO-CHAN! THIS ONE'S FANTASTIC!!
THK
NGH!
IT'S STRONG!!
GOOD! THEN I WON'T HOLD BACK...!
HYAH--!!

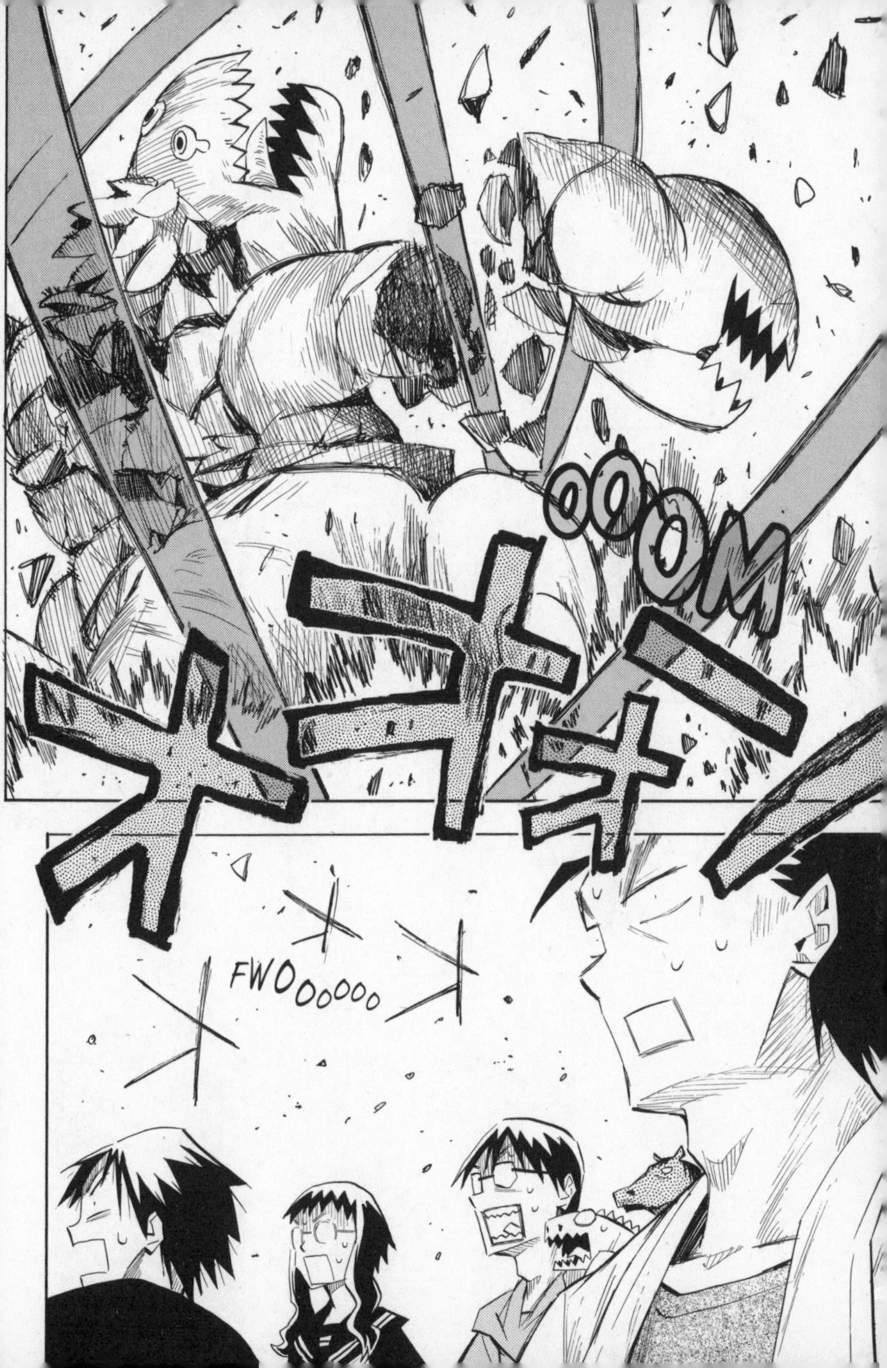
OOOOM
FWOoooooo

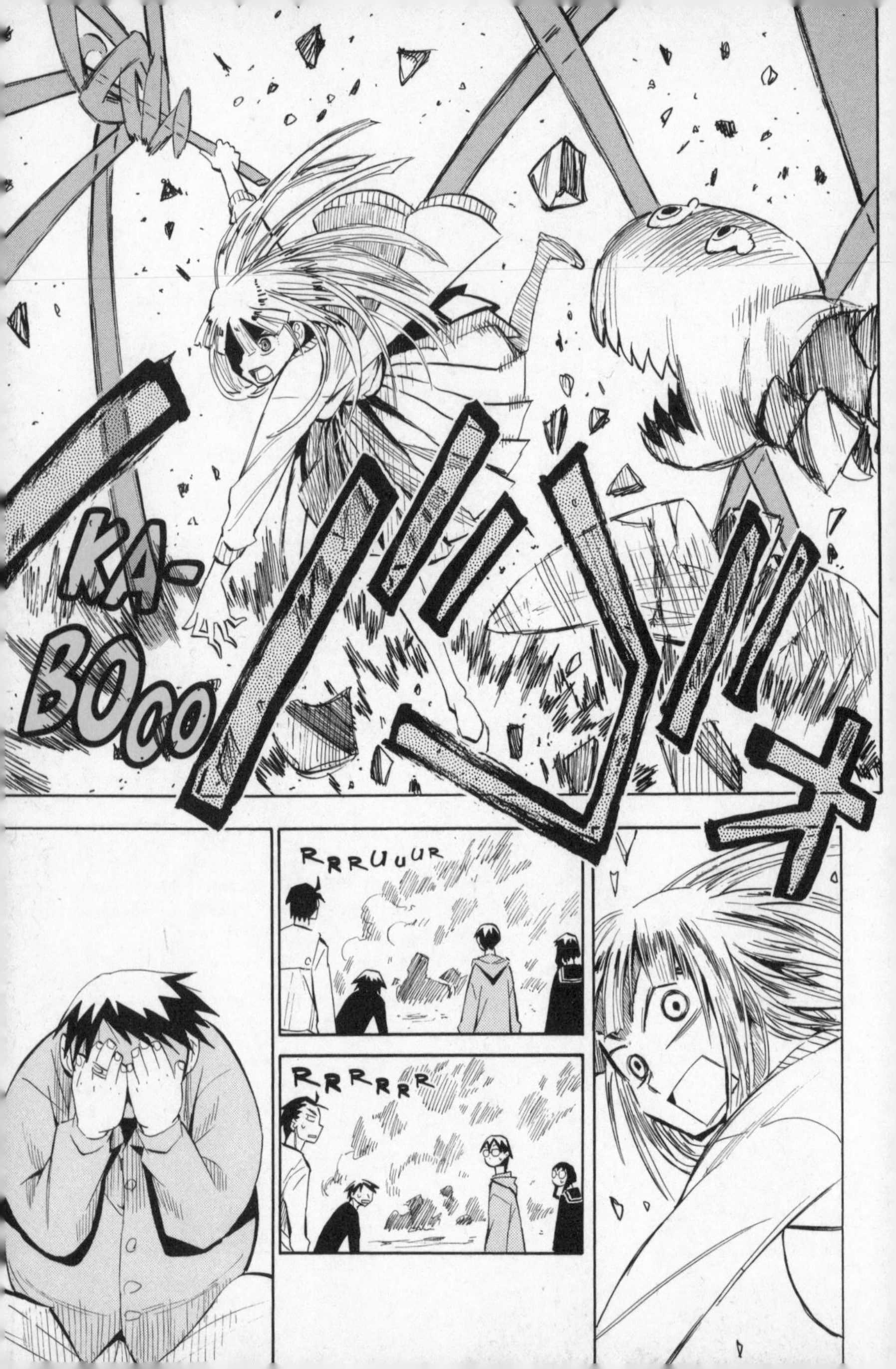
KA-BOOO
RRRUUUR
RRRRRR

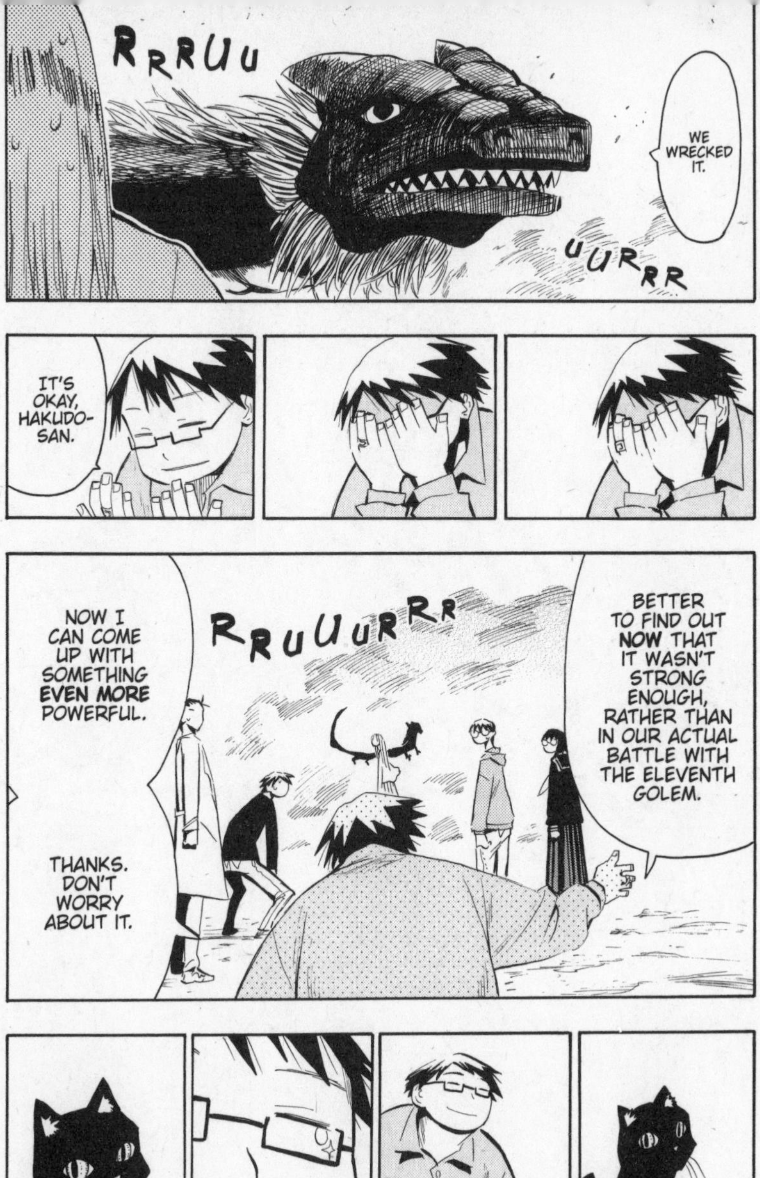
WE WRECKED IT.
RRRUU
UURRR
IT'S OKAY, HAKUDO-SAN.
BETTER TO FIND OUT NOW THAT IT WASN'T STRONG ENOUGH, RATHER THAN IN OUR ACTUAL BATTLE WITH THE ELEVENTH GOLEM.
RRUUURRR
NOW I CAN COME UP WITH SOMETHING EVEN MORE POWERFUL.
THANKS. DON'T WORRY ABOUT IT.

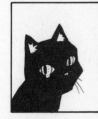

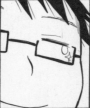

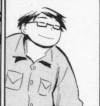

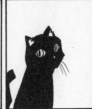

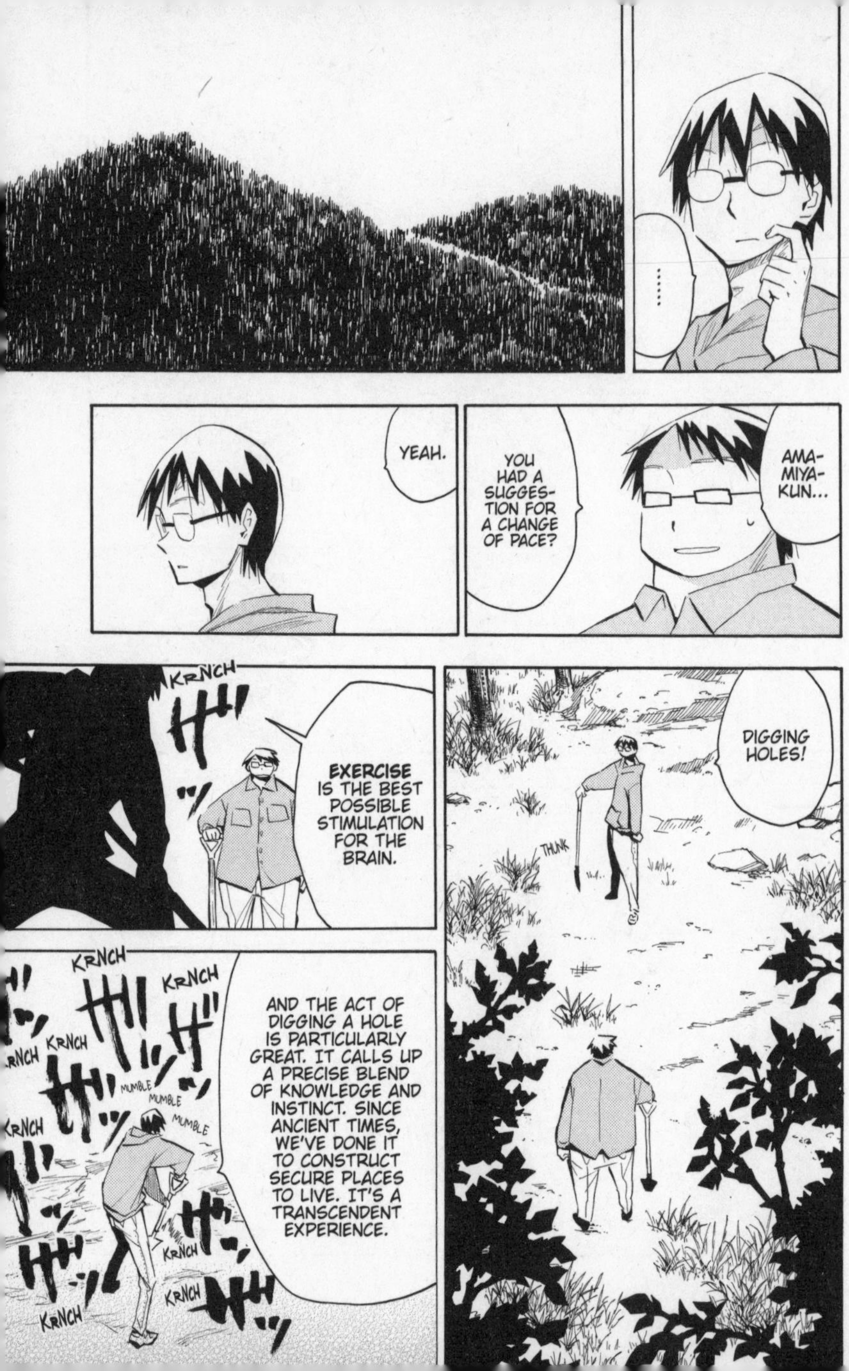
......
AMAMIYA-KUN...
YOU HAD A SUGGESTION FOR A CHANGE OF PACE?
YEAH.
DIGGING HOLES!
THUNK
KRNCH
EXERCISE IS THE BEST POSSIBLE STIMULATION FOR THE BRAIN.
KRNCH
KRNCH
KRNCH
KRNCH
MUMBLE MUMBLE MUMBLE
KRNCH
KRNCH
KRNCH
KRNCH
AND THE ACT OF DIGGING A HOLE IS PARTICULARLY GREAT. IT CALLS UP A PRECISE BLEND OF KNOWLEDGE AND INSTINCT. SINCE ANCIENT TIMES, WE'VE DONE IT TO CONSTRUCT SECURE PLACES TO LIVE. IT'S A TRANSCENDENT EXPERIENCE.

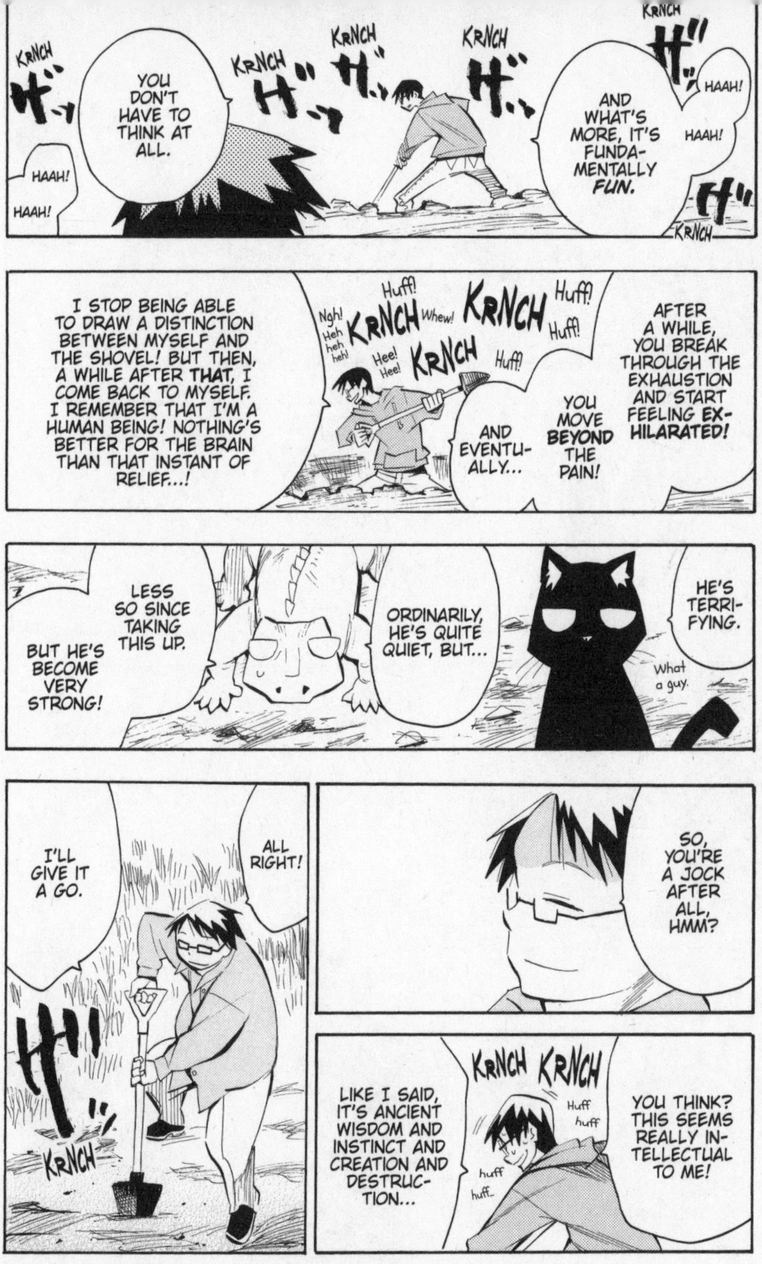
KRNCH
AND WHAT'S MORE, IT'S FUNDAMENTALLY **FUN.**
HAAH! HAAH!
KRNCH
KRNCH
KRNCH
KRNCH
YOU DON'T HAVE TO THINK AT ALL.
HAAH! HAAH!
AFTER A WHILE, YOU BREAK THROUGH THE EXHAUSTION AND START FEELING **EXHILARATED!**
YOU MOVE **BEYOND** THE PAIN!
AND EVENTUALLY...
Huff! Huff! Huff!
KRNCH
Whew!
KRNCH
Hee! Hee!
KRNCH
Ngh! Heh heh heh!
I STOP BEING ABLE TO DRAW A DISTINCTION BETWEEN MYSELF AND THE SHOVEL! BUT THEN, A WHILE AFTER **THAT**, I COME BACK TO MYSELF. I REMEMBER THAT I'M A HUMAN BEING! NOTHING'S BETTER FOR THE BRAIN THAN THAT INSTANT OF RELIEF...!
HE'S TERRIFYING.
What a guy.
ORDINARILY, HE'S QUITE QUIET, BUT...
LESS SO SINCE TAKING THIS UP.
BUT HE'S BECOME VERY STRONG!
SO, YOU'RE A JOCK AFTER ALL, HMM?
YOU THINK? THIS SEEMS REALLY INTELLECTUAL TO ME!
Huff huff
KRNCH KRNCH
huff huff...
LIKE I SAID, IT'S ANCIENT WISDOM AND INSTINCT AND CREATION AND DESTRUCTION...
ALL RIGHT!
I'LL GIVE IT A GO.
KRNCH

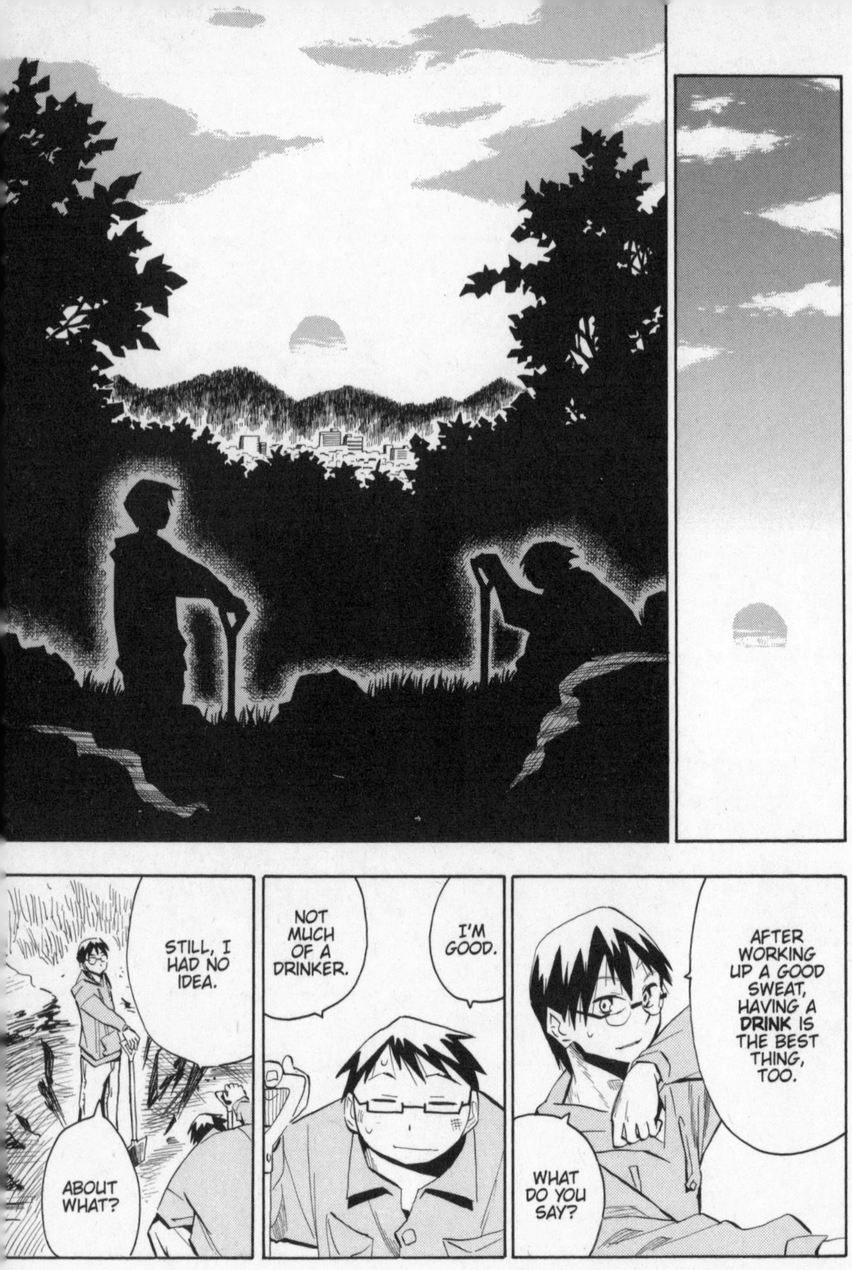
AFTER WORKING UP A GOOD SWEAT, HAVING A DRINK IS THE BEST THING, TOO.
WHAT DO YOU SAY?
I'M GOOD.
NOT MUCH OF A DRINKER.
STILL, I HAD NO IDEA.
ABOUT WHAT?

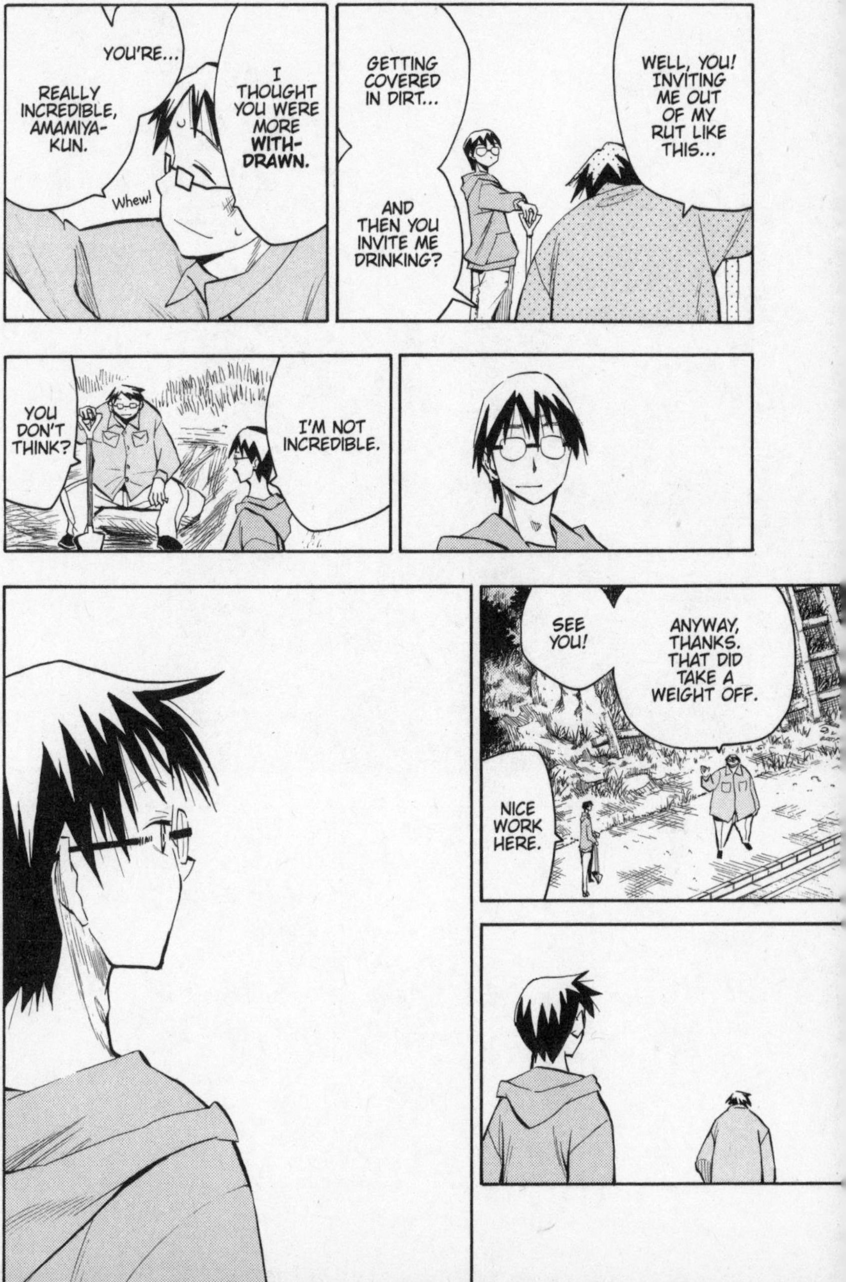
WELL, YOU! INVITING ME OUT OF MY RUT LIKE THIS...
GETTING COVERED IN DIRT...
AND THEN YOU INVITE ME DRINKING?
I THOUGHT YOU WERE MORE WITH-DRAWN.
YOU'RE...
REALLY INCREDIBLE, AMAMIYA-KUN.
Whew!
I'M NOT INCREDIBLE.
YOU DON'T THINK?
ANYWAY, THANKS. THAT DID TAKE A WEIGHT OFF.
SEE YOU!
NICE WORK HERE.

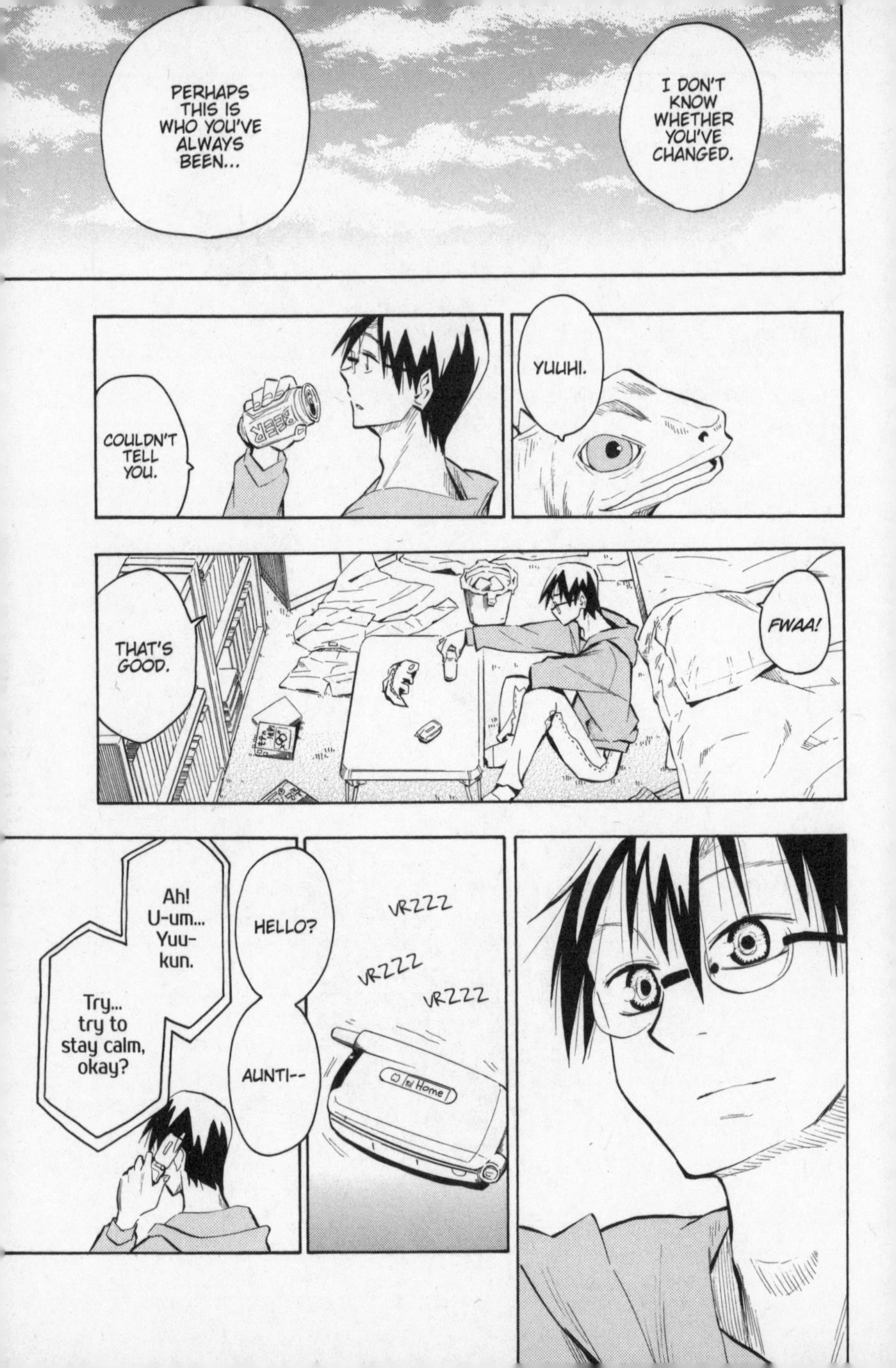
I DON'T KNOW WHETHER YOU'VE CHANGED.
PERHAPS THIS IS WHO YOU'VE ALWAYS BEEN...
YUUHI.
BEER
COULDN'T TELL YOU.
FWAA!
THAT'S GOOD.
VRZZZ
VRZZZ
VRZZZ
Home
HELLO?
AUNTI--
Ah! U-um... Yuu-kun.
Try... try to stay calm, okay?

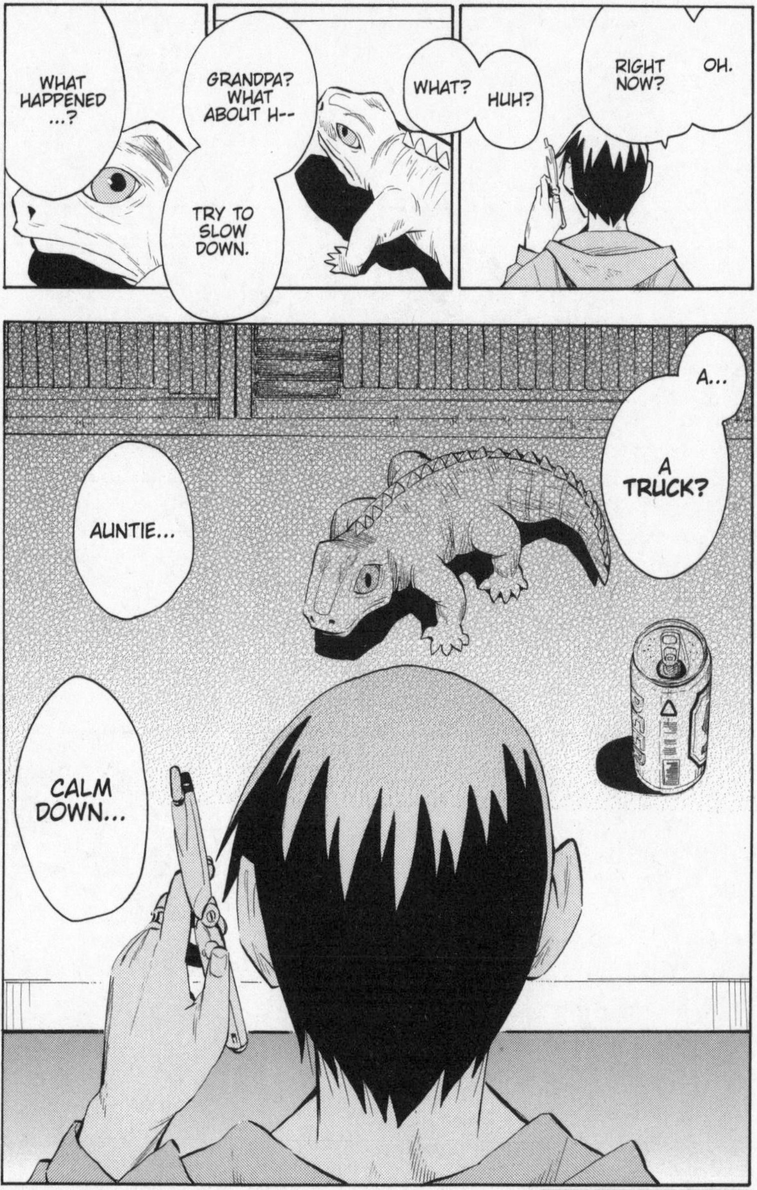
OH.
RIGHT NOW?
WHAT?
HUH?
GRANDPA? WHAT ABOUT H--
TRY TO SLOW DOWN.
WHAT HAPPENED ...?
A...
A TRUCK?
AUNTIE...
CALM DOWN...

Chapter 48/END

Lucifer and the Biscuit Hammer

Chapter 49

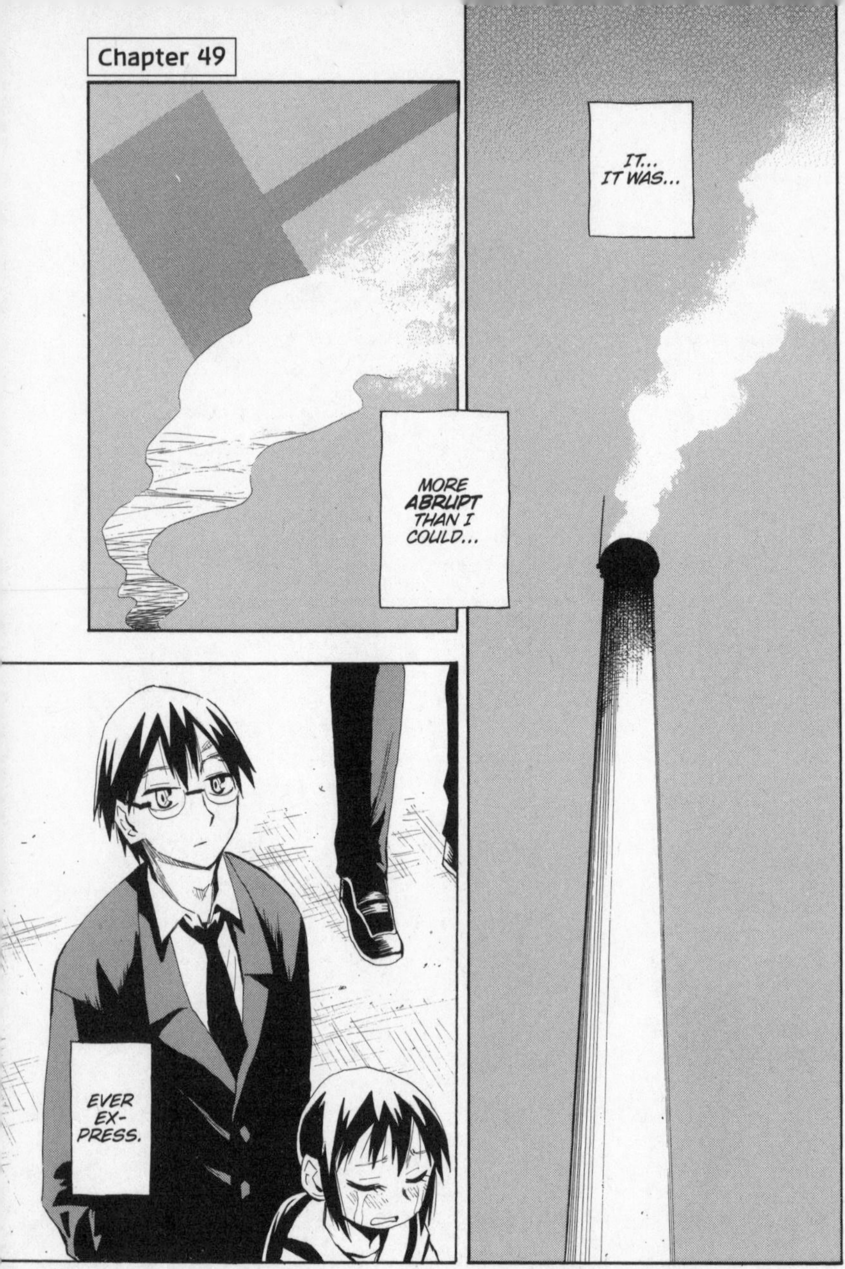
IT... IT WAS...
MORE ABRUPT THAN I COULD...
EVER EX-PRESS.

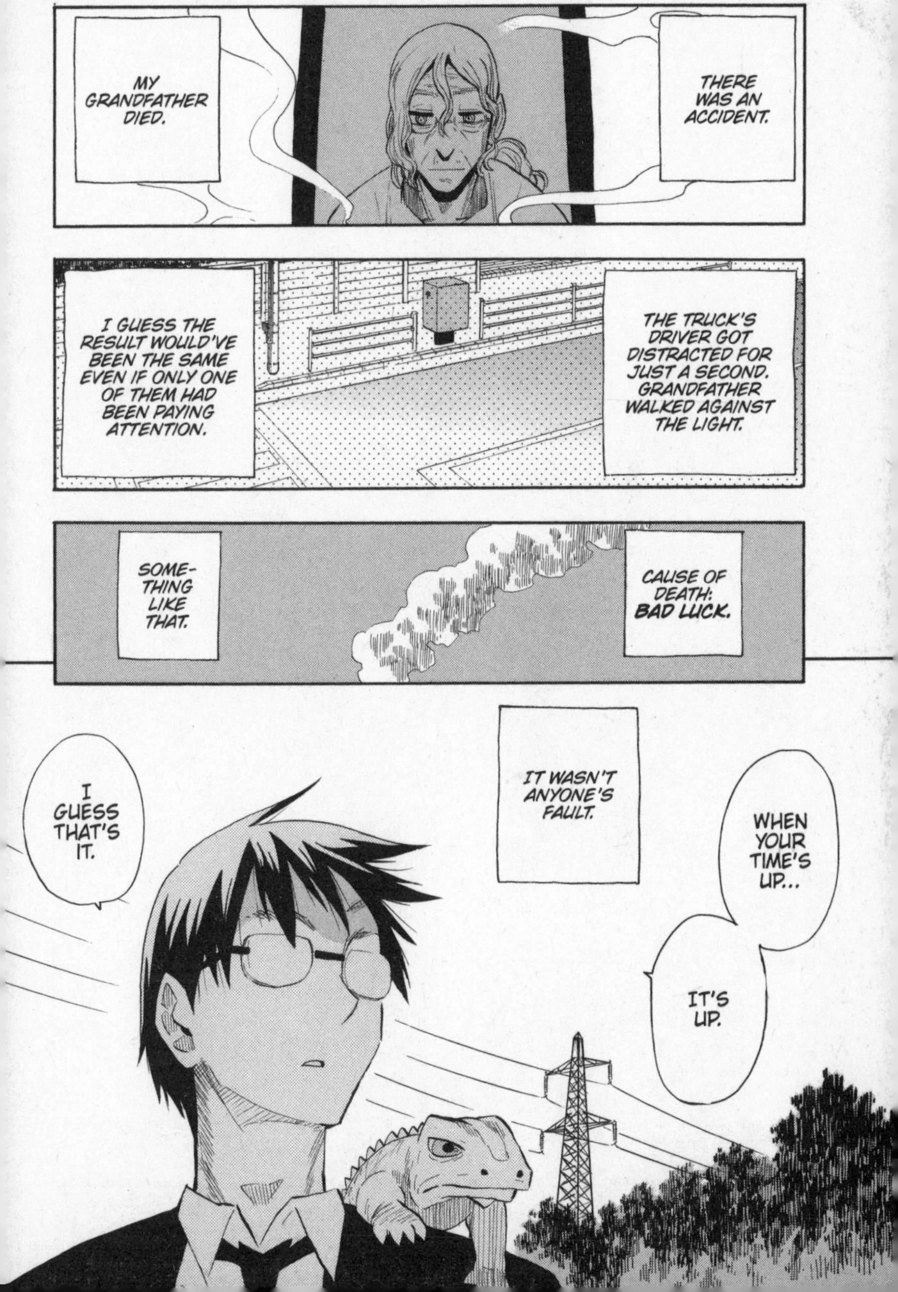
THERE WAS AN ACCIDENT.
MY GRANDFATHER DIED.
THE TRUCK'S DRIVER GOT DISTRACTED FOR JUST A SECOND. GRANDFATHER WALKED AGAINST THE LIGHT.
I GUESS THE RESULT WOULD'VE BEEN THE SAME EVEN IF ONLY ONE OF THEM HAD BEEN PAYING ATTENTION.
CAUSE OF DEATH: **BAD LUCK.**
SOME-THING LIKE THAT.
WHEN YOUR TIME'S UP...
IT'S UP.
IT WASN'T ANYONE'S FAULT.
I GUESS THAT'S IT.

Chapter 49: Before the Door

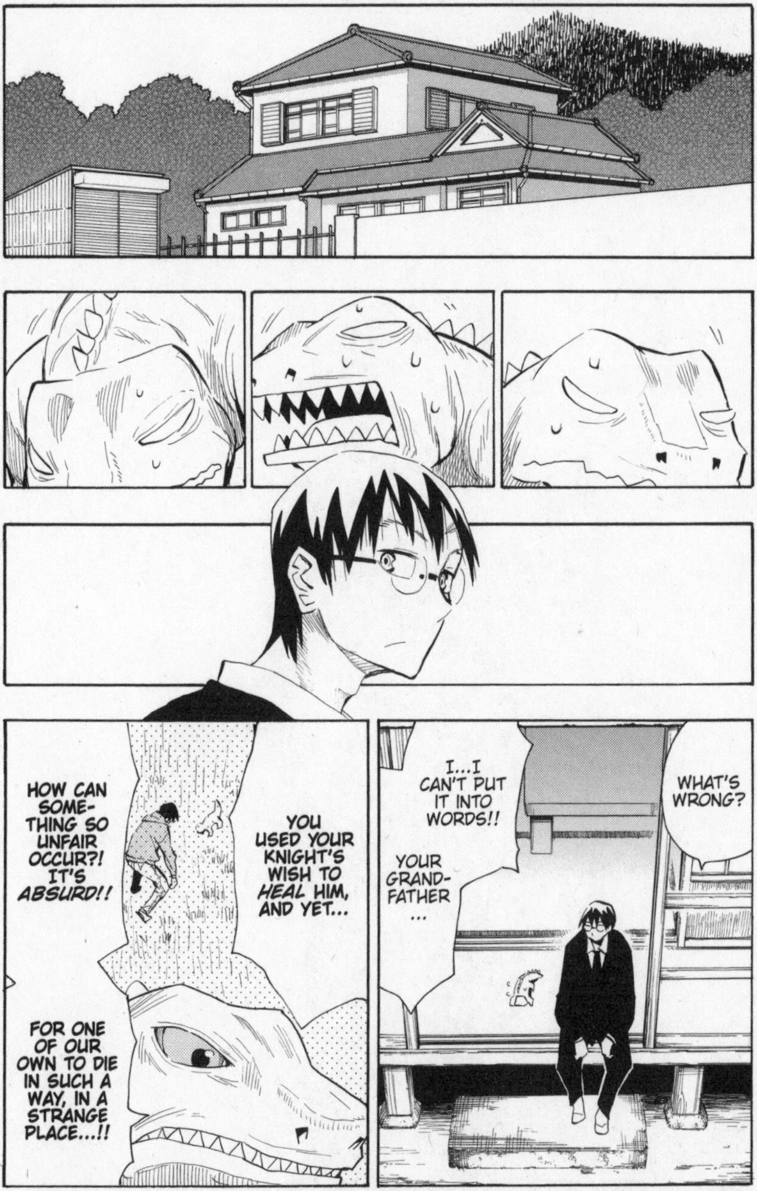
WHAT'S WRONG?
I...I CAN'T PUT IT INTO WORDS!!
YOUR GRAND-FATHER ...
YOU USED YOUR KNIGHT'S WISH TO *HEAL* HIM, AND YET...
HOW CAN SOME-THING SO UNFAIR OCCUR?! IT'S *ABSURD!!*
FOR ONE OF OUR OWN TO DIE IN SUCH A WAY, IN A STRANGE PLACE...!!

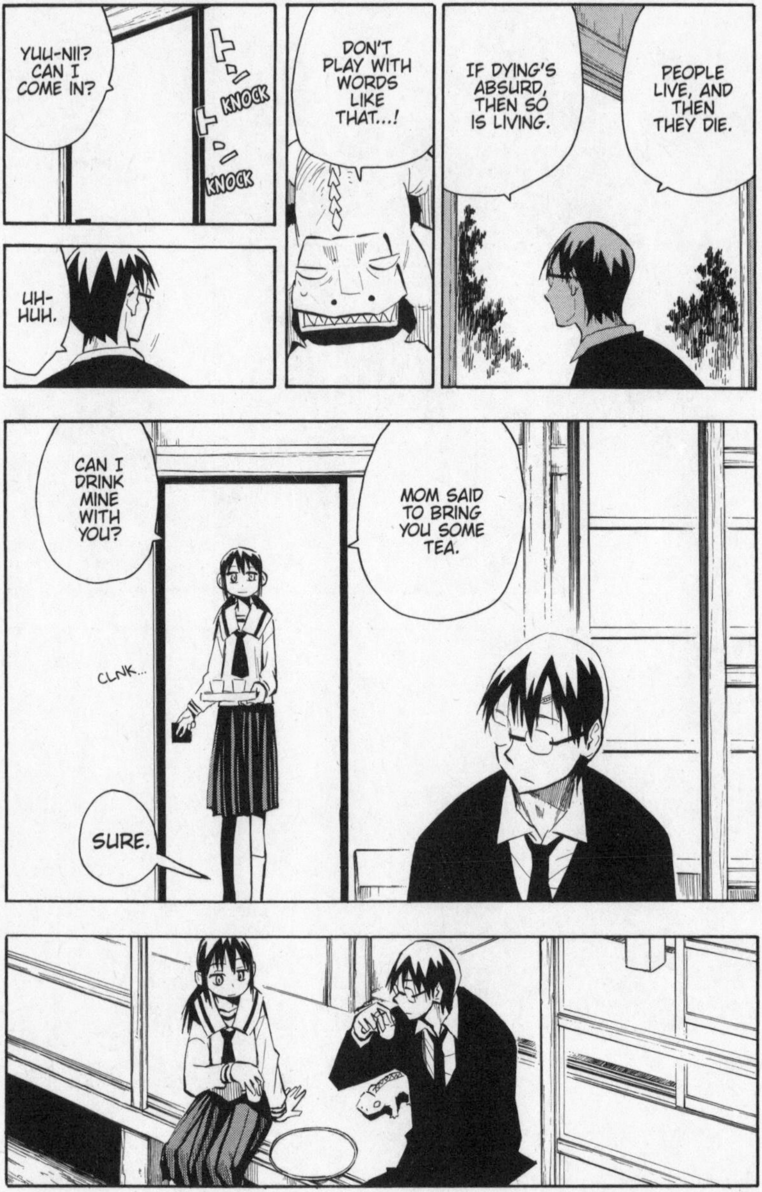
PEOPLE LIVE, AND THEN THEY DIE.
IF DYING'S ABSURD, THEN SO IS LIVING.
DON'T PLAY WITH WORDS LIKE THAT...!
KNOCK
KNOCK
YUU-NII? CAN I COME IN?
UH-HUH.
MOM SAID TO BRING YOU SOME TEA.
CAN I DRINK MINE WITH YOU?
CLNK...
SURE.

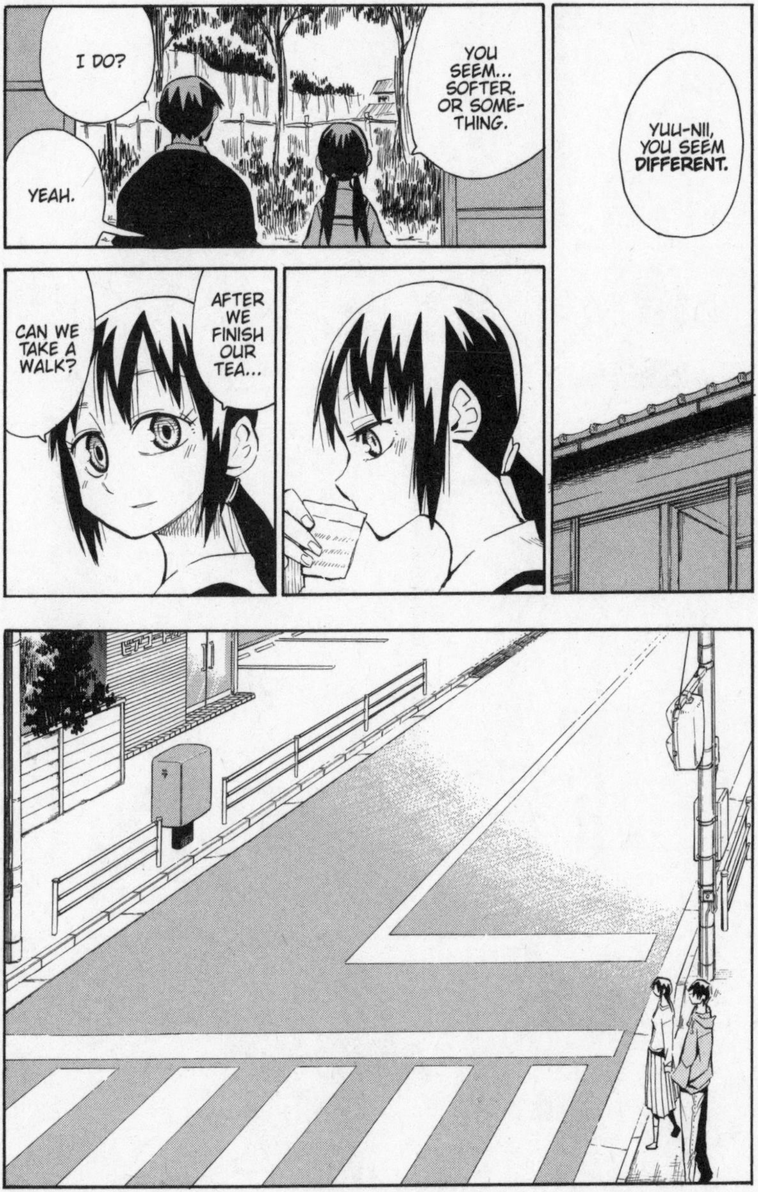
YUU-NII, YOU SEEM DIFFERENT.
YOU SEEM... SOFTER. OR SOME-THING.
I DO?
YEAH.
AFTER WE FINISH OUR TEA...
CAN WE TAKE A WALK?

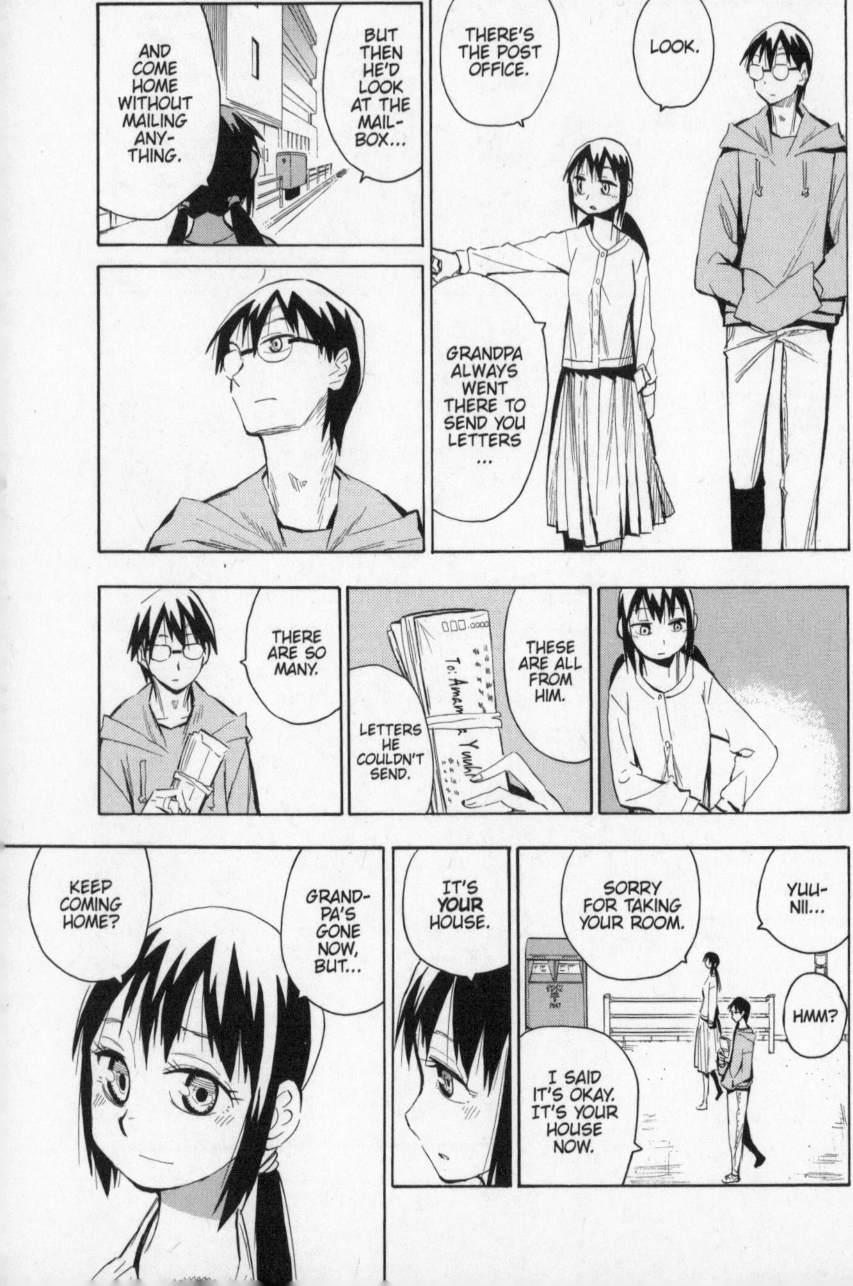
LOOK.
THERE'S THE POST OFFICE.
GRANDPA ALWAYS WENT THERE TO SEND YOU LETTERS ...
BUT THEN HE'D LOOK AT THE MAIL-BOX...
AND COME HOME WITHOUT MAILING ANY-THING.
THESE ARE ALL FROM HIM.
LETTERS HE COULDN'T SEND.
THERE ARE SO MANY.
YUU-NII...
SORRY FOR TAKING YOUR ROOM.
HMM?
I SAID IT'S OKAY. IT'S YOUR HOUSE NOW.
IT'S YOUR HOUSE.
GRAND-PA'S GONE NOW, BUT...
KEEP COMING HOME?

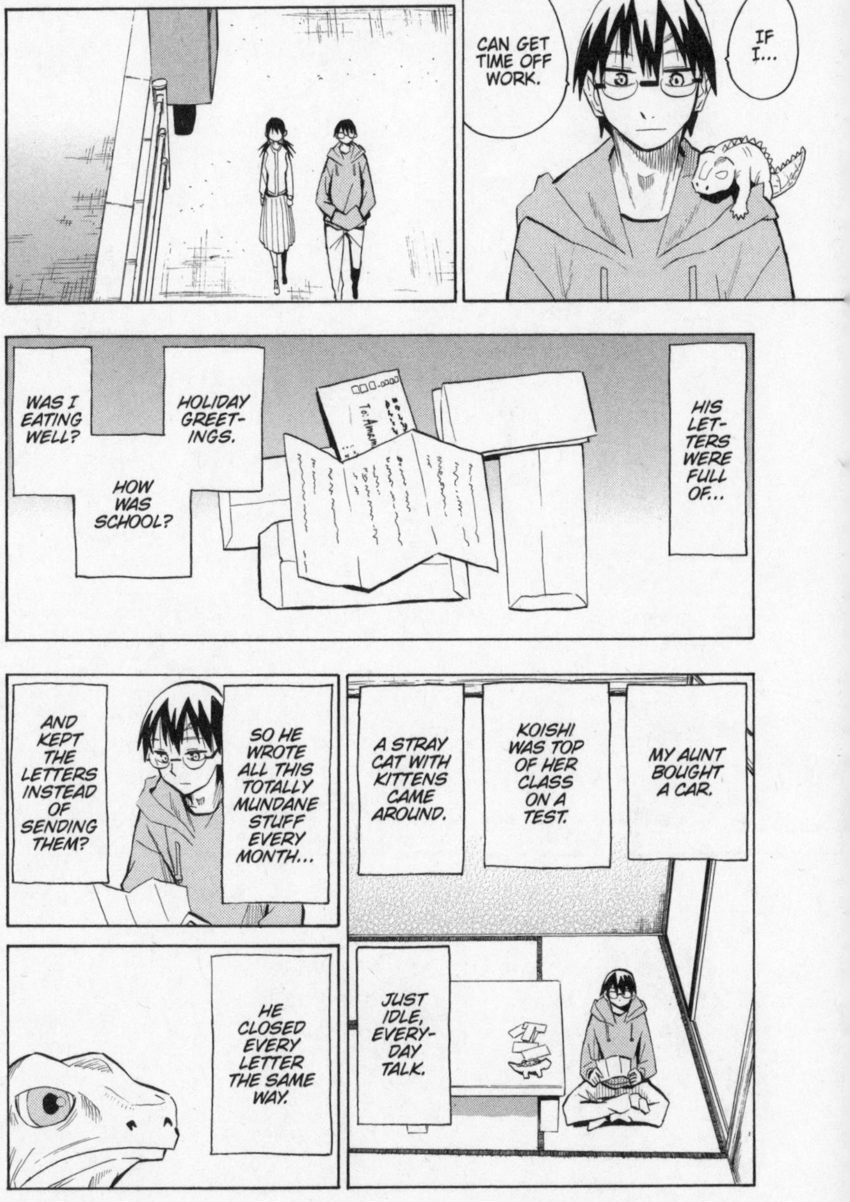
IF I...
CAN GET TIME OFF WORK.
HIS LETTERS WERE FULL OF...
HOLIDAY GREETINGS.
WAS I EATING WELL?
HOW WAS SCHOOL?
MY AUNT BOUGHT A CAR.
KOISHI WAS TOP OF HER CLASS ON A TEST.
A STRAY CAT WITH KITTENS CAME AROUND.
SO HE WROTE ALL THIS TOTALLY MUNDANE STUFF EVERY MONTH...
AND KEPT THE LETTERS INSTEAD OF SENDING THEM?
JUST IDLE, EVERYDAY TALK.
HE CLOSED EVERY LETTER THE SAME WAY.

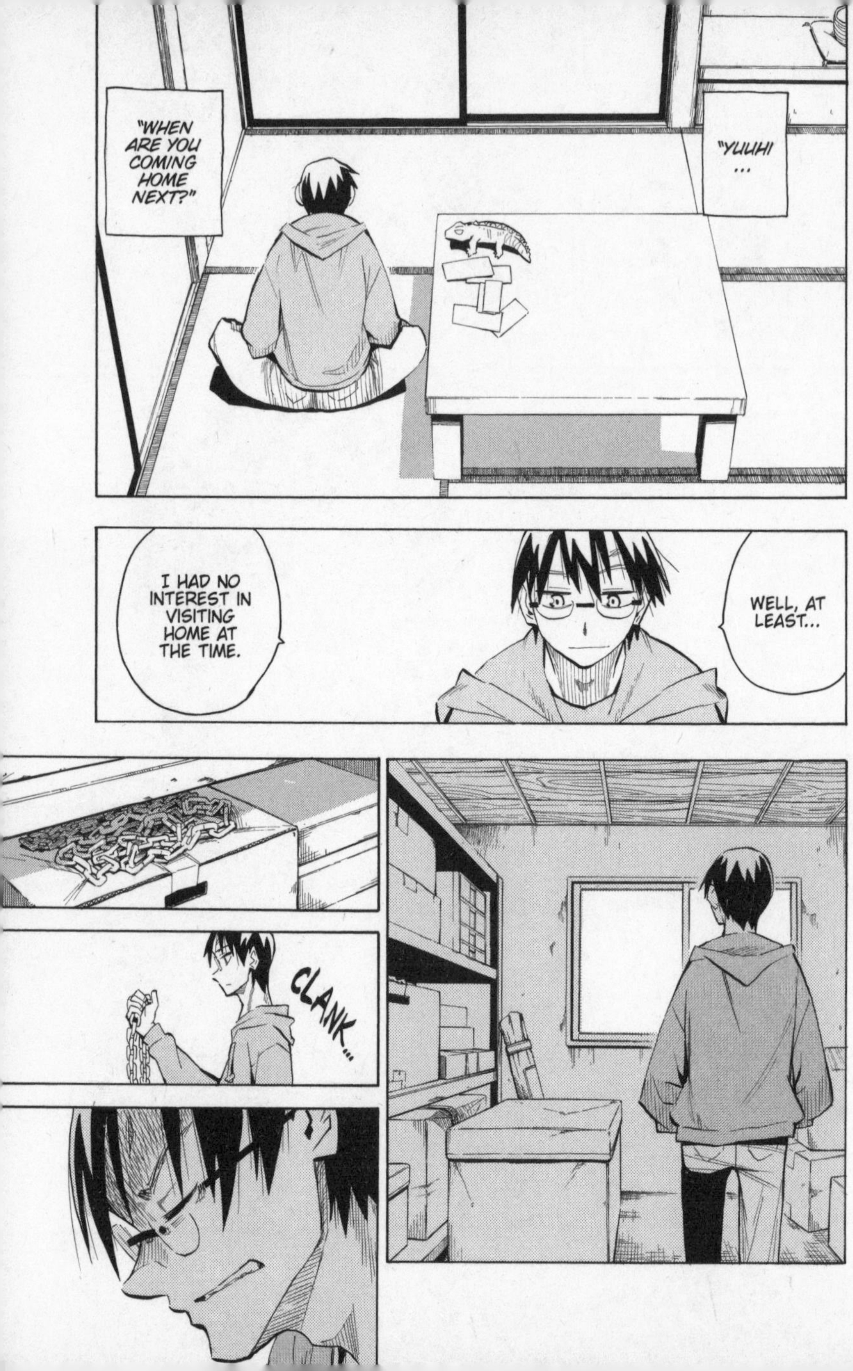
"YUUHI ...
"WHEN ARE YOU COMING HOME NEXT?"
WELL, AT LEAST...
I HAD NO INTEREST IN VISITING HOME AT THE TIME.
CLANK...

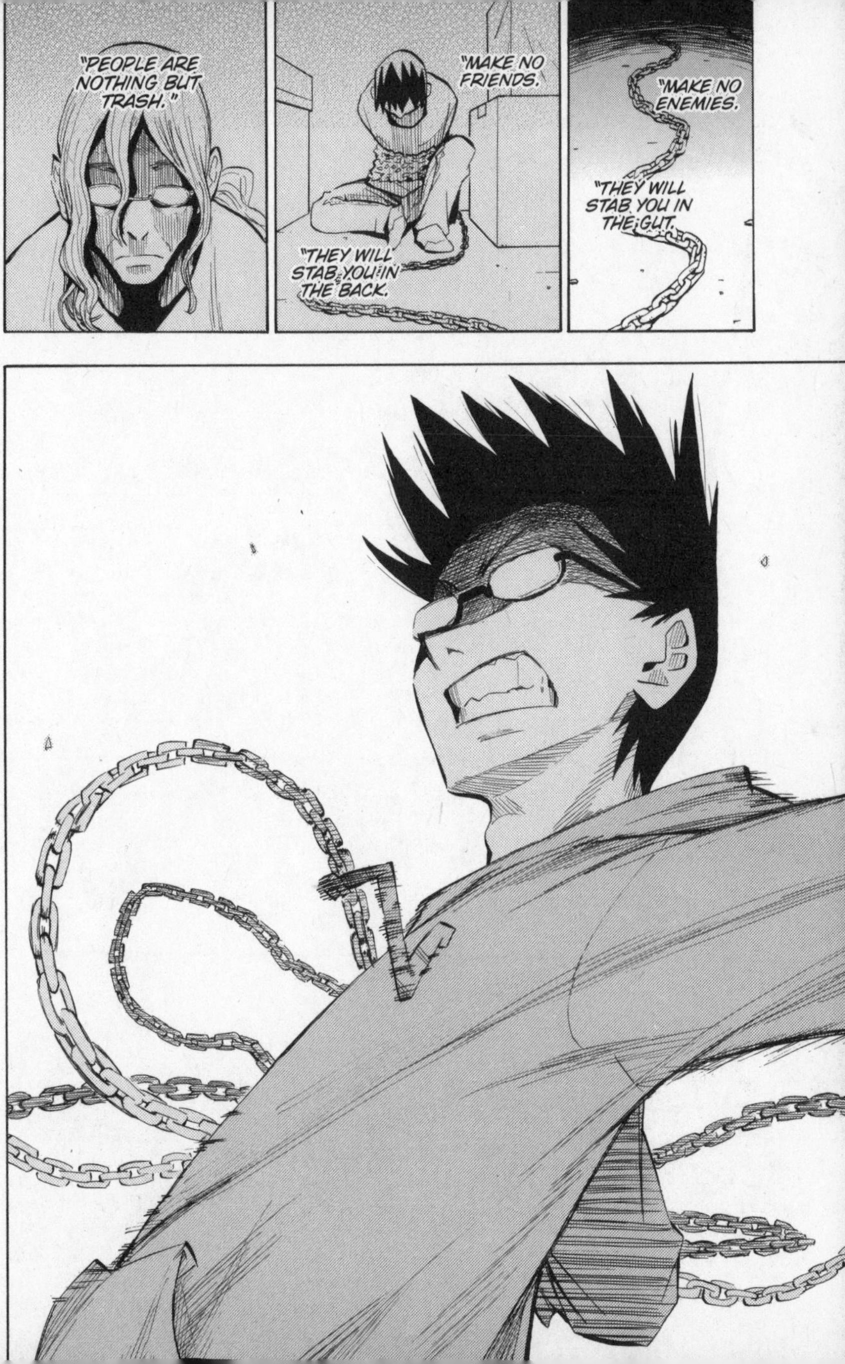
"MAKE NO ENEMIES.
"THEY WILL STAB YOU IN THE GUT.
"MAKE NO FRIENDS.
"THEY WILL STAB YOU IN THE BACK.
"PEOPLE ARE NOTHING BUT TRASH."

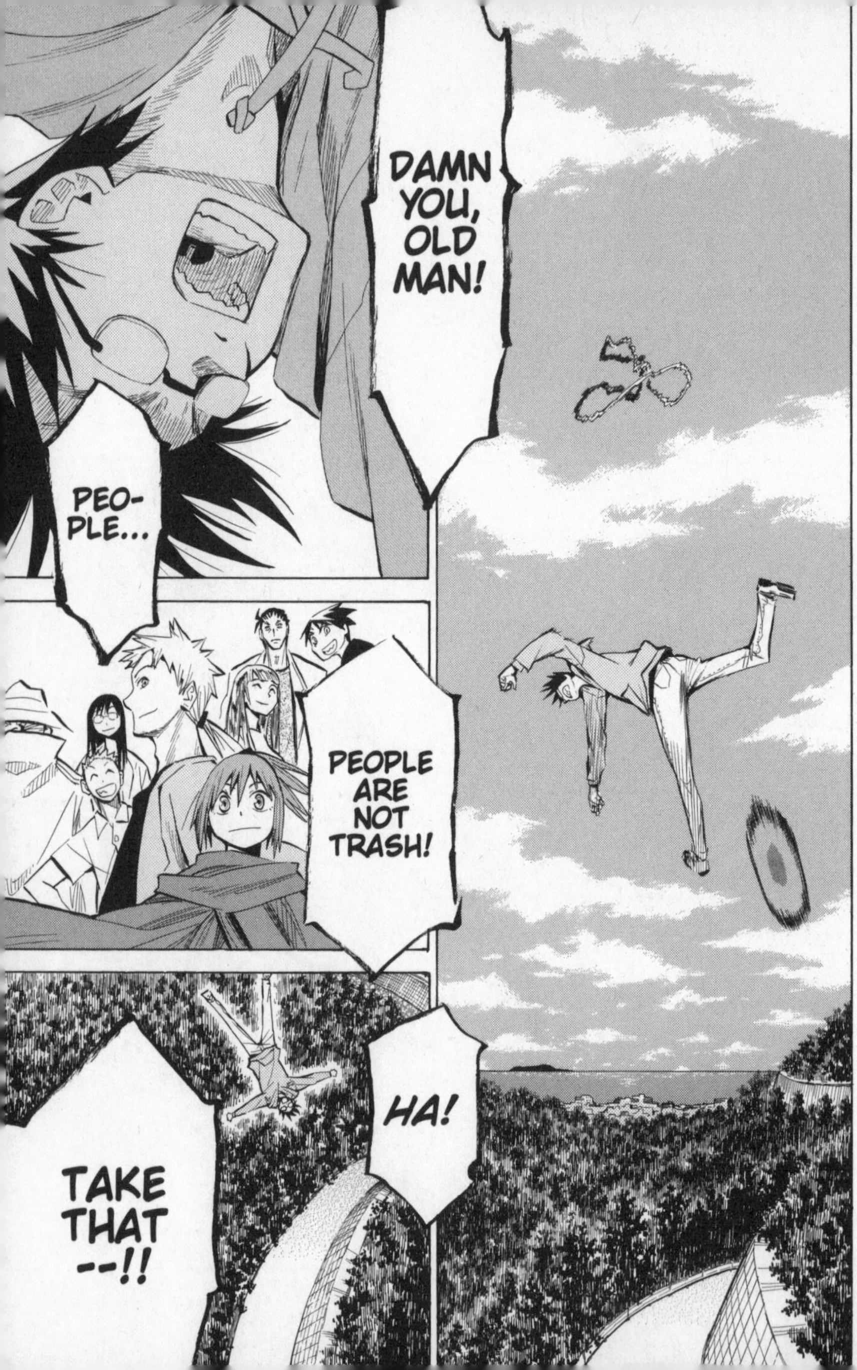
DAMN YOU, OLD MAN!
PEO- PLE...
PEOPLE ARE NOT TRASH!
HA!
TAKE THAT --!!

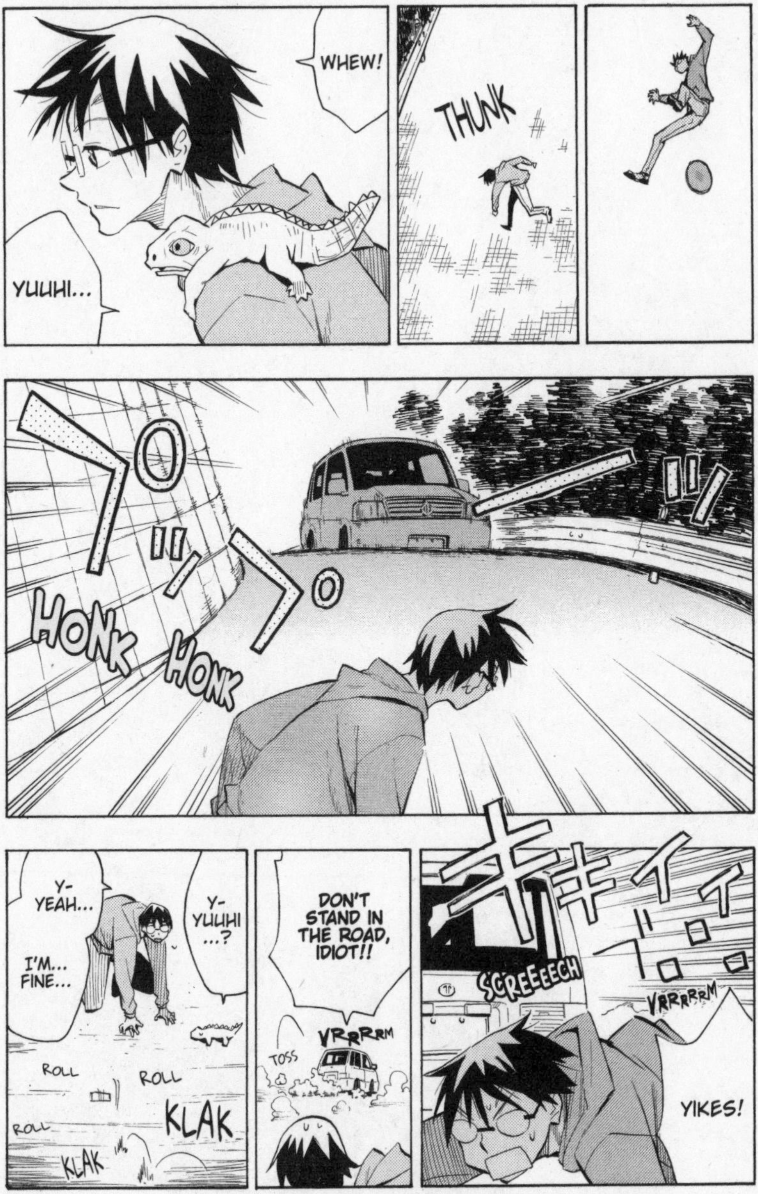
THUNK
WHEW!
YUUHI...
HONK
HONK
SCREEEECH
VRRRRRM
YIKES!
DON'T STAND IN THE ROAD, IDIOT!!
VRRRRM
TOSS
Y-YUUHI ...?
Y-YEAH...
I'M... FINE...
ROLL
ROLL
ROLL
KLAK
KLAK

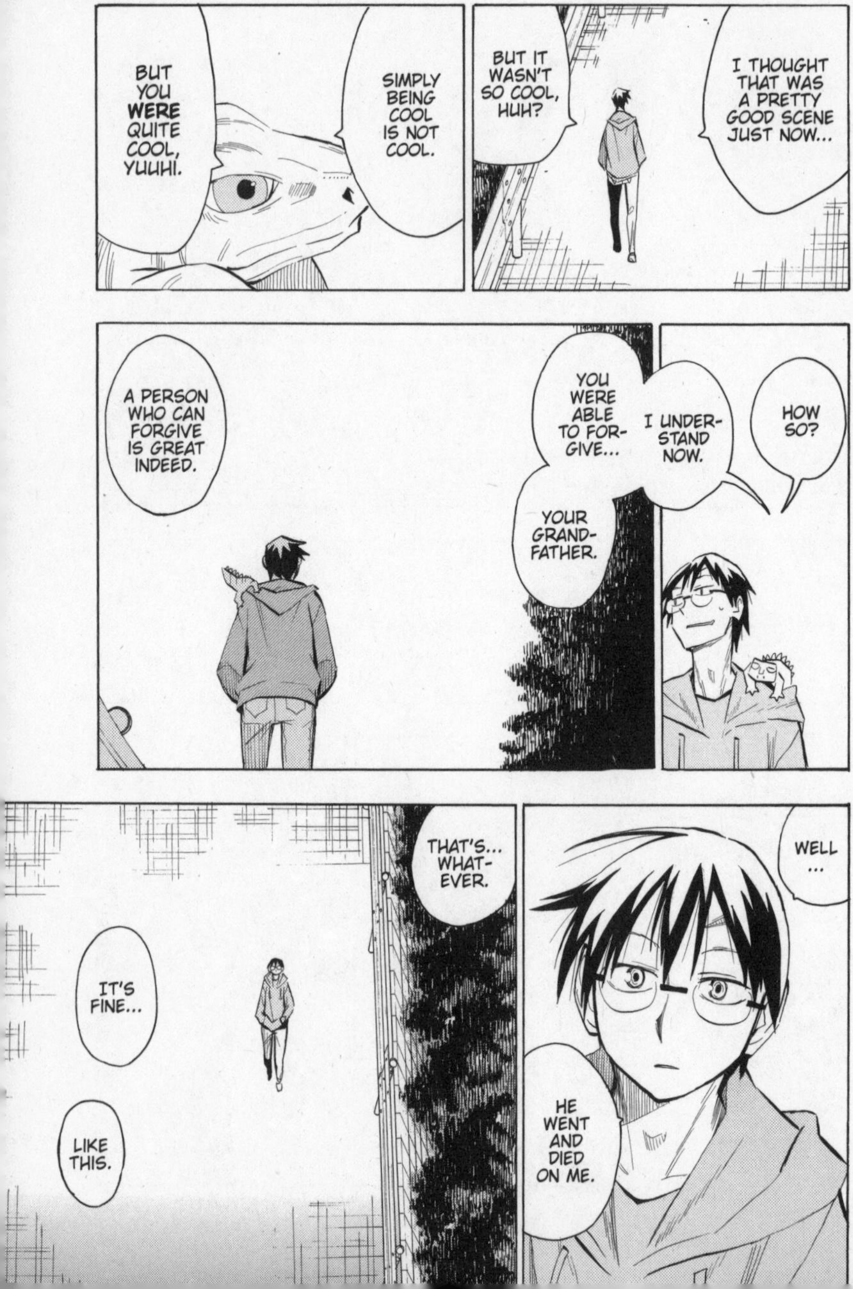
I THOUGHT THAT WAS A PRETTY GOOD SCENE JUST NOW...
BUT IT WASN'T SO COOL, HUH?
SIMPLY BEING COOL IS NOT COOL.
BUT YOU **WERE** QUITE COOL, YUUHI.
HOW SO?
I UNDER-STAND NOW.
YOU WERE ABLE TO FOR-GIVE...
YOUR GRAND-FATHER.
A PERSON WHO CAN FORGIVE IS GREAT INDEED.
WELL ...
HE WENT AND DIED ON ME.
THAT'S... WHAT-EVER.
IT'S FINE...
LIKE THIS.

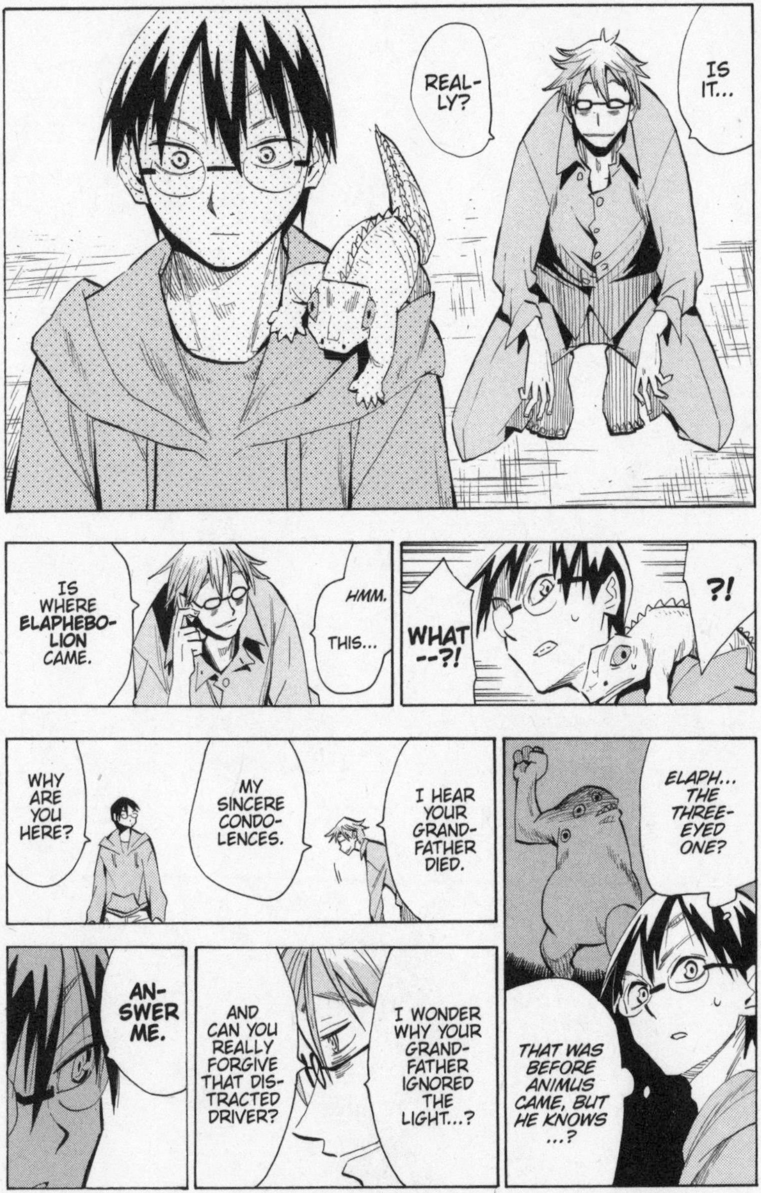
IS IT...
REAL-LY?
?!
WHAT--?!
HMM. THIS...
IS WHERE ELAPHEBOLION CAME.
ELAPH... THE THREE-EYED ONE?
THAT WAS BEFORE ANIMUS CAME, BUT HE KNOWS ...?
I HEAR YOUR GRAND-FATHER DIED.
MY SINCERE CONDO-LENCES.
WHY ARE YOU HERE?
I WONDER WHY YOUR GRAND-FATHER IGNORED THE LIGHT...?
AND CAN YOU REALLY FORGIVE THAT DIS-TRACTED DRIVER?
AN-SWER ME.

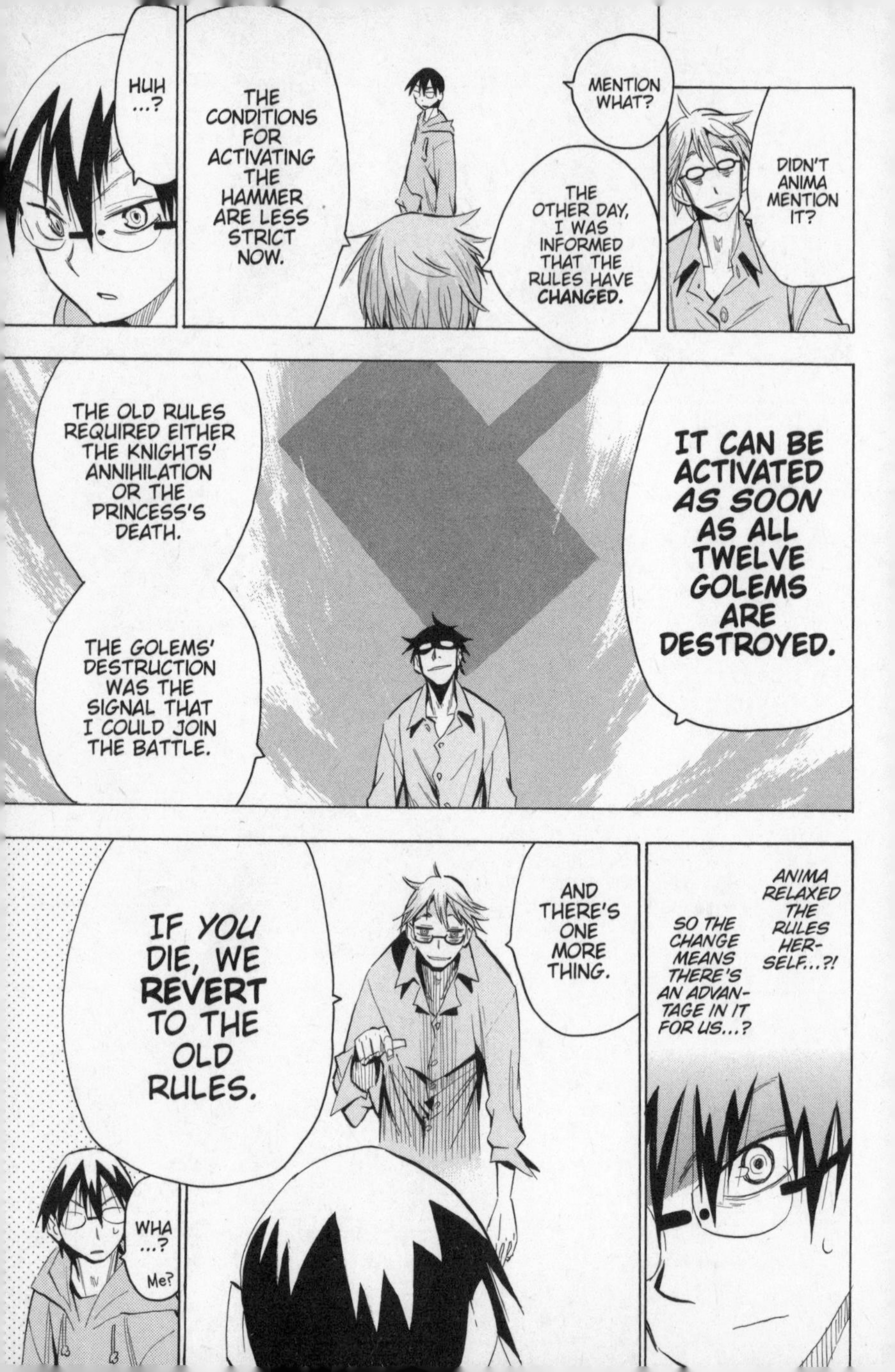

DIDN'T ANIMA MENTION IT?
MENTION WHAT?
THE OTHER DAY, I WAS INFORMED THAT THE RULES HAVE CHANGED.
THE CONDITIONS FOR ACTIVATING THE HAMMER ARE LESS STRICT NOW.
HUH...?
IT CAN BE ACTIVATED AS SOON AS ALL TWELVE GOLEMS ARE DESTROYED.
THE OLD RULES REQUIRED EITHER THE KNIGHTS' ANNIHILATION OR THE PRINCESS'S DEATH.
THE GOLEMS' DESTRUCTION WAS THE SIGNAL THAT I COULD JOIN THE BATTLE.
ANIMA RELAXED THE RULES HER-SELF...?!
SO THE CHANGE MEANS THERE'S AN ADVAN-TAGE IN IT FOR US...?
AND THERE'S ONE MORE THING.
IF YOU DIE, WE REVERT TO THE OLD RULES.
WHA...?
Me?

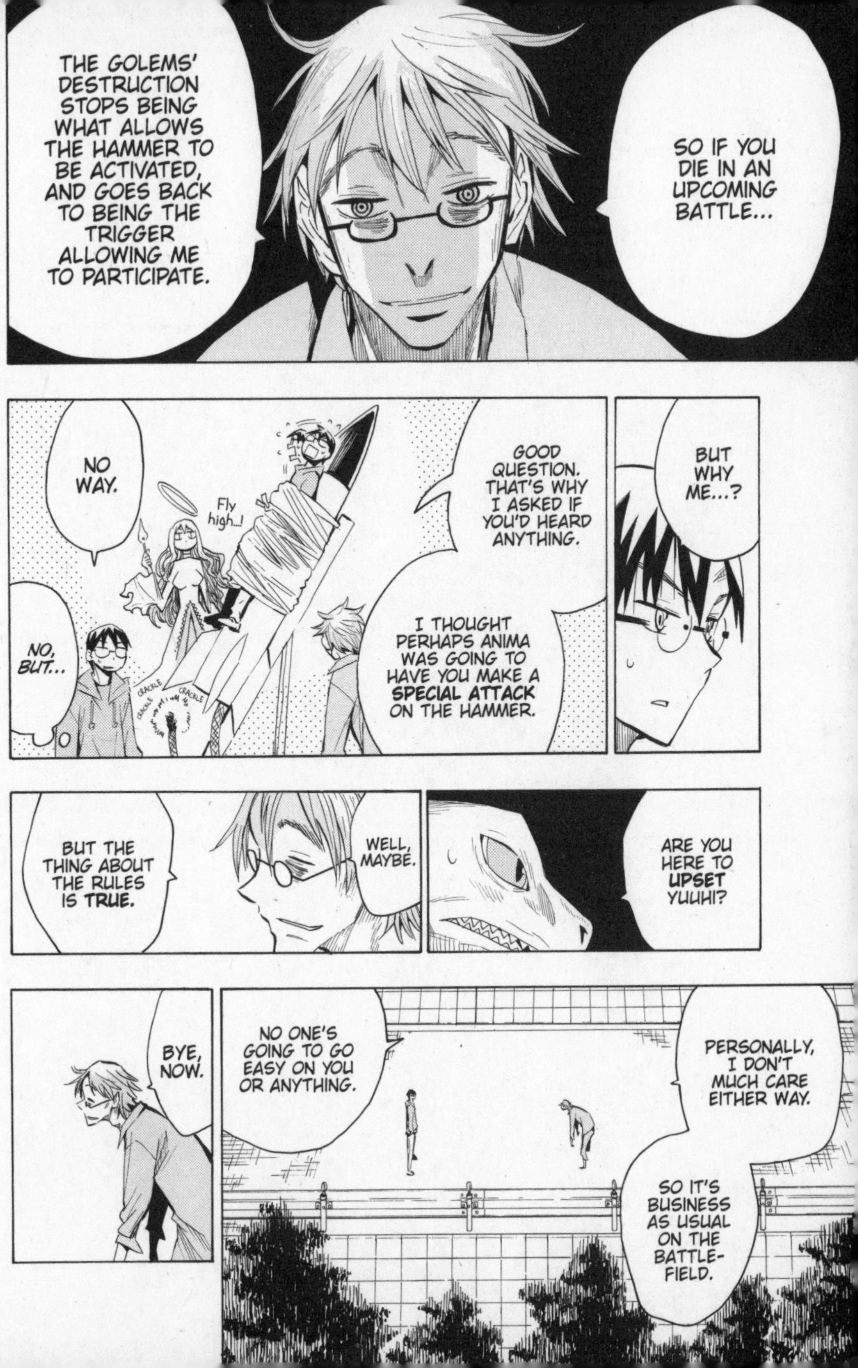
SO IF YOU DIE IN AN UPCOMING BATTLE...
THE GOLEMS' DESTRUCTION STOPS BEING WHAT ALLOWS THE HAMMER TO BE ACTIVATED, AND GOES BACK TO BEING THE TRIGGER ALLOWING ME TO PARTICIPATE.
BUT WHY ME...?
GOOD QUESTION. THAT'S WHY I ASKED IF YOU'D HEARD ANYTHING.
I THOUGHT PERHAPS ANIMA WAS GOING TO HAVE YOU MAKE A **SPECIAL ATTACK** ON THE HAMMER.
NO WAY.
Fly high...!
CRACKLE CRACKLE
NO, BUT...
ARE YOU HERE TO **UPSET** YUUHI?
WELL, MAYBE.
BUT THE THING ABOUT THE RULES IS **TRUE.**
PERSONALLY, I DON'T MUCH CARE EITHER WAY.
SO IT'S BUSINESS AS USUAL ON THE BATTLE-FIELD.
NO ONE'S GOING TO GO EASY ON YOU OR ANYTHING.
BYE, NOW.

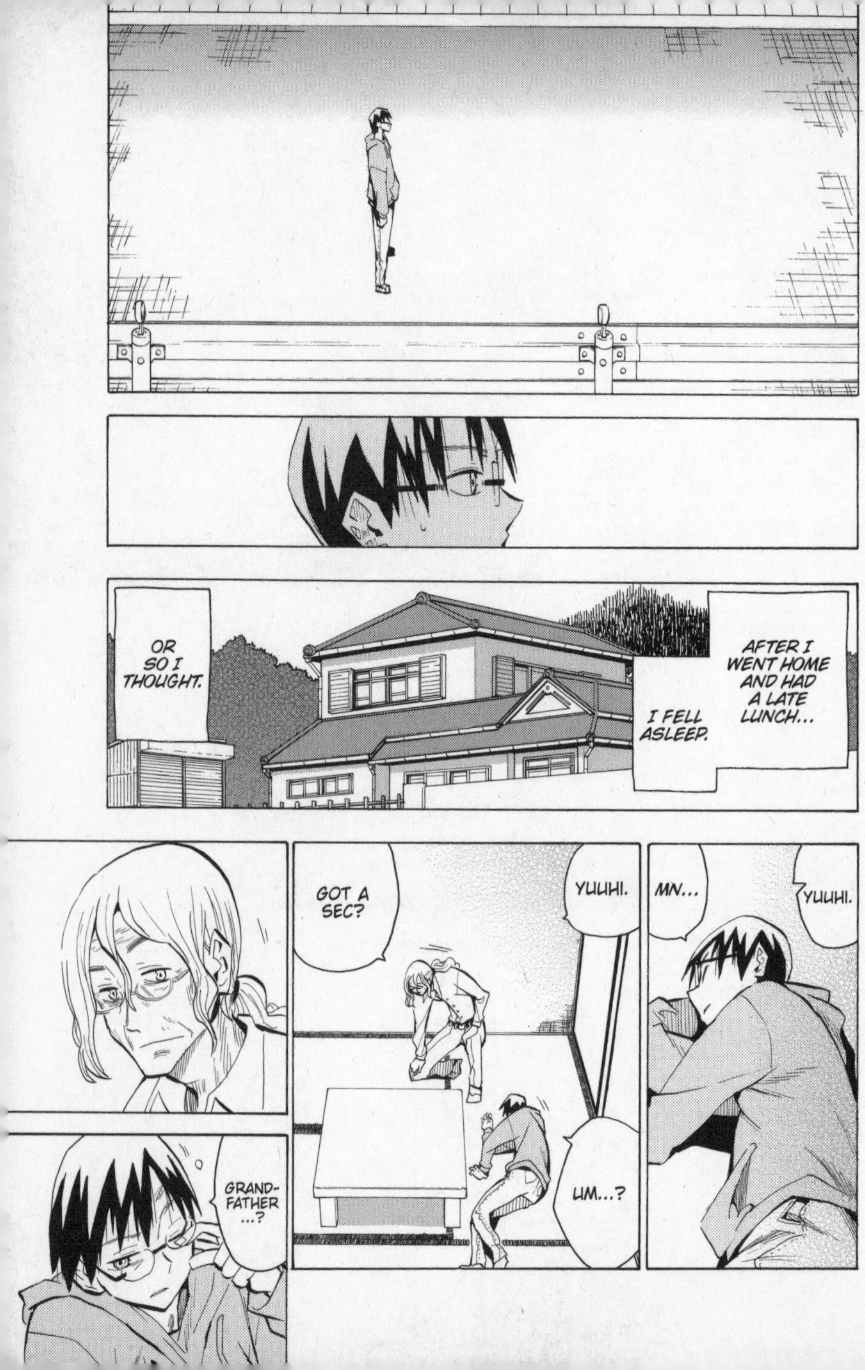
AFTER I WENT HOME AND HAD A LATE LUNCH...
I FELL ASLEEP.
OR SO I THOUGHT.
YUUHI.
MN...
YUUHI.
GOT A SEC?
UM...?
GRAND-FATHER ...?

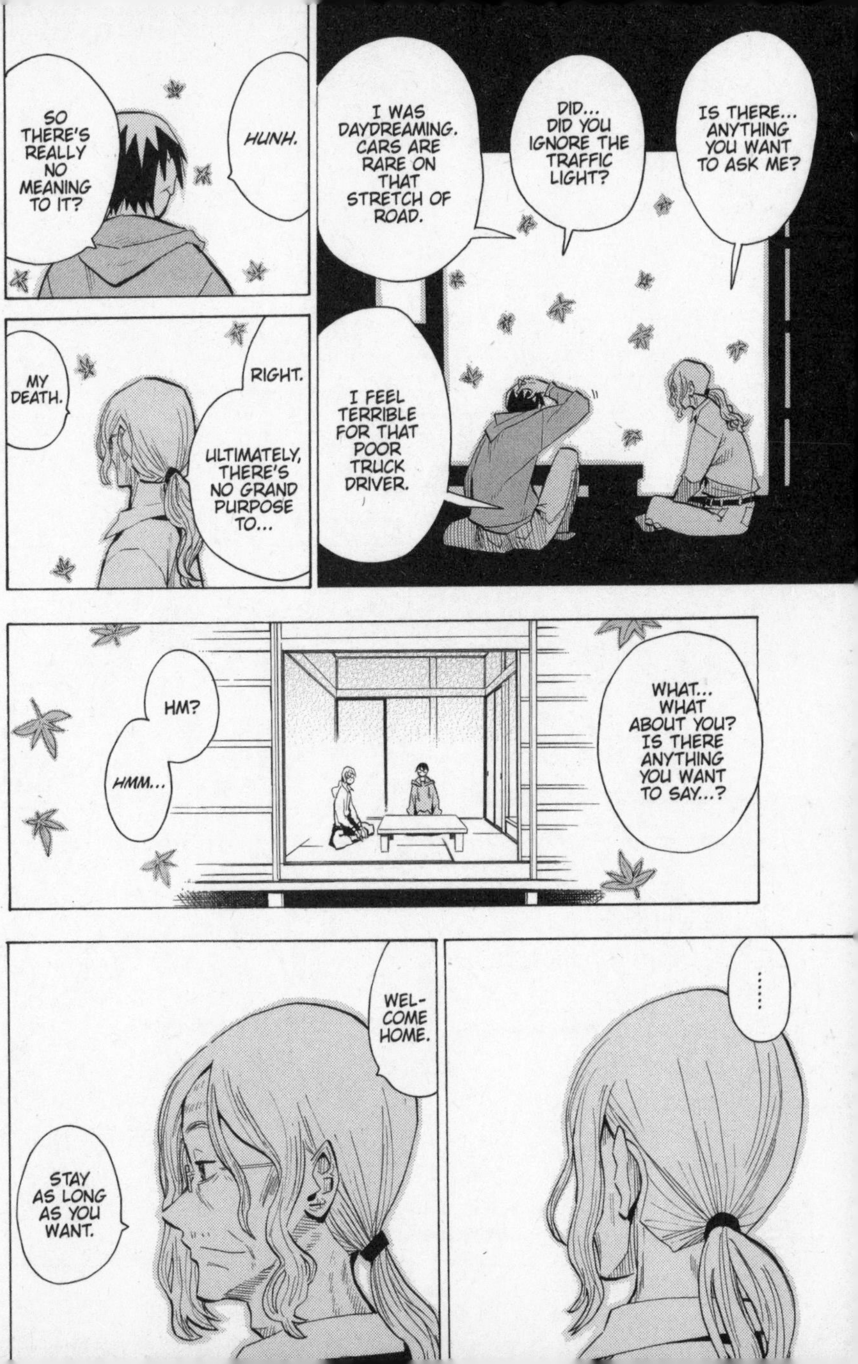
IS THERE... ANYTHING YOU WANT TO ASK ME?
DID... DID YOU IGNORE THE TRAFFIC LIGHT?
I WAS DAYDREAMING. CARS ARE RARE ON THAT STRETCH OF ROAD.
I FEEL TERRIBLE FOR THAT POOR TRUCK DRIVER.
HUNH.
SO THERE'S REALLY NO MEANING TO IT?
RIGHT.
ULTIMATELY, THERE'S NO GRAND PURPOSE TO...
MY DEATH.
WHAT... WHAT ABOUT YOU? IS THERE ANYTHING YOU WANT TO SAY...?
HM?
HMM...
......
WEL-COME HOME.
STAY AS LONG AS YOU WANT.

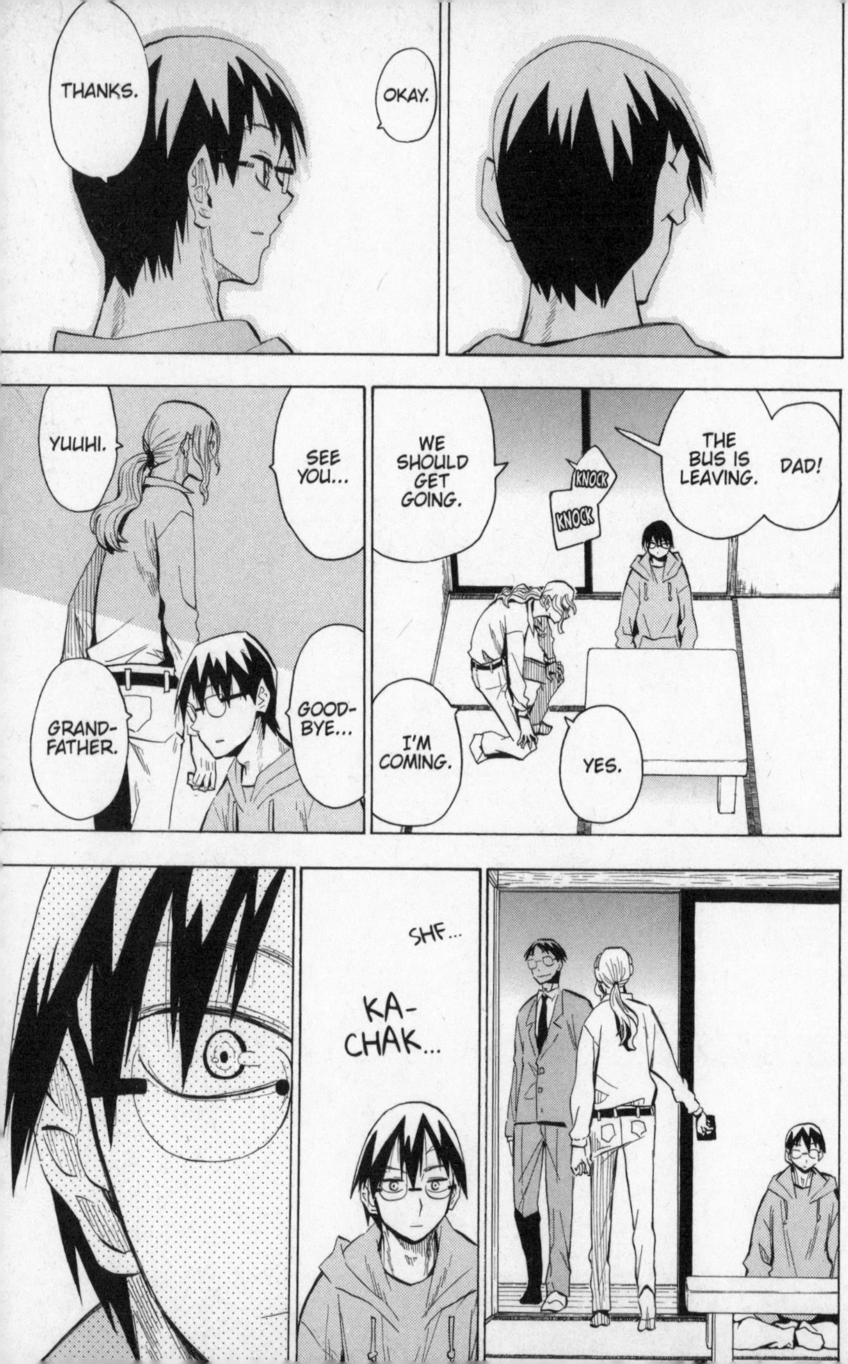
OKAY.
THANKS.
DAD!
THE BUS IS LEAVING.
KNOCK
KNOCK
WE SHOULD GET GOING.
YES.
I'M COMING.
SEE YOU...
YUUHI.
GOOD-BYE...
GRAND-FATHER.
SHF...
KA-CHAK...

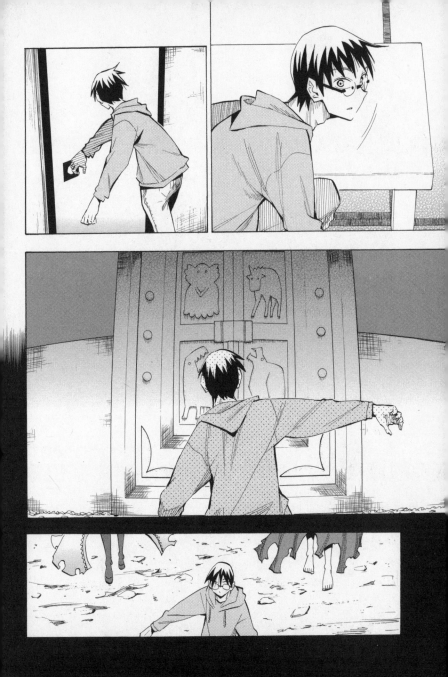

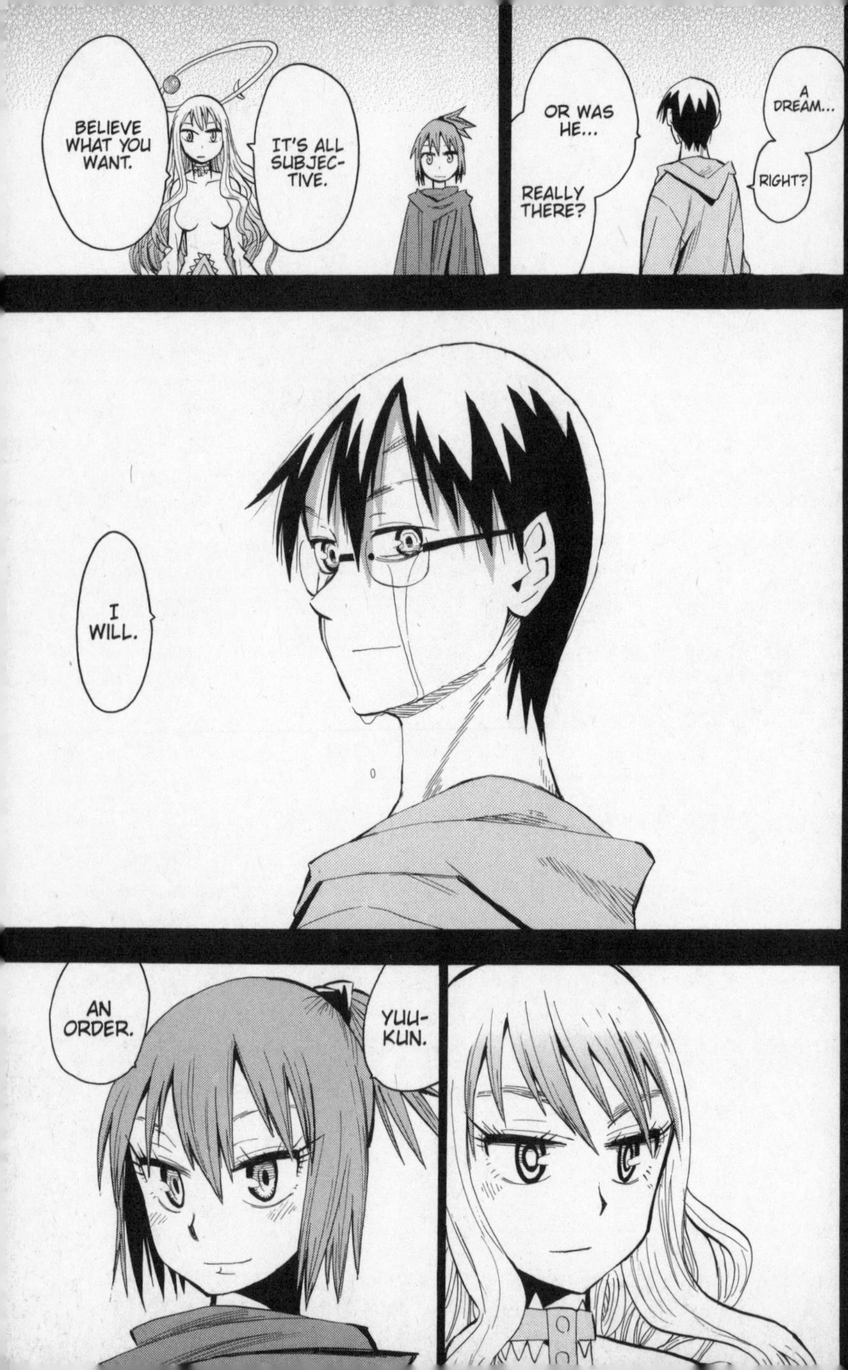
A DREAM...
RIGHT?
OR WAS HE...
REALLY THERE?
IT'S ALL SUBJECTIVE.
BELIEVE WHAT YOU WANT.
I WILL.
YUU-KUN.
AN ORDER.

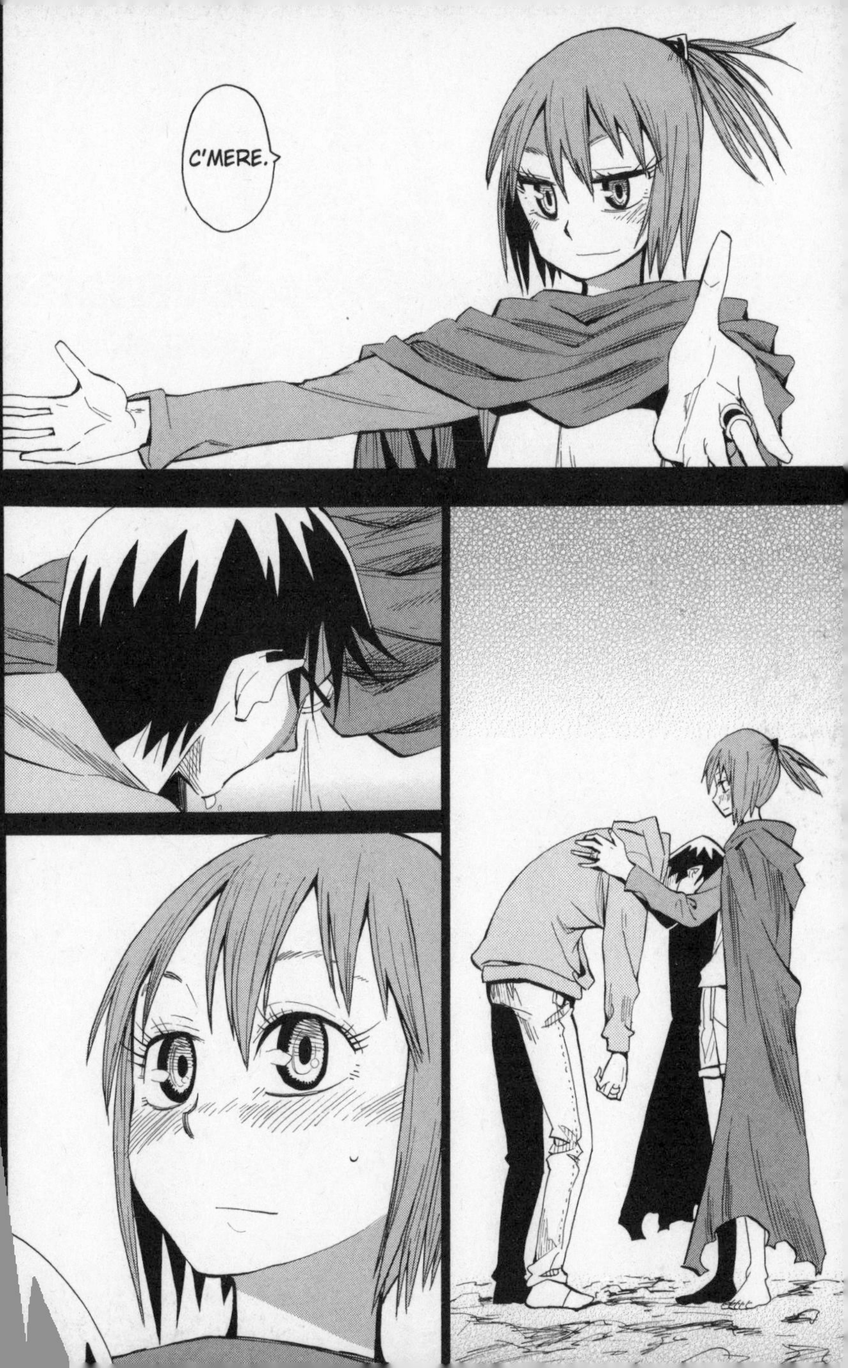
C'MERE.

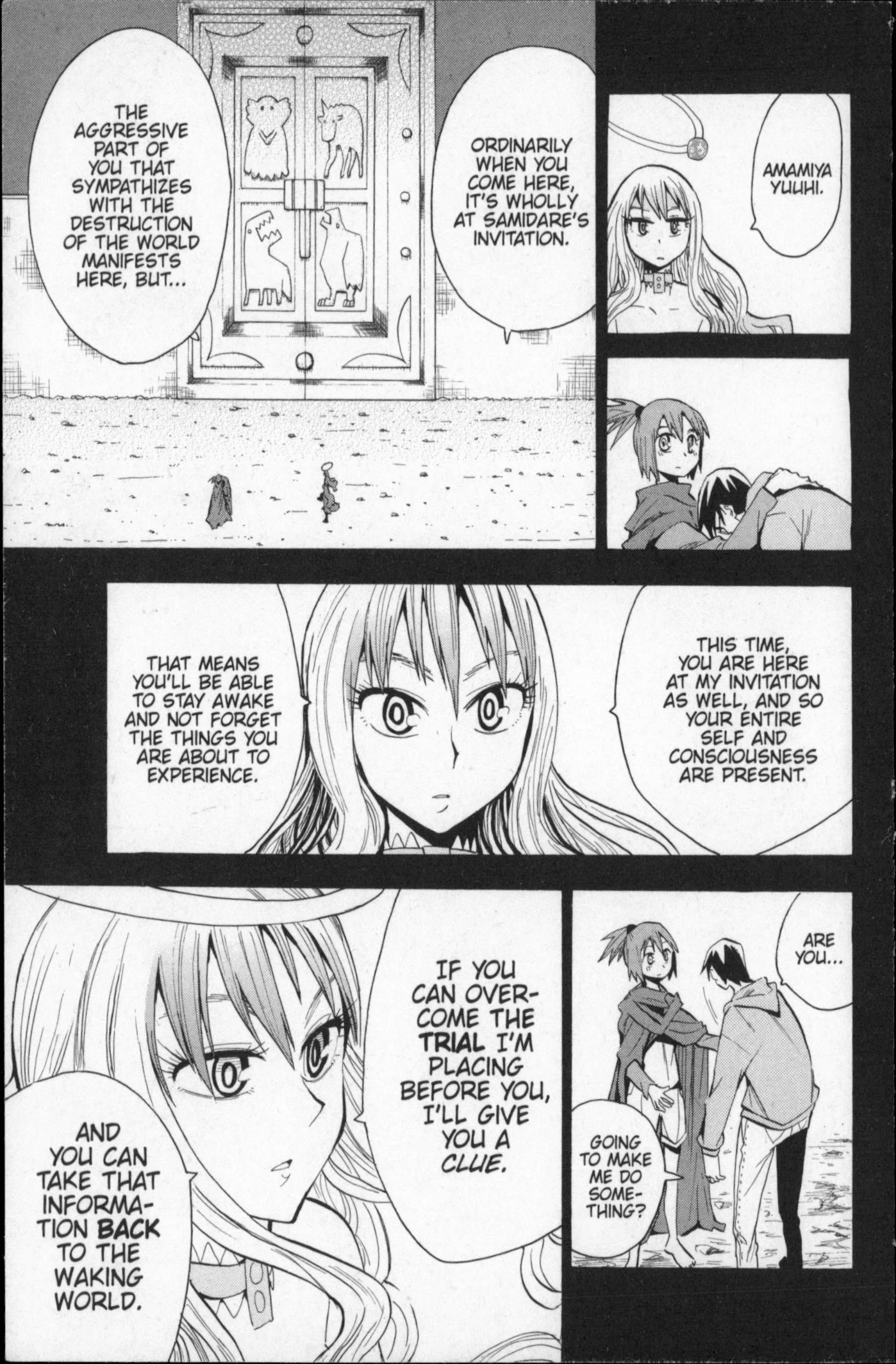
AMAMIYA YUUHI.
ORDINARILY WHEN YOU COME HERE, IT'S WHOLLY AT SAMIDARE'S INVITATION.
THE AGGRESSIVE PART OF YOU THAT SYMPATHIZES WITH THE DESTRUCTION OF THE WORLD MANIFESTS HERE, BUT...
THIS TIME, YOU ARE HERE AT MY INVITATION AS WELL, AND SO YOUR ENTIRE SELF AND CONSCIOUSNESS ARE PRESENT.
THAT MEANS YOU'LL BE ABLE TO STAY AWAKE AND NOT FORGET THE THINGS YOU ARE ABOUT TO EXPERIENCE.
ARE YOU...
GOING TO MAKE ME DO SOME-THING?
IF YOU CAN OVER-COME THE **TRIAL** I'M PLACING BEFORE YOU, I'LL GIVE YOU A *CLUE*.
AND YOU CAN TAKE THAT INFORMA-TION **BACK** TO THE WAKING WORLD.

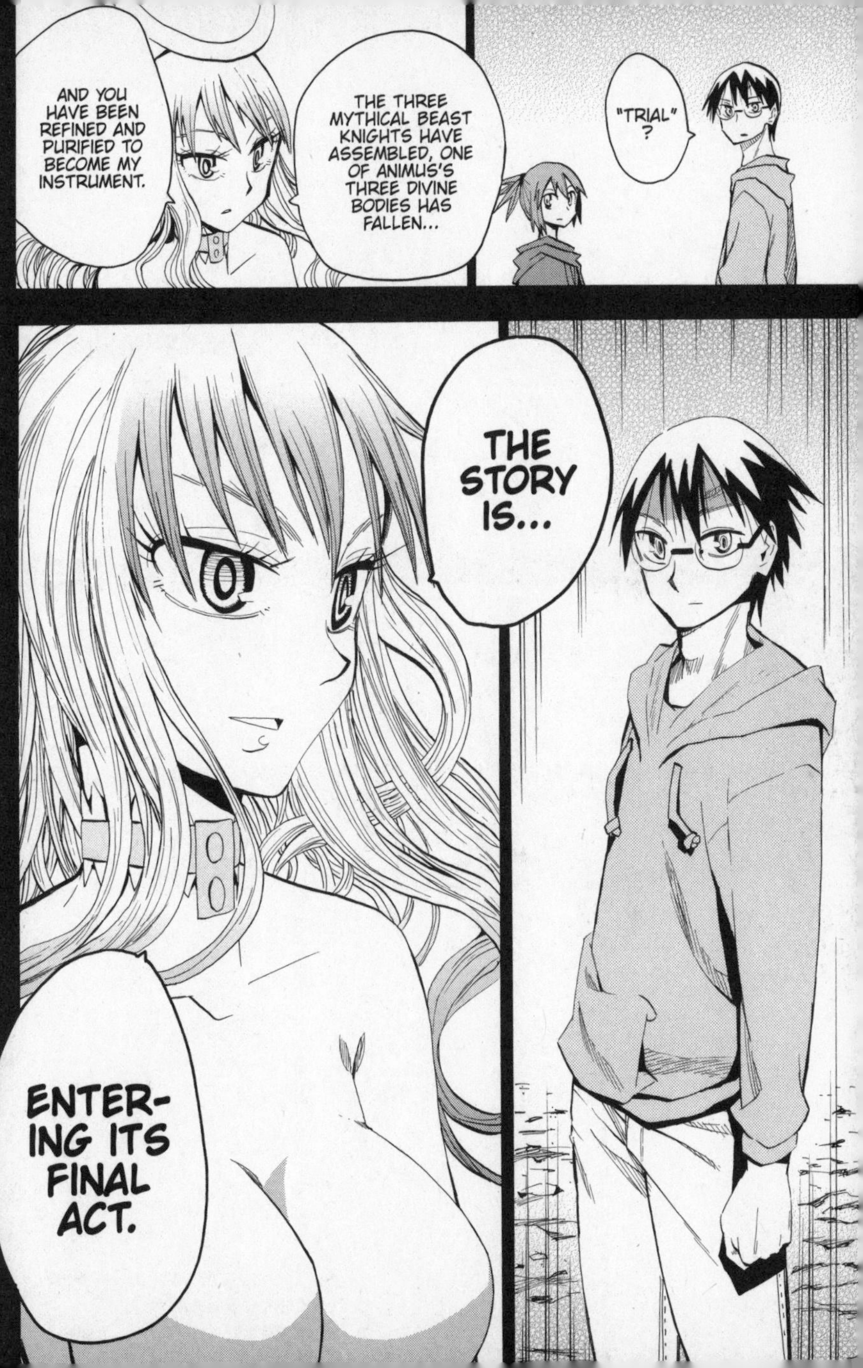
"TRIAL"?
THE THREE MYTHICAL BEAST KNIGHTS HAVE ASSEMBLED, ONE OF ANIMUS'S THREE DIVINE BODIES HAS FALLEN...
AND YOU HAVE BEEN REFINED AND PURIFIED TO BECOME MY INSTRUMENT.
THE STORY IS...
ENTER-ING ITS FINAL ACT.

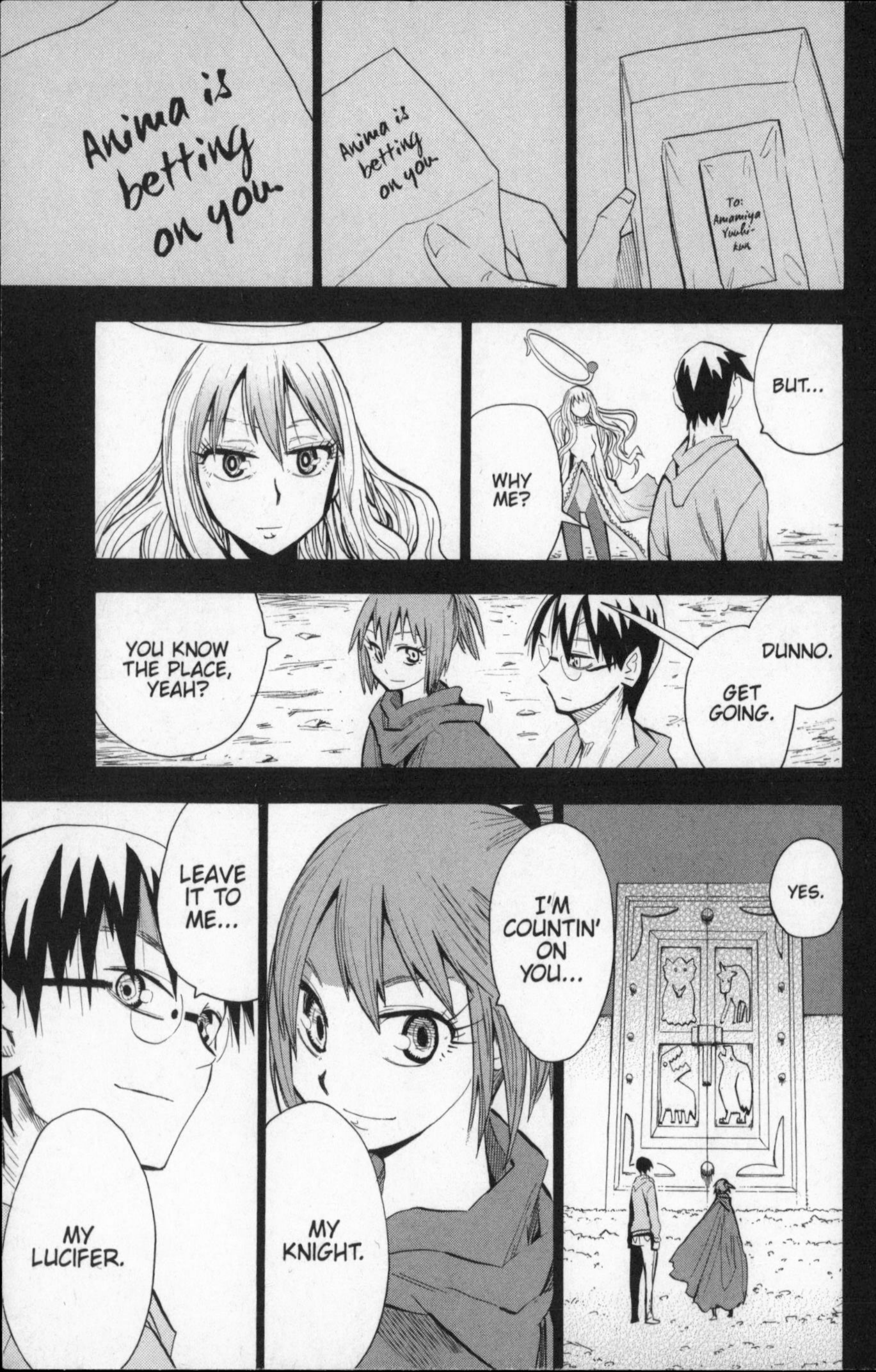
To: Amamiya Yuuhi-kun
Anima is betting on you
Anima is betting on you
BUT...
WHY ME?
DUNNO.
GET GOING.
YOU KNOW THE PLACE, YEAH?
YES.
I'M COUNTIN' ON YOU...
MY KNIGHT.
LEAVE IT TO ME...
MY LUCIFER.

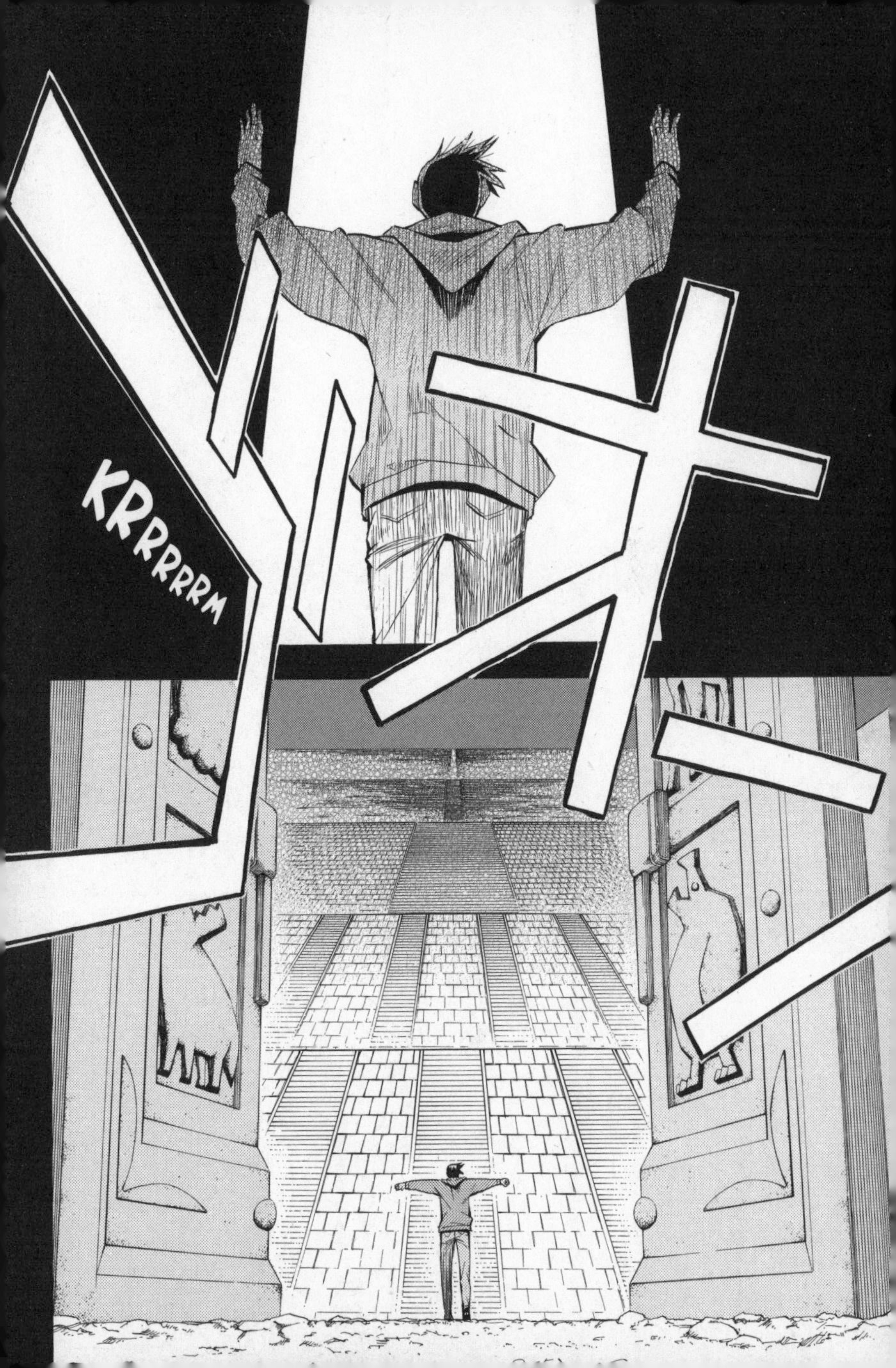
KRRRRRM

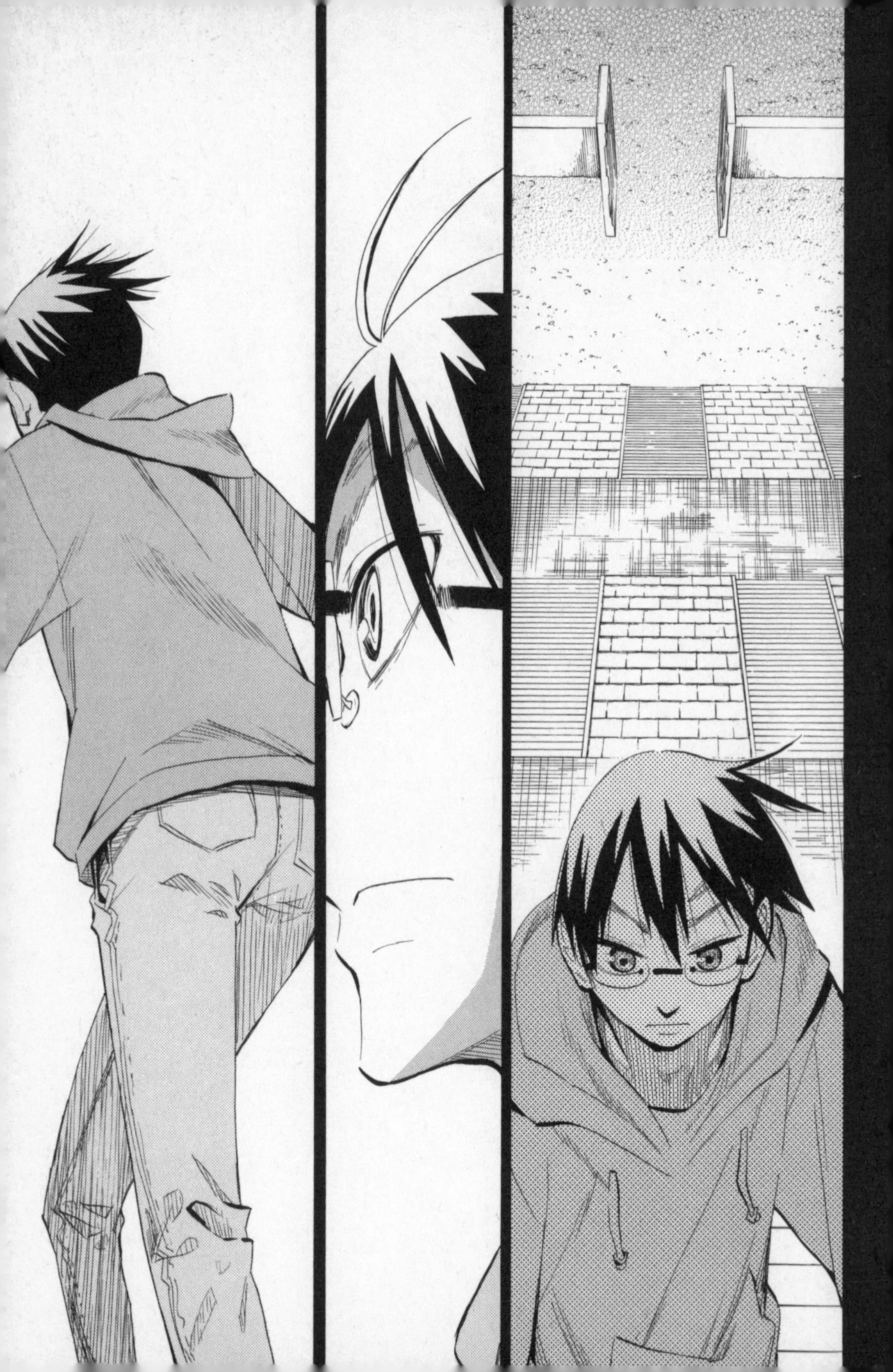

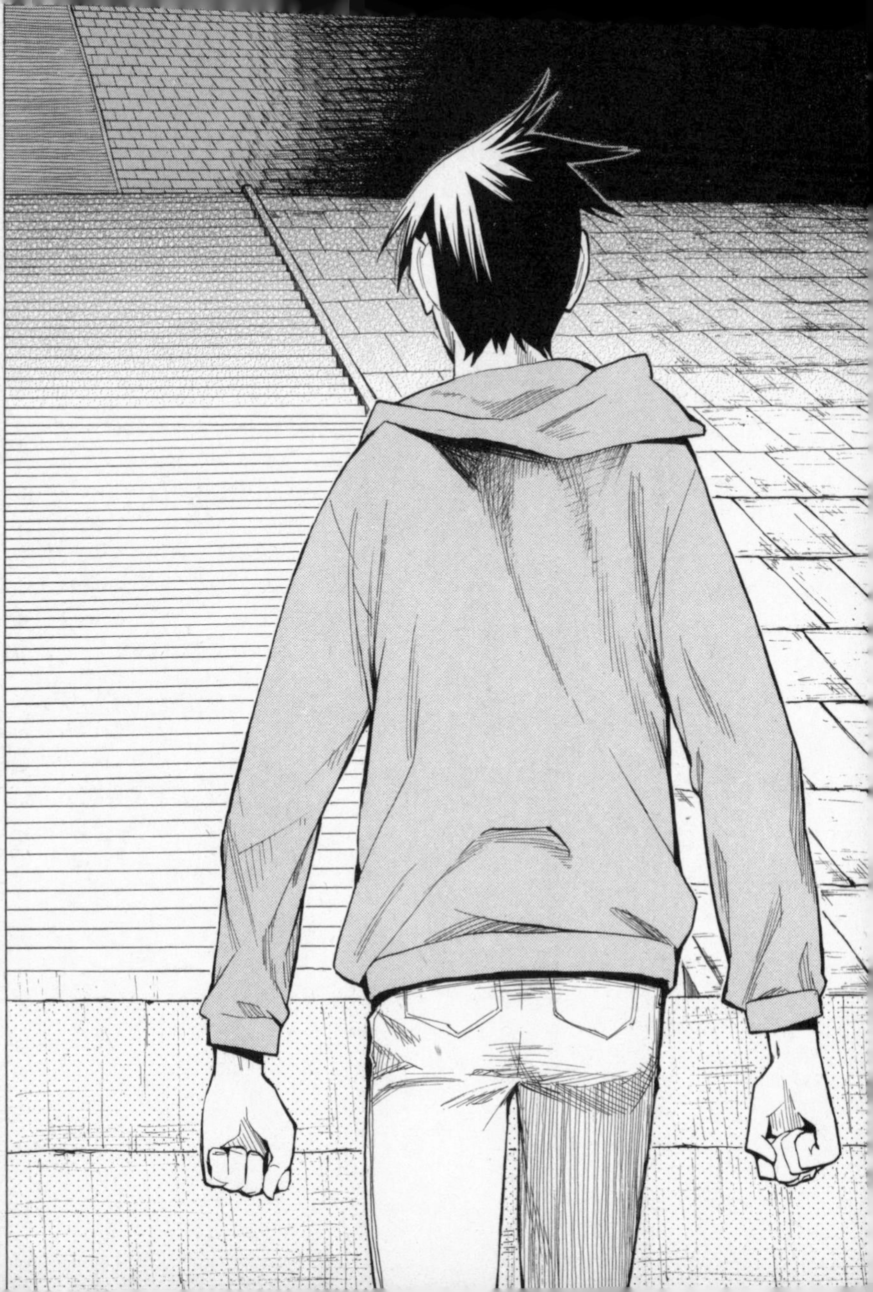

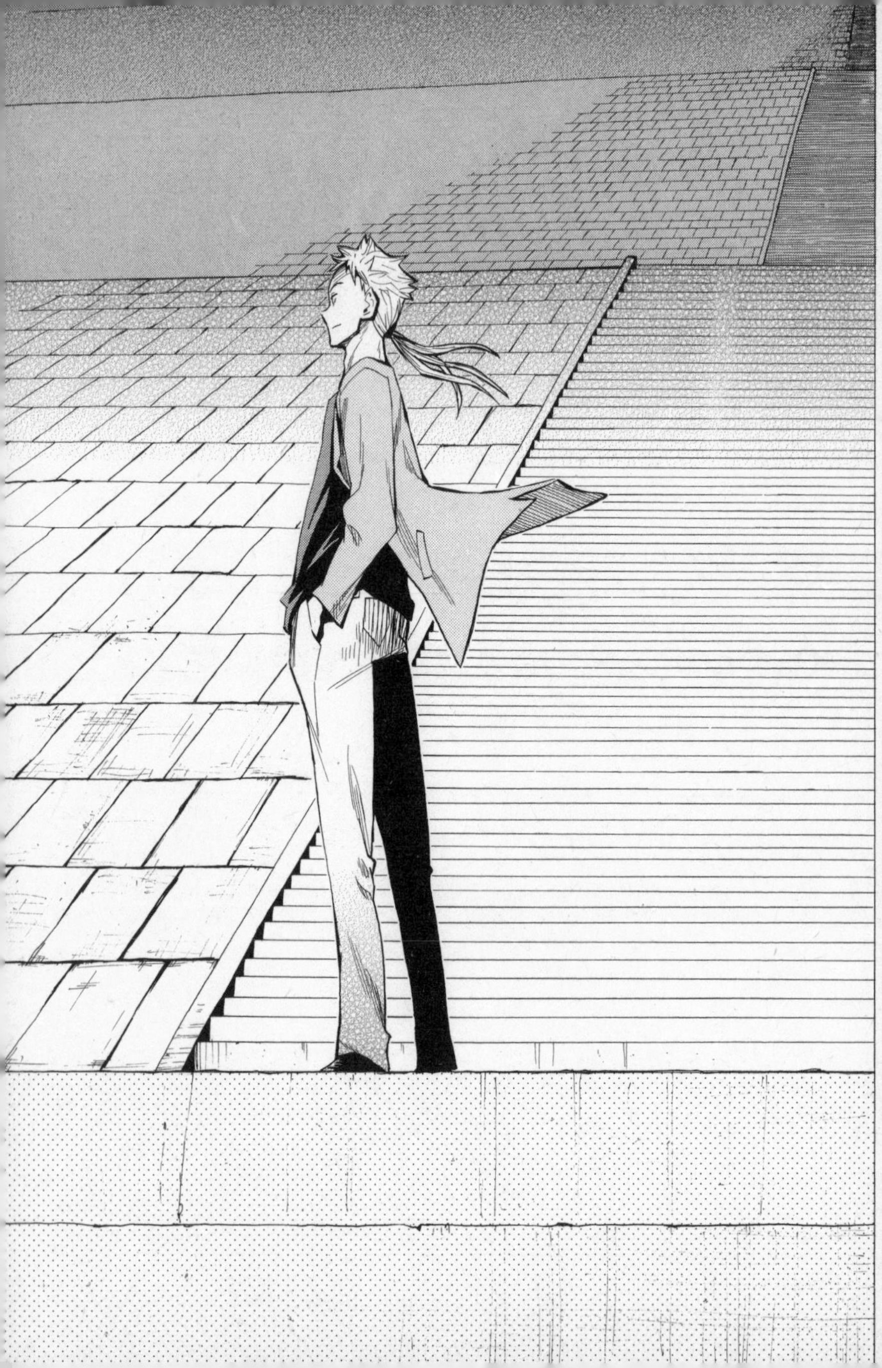

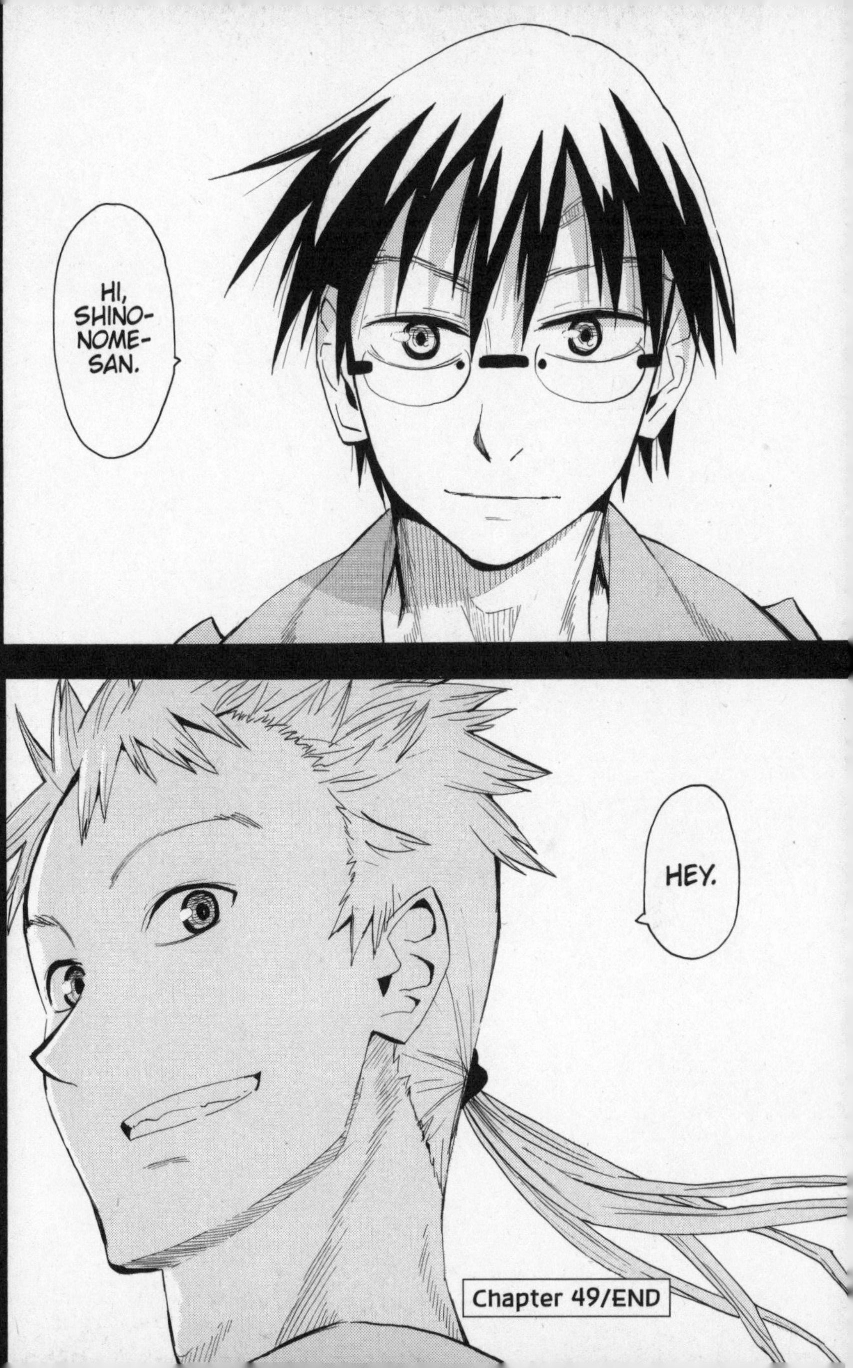
HI, SHINO-NOME-SAN.
HEY.
Chapter 49/END

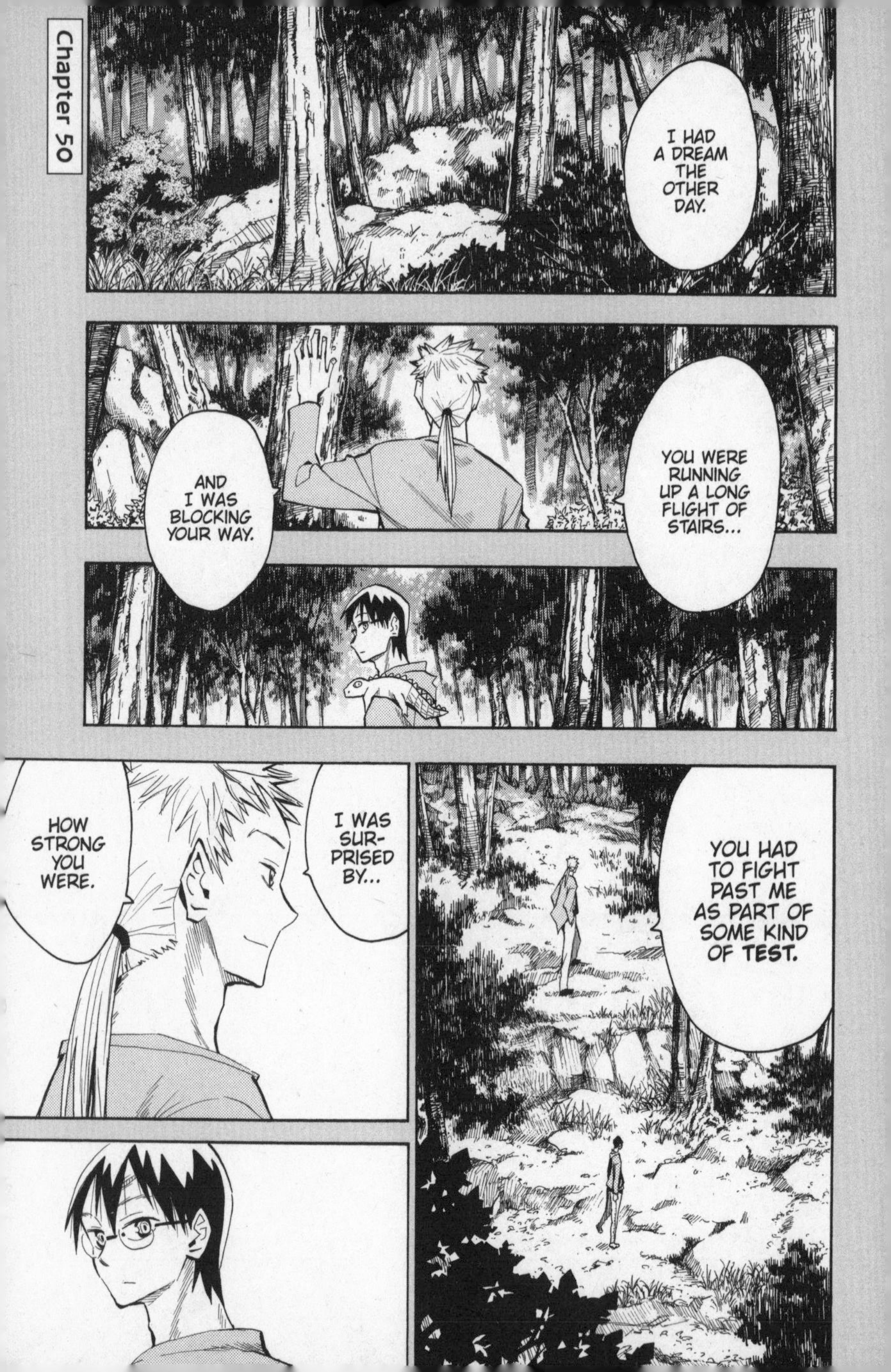
Chapter 50
I HAD A DREAM THE OTHER DAY.
YOU WERE RUNNING UP A LONG FLIGHT OF STAIRS...
AND I WAS BLOCKING YOUR WAY.
YOU HAD TO FIGHT PAST ME AS PART OF SOME KIND OF TEST.
I WAS SUR-PRISED BY...
HOW STRONG YOU WERE.

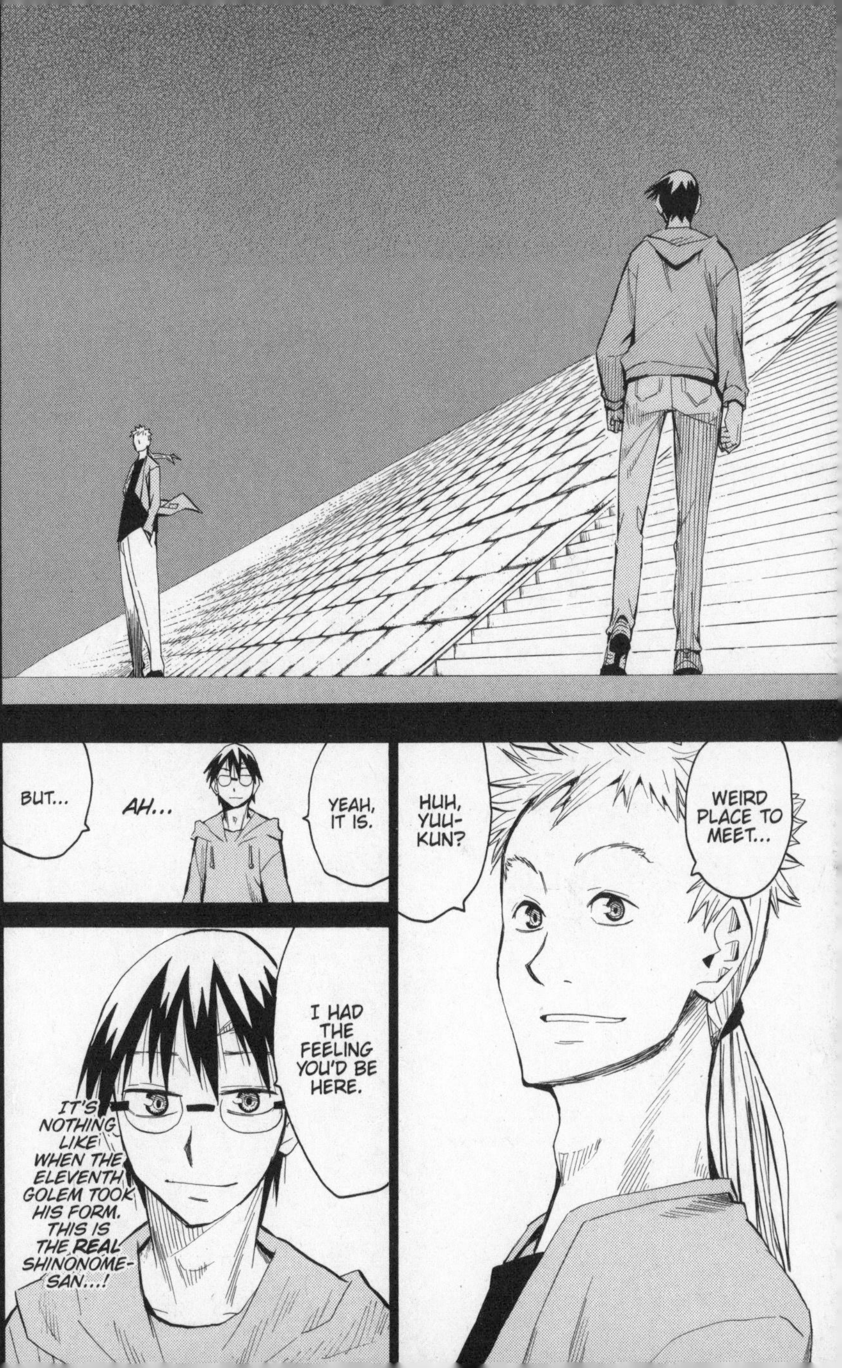
WEIRD PLACE TO MEET...
HUH, YUU-KUN?
YEAH, IT IS.
AH...
BUT...
I HAD THE FEELING YOU'D BE HERE.
IT'S NOTHING LIKE WHEN THE ELEVENTH GOLEM TOOK HIS FORM. THIS IS THE REAL SHINONOME-SAN...!

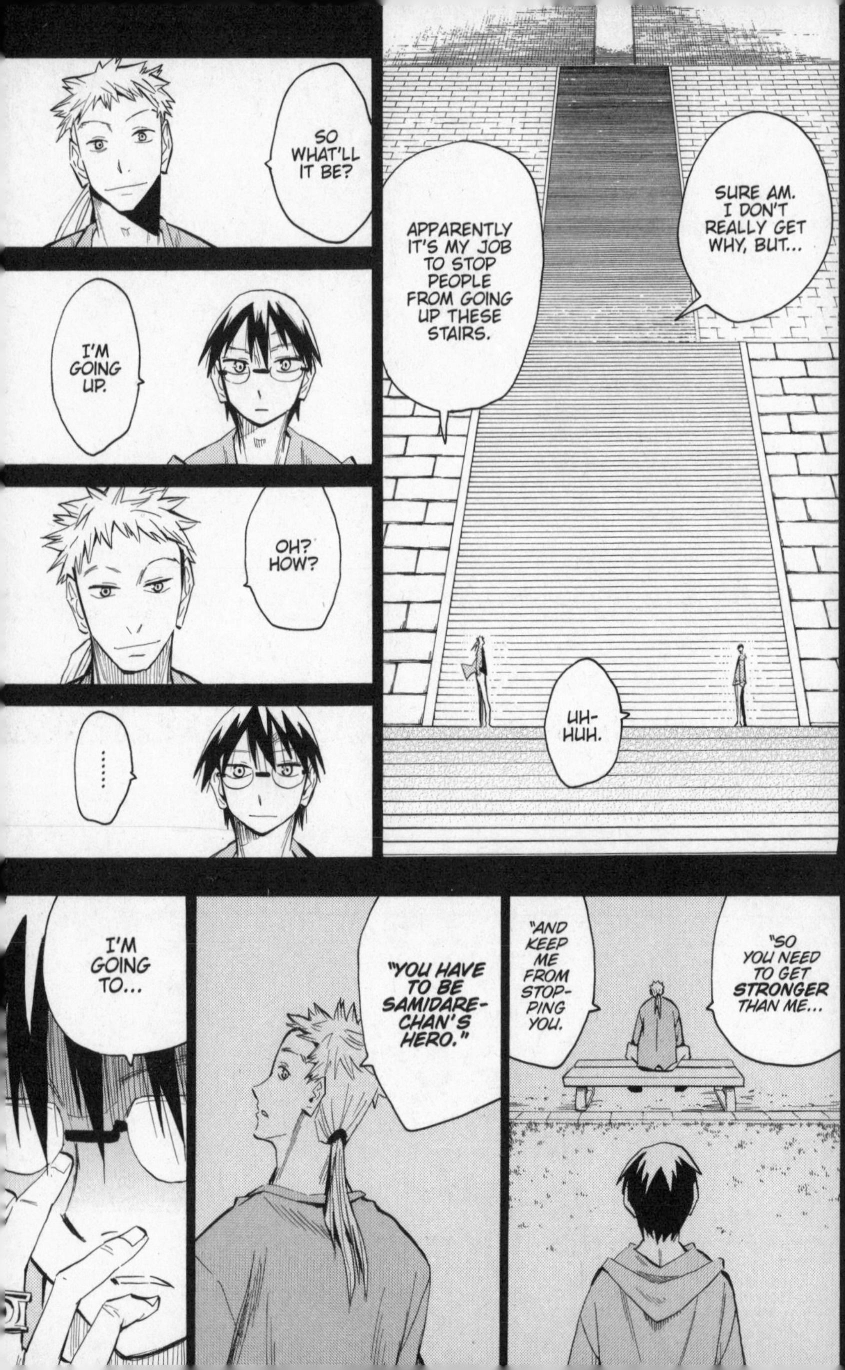
SURE AM. I DON'T REALLY GET WHY, BUT...
APPARENTLY IT'S MY JOB TO STOP PEOPLE FROM GOING UP THESE STAIRS.
UH-HUH.
SO WHAT'LL IT BE?
I'M GOING UP.
OH? HOW?
......
"SO YOU NEED TO GET STRONGER THAN ME...
"AND KEEP ME FROM STOP-PING YOU.
"YOU HAVE TO BE SAMIDARE-CHAN'S HERO."
I'M GOING TO...

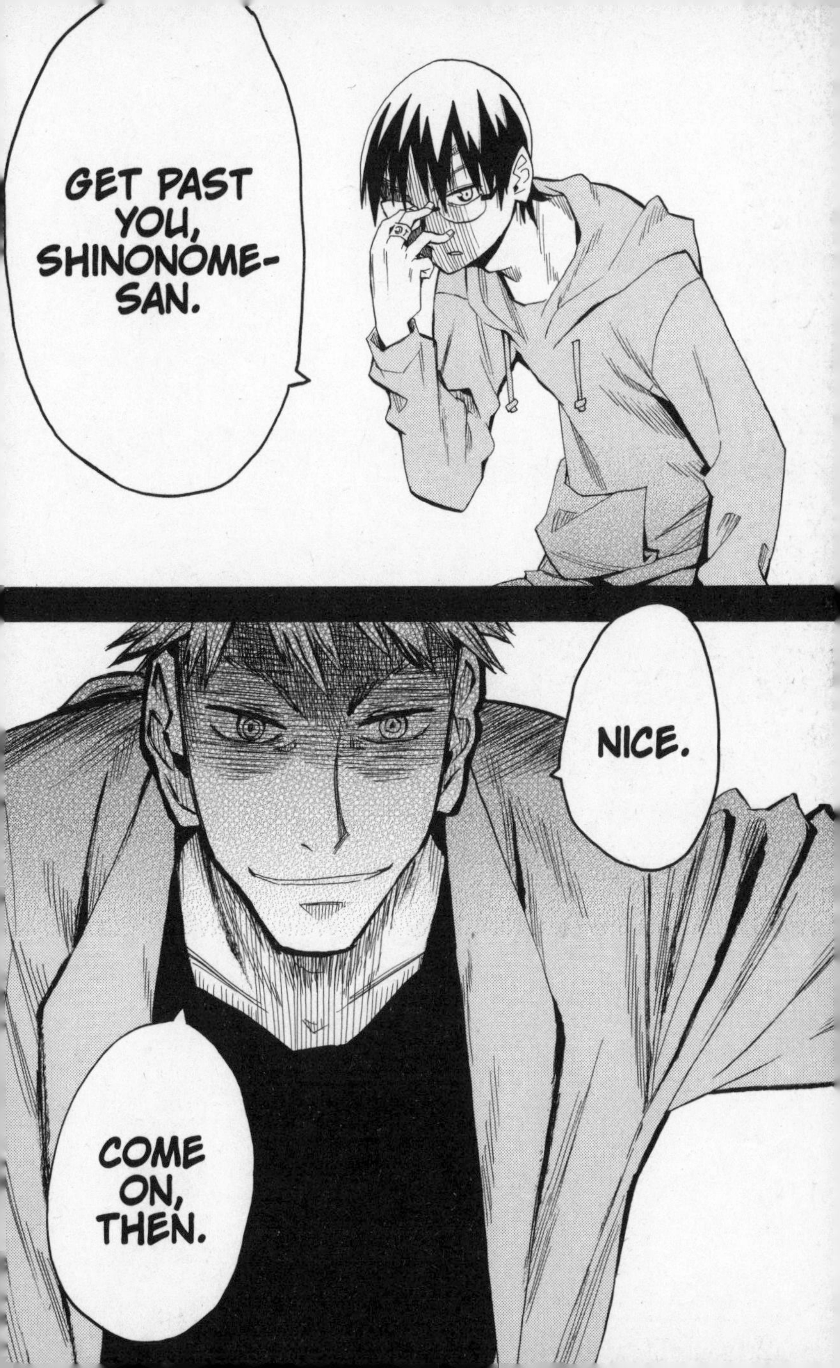
GET PAST YOU, SHINONOME-SAN.
NICE.
COME ON, THEN.

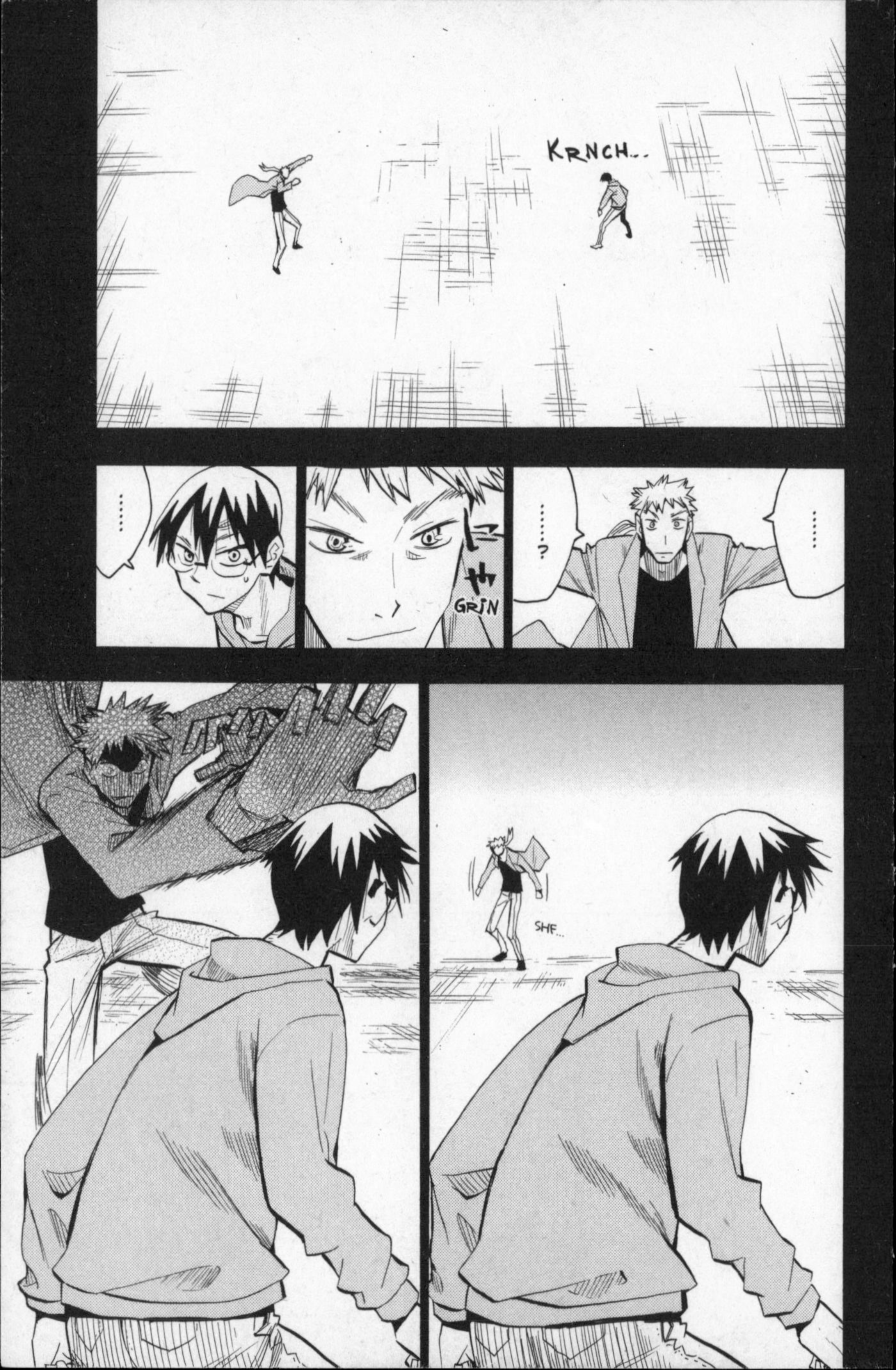
KRNCH...
......
......?
GRIN
......
SHF...

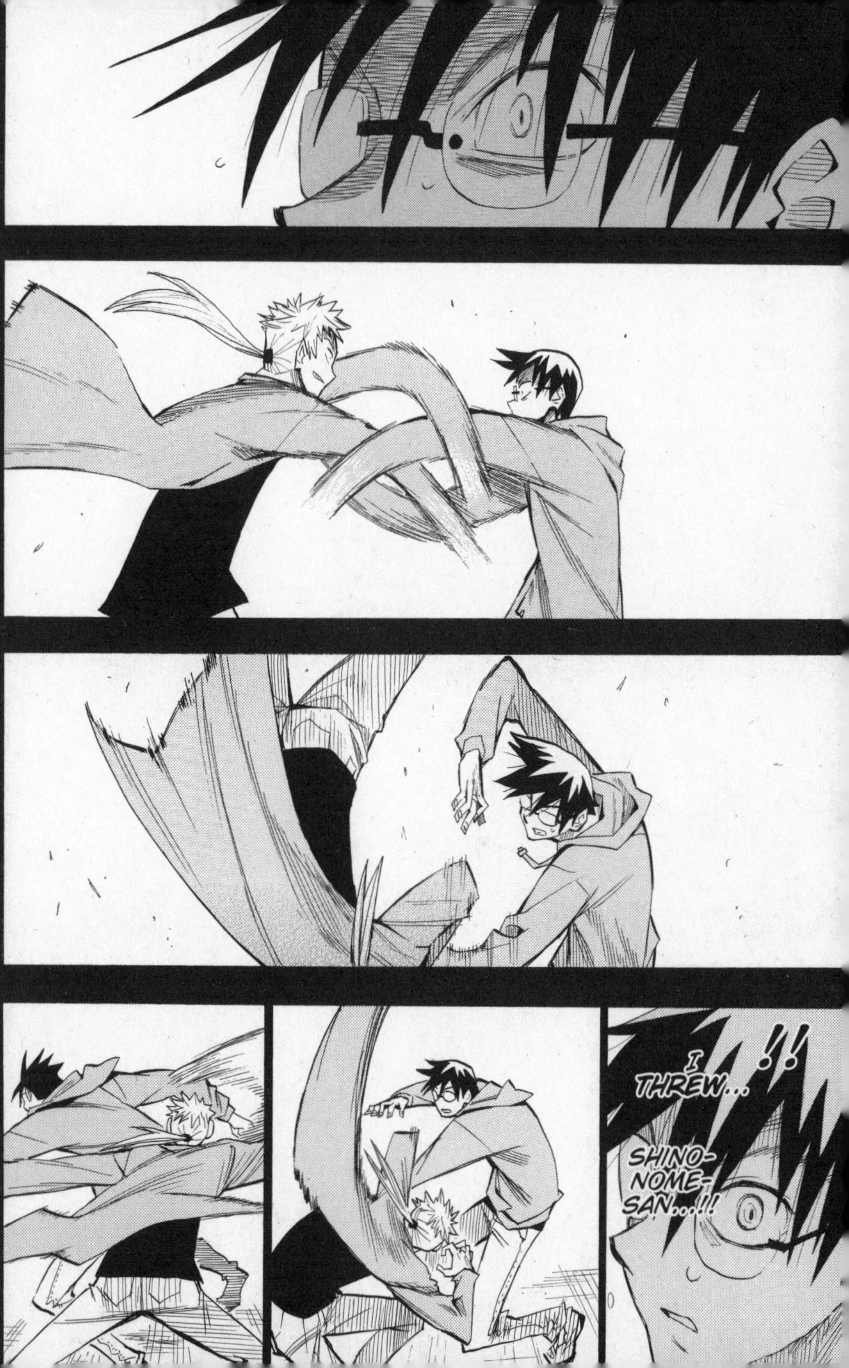
!!
I THREW...
SHINO-NOME-SAN...!!

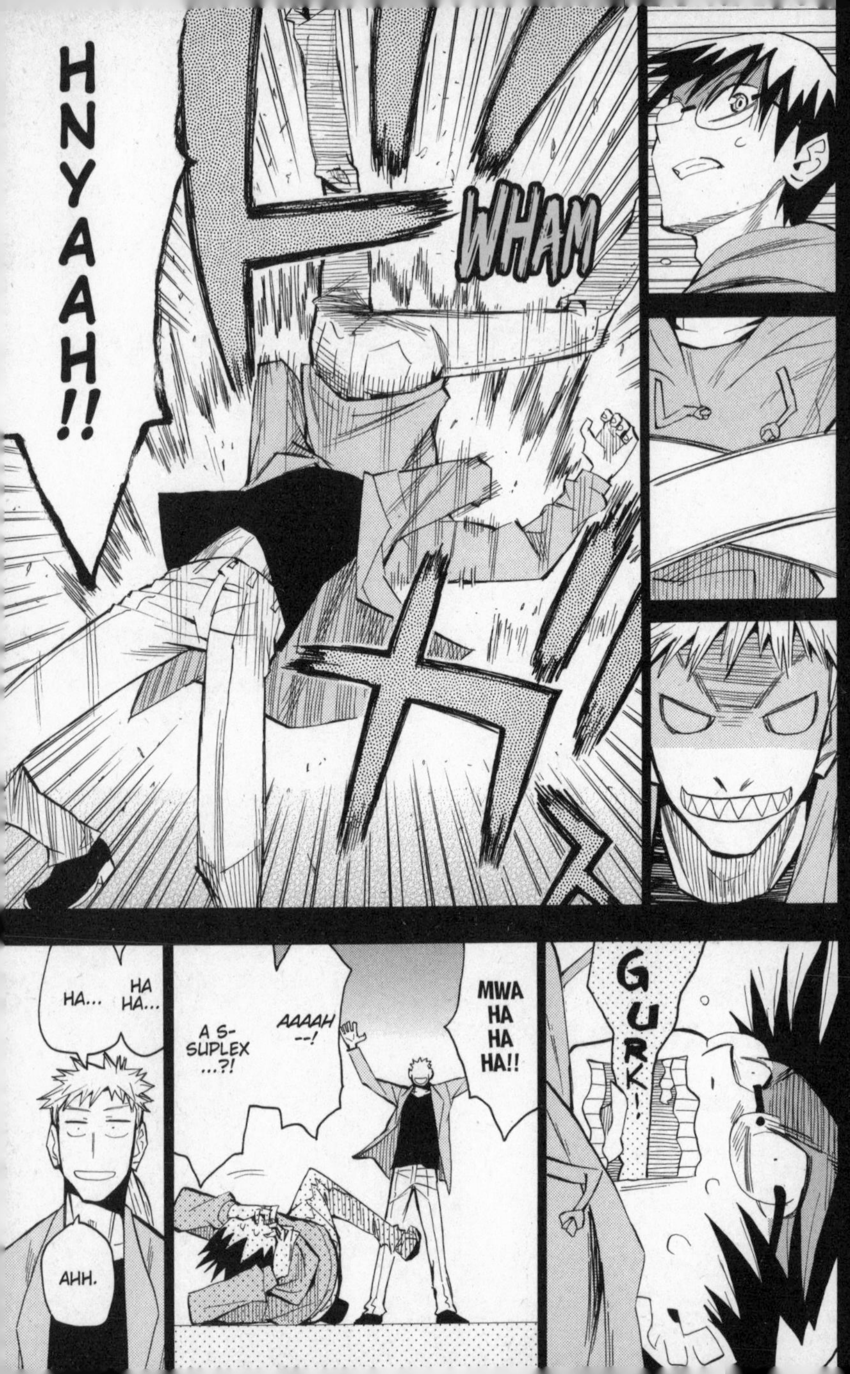
WHAM
HNYAAH!!
GURK!
MWA HA HA HA HA!!
AAAAH--!
A S-SUPLEX...?!
HA... HA HA...
AHH.

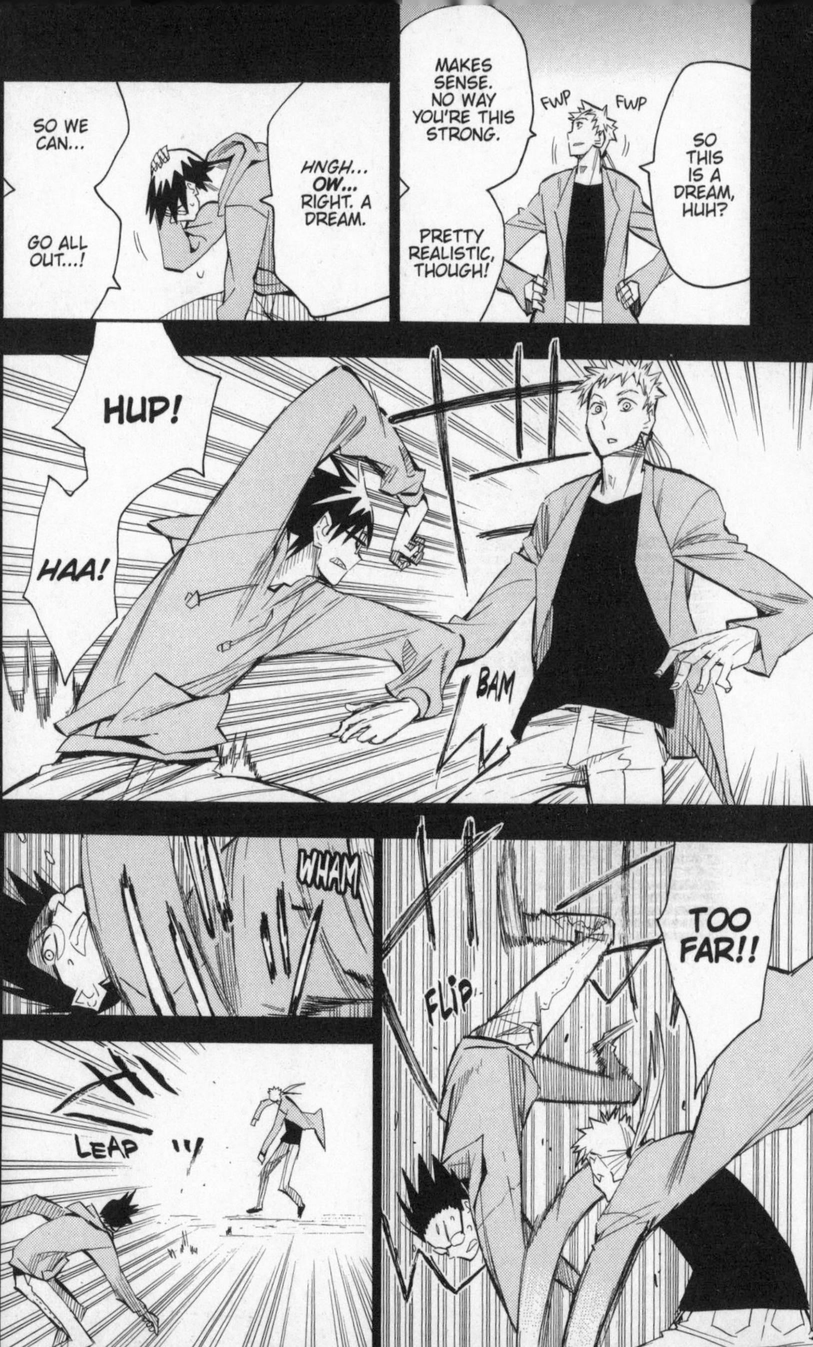
SO THIS IS A DREAM, HUH?
FWP
FWP
MAKES SENSE. NO WAY YOU'RE THIS STRONG.
PRETTY REALISTIC, THOUGH!
HNGH... OW... RIGHT. A DREAM.
SO WE CAN...
GO ALL OUT...!
HUP!
HAA!
BAM
TOO FAR!!
FLIP
WHAM
LEAP

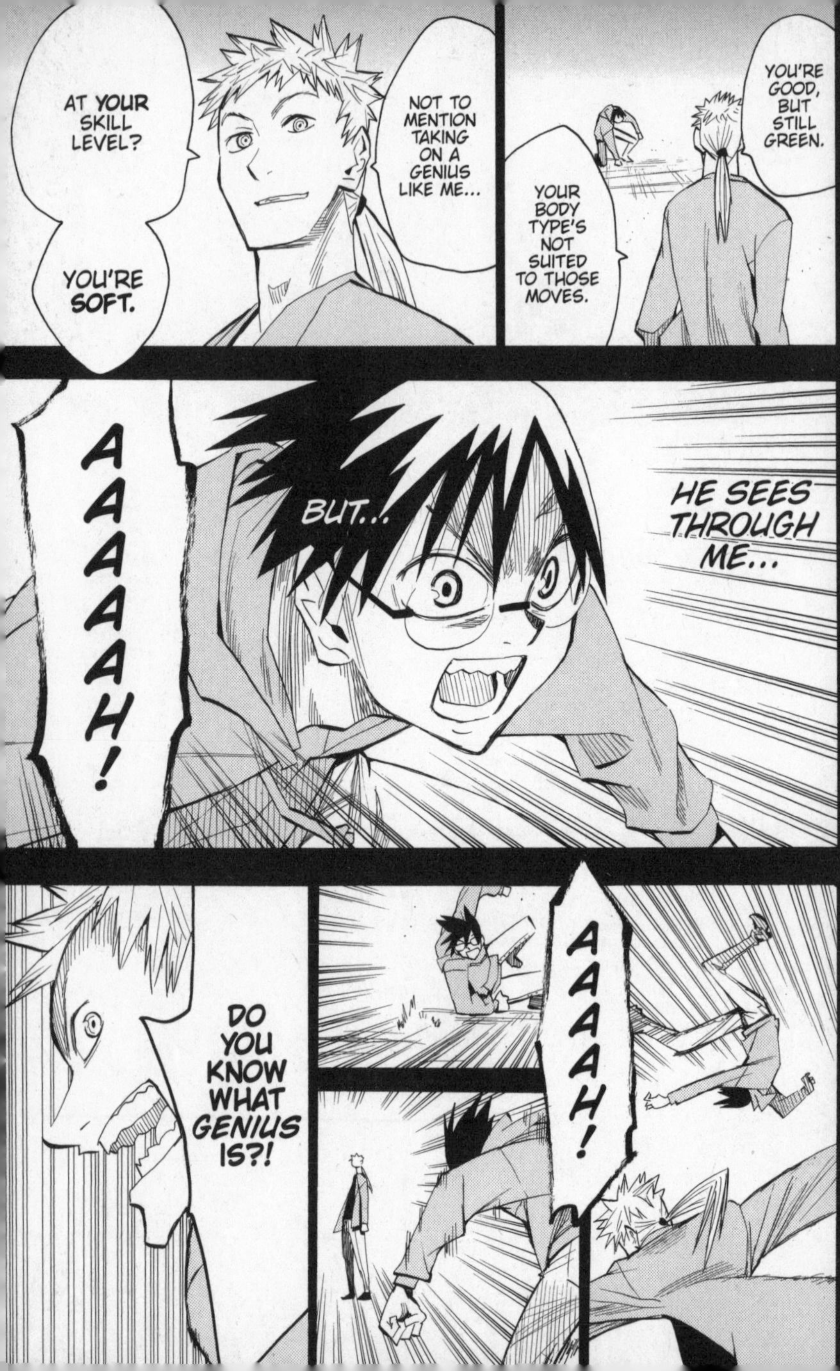
YOU'RE GOOD, BUT STILL GREEN.
YOUR BODY TYPE'S NOT SUITED TO THOSE MOVES.
NOT TO MENTION TAKING ON A GENIUS LIKE ME...
AT YOUR SKILL LEVEL?
YOU'RE SOFT.
HE SEES THROUGH ME...
BUT...
AAAAAH!
AAAAH!
DO YOU KNOW WHAT GENIUS IS?!

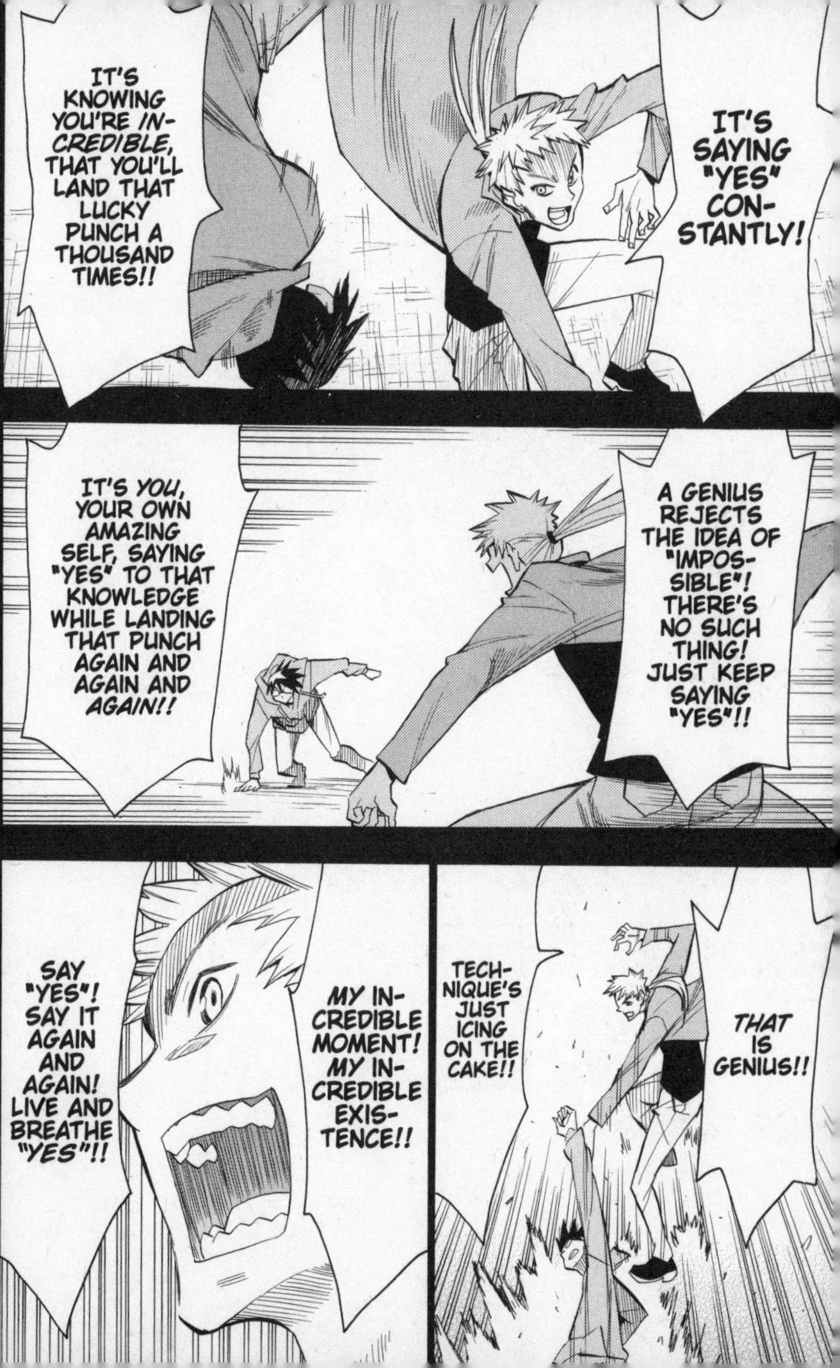
IT'S SAYING "YES" CONSTANTLY!
IT'S KNOWING YOU'RE *INCREDIBLE*, THAT YOU'LL LAND THAT LUCKY PUNCH A THOUSAND TIMES!!
A GENIUS REJECTS THE IDEA OF "IMPOSSIBLE"! THERE'S NO SUCH THING! JUST KEEP SAYING "YES"!!
IT'S *YOU*, YOUR OWN AMAZING SELF, SAYING "YES" TO THAT KNOWLEDGE WHILE LANDING THAT PUNCH AGAIN AND AGAIN AND *AGAIN*!!
THAT IS GENIUS!!
TECHNIQUE'S JUST ICING ON THE CAKE!!
MY INCREDIBLE MOMENT! *MY* INCREDIBLE EXISTENCE!!
SAY "YES"! SAY IT AGAIN AND AGAIN! LIVE AND BREATHE *"YES"*!!

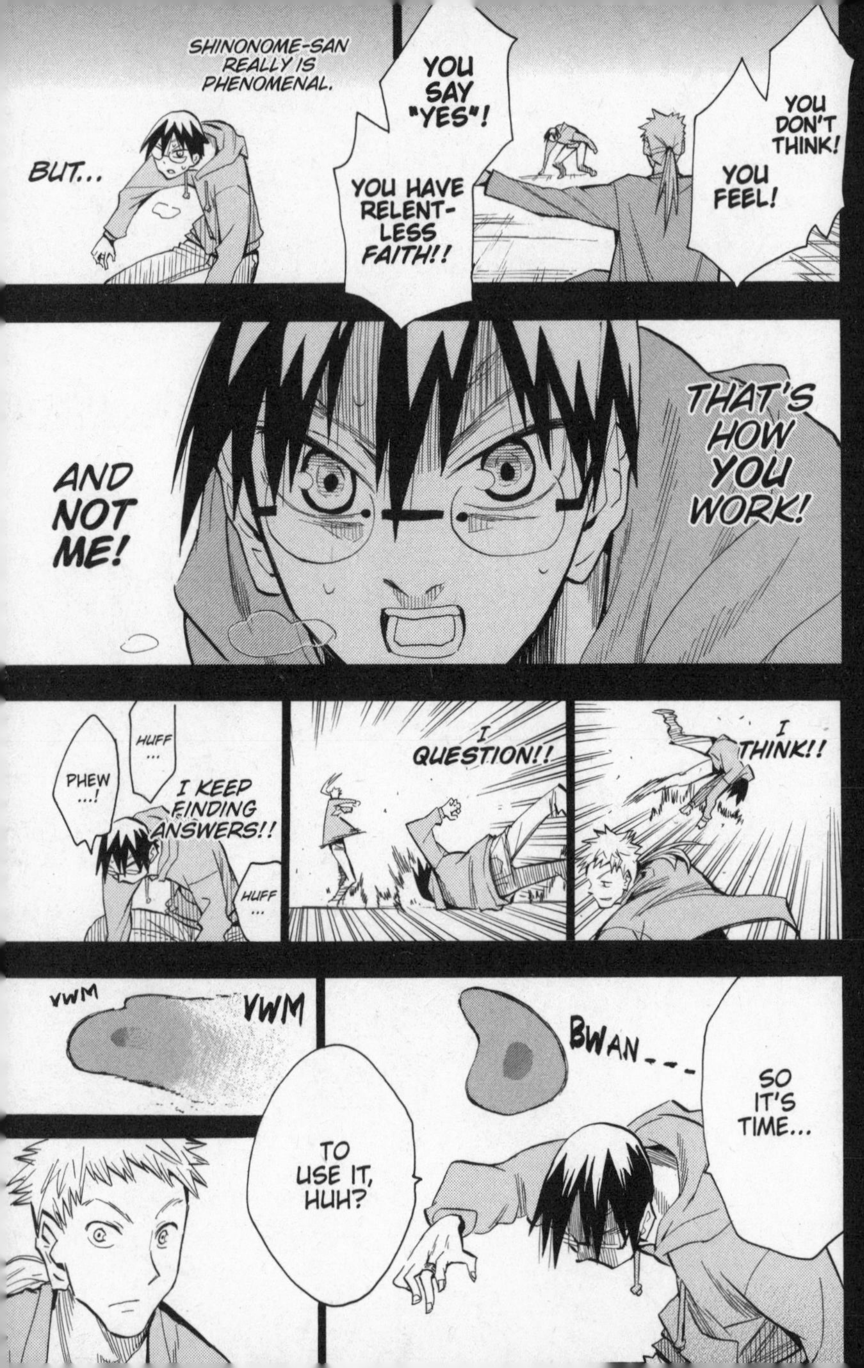
YOU DON'T THINK!
YOU FEEL!
YOU SAY "YES"!
YOU HAVE RELENTLESS FAITH!!
SHINONOME-SAN REALLY IS PHENOMENAL.
BUT...
THAT'S HOW YOU WORK!
AND NOT ME!
I THINK!!
I QUESTION!!
HUFF...
I KEEP FINDING ANSWERS!!
PHEW...!
HUFF...
SO IT'S TIME...
BWAN---
TO USE IT, HUH?
VWM
VWM

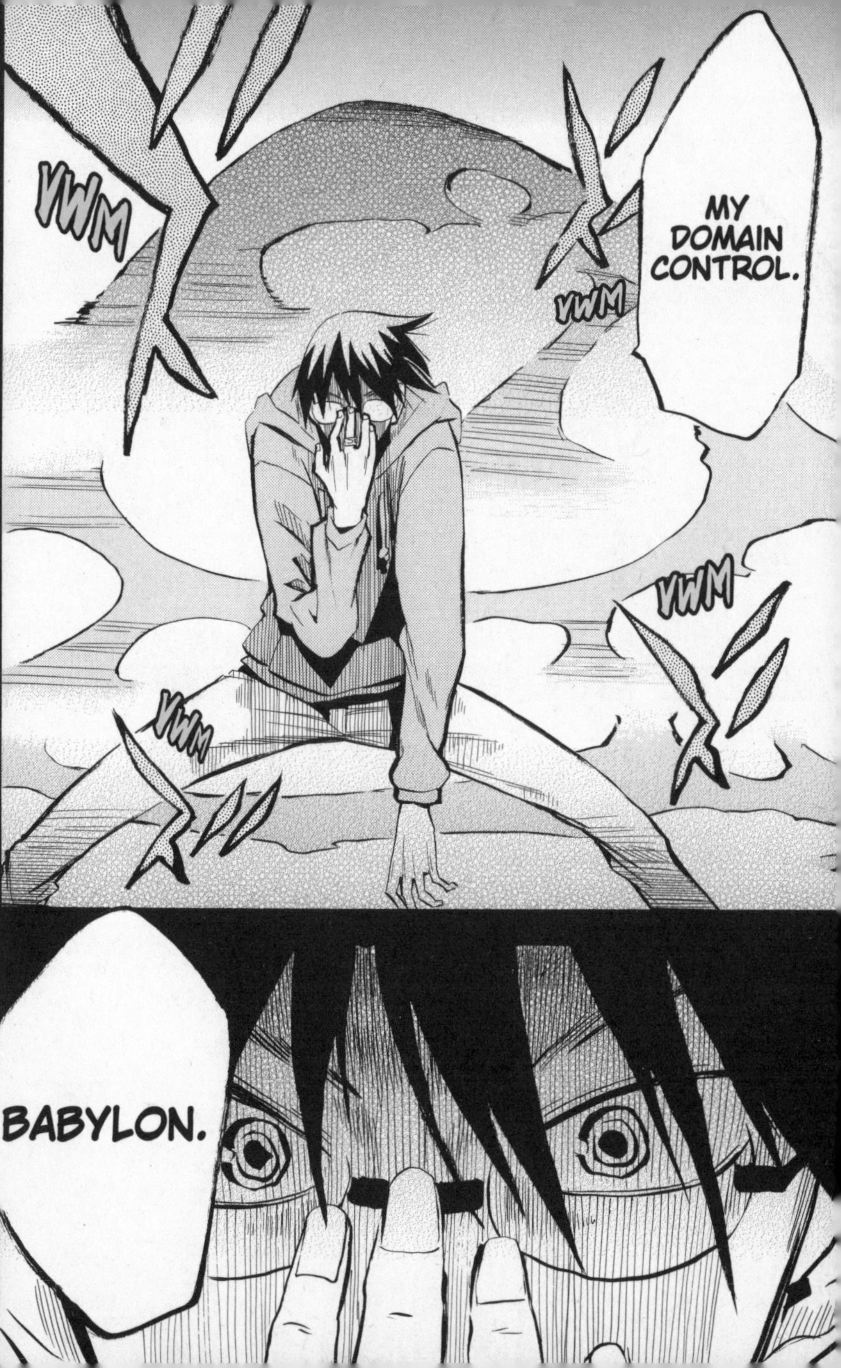
MY DOMAIN CONTROL.
VWM
VWM
VWM
VWM
BABYLON.

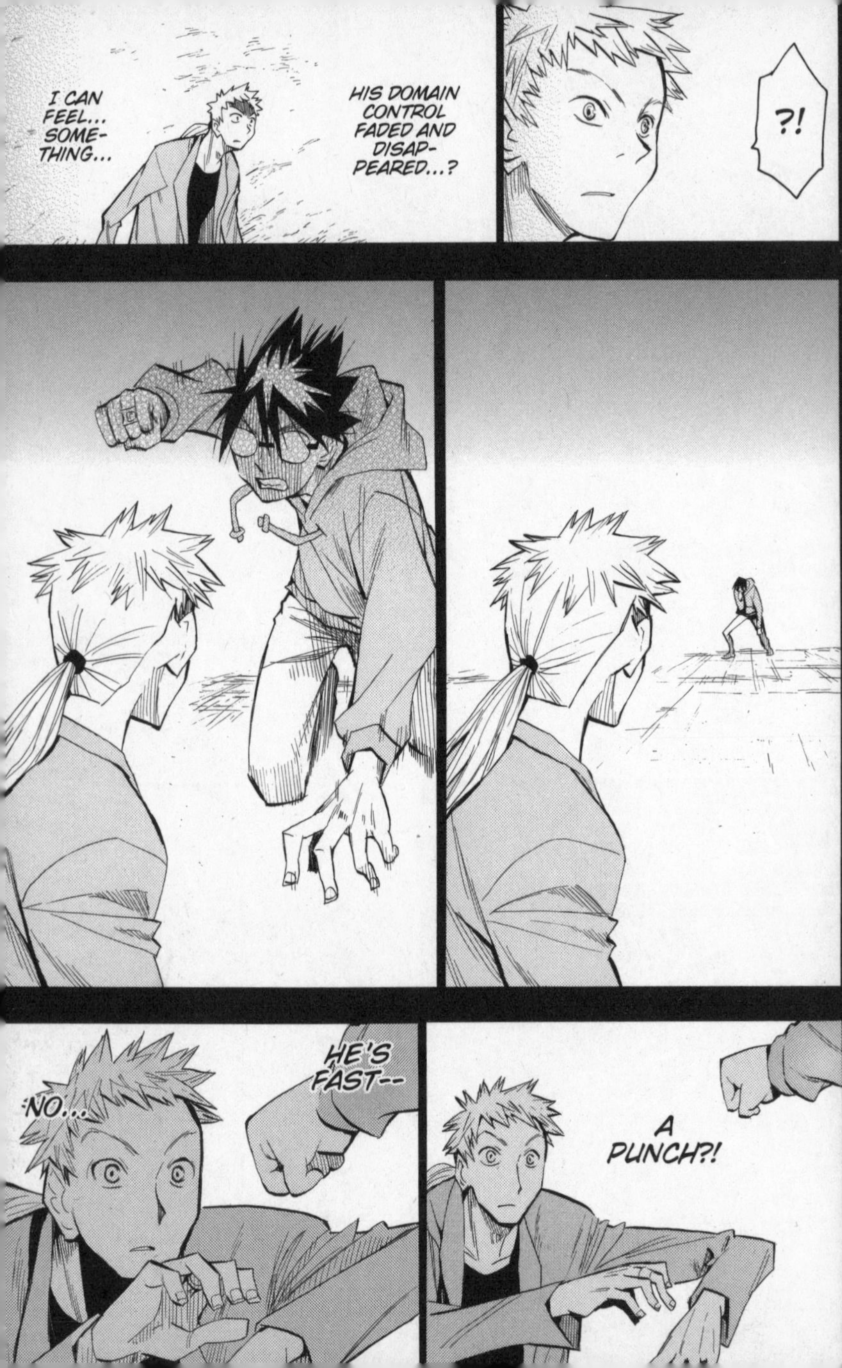
?!
HIS DOMAIN CONTROL FADED AND DISAP-PEARED...?
I CAN FEEL... SOME-THING...
A PUNCH?!
HE'S FAST--
NO...

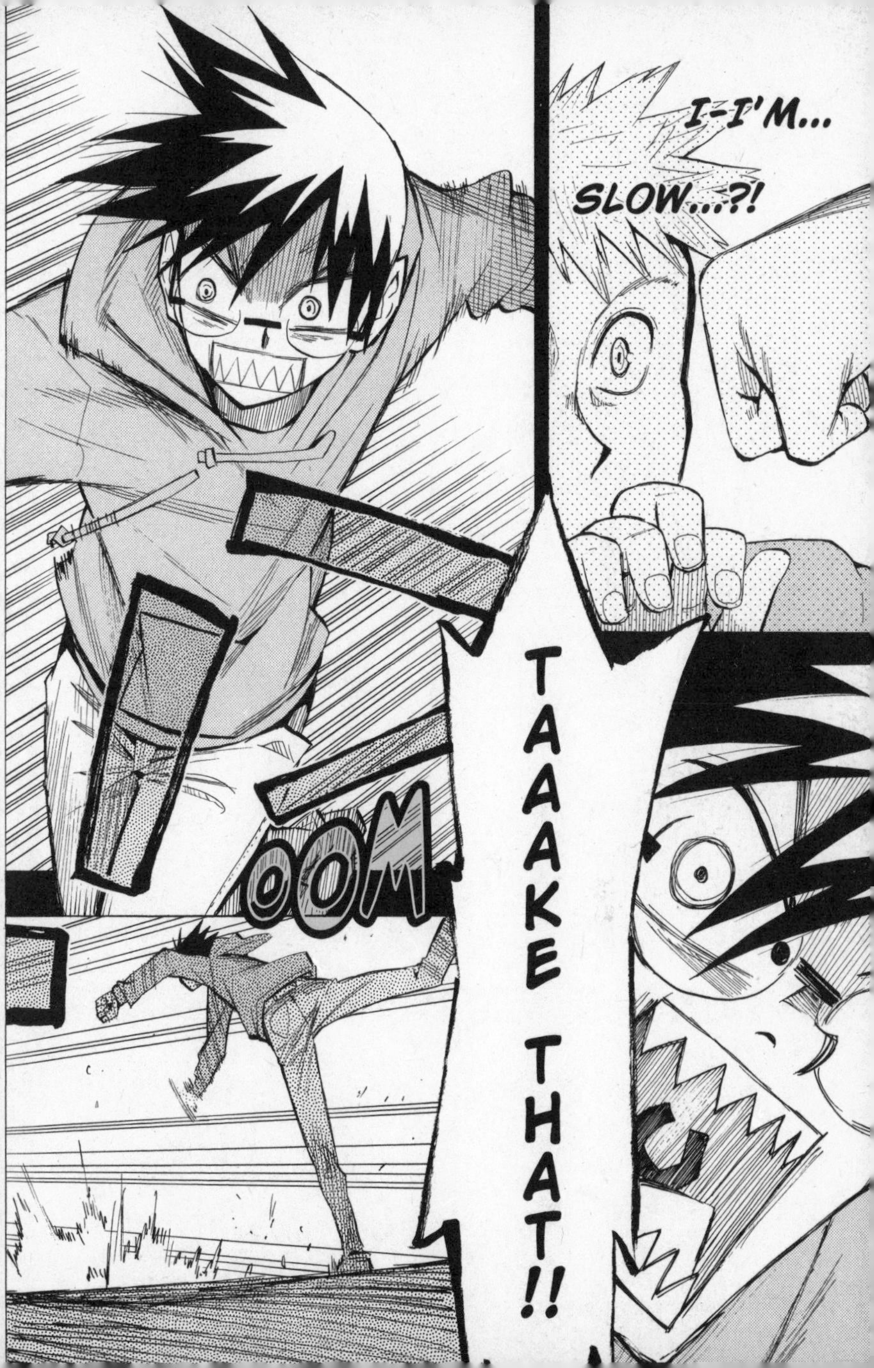
I-I'M...
SLOW...?!
TAAAKE THAT!!
OOM

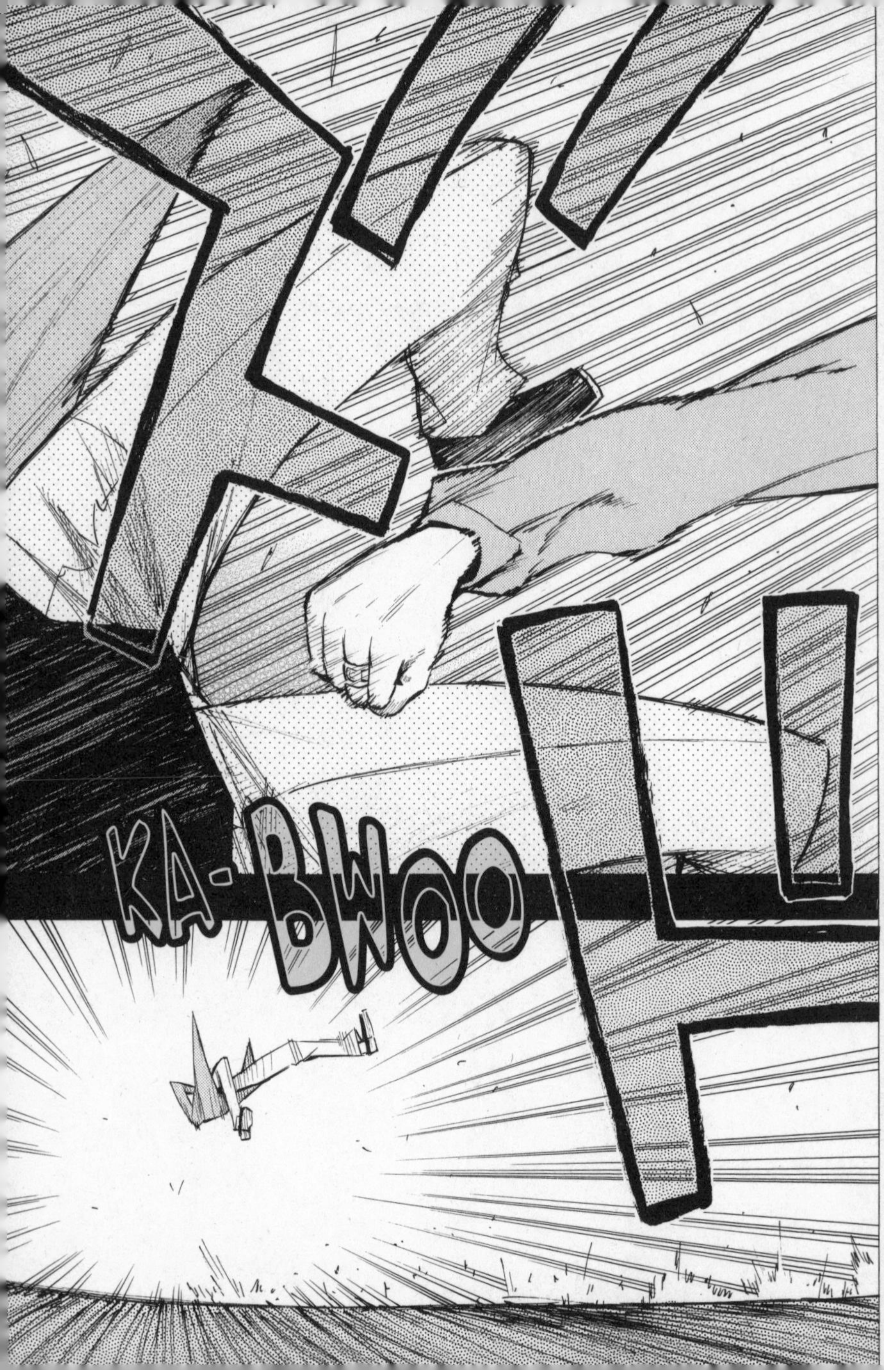
KA-BWOOM!

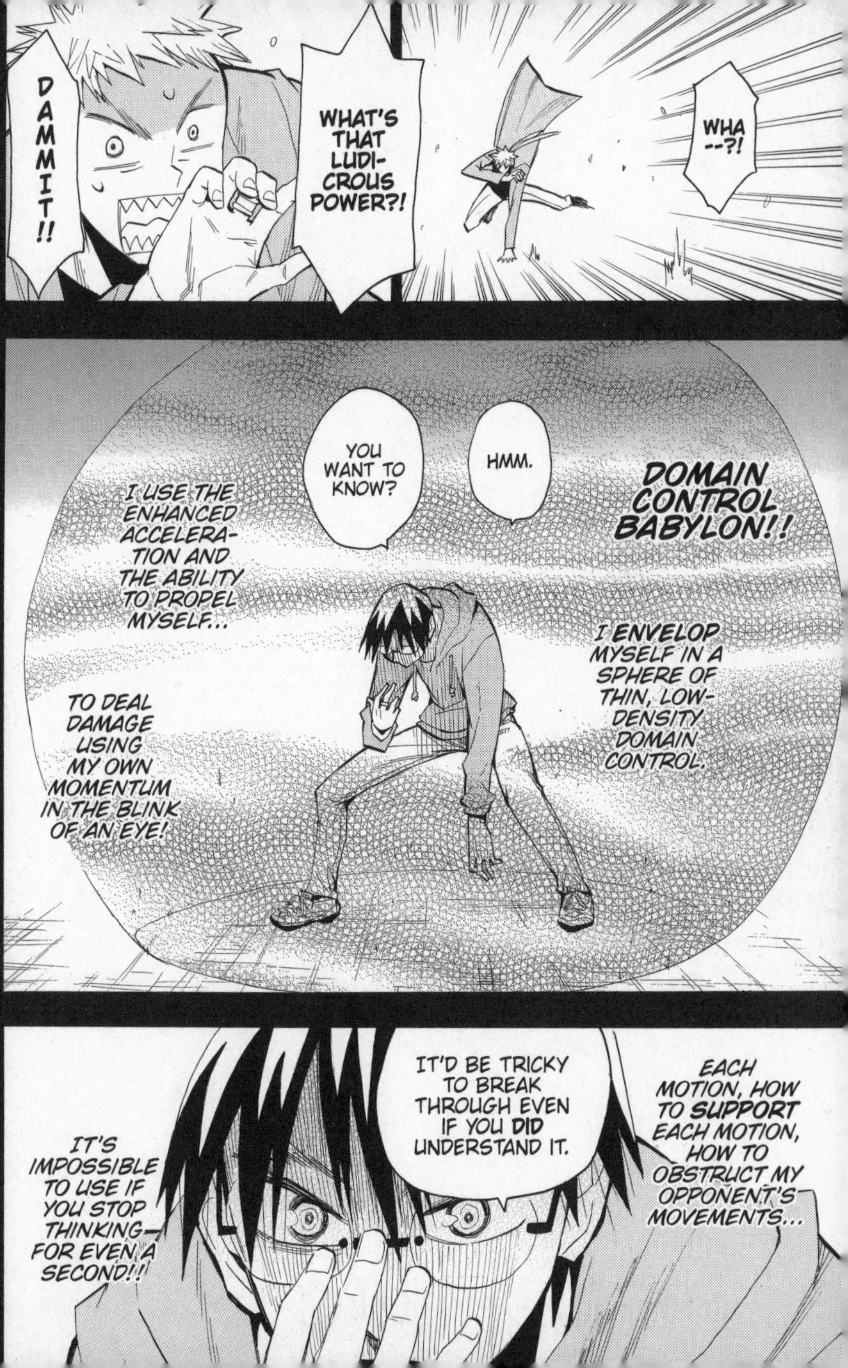
WHA--?!
WHAT'S THAT LUDI-CROUS POWER?!
DAMMIT!!
DOMAIN CONTROL BABYLON!!
HMM.
YOU WANT TO KNOW?
I ENVELOP MYSELF IN A SPHERE OF THIN, LOW-DENSITY DOMAIN CONTROL.
I USE THE ENHANCED ACCELERA-TION AND THE ABILITY TO PROPEL MYSELF...
TO DEAL DAMAGE USING MY OWN MOMENTUM IN THE BLINK OF AN EYE!
EACH MOTION, HOW TO SUPPORT EACH MOTION, HOW TO OBSTRUCT MY OPPONENT'S MOVEMENTS...
IT'D BE TRICKY TO BREAK THROUGH EVEN IF YOU DID UNDERSTAND IT.
IT'S IMPOSSIBLE TO USE IF YOU STOP THINKING FOR EVEN A SECOND!!

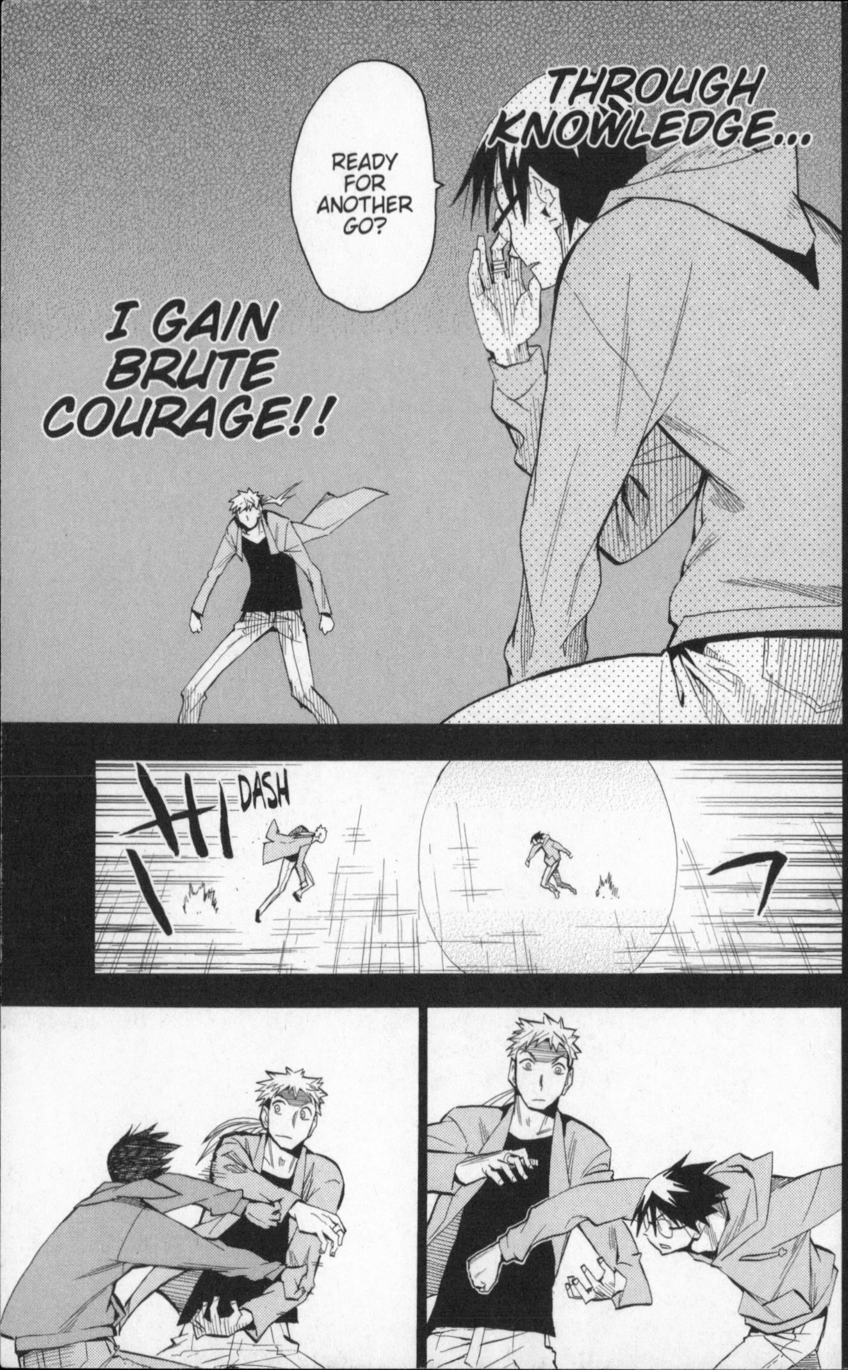
THROUGH KNOWLEDGE...
READY FOR ANOTHER GO?
I GAIN BRUTE COURAGE!!
DASH

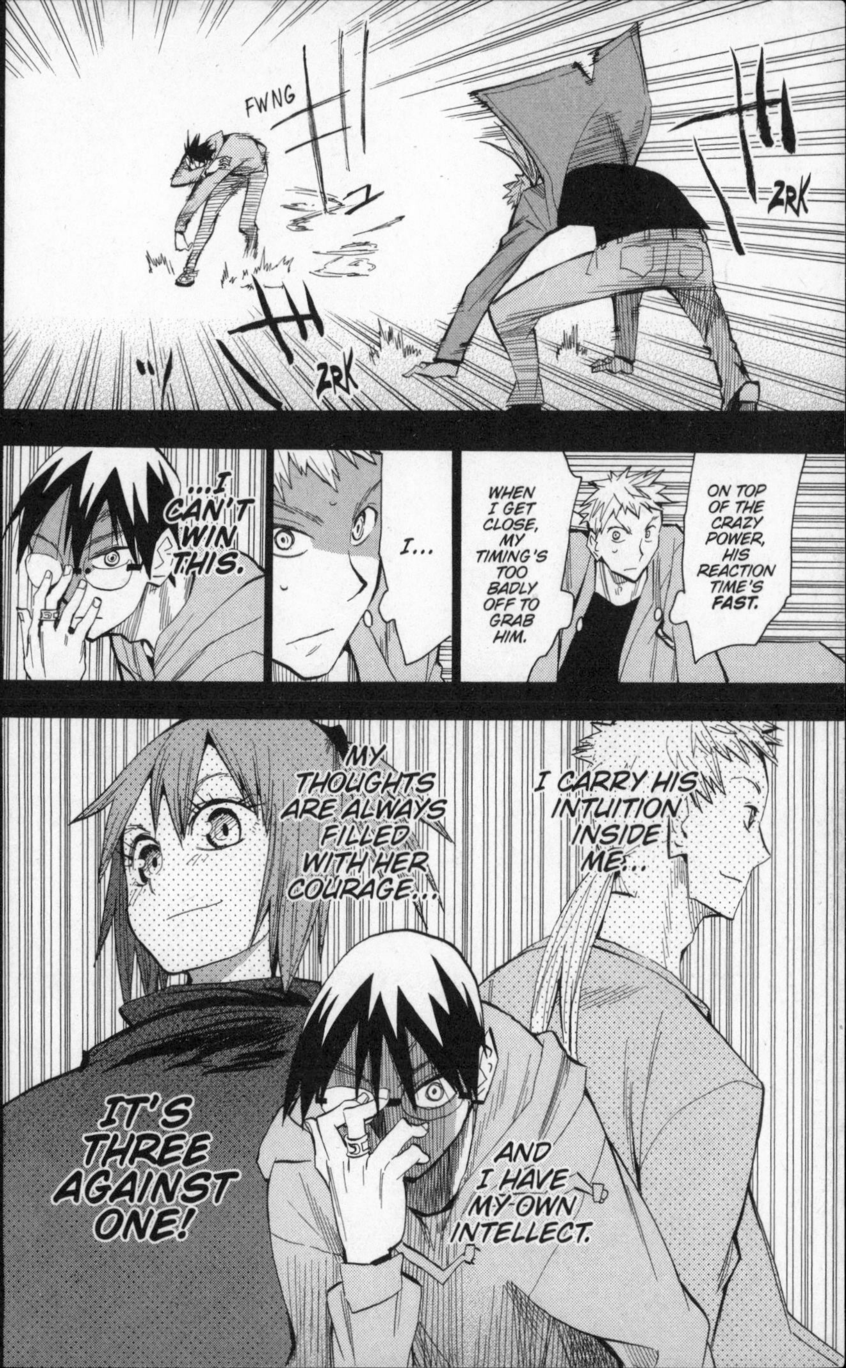
ZRK
FWNG
ZRK
ON TOP OF THE CRAZY POWER, HIS REACTION TIME'S FAST.
WHEN I GET CLOSE, MY TIMING'S TOO BADLY OFF TO GRAB HIM.
I...
...I CAN'T WIN THIS.
I CARRY HIS INTUITION INSIDE ME...
MY THOUGHTS ARE ALWAYS FILLED WITH HER COURAGE...
AND I HAVE MY OWN INTELLECT.
IT'S THREE AGAINST ONE!

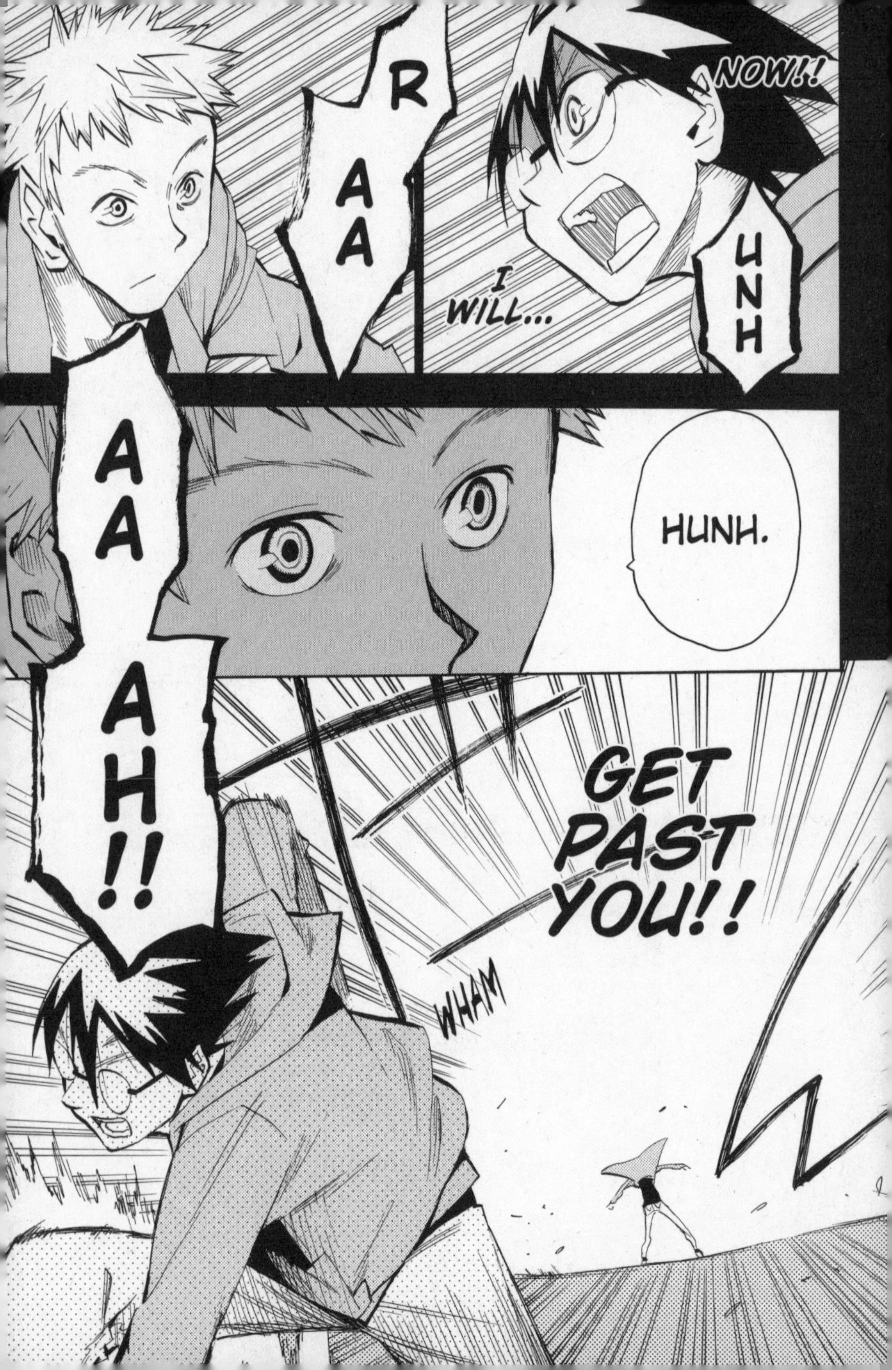

NOW!!
UNH
I WILL...
RAAAAAH!!
HUNH.
GET PAST YOU!!
WHAM

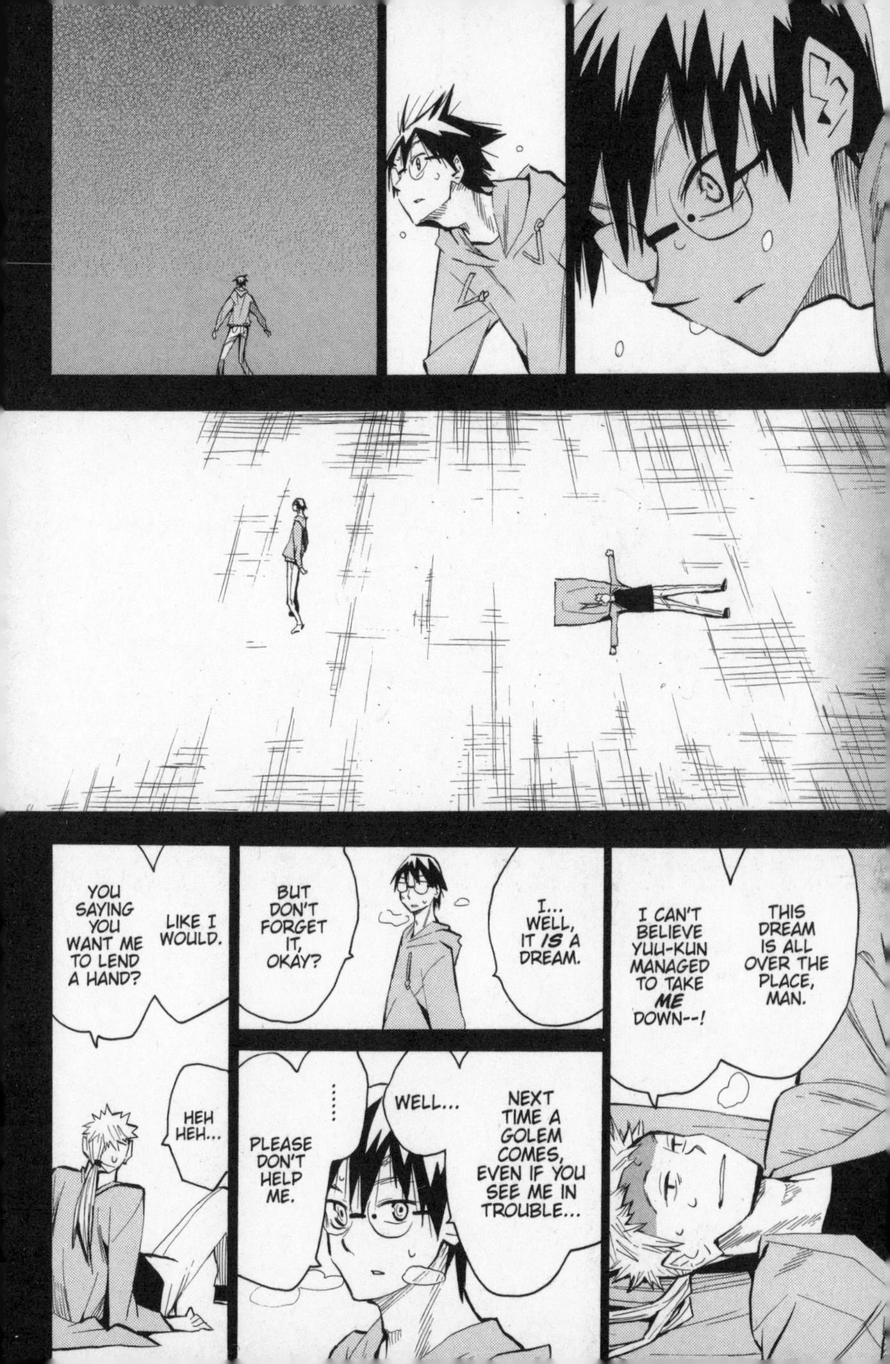
THIS DREAM IS ALL OVER THE PLACE, MAN.
I CAN'T BELIEVE YUU-KUN MANAGED TO TAKE *ME* DOWN--!
I... WELL, IT *IS* A DREAM.
BUT DON'T FORGET IT, OKAY?
WELL...
NEXT TIME A GOLEM COMES, EVEN IF YOU SEE ME IN TROUBLE...
......
PLEASE DON'T HELP ME.
LIKE I WOULD.
YOU SAYING YOU WANT ME TO LEND A HAND?
HEH HEH...

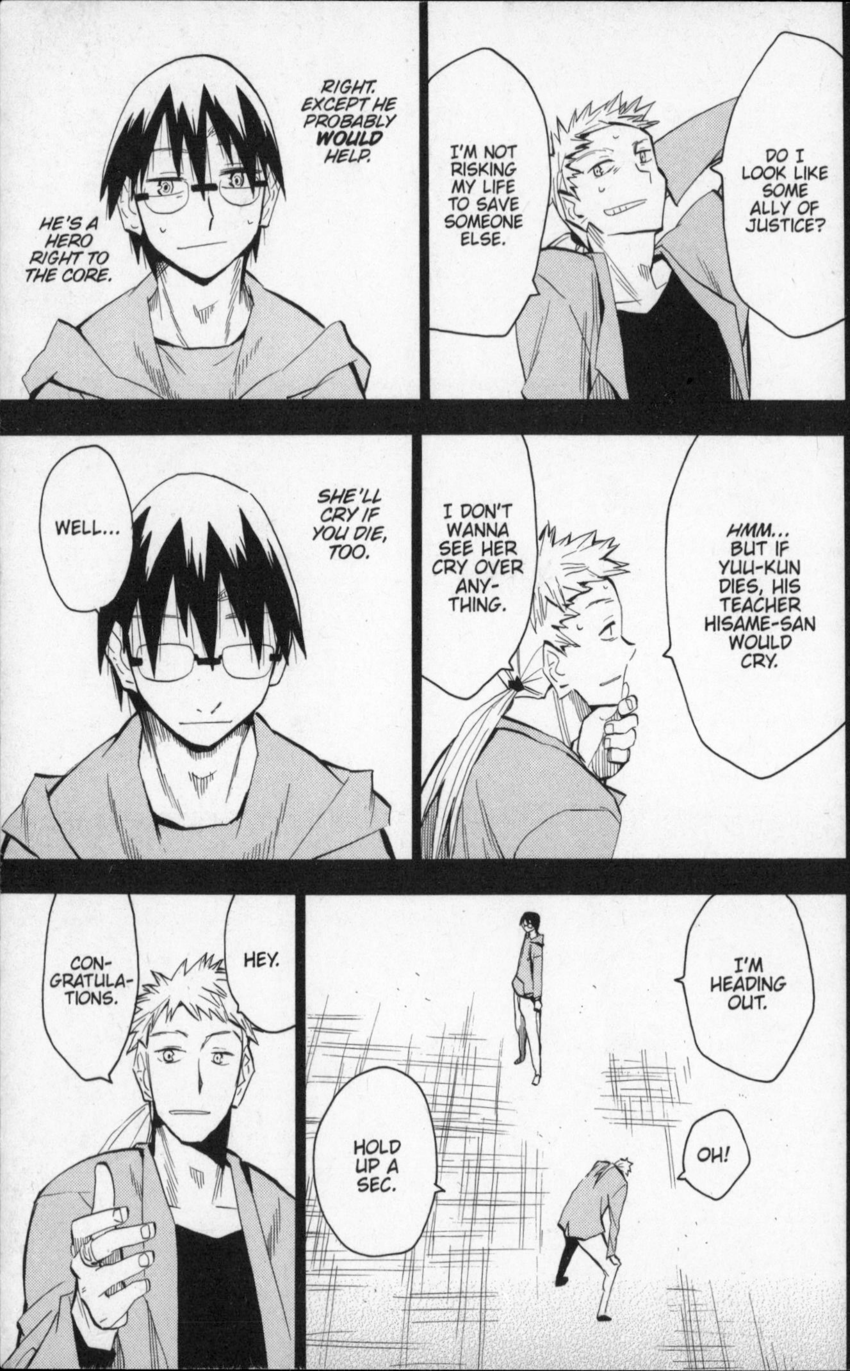
DO I LOOK LIKE SOME ALLY OF JUSTICE?
I'M NOT RISKING MY LIFE TO SAVE SOMEONE ELSE.
RIGHT. EXCEPT HE PROBABLY **WOULD** HELP.
HE'S A HERO RIGHT TO THE CORE.
HMM... BUT IF YUU-KUN DIES, HIS TEACHER HISAME-SAN WOULD CRY.
I DON'T WANNA SEE HER CRY OVER ANY-THING.
SHE'LL CRY IF YOU DIE, TOO.
WELL...
I'M HEADING OUT.
OH!
HOLD UP A SEC.
HEY.
CON-GRATULA-TIONS.

Chapter 50: Amamiya Yuuhi and Shinonome Hangetsu

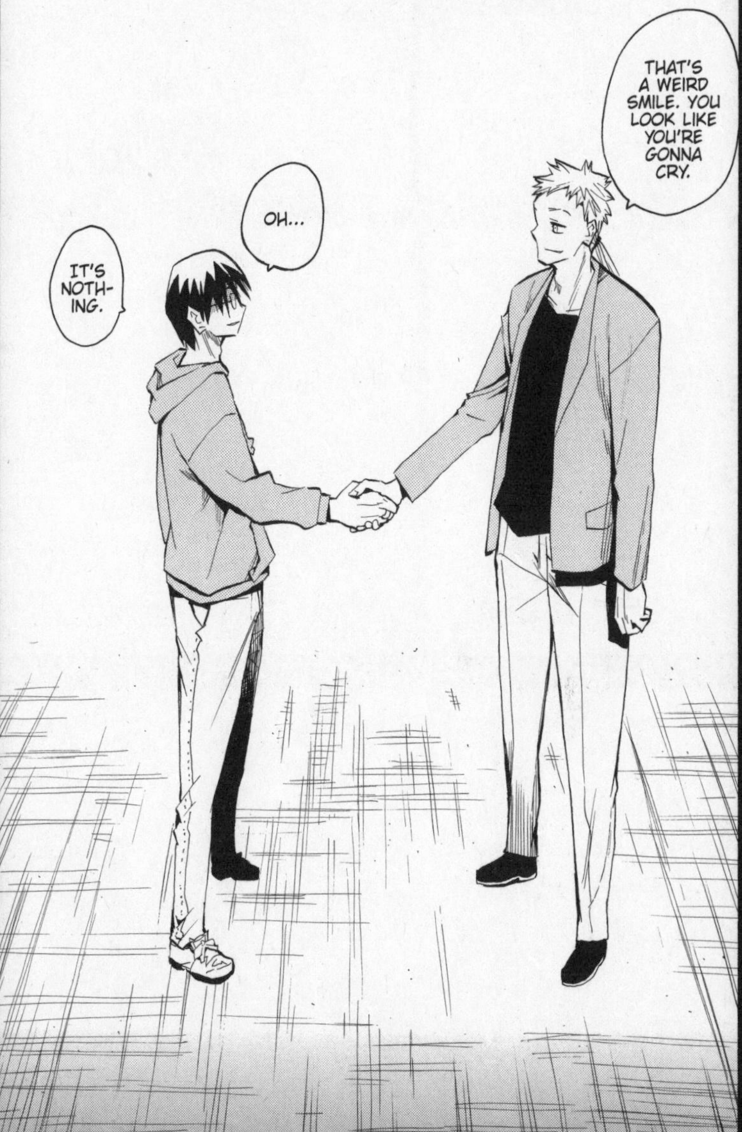
THAT'S A WEIRD SMILE. YOU LOOK LIKE YOU'RE GONNA CRY.
OH...
IT'S NOTH-ING.

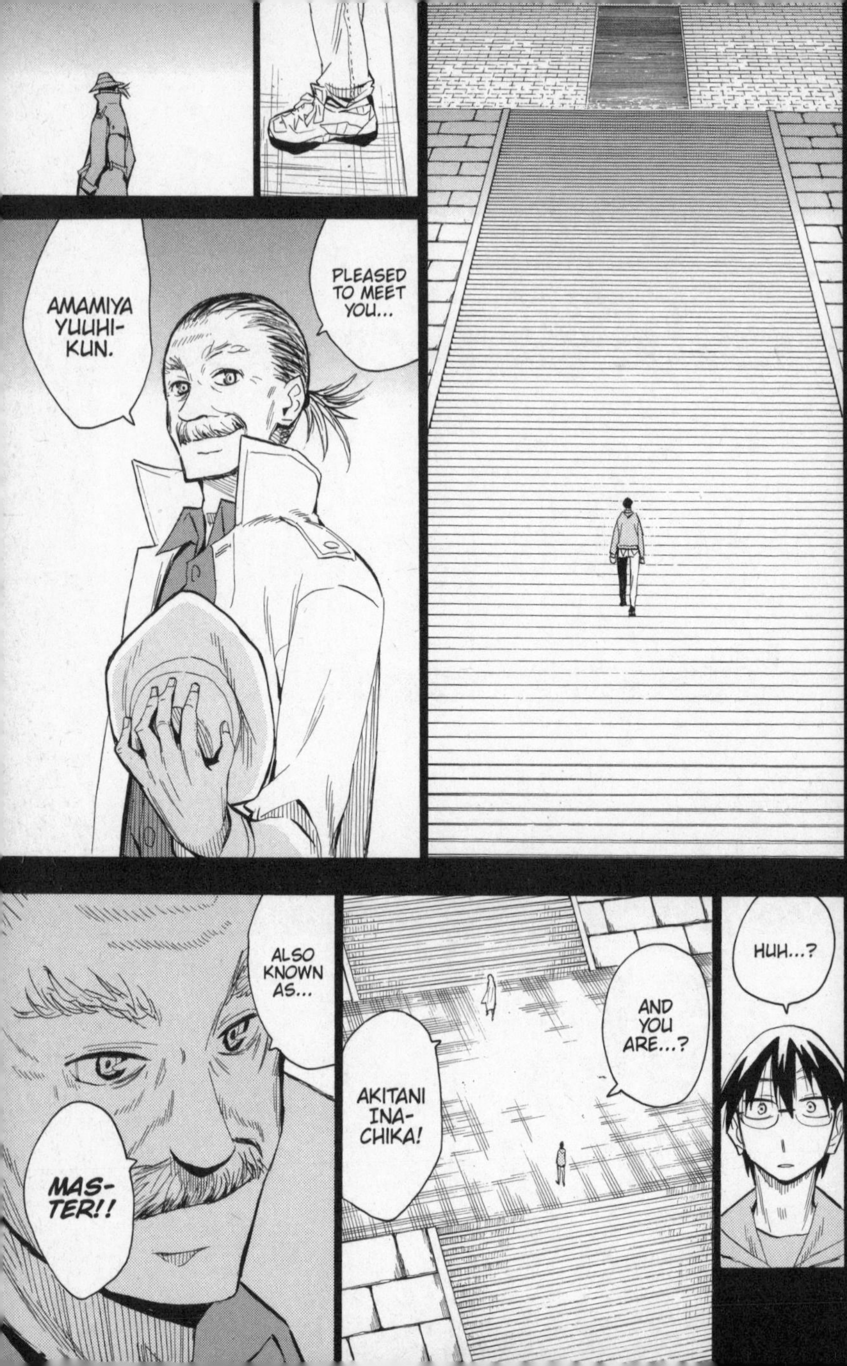
PLEASED TO MEET YOU...
AMAMIYA YUUHI-KUN.
HUH...?
AND YOU ARE...?
AKITANI INA-CHIKA!
ALSO KNOWN AS...
MAS-TER!!

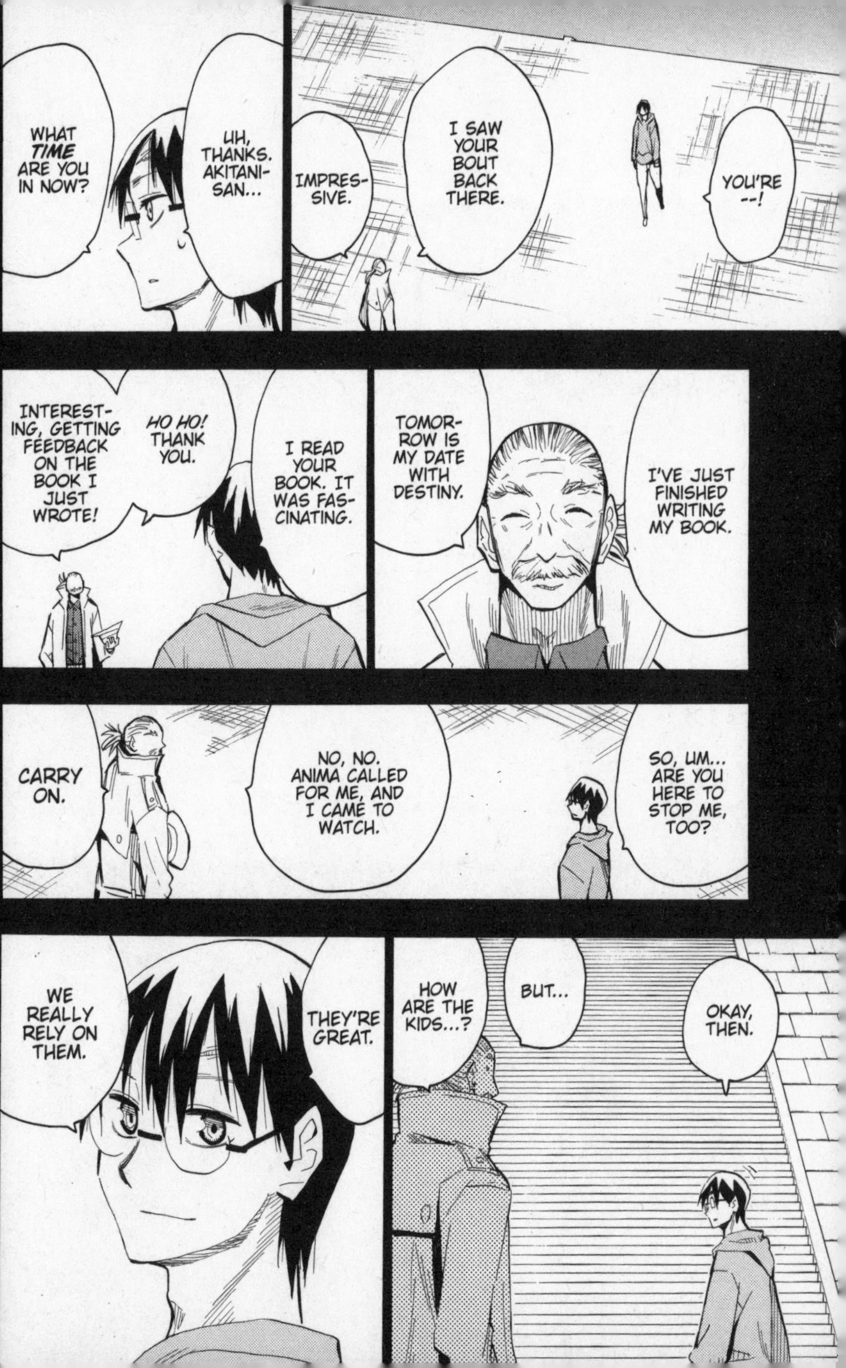
YOU'RE --!
I SAW YOUR BOUT BACK THERE.
IMPRESSIVE.
UH, THANKS. AKITANI-SAN...
WHAT *TIME* ARE YOU IN NOW?
I'VE JUST FINISHED WRITING MY BOOK.
TOMORROW IS MY DATE WITH DESTINY.
I READ YOUR BOOK. IT WAS FASCINATING.
HO HO! THANK YOU.
INTERESTING, GETTING FEEDBACK ON THE BOOK I JUST WROTE!
SO, UM... ARE YOU HERE TO STOP ME, TOO?
NO, NO. ANIMA CALLED FOR ME, AND I CAME TO WATCH.
CARRY ON.
OKAY, THEN.
BUT...
HOW ARE THE KIDS...?
THEY'RE GREAT.
WE REALLY RELY ON THEM.

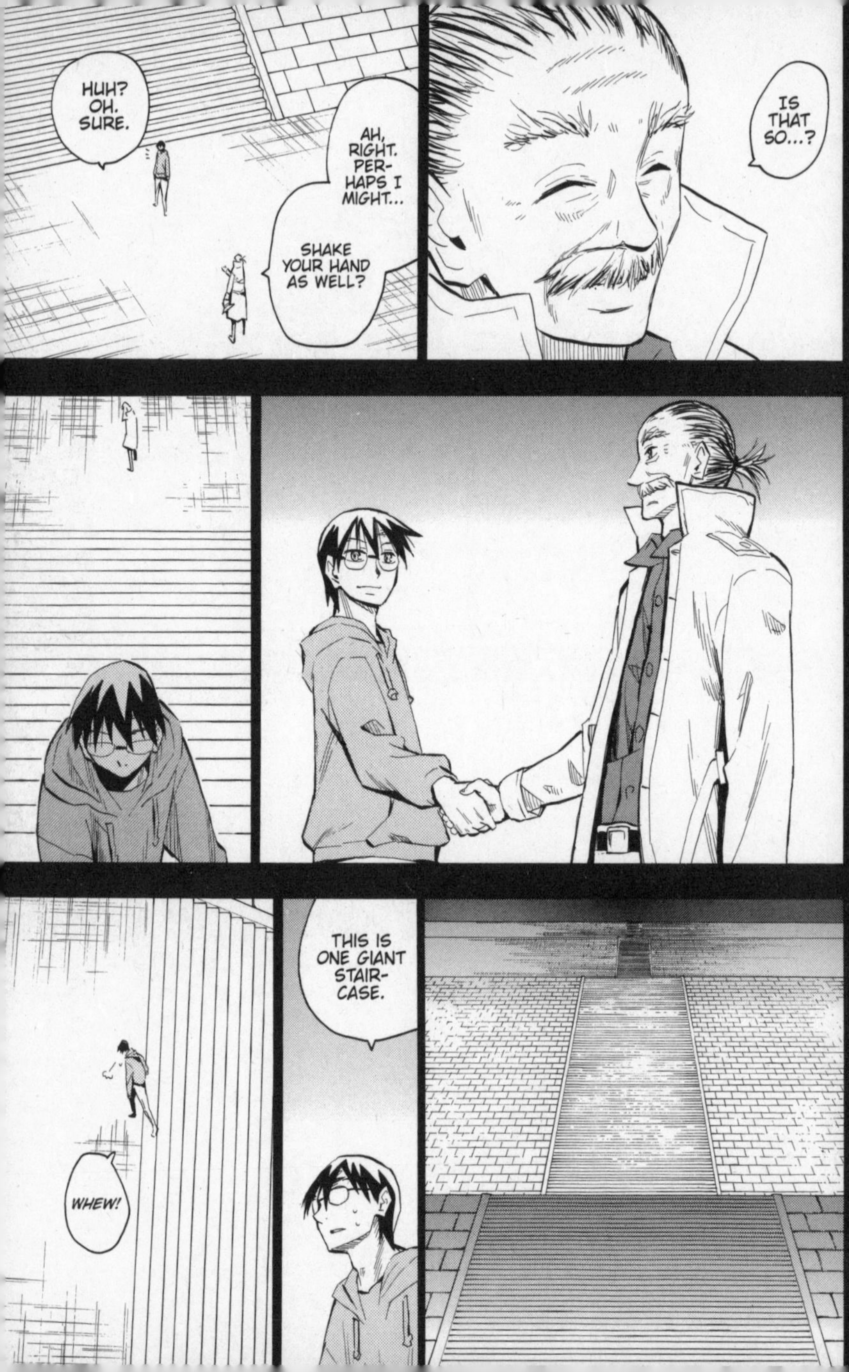
IS THAT SO...?
AH, RIGHT. PER-HAPS I MIGHT...
SHAKE YOUR HAND AS WELL?
HUH? OH. SURE.
THIS IS ONE GIANT STAIR-CASE.
WHEW!

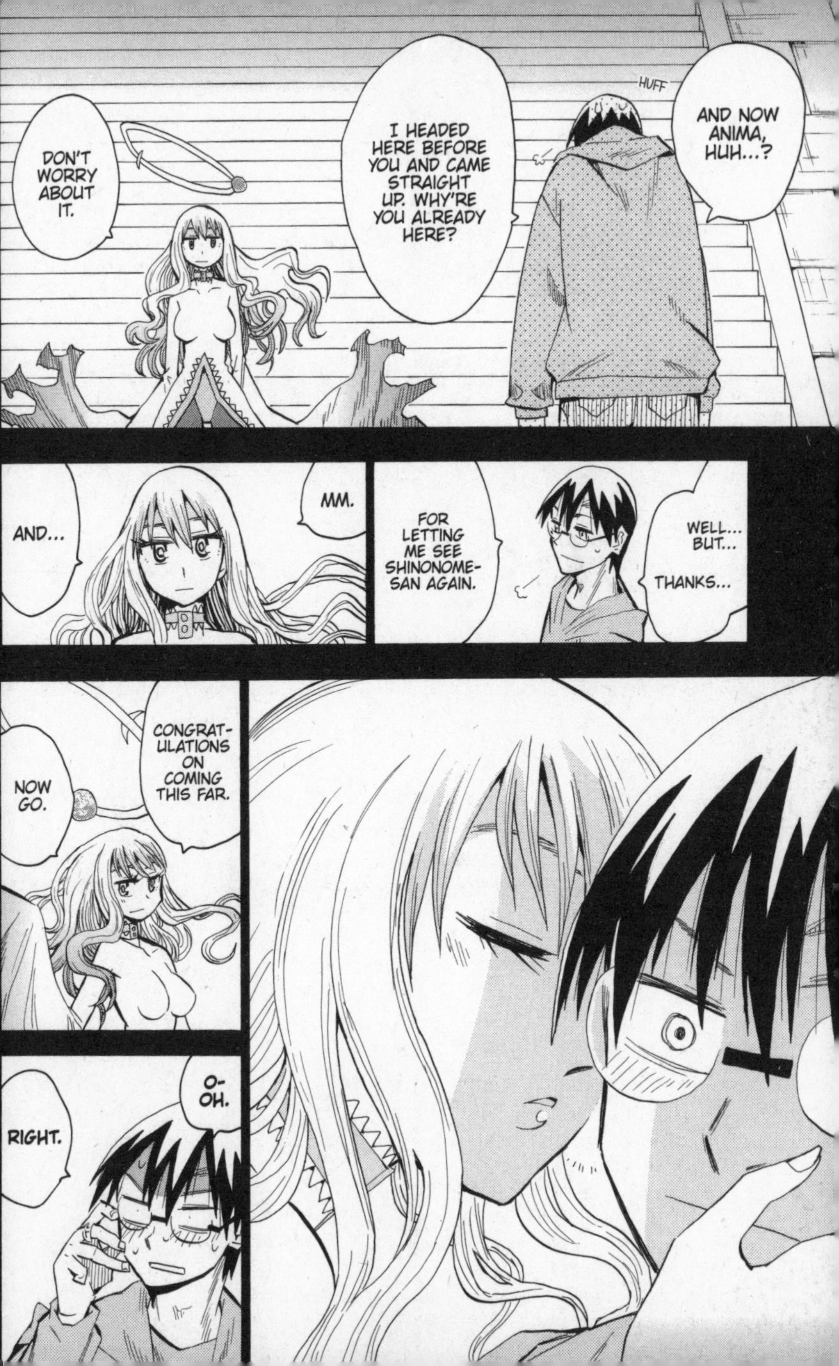
HUFF
AND NOW ANIMA, HUH...?
I HEADED HERE BEFORE YOU AND CAME STRAIGHT UP. WHY'RE YOU ALREADY HERE?
DON'T WORRY ABOUT IT.
WELL... BUT...
THANKS...
FOR LETTING ME SEE SHINONOME-SAN AGAIN.
MM.
AND...
CONGRAT-ULATIONS ON COMING THIS FAR.
NOW GO.
O-OH.
RIGHT.

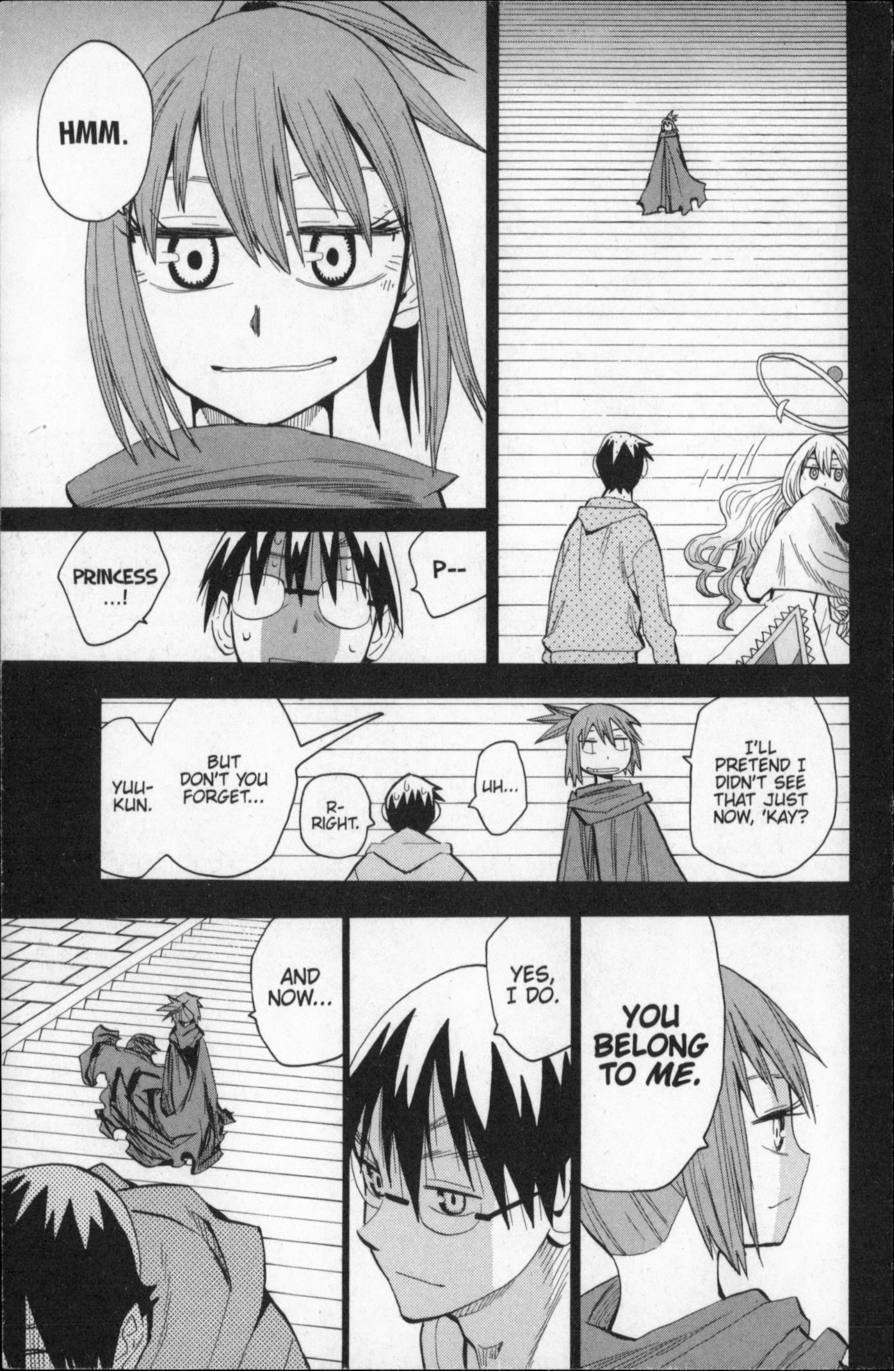
HMM.
P--
PRINCESS ...!
I'LL PRETEND I DIDN'T SEE THAT JUST NOW, 'KAY?
UH...
R- RIGHT.
BUT DON'T YOU FORGET...
YUU-KUN.
YOU BELONG TO ME.
YES, I DO.
AND NOW...

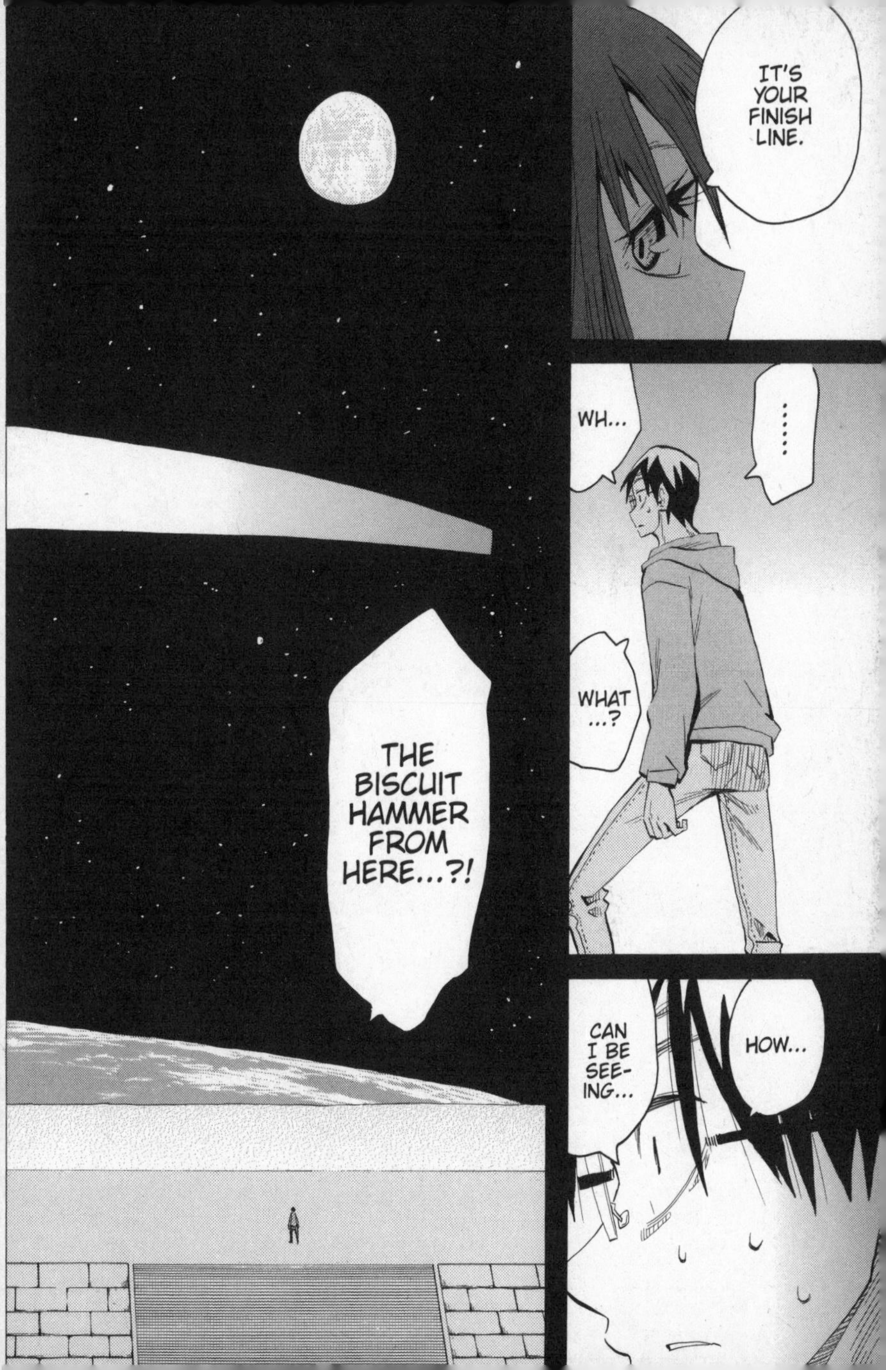
IT'S YOUR FINISH LINE.
......
WH...
WHAT ...?
HOW...
CAN I BE SEE-ING...
THE BISCUIT HAMMER FROM HERE...?!

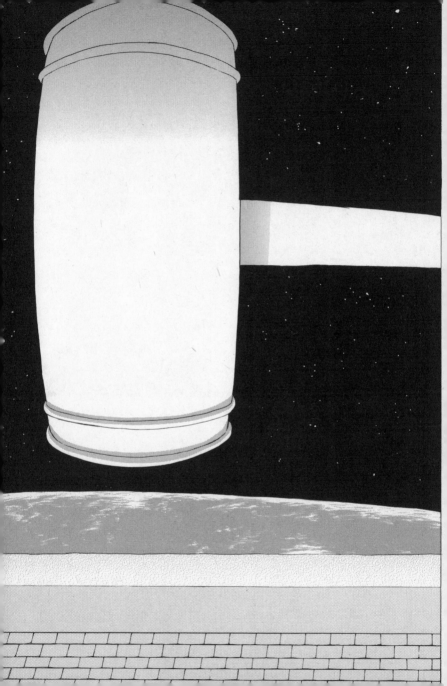

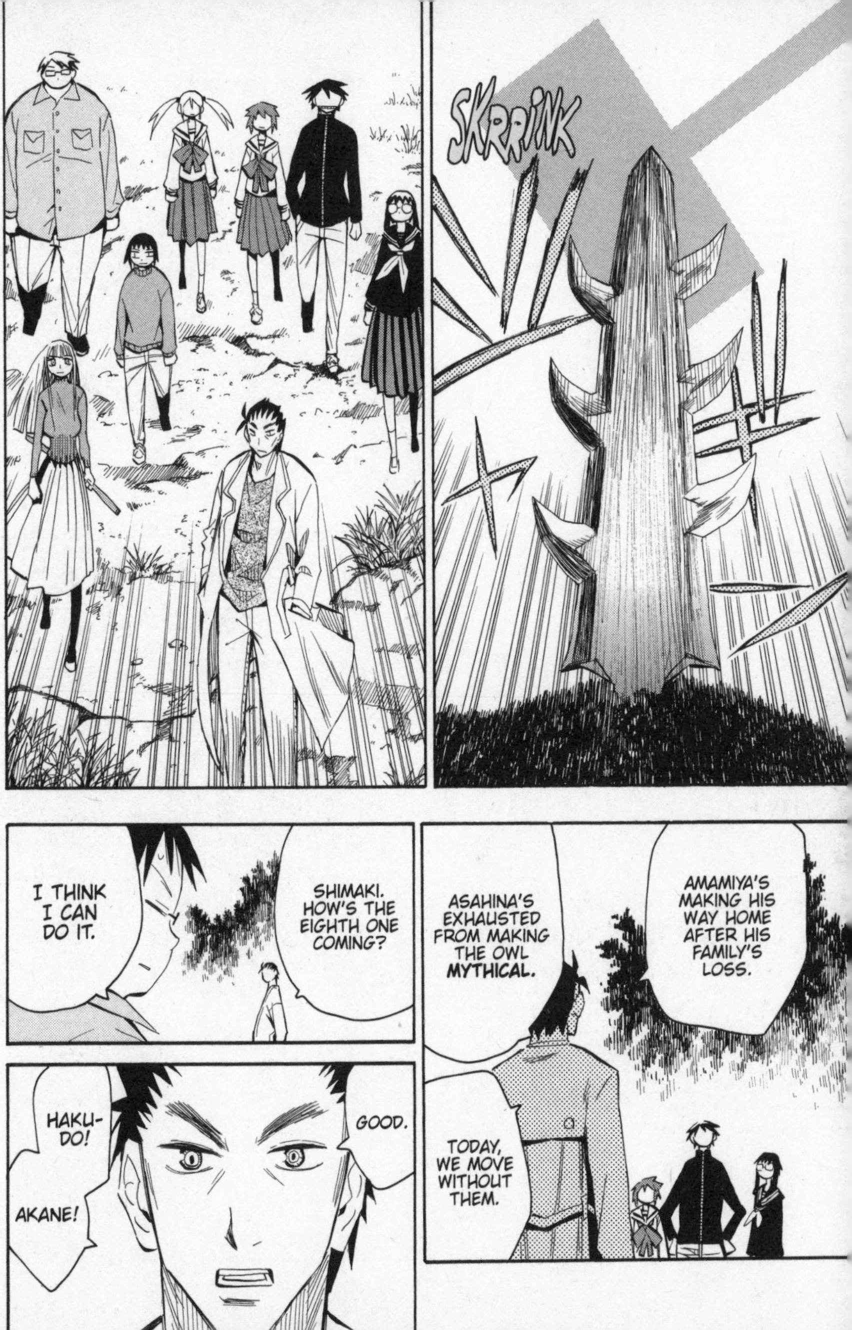
SKRRINK
AMAMIYA'S MAKING HIS WAY HOME AFTER HIS FAMILY'S LOSS.
ASAHINA'S EXHAUSTED FROM MAKING THE OWL **MYTHICAL**.
TODAY, WE MOVE WITHOUT THEM.
SHIMAKI. HOW'S THE EIGHTH ONE COMING?
I THINK I CAN DO IT.
GOOD.
HAKU-DO!
AKANE!

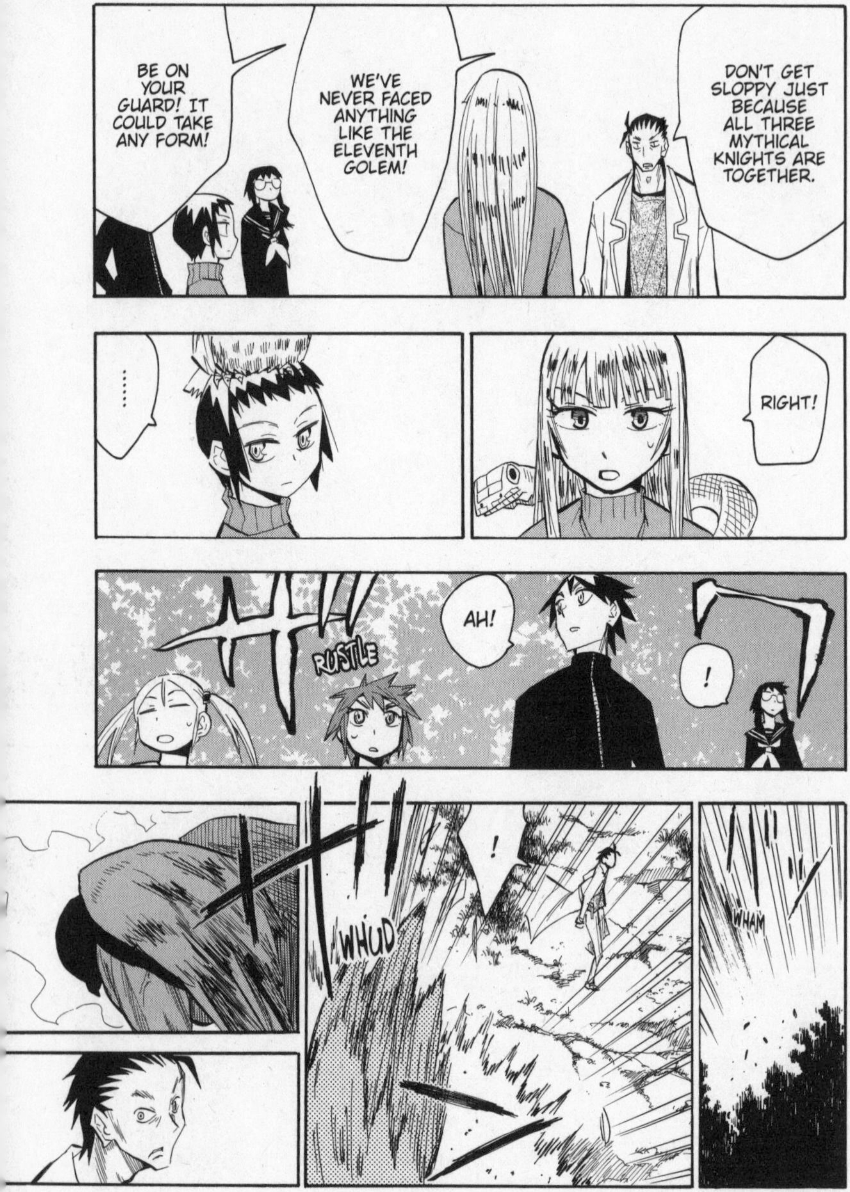
DON'T GET SLOPPY JUST BECAUSE ALL THREE MYTHICAL KNIGHTS ARE TOGETHER.
WE'VE NEVER FACED ANYTHING LIKE THE ELEVENTH GOLEM!
BE ON YOUR GUARD! IT COULD TAKE ANY FORM!
RIGHT!
......
!
AH!
RUSTLE
WHAM
!
WHUD

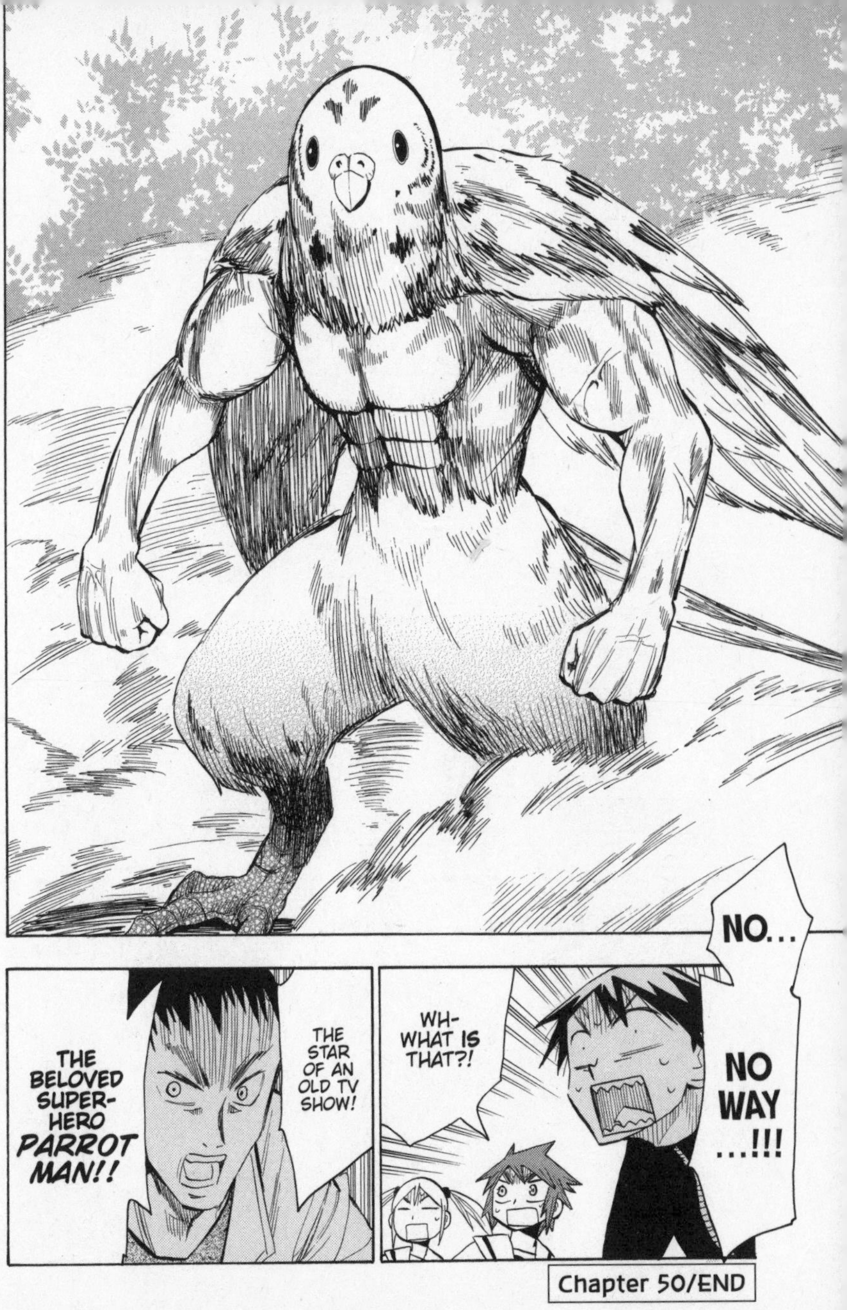
NO...
NO WAY ...!!!
WH-WHAT IS THAT?!
THE STAR OF AN OLD TV SHOW!
THE BELOVED SUPER-HERO *PARROT MAN!!*

Chapter 50/END

Lucifer and the Biscuit Hammer

Chapter 51

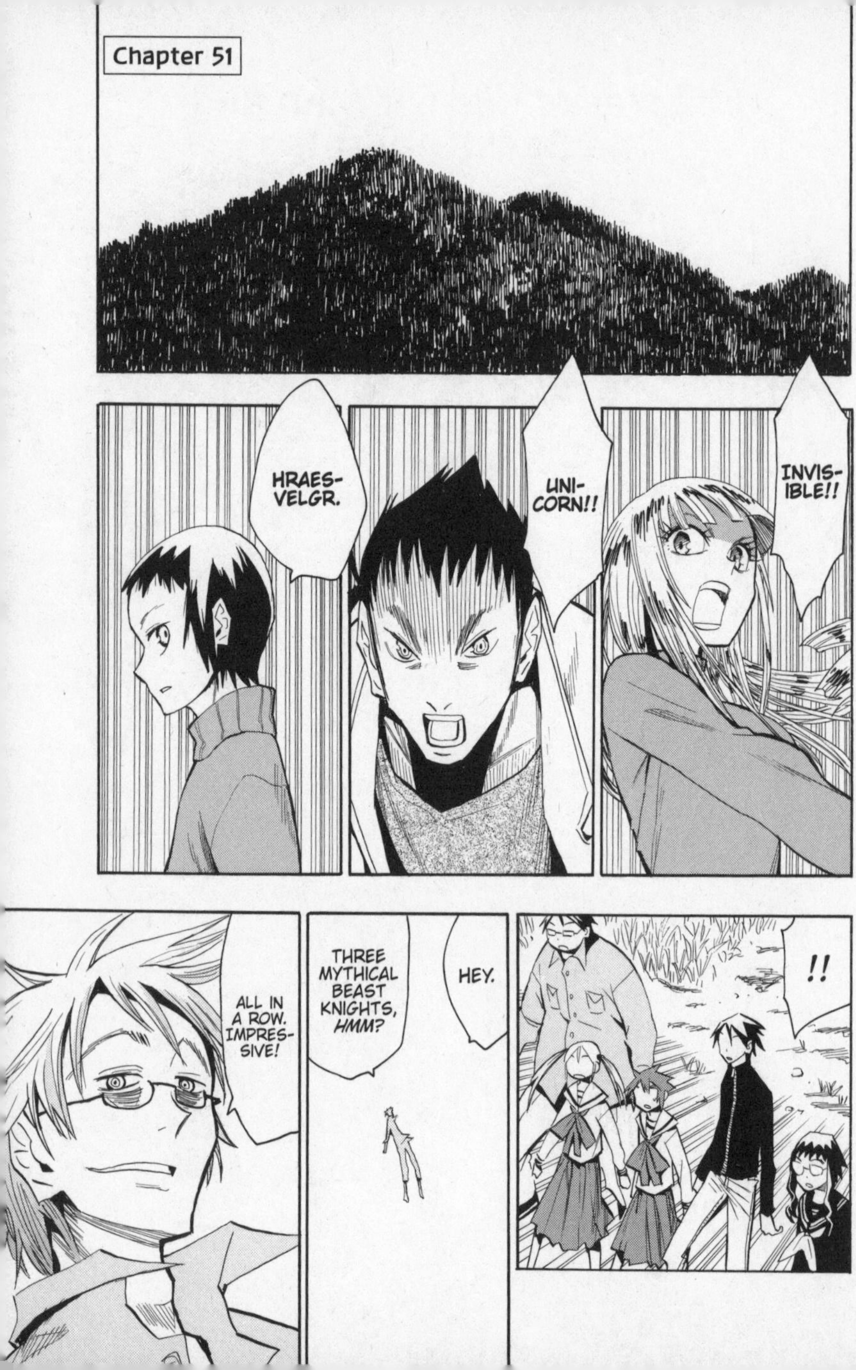
INVISIBLE!!
UNICORN!!
HRAESVELGR.
!!
HEY.
THREE MYTHICAL BEAST KNIGHTS, *HMM?*
ALL IN A ROW. IMPRESSIVE!

Chapter 51: Parrot Man and the Beast Knights

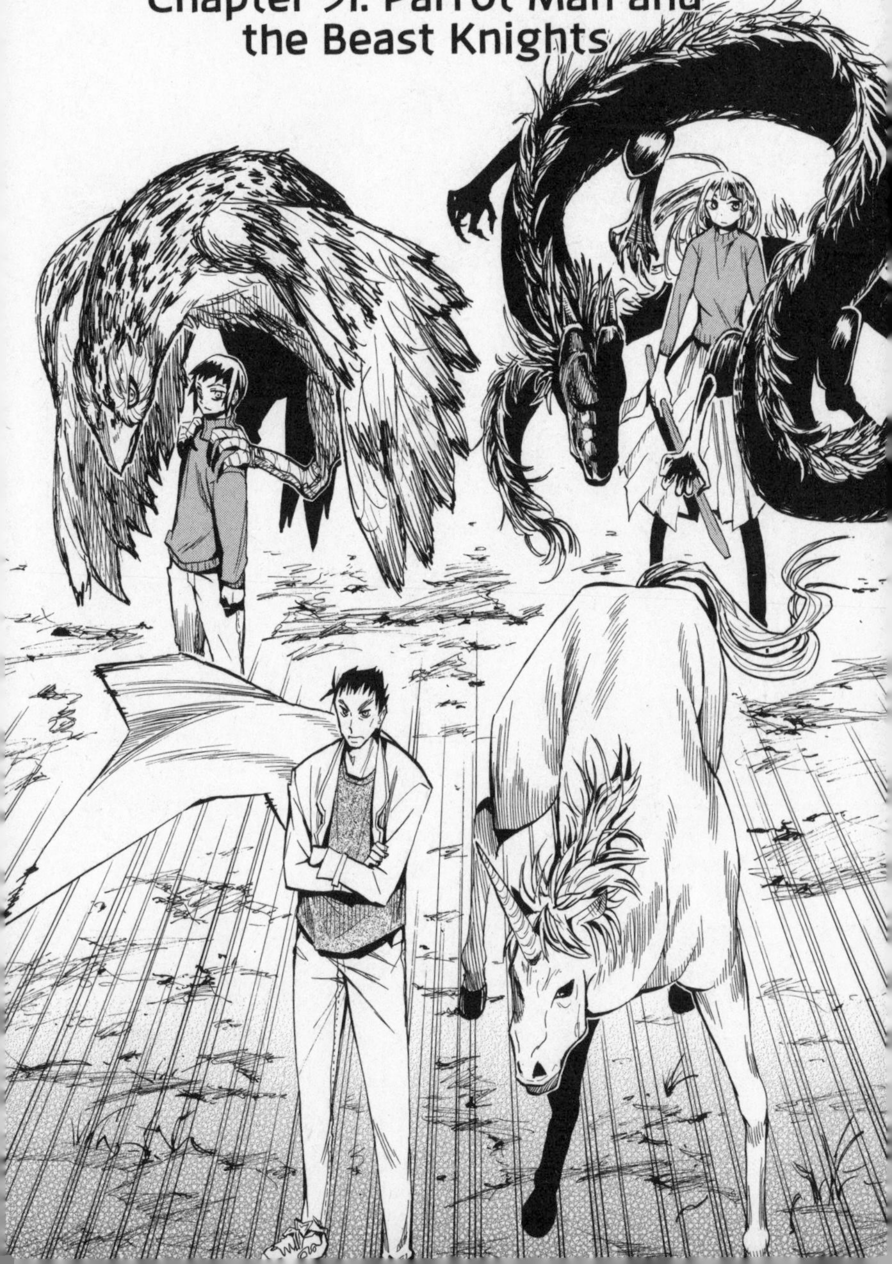

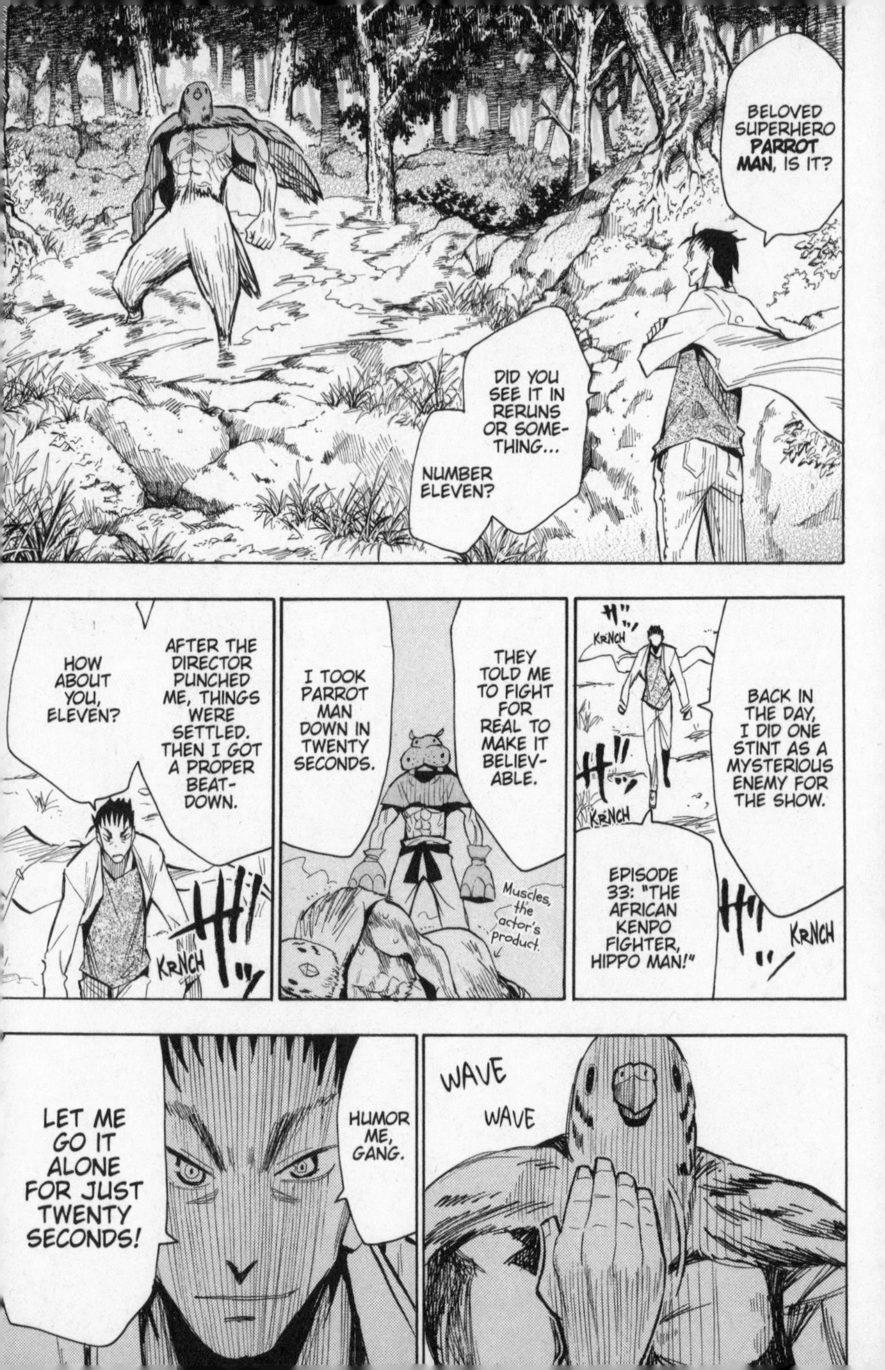
BELOVED SUPERHERO **PARROT MAN**, IS IT?
DID YOU SEE IT IN RERUNS OR SOMETHING...
NUMBER ELEVEN?
KRNCH
BACK IN THE DAY, I DID ONE STINT AS A MYSTERIOUS ENEMY FOR THE SHOW.
KRNCH
EPISODE 33: "THE AFRICAN KENPO FIGHTER, HIPPO MAN!"
KRNCH
THEY TOLD ME TO FIGHT FOR REAL TO MAKE IT BELIEVABLE.
I TOOK PARROT MAN DOWN IN TWENTY SECONDS.
Muscles, the actor's product.
AFTER THE DIRECTOR PUNCHED ME, THINGS WERE SETTLED. THEN I GOT A PROPER BEAT-DOWN.
HOW ABOUT YOU, ELEVEN?
KRNCH
WAVE
WAVE
HUMOR ME, GANG.
LET ME GO IT ALONE FOR JUST TWENTY SECONDS!

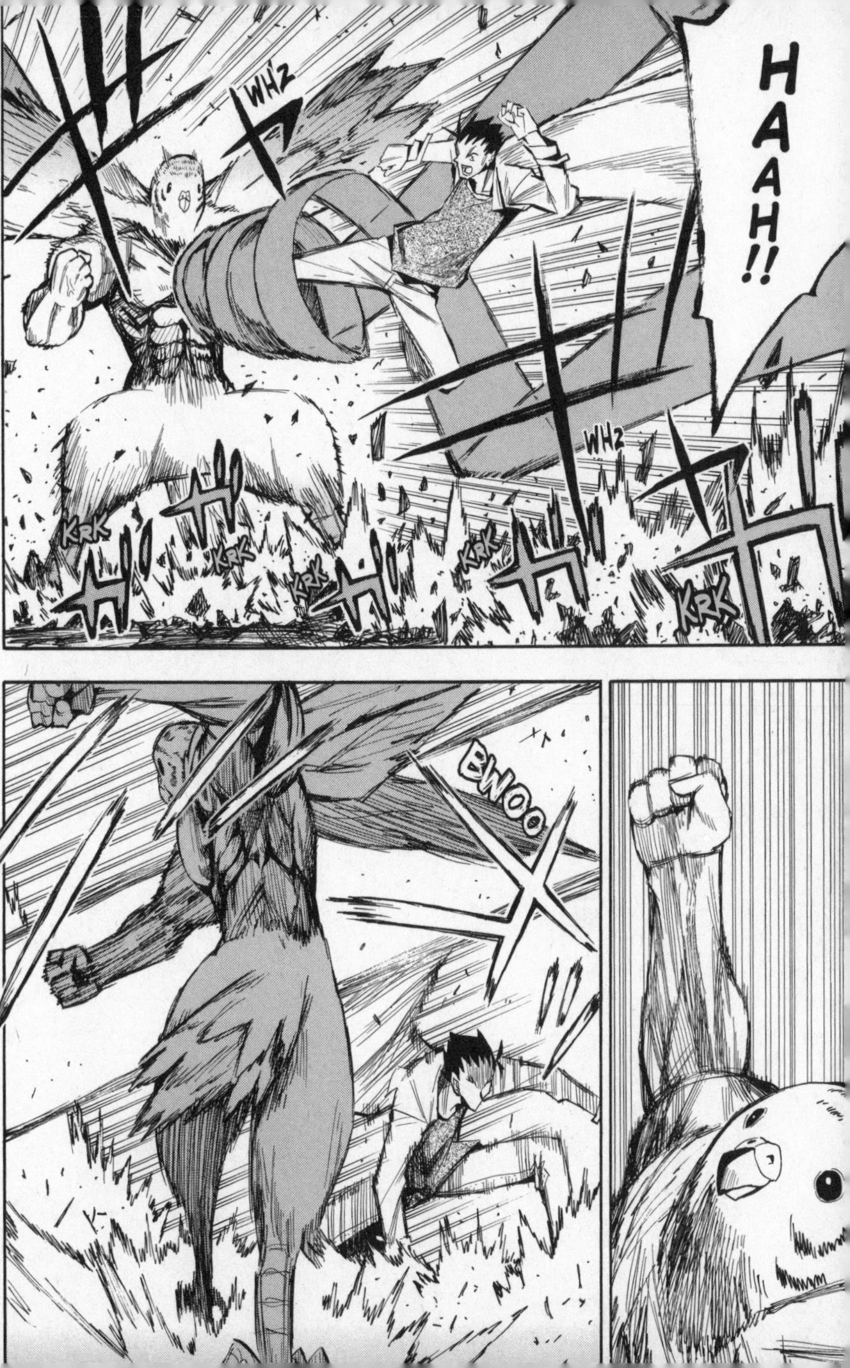
HAAAH!!
WHZ
WHZ
KRK
KRK
KRK
KRK
KRK
BWOO

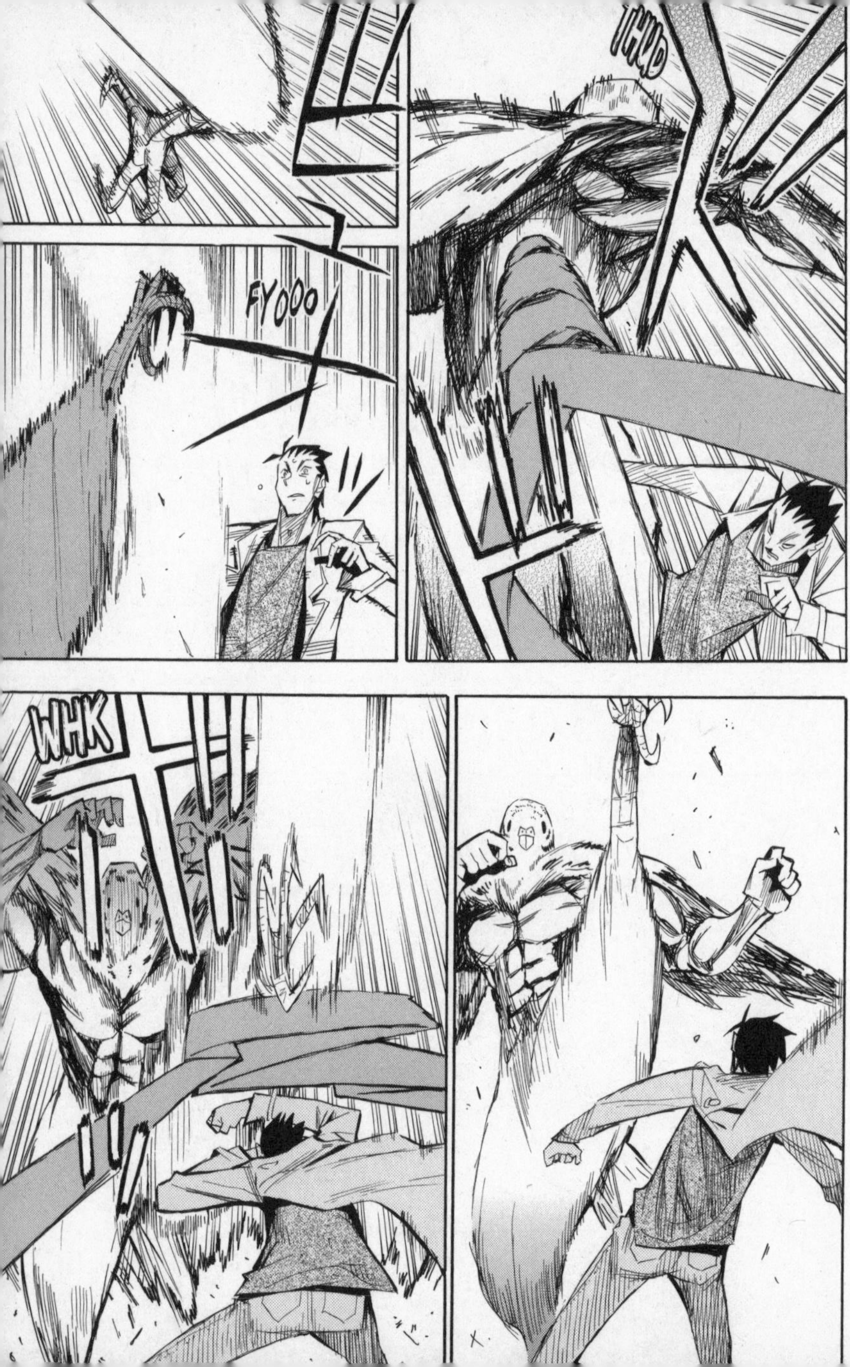
THUD
FYOOO
WHK

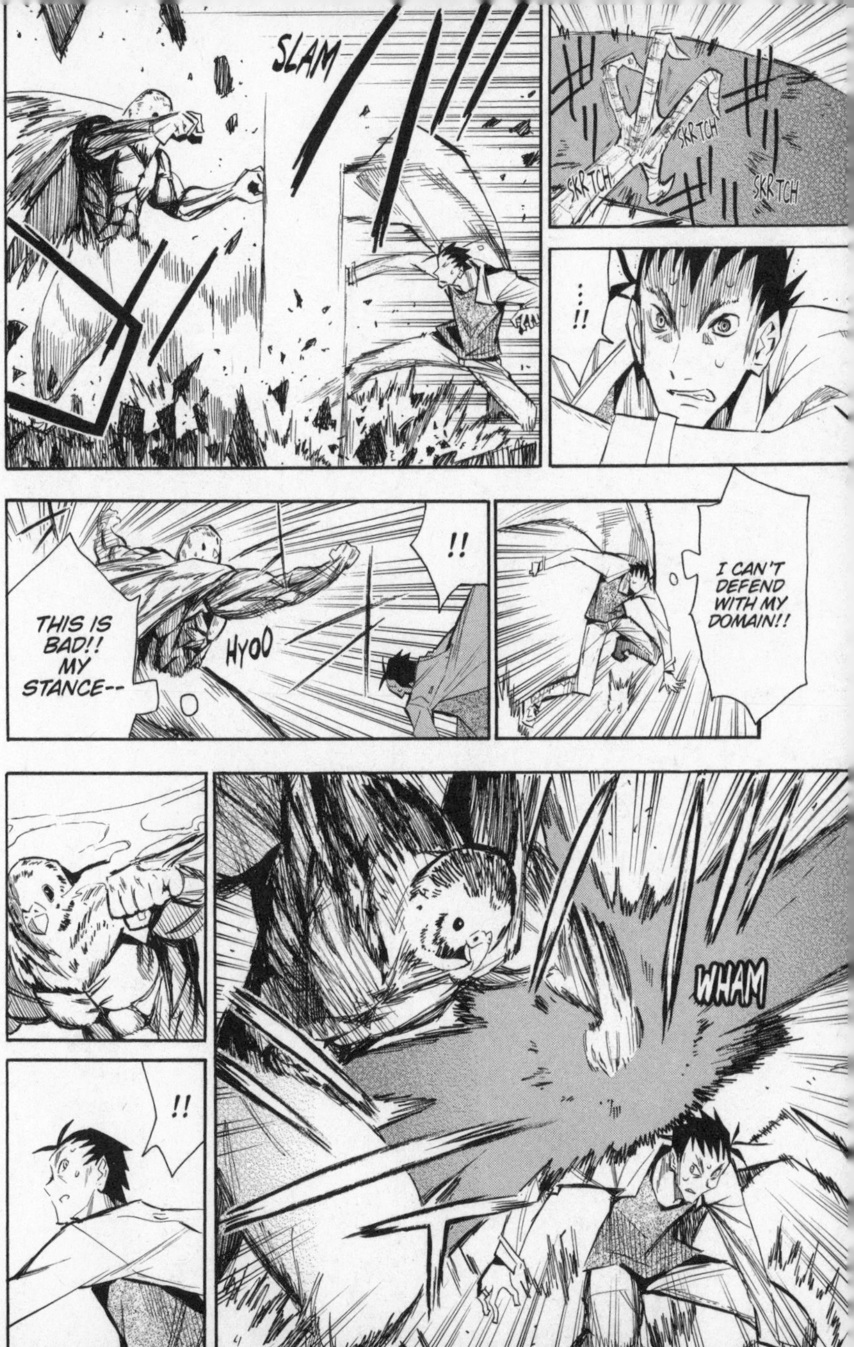
SKRTCH
SKRTCH
SKRTCH
...!!
SLAM
I CAN'T DEFEND WITH MY DOMAIN!!
!!
HYOO
THIS IS BAD!! MY STANCE--
WHAM
!!

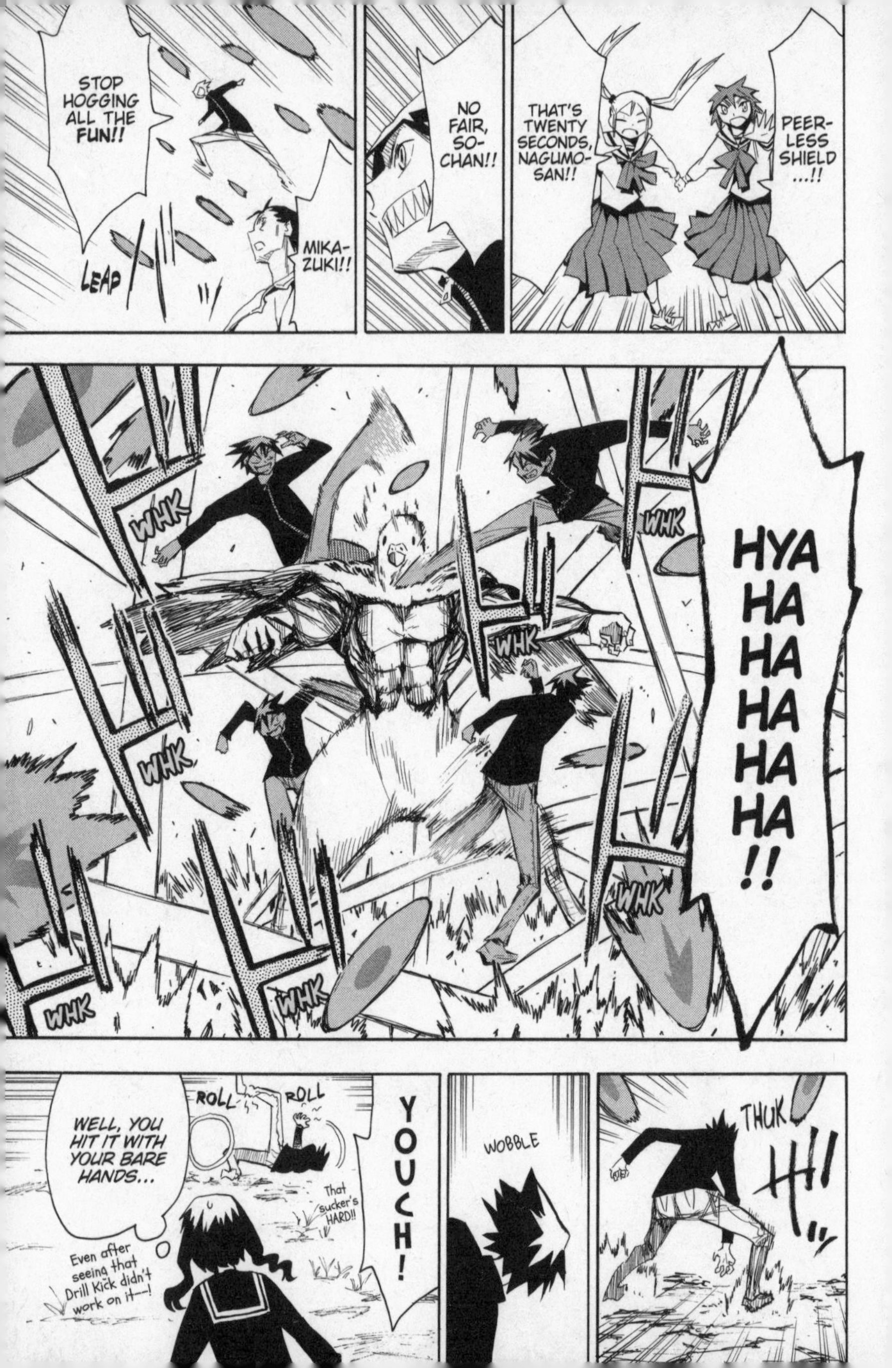
PEER-LESS SHIELD ...!!
THAT'S TWENTY SECONDS, NAGUMO-SAN!!
NO FAIR, SO-CHAN!!
STOP HOGGING ALL THE FUN!!
LEAP
MIKA-ZUKI!!
HYA HA HA HA HA HA HA!!
WHK
WHK
WHK
WHK
WHK
WHK
WHK
THUK
WOBBLE
YOUCH!
ROLL
ROLL
That sucker's HARD!!
WELL, YOU HIT IT WITH YOUR BARE HANDS...
Even after seeing that Drill Kick didn't work on it—!

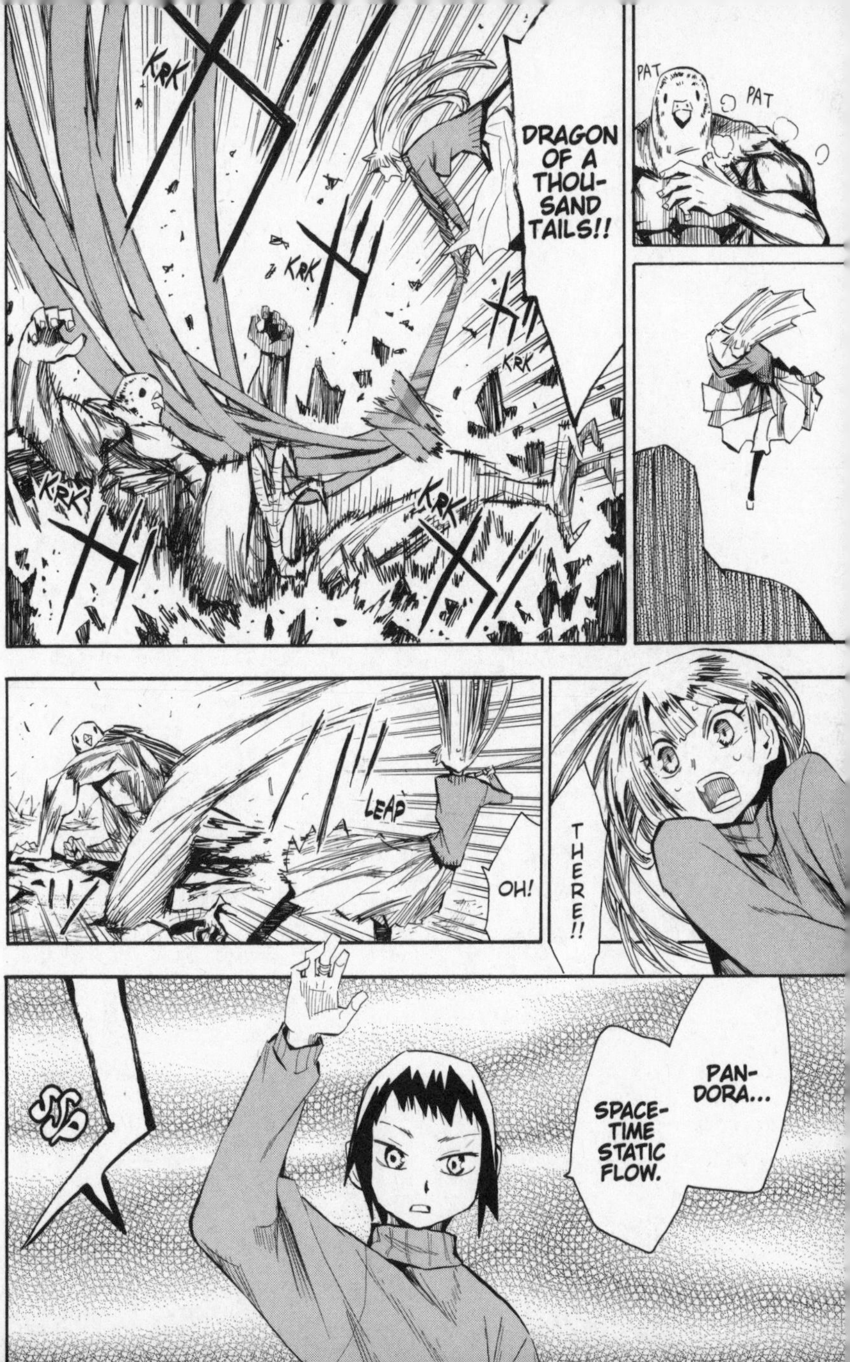
PAT
PAT
DRAGON OF A THOU-SAND TAILS!!
KRK
KRK
KRK
KRK
KRK
THERE!!
OH!
LEAP
PAN-DORA...
SPACE-TIME STATIC FLOW.

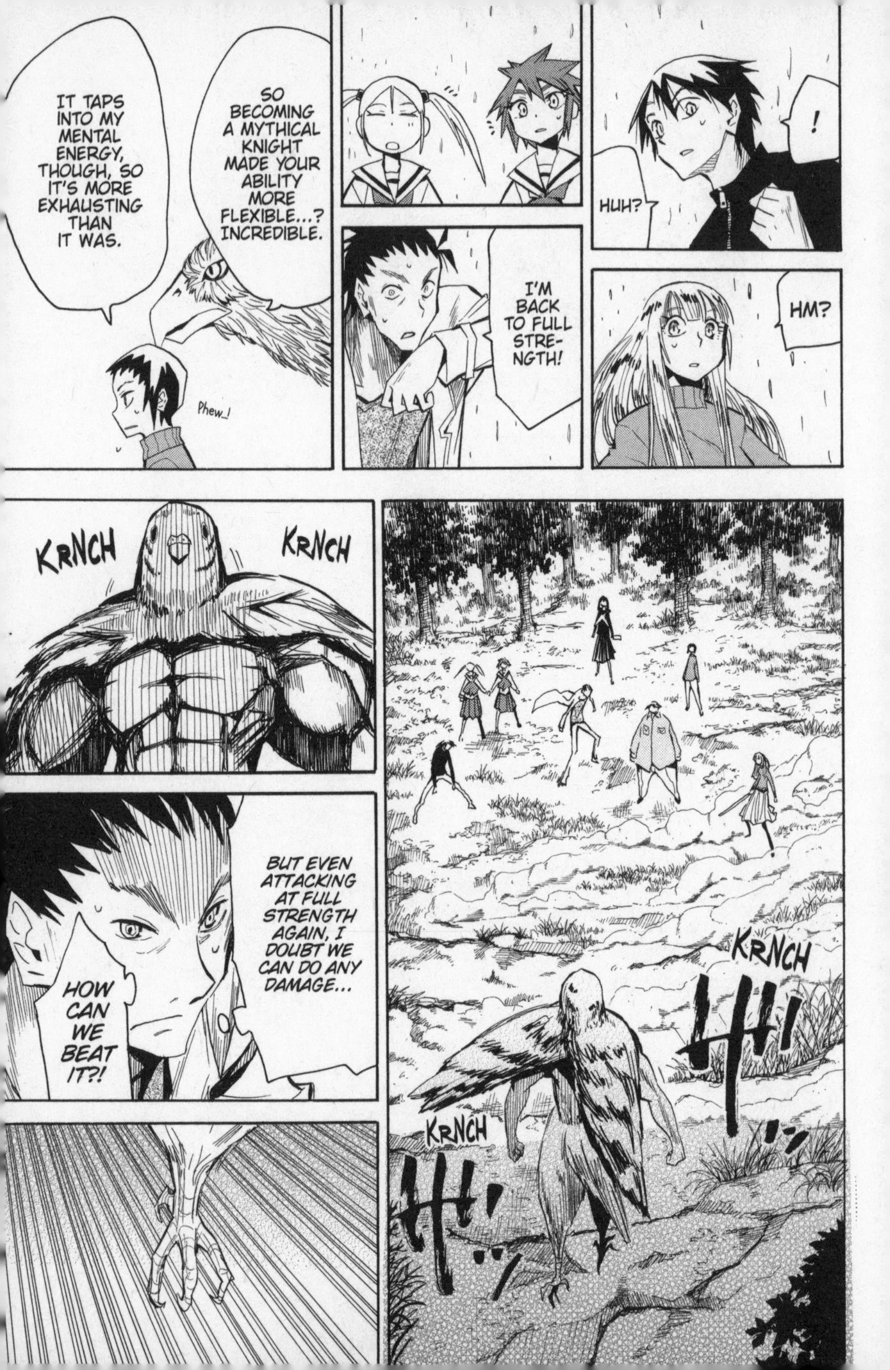
!
HUH?
HM?
I'M BACK TO FULL STRE-NGTH!
SO BECOMING A MYTHICAL KNIGHT MADE YOUR ABILITY MORE FLEXIBLE...? INCREDIBLE.
IT TAPS INTO MY MENTAL ENERGY, THOUGH, SO IT'S MORE EXHAUSTING THAN IT WAS.
Phew...!
KRNCH
KRNCH
KRNCH
KRNCH
BUT EVEN ATTACKING AT FULL STRENGTH AGAIN, I DOUBT WE CAN DO ANY DAMAGE...
HOW CAN WE BEAT IT?!

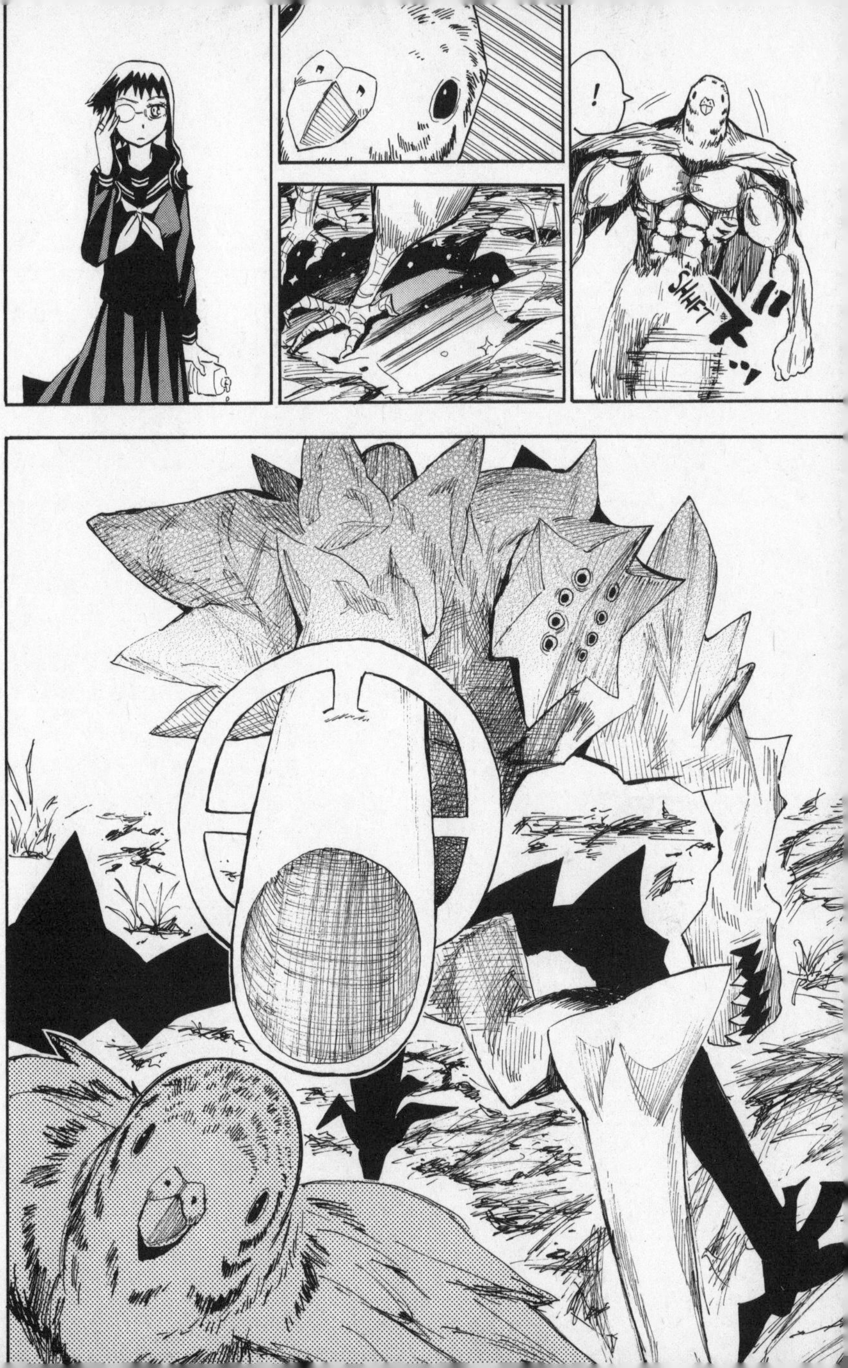
!
SHIFT

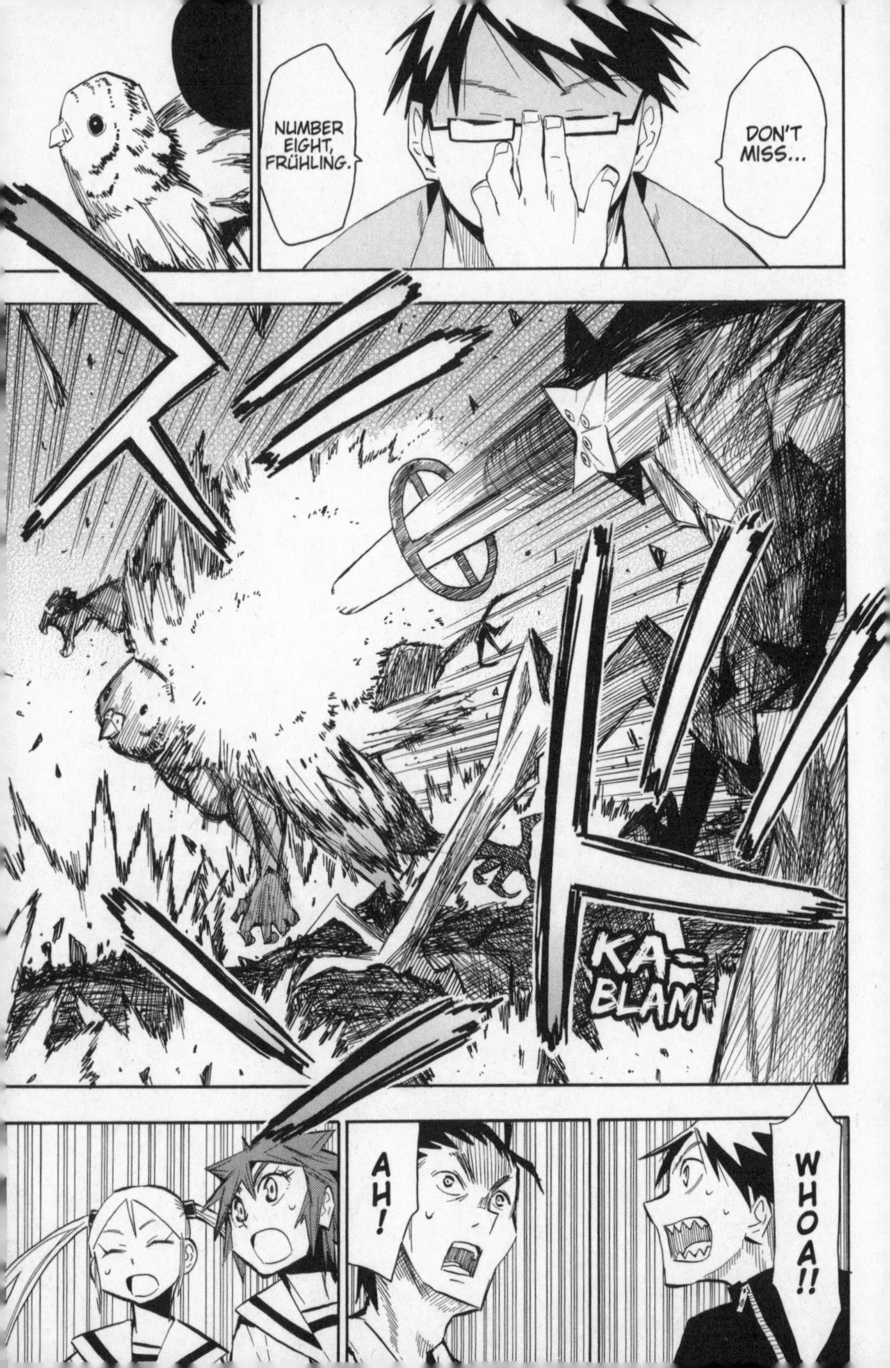

DON'T MISS...
NUMBER EIGHT, FRÜHLING.
KA-BLAM
WHOA!!
AH!

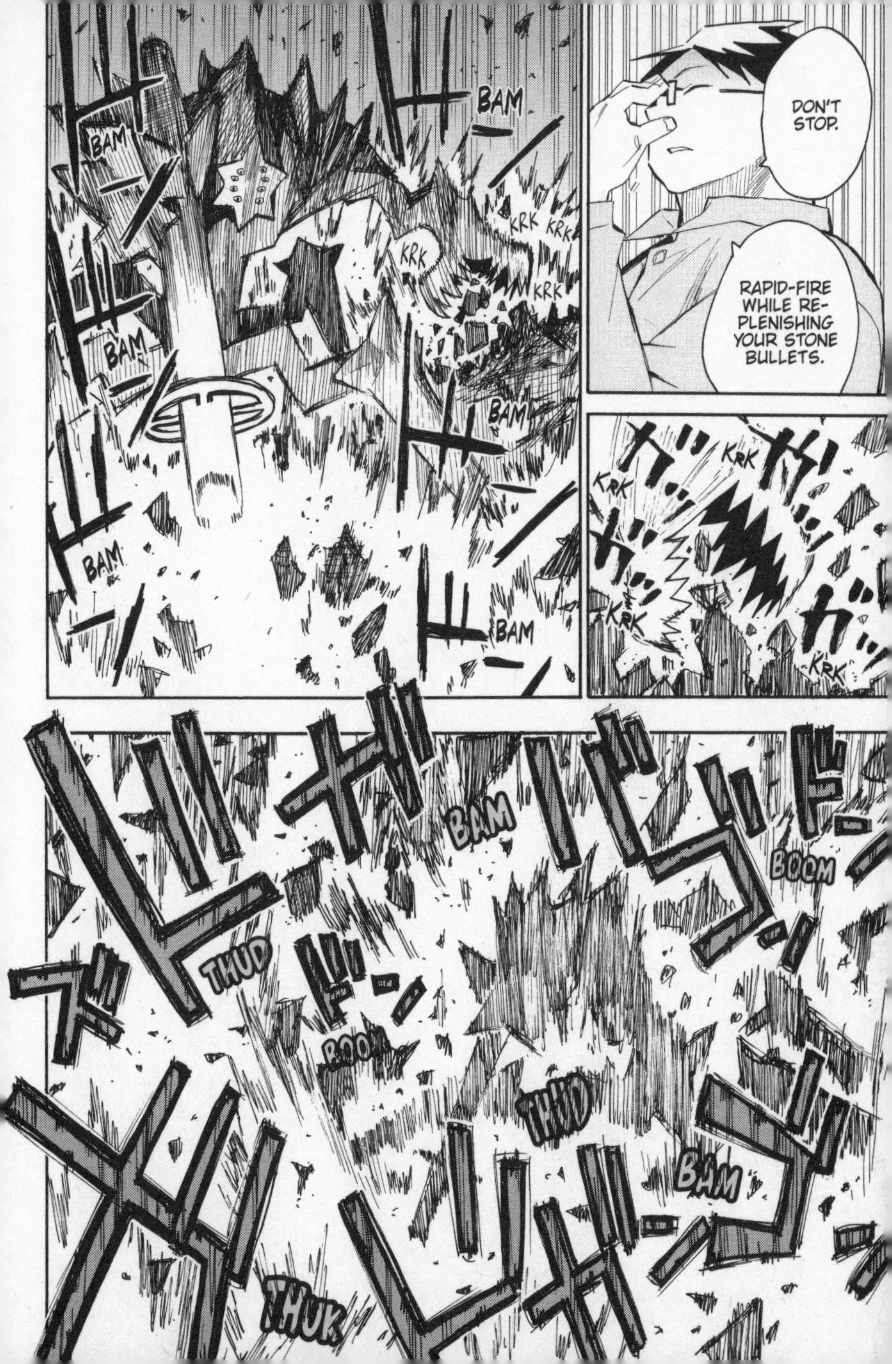
DON'T STOP.
RAPID-FIRE WHILE RE-PLENISHING YOUR STONE BULLETS.
KRK
KRK
KRK
KRK
BAM
BAM
KRK
KRK
KRK
KRK
BAM
BAM
BAM
BAM
BAM
BAM
BOOM
THUD
THUD
BAM
THUK

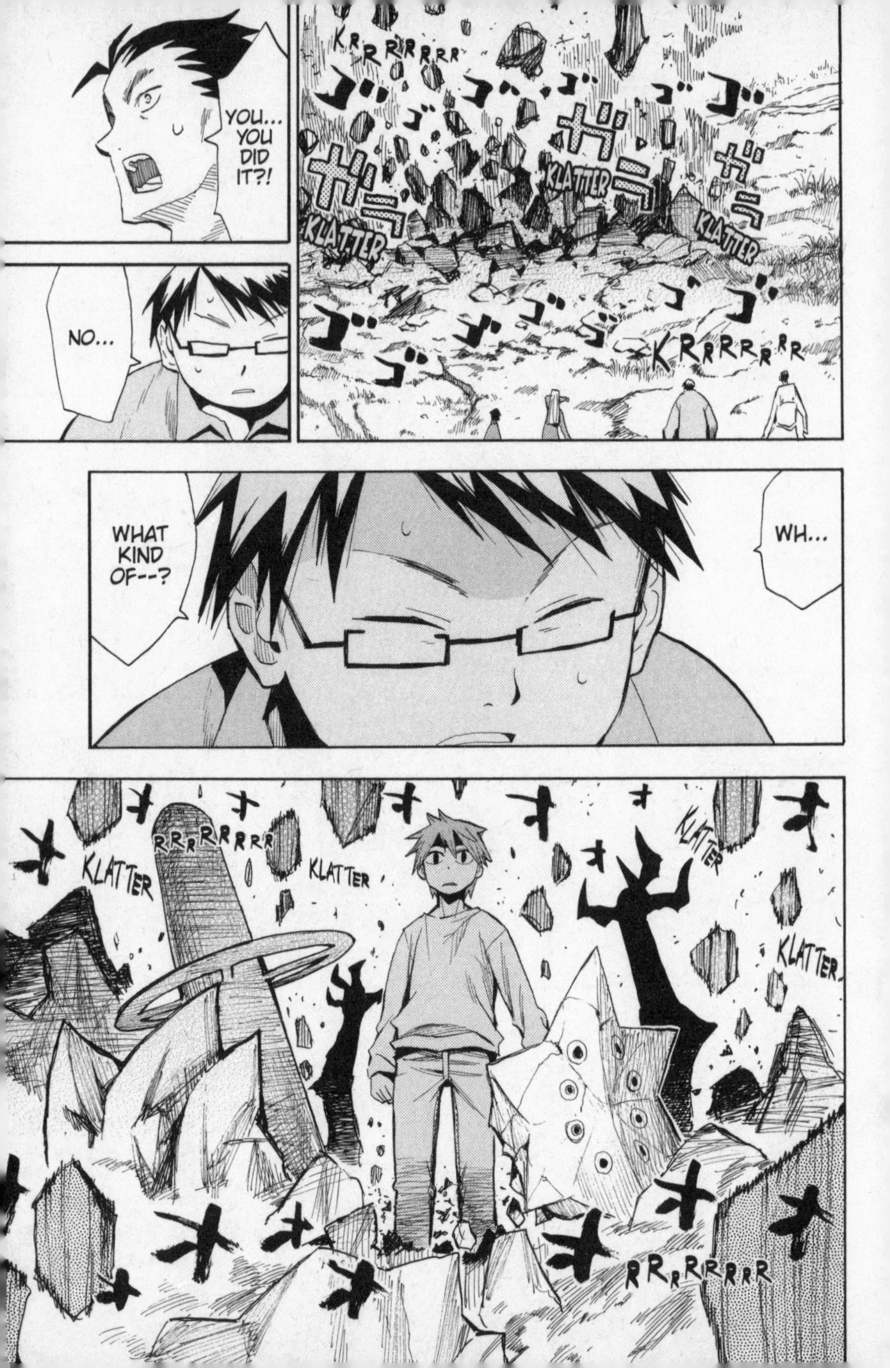
KRRRRRRRR
KLATTER
KLATTER
KLATTER
KRRRRRRR
YOU... YOU DID IT?!
NO...
WH...
WHAT KIND OF--?
RRRRRRRR
KLATTER
KLATTER
KLATTER
KLATTER
RRRRRRRR

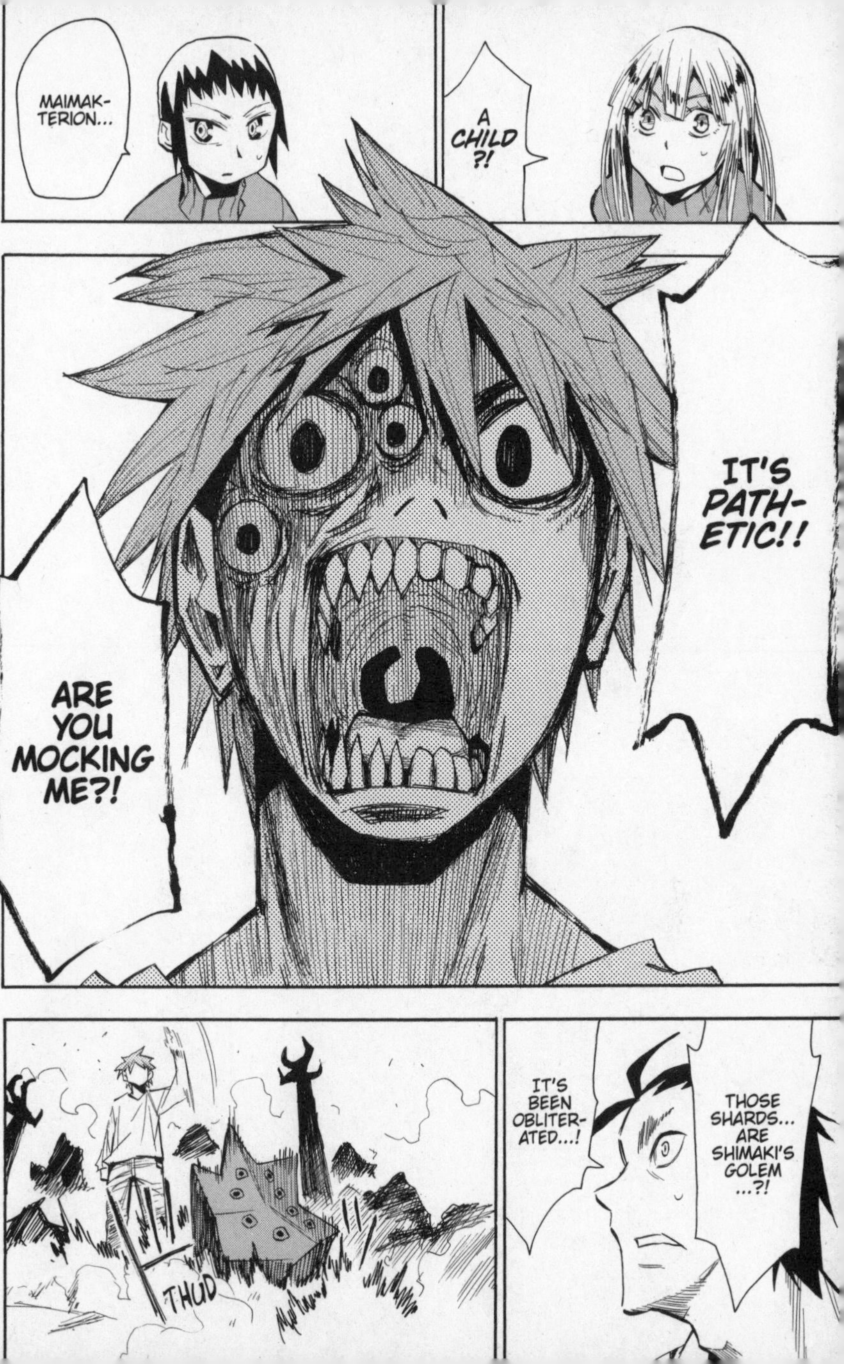
A CHILD?!
MAIMAK-TERION...
IT'S PATH-ETIC!!
ARE YOU MOCKING ME?!
THOSE SHARDS... ARE SHIMAKI'S GOLEM...?!
IT'S BEEN OBLITER-ATED...!
THUD

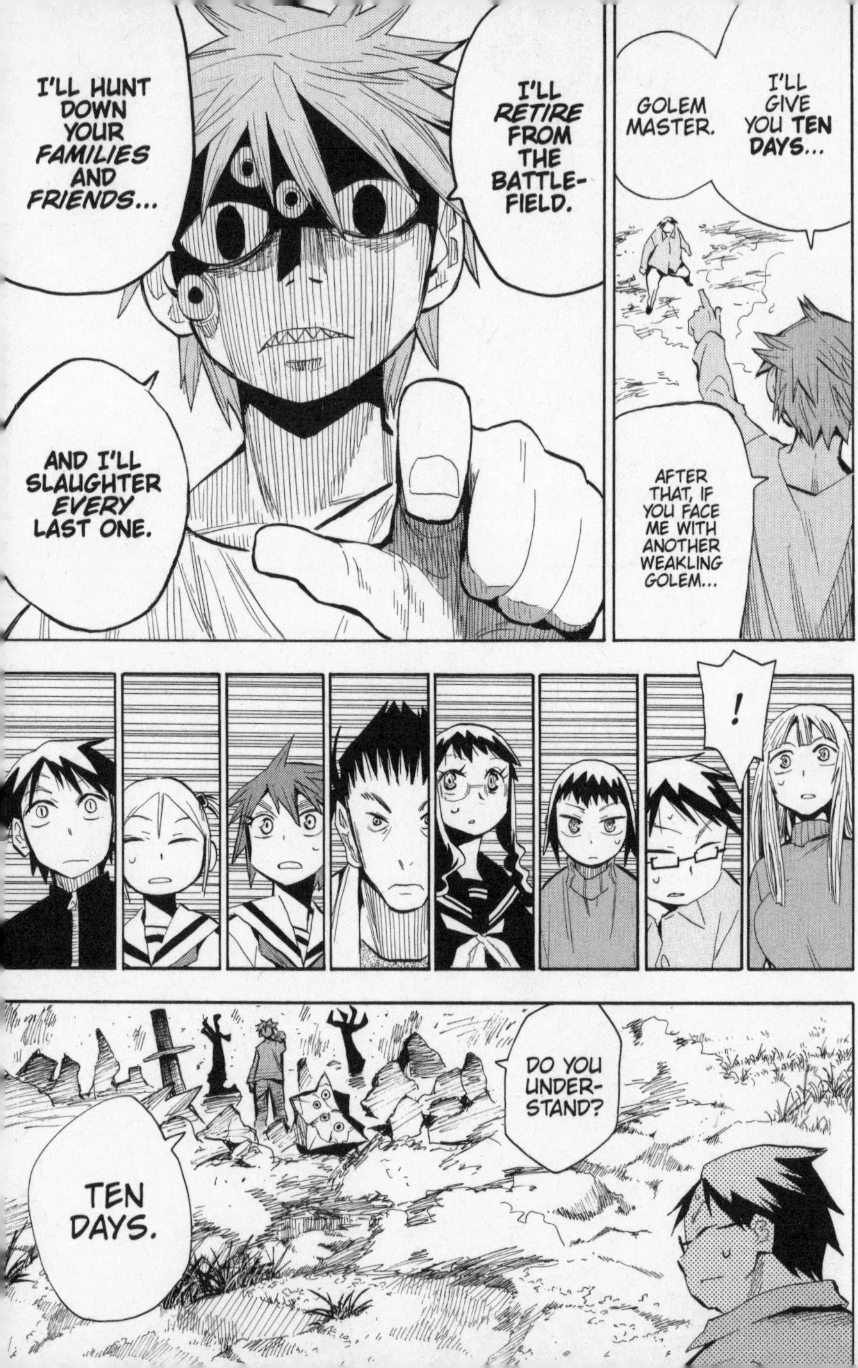
I'LL GIVE YOU TEN DAYS...
GOLEM MASTER.
AFTER THAT, IF YOU FACE ME WITH ANOTHER WEAKLING GOLEM...
I'LL *RETIRE* FROM THE BATTLE-FIELD.
I'LL HUNT DOWN YOUR *FAMILIES* AND *FRIENDS*...
AND I'LL SLAUGHTER *EVERY* LAST ONE.
!
DO YOU UNDER-STAND?
TEN DAYS.

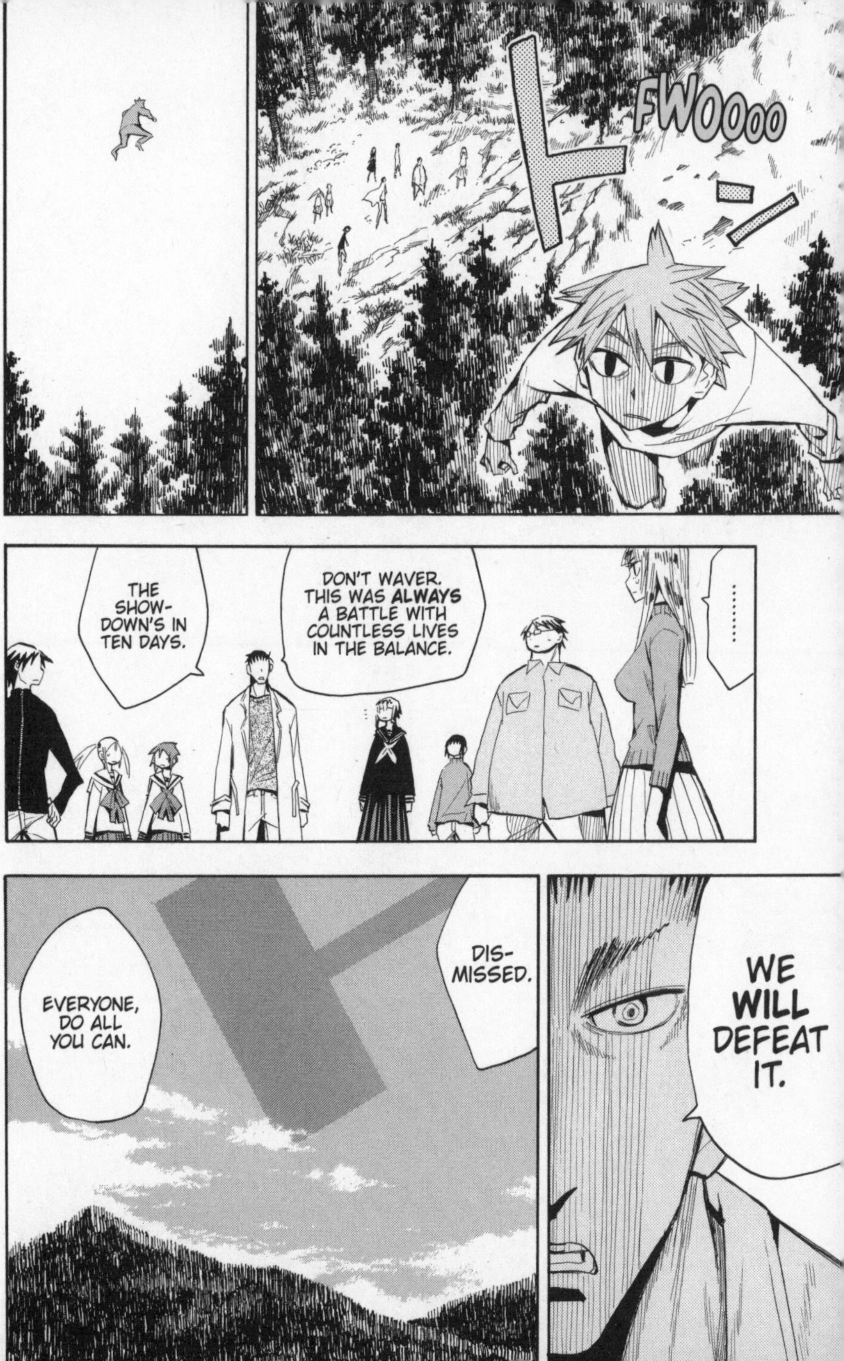
FWOOoo
……
DON'T WAVER. THIS WAS **ALWAYS** A BATTLE WITH COUNTLESS LIVES IN THE BALANCE.
THE SHOW-DOWN'S IN TEN DAYS.
WE **WILL** DEFEAT IT.
DIS-MISSED.
EVERYONE, DO ALL YOU CAN.

· · · · · ·

HYO-KUN...

A GOLEM...

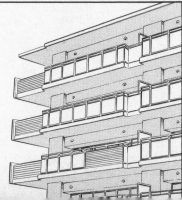

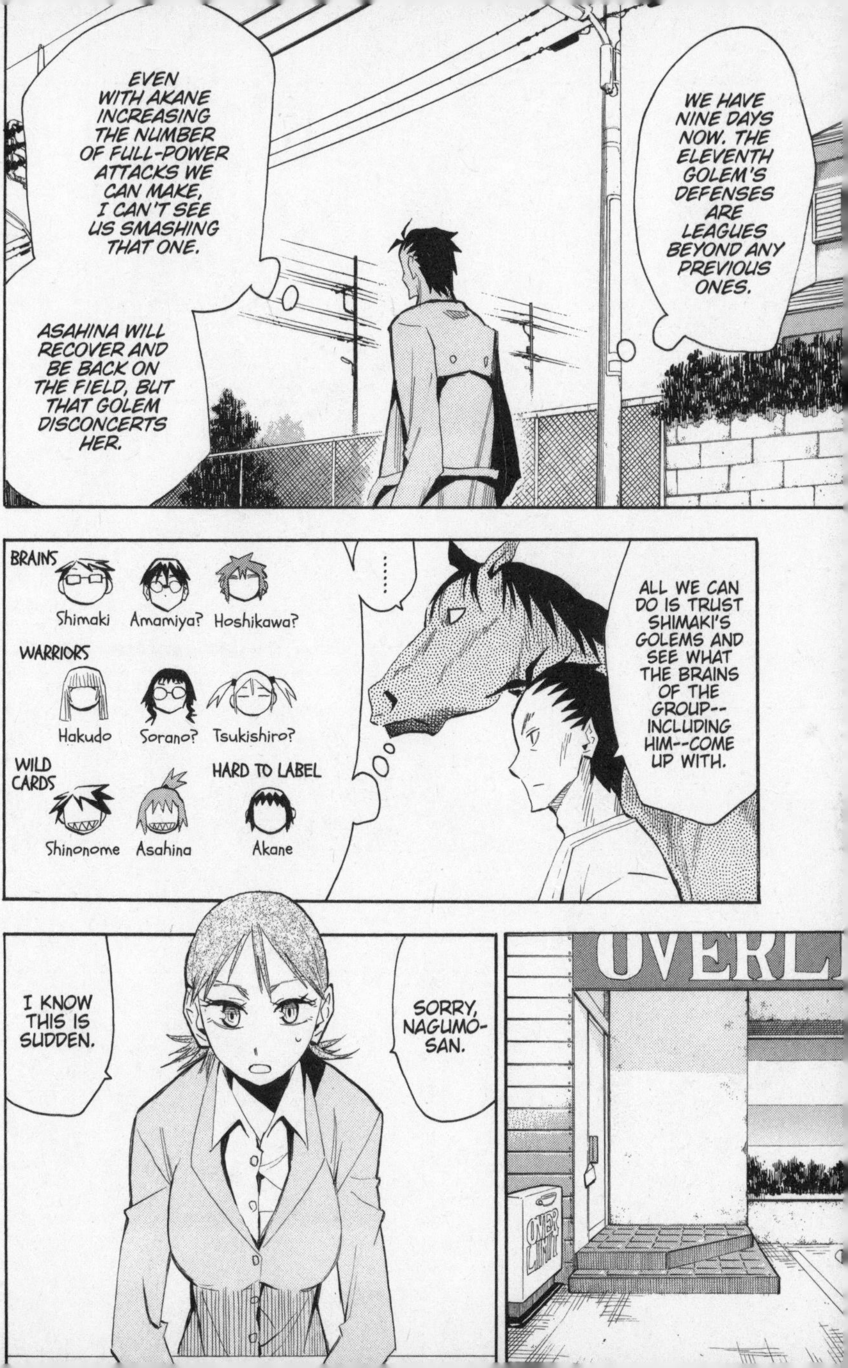
WE HAVE NINE DAYS NOW. THE ELEVENTH GOLEM'S DEFENSES ARE LEAGUES BEYOND ANY PREVIOUS ONES.
EVEN WITH AKANE INCREASING THE NUMBER OF FULL-POWER ATTACKS WE CAN MAKE, I CAN'T SEE US SMASHING THAT ONE.
ASAHINA WILL RECOVER AND BE BACK ON THE FIELD, BUT THAT GOLEM DISCONCERTS HER.
ALL WE CAN DO IS TRUST SHIMAKI'S GOLEMS AND SEE WHAT THE BRAINS OF THE GROUP--INCLUDING HIM--COME UP WITH.
......
BRAINS
Shimaki
Amamiya?
Hoshikawa?
WARRIORS
Hakudo
Sorano?
Tsukishiro?
WILD CARDS
Shinonome
Asahina
HARD TO LABEL
Akane
OVERL
SORRY, NAGUMO-SAN.
I KNOW THIS IS SUDDEN.

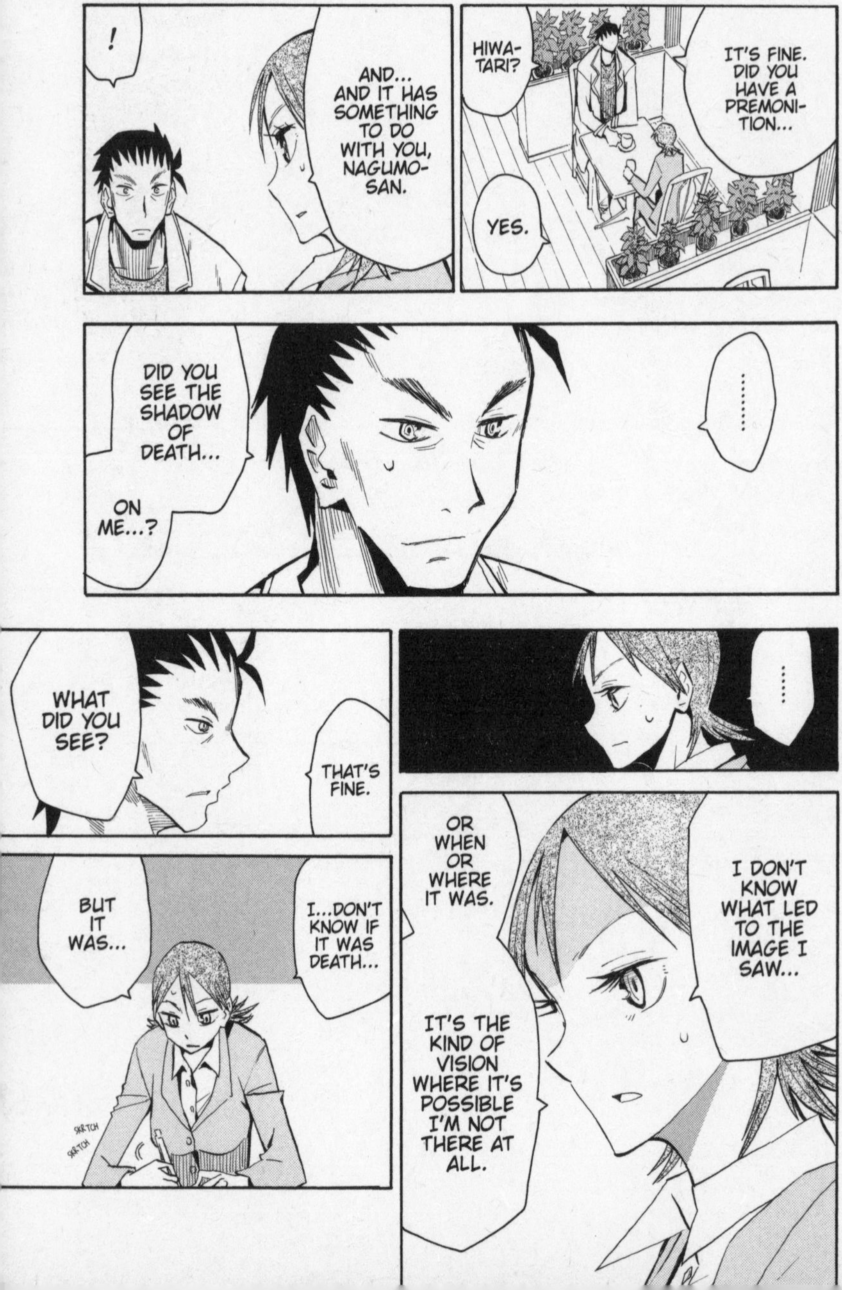
IT'S FINE. DID YOU HAVE A PREMONITION...
HIWATARI?
YES.
AND... AND IT HAS SOMETHING TO DO WITH YOU, NAGUMO-SAN.
!
......
DID YOU SEE THE SHADOW OF DEATH...
ON ME...?
......
I DON'T KNOW WHAT LED TO THE IMAGE I SAW...
OR WHEN OR WHERE IT WAS.
IT'S THE KIND OF VISION WHERE IT'S POSSIBLE I'M NOT THERE AT ALL.
THAT'S FINE.
WHAT DID YOU SEE?
I...DON'T KNOW IF IT WAS DEATH...
BUT IT WAS...
SKRTCH
SKRTCH

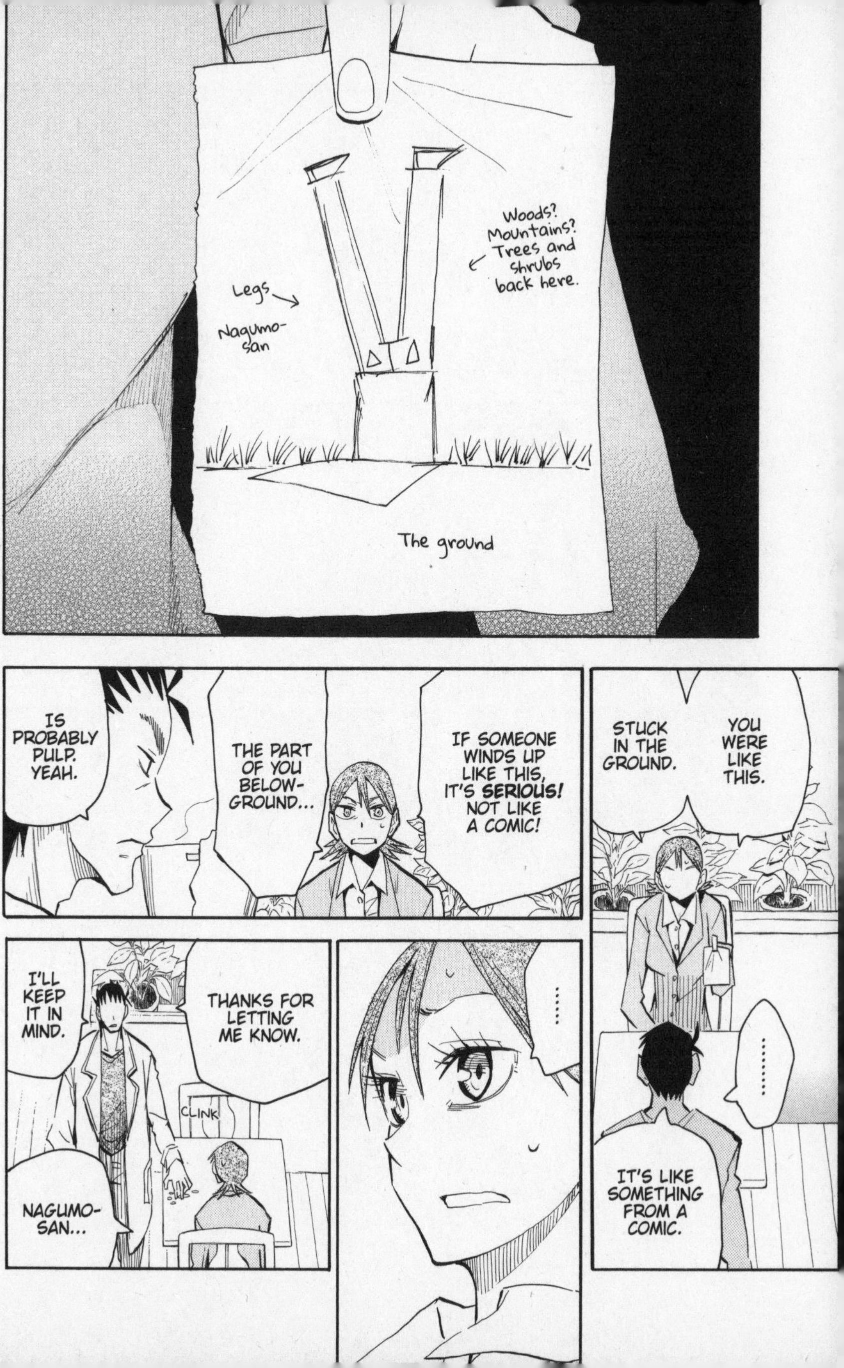
Woods? Mountains? Trees and shrubs back here.
Legs
Nagumo-san
The ground
YOU WERE LIKE THIS.
STUCK IN THE GROUND.
......
IT'S LIKE SOMETHING FROM A COMIC.
IF SOMEONE WINDS UP LIKE THIS, IT'S **SERIOUS!** NOT LIKE A COMIC!
THE PART OF YOU BELOW-GROUND...
IS PROBABLY PULP. YEAH.
......
THANKS FOR LETTING ME KNOW.
I'LL KEEP IT IN MIND.
CLINK
NAGUMO-SAN...

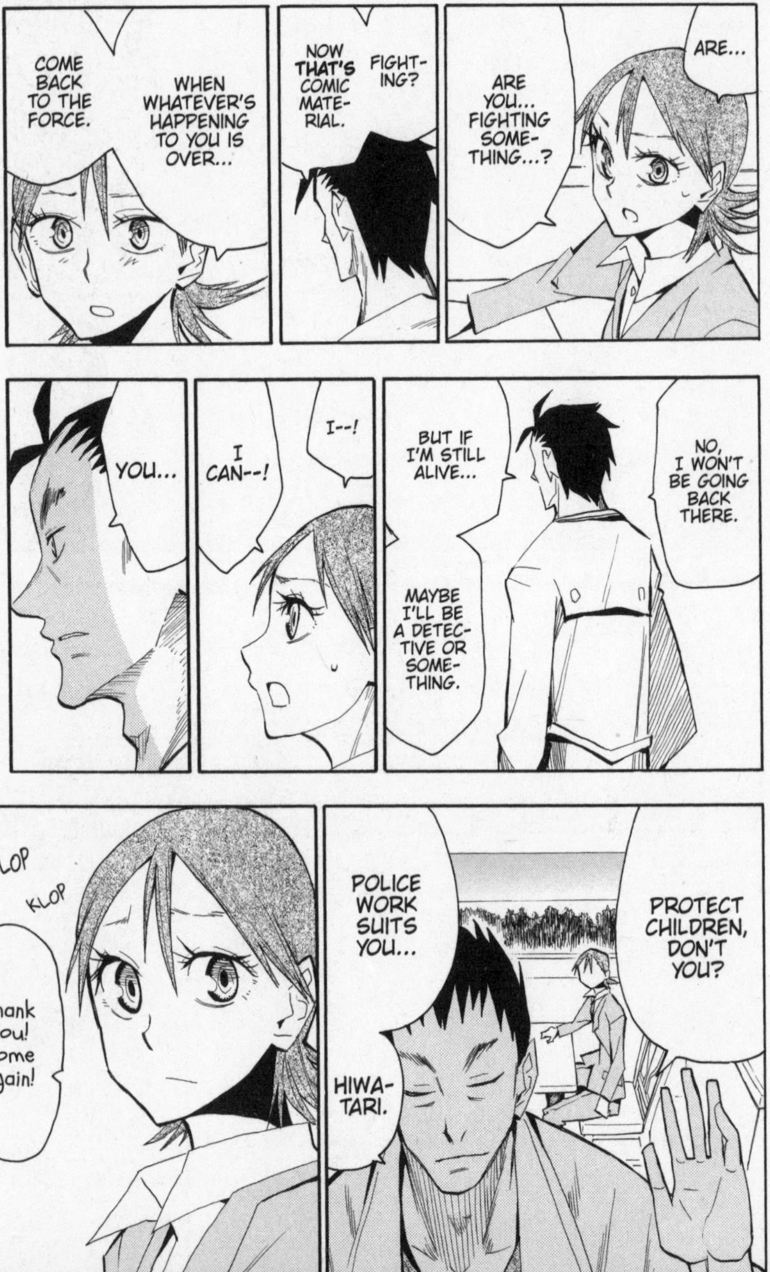
ARE...
ARE YOU... FIGHTING SOMETHING...?
FIGHTING?
NOW THAT'S COMIC MATERIAL.
WHEN WHATEVER'S HAPPENING TO YOU IS OVER...
COME BACK TO THE FORCE.
NO, I WON'T BE GOING BACK THERE.
BUT IF I'M STILL ALIVE...
MAYBE I'LL BE A DETECTIVE OR SOMETHING.
I--!
I CAN--!
YOU...
PROTECT CHILDREN, DON'T YOU?
POLICE WORK SUITS YOU...
HIWATARI.
KLOP
KLOP
Thank you! Come again!

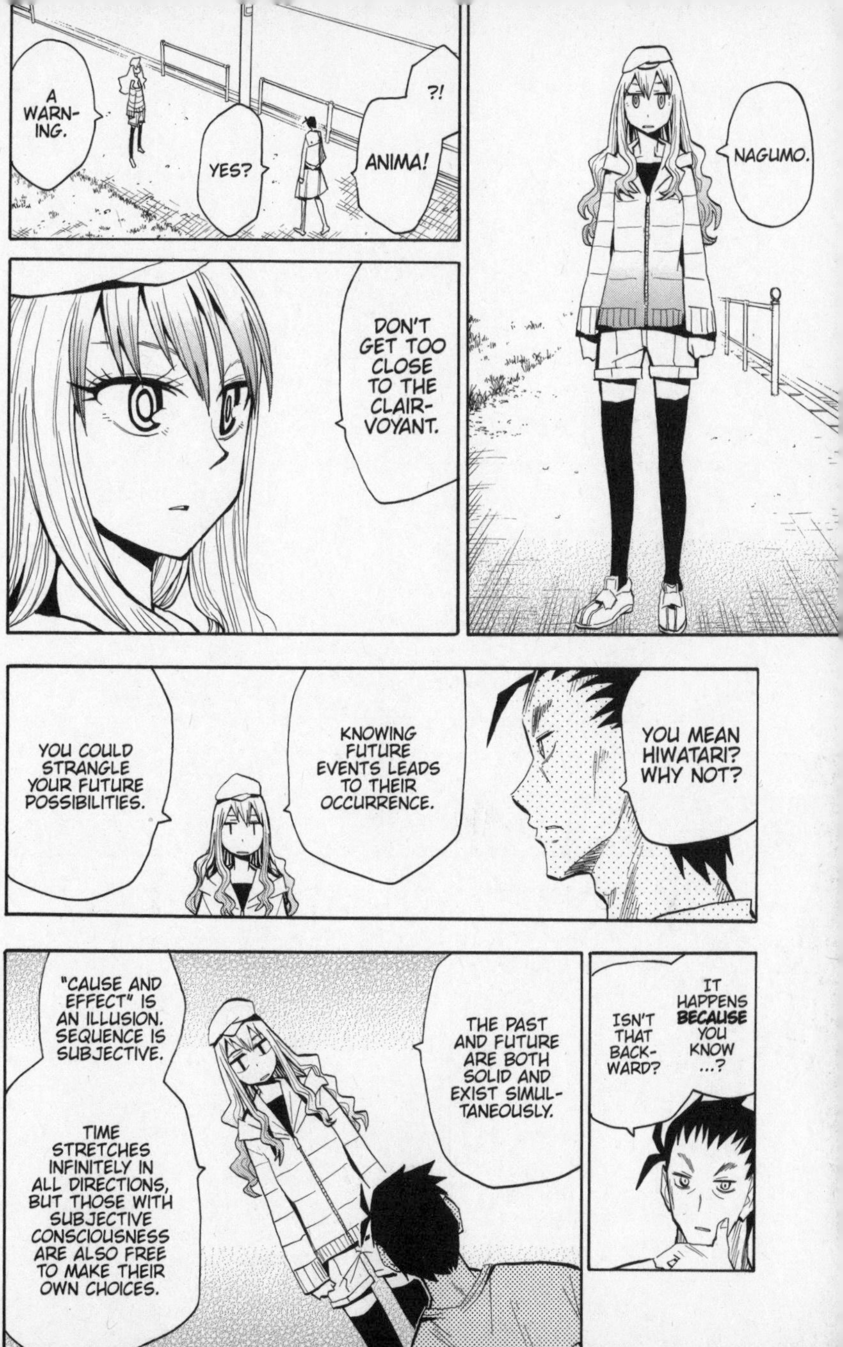
NAGUMO.
?!
ANIMA!
YES?
A WARNING.
DON'T GET TOO CLOSE TO THE CLAIRVOYANT.
YOU MEAN HIWATARI? WHY NOT?
KNOWING FUTURE EVENTS LEADS TO THEIR OCCURRENCE.
YOU COULD STRANGLE YOUR FUTURE POSSIBILITIES.
IT HAPPENS **BECAUSE** YOU KNOW ...?
ISN'T THAT BACKWARD?
THE PAST AND FUTURE ARE BOTH SOLID AND EXIST SIMULTANEOUSLY.
"CAUSE AND EFFECT" IS AN ILLUSION. SEQUENCE IS SUBJECTIVE.
TIME STRETCHES INFINITELY IN ALL DIRECTIONS, BUT THOSE WITH SUBJECTIVE CONSCIOUSNESS ARE ALSO FREE TO MAKE THEIR OWN CHOICES.

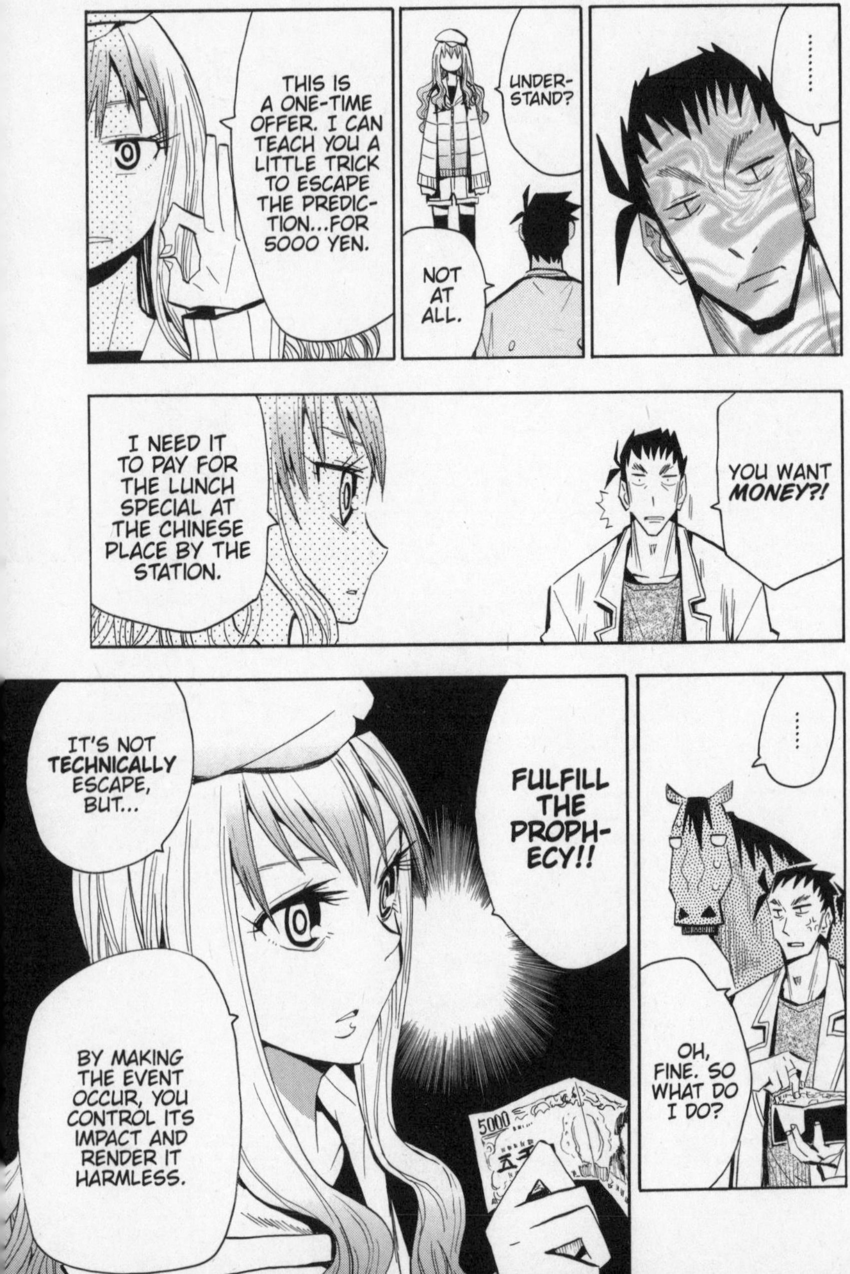
......
UNDER-STAND?
NOT AT ALL.
THIS IS A ONE-TIME OFFER. I CAN TEACH YOU A LITTLE TRICK TO ESCAPE THE PREDICTION...FOR 5000 YEN.
YOU WANT MONEY?!
I NEED IT TO PAY FOR THE LUNCH SPECIAL AT THE CHINESE PLACE BY THE STATION.
......
OH, FINE. SO WHAT DO I DO?
FULFILL THE PROPHECY!!
IT'S NOT TECHNICALLY ESCAPE, BUT...
BY MAKING THE EVENT OCCUR, YOU CONTROL ITS IMPACT AND RENDER IT HARMLESS.

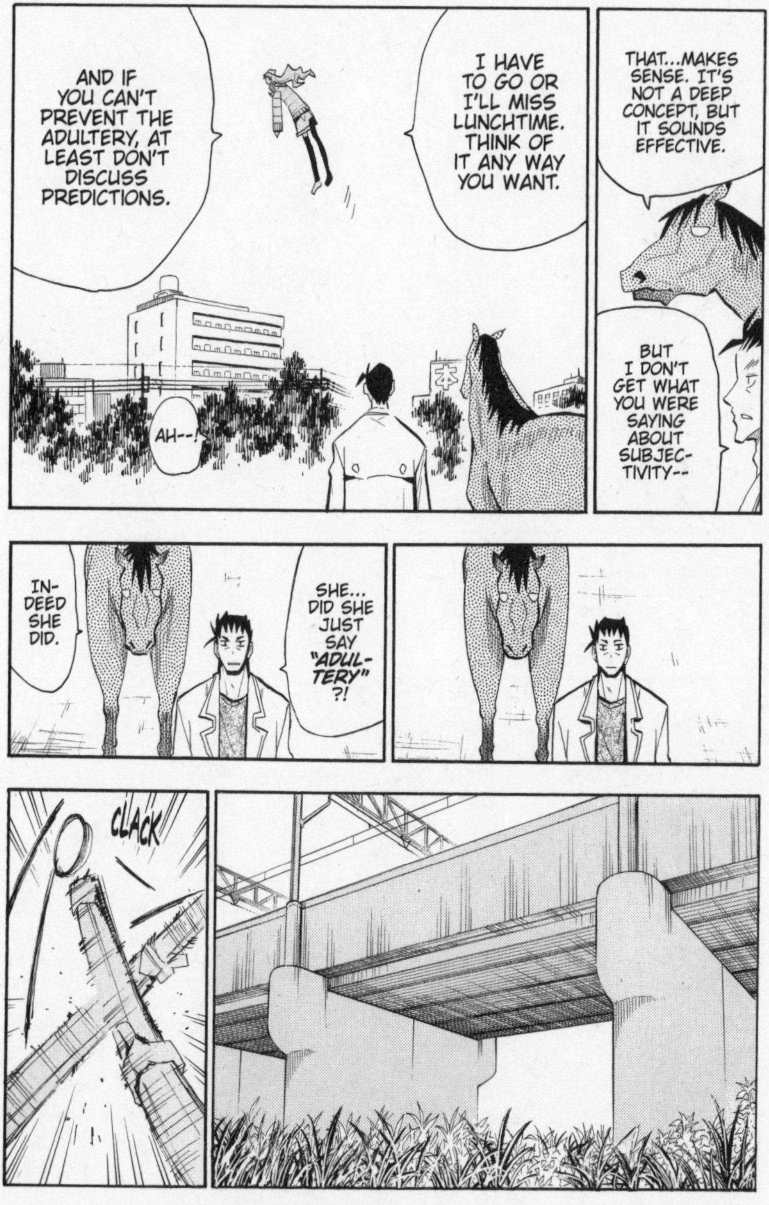
THAT...MAKES SENSE. IT'S NOT A DEEP CONCEPT, BUT IT SOUNDS EFFECTIVE.
BUT I DON'T GET WHAT YOU WERE SAYING ABOUT SUBJECTIVITY--
I HAVE TO GO OR I'LL MISS LUNCHTIME. THINK OF IT ANY WAY YOU WANT.
AND IF YOU CAN'T PREVENT THE ADULTERY, AT LEAST DON'T DISCUSS PREDICTIONS.
本
AH--!
SHE... DID SHE JUST SAY "ADULTERY"?!
INDEED SHE DID.
CLACK

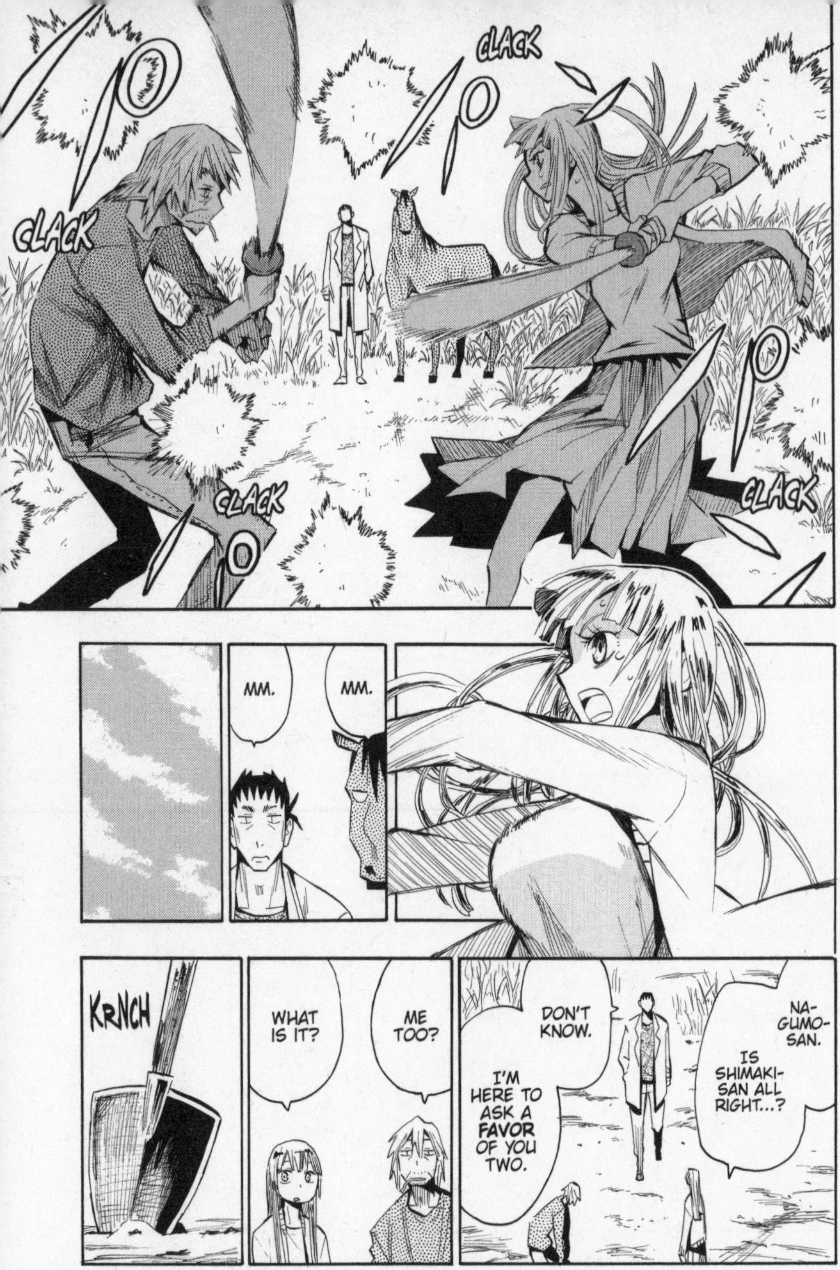
CLACK
CLACK
CLACK
CLACK
MM.
MM.
NA-GUMO-SAN.
IS SHIMAKI-SAN ALL RIGHT...?
DON'T KNOW.
I'M HERE TO ASK A FAVOR OF YOU TWO.
ME TOO?
WHAT IS IT?
KRNCH

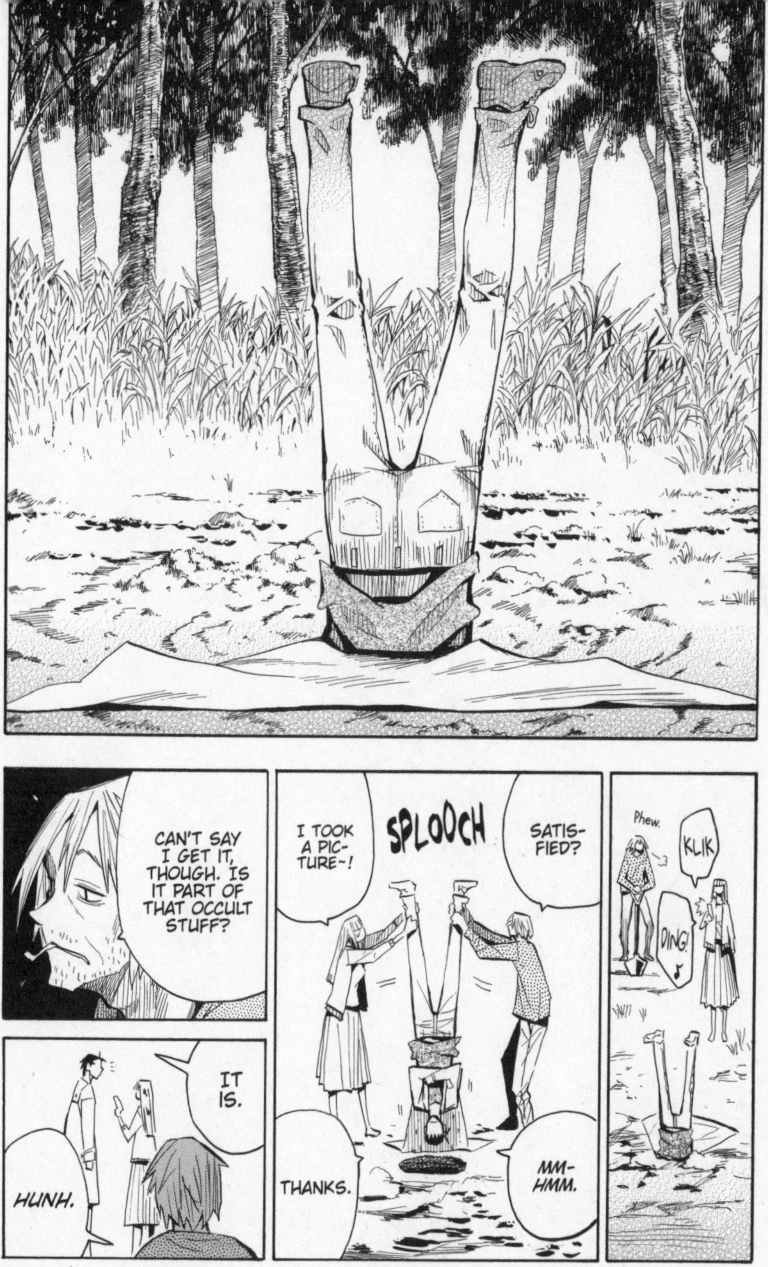
KLIK
Phew.
DING!
SATIS-FIED?
SPLOOCH
I TOOK A PIC-TURE~!
MM-HMM.
THANKS.
CAN'T SAY I GET IT, THOUGH. IS IT PART OF THAT OCCULT STUFF?
IT IS.
HUNH.

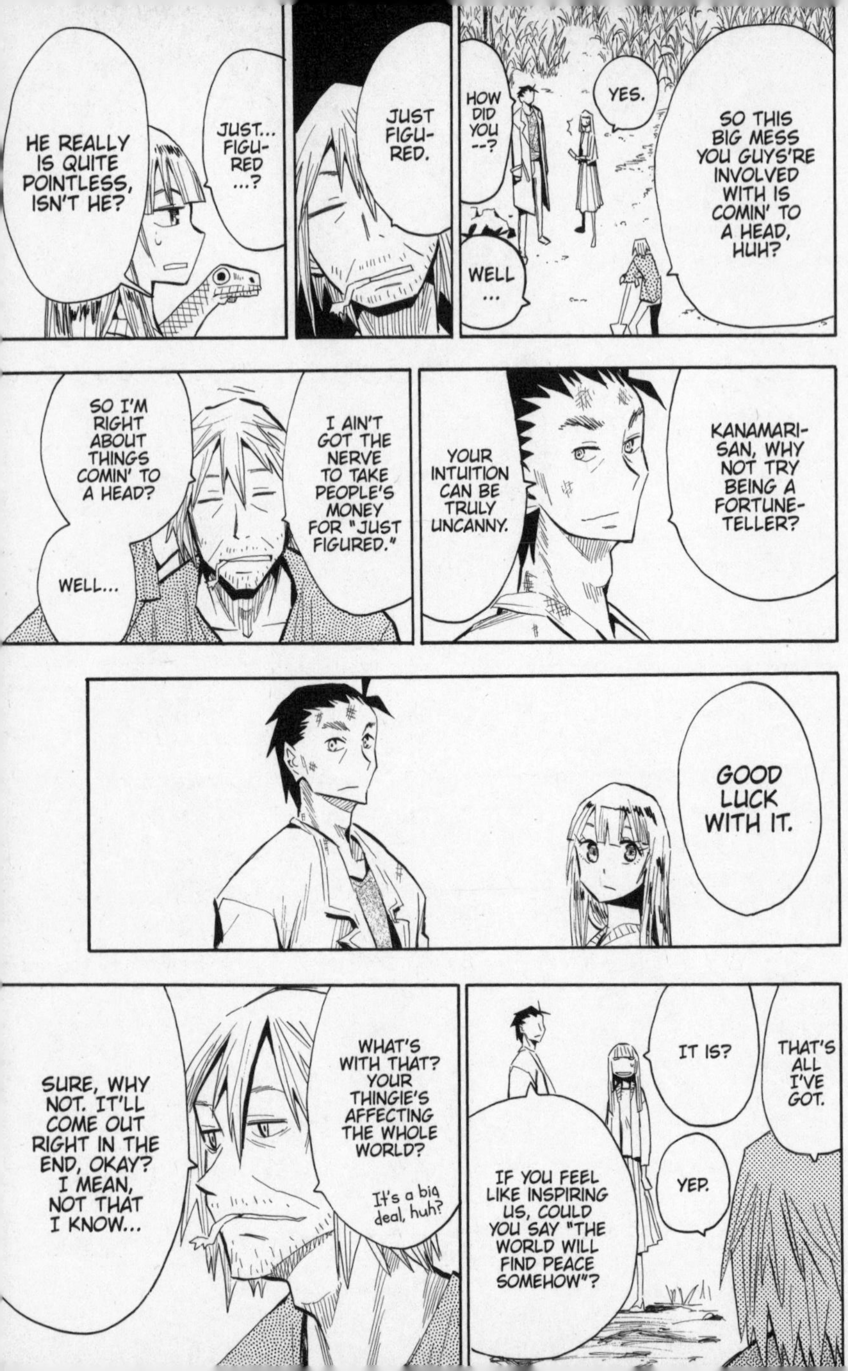
SO THIS BIG MESS YOU GUYS'RE INVOLVED WITH IS COMIN' TO A HEAD, HUH?
YES.
HOW DID YOU --?
WELL ...
JUST FIGU-RED.
JUST... FIGU-RED ...?
HE REALLY IS QUITE POINTLESS, ISN'T HE?
KANAMARI-SAN, WHY NOT TRY BEING A FORTUNE-TELLER?
YOUR INTUITION CAN BE TRULY UNCANNY.
I AIN'T GOT THE NERVE TO TAKE PEOPLE'S MONEY FOR "JUST FIGURED."
SO I'M RIGHT ABOUT THINGS COMIN' TO A HEAD?
WELL...
GOOD LUCK WITH IT.
THAT'S ALL I'VE GOT.
IT IS?
YEP.
IF YOU FEEL LIKE INSPIRING US, COULD YOU SAY "THE WORLD WILL FIND PEACE SOMEHOW"?
WHAT'S WITH THAT? YOUR THINGIE'S AFFECTING THE WHOLE WORLD?
It's a big deal, huh?
SURE, WHY NOT. IT'LL COME OUT RIGHT IN THE END, OKAY? I MEAN, NOT THAT I KNOW...

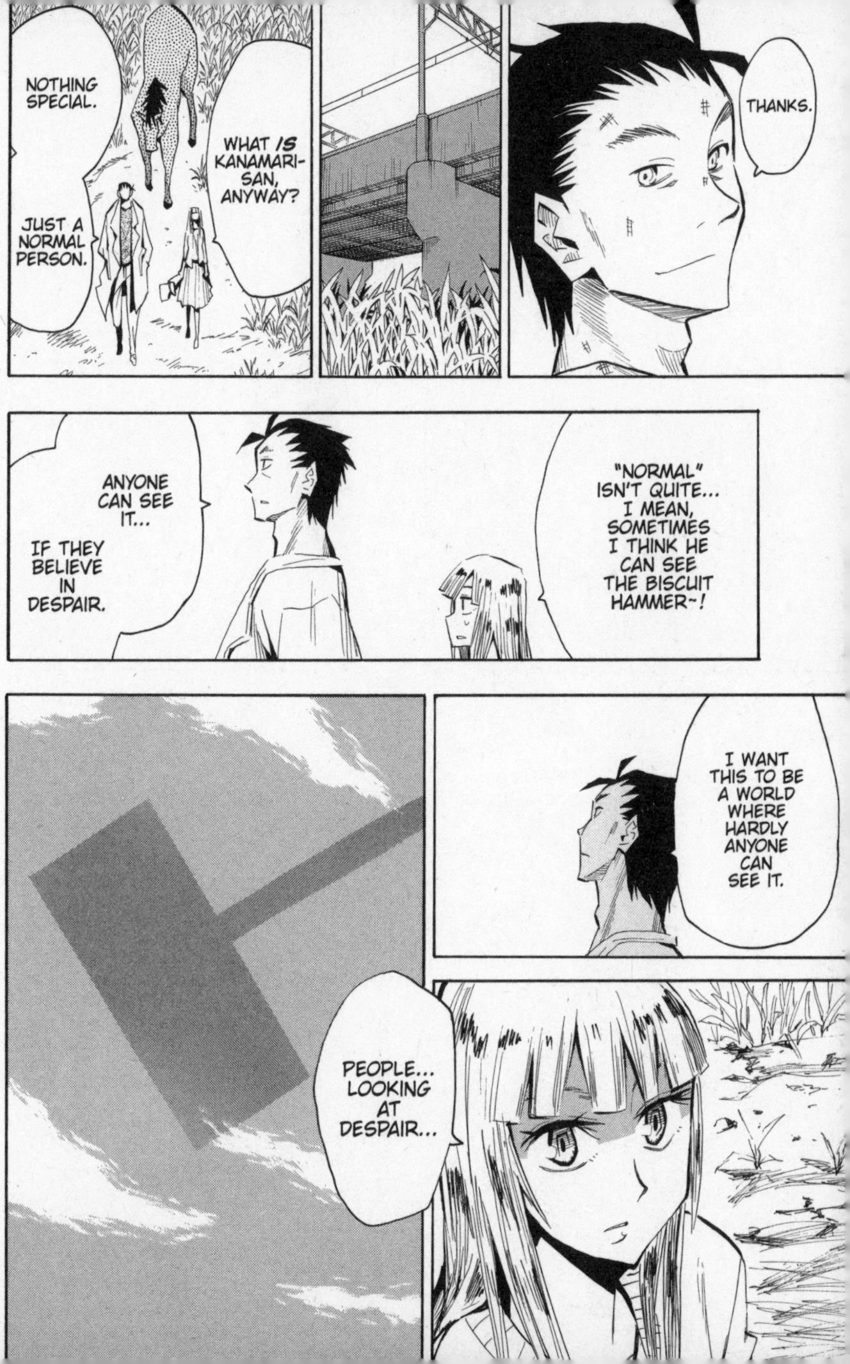
THANKS.
WHAT *IS* KANAMARI-SAN, ANYWAY?
NOTHING SPECIAL.
JUST A NORMAL PERSON.
"NORMAL" ISN'T QUITE... I MEAN, SOMETIMES I THINK HE CAN SEE THE BISCUIT HAMMER~!
ANYONE CAN SEE IT...
IF THEY BELIEVE IN DESPAIR.
I WANT THIS TO BE A WORLD WHERE HARDLY ANYONE CAN SEE IT.
PEOPLE... LOOKING AT DESPAIR...

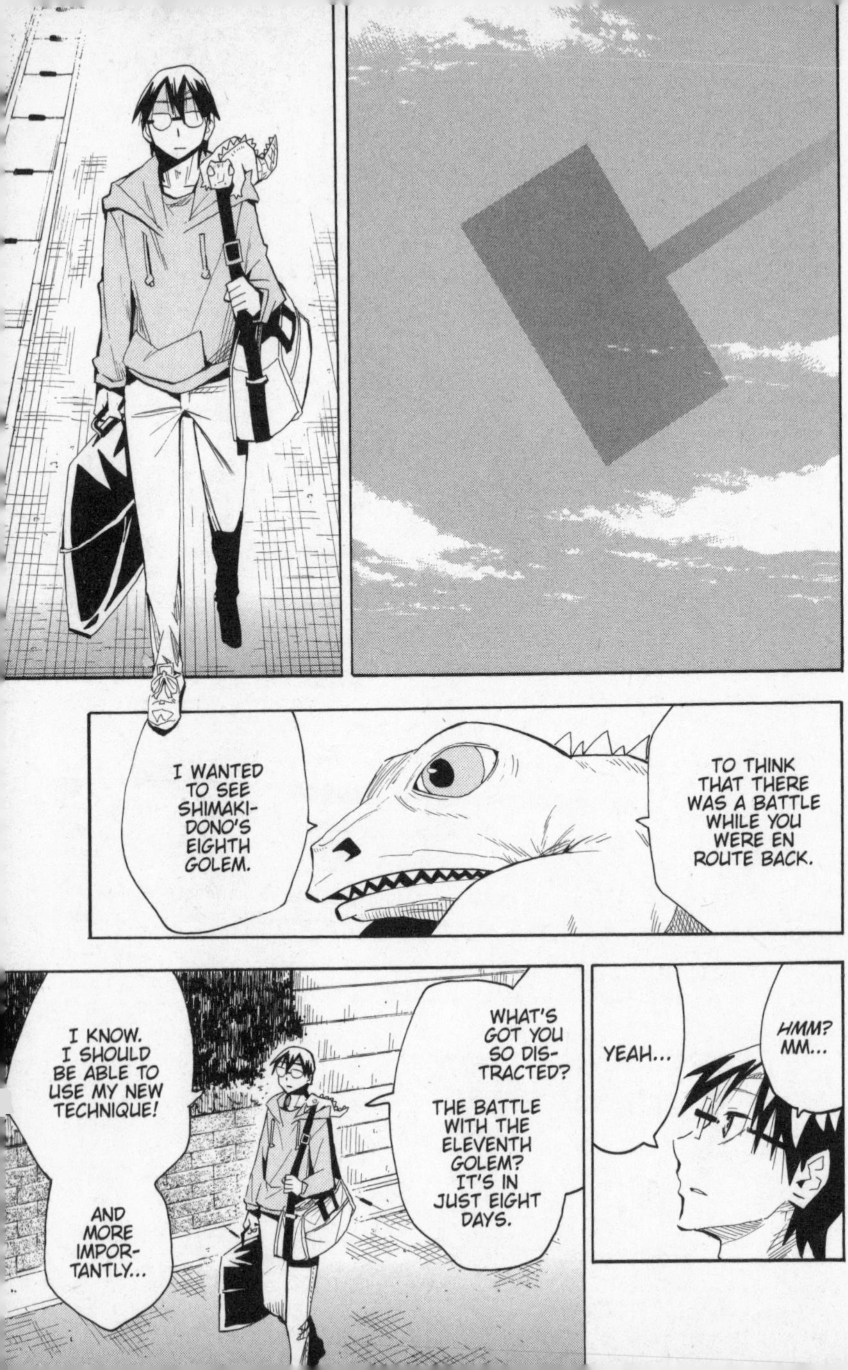
TO THINK THAT THERE WAS A BATTLE WHILE YOU WERE EN ROUTE BACK.
I WANTED TO SEE SHIMAKI-DONO'S EIGHTH GOLEM.
HMM? MM...
YEAH...
WHAT'S GOT YOU SO DIS-TRACTED?
THE BATTLE WITH THE ELEVENTH GOLEM? IT'S IN JUST EIGHT DAYS.
I KNOW. I SHOULD BE ABLE TO USE MY NEW TECHNIQUE!
AND MORE IMPOR-TANTLY...

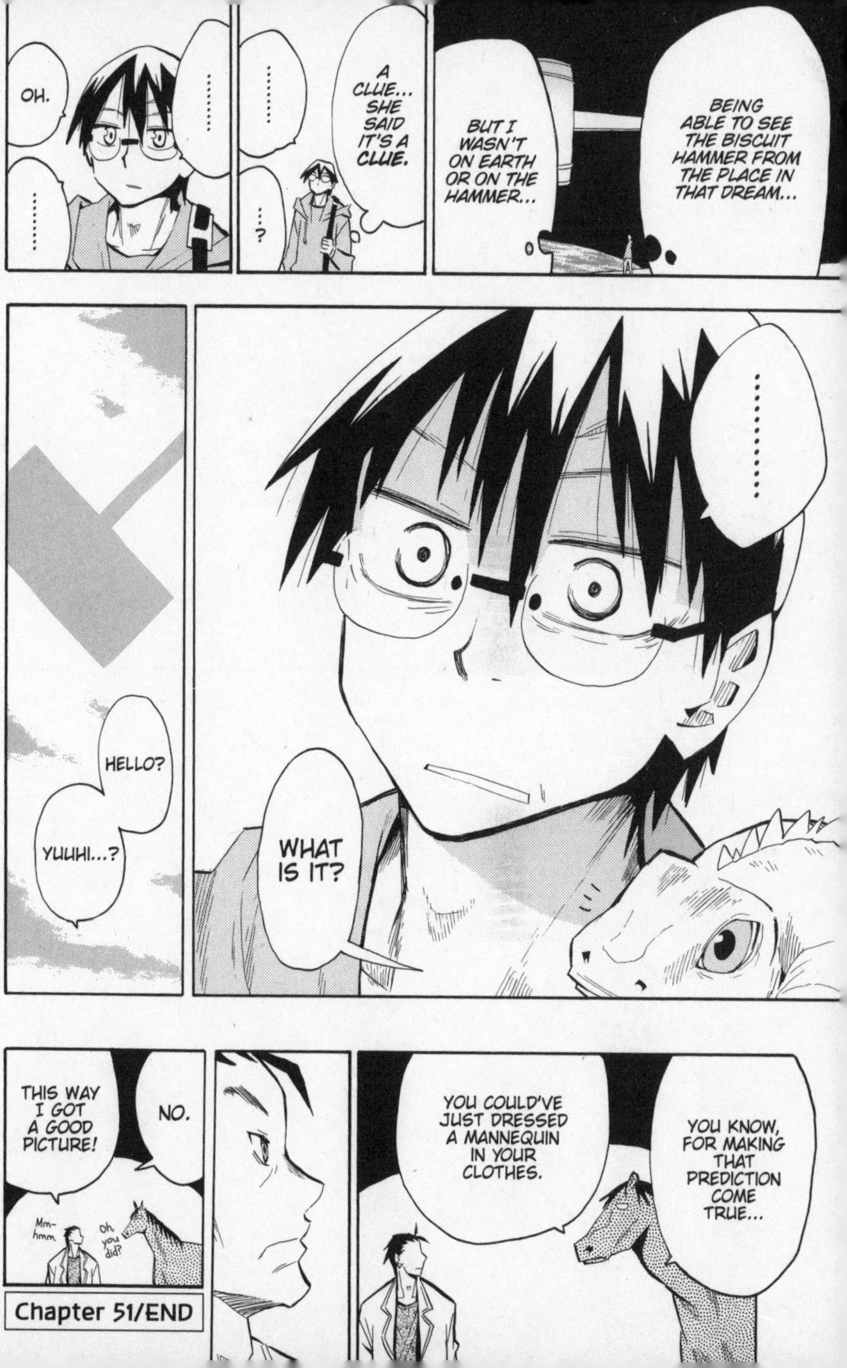
BEING ABLE TO SEE THE BISCUIT HAMMER FROM THE PLACE IN THAT DREAM...
BUT I WASN'T ON EARTH OR ON THE HAMMER...
A CLUE... SHE SAID IT'S A CLUE.
......
...?
......
OH.
......
......
WHAT IS IT?
HELLO?
YUUHI...?
YOU KNOW, FOR MAKING THAT PREDICTION COME TRUE...
YOU COULD'VE JUST DRESSED A MANNEQUIN IN YOUR CLOTHES.
NO.
THIS WAY I GOT A GOOD PICTURE!
Oh, you did?
Mm-hmm

Chapter 51/END

Lucifer and the Biscuit Hammer

Chapter 52

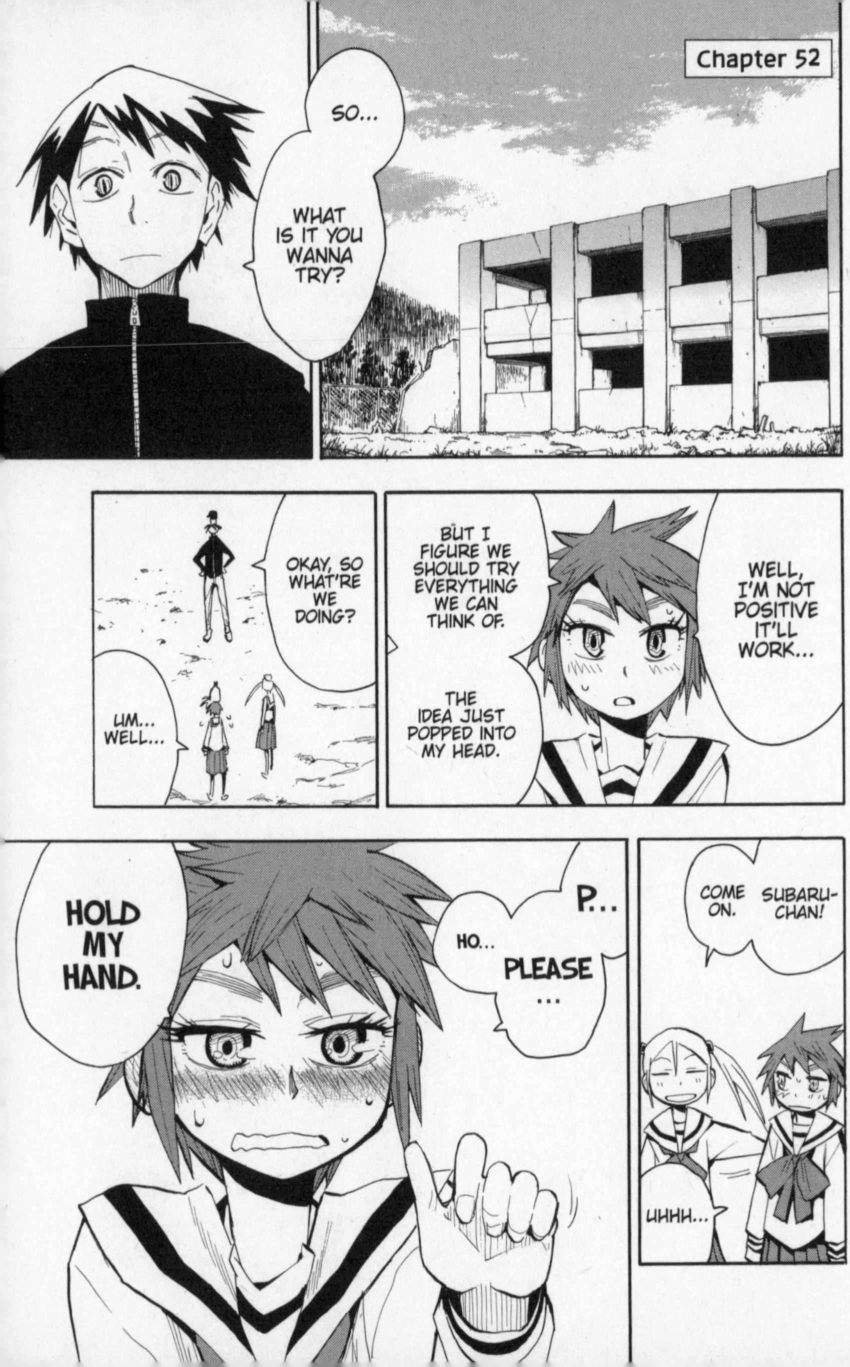
SO...
WHAT IS IT YOU WANNA TRY?
WELL, I'M NOT POSITIVE IT'LL WORK...
BUT I FIGURE WE SHOULD TRY EVERYTHING WE CAN THINK OF.
THE IDEA JUST POPPED INTO MY HEAD.
OKAY, SO WHAT'RE WE DOING?
UM... WELL...
SUBARU-CHAN!
COME ON.
UHHH...
P... PLEASE ...
HO...
HOLD MY HAND.

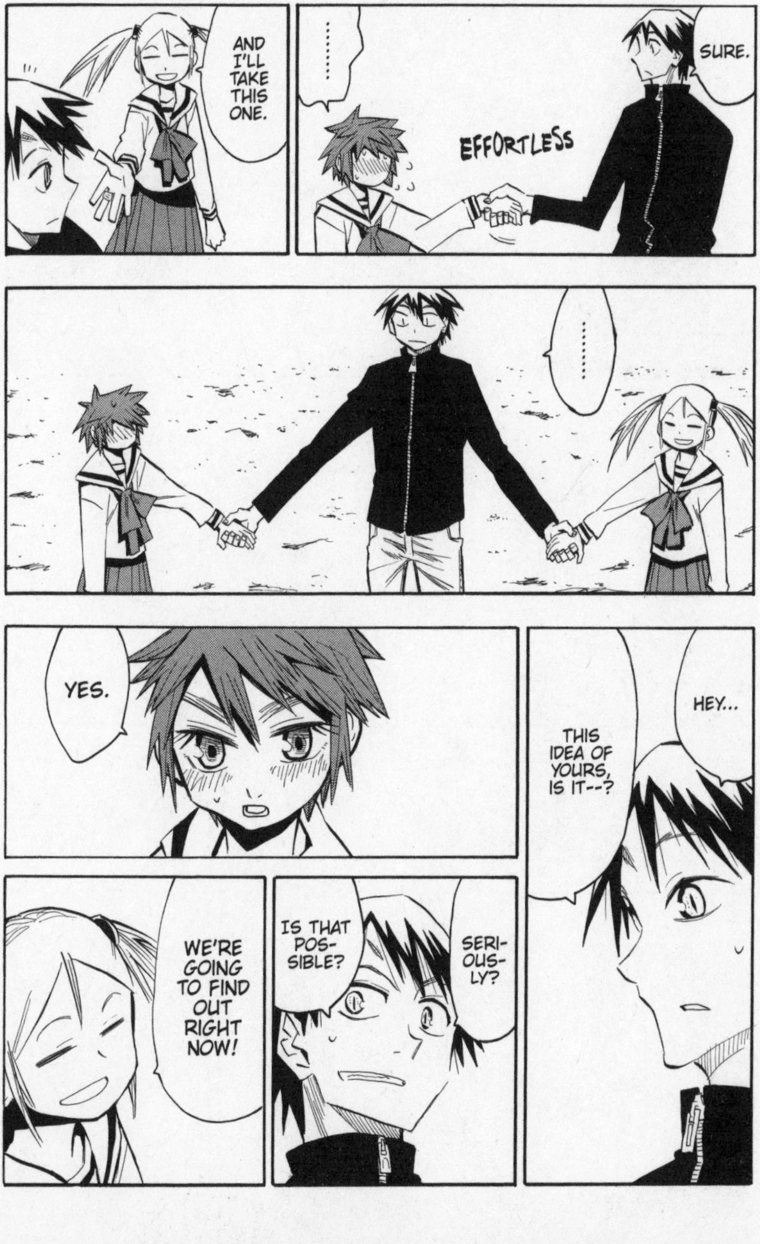
SURE.
......
EFFORTLESS
AND I'LL TAKE THIS ONE.
......
HEY...
THIS IDEA OF YOURS, IS IT--?
YES.
SERI-OUS-LY?
IS THAT POS-SIBLE?
WE'RE GOING TO FIND OUT RIGHT NOW!

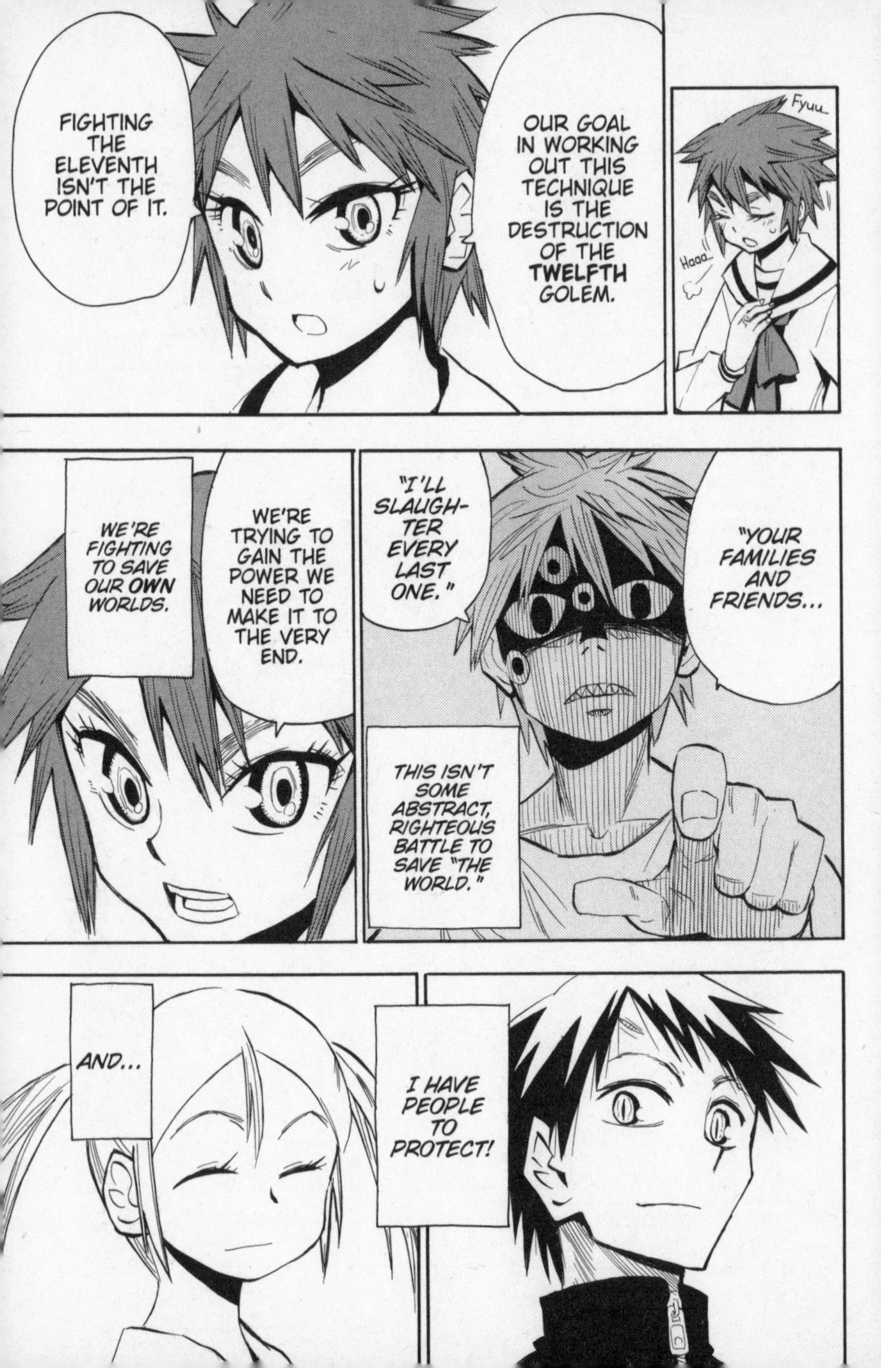
Fyuu...
Haaa...
OUR GOAL IN WORKING OUT THIS TECHNIQUE IS THE DESTRUCTION OF THE TWELFTH GOLEM.
FIGHTING THE ELEVENTH ISN'T THE POINT OF IT.
"YOUR FAMILIES AND FRIENDS...
"I'LL SLAUGHTER EVERY LAST ONE."
THIS ISN'T SOME ABSTRACT, RIGHTEOUS BATTLE TO SAVE "THE WORLD."
WE'RE TRYING TO GAIN THE POWER WE NEED TO MAKE IT TO THE VERY END.
WE'RE FIGHTING TO SAVE OUR OWN WORLDS.
I HAVE PEOPLE TO PROTECT!
AND...

Chapter 52: Maimakterion and the Beast Knights (Part 1)

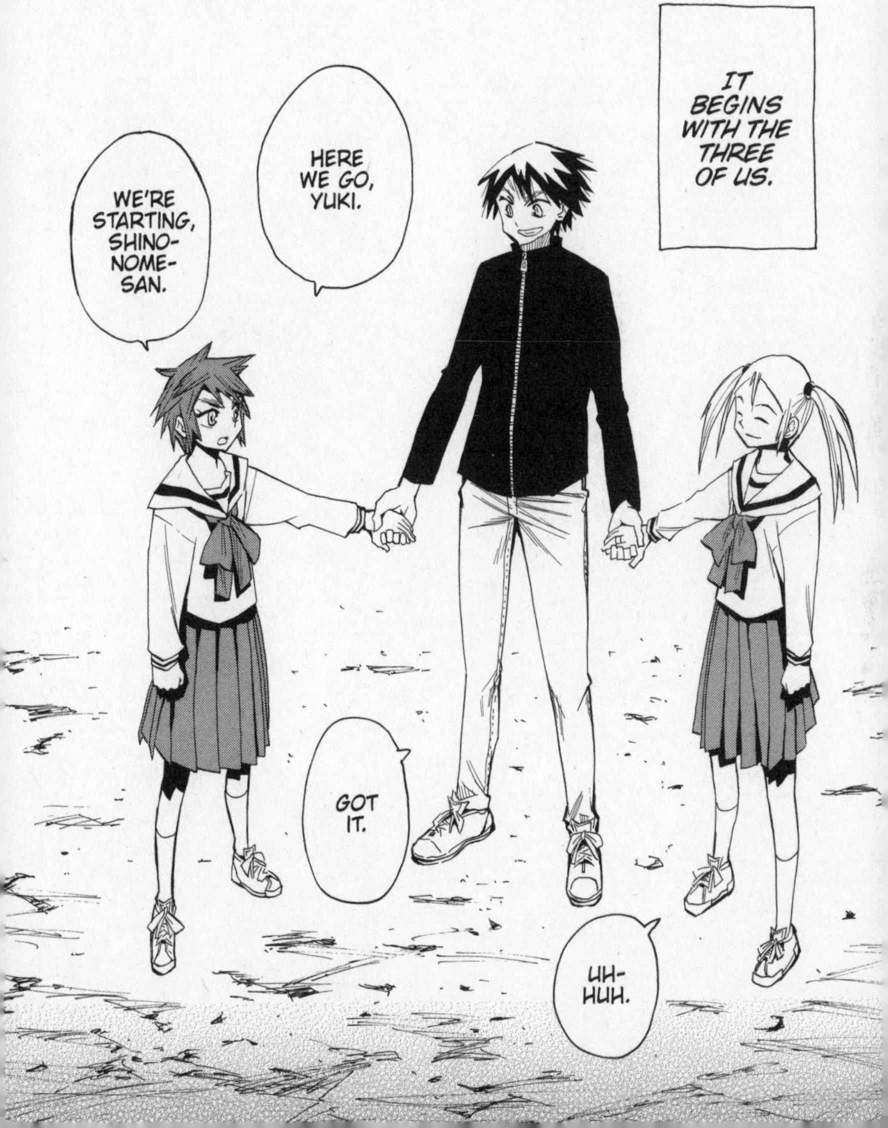

IT BEGINS WITH THE THREE OF US.
HERE WE GO, YUKI.
WE'RE STARTING, SHINONOME-SAN.
UH-HUH.
GOT IT.

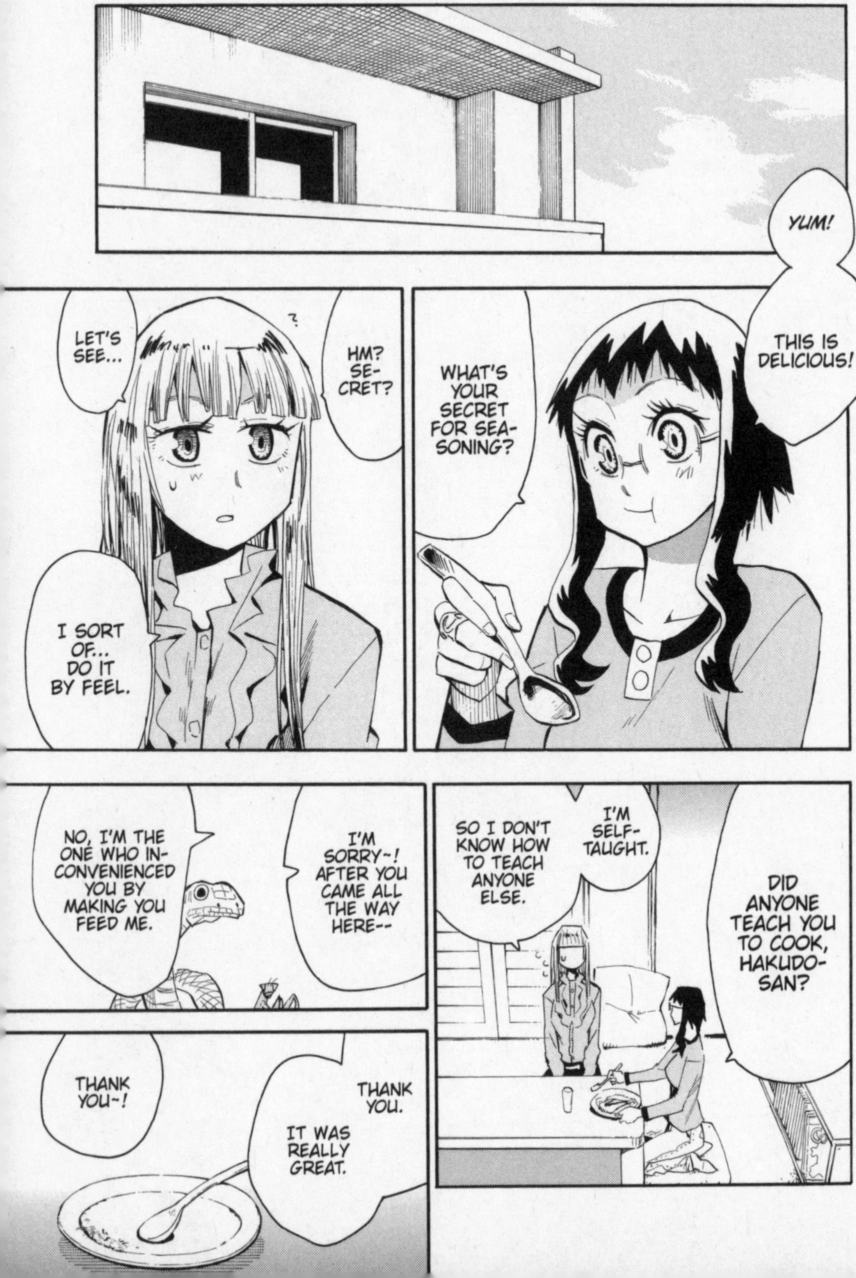
YUM!
THIS IS DELICIOUS!
WHAT'S YOUR SECRET FOR SEA-SONING?
HM? SE-CRET?
LET'S SEE...
I SORT OF... DO IT BY FEEL.
DID ANYONE TEACH YOU TO COOK, HAKUDO-SAN?
I'M SELF-TAUGHT.
SO I DON'T KNOW HOW TO TEACH ANYONE ELSE.
I'M SORRY~! AFTER YOU CAME ALL THE WAY HERE--
NO, I'M THE ONE WHO IN-CONVENIENCED YOU BY MAKING YOU FEED ME.
THANK YOU.
IT WAS REALLY GREAT.
THANK YOU~!

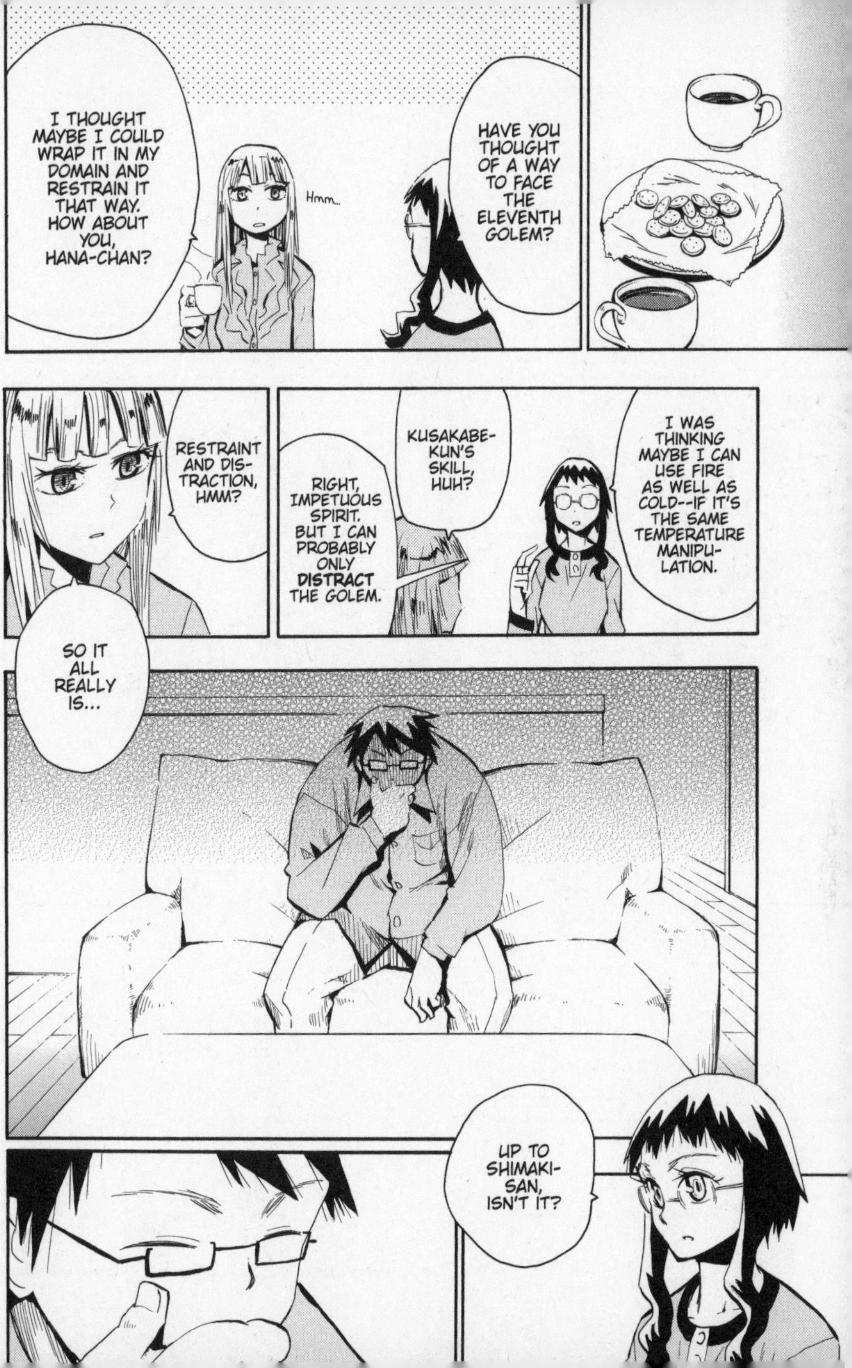
HAVE YOU THOUGHT OF A WAY TO FACE THE ELEVENTH GOLEM?
Hmm..
I THOUGHT MAYBE I COULD WRAP IT IN MY DOMAIN AND RESTRAIN IT THAT WAY. HOW ABOUT YOU, HANA-CHAN?
I WAS THINKING MAYBE I CAN USE FIRE AS WELL AS COLD--IF IT'S THE SAME TEMPERATURE MANIPU-LATION.
KUSAKABE-KUN'S SKILL, HUH?
RIGHT, IMPETUOUS SPIRIT. BUT I CAN PROBABLY ONLY **DISTRACT** THE GOLEM.
RESTRAINT AND DIS-TRACTION, HMM?
SO IT ALL REALLY IS...
UP TO SHIMAKI-SAN, ISN'T IT?

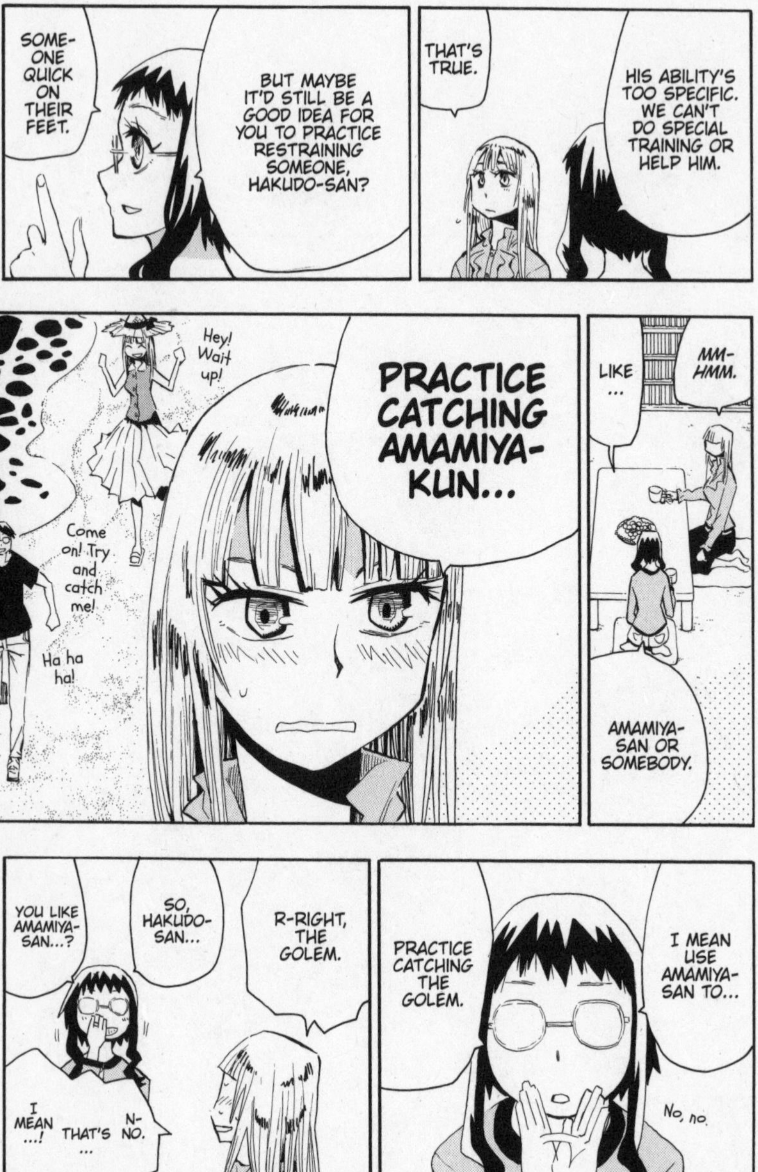
HIS ABILITY'S TOO SPECIFIC. WE CAN'T DO SPECIAL TRAINING OR HELP HIM.
THAT'S TRUE.
BUT MAYBE IT'D STILL BE A GOOD IDEA FOR YOU TO PRACTICE RESTRAINING SOMEONE, HAKUDO-SAN?
SOME-ONE QUICK ON THEIR FEET.
MM-HMM.
LIKE ...
AMAMIYA-SAN OR SOMEBODY.
PRACTICE CATCHING AMAMIYA-KUN...
Hey! Wait up!
Come on! Try and catch me!
Ha ha ha!
I MEAN USE AMAMIYA-SAN TO...
PRACTICE CATCHING THE GOLEM.
No, no.
R-RIGHT, THE GOLEM.
SO, HAKUDO-SAN...
YOU LIKE AMAMIYA-SAN...?
N-NO.
THAT'S ...
I MEAN ...!

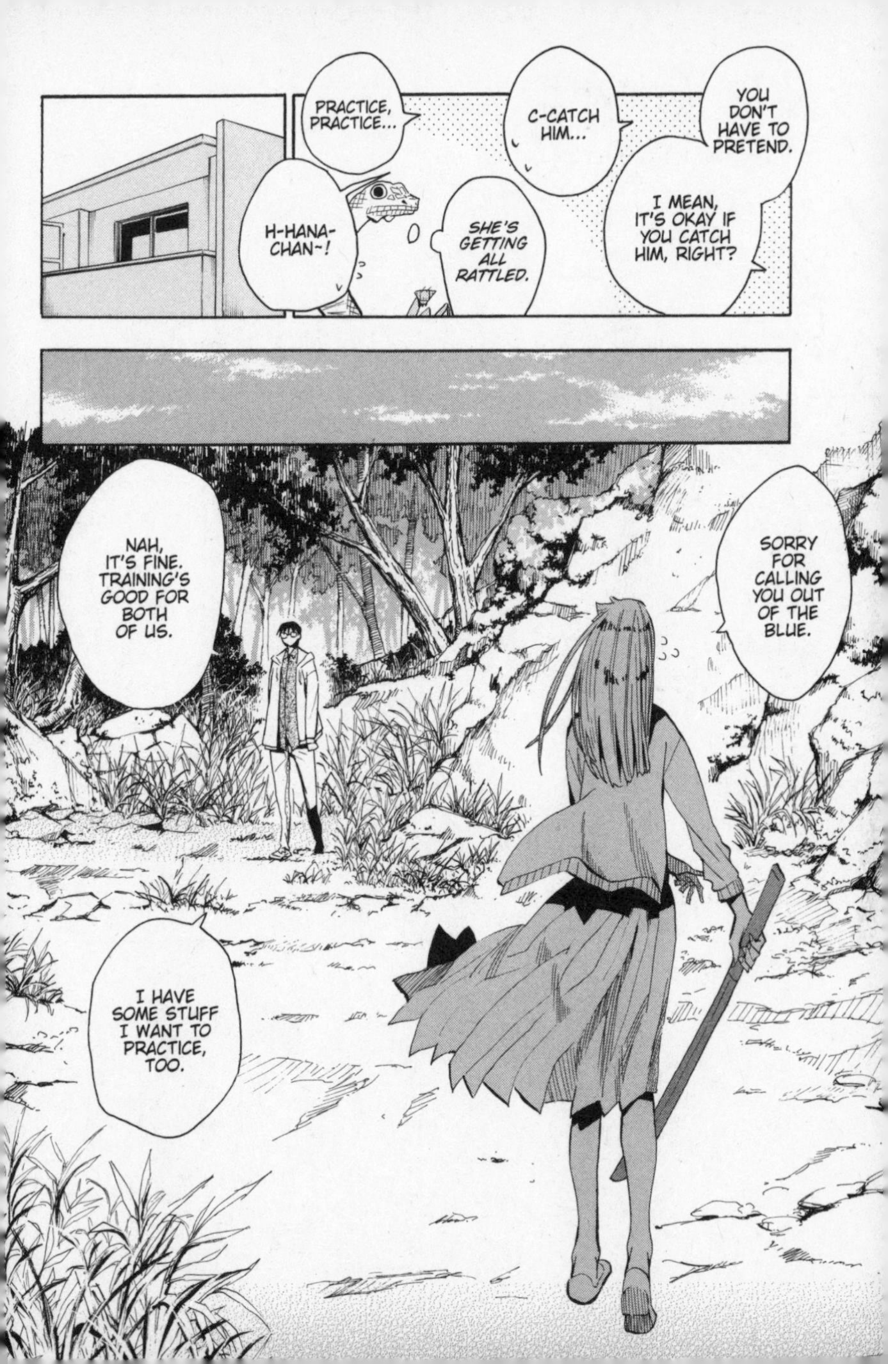
YOU DON'T HAVE TO PRETEND.
I MEAN, IT'S OKAY IF YOU CATCH HIM, RIGHT?
C-CATCH HIM...
SHE'S GETTING ALL RATTLED.
PRACTICE, PRACTICE...
H-HANA-CHAN~!
SORRY FOR CALLING YOU OUT OF THE BLUE.
NAH, IT'S FINE. TRAINING'S GOOD FOR BOTH OF US.
I HAVE SOME STUFF I WANT TO PRACTICE, TOO.

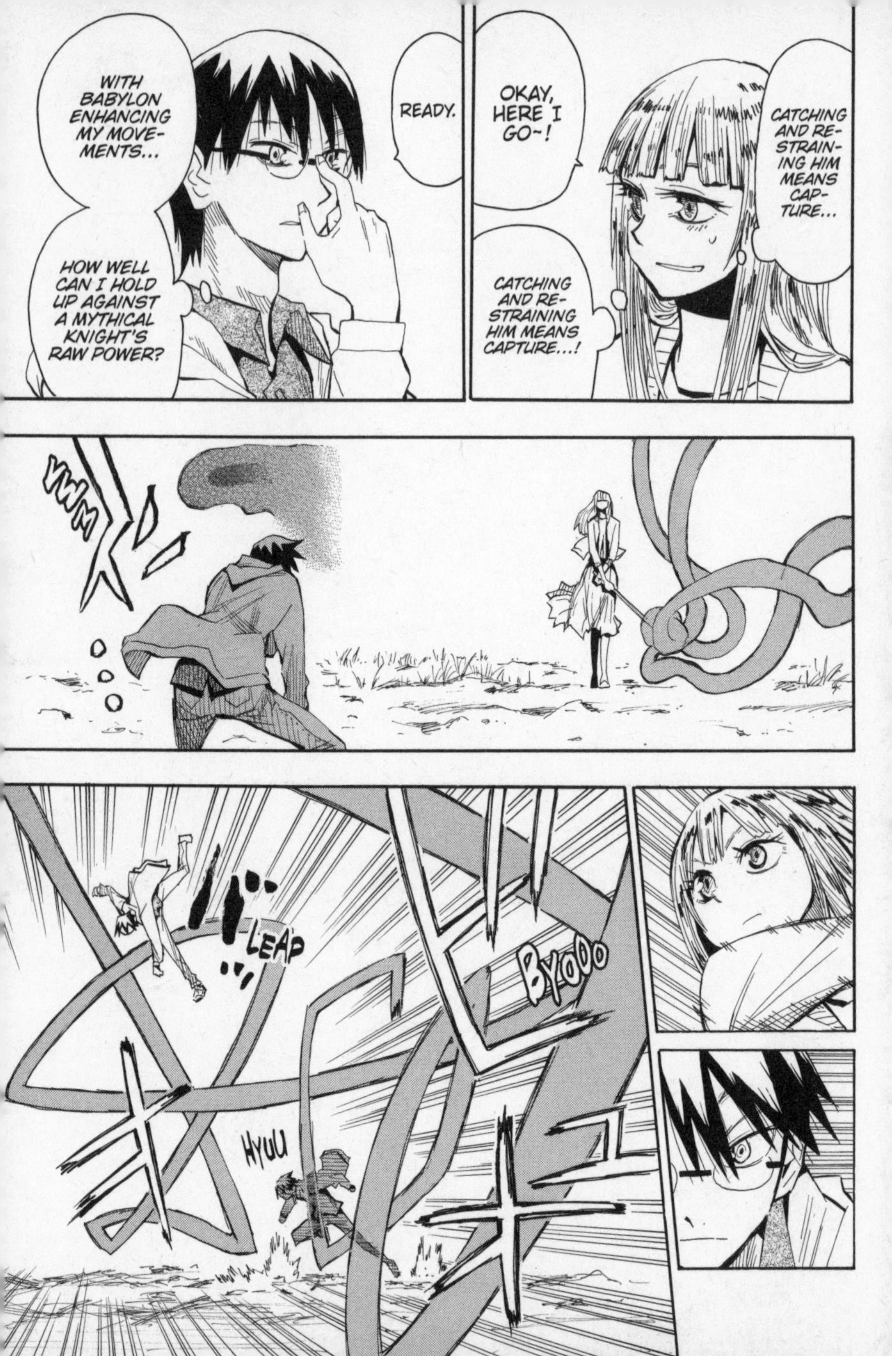
CATCHING AND RE-STRAINING HIM MEANS CAP-TURE...
OKAY, HERE I GO~!
CATCHING AND RE-STRAINING HIM MEANS CAPTURE...!
READY.
WITH BABYLON ENHANCING MY MOVE-MENTS...
HOW WELL CAN I HOLD UP AGAINST A MYTHICAL KNIGHT'S RAW POWER?
VWM
BYOOO
LEAP
HYUU

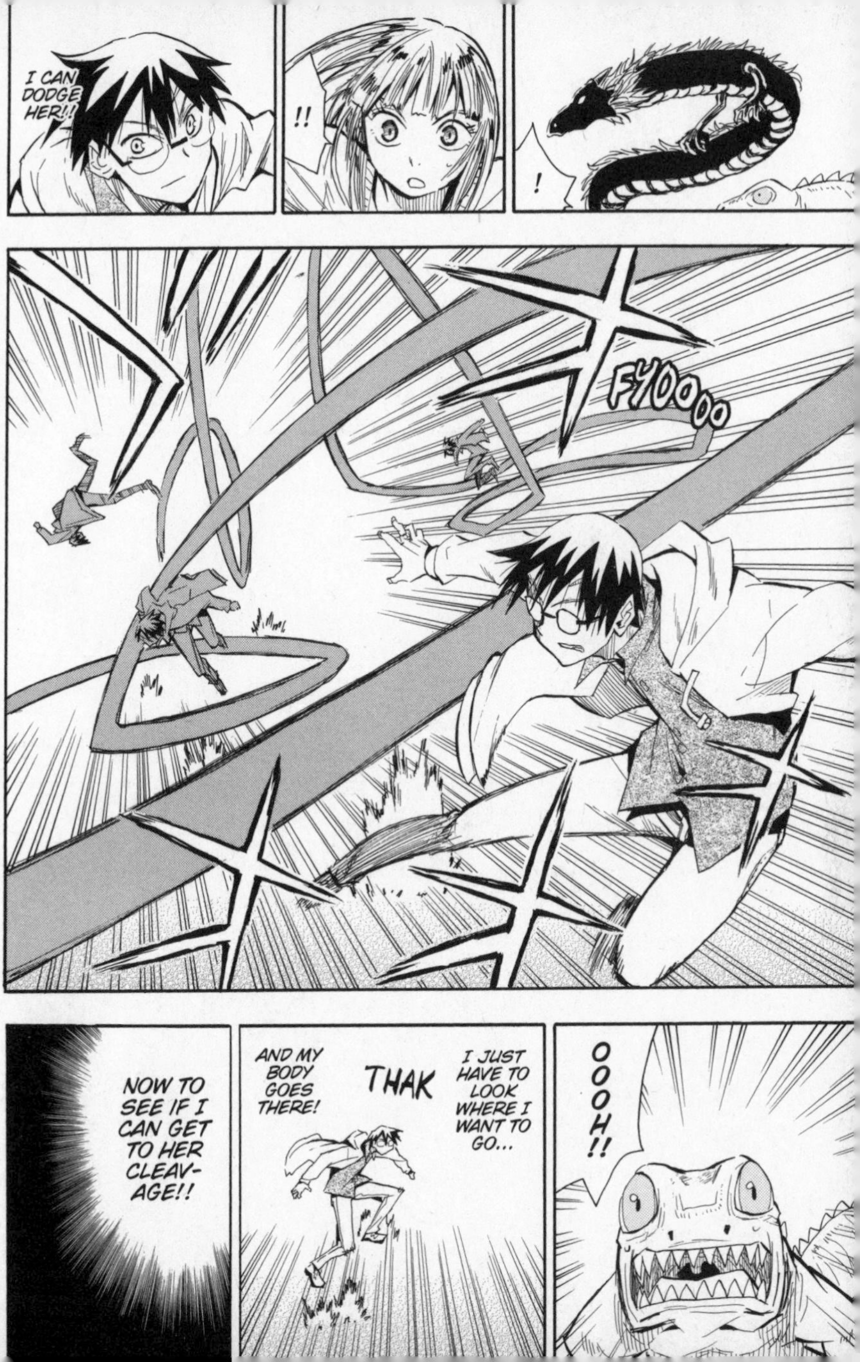
!
!!
I CAN DODGE HER!!
FYOOOO
OOOOH!!
I JUST HAVE TO LOOK WHERE I WANT TO GO...
THAK
AND MY BODY GOES THERE!
NOW TO SEE IF I CAN GET TO HER CLEAV-AGE!!

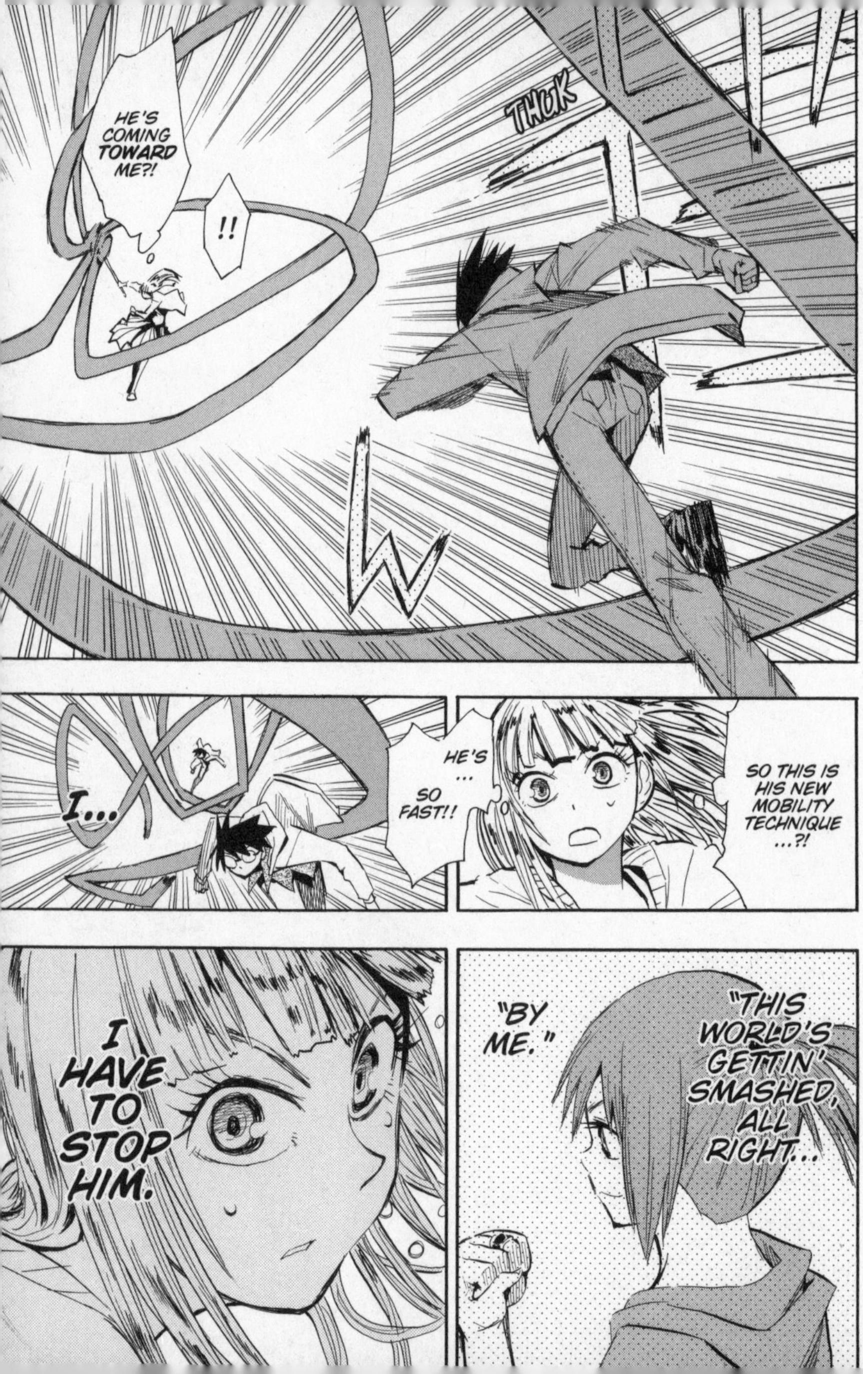
THUK
HE'S COMING TOWARD ME?!
!!
W
SO THIS IS HIS NEW MOBILITY TECHNIQUE ...?!
HE'S ... SO FAST!!
I...
"THIS WORLD'S GETTIN' SMASHED, ALL RIGHT...
"BY ME."
I HAVE TO STOP HIM.

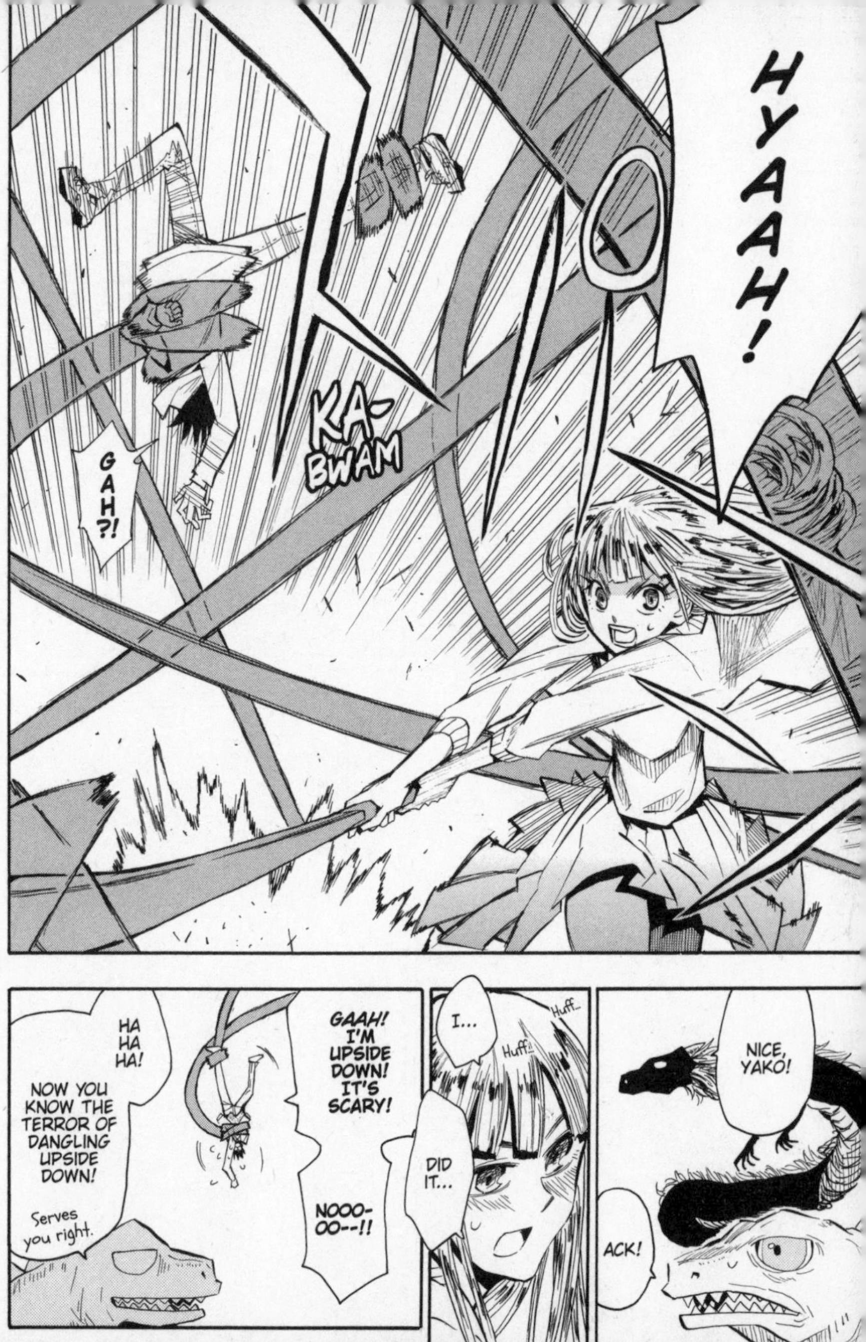
HYAAAH!
KA-BWAM
GAH?!
NICE, YAKO!
ACK!
Huff...
Huff!!
I...
DID IT...
GAAH! I'M UPSIDE DOWN! IT'S SCARY!
HA HA HA! NOW YOU KNOW THE TERROR OF DANGLING UPSIDE DOWN!
NOOO-OO--!!
Serves you right.

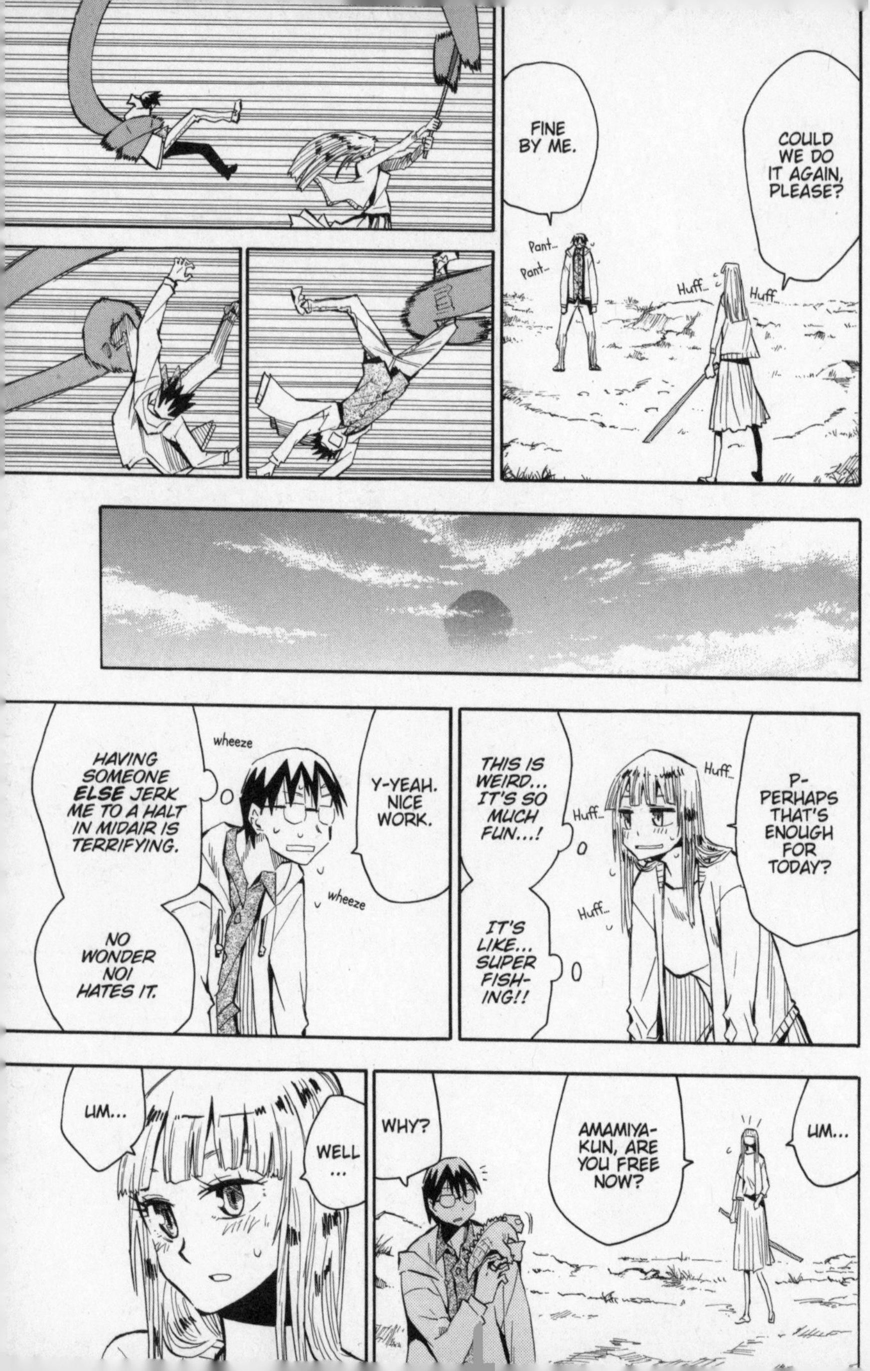
COULD WE DO IT AGAIN, PLEASE?
FINE BY ME.
Huff... Huff...
Pant... Pant...
P-PERHAPS THAT'S ENOUGH FOR TODAY?
Huff...
THIS IS WEIRD... IT'S SO MUCH FUN...!
Huff...
Huff...
IT'S LIKE... SUPER FISHING!!
Y-YEAH. NICE WORK.
wheeze
HAVING SOMEONE ELSE JERK ME TO A HALT IN MIDAIR IS TERRIFYING.
wheeze
NO WONDER NOI HATES IT.
UM...
AMAMIYA-KUN, ARE YOU FREE NOW?
WHY?
WELL ...
UM...

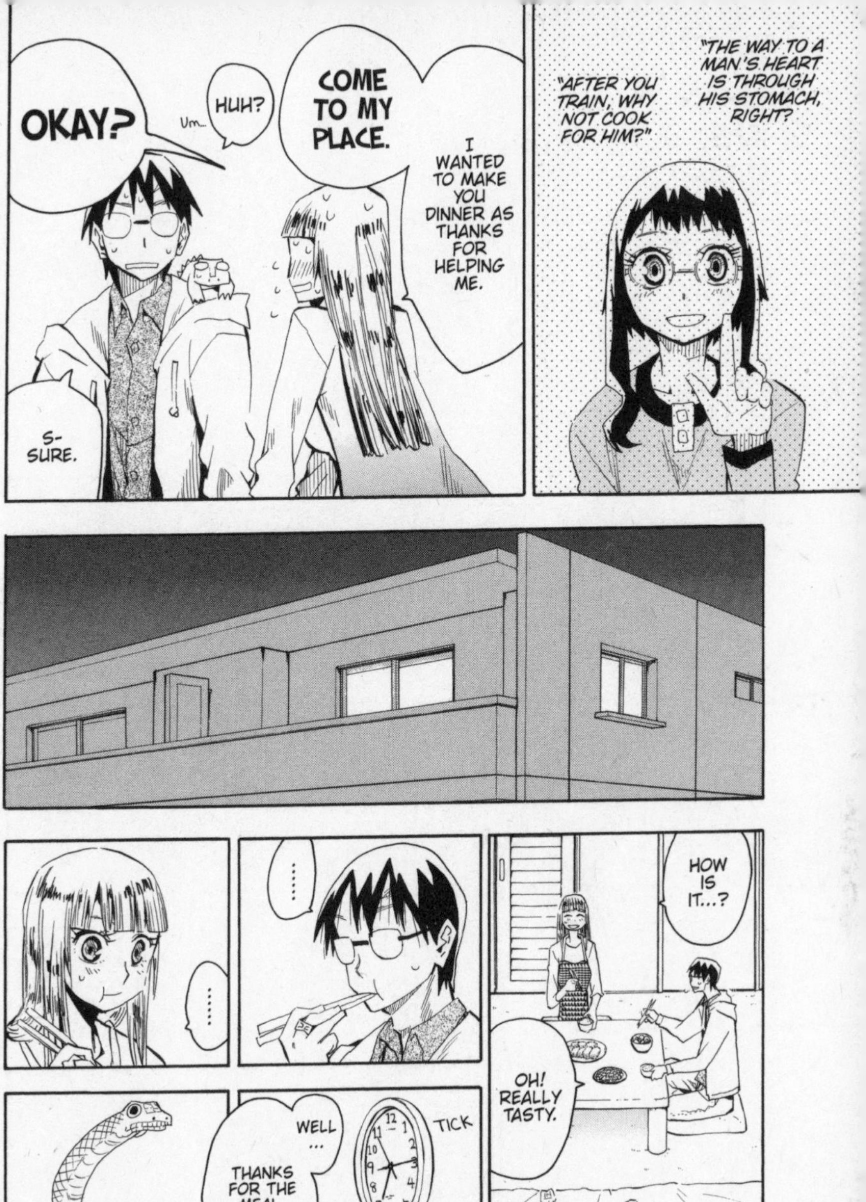
"THE WAY TO A MAN'S HEART IS THROUGH HIS STOMACH, RIGHT?
"AFTER YOU TRAIN, WHY NOT COOK FOR HIM?"
COME TO MY PLACE.
I WANTED TO MAKE YOU DINNER AS THANKS FOR HELPING ME.
HUH?
Um...
OKAY?
S-SURE.
HOW IS IT...?
OH! REALLY TASTY.
......
......
TICK
WELL ...
THANKS FOR THE MEAL.
TOCK

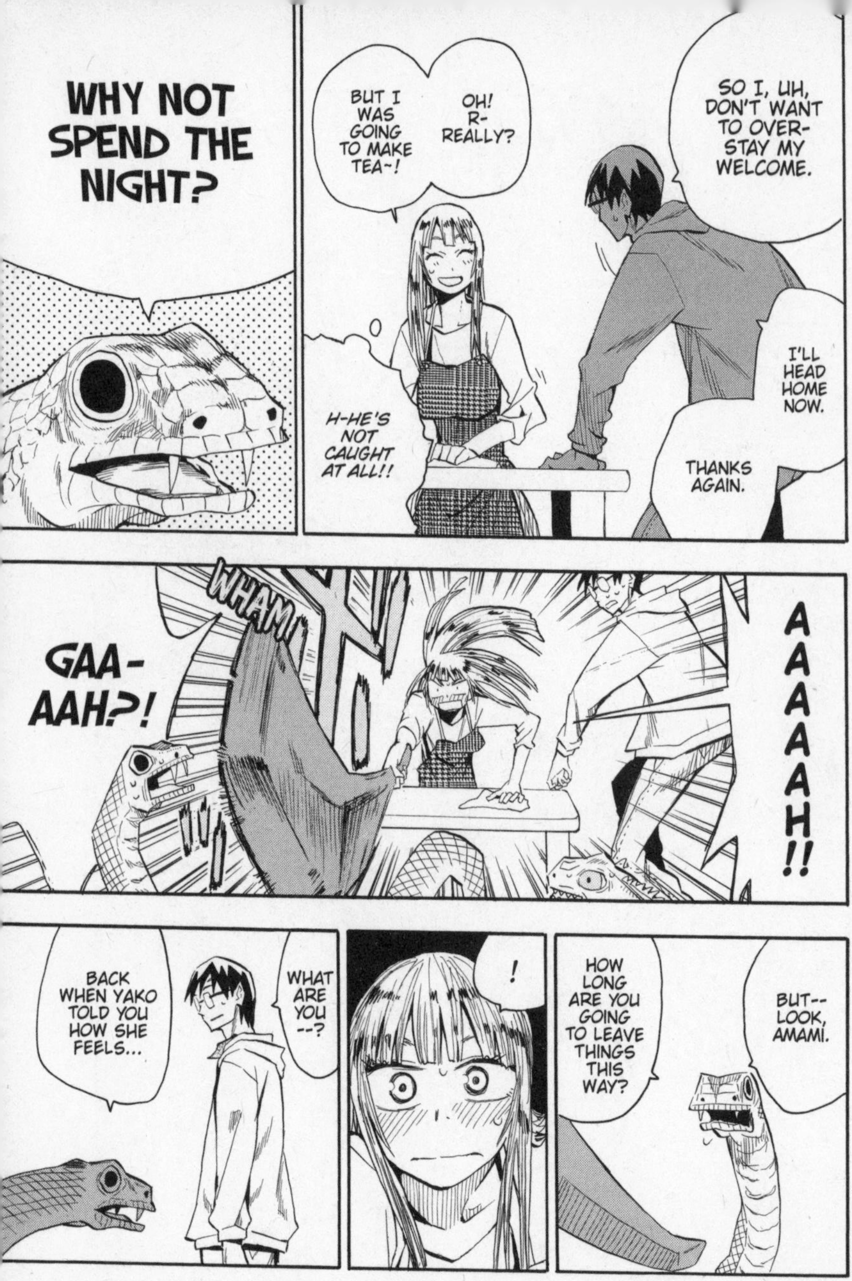
SO I, UH, DON'T WANT TO OVER-STAY MY WELCOME.
I'LL HEAD HOME NOW.
THANKS AGAIN.
OH! R-REALLY?
BUT I WAS GOING TO MAKE TEA~!
H-HE'S NOT CAUGHT AT ALL!!
WHY NOT SPEND THE NIGHT?
AAAAAAH!!
WHAM
GAA-AAH?!
BUT-- LOOK, AMAMI.
HOW LONG ARE YOU GOING TO LEAVE THINGS THIS WAY?
!
WHAT ARE YOU --?
BACK WHEN YAKO TOLD YOU HOW SHE FEELS...

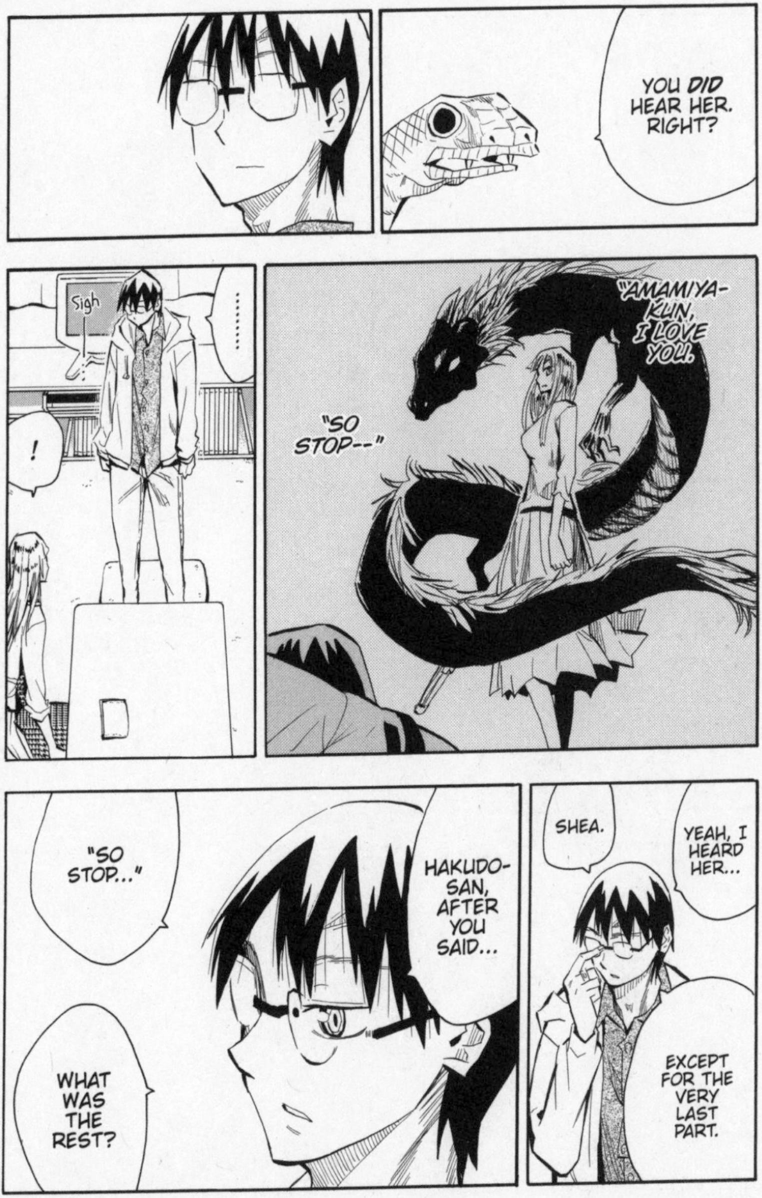
YOU DID HEAR HER. RIGHT?
"AMAMIYA-KUN, I LOVE YOU."
"SO STOP--"
....
Sigh
!
SHEA.
YEAH, I HEARD HER...
EXCEPT FOR THE VERY LAST PART.
HAKUDO-SAN, AFTER YOU SAID...
"SO STOP..."
WHAT WAS THE REST?

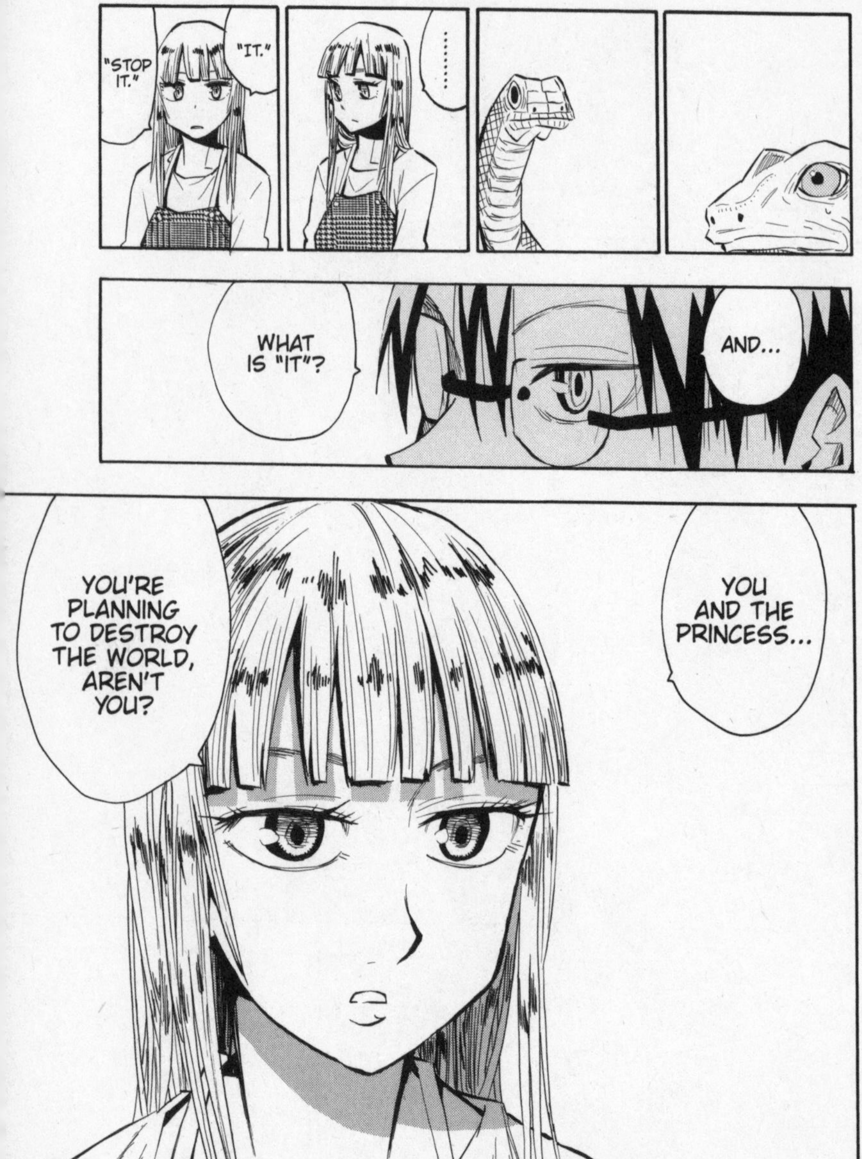
......
"IT."
"STOP IT."
AND...
WHAT IS "IT"?
YOU AND THE PRINCESS...
YOU'RE PLANNING TO DESTROY THE WORLD, AREN'T YOU?

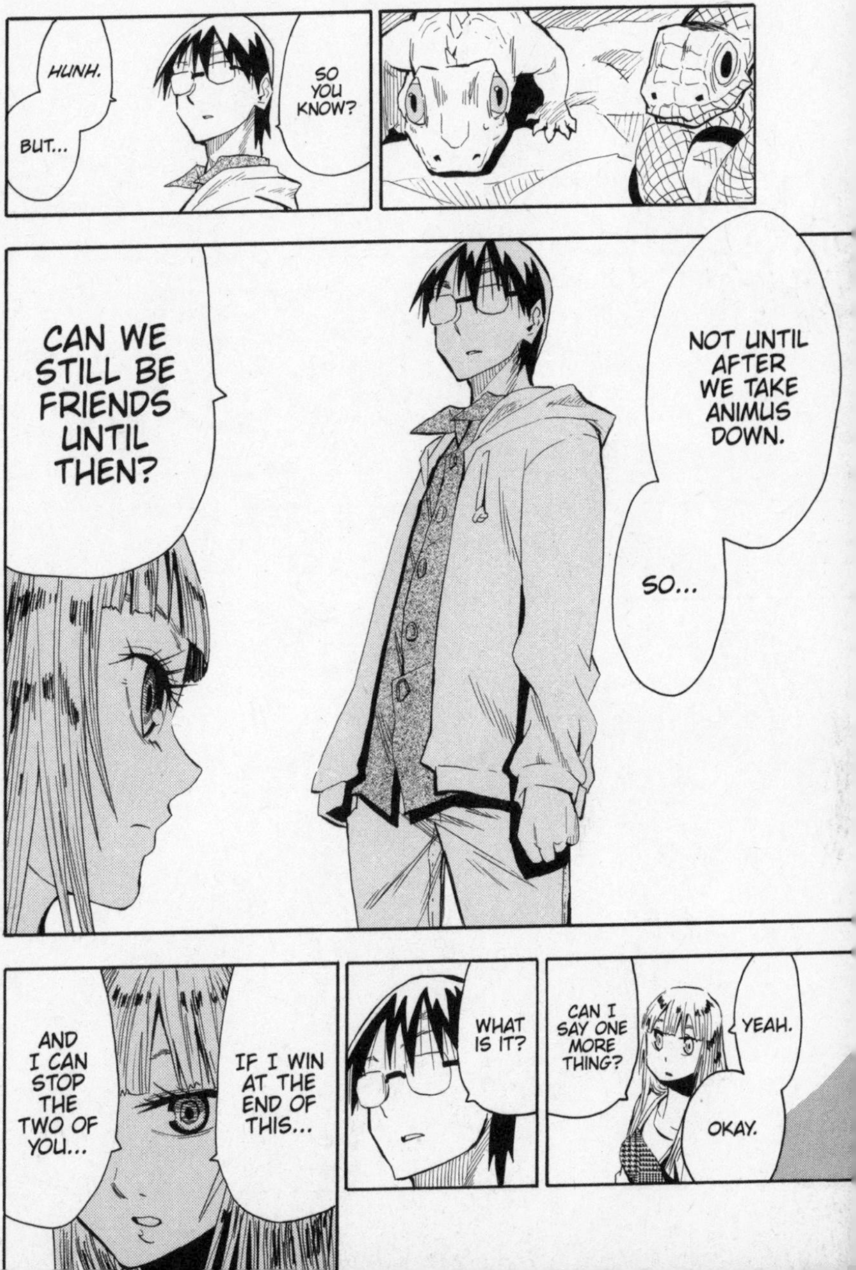
SO YOU KNOW?
HUNH.
BUT...
NOT UNTIL AFTER WE TAKE ANIMUS DOWN.
SO...
CAN WE STILL BE FRIENDS UNTIL THEN?
YEAH.
CAN I SAY ONE MORE THING?
OKAY.
WHAT IS IT?
IF I WIN AT THE END OF THIS...
AND I CAN STOP THE TWO OF YOU...

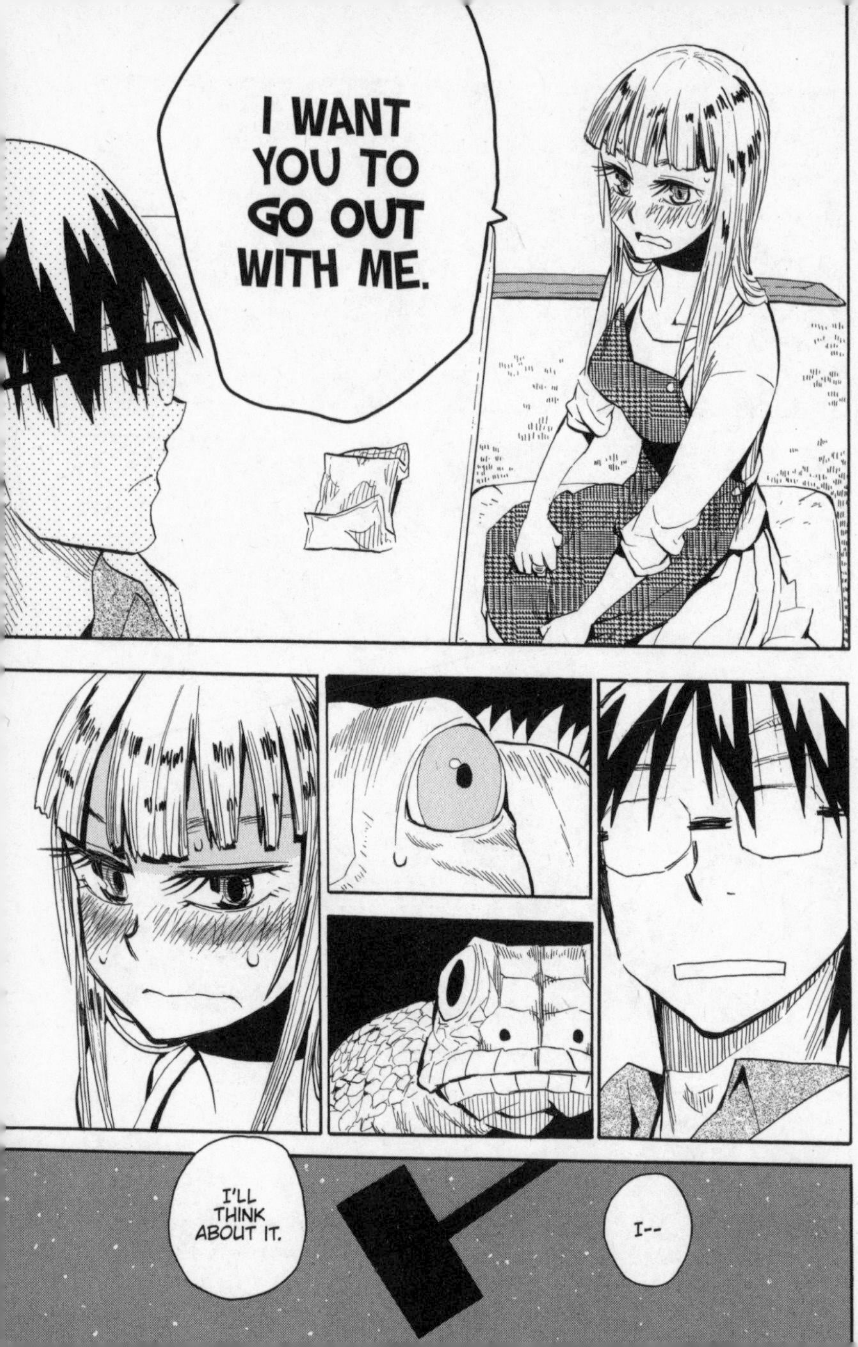
I WANT YOU TO GO OUT WITH ME.
I--
I'LL THINK ABOUT IT.

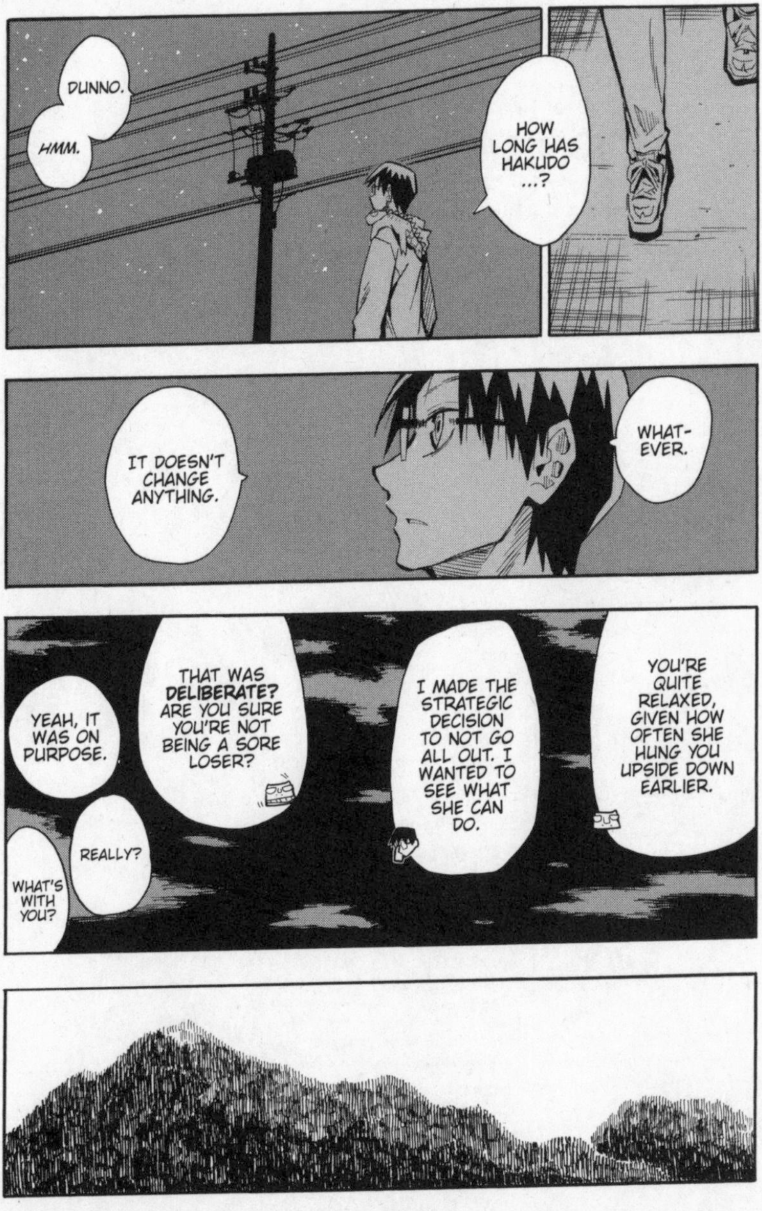
HOW LONG HAS HAKUDO ...?
DUNNO.
HMM.
WHAT-EVER.
IT DOESN'T CHANGE ANYTHING.
YOU'RE QUITE RELAXED, GIVEN HOW OFTEN SHE HUNG YOU UPSIDE DOWN EARLIER.
I MADE THE STRATEGIC DECISION TO NOT GO ALL OUT. I WANTED TO SEE WHAT SHE CAN DO.
THAT WAS DELIBERATE? ARE YOU SURE YOU'RE NOT BEING A SORE LOSER?
YEAH, IT WAS ON PURPOSE.
REALLY?
WHAT'S WITH YOU?

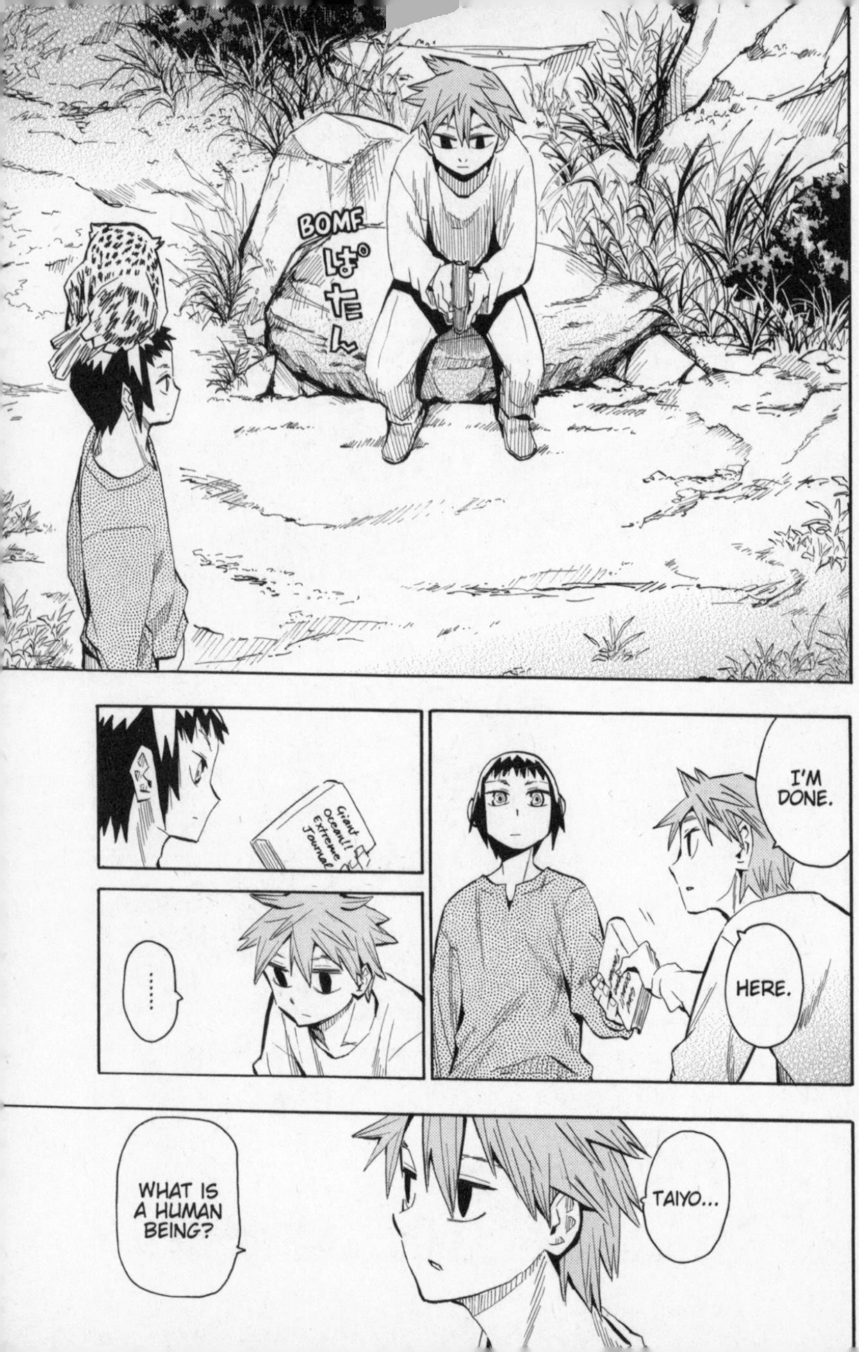
BOMF
ぱたん
I'M DONE.
HERE.
Giant Ocean!! Extreme Journal
......
TAIYO...
WHAT IS A HUMAN BEING?

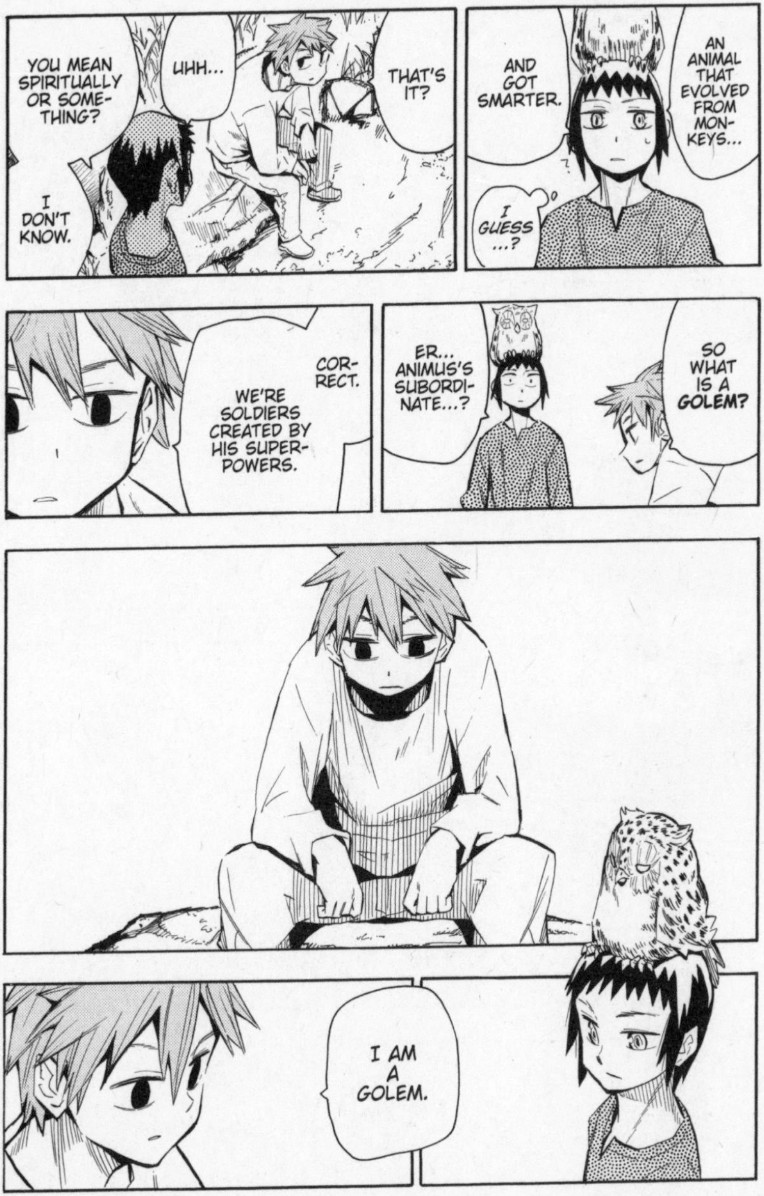
AN ANIMAL THAT EVOLVED FROM MON-KEYS...
AND GOT SMARTER.
I GUESS ...?
THAT'S IT?
UHH...
YOU MEAN SPIRITUALLY OR SOME-THING?
I DON'T KNOW.
SO WHAT IS A GOLEM?
ER... ANIMUS'S SUBORDI-NATE...?
COR-RECT.
WE'RE SOLDIERS CREATED BY HIS SUPER-POWERS.
I AM A GOLEM.

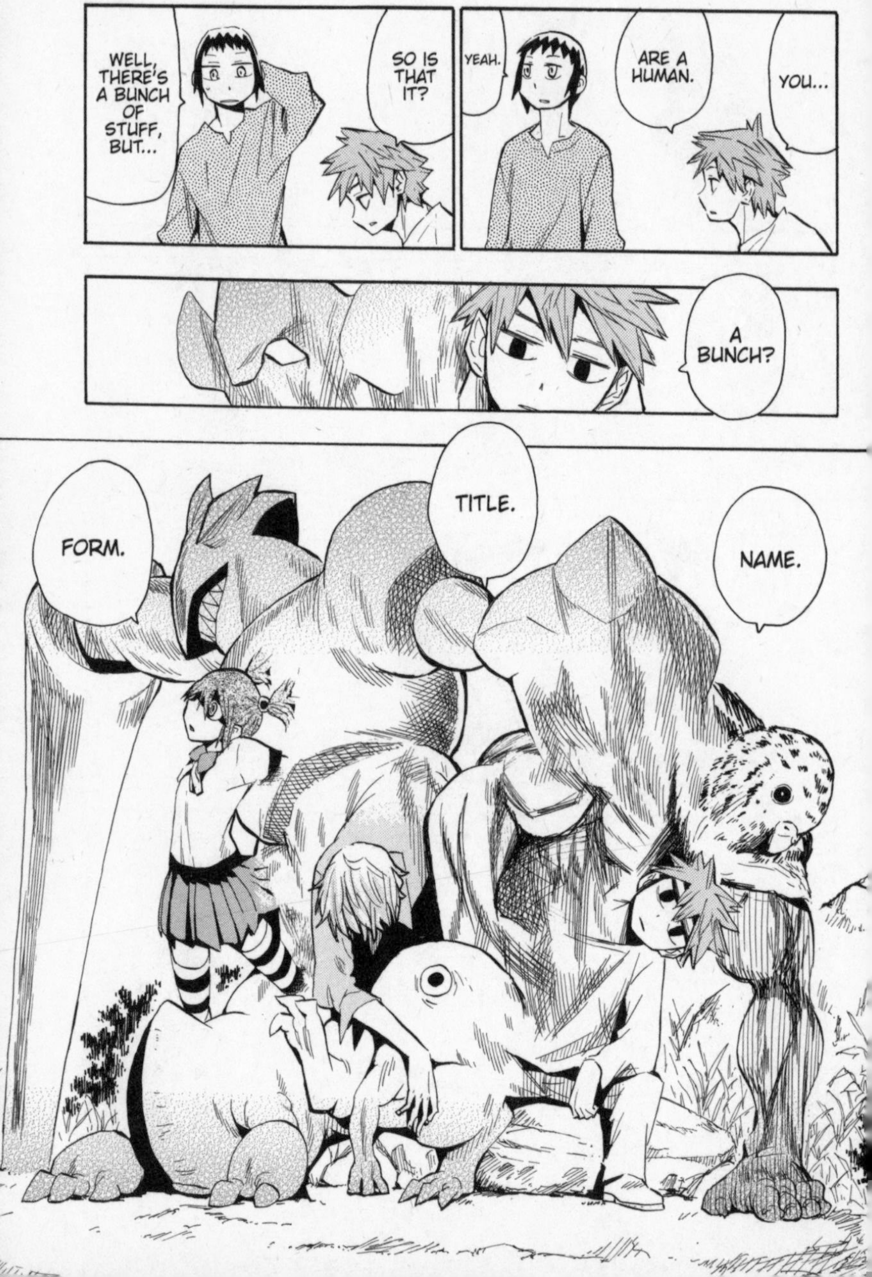
YOU...
ARE A HUMAN.
YEAH.
SO IS THAT IT?
WELL, THERE'S A BUNCH OF STUFF, BUT...
A BUNCH?
NAME.
TITLE.
FORM.

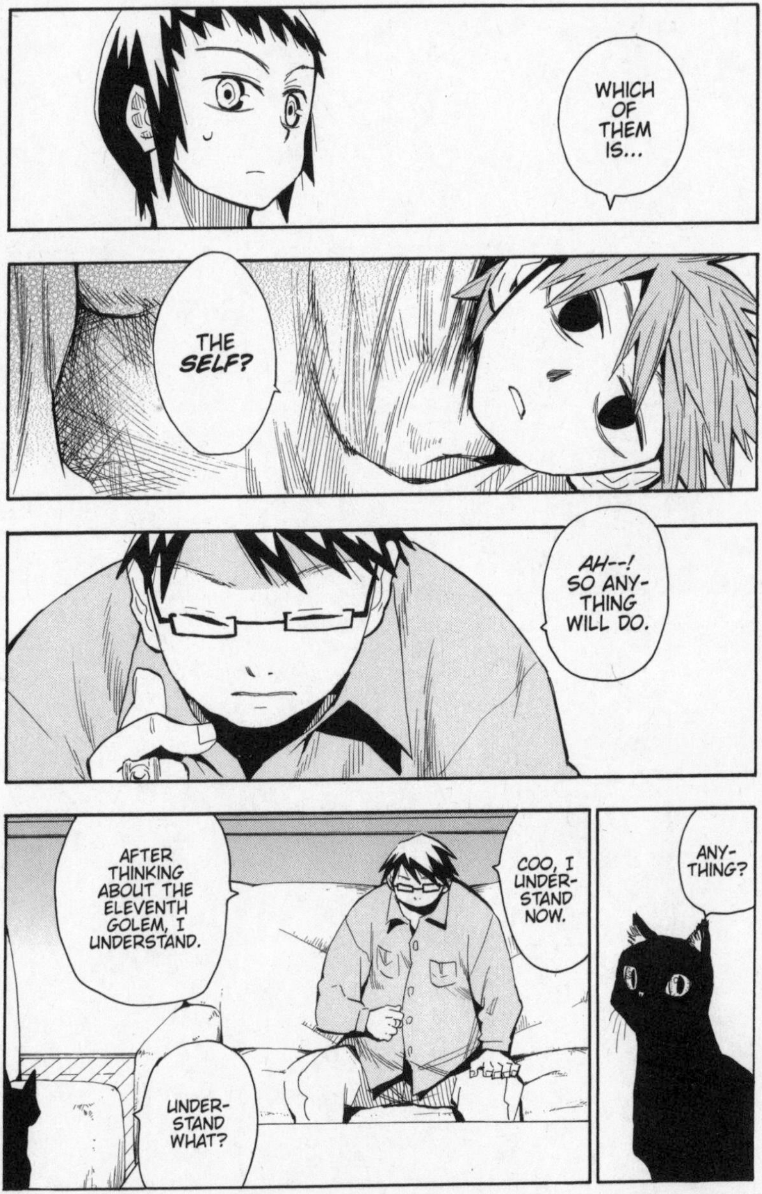
WHICH OF THEM IS...
THE *SELF?*
AH--! SO ANY-THING WILL DO.
ANY-THING?
COO, I UNDER-STAND NOW.
AFTER THINKING ABOUT THE ELEVENTH GOLEM, I UNDERSTAND.
UNDER-STAND WHAT?

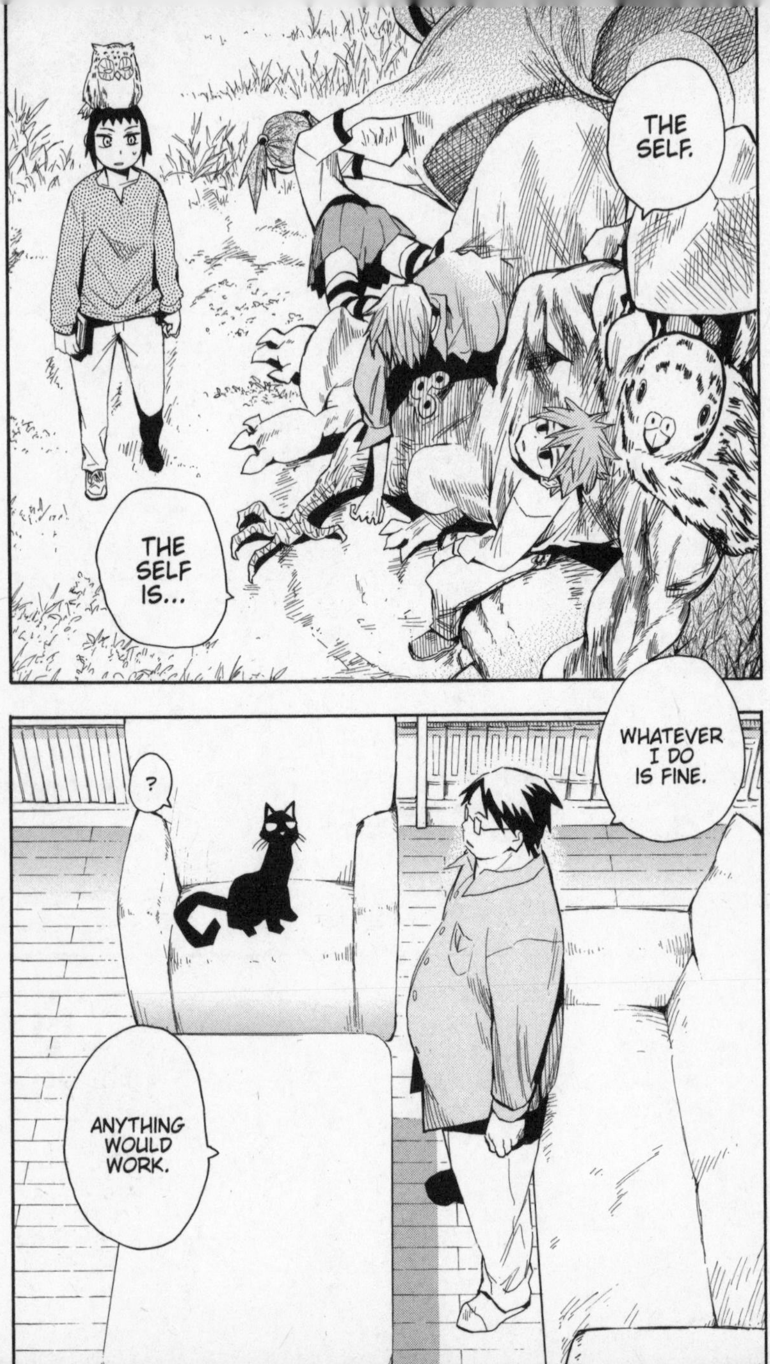
THE SELF.
THE SELF IS...
WHATEVER I DO IS FINE.
?
ANYTHING WOULD WORK.

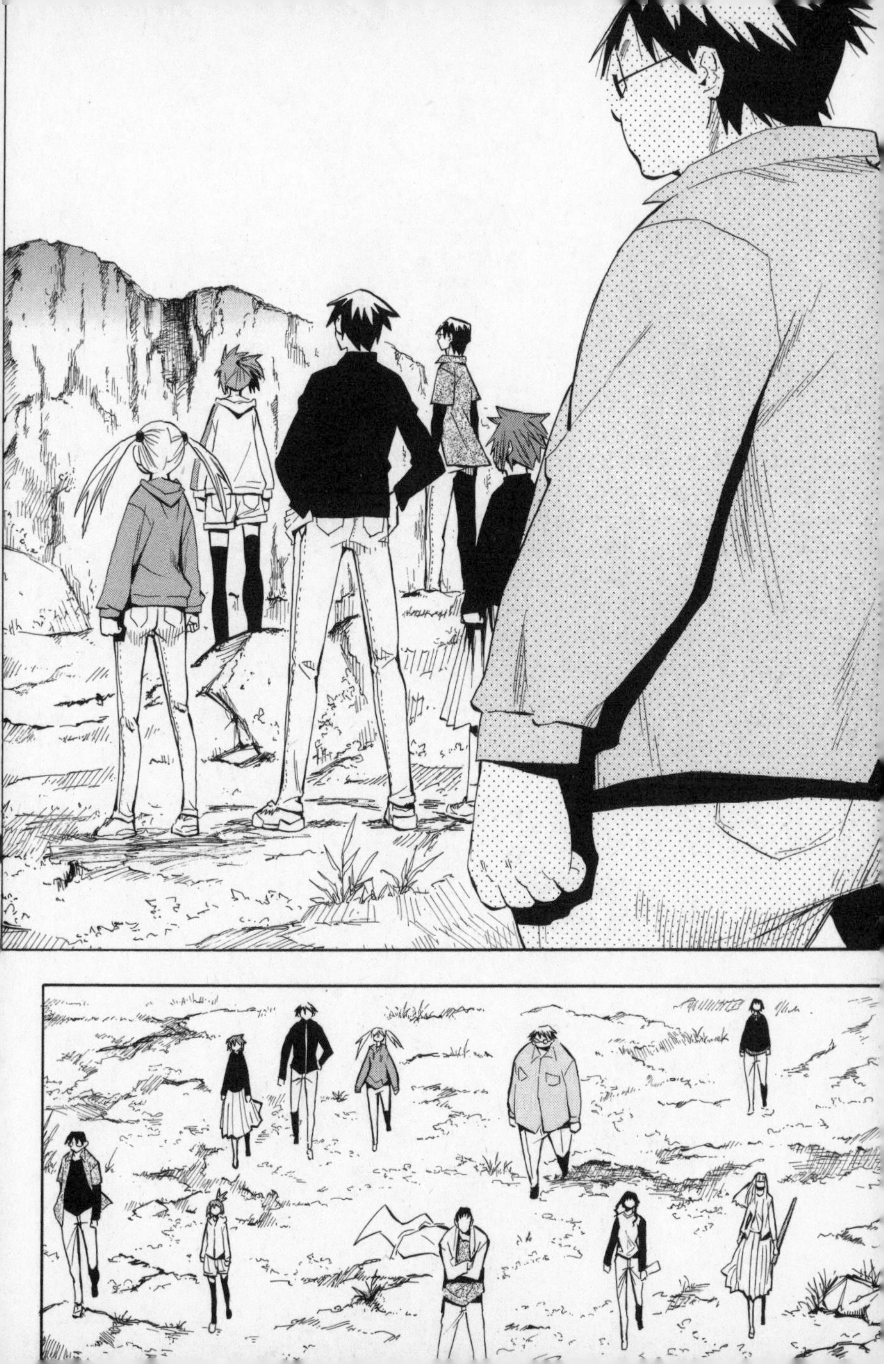

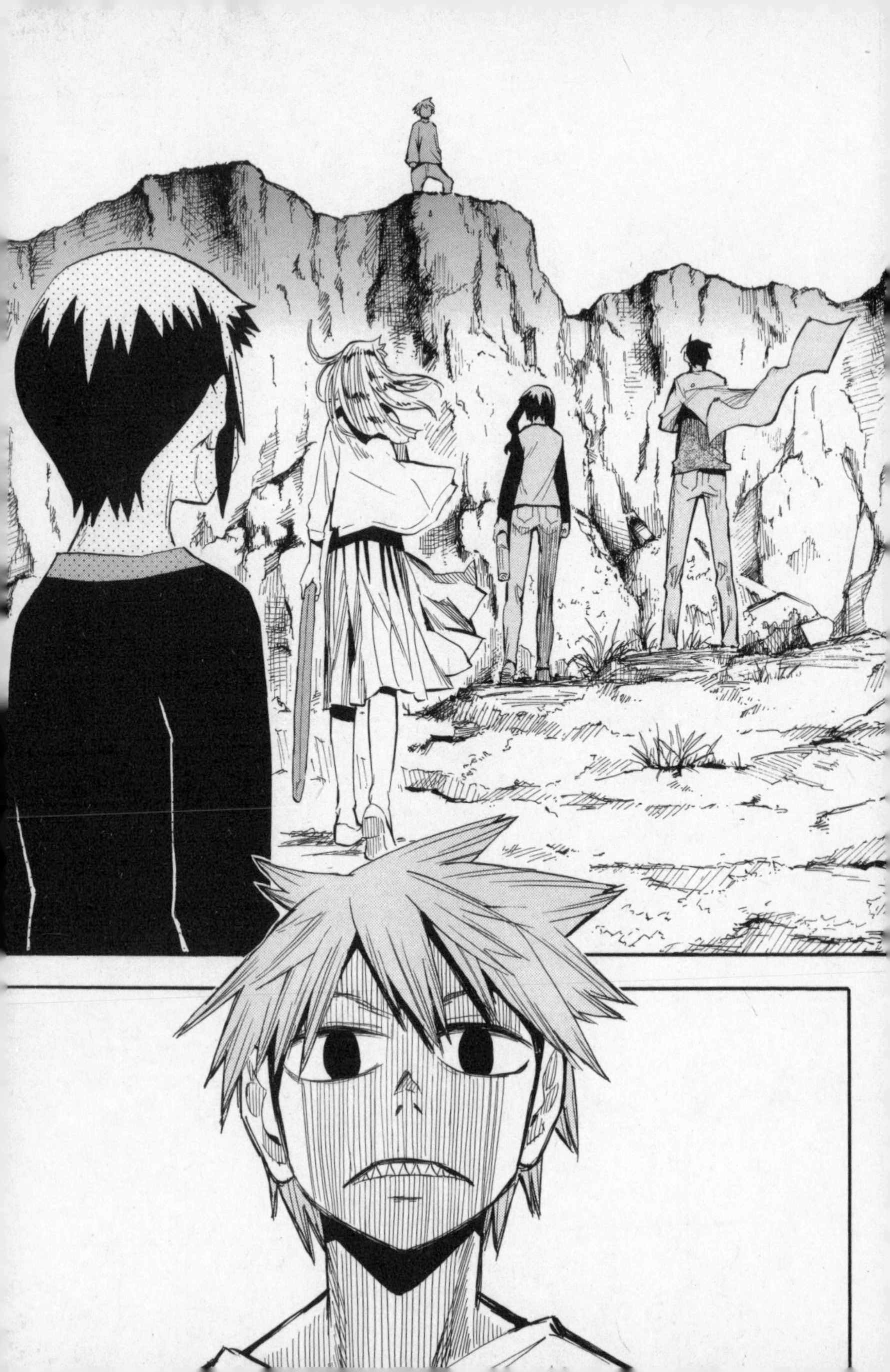

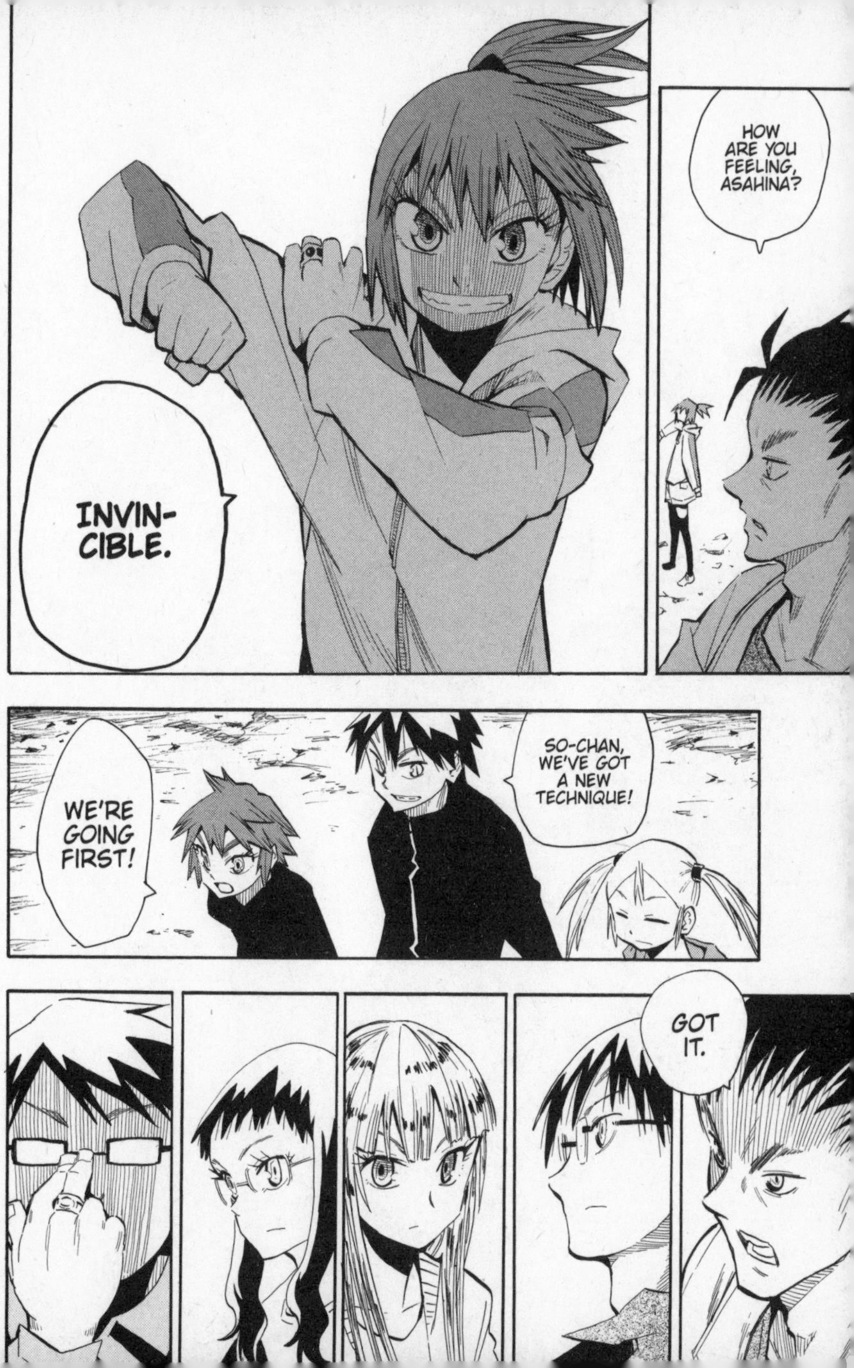
HOW ARE YOU FEELING, ASAHINA?
INVINCIBLE.
SO-CHAN, WE'VE GOT A NEW TECHNIQUE!
WE'RE GOING FIRST!
GOT IT.

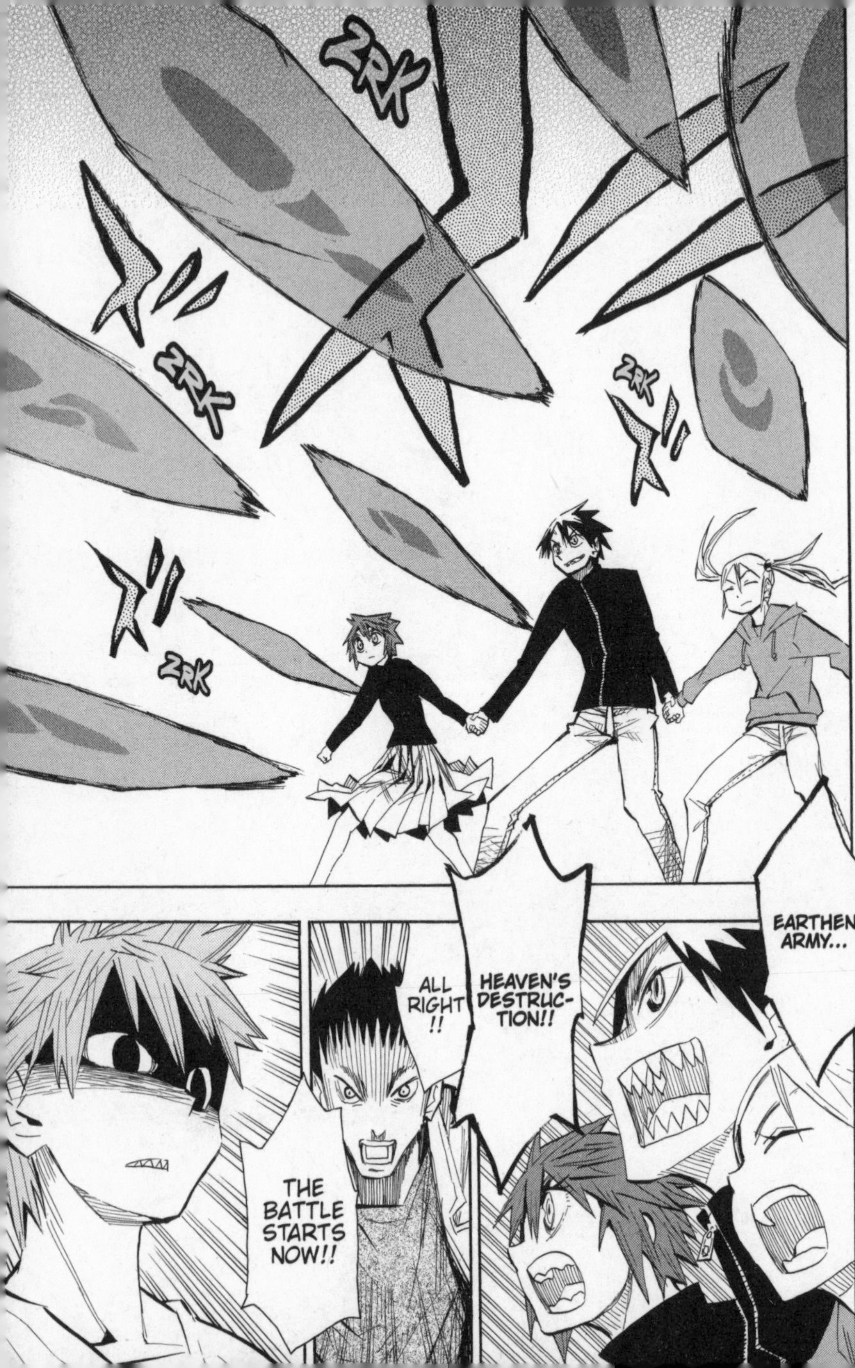
ZRK
ZRK
ZRK
ZRK
EARTHEN ARMY...
HEAVEN'S DESTRUC-TION!!
ALL RIGHT!!
THE BATTLE STARTS NOW!!

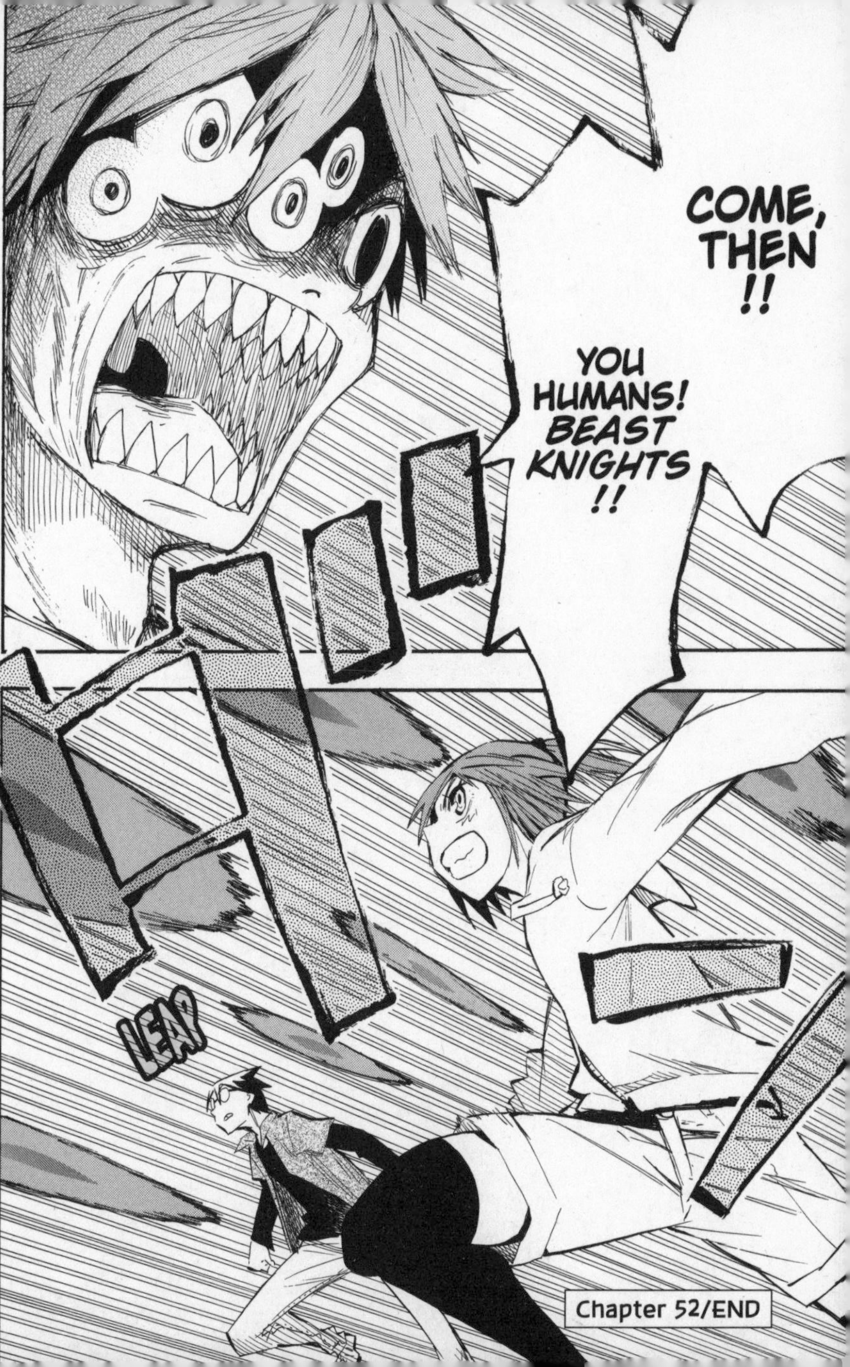
COME, THEN !!
YOU HUMANS! BEAST KNIGHTS !!
LEAP
Chapter 52/END

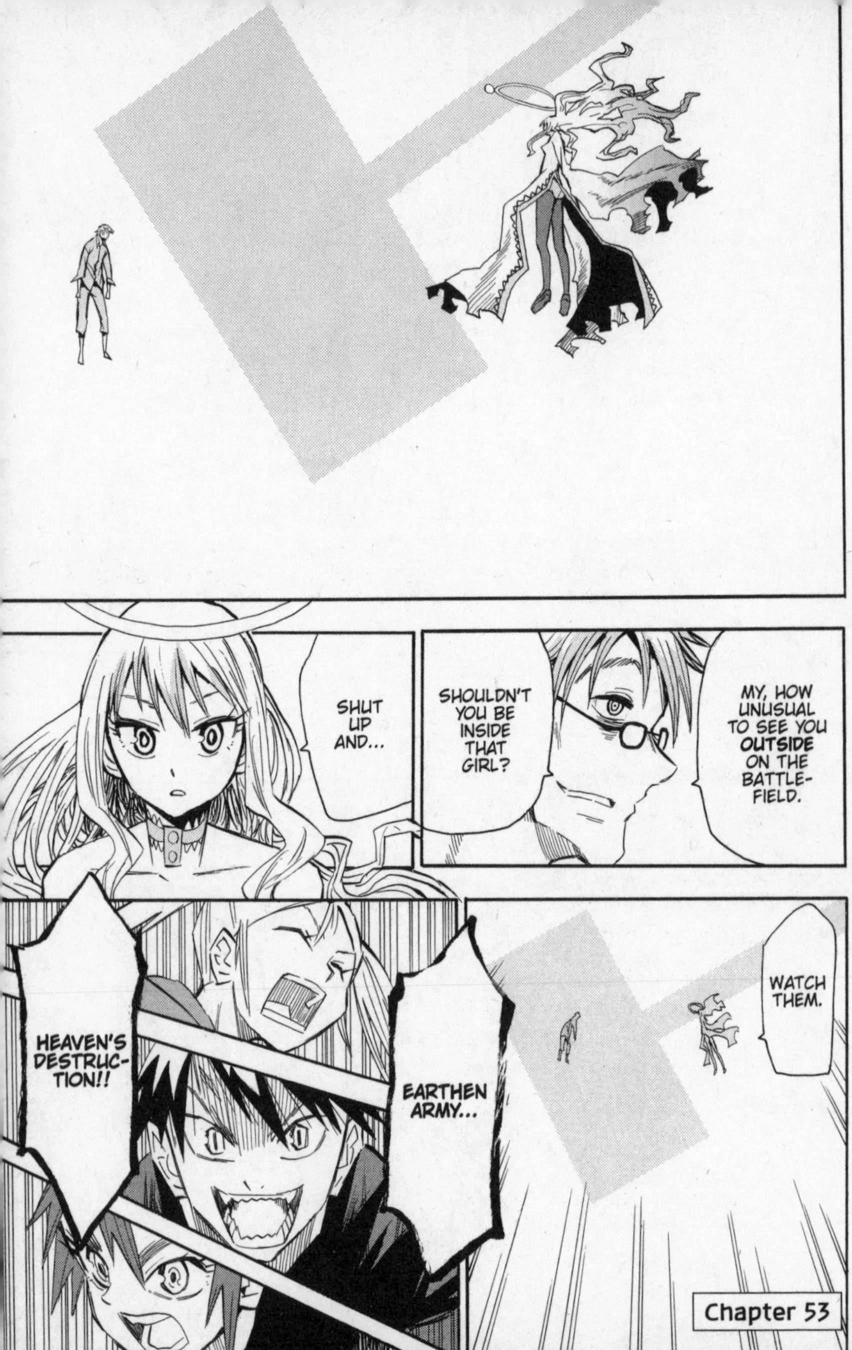
MY, HOW UNUSUAL TO SEE YOU OUTSIDE ON THE BATTLE-FIELD.
SHOULDN'T YOU BE INSIDE THAT GIRL?
SHUT UP AND...
WATCH THEM.
EARTHEN ARMY...
HEAVEN'S DESTRUC-TION!!
Chapter 53

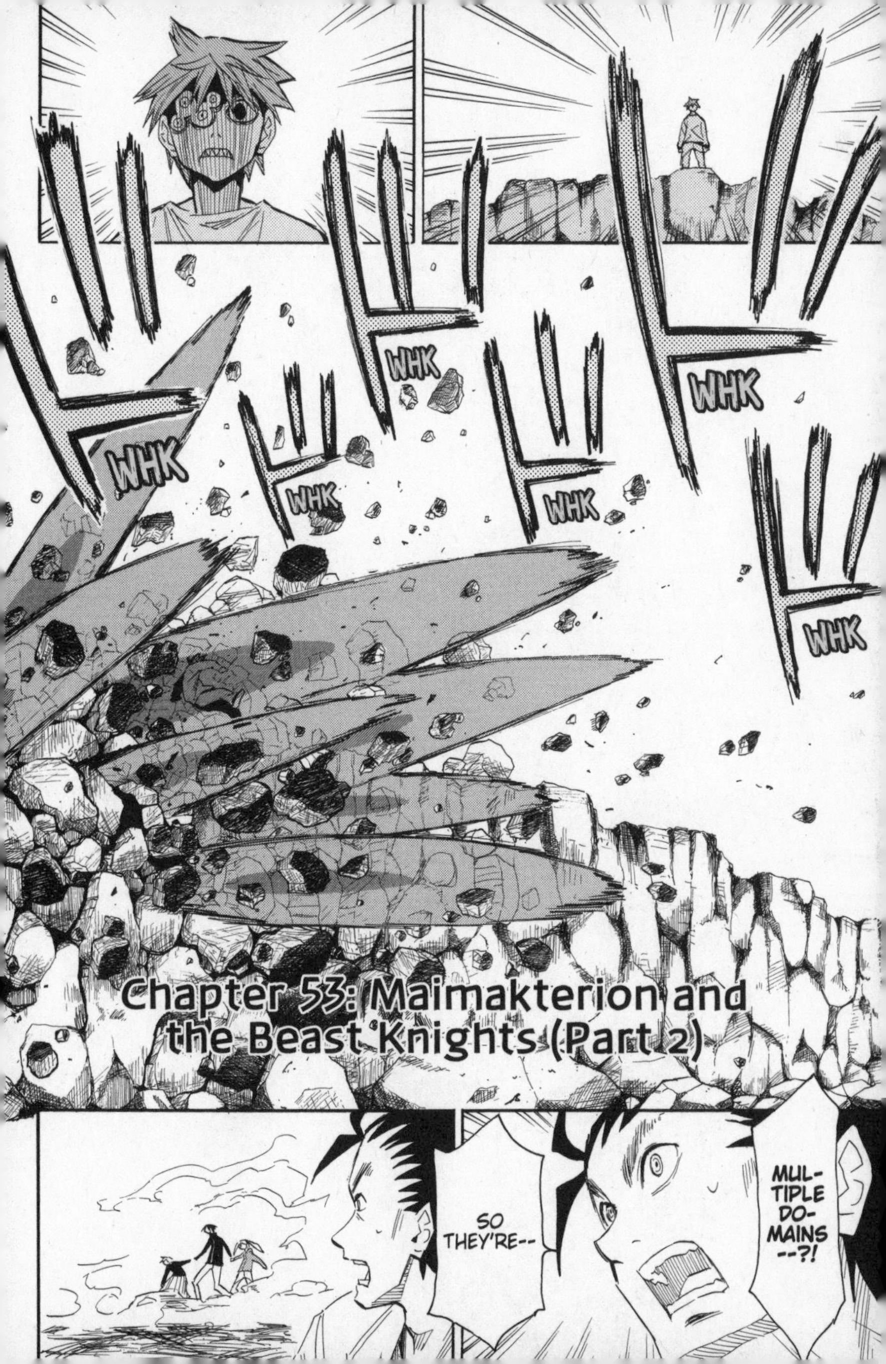
WHK
WHK
WHK
WHK
WHK
WHK
Chapter 53: Maimakterion and the Beast Knights (Part 2)
MUL-
TIPLE
DO-
MAINS
--?!
SO
THEY'RE--

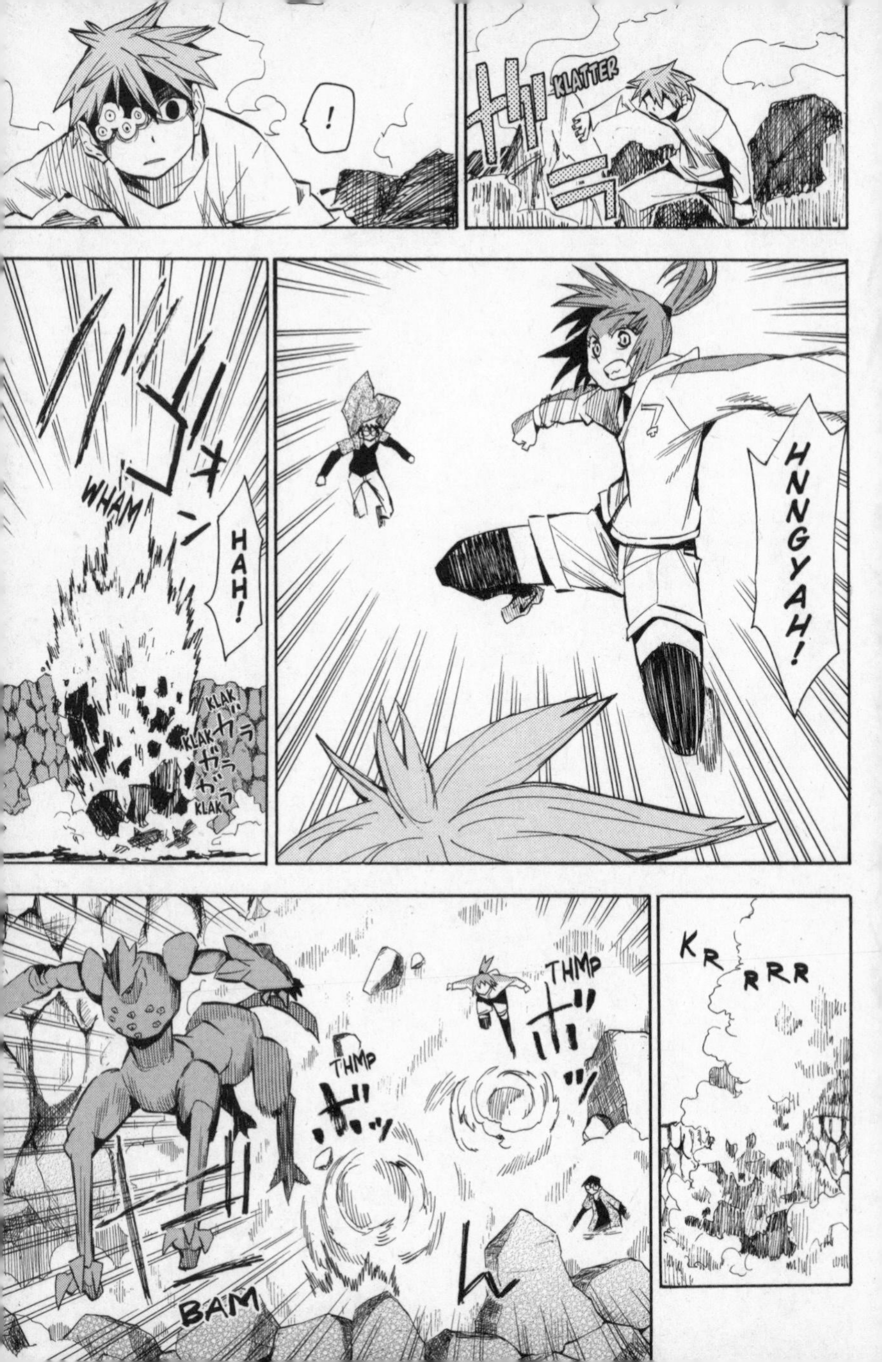
KLATTER
!
HNNGYAH!
WHAM
HAH!
KLAK
KLAK
KLAK
KR RRRR
THMP
THMP
BAM

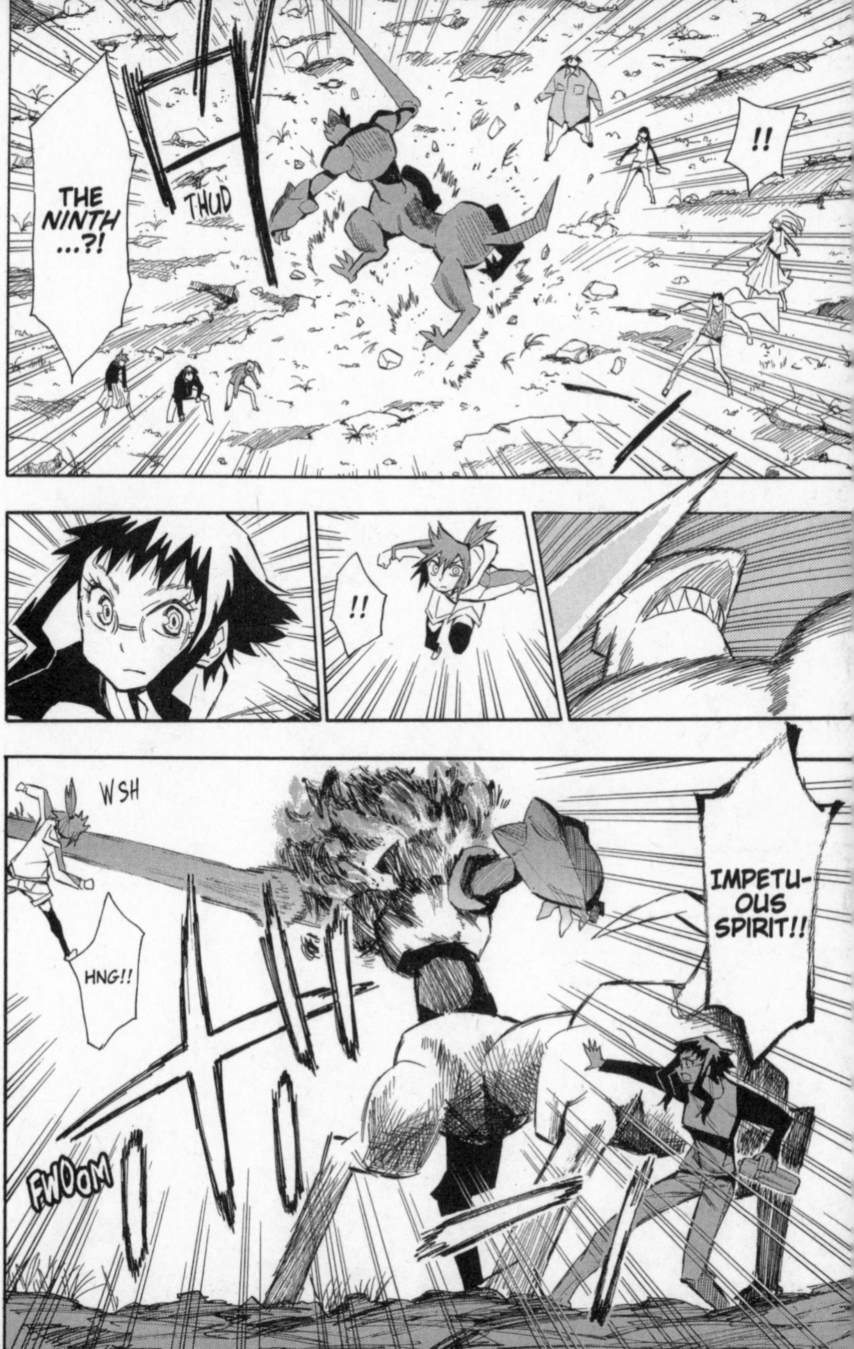
!!
THUD
THE NINTH ...?!
!!
IMPETU-OUS SPIRIT!!
WSH
HNG!!
FWOOM

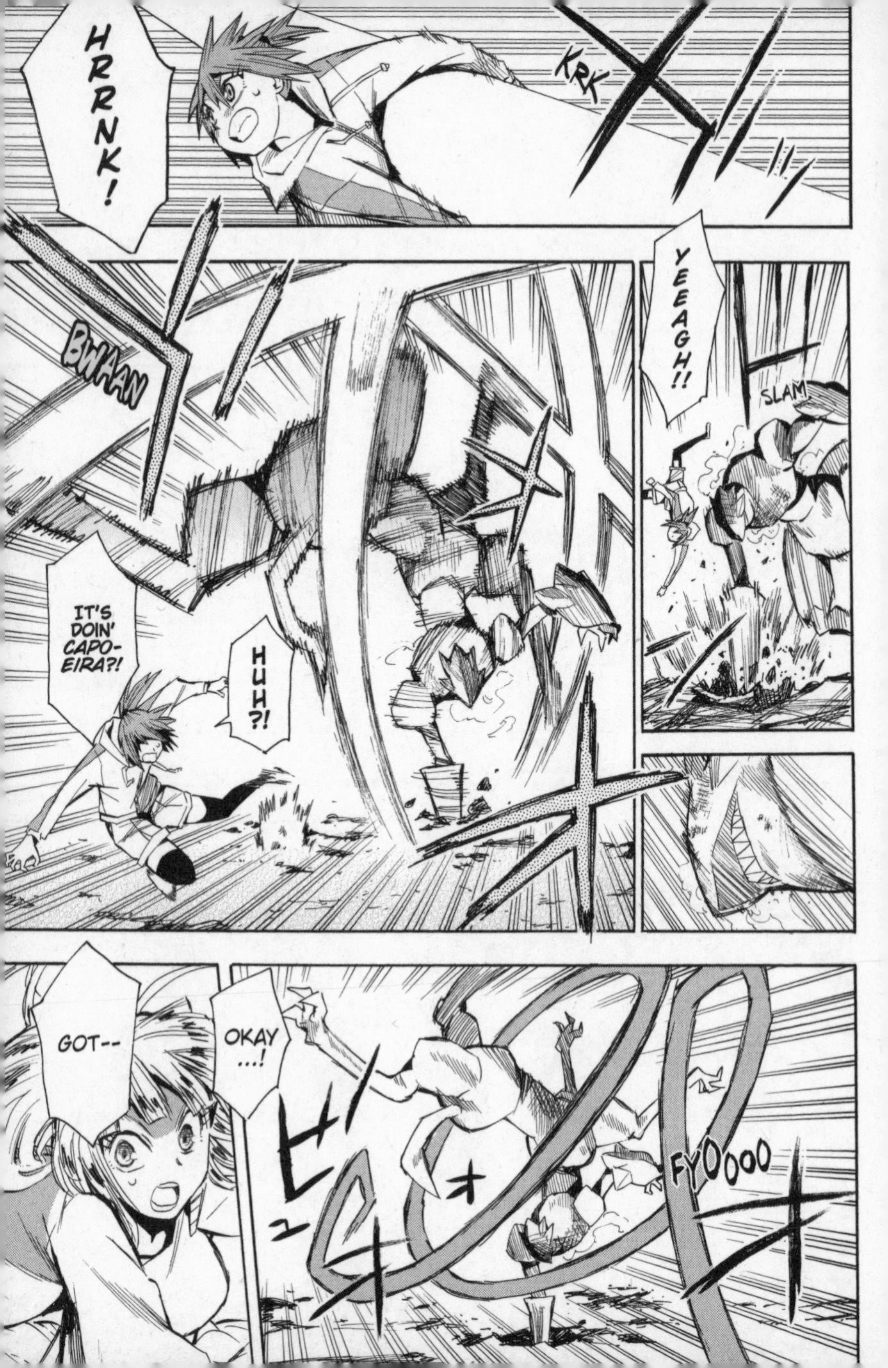
KRK
HRRNK!
YEEEAGH!!
SLAM
BWAAN
HUH?!
IT'S DOIN' CAPOEIRA?!
FYOOOO
OKAY ...!
GOT--

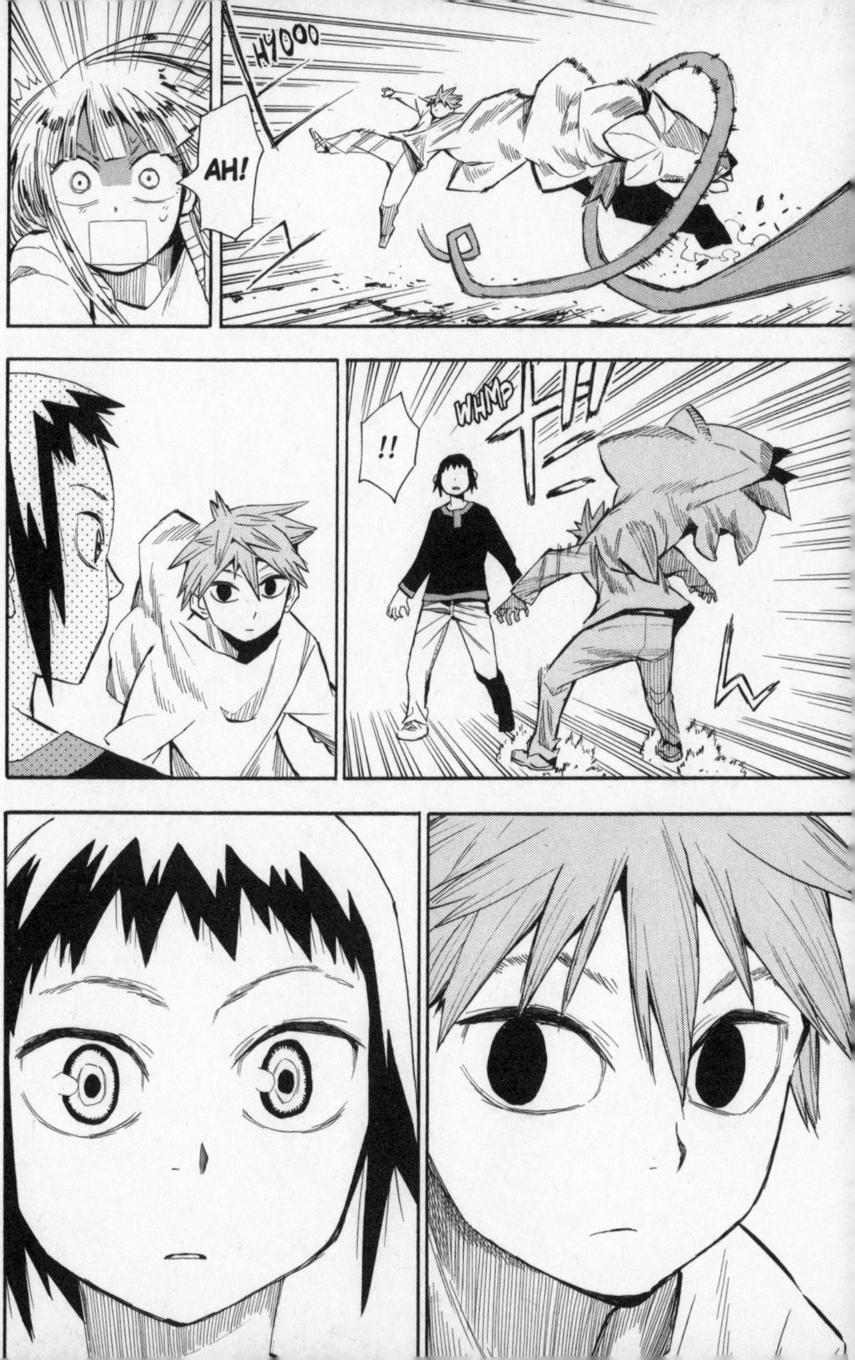
HYOOO
AH!
WHMP
!!

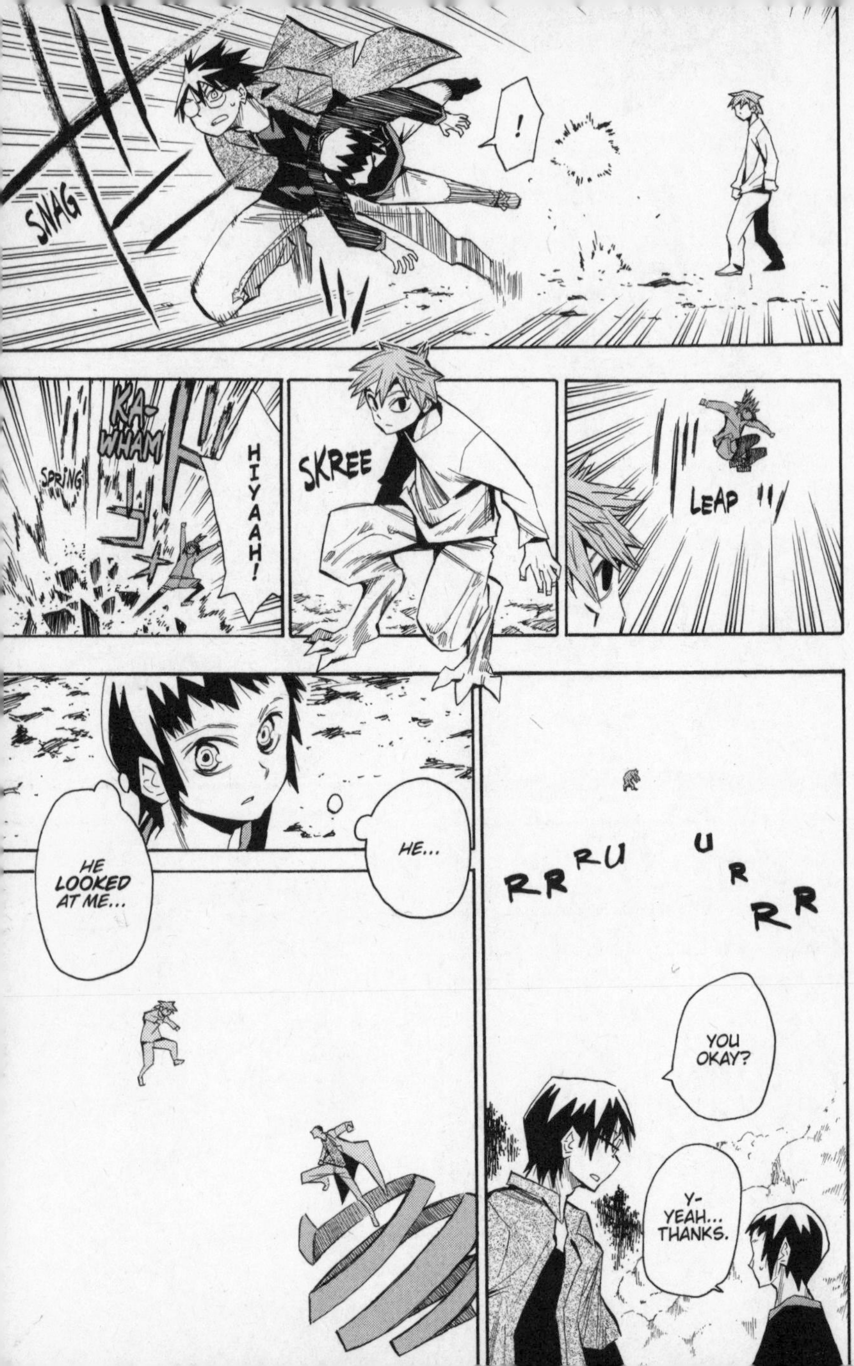
!
SNAG
LEAP
SKREE
KA-WHAM
SPRING
HIYAAH!
RRRU URRRR
YOU OKAY?
Y-YEAH... THANKS.
HE...
HE LOOKED AT ME...

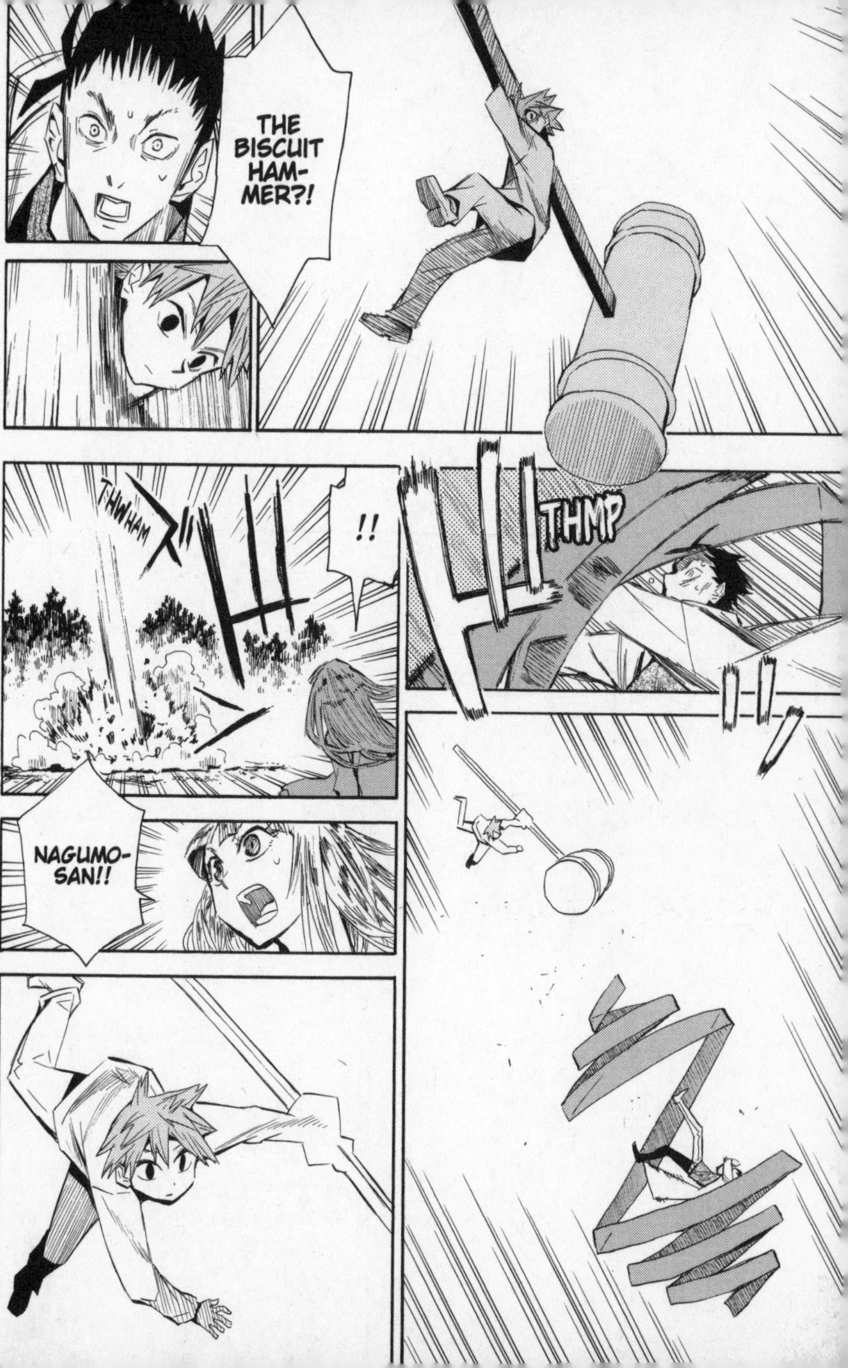
THE BISCUIT HAM-MER?!
THMP
THWHAM
!!
NAGUMO-SAN!!

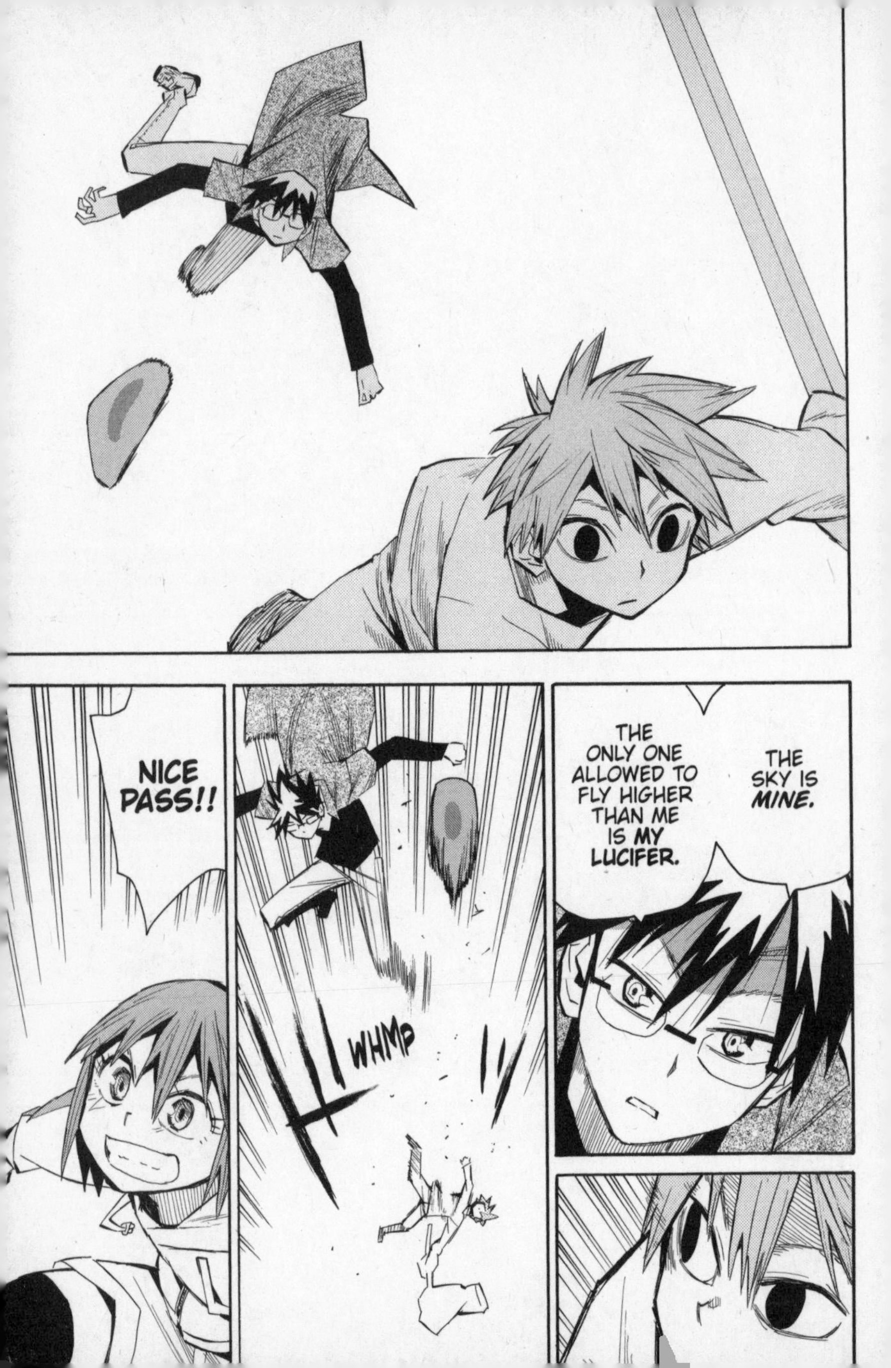
THE SKY IS MINE.
THE ONLY ONE ALLOWED TO FLY HIGHER THAN ME IS MY LUCIFER.
WHMP
NICE PASS!!

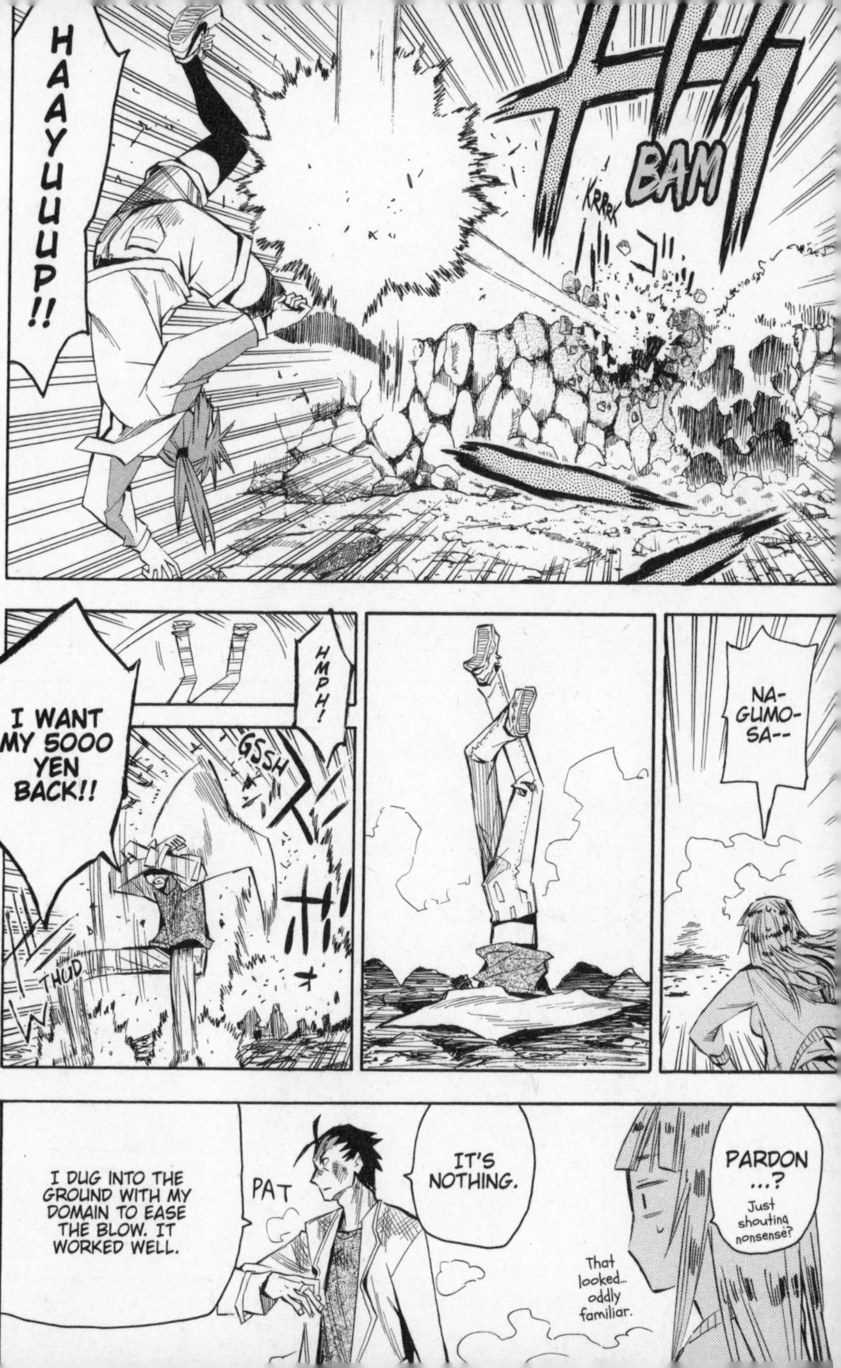

BAM
KRRRK
HAAYUUUUP!!
NA-GUMO-SA--
HMPH!
GSSH
I WANT MY 5000 YEN BACK!!
THUD
PARDON ...?
Just shouting nonsense?
That looked... oddly familiar.
IT'S NOTHING.
PAT
I DUG INTO THE GROUND WITH MY DOMAIN TO EASE THE BLOW. IT WORKED WELL.

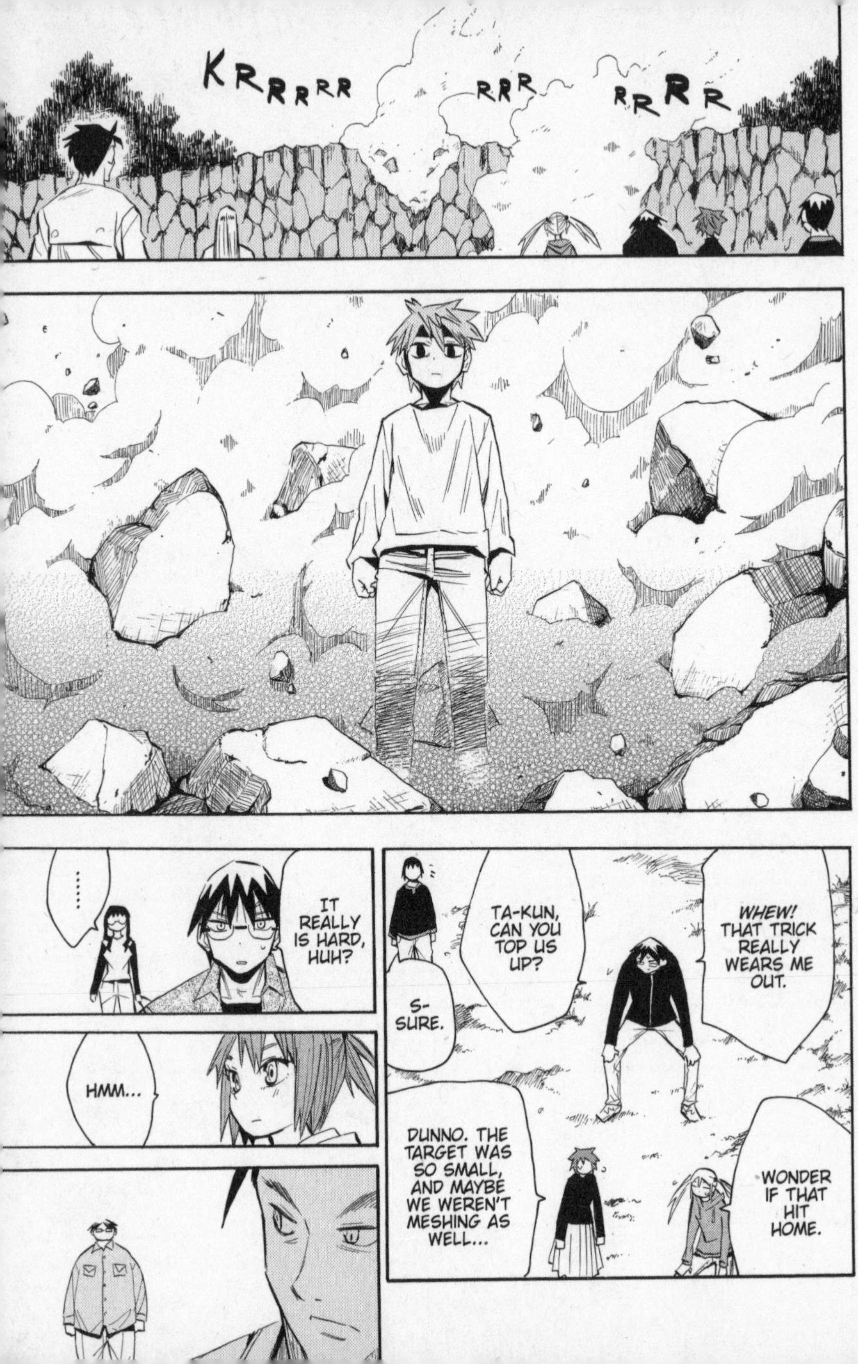
RRRRR
RRR
KRRRRRR
WHEW! THAT TRICK REALLY WEARS ME OUT.
TA-KUN, CAN YOU TOP US UP?
S-SURE.
WONDER IF THAT HIT HOME.
DUNNO. THE TARGET WAS SO SMALL, AND MAYBE WE WEREN'T MESHING AS WELL...
IT REALLY IS HARD, HUH?
......
HMM...

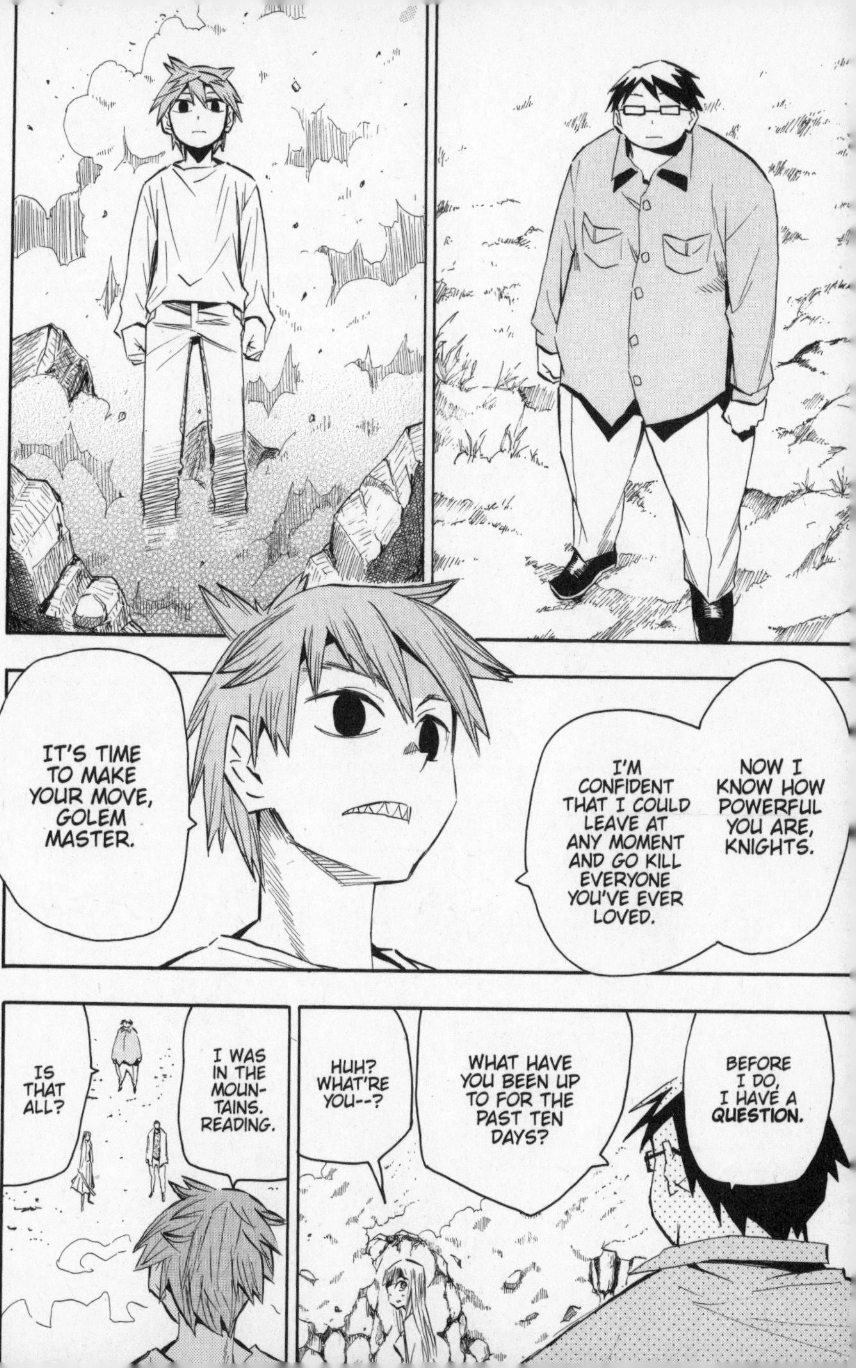
NOW I KNOW HOW POWERFUL YOU ARE, KNIGHTS.
I'M CONFIDENT THAT I COULD LEAVE AT ANY MOMENT AND GO KILL EVERYONE YOU'VE EVER LOVED.
IT'S TIME TO MAKE YOUR MOVE, GOLEM MASTER.
BEFORE I DO, I HAVE A QUESTION.
WHAT HAVE YOU BEEN UP TO FOR THE PAST TEN DAYS?
HUH? WHAT'RE YOU--?
I WAS IN THE MOUN-TAINS. READING.
IS THAT ALL?

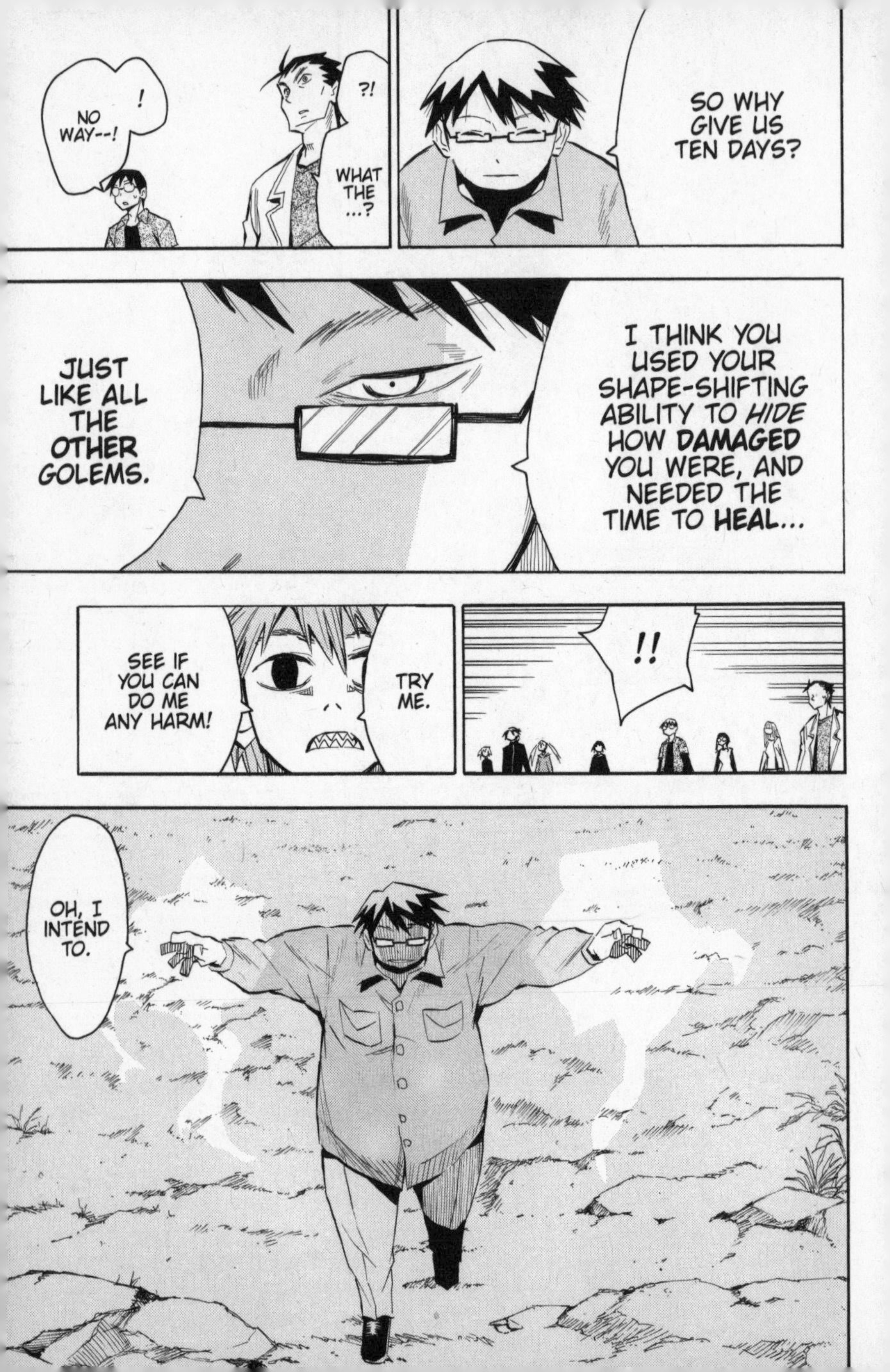
SO WHY GIVE US TEN DAYS?
?!
WHAT THE ...?
!
NO WAY--!
I THINK YOU USED YOUR SHAPE-SHIFTING ABILITY TO HIDE HOW DAMAGED YOU WERE, AND NEEDED THE TIME TO HEAL...
JUST LIKE ALL THE OTHER GOLEMS.
!!
TRY ME.
SEE IF YOU CAN DO ME ANY HARM!
OH, I INTEND TO.

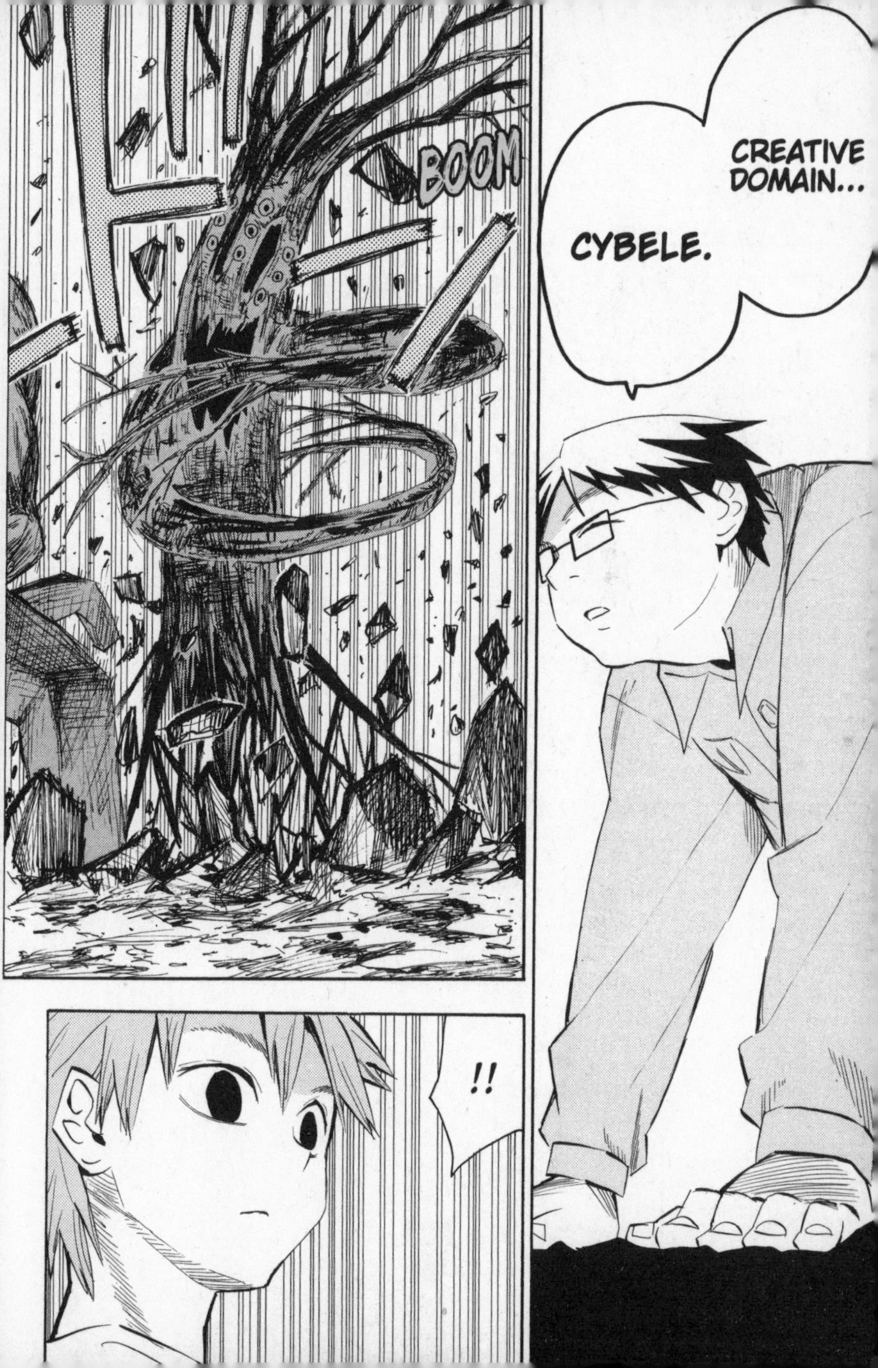
CREATIVE DOMAIN...
CYBELE.
BOOM
!!

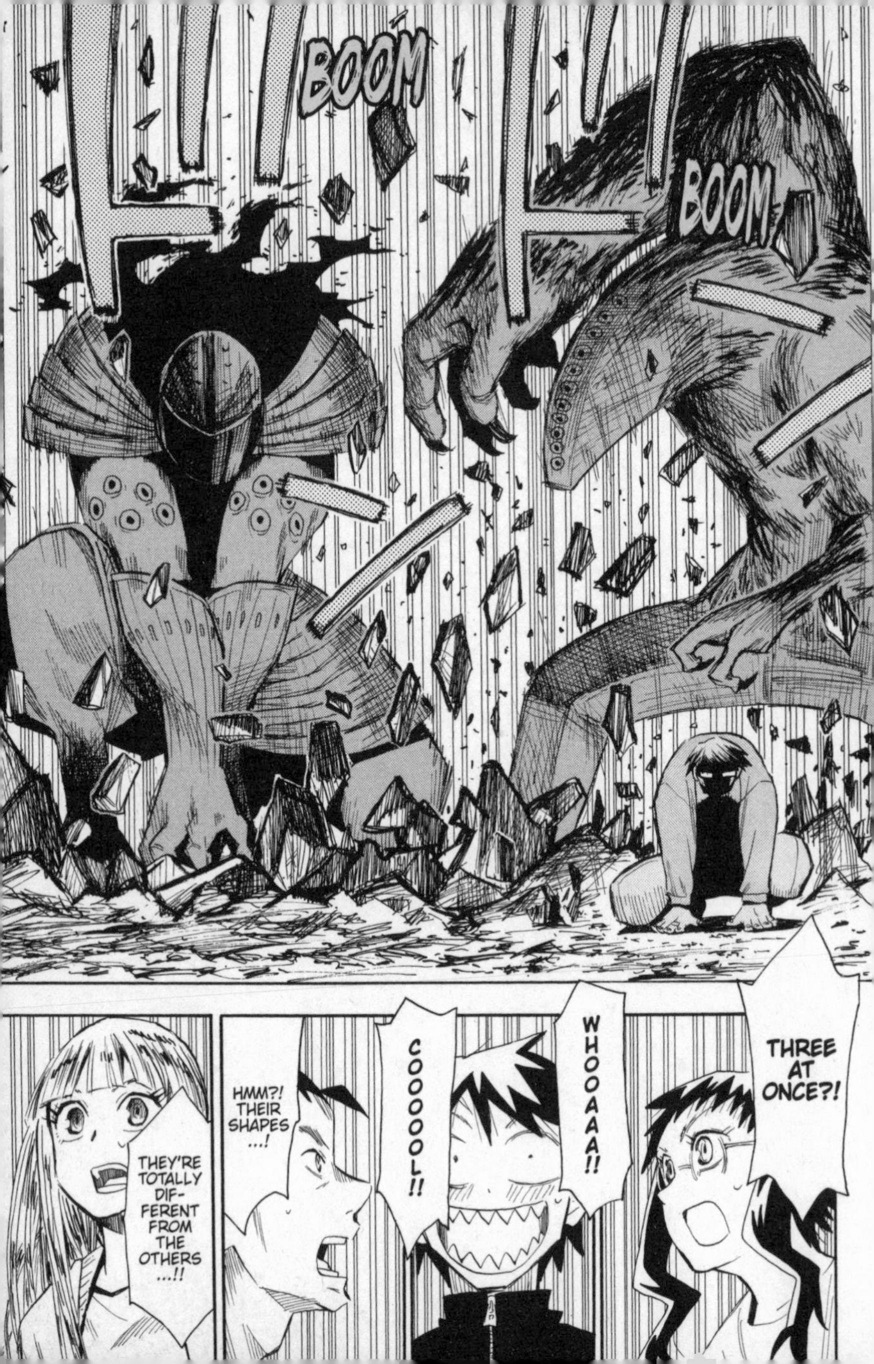
BOOM
BOOM
THREE AT ONCE?!
WHOOOAAA!!
COOOOOOL!!
HMM?! THEIR SHAPES ...!
THEY'RE TOTALLY DIF-FERENT FROM THE OTHERS ...!!

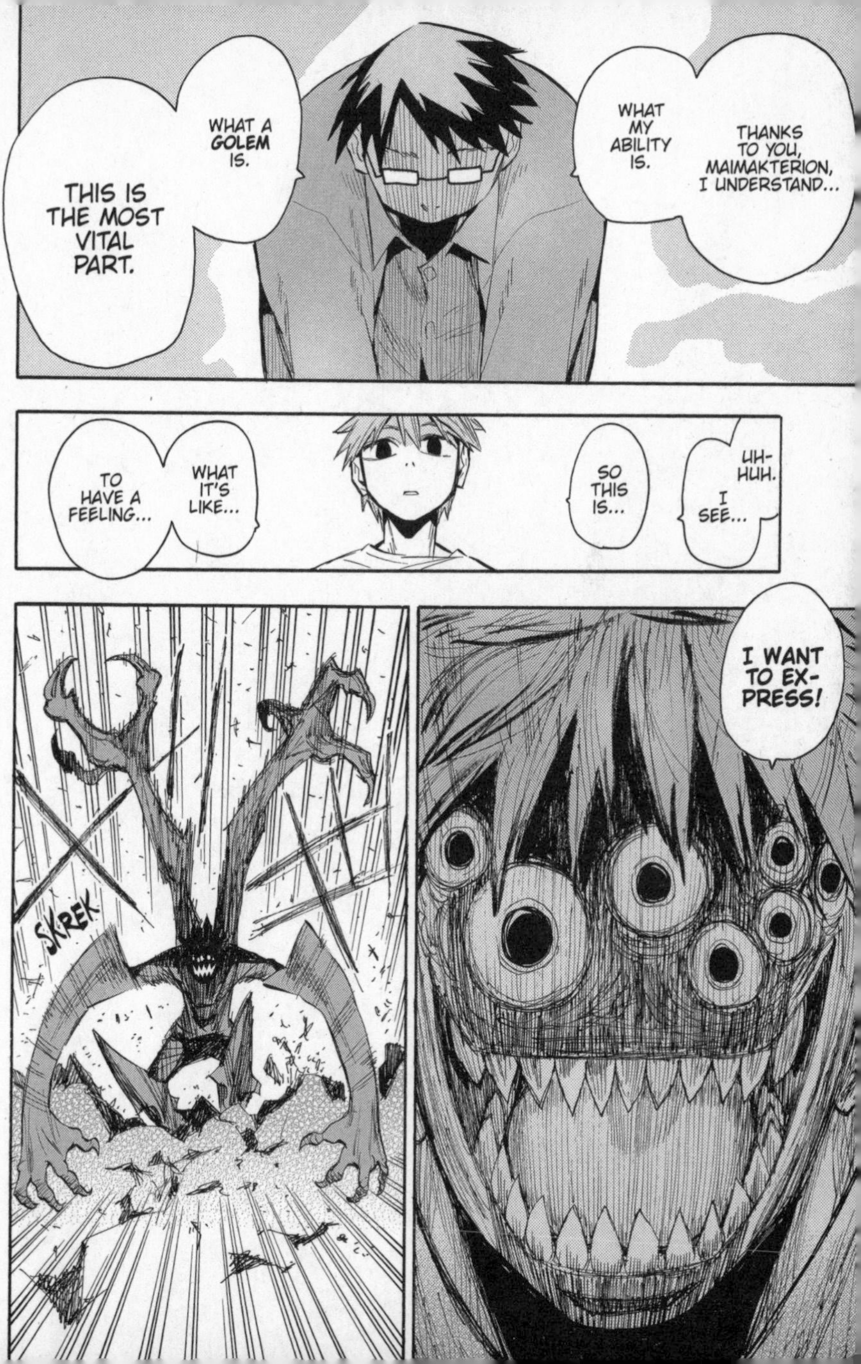
THANKS TO YOU, MAIMAKTERION, I UNDERSTAND...
WHAT MY ABILITY IS.
WHAT A GOLEM IS.
THIS IS THE MOST VITAL PART.
UH-HUH. I SEE...
SO THIS IS...
WHAT IT'S LIKE...
TO HAVE A FEELING...
I WANT TO EX-PRESS!
SKREK

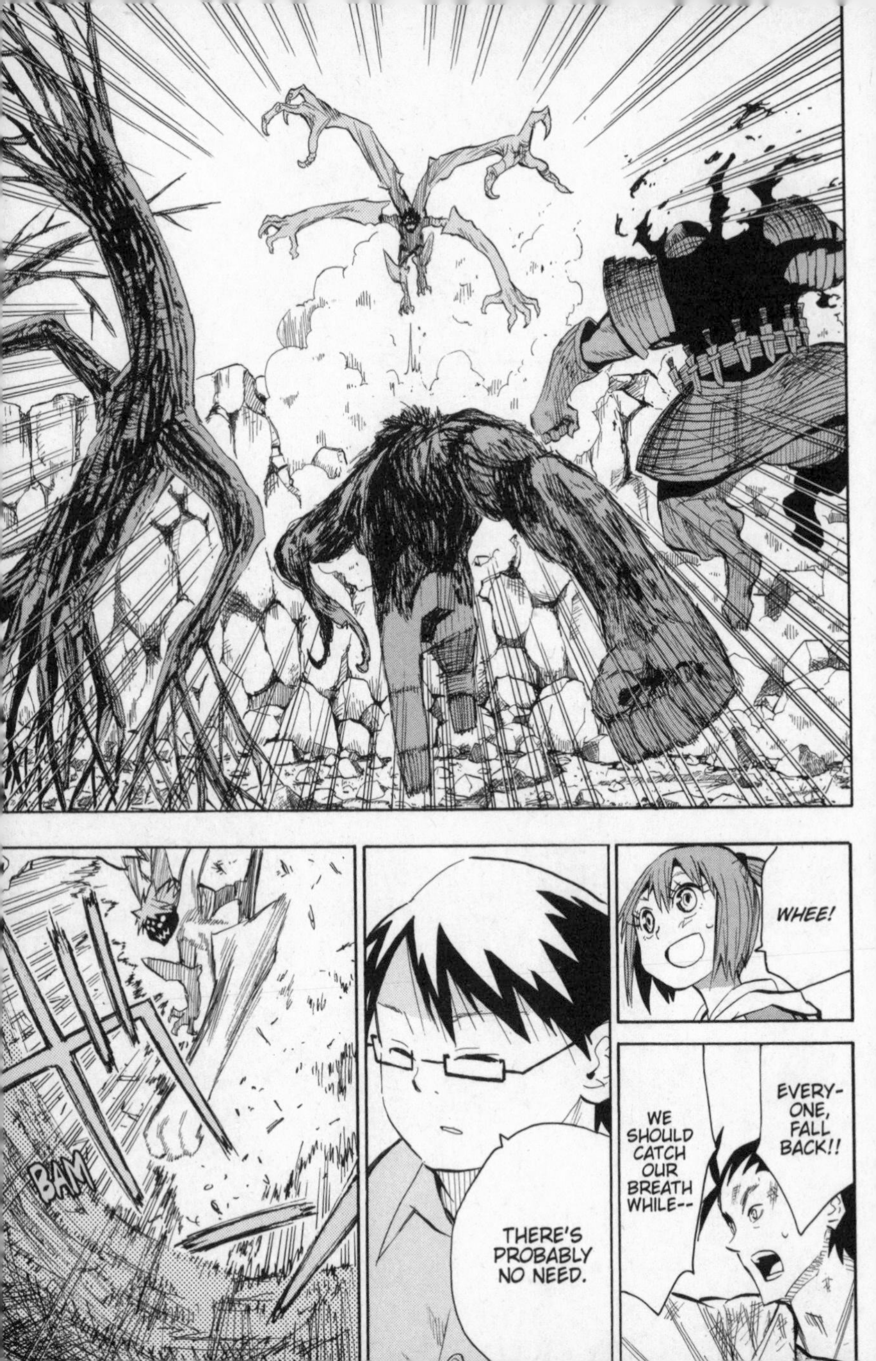
WHEE!
EVERY-ONE, FALL BACK!!
WE SHOULD CATCH OUR BREATH WHILE--
THERE'S PROBABLY NO NEED.
BAM

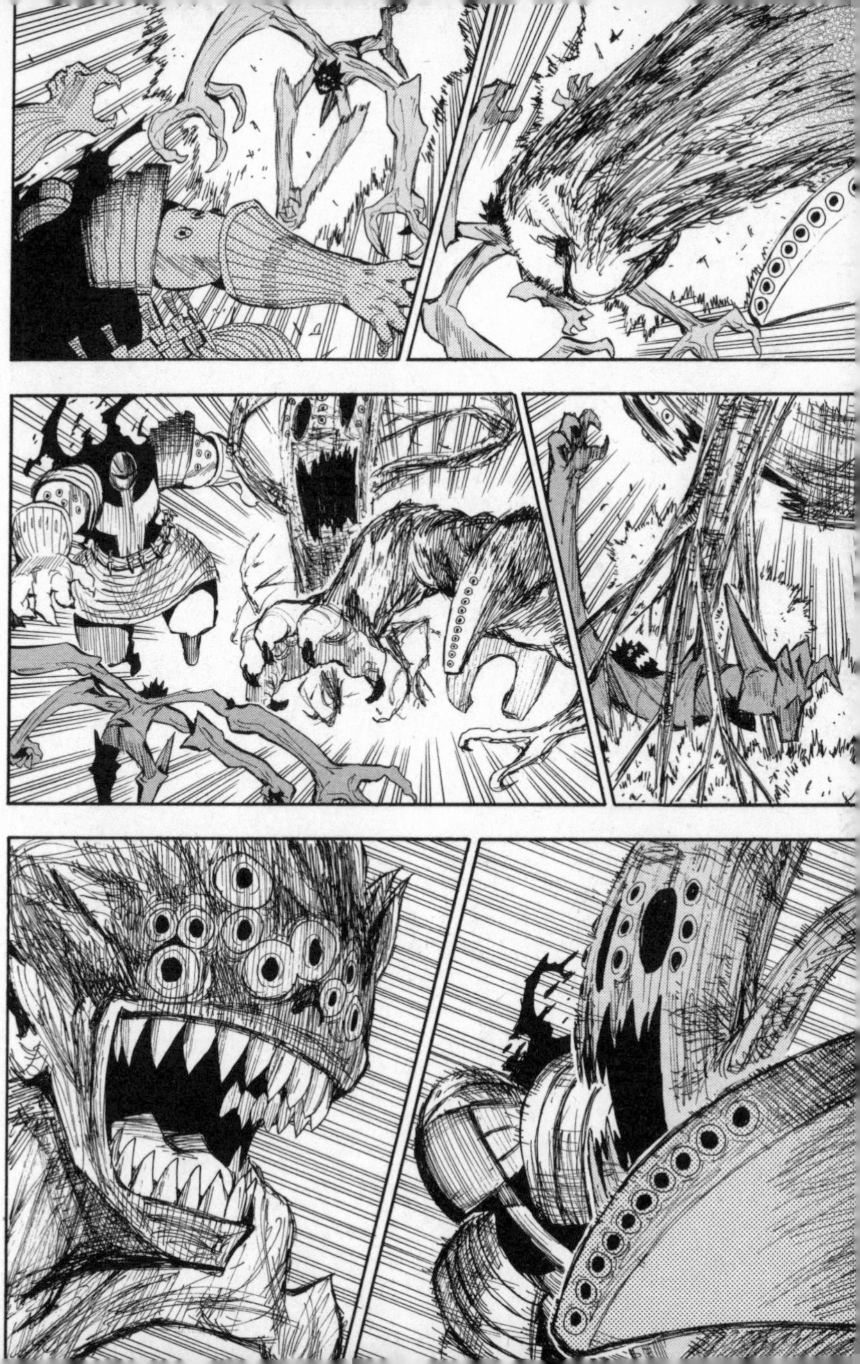

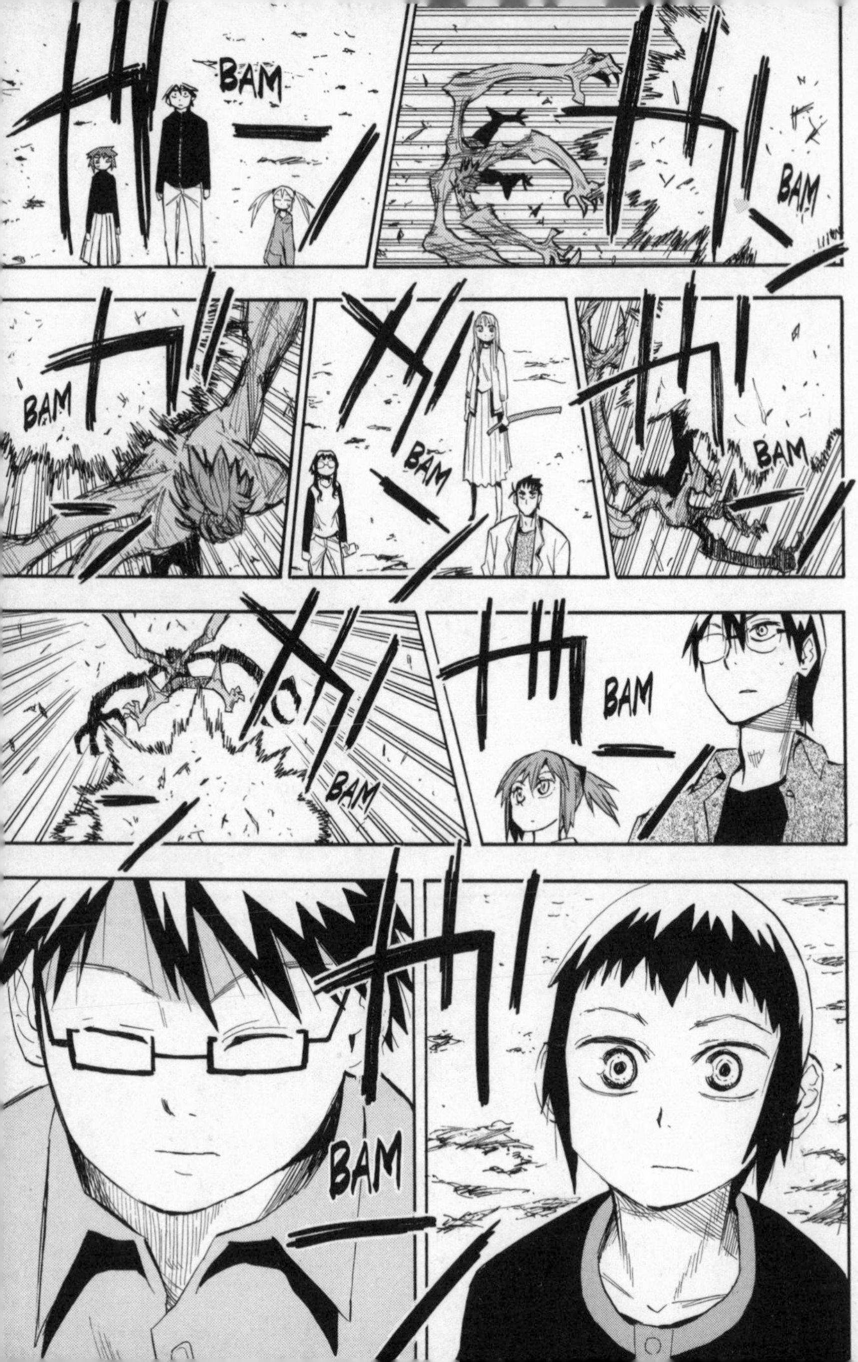
BAM
BAM
BAM
BAM
BAM
BAM
BAM
BAM

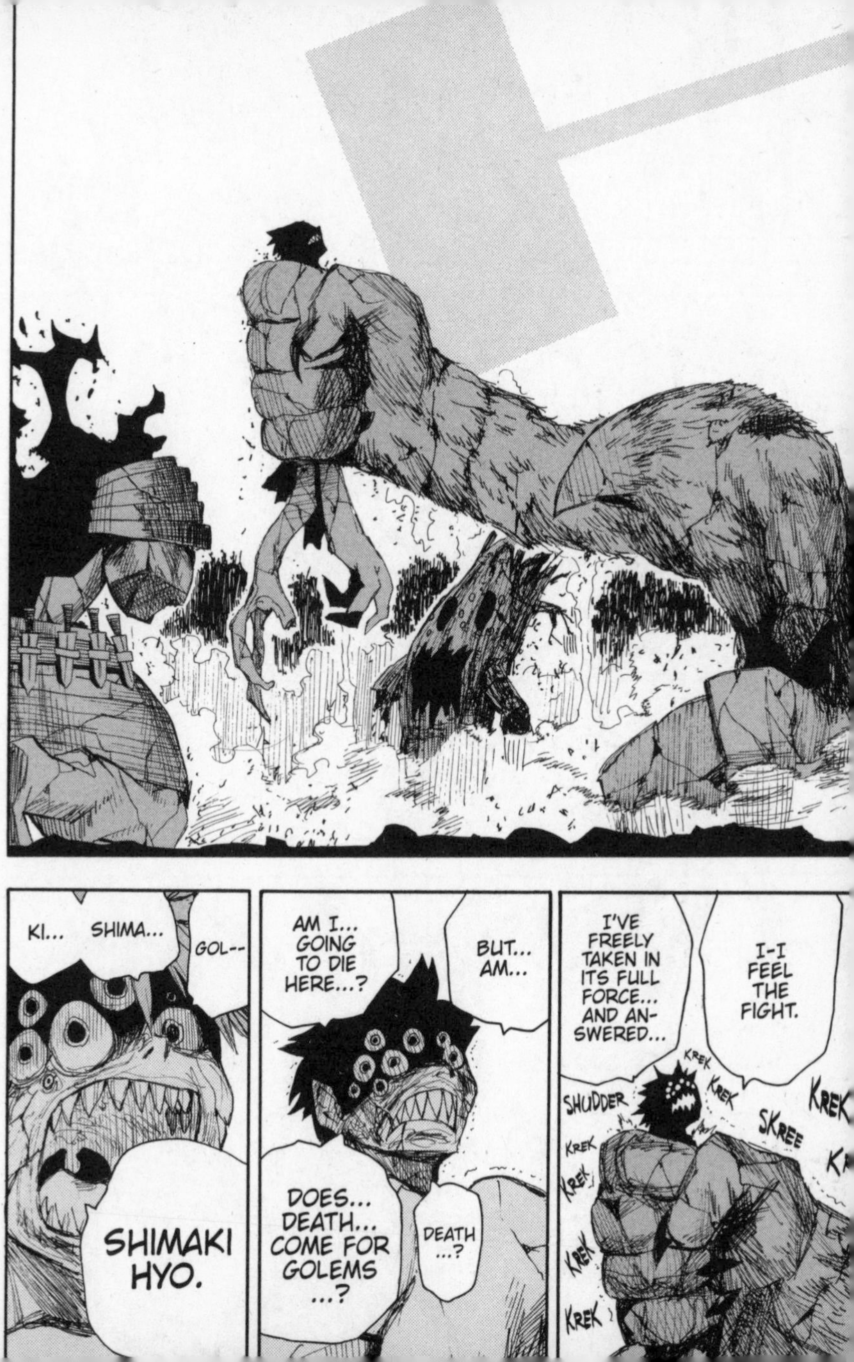
I-I FEEL THE FIGHT.
I'VE FREELY TAKEN IN ITS FULL FORCE... AND AN-SWERED...
KREK
KREK
KREK
SKREE
SHUDDER
KREK
KREK
KREK
KREK
BUT... AM...
AM I... GOING TO DIE HERE...?
DEATH ...?
DOES... DEATH... COME FOR GOLEMS ...?
GOL--
SHIMA...
KI...
SHIMAKI HYO.

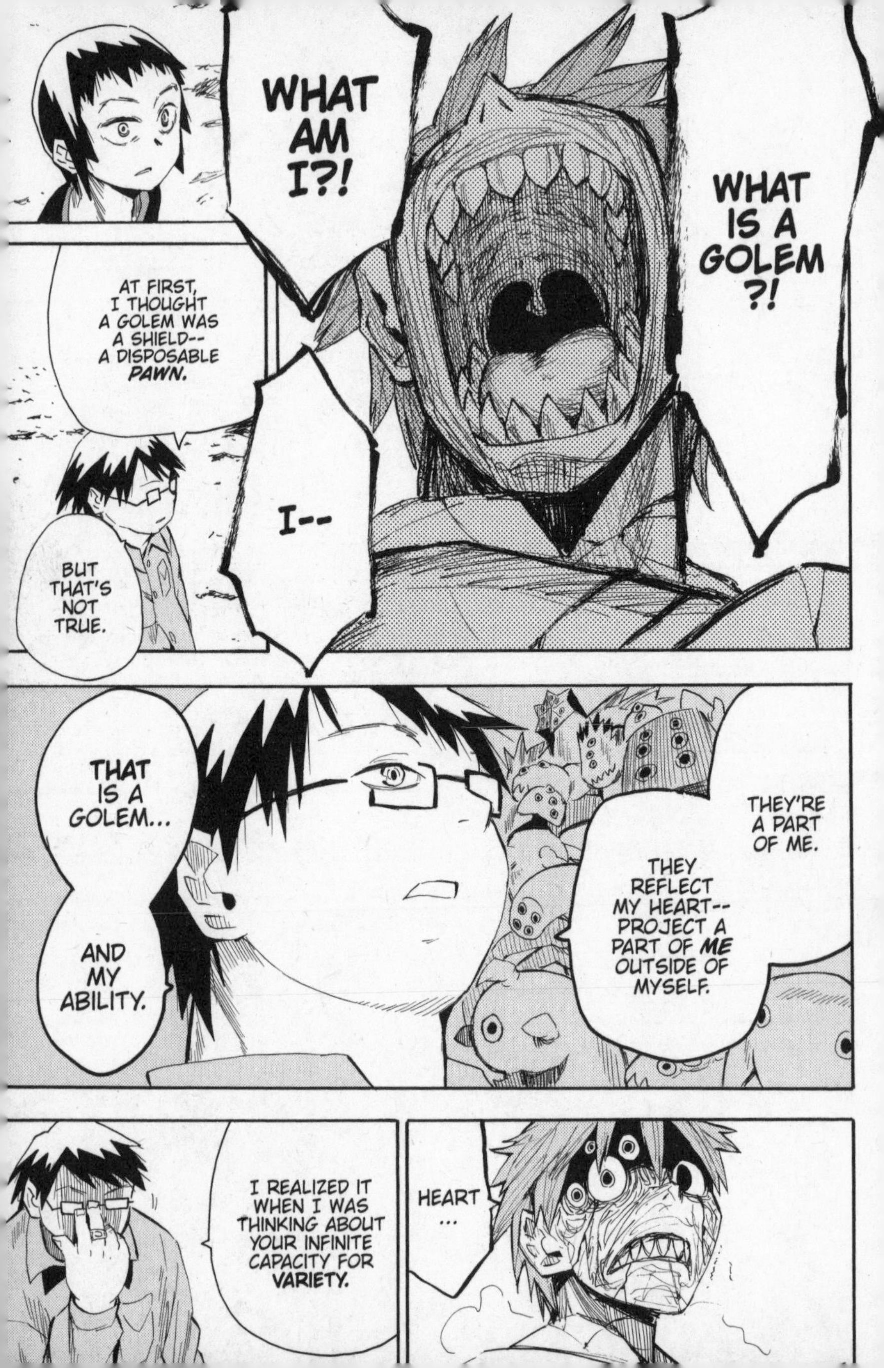
WHAT AM I?!
WHAT IS A GOLEM ?!
I--
AT FIRST, I THOUGHT A GOLEM WAS A SHIELD-- A DISPOSABLE PAWN.
BUT THAT'S NOT TRUE.
THEY'RE A PART OF ME.
THEY REFLECT MY HEART-- PROJECT A PART OF ME OUTSIDE OF MYSELF.
THAT IS A GOLEM...
AND MY ABILITY.
HEART ...
I REALIZED IT WHEN I WAS THINKING ABOUT YOUR INFINITE CAPACITY FOR VARIETY.

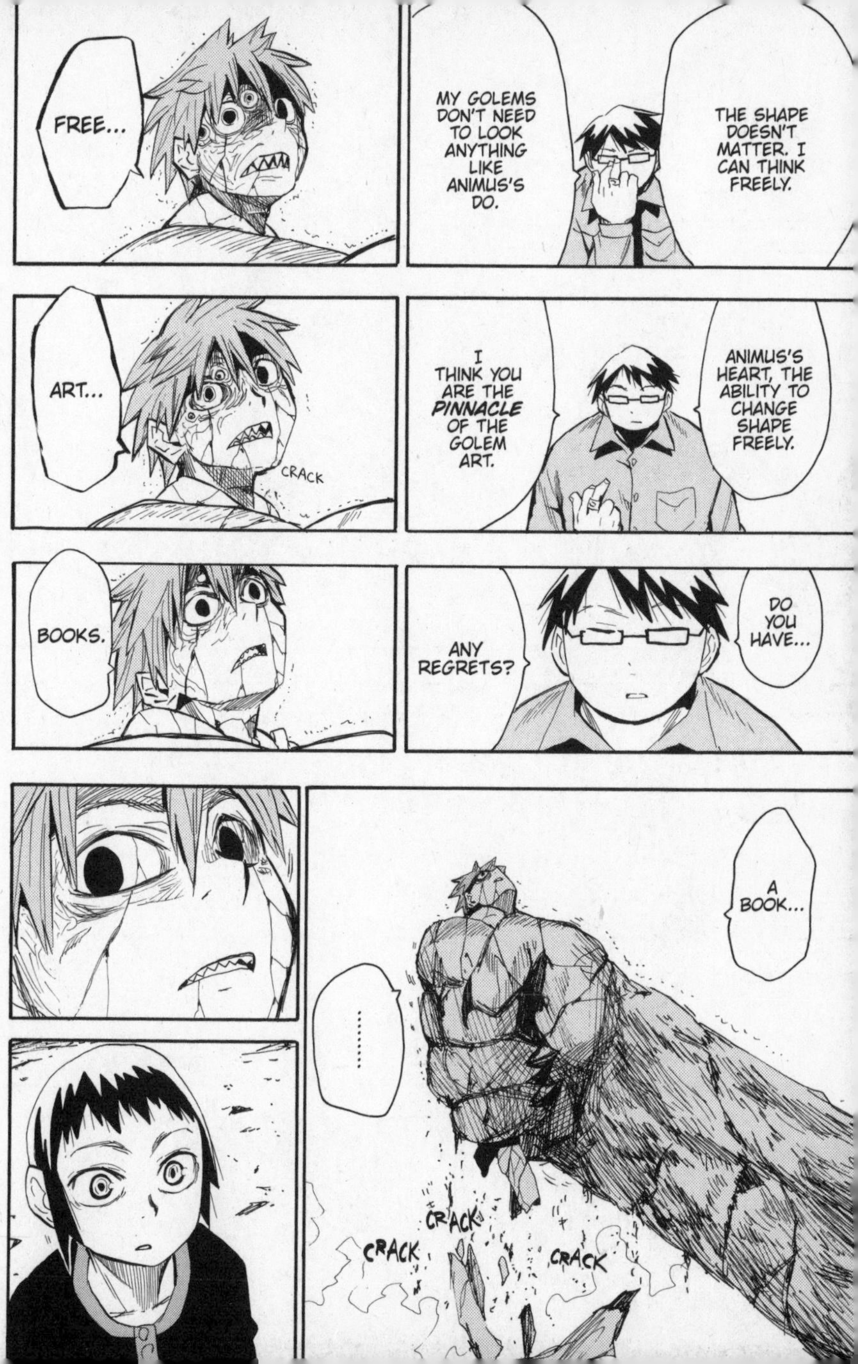
THE SHAPE DOESN'T MATTER. I CAN THINK FREELY.
MY GOLEMS DON'T NEED TO LOOK ANYTHING LIKE ANIMUS'S DO.
FREE...
ANIMUS'S HEART, THE ABILITY TO CHANGE SHAPE FREELY.
I THINK YOU ARE THE *PINNACLE* OF THE GOLEM ART.
ART...
CRACK
DO YOU HAVE...
ANY REGRETS?
BOOKS.
A BOOK...
......
CRACK
CRACK
CRACK

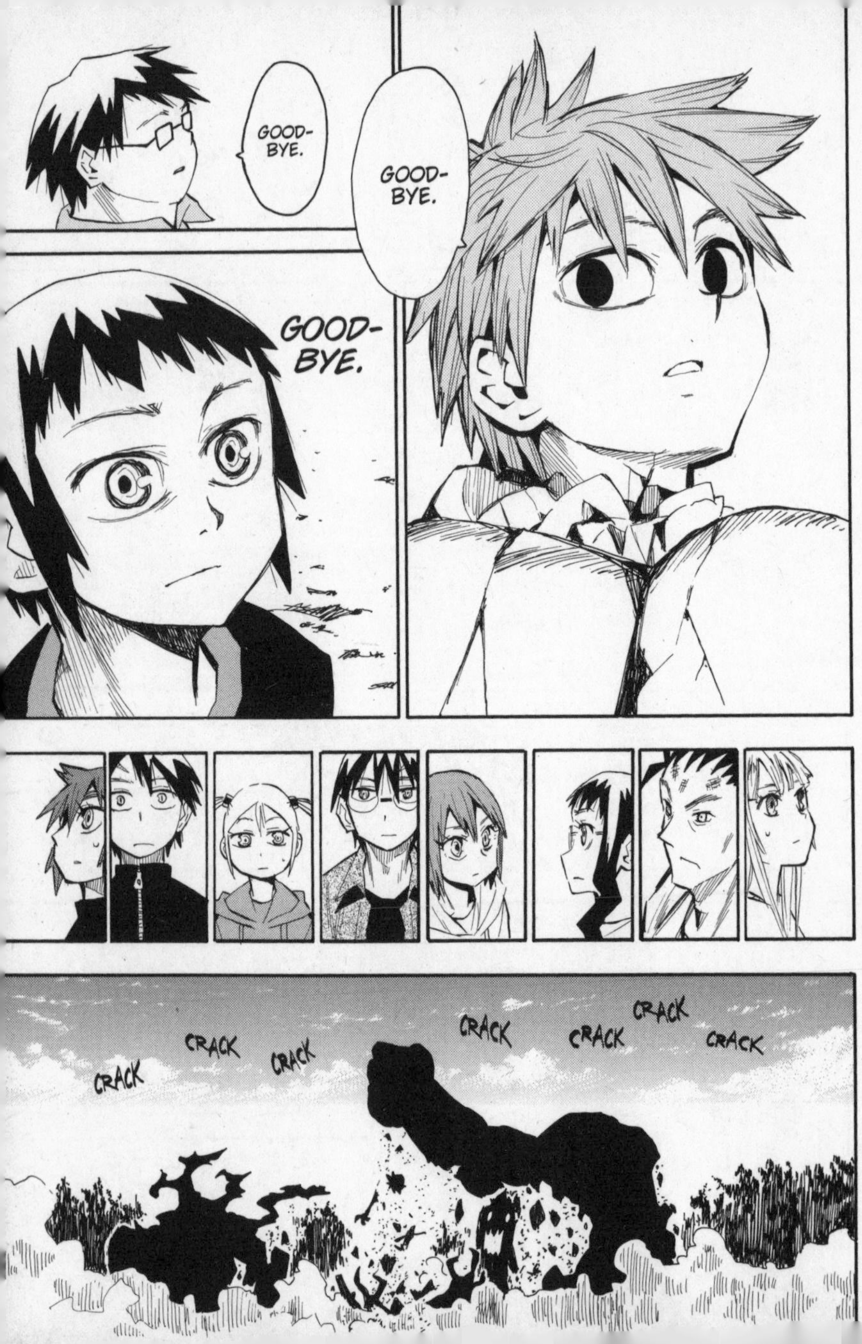
GOOD-BYE.
GOOD-BYE.
GOOD-BYE.
CRACK
CRACK
CRACK
CRACK
CRACK
CRACK
CRACK

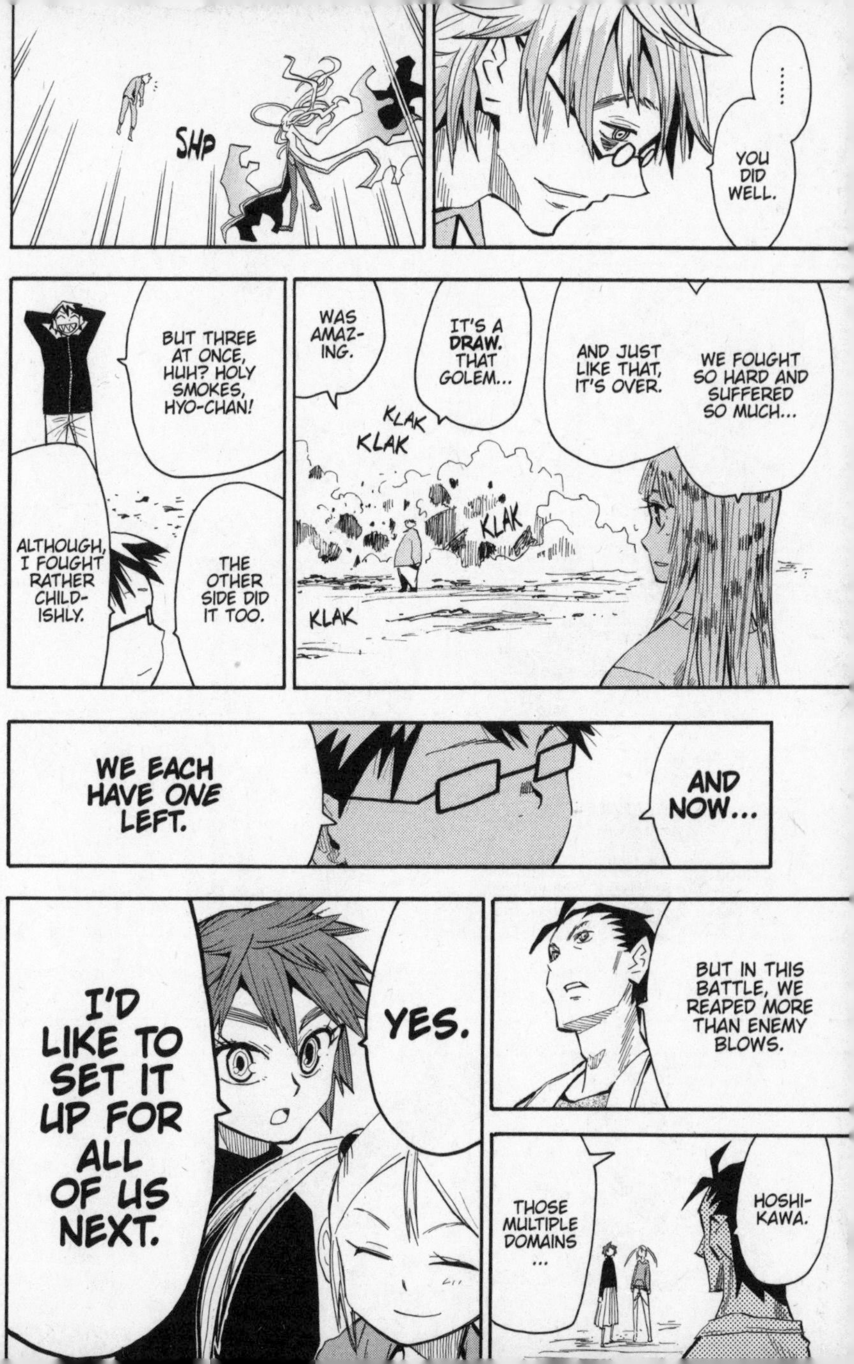
......
YOU DID WELL.
SHP
WE FOUGHT SO HARD AND SUFFERED SO MUCH...
AND JUST LIKE THAT, IT'S OVER.
IT'S A DRAW. THAT GOLEM...
WAS AMAZING.
KLAK
KLAK
KLAK
KLAK
BUT THREE AT ONCE, HUH? HOLY SMOKES, HYO-CHAN!
THE OTHER SIDE DID IT TOO.
ALTHOUGH, I FOUGHT RATHER CHILDISHLY.
AND NOW...
WE EACH HAVE ONE LEFT.
BUT IN THIS BATTLE, WE REAPED MORE THAN ENEMY BLOWS.
HOSHIKAWA.
THOSE MULTIPLE DOMAINS...
YES.
I'D LIKE TO SET IT UP FOR ALL OF US NEXT.

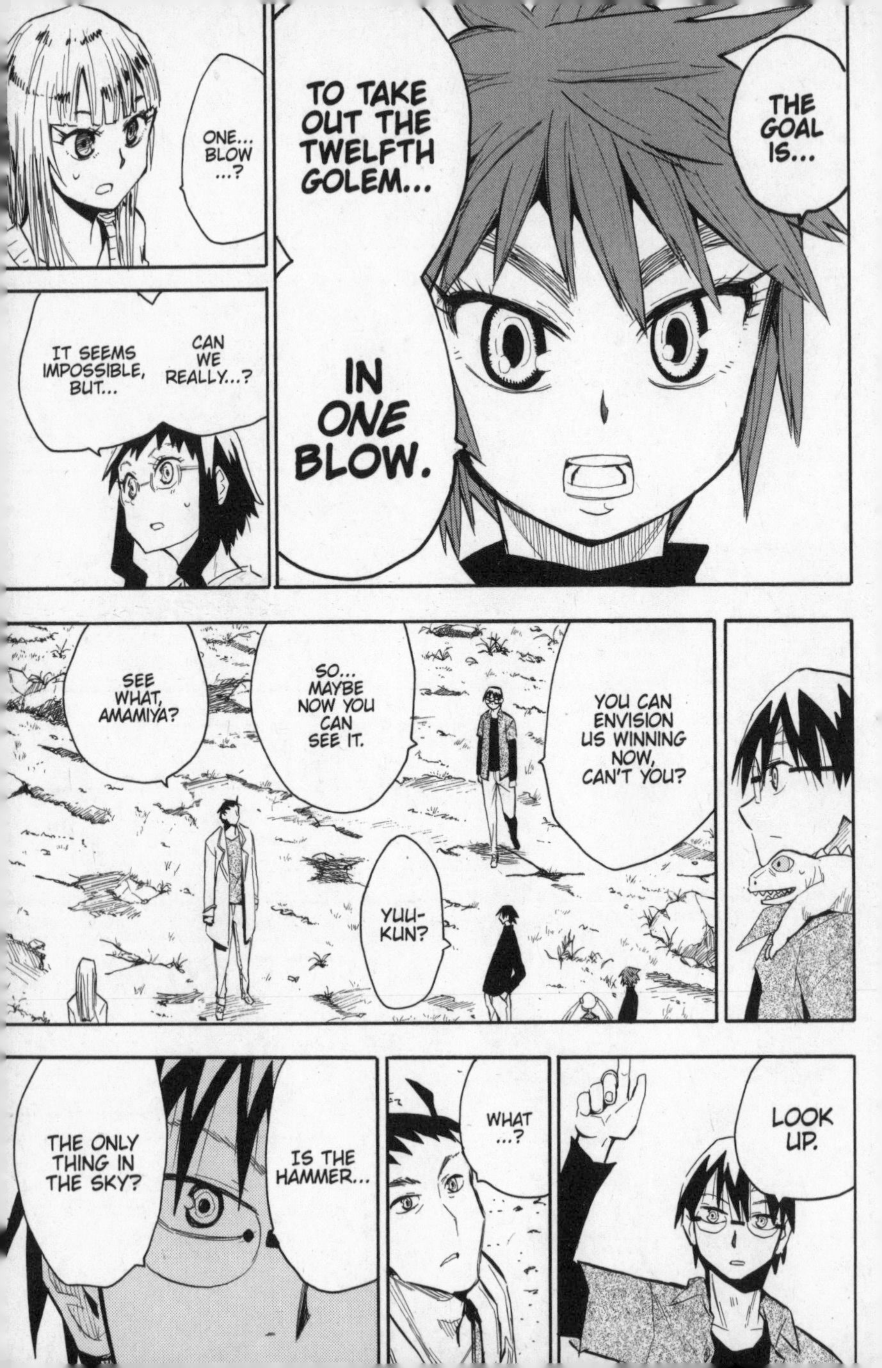
THE GOAL IS...
TO TAKE OUT THE TWELFTH GOLEM...
IN ONE BLOW.
ONE... BLOW ...?
CAN WE REALLY...?
IT SEEMS IMPOSSIBLE, BUT...
YOU CAN ENVISION US WINNING NOW, CAN'T YOU?
SO... MAYBE NOW YOU CAN SEE IT.
YUU-KUN?
SEE WHAT, AMAMIYA?
LOOK UP.
WHAT ...?
IS THE HAMMER...
THE ONLY THING IN THE SKY?

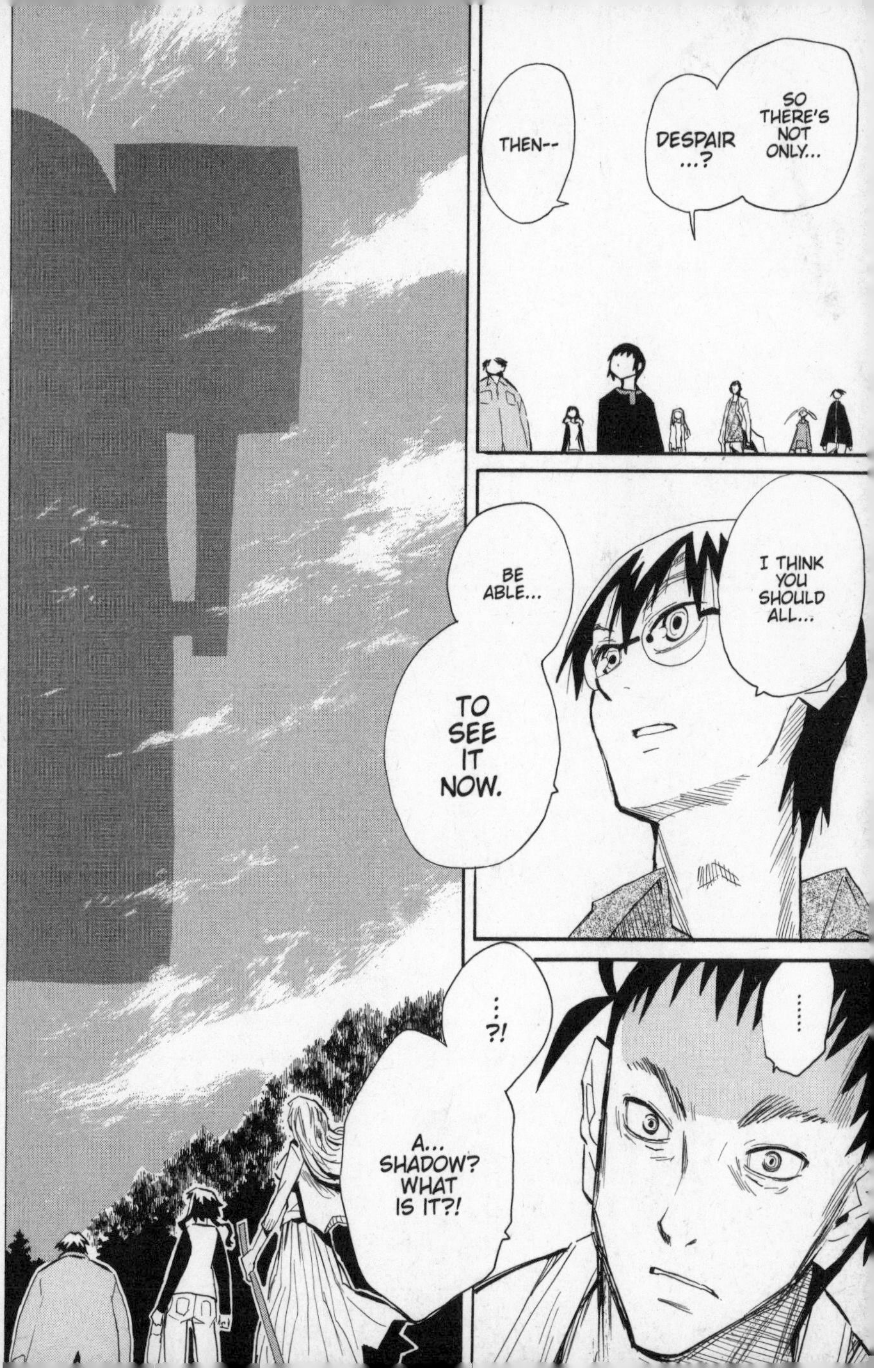
SO THERE'S NOT ONLY...
DESPAIR ...?
THEN--
I THINK YOU SHOULD ALL...
BE ABLE...
TO SEE IT NOW.
......
...?!
A... SHADOW? WHAT IS IT?!

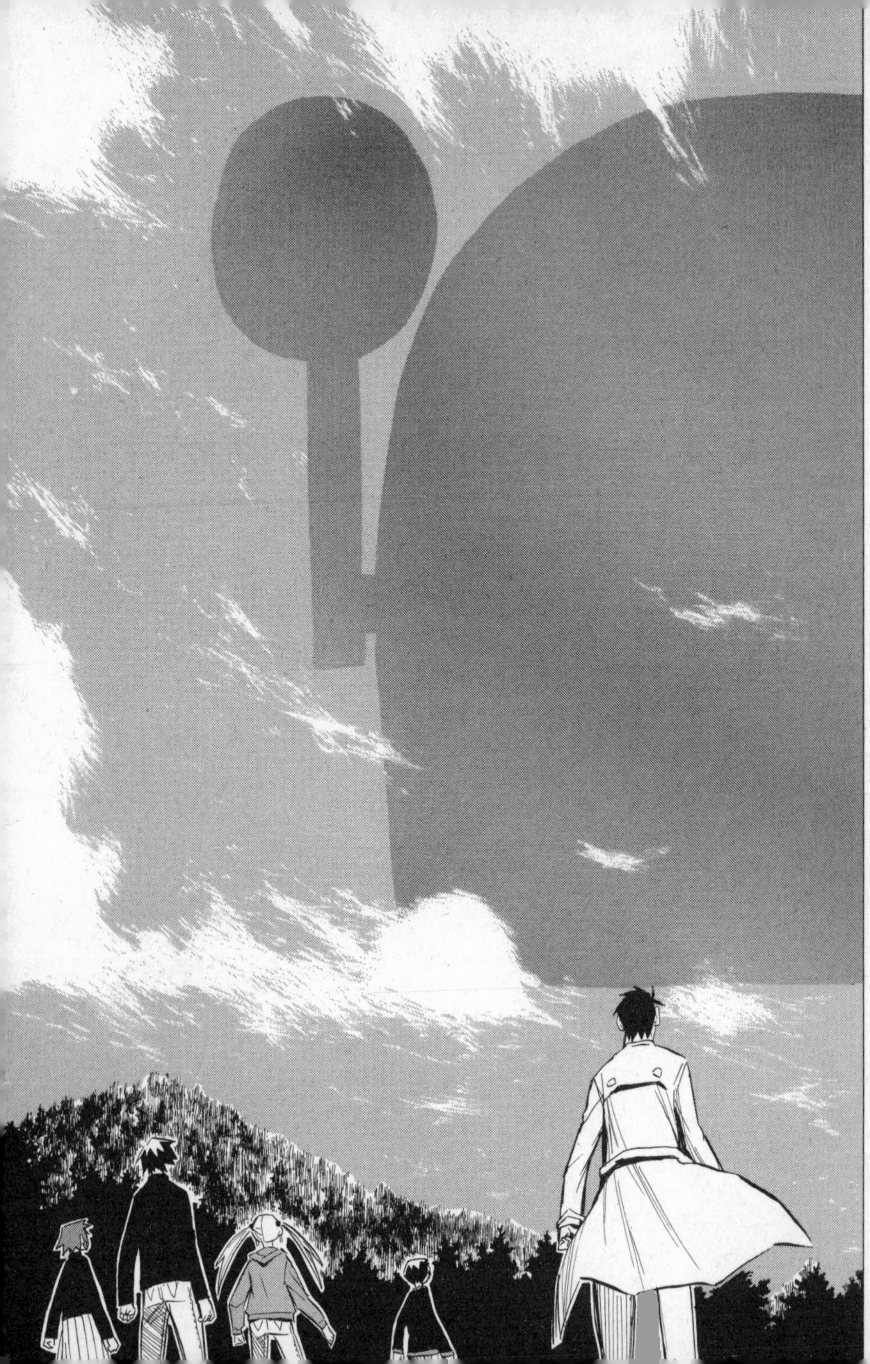

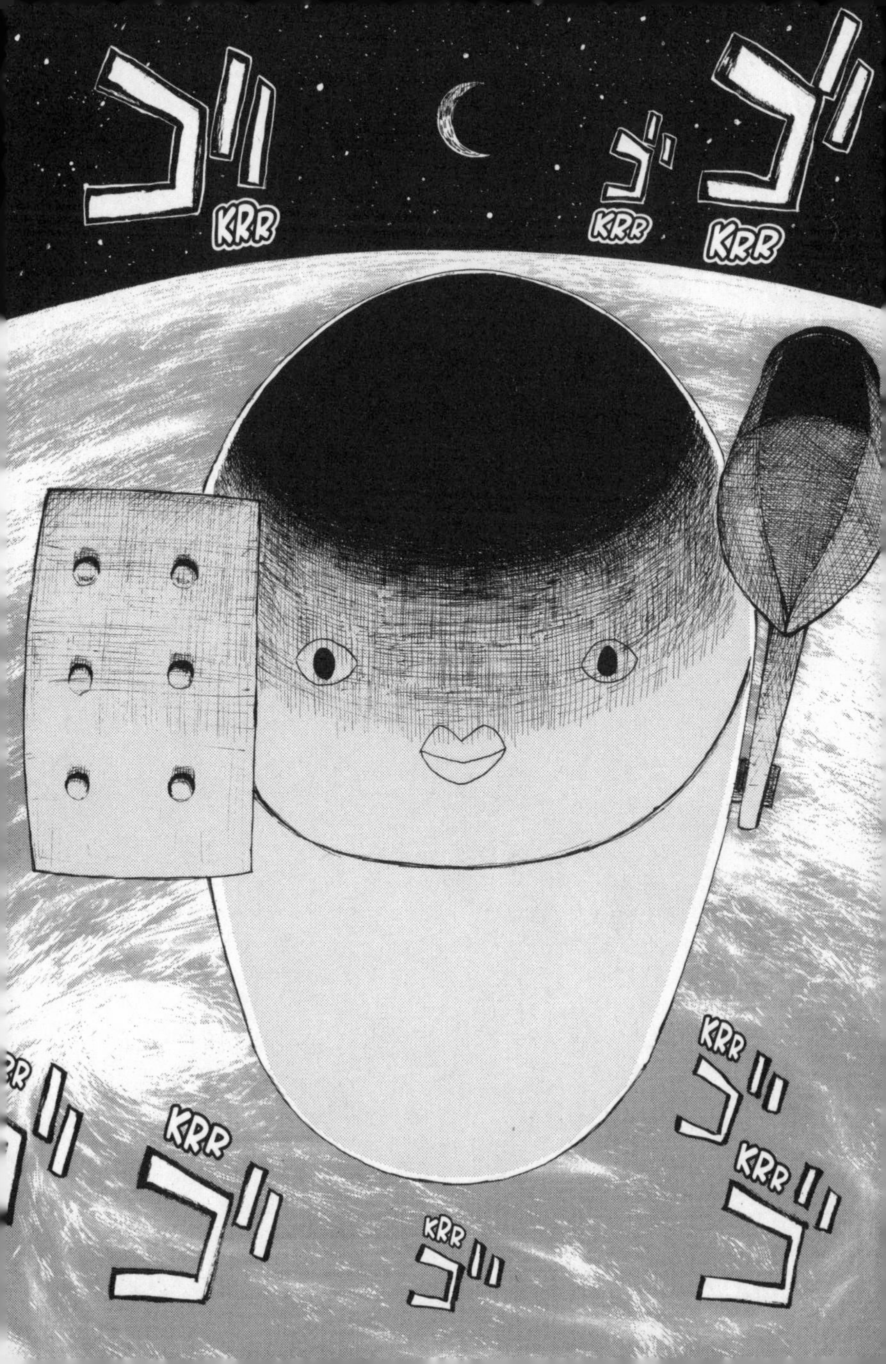
ゴ
KRR
ゴ
KRR
ゴ
KRR
ゴ
KRR
ゴ
KRR
ご
KRR
ゴ
KRR
ゴ
RR

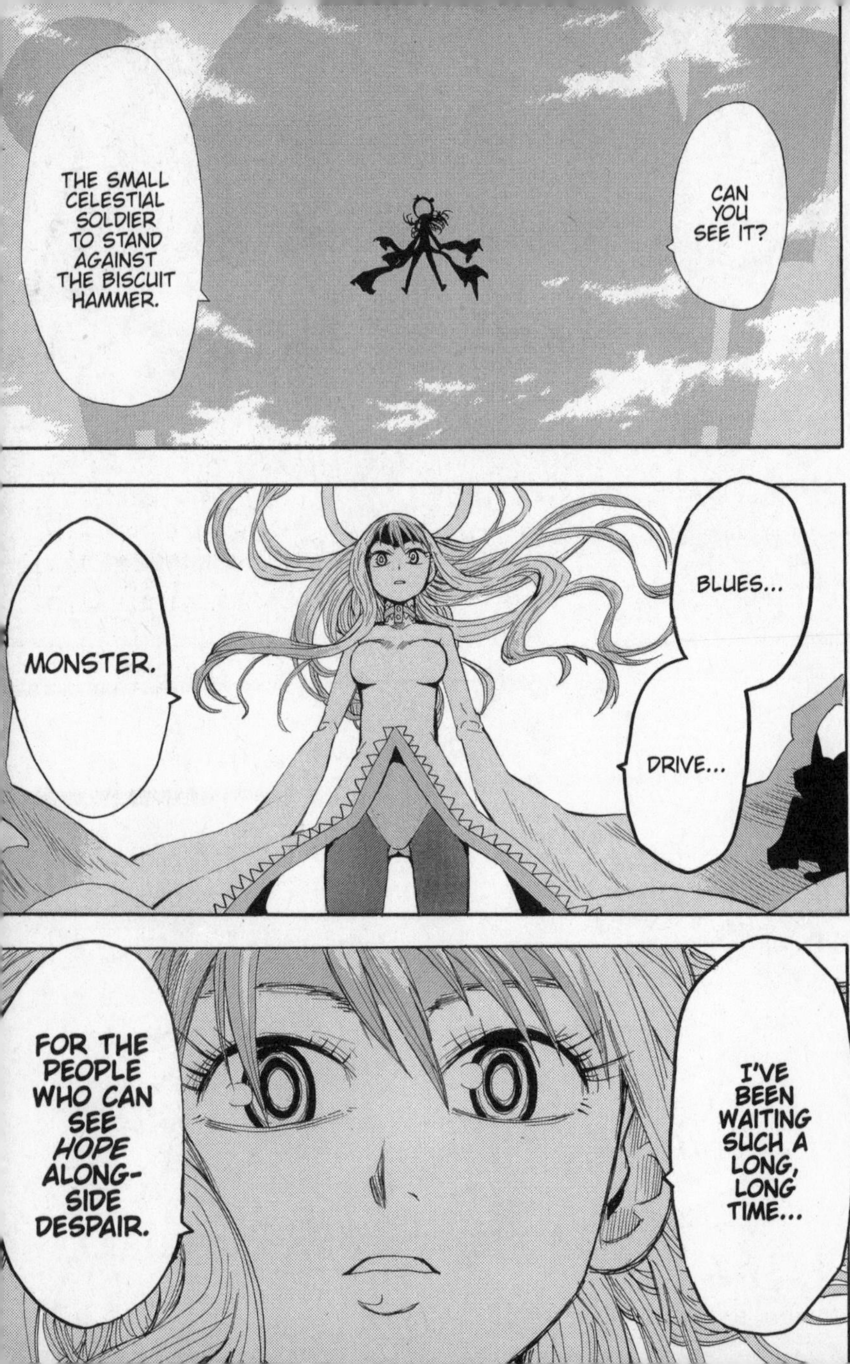
CAN YOU SEE IT?
THE SMALL CELESTIAL SOLDIER TO STAND AGAINST THE BISCUIT HAMMER.
BLUES...
DRIVE...
MONSTER.
I'VE BEEN WAITING SUCH A LONG, LONG TIME...
FOR THE PEOPLE WHO CAN SEE *HOPE* ALONG-SIDE DESPAIR.

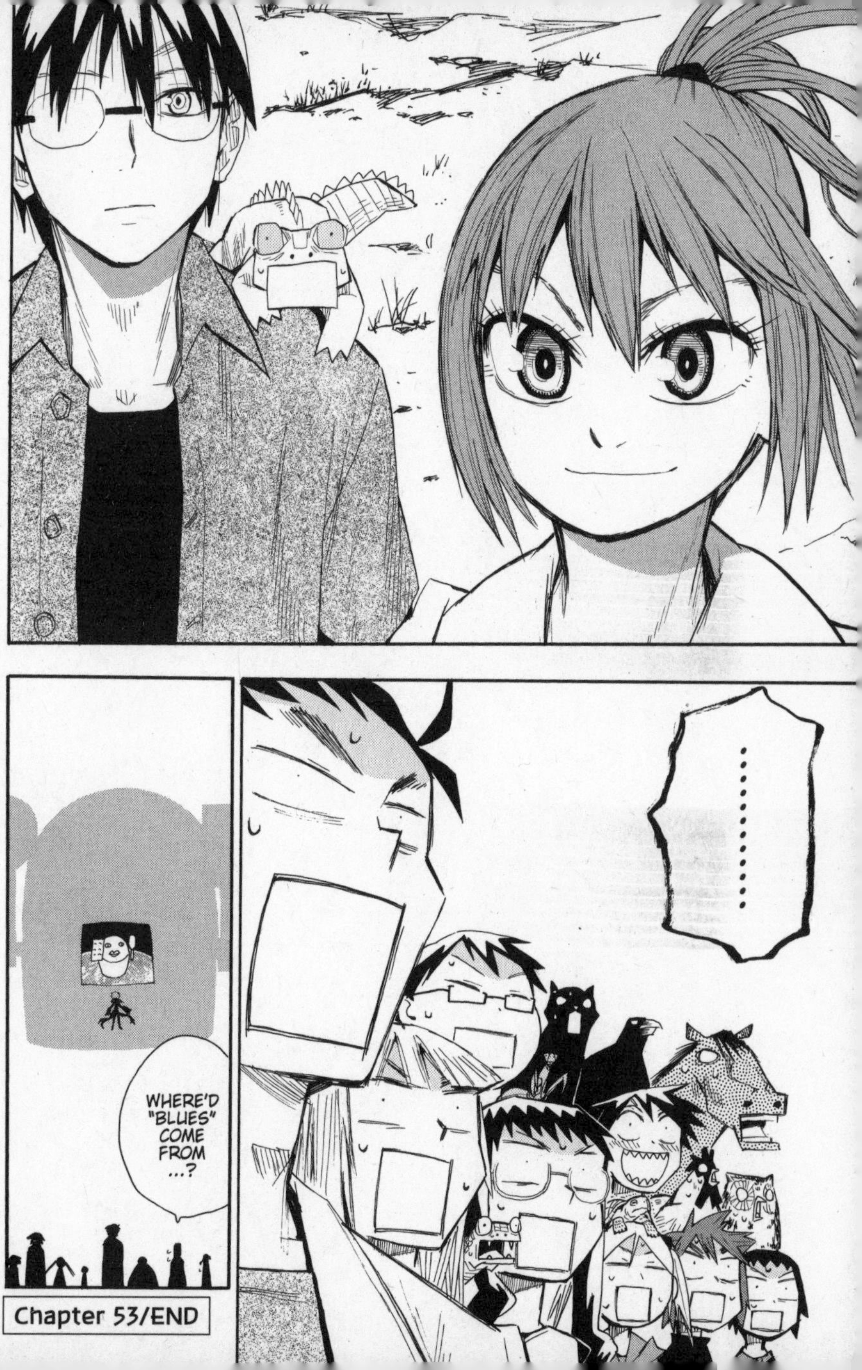
....
WHERE'D "BLUES" COME FROM ...?
Chapter 53/END

Lucifer and the Biscuit Hammer

Lucifer and the Biscuit Hammer
Volume 8
"Spirit"

Production staff
  Tonpu
  Abeshi Kobayashi
  Kenta Ishizaka
  Jueru Choden

Japanese logo/Cover design
  Eiichi Hagiwara (big body)

Supervising editor
  Ami Adachi

VOLUME 8
AFTERWORD

LAST TIME I WROTE ABOUT THE WHOLE DEBT
THING, BUT NOT TO WORRY——IT'S JUST A NORMAL
MORTGAGE. I WROTE DOWN THE ACTUAL AMOUNT
BECAUSE I WAS THINKING ABOUT DRAWING AN
ESSAY-TYPE MANGA ABOUT A HOUSE OR A CONDO
OR SOMETHING SOMEDAY, SO I FIGURED THERE
WAS NO POINT HIDING IT, BUT I PROBABLY WON'T
EVER ACTUALLY DO THAT. SO IT WOUND UP BEING
JUST A BIT OF INFO I TOSSED OUT THERE. I DON'T
REALLY REMEMBER WHAT WAS GOING ON.

BUT THAT REMINDS ME: THE BOOK 8 COVER HAS
ALL OF THE BEAST KNIGHTS TOGETHER, SO IT KINDA
LOOKS LIKE THE FINAL VOLUME. BUT IT'S NOT!
WE'RE GETTING CLOSE, THOUGH.

MAYBE I'LL WRITE A BIT MORE. THE TRICK TO
OUT-OF-BODY EXPERIENCES IS THE POWER THAT
COMES FROM SLEEP PARALYSIS. YOU HAVE PLENTY
OF OPPORTUNITIES WHEN YOU'RE GOING BACK
TO SLEEP. WHEN YOU START HEARING TERRIFYING
AUDITORY HALLUCINATIONS WHILE YOU'RE
PARALYZED, THAT'S YOUR CHANCE!

WELL, SEE YOU.

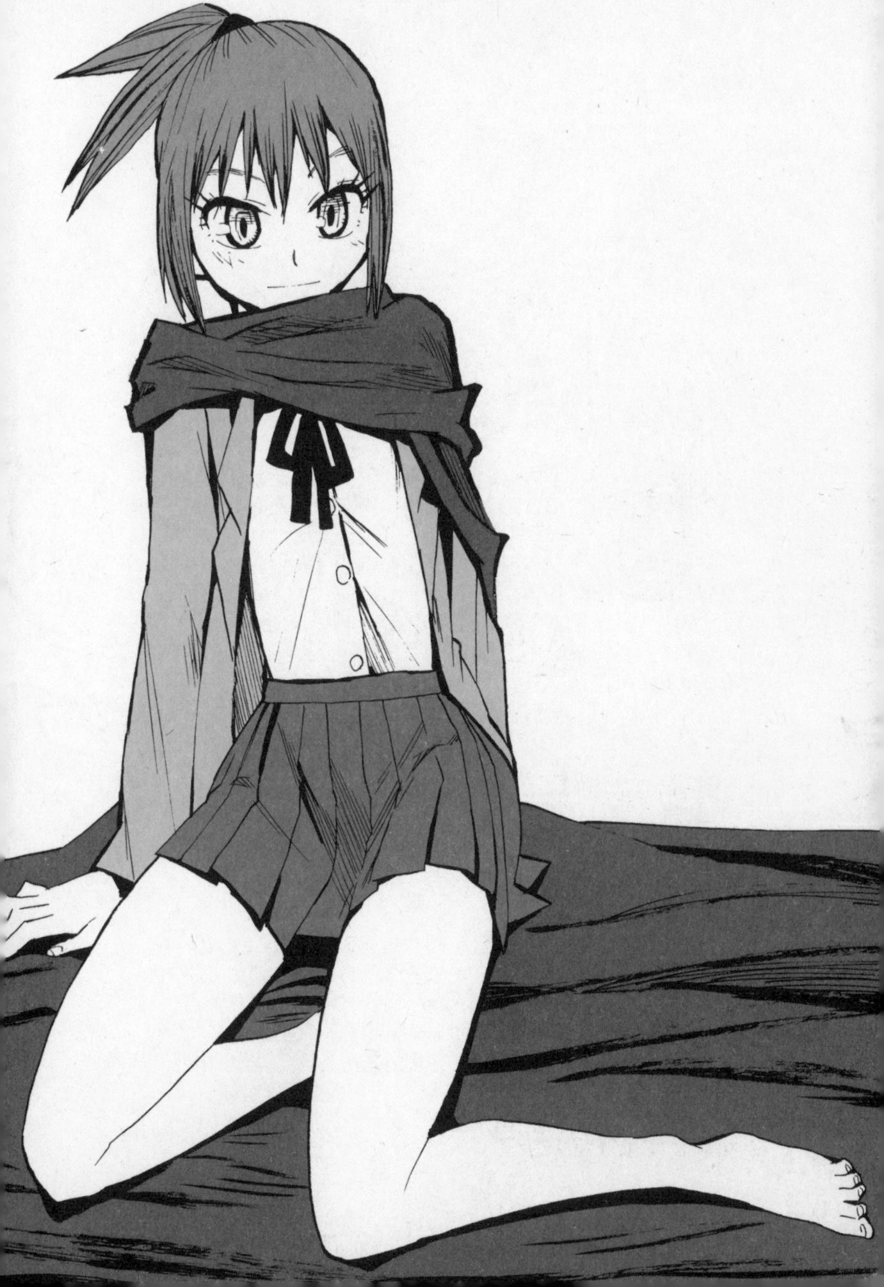

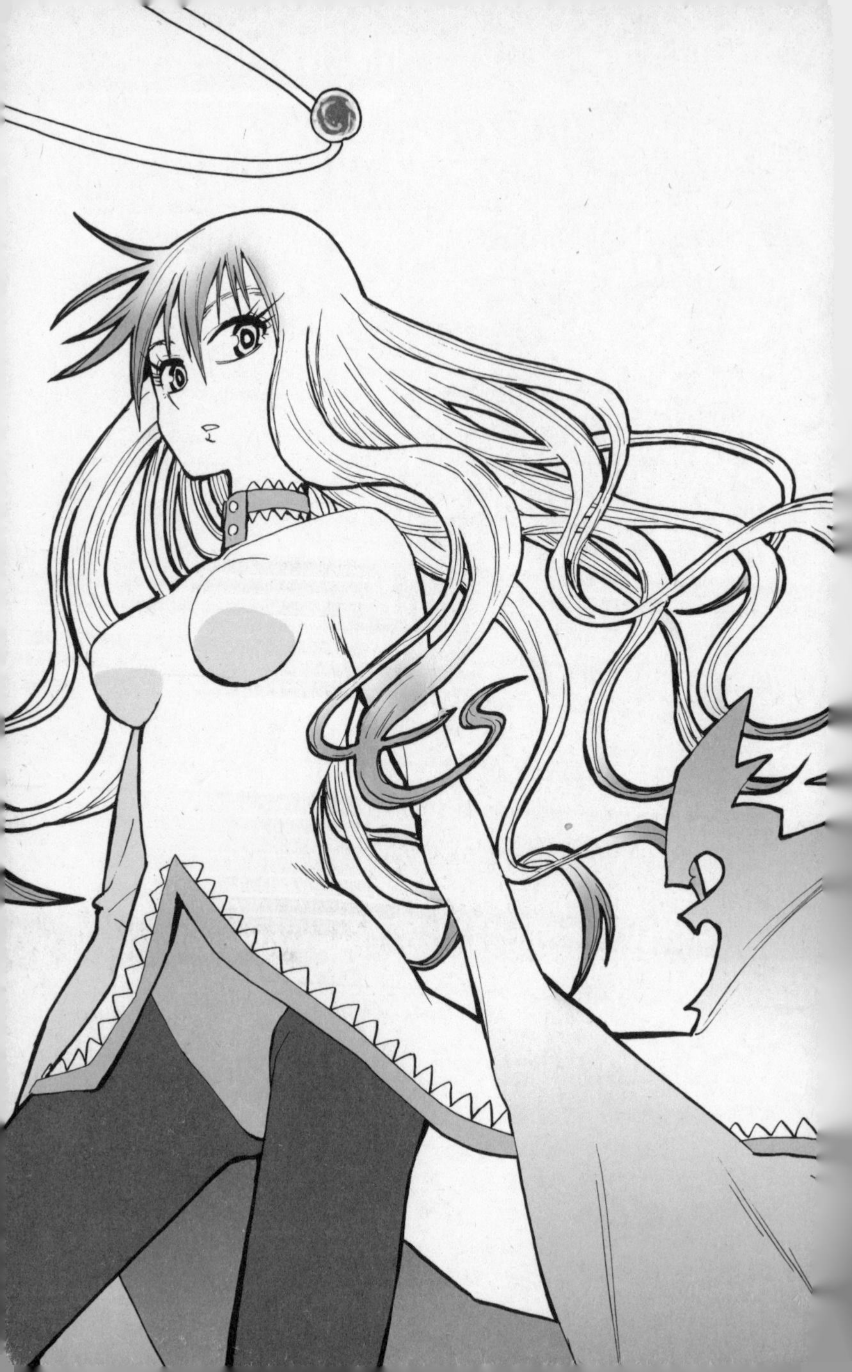

SEVEN SEAS ENTERTAI...

W9-CLP-943

JUL 10/24

Lucifer and the BISCUIT HAMMER

story and art by **SATOSHI MIZUKAMI**

VOLUMES 7-8

TRANSLATION
Jocelyne Allen

ADAPTATION
sabet Reinhardt MacFarlane

LETTERING AND LAYOUT
Lys Blakeslee

LOGO DESIGN
Phil Balsman

COVER DESIGN
Nicky Lim

PROOFREADER
Rebecca Scoble

ASSISTANT EDITOR
Lissa Pattillo

MANAGING EDITOR
Adam Arnold

PUBLISHER
Jason DeAngelis

HOSHI NO SAMIDARE volumes 7-8
© SATOSHI MIZUKAMI 2009
Originally published in Japan in 2009 by SHONENGAHOSHA Co., Ltd., Tokyo.
English translation rights arranged through TOHAN CORPORATION, Tokyo.

Seven Seas books may be purchased in bulk for educational, business, or
promotional use. For information on bulk purchases, please contact Macmillan
Corporate & Premium Sales Department at 1-800-221-7945 (ext 5442)
or write specialmarkets@macmillan.com.

Seven Seas and the Seven Seas logo are trademarks of
Seven Seas Entertainment, LLC. All rights reserved.

ISBN: 978-1-626921-69-6

Printed in Canada

First Printing: August 2015

10 9 8 7 6 5 4 3 2 1

FOLLOW US ONLINE: *www.gomanga.com*

READING DIRECTIONS

This book reads from *right to left*, Japanese style.
If this is your first time reading manga, you start
reading from the top right panel on each page and
take it from there. If you get lost, just follow the
numbered diagram here. It may seem backwards at
first, but you'll get the hang of it! Have fun!!

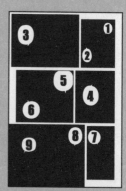